Configuring Cisco Unified Communications Manager and Unity Connection:
A Step-by-Step Guide

David Bateman

Cisco Press

800 East 96th Street

Indianapolis, IN 46240

Configuring Cisco Unified Communications Manager and Unity Connection: A Step-by-Step Guide

David Bateman

Copyright © 2011 Cisco Systems, Inc.

Cisco Press logo is a trademark of Cisco Systems, Inc.

Published by:
Cisco Press
800 East 96th Street
Indianapolis, IN 46240 USA

Printed in the United States of America   1 2 3 4 5 6 7 8 9 0

First Printing   May 2011

Library of Congress Cataloging-in-Publication Number is on file.

ISBN-10: 1-58714-226-0

ISBN-13: 978-1-58714-226-0

Warning and Disclaimer

This book is designed to provide information about configuration and administrative tasks related to Communications Manager and Unity. Every effort has been made to make this book as complete and as accurate as possible, but no warranty or fitness is implied.

The information is provided on an "as is" basis. The author, Cisco Press, and Cisco Systems, Inc. shall have neither liability nor responsibility to any person or entity with respect to any loss or damages arising from the information contained in this book or from the use of the discs or programs that may accompany it.

The opinions expressed in this book belong to the author and are not necessarily those of Cisco Systems, Inc.

Trademark Acknowledgments

All terms mentioned in this book that are known to be trademarks or service marks have been appropriately capitalized. Cisco Press or Cisco Systems, Inc. cannot attest to the accuracy of this information. Use of a term in this book should not be regarded as affecting the validity of any trademark or service mark.

Corporate and Government Sales

Cisco Press offers excellent discounts on this book when ordered in quantity for bulk purchases or special sales.

For more information please contact: U.S. Corporate and Government Sales
1-800-382-3419 corpsales@pearsontechgroup.com

For sales outside the U.S. please contact: International Sales international@pearsoned.com

Feedback Information

At Cisco Press, our goal is to create in-depth technical books of the highest quality and value. Each book is crafted with care and precision, undergoing rigorous development that involves the unique expertise of members from the professional technical community.

Readers' feedback is a natural continuation of this process. If you have any comments regarding how we could improve the quality of this book, or otherwise alter it to better suit your needs, you can contact us through e-mail at feedback@ciscopress.com. Please make sure to include the book title and ISBN in your message.

We greatly appreciate your assistance.

Publisher: Paul Boger	**Cisco Representative:** Erik Ullanderson
Associate Publisher: Dave Dusthimer	**Cisco Press Program Manager:** Anand Sundaram
Executive Editor: Brett Bartow	**Development Editor:** Marianne Bartow
Managing Editor: Sandra Schroeder	**Technical Editors:** David Mallory, Toby Sauer
Project Editor: Mandie Frank	**Copy Editor:** John Edwards
Editorial Assistant: Vanessa Evans	**Proofreader:** Apostrophe Editing Services
Designer: Sandra Schroeder	**Composition:** Mark Shirar
Indexer: Tim Wright	

CISCO.

Americas Headquarters	Asia Pacific Headquarters	Europe Headquarters
Cisco Systems, Inc.	Cisco Systems (USA) Pte. Ltd.	Cisco Systems International BV
San Jose, CA	Singapore	Amsterdam, The Netherlands

Cisco has more than 200 offices worldwide. Addresses, phone numbers, and fax numbers are listed on the Cisco Website at **www.cisco.com/go/offices**.

CCDE, CCENT, Cisco Eos, Cisco HealthPresence, the Cisco logo, Cisco Lumin, Cisco Nexus, Cisco StadiumVision, Cisco TelePresence, Cisco WebEx, DCE, and Welcome to the Human Network are trademarks; Changing the Way We Work, Live, Play, and Learn and Cisco Store are service marks; and Access Registrar, Aironet, AsyncOS, Bringing the Meeting To You, Catalyst, CCDA, CCDP, CCIE, CCIP, CCNA, CCNP, CCSP, CCVP, Cisco, the Cisco Certified Internetwork Expert logo, Cisco IOS, Cisco Press, Cisco Systems, Cisco Systems Capital, the Cisco Systems logo, Cisco Unity, Collaboration Without Limitation, EtherFast, EtherSwitch, Event Center, Fast Step, Follow Me Browsing, FormShare, GigaDrive, HomeLink, Internet Quotient, IOS, iPhone, iQuick Study, IronPort, the IronPort logo, LightStream, Linksys, MediaTone, MeetingPlace, MeetingPlace Chime Sound, MGX, Networkers, Networking Academy, Network Registrar, PCNow, PIX, PowerPanels, ProConnect, ScriptShare, SenderBase, SMARTnet, Spectrum Expert, StackWise, The Fastest Way to Increase Your Internet Quotient, TransPath, WebEx, and the WebEx logo are registered trademarks of Cisco Systems, Inc. and/or its affiliates in the United States and certain other countries.

All other trademarks mentioned in this document or website are the property of their respective owners. The use of the word partner does not imply a partnership relationship between Cisco and any other company. (0812R)

About the Author

David J. Bateman is a certified Cisco Systems instructor and the director of curriculum development for Skyline-ATS. He has more than 20 years of internetworking experience. For more than 10 years, David was a senior LAN/WAN engineer, working on small, medium, and large networks. Later in his career, he took on the responsibility of running the business operations of a technical services company, while maintaining his existing client base. David has always enjoyed sharing his knowledge, and in 1999, he added to his list of accomplishments by becoming a technical seminar leader. After many successful seminars, he decided to become a full-time Cisco instructor for Skyline Advanced Technology Services. He has been teaching and implementing Cisco voice technologies since 2000. David's years of real-world technical and business knowledge allow him to bring a unique perspective to the classroom, where he not only delivers critical technical knowledge but can also explain how technologies can be used to address various business issues.

About the Technical Reviewers

David L Mallory, CCIE No. 1933, is a technical leader for Learning@Cisco, where he is responsible for content development strategy. For the last seven years, David has been primarily focused on UC certifications and was the technical lead for the Cisco 360 Learning Program for CCIE Voice. Prior to joining Learning@Cisco, David was a systems engineer supporting global accounts. David is a frequent presenter at Cisco Live and has obtained four CCIEs—Routing & Switching, WAN Switching, Security, and Voice.

Toby Sauer is the lead voice instructor and voice curriculum manager for Skyline Advanced Technology Services. He brings 30 years of experience in the traditional voice, data, and VoIP arenas. Toby has been involved in Cisco VoIP since the beginning, working with traditional VoIP, and he was involved in the earliest installations of Cisco Communications Manager. He has installed many different implementations of Communications Manager and was responsible for converting most of the Midwest's Cisco offices from traditional PBX to Communications Manager.

Toby became a Cisco voice instructor in 2000. As the Communications Manager product continued to grow and develop, he was a key instructor to many of the original deployment partners.

Toby currently holds CCNP-Voice, CCNA-Voice, CCNA-RS, CCSI, and various partner-level certifications. He teaches all the Cisco Standard Voice courses and many custom variations of these courses.

Dedications

I'd like to dedicate this book to my parents, who taught me unconditional love; to my wife, Nikki, who is my life, my love, my all; and to Matthew, a young man that I am proud to call my son.

Acknowledgments

There are a number of people that I would like to thank in helping me complete this book. Often the greatest help that can be received is when someone is willing to sacrifice so that you can succeed. With this in mind, I would like to thank my wife, Nikki. She has sacrificed many beautiful summer days that we could have spent out on the motorcycle so that I could work on this book. She sacrificed hours each week reading what I had written in order that I might deliver a more readable copy to the editors. I know it was not always fun for her, but it helped me complete this book. Without her sacrifice, this book would not have been possible.

I would also like to thank the technical editors. Their keen insight and willingness to ask me what the heck I was thinking on some subjects have helped make this a much better book than it was when I first wrote it.

Of course I'd like to thank those at Skyline-ATS, where I work. I would especially like to thank them for the skill they showed in increasing my workload as deadlines for the book drew near. I guess they figured I would do better under pressure. But seriously, I would like to thank Mike Maudlin and Mike Zanatto for their understanding and cooperation during this project. I also need to thank all the others that I worked with at Skyline-ATS. The awesome amount of knowledge that we hold as a team is incredible, and to have such a resource at my disposal has been invaluable.

A big thank-you to the folks at Cisco Press: Brett Bartow, who assisted from the beginning of this project and was always there to remind me of upcoming deadlines long enough in advance so that I had time to either meet the deadline or come up with a really good excuse. Also Marianne Bartow, who acted as my development editor and was always helpful and encouraging.

Thanks one and all for all you've done.

Contents at a Glance

Table of Contents

Icons Used in This Book

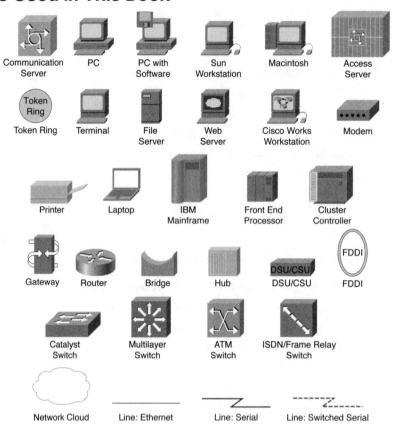

Command Syntax Conventions

The conventions used to present command syntax in this book are the same conventions used in the IOS Command Reference. The Command Reference describes these conventions as follows:

- **Boldface** indicates commands and keywords that are entered literally as shown. In actual configuration examples and output (not general command syntax), boldface indicates commands that are manually input by the user (such as a **show** command).

- *Italics* indicate arguments for which you supply actual values.

- Vertical bars (|) indicate separate alternative, mutually exclusive elements.

- Square brackets [ ] indicate optional elements.

- Braces { } indicate a required choice.

- Braces within brackets [{ }] indicate a required choice within an optional element.

Introduction

On March 10, 1876, Alexander Graham Bell made the first successful telephone call. As with many things, the test was purely accidental. Graham spilled acid on his leg, and Watson, his assistant, heard his call for help through the telephone. So, what has changed over the last 129 years? It would be easier to discuss what hasn't changed. The world of telephony has undergone some significant changes but none as exciting as Voice over IP (VoIP) solutions from Cisco. There are still those who believe we were all a lot better off in an analog world, but you can't stop progress, and the Cisco Unified Communications solutions are starting to grow faster than many had believed.

This new technology brings with it the need for individuals to learn how it works. Although there are many fine Cisco Press books on this technology, I noticed many of my students requesting a task-oriented book. They were looking for a book in which they could look up a specific task and be walked through it. This was the initial goal of the book. Through the writing process, the book evolved from offering only a step-by-step guide into also offering easy-to-understand explanations for many of the Cisco Unified Communications concepts and components.

Goals and Methods

New technologies bring new opportunities and challenges. One of the challenges that we are faced with in the Cisco Unified Communications world is the capability to easily understand the many facets of the configuration and integration process. Because this platform can be deployed in so many different configurations and environments, system administrators and system engineers need a resource that offers quick access to step-by-step solutions. In an environment such as this, it is nearly impossible to keep track of the exact steps for each configuration task. Those tasks that you do on a daily basis are easy to perform, but when you are called upon to perform unfamiliar tasks, you don't always have the time to learn the proper steps. *Configuring Communication Manager and Unity Connection* shows readers how to complete many of the common tasks, and some not-so-common tasks, performed within a Cisco Unified Communications solution.

Who Should Read This Book

The book is aimed at individuals who are required to configure Communications Manager and Unity and Unity Connection solutions as a primary part of their jobs. The book is unique because it covers Communications Manager, Unity, and Unity Connection.

Although this book focuses on the tasks that must be performed, it also offers easy-to-understand explanations for many of the technologies that are commonly found with Cisco Unified Communications environments, which makes it an excellent resource for individuals who are new to this technology.

How This Book Is Organized

Within the book, tasks are organized in the same order in which they would naturally be performed. Some tasks include cross-references to prerequisite tasks. Whenever possible, however, all tasks are presented within the same section.

Different people, depending on their knowledge and background, will use this book in different ways. Many will find it a useful reference tool when completing an unfamiliar task, and those new to this technology will find that reading this book from cover to cover will help them gain a solid understanding of this technology. Although the step-by-step guides were written with the assumption that you have access to a Communications Manager while reading the steps, this is not required. This book includes numerous screen shots, which enable you to see what is happening in the administration interface even if you do not have access to a Communications Manager.

Chapter 1 offers you a high-level overview of most of the concepts and components that are found within Communications Manager and Unity. Basically, the information found in two weeks of classes has been compressed to quickly bring you up to speed. This by no means is a replacement for these classes—just a quick overview.

Chapters 2 through 6 cover Communications Manager configuration, whereas Chapters 7 through 11 discuss Unity and Unity Connection configuration. The last chapter speaks to more advanced features of both technologies and offers a few ways to leverage the strengths of both to create a more feature-rich environment.

The following is a brief description of each chapter.

Chapter 1: CUCM and Unity Connection Overview

This chapter offers a broad overview of the Cisco Unified Communications solutions to ensure that you are comfortable with what follows in the book. The intent of this chapter is to offer you an overview of the various components of a Cisco Voice over IP solution. You are strongly encouraged to refer to suggested reference material for additional information on any topic with which you might be unfamiliar. You can find this material in the appendix.

Chapter 2: Preparing CUCM for Deployment

To ensure a smooth deployment, tasks must be performed in a certain order. In this chapter, you learn what tasks must be completed before adding devices. As with most things, if you fail to create a solid foundation, you will encounter problems in the future. This chapter ensures that the proper foundation is created and future problems are avoided. Topics covered include services configuration, enterprise parameters, and device registration tasks. Additionally, this chapter includes step-by-step instructions for each task.

Chapter 3: Deploying Devices

After the predeployment tasks are completed, you are ready to add devices. This chapter focuses on the tasks required to add various devices to your Communications Manager environment. Devices have been divided into two major categories: clients (IP phones, softphones, and so on) and gateways. The chapter includes step-by-step instructions for adding each device.

Chapter 4: Implementing a Route Plan

Before you can place calls to destinations that are not directly connected to your
Communications Manager environment, you must configure a route plan. This chapter discusses all the components of a route plan, such as route patterns, route lists, and route
groups and the tasks that are needed to implement an efficient dial plan. The step-by-step
tasks show how to create and configure route patterns, route lists, and route groups and
more advanced components, such as CTI route points, translation patterns, and route filters.

Chapter 5: Configuring Class of Service and Call Admission Control

After a dial plan is created, you might want to limit what destinations certain devices can
reach. This chapter discusses how to do this by configuring Calling Search Spaces and
partitions. It is also necessary that some types of Call Admission Control be deployed on
WAN links so that the quality of voice is maintained. To this end, Call Admission Control
features are covered. Finally, this chapter discusses the importance of special services,
such as 911, and describes how to properly configure the dial plan to handle these types
of calls.

Chapter 6: Configuring CUCM Features and Services

After basic call-processing functions are configured and working properly, you need to
add new features and monitor the health of the system. This chapter explores a number
of the features that can be implemented, including IP phone service, media resources, and
Extension Mobility. The need for, and the functions of, SRST is also covered in this chapter. Furthermore, this chapter examines some of the monitoring services that are included
in Communications Manager. Step-by-step instructions that explain how to add each feature and service are included.

Chapter 7: Unity Predeployment Tasks

The first step to proper configuration is verifying that the integration is correct and that
all predeployment tasks are complete. This chapter includes step-by-step instructions for
completing predeployment tasks, such as verifying integration, defining system parameters, and creating templates, distribution lists, and CoS.

Chapter 8: User Reference

After a proper integration between Unity/Connection and Communications Manager is
achieved and the predeployment tasks discussed in the previous chapter are completed,
the user can be added. In this chapter, the different types of users are examined. Then,
the process for adding, importing, and managing users is explored. Within the "Managing
Users" section, various administrative tasks are discussed, which range from "How to
reset a user's password" to "How to properly remove users." Each task includes step-by-
step instructions.

Chapter 9: Call Management

One of the system's most useful and often underutilized features is call management. This
chapter ensures that the reader understands the way that the system processes a call. The
most basic object of the call management system is a call handler. A brief review of how

call handlers work is included in the beginning of this chapter. Additionally, a common use of the system's call management feature is to deploy a basic auto-attendant, which is described within this text. The chapter also addresses some of the more advanced call management features, such as call routing rules and audio-text applications. Complete step-by-step instructions are included within this chapter.

Chapter 10: Implementing Unity Networking

Because many organizations are migrating to Unity/Connection from a voicemail system or have other voicemail systems deployed at other locations, Unity/Connection must communicate with them. Unity can be integrated with these systems through a number of industry-standard protocols. This chapter discusses the different types of networking that can be deployed and looks at how to determine the proper one to use.

Chapter 11: Exploring Additional Tools

Although most day-to-day tasks can be accomplished using the system administrative interface, it is often more efficient to use one of the many tools that are included with Unity/Connection. The tools help accomplish tasks that range from making bulk user changes to migrating users to another server. This chapter introduces the reader to these tools and includes step-by-step details on how to use each of them.

Chapter 12: Maximizing CUCM and Unity Connection Capabilities

As Communications Manager and Unity/Connection evolve, more and more advanced features are added. This chapter looks at a few of these more advanced features, such time-of-day routing and call queuing. In addition, the chapter offers a few examples of features that can be created by taking existing features of each application and adding a new twist to them, such as using Unity as a conference manager.

Target Version

This book was written for Communications Manager, Unity, and Unity Connection versions 8.0 and 8.5. This is not to say that you must run any of these versions for this book to be of value to you. It does, however, mean that some of the step-by-step guides might be slightly different. With each new version, the menus are sometimes moved or slightly changed, or there might be an additional field in the new version. However, none of these issues should cause you great concern. If the field isn't there, don't worry about it. If a menu isn't exactly where you expect it, just look above or below, and you are sure to find it. Including the exact steps for every version of these applications would have made the book larger than you would care to lift, let alone read. Remember that the value of this book goes beyond the step-by-step guides, because it also provides easy-to-understand explanations of many Cisco Unified Communications concepts.

Chapter 1

CUCM and Unity Connection Overview

Before embarking on any worthwhile adventure, it is important that you have a good map and a solid understanding of the purpose of your trip. This chapter provides just that—an introduction to some of the many components that make up a Cisco Unified Communications environment.

Technical books can be divided into one of two categories: "why" books and "how-to" books. Why books provide you with a solid understanding of the technology and explain why you would want to deploy it. How-to books tell you how to deploy a given technology. This is a how-to book. The main purpose of this book is that of a configuration reference. However, it is important that you have a solid understanding of the technology. This chapter provides you with a broad overview of this technology and references to further information. If you are new to this technology, you are strongly encouraged to pursue more in-depth information than is presented in this chapter before deploying this technology. If you haven't been involved in this technology for a while, you might be thinking of skipping this chapter and moving on to the meat of the book. This, of course, is your decision, but reading this chapter can give you a better understanding of the specific technologies discussed later in this book.

After reading this chapter, you should have a high-level understanding of the Communications Manager, Unity, and Unity Connection components and how they fit into a Cisco Voice over IP (VoIP) solution. This chapter has been divided into the following sections:

- Reliable foundation

- Communications Manager overview

- Unity overview

- Unity Connection overview

- Security concerns

Because this technology is a mixture of two preexisting technologies, traditional telcom and traditional data, it is likely that you started out solely in one of these disciplines. Often when you start to learn a new technology, you try to compare it to technologies you've learned. This sometimes causes learners to miss an important point because they were preoccupied with trying to make this new information fit in with previous learning. If you are new to this technology, you should take any current knowledge you have and place it aside while reading. After you have read this chapter and feel that you understand it, you should then integrate it with your current knowledge base.

At first, this can be difficult because we all seem to want to fall back on what we already know. So each time you find yourself doing this, just stop reading for a moment and refocus on acquiring new information, knowing that later you can integrate it with what you already know. Also, try not to make judgments while reading. Many times people have made up their minds about a product or technology before they have even seen it. Even if you are learning this technology because "you have to," be as open to it as possible. Regardless of any person's resistance, technology will not stop or even slow down.

Ensuring a Reliable Foundation

Whether you are building a house or a network, a solid foundation is crucial. In a VoIP network, the foundation is even more crucial because both data and voice will use the same network. This means that you need to implement an even higher level of redundancy than you feel is necessary in a traditional data network. The term *five 9s* is used a lot in the traditional telcom world; this stands for 99.999 percent uptime. The expectation is that any network that carries voice should be up 99.999 percent of the time. This calculates to just a little more than 5 minutes a year of downtime, not including planned downtime for upgrades and maintenance. You might be saying, "That's impossible," but actually it is possible. With the proper planning and design, you can expect to see nearly no downtime. Make note that I said, "with the proper planning and design." There have been a number of VoIP deployments that failed solely because a proper infrastructure was not implemented. Typically, a VoIP environment is broken into four layers. Each layer plays a vital role. An example of the devices that are in each layer follows:

- **Clients:** IP phones

- **Applications:** Unity

- **Call processing:** Communications Manager

- **Infrastructure:** Switches and gateways

Note   Calculations of five 9s varied by telephony vendor and typically discounted issues that affected a single user or a small group of users. For example, if you lost a desktop switch and 24 users had no phone service for 3 hours, this wouldn't count against your five 9s.

The foundation of the network is at the infrastructure level, where components such as switches, routers, and gateways reside. A solid understanding of these components is needed to design a solution that can withstand common day-to-day problems that arise on most networks. The discussion begins with a look at these components.

Infrastructure Overview

A properly deployed infrastructure is the key to a reliable network. This section begins by examining the foundation of the infrastructure. The cable is one of the most often overlooked components of the network. This is often because it rarely causes problems after it is installed. Cabling problems normally don't appear until some new type of technology is added to the network. I remember one client that was running a 4-megabit network with no trouble. When he upgraded to 16 megabits, the network started failing and he had to rewire the entire network.

Nowadays, twisted-pair Ethernet is installed in most environments. The Cisco VoIP solution is designed with the assumption that twisted-pair Ethernet is installed at each desktop.

One of the common issues that arises with cabling is when the installer takes a few short-cuts. A common shortcut is failing to terminate all the pairs of the cable. The installer assumes that because Ethernet uses only pins 1, 2, 3, and 6, there is no need to terminate the others. In most cases, the network can function when cabled this way. The problem is, however, that such a network is not installed to industry standards, and all Cisco solutions are based on the assumption that the existing infrastructure is installed according to industry standards. In an environment such as this, you cannot use the Cisco power patch panel because it relies on pins 4, 5, 7, and 8 to deliver power to the phone. Ensure that you have all cabling tested and certified before the deployment begins. As the saying goes, "An ounce of prevention is worth a pound of dropped calls" (or something like that).

After you have the cabling under control, you need to look at the equipment to which the cabling connects. On the one end of the cable you have phones, which is quite straight-forward. On the other end, you have the phone plugged into a switch.

Note   This discussion assumes that the phone is plugged into a switch, not a hub. Plugging phones into hubs is not advised because all devices on a hub share the same bandwidth, and this can lead to poor voice quality. In addition, do not daisy-chain phones (plug one phone into another).

When deciding which switch to use, a few things must be considered. First, it is recommended that all switches you plan to use within the Cisco VoIP solution are Cisco switches. This is not simply because Cisco wants to sell more switches, but because certain Cisco switches include special features that allow greater functionality within your network. These features include inline power, voice virtual LANs (VLAN), and Cisco Discovery Protocol (CDP) support. This does not mean that switches from other manufacturers cannot be used. It simply means that some features discussed in the following sections might not be supported.

Inline Power

This is the ability to provide power to the phones through the Ethernet cable. There are two inline power schemes:

- The Cisco inline power convention, which uses pins 1, 2, 3, and 6 to provide power. These same wires are used for the transfer of data.

- Power over Ethernet (PoE), as defined in IEEE Standard 802.3af. This is an approved industry standard, which uses pins 1, 2, 3, and 6 or 4, 5, 7, and 8 to provide power. The standard differs from the Cisco inline power scheme in a number of ways, the most significant being the way that power requirement is detected. Current Cisco phones support the 802.3af standard, but keep in mind that older models might not.

The net effect of either standard is the same—power is supplied to the phone through the Ethernet cable. The switches that support either of these conventions can detect whether the attached device requires inline power, and if the device does require inline power, the switch provides it. Having two methods of supplying inline power can be confusing, so it is best that the phones and switches you purchase use the same method.

Voice VLANs

This allows the use of a single switch port to simultaneously support both a phone and a PC by allowing a single port to recognize two VLANs. The PC is plugged into the back of the phone, and the phone is plugged into the switch. The switch then advertises both VLANs. The phone can recognize the voice VLAN and use it. PCs cannot recognize voice VLANs and use the native VLAN.

CDP Support

CDP is a Cisco-proprietary protocol that allows Cisco equipment to share certain information with other Cisco equipment. The phones use CDP to determine whether a voice VLAN is present on that port. It also shares other information such as port power information and quality of service (QoS) information with the Cisco Catalyst switch.

Make sure that the switch you choose supports these features. Most currently shipping Catalyst switches are capable of supporting all these features.

Voice Gateways

After you ensure that the cabling and switches are adequate for a VoIP solution, you are ready to deploy the endpoints. Endpoints can be any of the following: phones, soft clients, or gateways. Of these devices, only gateways are considered to reside at the infrastructure level. Phones and Communications Managers are covered later in this chapter.

In its simplest form, a gateway is a device that allows connectivity of dissimilar networks. In the VoIP world, a gateway connects the Communications Manager voice network to another network. The public switched telephone network (PSTN) is the most popular network with which IP phones must communicate. The job of the gateway is to convert the data traveling through it to a format that the other side understands. Just as a translator is needed when a person speaks German to someone who understands only Spanish, a gateway is needed to convert VoIP to a signal that the PSTN understands.

The hardware that acts as a gateway varies, depending on what type of network you connect to and what features you require. When choosing a gateway, ensure that it supports the following four core gateway requirements:

- **DTMF relay:** Dual-tone multifrequency (DTMF) are the tones that are played when you press the dial pad on a phone. Many people refer to this as touch tones. Because voice is often compressed, the DTMF can become distorted. The DTMF relay feature allows the DTMF to be sent out of band, which resolves the distortion problem.

- **Supplementary services:** Include hold, transfer, and conferencing.

- **Cisco Unified Communications Manager (CUCM) redundancy:** Supports the capability to fail over to a secondary Communications Manager if the primary Communications Manager fails.

- **Call survivability:** Ensures that the call will not drop if the Communications Manager, to which either endpoint is registered, fails.

Later, the various types of gateways are discussed. For now, understand the purpose of a gateway and the required features.

Creating a Reliable VoIP Infrastructure

In the summer of 2003, the northeastern portion of the United States experienced a widespread power outage. The power outage lasted from 6 hours to 3 days depending upon the area. One of the most impressive and yet understated events that occurred during this time is what didn't happen. For the most part, the PSTN didn't fail, and no one even noticed. Because no one actually noticed shows how much people expect the phones to always work. The power was out, and yet most people didn't think for a second that the PSTN might fail. The system didn't fail because of the highly reliable and redundant infrastructure that has been developed over the years. This is the type of reliability that people have come to expect from the phone system. It has been stated that many people view dial tone as a God-given right, or even one of the inalienable rights in the constitution. (I doubt anyone thinks that, but you get the idea.) With this in mind, you must make every effort to ensure that nothing short of a natural disaster prevents your customer from having dial tone.

The most important thing to keep in mind is that individual components of the system will fail. It is not a question of if something will fail, but when. Because components will fail, it is up to you to determine how to prevent the failure from affecting dial tone. This is done during the design phase of the project.

Note The design phase is perhaps the single most important part of any deployment. Countless times I've had panicked customers, whom I inherited from other integrators, calling me with problems that could have been averted if dealt with during the design phase. Often when I ask clients how this problem was dealt with during the design phase, they answer, "What design phase?" Make certain that you cover as many foreseen and unforeseen eventualities as possible during the design phase. Although your customers might never see how good you are at fixing a system when it fails, they will know how good you are because it doesn't fail.

Redundancy is the core component in a reliable infrastructure. The system design should include redundancy at every level. This starts in the wiring closet.

Reducing the cable infrastructure and allowing ease of cable management are two of the motivating factors for migrating to a VoIP solution. Therefore, it does not make sense that redundancy is extended to the cable level. Remember, your goal is to achieve the same level of reliability that people expect from a phone system. People understand that if there is a cabling problem, the phone won't work. This is one of the few acceptable reasons for a phone system to fail. So, as far as the cabling goes, you just need to ensure that the existing network cabling infrastructure is certified as previously mentioned.

Switches are the next piece of the infrastructure that needs to be considered. Redundancy at the switch level is nothing new. Although redundancy has always been encouraged in data networks, it is no longer just a suggestion; it is required to achieve the expected level of reliability. In smaller environments that might have only a single switch, redundancy at the switch level doesn't apply; however, in large networks, make sure that you design a highly available network by building redundancy in at the core and distribution switch level. This means that there will be multiple paths a packet can take to get to its destination. Because of a protocol called Spanning Tree Protocol (STP), only one path is available at any given time. STP ensures that if a link fails, an alternative path will be opened. To find out more about STP, see the additional references listed in the appendix "Additional Reference Resources."

A redundant path can ensure that a packet reaches its destination, but it is also important that it gets there in a timely manner. Voice traffic does not handle delay very well. If too much delay is introduced, the quality of the conversation tends to degrade rapidly. You have probably noticed the effect delay can have on a conversation when watching a TV news reporter through a satellite link. It seems to take the reporter a few seconds to respond to a news anchor's question. This is because there is a several-second delay between the time the question is asked and the time when it reaches the reporter's destination.

Many things can affect the delay that is introduced into a conversation. One of the most common is the competition between voice and other traffic for bandwidth. To help alleviate this, QoS must be implemented within the network. QoS gives certain traffic priority over other traffic. The proper configuration of QoS is essential for any network that has both voice and data on the same wire. A detailed discussion on QoS is beyond the scope of this book. Refer to Appendix A, for suggested references on this subject.

Before leaving the wiring closet, one more thing requires attention: power. Remember that a power failure is not an acceptable reason to lose dial tone. A power outage is not necessarily an acceptable reason for data networks to fail. There was a time when people expected and accepted the loss of data during a power outage. They were never happy about it, but they weren't surprised either. Nowadays with the reasonable price of uninterruptible power supplies (UPS), data networks are no longer as susceptible to power outages as they were in the past. It is nearly unheard of not to have a UPS on file servers and, in many cases, throughout the network. Switches are no exception. As with any equipment, you need to do some research to determine the proper size of the UPS you need. To do this, determine the amount of power that the switch draws and then determine the amount of time you want the switch to run without power. You don't need to worry about redundant power at the phone if you use inline power. Keep in mind that the more phones that draw power from the switch, the larger the UPS you need.

As mentioned previously, gateways are also considered part of the infrastructure. Therefore, whenever possible, redundancy should be included at the gateway level. In some cases, such as an environment that has only a single trunk from the PSTN, redundancy is not feasible. If the environment has other Cisco routers, try to use the same model router for your PSTN gateway. This way, if the PSTN gateway does fail, you might swap equipment for a short-term solution or, at the very least, use the other router for testing purposes after hours. If you do have multiple trunks, it is a good idea to have at least two physical gateways connecting the network to the PSTN. A level of redundancy can be added by using multiple service providers. For example, if you have two trunks, use a different service provider for each. This way, if either of the service providers has a widespread outage, the other trunk will still be functional.

This section dealt with the reliability of the infrastructure. This is only a portion of the solution that must be considered when implementing a reliable system. A system is only as good as its weakest link, so you need to ensure that the entire system is designed with the same goal in mind—"Don't affect dial tone." In the next section, you look at the call-processing layer, more specifically, the Communications Manager.

Communications Manager Overview

In the previous section, the infrastructure was discussed, and you learned what was necessary to create a solid foundation on which to build the rest of the system. As when building a house, you can move to the heart of the project after the foundation is set.

The Communications Manager is considered the heart of the Cisco Unified Communications solution. It is responsible for device registrations and call control. Communications Manager is an application that runs on a media convergence server (MCS). Often the term *Communications Manager* is used to refer to the physical device that the application runs on, but the hardware should be referred to as the MCS. Communications Manager is the software running on the hardware.

Note   Cisco has certified certain servers for use as MCSs. Currently only certain HP and IBM servers are certified. Servers can be purchased from Cisco or directly from IBM or HP. The different platforms offer various features, such as redundant hard drives and power supplies. Be sure to take this into consideration when choosing a server. Keep in mind that not all IBM and HP servers are approved, so be certain to check with Cisco to ensure that the server you choose is approved. Also be aware that the HP servers that are supported are older models, and Cisco does not plan on approving newer HP models. Many integrators choose to purchase the MCS from Cisco to have a single-vendor solution.

Every system should have at least two Communications Managers, and the two are referred to as a Communications Manager cluster. The exception to this rule is if you run Communications Manager Business Edition. Later in this chapter, you learn why a minimum of two Communications Managers is strongly recommended. Based on the previous section, you might guess for yourself. Does the word *redundancy* come to mind?

Defining Communications Manager Components

Communications Manager is responsible for all device registration and call control. Much of the configuration is performed through the Communications Manager administrative interface. This section introduces you to the various components of Communications Manager and the devices that it controls.

Most configuration and administration is performed through Communications Manager's web browser interface. Using this interface, you can configure phones, add users to Communications Manager's directory, define the dial plan, and perform various other tasks. The majority of the tasks that you learn how to perform later will be done using this interface. The interface is fairly simple to navigate, and after a short time, most people are quite comfortable using it. It is important to remember that it is a web-based interface and hence might sometimes not be as responsive as you would expect. The delays are more noticeable when you access a remote Communications Manager over a WAN link. Each evolution of this interface improves the end-user experience, and nowadays it is much more enjoyable to use than in years past.

All the information that you enter through the web interface must be stored. Communications Manager uses IBM Informix to store this information. All configuration information is stored in this database.

As mentioned earlier, each Communications Manager cluster should have at least two Communications Managers. The reason for this is redundancy. Remember, the system needs to deliver the same level of reliability that people are used to with a traditional phone system. Having multiple Communications Managers also provides a more scalable system, which will be explained shortly. For now, the focus is on the role that the various Communications Managers play in regard to the database. A Communications Manager is referred to as either a publisher or a subscriber. Each Communications Manager cluster has only one publisher. All other Communications Managers within that cluster are referred to as subscribers.

The job of the publisher is to maintain the most current copy of the database. Whenever anything is added to the database, the information is sent from the publisher to all the subscribers. The data is never written to the subscribers first and then transferred to the publisher.

So far, we have discussed only the roles that the Communications Managers play in the database. The other job of the Communications Manager is device control. All devices register to a Communications Manager. This Communications Manager is known as that device's primary Communications Manager. Each device also has a secondary Communications Manager that it can register to if the primary fails. Devices use a subscriber as their primary Communications Manager. This leaves the publisher alone so that it can take care of its main responsibility, which is to maintain the database. In some cases, a device can have a tertiary server to which it can fail over if both the primary and secondary are not available. In most cases, primary, secondary, and tertiary Communications Managers should be subscribers.

If the primary Communications Manager fails, the device registers to the secondary. The device registers with the secondary Communications Manager only if it is not on a call when the Communications Manager fails. If the device is active when the Communications Manager fails, it registers with the secondary Communications Manager when the call ends. In most cases, a call stays up even if the participating Communications Manager that is controlling devices in the call fails. The reason is that during a call, the communication is point to point, meaning that the Communications Manager is not involved with the actual voice stream. The device has no idea that the Communications Manager has failed because it does not communicate with the device again until either the call is over or a feature that requires Communications Manager is invoked, such as hold or transfer. If a device whose Communications Manager has failed tries to invoke such a feature, the phone display indicates a Communications Manager failure. The feature either fails or is unavailable (grayed out), depending on phone type. The call itself is not affected. A message also appears on the phone stating that the Communications Manager is down and the feature is not available.

Note   In certain cases, the failure of a Communications Manager could cause the call to drop. One example is if the call were connected through a Media Gateway Control Protocol (MGCP) PRI.

In small environments where there are only two Communications Managers, it is acceptable to use the publisher as a secondary Communications Manager. If you have more than 1250 users, it is not recommended to use the publisher as a secondary Communications Manager. Figure 1-1 shows a typical Communications Manager environment that can support up to 5000 phones. This figure is an example of what is referred to as one-to-one redundancy. In this configuration, 2500 phones register to Communications Managers B and C. Communications Managers D and E are secondary servers for these phones. Communications Manager A is the publisher, and no phones register to it. This example is based on the assumption that all the servers on which the Communications Manager is loaded are MCS-7835s or equivalent. Other server models support a different number of phones per server. For example, the MCS 7845 supports up to 7500 phones per server.

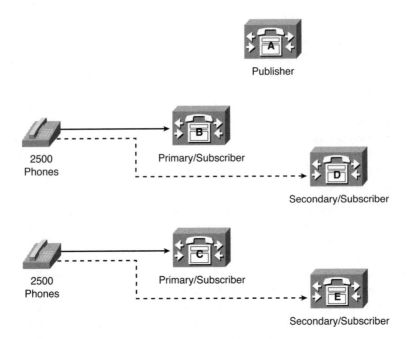

Figure 1-1   *One-to-One Redundancy Communications Manager Cluster*

Communications Manager Business Edition

Cisco offers a version of Communications Manager that is called Communications Manager Business Edition (CMBE). It is just like the standard Communications Manager with a few limitations. CMBE can only support up to 575 phones and does not support redundancy. In other words, there are no subscribers and only one publisher. It comes packaged with Unity Connection, which runs coresident (on the same server). This is an excellent "all in one" solution for small- to medium-size companies. All administration tasks and features configurations are performed the same as they are on the standard Communications Manager. They both use the same administration interface, and the software architecture is identical.

Communications Manager Devices

A large number of devices register with a Communications Manager, but they typically fall into one of the following categories:

■   Phones

■   Gateways

- Gatekeeper

- Media resources

Each of these devices has its own unique role within the Communications Manager environment, and this section briefly describes each one. For more information on these devices, refer to Appendix A.

Phones

A number of different model phones can be used in a Communications Manager environment. Table 1-1 lists and describes some of the more popular models.

Table 1-1 *Phone Models Used in a Communications Manager Environment*

Phone	Description
Model 7911	The 7911 is a single-line, entry-level phone. It offers a switch port in the back to which you can attach a PC. It only supports audio and text eXtensible Markup Language (XML) support.
Model 7942/7945	These phones support two lines and XML applications. These are considered midrange phones and are typically used in environments where two lines are adequate. They also have a switch port in the back for attaching a PC. The main difference between these phones is that the 7945 offers a color screen and the 7942 is only grayscale.
Model 7962/7965	These phones support four lines and XML applications. They also have a switch port in the back for attaching a PC. The main difference between these phones is that the 7965 offers a color screen while the 7962 is only grayscale.
Model 7975	This is an eight-line phone that offers a touch screen; this allows you to invoke certain features by touching the screen. It also supports XML applications.
Model 7925	The 7925 is a color-screen wireless phone that connects to the network through a wireless access point. The phone's shape and size are similar to a cell phone, but it only works in a Communications Manager environment.
IP Communicator	The Cisco IP Communicator is an application that runs on a PC and allows the PC to be used as a phone. Typically, a headset is attached to the PC, and the user can make and receive calls using the PC.
6900 Series	This is a series of cost-effective phones that work well for companies that are switching from a traditional analog phone system. While not as feature-rich as other phones, they offer a lower-cost entry yet still provide access to many Cisco Communication Manager's features.

Table 1-1 *Phone Models Used in a Communications Manager Environment*

Phone	Description
8900 Series	The 8900 series is a newer series of phone from Cisco that offers high-definition voice in addition to a high-resolution adjustable display. This series also includes USB ports, which support wired headsets.
9900 Series	This series is very similar to the 8900 but also supports a directly attached USB camera for video calls and Bluetooth. The 9971 also offers Wi-Fi.

Note One of the advanced features of many Cisco IP Phones is their capability to parse XML. These phones have an LCD screen on which the user can look up others in the directory, receive messages, log in and out of services, and perform many other functions. Through the use of XML programming, many companies have developed a variety of applications such as time clocks and inventory lookup.

Gateways Overview

As mentioned earlier, gateways are used to connect dissimilar systems together, such as connecting Communications Manager to the public switched telephone network (PSTN). The core requirements were discussed earlier, so this section examines the different types of gateways and how they communicate, meaning the protocol they use. There are three main protocols that are used today for communicating between Communications Manager and gateways. They are Media Gateway Control Protocol (MGCP), H.323, and Session Initiation Protocol (SIP). These are industry-standard protocols and offer similar features.

The type and number of trunks that a customer has also affects the type of gateway you select. Communications Manager is connected to the PSTN using either an analog or a digital trunk. The trunk used also affects the type of equipment you use for the gateway. Gateways differ in interface types and capacities. If analog trunks are used, typically a Foreign Exchange Office (FXO) port is used for each line. With analog lines, each call takes up a port on a gateway. This is not always a practical solution in a large environment. Typically, a T1 or E1 line is used to connect to the PSTN if a company needs more than a few lines. These types of trunks are normally more cost-effective if more than eight simultaneous connections to the PSTN are required.

So far, only using gateways as a way to connect to the PSTN has been discussed. Gateways are also needed to connect Communications Manager to traditional phones systems. In many cases, customers choose to integrate the Communications Manager into their existing voice solution and slowly replace the traditional PBX. This is done by connecting the Communications Manager to the traditional PBX through either analog or digital interfaces. The interface used depends on the volume of traffic expected to travel between the two phone systems and the interface available. For environments that expect large volumes of calls to travel between the phone systems, a T1 or E1 line is used. Figure 1-2 shows how this integration might look.

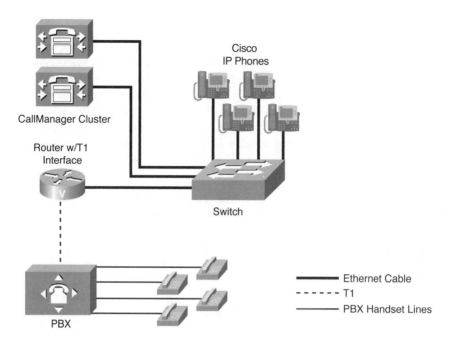

Figure 1-2   *Communications Manager–to–PBX Integration*

Note   The physical connection used to connect a traditional PBX with Communications Manager through T1 interfaces is a crossover T1 cable from the T1 interface of the traditional PBX to the T1 interface on the Communications Manager gateway.

Gateways are used not only to connect Communications Manager to traditional PBXs but also to connect multiple Communications Manager environments together. As mentioned earlier, two or more Communications Managers are known as a Communications Manager cluster. All the IP devices within a cluster can communicate with each other without a gateway. However, when two Communications Manager clusters need to be connected, a gateway must be configured. The connection between the two Communications Manager clusters is called an ICT (Intercluster Trunk). In earlier versions of Communications Manager, these were configured under gateways. Now they are referred to as trunks in the configuration menu. Chapter 3, "Deploying Devices," discusses these gateways more fully.

Gateways are also used to provide analog connectivity within a Communications Manager environment. Although the goal of VoIP is to use IP to transport voice whenever possible, there are times when an analog connection is required; modems and fax machines are examples. To connect an analog device such as a fax machine, a Foreign Exchange Station (FXS) port is required. A gateway with FXS ports allows analog devices to operate within a VoIP network.

Gatekeepers

Now that you understand how to connect Communications Manager to the other systems, you need to make sure that the path used to connect to another system does not become congested. It is not possible to allow more calls than a connection can handle when connecting to the PSTN or a traditional PBX using analog lines or voice T1s. However, when connecting devices using an IP connection, oversubscribing is possible. Oversubscribing occurs when more calls connect across a link than the link can adequately handle. When connecting multiple Communications Manager clusters together, you can use gatekeepers to prevent oversubscribing. This is referred to as Call Admission Control (CAC).

A gatekeeper is an H.323 device and typically runs on a router such as a 2800. Hence, Communications Manager communicates with it using H.323. Figure 1-3 shows a typical deployment. This diagram shows two Communications Manager clusters connected through an ICT. The gatekeeper manages the available bandwidth between the sites. The total allowable bandwidth for voice calls is configured in the gatekeeper.

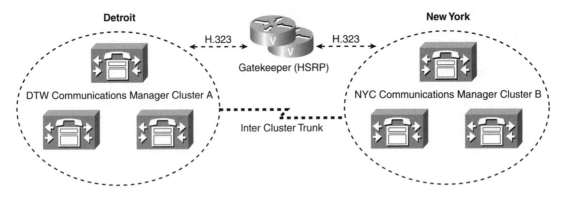

Figure 1-3 *Gatekeeper*

An example call flow would go something like this:

Step 1. Joe, who resides in Detroit, attempts to place a call to Fred, who resides in New York. The Communications Manager in Detroit sends a request to the gatekeeper to see whether there is enough bandwidth to place the call.

Step 2. The gatekeeper replies with either a confirmation (bandwidth is available) or a rejection (bandwidth is not available).

Step 3. If the bandwidth is available, the call setup proceeds and the Communications Manager in New York is informed that a call is being placed to Fred.

Step 4. The Communications Manager in New York then sends a request to the gatekeeper to see whether there is enough bandwidth for its side of the call.

Step 5. If the gatekeeper sends a confirmation, the call setup is complete, and Joe and Fred can talk about how the Lions actually won a game that weekend.

Much more occurs during setup. The previous example was presented to help you understand how a gatekeeper enforces CAC.

Assume for a moment that the gatekeeper in the previous example failed. What happens when the Detroit Communications Manager sends a request to the gatekeeper? Because the gatekeeper isn't working, the Communications Manager does not receive a confirmation and the call does not go through. How do you prevent a failed gatekeeper from negatively affecting call setup? The best solution is to have two gatekeepers. Once again, the theme running throughout this chapter is redundancy. Redundant gatekeepers can be configured by using Hot Standby Router Protocol (HSRP) or gatekeeper clustering. It is recommended that one of these solutions be implemented.

Not only can the gatekeeper be used for CAC purposes, but it can also determine the location of a requested device. This feature is discussed more fully in the CAC sections of Chapter 5, "Configuring Class of Service and Call Admission Control."

There are times when CAC is needed within a cluster. Because the gatekeeper is used when communicating outside a cluster, some other type of CAC must be implemented. For example, some type of CAC is needed within a cluster when a number of offices use the same Communications Manager at a central site.

CAC is accomplished in an IP WAN with centralized call processing deployment by configuring *locations* in Communications Manager. When configuring locations, the amount of bandwidth that is available for voice calls is entered in each location. When calls are placed between locations, bandwidth is deducted from the available bandwidth and calls are allowed or disallowed based on the available bandwidth. Locations are configured within Communications Manager, and no additional hardware is required. Often people ask whether they can use locations instead of a gatekeeper to save money. Remember that locations are designed to be used when the call is placed between two devices within the same cluster. It is best to use a gatekeeper for calls placed between separate networks.

Media Resources

To accomplish certain tasks such as conferencing and Music on Hold (MoH), Communications Manager needs to call upon additional resources. The core Communications Manager application does not have the capability to perform these tasks, so it relies on other resources, which are either hardware or software. Some resources reside on the same server as Communications Manager and others require additional hardware. The sections that follow describe the various resources.

Conference Bridge (CFB)

Conference bridges (CFB) are required for a caller to have a conference call with at least two other callers. CFBs can be either software or hardware; however, hardware is recommended. Software CFBs run as a process in Communications Manager, whereas hardware CFBs require additional equipment. Hardware CFBs require digital signal processors

(DSP). Not all devices that have DSPs can be configured as a CFB. The following devices can be configured as CFBs:

- Catalyst 6000 T1/E1 ports
- Catalyst 4000 Access Gateway Modules
- Supported Cisco routers with DSP farms

Note   The Catalyst 600 and 4000 can no longer be purchased from Cisco.

Transcoders

A transcoder allows devices that are using different codecs to communicate. Transcoders can change an incoming codec to another codec that the destination device can understand.

Note   A codec (which stands for compression/decompression) is used to express the format used to compress voice. An algorithm is used to compress voice so that it requires less bandwidth. The two most common codecs used in a Communications Manager environment are G.711 and G.729a.

MoH

Music on Hold (MoH) allows an audio source to be streamed to devices that are on hold. It is a process that runs on a Communications Manager. The audio can be streamed either multicast or unicast, and the codec can be configured. Up to 51 audio sources can be configured, including live audio that is plugged into a sound card (USB device) installed in the Communications Manager. It is also possible to configure the audio source to be streamed from a router.

Annunciator

The Annunciator is a software service that runs on the Communications Manager and provides audio announcements to callers. An example of this is if a caller dialed a number that Communications Manager could not process, the caller would hear a message something like, "The number you have dialed cannot be reached; please hang up and try your call again."

Now that you have an overview of the components required in a Communications Manager environment, you should review various deployment models. As this technology matures, the way it is deployed continues to evolve. It is essential that it be deployed only in a supported fashion. The next section discusses the various supported deployment models.

Understanding Communications Manager Deployment Models

There are essentially three main Communications Manager deployment models currently supported by Cisco. Although during the past few years these models have evolved to create what appear to be new deployment models, all support models fit into one of the following three categories of sites as described in the sections that follow:

- Single-site

- Multisite WAN with centralized call processing

- Multisite WAN with distributed call processing

Single-Site

In this model, a Communications Manager is deployed within a single building or perhaps in a campus area. However, some would argue a campus area would typically fall into the centralized model. In the past, the core theme behind this model was exclusive connectivity. There was no VoIP connectivity to any system outside its own. At present, service provides are offering SIP trunks that allow you to send calls outside of your system using VoIP. Any call placed to a destination outside its own is sent to the PSTN or an Internet Telephony Service Provider (ITSP).

Multisite WAN with Centralized Call Processing

A centralized deployment includes remote locations that have IP phones registering to the Communications Manager at the main site. Normally, there is only one Communications Manager cluster in a deployment such as this. Remote phones send all requests across the WAN to the Communications Manager. If the WAN fails and the phones have no local device to which to register, the phones are unusable.

Note Technology called Survivable Remote Site Telephony (SRST) has been developed that allows enables remote offices to have dial tone and make calls across the PSTN if the WAN or remote network fails. SRST runs on a router such as a 3800. The number of phones that can register to an SRST system depends on the hardware on which it is running. SRST is discussed in Chapter 6, "Configuring CUCM Features and Services."

Multisite WAN with Distributed Call Processing

There are multiple sites in this model, each having its own Communications Manager cluster. There is IP connectivity between them, and ICTs are configured to send the voice across. A gatekeeper is highly recommended in this deployment to prevent oversubscribing and assist in call routing.

Often companies that need distributed deployment also have remote sites with just a few phones. A Communications Manager cannot be justified for the remote site, so the phones register to a remote Communications Manager just as they would in a centralized deployment. When centralized and distributed deployments are merged together like this, it is referred to as a *hybrid deployment*.

Another form of this deployment is referred to as a Clustering over the IP WAN. In this scenario, a single Communications Manager cluster is split among multiple sites. For example, a publisher and a subscriber are in the Detroit office and a subscriber is at the New York office. The phones within the respective offices register with the local Communications Manager.

One of the major requirements in a deployment such as this is that, as of Communications Manager 6.1, the round-trip delay can be no greater than 80 ms (no greater than 40 ms one delay). The standard one-way delay allowed enabled for voice is 150 ms, so the requirements in this type of deployment are much more stringent. Figure 1-4 shows an example of a Clustering over the IP WAN deployment.

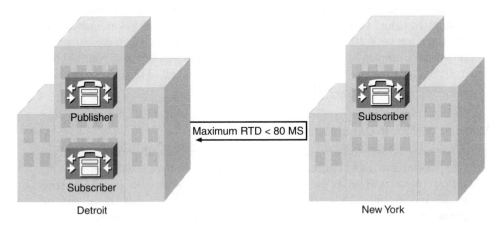

Figure 1-4   *Distributed Single Cluster*

The environment in which you deploy Communications Manager typically dictates which deployment model you choose. Regardless of which model is being deployed, it will most likely connect to an outside system such as the PSTN. When a call is placed outside the local system, the Communications Manager must know where to send the call based on the numbers dialed. The next section discusses how these call-routing decisions are made.

Route Plan Overview

Communications Manager knows about all devices that are registered within the cluster and knows how to route calls to any destination within the cluster. However, if a call is placed to a destination outside the cluster, Communications Manager needs to know where to send the call. This is the purpose of a route plan. A route plan is configured with Communications Manager to determine where to send calls based on the number that is dialed.

A route plan consists of a number of components, which are discussed in this section. Here Following is a brief description of each of the components that make up a dial plan. The list is in the order in which these devices must be configured. Later, the actual flow will be discussed.

Step 1.   **Device (gateway):** Gateways were explained earlier as devices that connect dissimilar systems. The gateway is the last component in a route plan because it sends the call to an outside system. As mentioned before, the gateway connects the Communications Manager system to the PSTN and to other destinations.

Step 2.   **Route group:** A route group is used to route the call to a gateway. Each route group includes at least one gateway, but because there is often more than one gateway, a call can be routed through a route group that can point to multiple gateways. The order in which the gateways appear in the route group determines which gateway the call is routed to first. If the intended gateway is not available, the route group sends the call to the next gateway in its list.

Step 3.   **Route list:** A route list is used to route the call to a route group. Each route list must have at least one route group in it. Just as a route group can point to multiple gateways, a route list can point to multiple route groups. The order in which the route groups appear in the route list determines which route group the call is routed to first. If all the devices in the first route group are unavailable, the route list routes the call to the next route group in the list. If all gateways in the route groups within the list are unavailable, the call fails.

Step 4.   **Route pattern:** When a user dials a number, Communications Manager compares the digits dialed against all the patterns it knows. As mentioned earlier, Communications Manager knows about all devices within the cluster. If the number dialed matches the number assigned to a device in the cluster, Communications Manager sends the call to that device. If the call is placed to a device outside the cluster, a matching route pattern must be configured in the Communications Manager. Because it is impossible to enter every possible number that might be dialed, wildcards are used to allow a single route to pattern-match multiple numbers. An example of one of the wildcards used in Communications Manager is an X. In a route pattern, an X matches any single digit 0–9. For example, a route pattern of 5XXX would match all numbers from 5000 to 5999.

Typical Call Flow

Now that you understand the basic components of a dial plan, examining a typical call flow is in order. Communications Manager in this example has the route pattern 9.1248547XXXX:

Step 1.   A user dials 912485479000.

Step 2.   Communications Manager analyzes the dialed digits and determines that the closest match it knows of is 91248547XXXX.

Step 3.   Communications Manager routes the call to the route list that has been configured for the route pattern 91248547XXXX.

Step 4.   The call is then routed to the first route group in the route list.

Step 5.   If there is more than one gateway in the route group, the call is sent to the first
gateway in the list. If the gateway is available, the call is sent out that gateway.

At times, a dialed number matches more than one pattern. When this occurs,
Communications Manager selects the closest match. For example, if a user dials 5010 and
Communications Manager has 5XXX and 50XX as route patterns, 50XX is selected
because there are only 100 possible matches, whereas there are 1000 matches with the
route pattern 5XXX.

Wildcards

Up to this point, the only route pattern wildcard that has been discussed is the X.
Chapter 4, "Implementing a Route Plan," discusses wildcards further. For now, the following sections present wildcards that can be used in route patterns.

The Wildcard @

This wildcard matches any phone number that is part of a public number plan such as the
North American Numbering Plan (NANP). The easiest way to understand what numbers
are part of NANP is that any number you can dial from a home phone in North America
would be part of the NANP. This includes numbers such as 911 and all international numbers. The NANP is installed by default, but other numbering plans can be
downloaded/installed.

The Wildcard !

This wildcard represents any digit and any number of digits. At first, people think that "!"
is the same thing as the X wildcard, but remember that the X represents only a single
digit. The "!" can represent any number of digits.

The Wildcard [x-y]

This wildcard represents a single digit range. For example, 5[3-5] would match 53, 54, or
55. The numbers inside the brackets always represent a range and match only a single digit.

> **Note**   In a pattern such as 5[25-7], the only matches are 52, 55, 56, and 57. When people
> first look at this pattern, they think it matches 525, 526, and 527, but remember that the
> brackets can only represent a single digit.

The Wildcard [^x-y]

This wildcard represents an exclusion range, that is, any single digit that is not included in
the range matches. For example, the pattern 5[^3-8] matches 50, 51, 52, and 59.

Calling Privileges

While creating a dial plan, you will find that some individuals within the company are allowed to place calls that others are not. For example, some companies do not allow all employees to make long-distance calls. Also, it is highly unlikely that you would want to allow international calls to be placed from a lobby phone. These issues are addressed by assigning calling privileges to devices. Calling privileges are configured by creating what is referred to as a class of control. The term class of service (CoS) was used in previous versions of Communications Manager, but it is now configured within the class of control area.

Note   The terms *class of service (CoS)* and *class of control* are often used when talking about calling privileges. These two terms are synonymous with calling privileges. Those of you that come from a data background should not confuse this with the QoS component known as CoS. Although it stands for the same thing, class of service, it does not mean the same thing. Think of it this way: CoS in the data world is about prioritizing; CoS in the IP telephony world involves rights and restrictions.

Class of control is essentially a way to determine what destinations a given device can reach. For example, if you want to call someone in Germany, your CoS would have to allow international calls. In the same regard, if you want to prevent a device from calling Germany, you would assign a CoS that does not allow international dialing.

A class of control comprises two components, a Calling Search Space (CSS) and partitions. A solid understanding of these two components is essential to create an effective class of control. These two components seem to cause some confusion for those who are new to the concept, but at the core, they are simple concepts.

The simplest way to view this concept is to imagine a partition as a lock and a CSS as a key chain. If a number has a lock on it, you need the key on your key chain to reach that number. Simple, right? Well, as with anything, as things grow they can become more complex.

Partitions are assigned to anything that can be called, such as a directory number or a route pattern. Calling search spaces are assigned to anything that can place a call, such as phones and gateways. The configuration of these components is discussed in Chapter 5. Taking a closer look at how the components are configured can help clarify the concept.

Figure 1-5 shows how assigning partitions to a pattern and CSS to phones affect dialing privileges.

The two phones in Figure 1-5, Phone A and Phone B, each have a different CSS that determines where they can call. They both dial 912485479000. Based on the CSS of the phone, a match is determined. The only pattern that the dialed digits match is the 9.1248547XXXX pattern, which has the LocalLD partition. Because Phone A's CSS allows access to the LocalLD partition, its call goes through. However, Phone B's CSS does not allow access to the LocalLD partition, so that call fails.

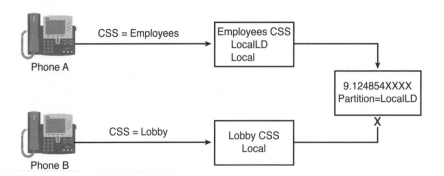

Figure 1-5   *CoS Example*

> **Note**   If you feel a little uncertain on this concept, fear not. I have had many students who worked with CSS and partitions for years and still didn't have a handle on it. The best advice is to start small, such as the example in Figure 1-5, and build on that. Although the design can become complex, the way that CSS and partitions work does not change and is simple.

As you can see, the components that are required to implement a Cisco Communications Manager solution are quite extensive. This section has presented only a high-level overview. By now, you should understand the importance of a solid infrastructure and be able to describe the role that redundancy plays in providing reliable service. Furthermore, you should be comfortable with the various devices that can register to Communications Manager and the various deployment models of Communications Manager. Finally, you should understand the basics behind dial plans and see how CoS can affect a device's capability to reach certain destinations.

Unified Messaging Overview

Typically, when you have a phone, you want to have a way for someone to leave a message when you cannot take the call. This means that most Communications Manager environments will have some type of voicemail system. Cisco offers three voicemail solutions: Unity, Unity Connection, and Unity Express. That is right; they all contain the word Unity in their name. This sometimes causes some confusion. This section looks at the two systems that are most often deployed with CUCM. Unity Express is a solution more often found in environments that have CUCM Express deployed and, for that reason, is outside of the scope of this course.

First, there is Unity. Many people view Unity as a voicemail solution, and although it does handle all the functions of a voicemail system, it is much more than that. Unity is a completely unified communication system. That is, it not only handles voicemail functions for a company, but it also can integrate into an existing email and faxing infrastructure. Because the voicemail, email, and faxing systems can be integrated with one another, they can use a single message store. This means that end users can now retrieve all their voicemail, email, and faxes from one location. In the past, users would have to use the phone to get their voicemail, the PC to get their email, and a fax machine to retrieve their faxes. With unified messaging, all these messages can be retrieved from a single device, be it a PC or a phone. Using a PC, users can read their email and faxes or listen to their voicemail over the PC speakers. The users can also use a phone to retrieve their voicemail and email, because Unity's text-to-speech engine converts the email to a synthesized voice and streams it over the phone.

The other voicemail system is Unity Connection. Recently it has risen in popularity. It offers many of the same features as Unity and a few that Unity does not. The main difference, though, is not in the features it offers but rather in its infrastructure. Although Unity requires an external mail store (Exchange or Dominos), Unity Connection does not. It stores the messages on-box within its own store. However, even though Unity Connection does not require an email server such as Exchange, it can still integrate with an email server so that features such as listening to your email over the phone or checking your voicemail from your email client are still available.

Both products are powerful applications that require a variety of components to accomplish its tasks. The topics covered in this section provide you with a good understanding of the components within these systems and how these components fit into the solution. The areas covered in this section are as follows:

- Software architecture

- Call flow

- Call handlers

- Subscribers

- Networking

Software Architecture

Although Unity and Unity Connection offer similar services and features, their software architecture is not similar at all, as you see in the following sections.

Unity Software Architecture

Unlike some applications, Unity is not a standalone application. That is, in and of itself, it cannot provide voicemail services. Unity depends on a number of other applications to provide its array of services. If Unity were merely a voicemail system, it could have been designed not to require other applications. However, because it is a unified communications solution requires that it integrate with a company's email server. Because both a voicemail system and an email server have to send, receive, and store messages, Unity simply uses the existing email server to handle these functions. This is not to say that Unity does not handle the messages. This is discussed later. The various software components with which Unity interfaces include a mail store; a directory, such as Active Directory (AD); Structured Query Language (SQL); and Internet Information Server (IIS).

A closer look at the software architecture can help you understand the need for each component.

The discussion begins at the lowest level of the software architecture. The first layer of any software architecture is the operating system (OS). The current version of Unity requires Windows 2003 Server OS. Unity integrates tightly with Microsoft's AD when using Exchange 2003. Previous versions of Unity supported Windows 2000, so don't worry if the version you run isn't on Windows 2003.

Note   Much like Communications Manager, Unity is supported only on Cisco-approved servers. Currently there are a number of models approved by Cisco. These servers can be purchased from Cisco or directly from HP or IBM. You can find the most current list of approved servers by searching for "Cisco Unity supported platforms list" at Cisco.com.

After the OS is on the server, other supporting applications have to be available before Unity can be configured. Unity depends on an outside message store to store messages. Currently you can use Microsoft Exchange or Lotus Notes as the message store. If Exchange is used, it can run on the same server as Unity, but this should be done only if you use Unity as a voicemail-only solution. If Unity is used as a unified communications solution, Exchange should be loaded on a separate server. If Notes is the message store, it must run on a separate server.

Note   As of Unity 8.0, Domino is no longer supported as a mail store.

Note   If Notes is the message store, an additional piece of software is required. It is called Domino Unified Communication Services (DUCS). This can be purchased from IBM and is used to allow the transfer of information between Unity and the Domino environment.

All the information entered into Unity must be stored. Unity uses SQL as its database, and most of the information you enter, such as usernames and phone passwords, are stored in SQL. Hence, SQL must run on the Unity server.

As mentioned earlier, Unity integrates with AD when using Exchange 2003, so the server must be part of an AD. If the Unity server is a standalone computer, that is, it is not part of an existing AD, it must be configured with AD and act as its own domain controller. Some of the information—for example, name, telephone number, and alias stored in SQL—is replicated to the AD.

Unity is similar to Communications Manager in that most of the configuration of Unity is done through a web browser interface. This requires that IIS run on the Unity server. During the installation process, IIS is installed. Additional tools perform many of the same tasks that are accomplished using the web browser interface. These tools are discussed in Chapter 11, "Exploring Unity/Connection Tools." The main advantage to using

the browser interface is that no additional software has to be loaded on a PC to adminis-
ter Unity. This is a useful feature when you find yourself away from your desk needing to
change something in Unity.

Unity Connection Architecture

In contrast to Unity, Unity Connection is a standalone application. That is, it can be a
self-contained voicemail solution without any dependency on any separately installed
third-party software. Installing Unity Connection is as simple as inserting the disk into a
new server, powering it up, and answering a few questions. This install process installs the
OS and all required applications. The install for Unity Connection is much easier and
faster than that of Unity.

The OS that is used is often referred to as the VTG OS. VTG is an acronym for Voice
Technology Group. This is the same Linux-based OS that is used for Communications
Manager. Unity Connection stores all its information in an Informix database, just as
Communications Manager does. Unity Connection and Communications Manager share
a lot of the same software infrastructure. This is one reason why Unity Connection and
Communications Manager can run on the same server if you deploy Communications
Manager Business Edition.

Just as with Communications Manager and Unity, most of the configuration for Unity
Connection is done through a web browser.

Following the Call Flow

Before discussing the actual components that determine the path a call takes, now take a
high-level look at the various ways that a call can enter either of these systems and see
how each type is dealt with. Because Unity and Unity Connection handle calls in much
the same way, this section applies to both products. To keep things simple, both Unity
and Unity Connection are referred to as "the system" for the rest of this section.

Typically, calls are forwarded to voicemail systems because the phone called is either
busy or unanswered. When the system receives a call, it examines the reason that it is
receiving the call. The phone system that forwarded the call includes a call-forwarded reason to the system. In this case, it was forwarded because the called party was busy or did
not answer. If the call is forwarded because the caller did not answer, the system plays
the called party's standard greeting. If the call were forwarded because the called party
was on the phone, the system plays the called party's busy greeting.

In Unity, each user is known as a subscriber, but in Unity Connection, each user is known
as a user. To keep consistent in this section, they are referred to as users. Each user can
have five different greetings, which are as follows:

- **Standard:** Played during open hours when the user does not answer the phone. This is
  the default greeting and is always enabled.

- **Busy:** Played when the user is on another call.

- **Closed:** Played after hours.

- **Internal:** Played when another user reaches voicemail.

- **Alternate/holiday:** If enabled, always plays regardless of the forwarded reason or time of day. This greeting can be used as a vacation greeting. Note: Unity refers to this greeting as the Alternate; UC refers to it as the Holiday.

The system is often used as an auto-attendant, which allows all incoming calls to be answered by the system and then forwarded to the desired destination. In this instance, the call is not forwarded and is considered a direct call. The system handles direct calls differently than forwarded calls. The first thing the system does is attempt to determine whether the caller is a user. It does this by identifying whether the caller ID matches any phone number that is associated with a user. If it finds a match, it assumes that the user is calling and asks for the user's password.

Note   All users have at least one phone number associated with them. This is their phone extension. Additional numbers can be assigned to subscribers. They are referred to as alternate extensions. A common use for alternate extensions is to associate a subscriber's cell phone or home number so that when they call in to check messages they are taken directly to the login prompt.

If the system determines that the caller ID is not associated with a user, the call is sent to the system's opening greeting. An opening greeting is the main greeting that outside callers hear when they reach the auto-attendant. It might say something like "Thank you for calling Bailey, Inc. If you know your party's extension, you can dial it at any time during this greeting." The options offered to the caller are determined by the system administrator based on the company's needs.

Exploring Call Handlers

Often companies that use the system as an auto-attendant create a menu that can lead outside callers to the proper department. You have probably experienced memorably frustrating menus. To create menus in the system, objects titled *call handlers* are created. One call handler was mentioned in the previous section. The opening greeting is a call handler. The easiest way to think of a call handler is as an object that can be used to help route calls. You can also think of call handlers as the building blocks that make up the menu system.

There are primarily three types of call handlers that can be used within the system:

- System call handlers
- Interview handlers
- Directory handlers

Table 1-2 *Call Handler Parameters*

Configuration Page	Parameter
Profile (Handler Basics in Unity Connection)	Name, Creation date, Owner (Unity only), Recorded voice, Schedule, Extension, Language, Switch (PBX)
Transfer	Status, Transfer incoming call, Transfer type, Rings to wait, If busy, Announce, Introduce, Confirm, Ask caller's name
Greeting	Greeting, Status, Source, Allow caller input, After greeting action, Reprompt, Number of reprompts
Caller Input	Allow extension dialing during greeting, Milliseconds to wait, Lock key, Action
Message	Message recipient, Max message length, After message action, Caller edit, Urgent marking
Call Handler Owners (Unity Connection only)	Owner of the call handler

The system call handler is used to build the menu system and typically contains a recorded prompt and asks the caller for input, such as "Press 1 for sales, press 2 for technical support, or hold on the line for further assistance." Within Unity, these types of call handlers have no special classification and can be referred to as general call handlers. They are simply known as call handlers. Within Unity Connection, they are called system call handlers. Table 1-2 lists five configurable pages for a call handler and some of the parameters found in each. These parameters vary slightly between Unity and Unity Connection, but this table gives you a good idea of the number of parameters that need to be configured for each call handler. More detail is given to these parameters in the "Configuring Call Handlers" section found in Chapter 9, "Call Management."

The next type of call handler is called an interview handler. It is used to extract information from the caller that requires asking more than one question. An interview handler can contain up to 20 questions. It allows the user time to answer between the questions. Unlike the call handler described previously, there are only two sets of parameters that need to be configured for the interview handler. Table 1-3 shows these parameters in the "Creating Advanced Call Routing Systems" section found in Chapter 9.

Note An example used for an interview handler would be a class survey hotline. After students take a class, they can call a number and answer five questions. The answers are later transcribed and entered into the school's database.

Table 1-3 *Interview Handler Parameters*

Parameter	Description
Profile (Handler Basics in Unity Connection)	Name, Creation date, Owner (Unity only), Recorded voice, Extension, Language, Deliver response to, Response urgency, After interview action
Question	Questions number, Question text, Maximum length in seconds (for response), Recorded question

The third type of call handler is known as a directory handler. The directory handler allows callers to dial by name. As the caller spells the person's name using the dial pad, the system searches to find all matching names. The system then offers the caller name choices and allows the caller to choose the party to which they would like to be forwarded. The system allows multiple directory handlers so that each department could have a separate one if wanted. Directory handlers have four sets of configurable parameters, as shown in Table 1-4. More detail is given to these parameters in the "Configuring Directory Handlers" section found in Chapter 9.

Figure 1-6 shows a typical system menu system flow chart. The various types of call handlers that have been discussed are shown in this figure. Each of the boxes represents a call handler.

Table 1-4 *Directory Handler Parameters*

Parameter	Description
Profile (Handler Basics in Unity Connection)	Name, Creation date, Owner, Recorded voice, Extension, Language, Play all names, Search scope (Unity Connection only), Search result behavior (Unity Connection only)
Search Options (Unity only)	Search in, Search by
Match List Options (Unity only)	On unique, Announce matched using, Announce extension
Caller Input	No input timeout, Last input timeout, Repeat prompt, Send on to exit
Greeting (Unity Connection only)	Greeting

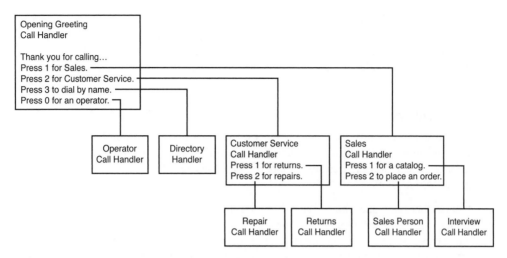

Figure 1-6   *Example Menu System Flow Chart*

> Tip   It is a good idea to draw your menu system in a flow chart form before creating it on the system. This helps ensure that all the call handlers are linked and that the flow makes sense.

Typically call handlers are used to route a call through the system. However, they can be configured to take messages. If a call handler is configured to take a message, the message must be sent to a user. Call handlers are simply database objects and do not have mailboxes.

As you can see, call handlers are a fundamental part of the system. Even the most basic system contains a number of call handlers. So a solid understanding of how they are configured and work is essential. This section has only touched the surface of the power and flexibility of call handlers. Once again, you are encouraged to review the listed references in Appendix A for further study of this technology.

Defining Various Types of Users

Now that you have a good understanding of how calls are routed through a system, we take a look at the users. As mentioned earlier, in Unity, users are referred to as subscribers, while in Unity Connection, they are simply referred to as users. The following sections look at each type separately to help you better understand the differences.

Unity Connection Users

Within Unity Connection there are three types of users: those with voice mailboxes, those without voice mailboxes, and contacts. Users with voice mailboxes are the type of users that you will be creating the majority of the time. Users without voice mailboxes are users for people that need administrative access to the system but do not need voice-mail on the system. The main purpose of contacts is to add someone to the directory who does not have an account on the system. It is common to list users who have a voice-mail account on a different system. This allows voicemails to be forwarded to them.

Unity Subscribers

When it comes to Unity, there are a number of different types of subscribers. This is because Unity relies on another application such as Exchange or Dominos to store the messages. The following sections explore the various types of subscribers that can be created within Unity.

A subscriber is anyone who has an account on the Unity system. Typically, Unity sub-scribers' messages are stored on the message store that is associated with Unity. However, subscribers are sometimes created where the mailbox actually resides on a dif-ferent voicemail system. The following sections explore all the types of users who can be configured in Unity and indicate the appropriate uses for each. Six different types of subscribers can be configured as follows: Exchange, Domino, Internet, AMIS-a, VPIM, and bridge.

Exchange Subscriber

An Exchange subscriber is the most common type of subscriber. This subscriber, as the name implies, has its messages stored on an Exchange server. Exchange subscribers have access to voicemail using the phone, also called the telephone user interface (TUI). If licensed, they might also have access to voicemail using a PC. This is referred to as the graphical user interface (GUI).

Note   Exchange subscribers can be divided into two subtypes of subscribers. One type is referred to as voicemail-only. These subscribers use the Exchange server for voicemail messaging purposes only. Furthermore, they cannot retrieve their email through Unity or their voicemail through a PC. The other type is known as unified messaging. These sub-scribers have both their email and voicemail stored on the Exchange server and can access both from either a phone or a PC.

Domino Subscriber

A Domino subscriber is similar to an Exchange subscriber except that it uses Domino as the message store, not Exchange. Unlike Exchange subscribers, a Domino subscriber must be a unified messaging user. Domino is not supported as a voicemail-only solution.

Note   As of Unity 8.0 Domino is no longer supported.

Internet Subscriber

An Internet subscriber does not have a mailbox on the message store associated with Unity. The mailbox is an Internet email account. This type of account allows outside workers to be listed in the directory and receive voicemail without any type of access to Unity. This type of subscriber is generally used to provide voicemail for contract employees who work from their homes. When messages are left for Internet subscribers, they are delivered to the Internet email account as WAV file attachments, and the subscribers retrieve them when they download their mail.

AMIS-a (Audio Messaging Interchange Specification–Analog) Subscriber

This type of subscriber is used when Unity is connected to a non-Unity voicemail system using the AMIS protocol. The subscriber's mailbox is located on the non-Unity voicemail system. This type of subscriber has no direct access to Unity.

Voice Profile for Internet Mail (VPIM) Subscriber

This type of subscriber is used when Unity is connected to a non-Unity voicemail system using the VPIM protocol. The subscriber's mailbox is located on the non-Unity voicemail system. This type of subscriber has no direct access to Unity.

Bridge Subscriber

This type of subscriber is used when Unity is connected to an Octel voicemail system using bridge networking. The subscriber's mailbox is located on the Octel voicemail system. This type of subscriber has no direct access to Unity.

User Parameters

When creating and configuring a user, you notice that a number of the parameters are similar to those found in a call handler. This is because each user has an associated call handler. When you create a user, a call handler is also created. So, when you are configuring certain user parameters, you are actually configuring the call handler associated with that user. To help illustrate this, Table 1-5 shows all the Unity parameter sets. Those marked with an asterisk (*) are the parameters used to create the call handler. While the names of the parameters in Unity Connection vary slightly, the concept is the same.

Note   Not all Unity subscribers have all the parameters listed in Table 1-5. The parameters available depend on the type of subscriber that you are creating. In some cases, there are some parameters that are not listed in this table. Only the most common parameters are listed.

A user is more than just a call handler, as you can see by the additional parameters that need to be configured. A user can be seen as a collection of objects, one being the call handler. It is the call handler's job to offer the caller any available choices and play the greeting. Another piece of a user is the mailbox where the voice messages are stored. For a Unity subscriber, the mailbox typically resides on an Exchange server. There are also additional user settings. These settings are not part of the mailbox or the call handler. These attributes deal with things such as phone passwords, message notification, and CoS. These settings, much like the call handlers, are stored in the database.

Table 1-5 *Subscriber Parameters*

Parameter	Description
Profile*	Name, Display name, CoS, Extension, FAX ID, Recorded voice, Schedule, Time zone, Self-enrollment setting, Directory, Language, Switch (PBX)
Account	Account status, GUI access status, Creation date, Last phone contact, Billing ID, Call handlers owned, Windows NT account status
Phone Password	User cannot change password, Must change on next login, Never expires, Password, Date of last change
Private Lists	Private list number, Name of list, Recorded name, Current members
Conversation	Menu style, Volume, Language, Time format, Send to, Identify by, Play recorded name, Message counts, Message type menus, Sort by, Message number, Time Message was sent
Call Transfer*	Transfer to, Transfer type, Rings to wait, If busy, Announce, Introduce, Confirm, Ask caller's name
Greetings*	Greeting, Status, Source, Allow caller input, After greeting action, Reprompt, Number of reprompts
Caller Input*	Allow extension dialing during greeting, Milliseconds to wait, Lock key, Action
Messages*	Max message length, After message action, Caller edit, Urgent marking, Language, MWI
Message Notification	Device, Phone number, Extra digits, Dialing options, Status, Schedule
Alternate Extensions	Alternate extensions
Alternate Names	Alternate name
Features	Broadcast messages, Message locator, Message security

*Parameters used to create the call handler

Note The term *class of service (CoS)* is sometimes confusing because it means different things depending on the technology it is referring to. When the term is used with Unity/Connection, it is referring to rights and access, such as what features a user has access to.

As you can see, many parameters need to be configured for each user. If you had to con-figure each parameter for every user, it would take far too long. To simplify this task, objects known as *templates* are used when creating users. A template defines how the parameters should be set by default. Typically there are large groups of users that need similar settings. A template is created for each group, and after creation, a user can be edited as needed.

Note   It is important to understand that templates are significant only at the point of user creation. Changing a template after a user is created has no effect on that user.

As previously stated, not all subscribers have all the parameters listed in Table 1-5. Parameters depend on the type of subscriber that is being created.

Networking Overview

Both Unity and Unity Connection have the capability to network with each other and other voicemail systems. The following sections explore the types of networking that are supported by each system.

Unity Networking

Unity has the capability to network with other types of voicemail systems. This feature allows employees of large companies that have multiple voicemail systems to efficiently exchange voicemails regardless of the system on which they are homed. Cisco under-stands that companies have a substantial investment in current solutions and might not be ready to do a total cut-over. Often Unity is deployed for a portion of the users as a pilot. It is easier to convince the client to start with a pilot because Unity can talk with other systems and allow the end user to use the most common features.

Following are four types of Unity networking:

- Digital
- VPIM
- AMIS
- Bridge

Typically, people think of networking as plugging two PCs into an Ethernet jack that allows enables them to communicate. Unity networking is not just plugging an Ethernet cable into the Unity server. Unity networking refers to connecting Unity to another voice-mail system. This can be done in a variety of ways, which are described in the following sections. The overall goal is to have Unity interface with another voicemail system as seamlessly as possible.

Digital Networking

Digital networking allows multiple Unity systems within the same directory, such as AD, to seamlessly interact with one another. When using digital networking, the Unity systems have the ability to share the directories of each other. This allows outside callers to search for any subscriber, regardless of which Unity server they are associated with. This type of networking offers many other features, which is discussed in Chapter 10, "Implementing Unity Networking."

VPIM Networking

VPIM networking allows Unity to interface with non-Unity voicemail servers through a TCP/IP link. This link can be an Internet connection or a private network. The non-Unity voicemail system must support VPIM, which is often an add-on that requires an additional investment.

AMIS Networking

AMIS networking allows Unity to interface with a non-Unity voicemail system across analog lines. This is typically done across the PSTN, but it might also be used for in-house migration. AMIS is not as efficient as VPIM, because it uses analog lines, so trans-missions can be more time-consuming. For example, a 5-minute message sent to five peo-ple through AMIS takes 25 minutes, plus setup and teardown time. With VPIM, the transmission time is much shorter. (The actual transmission time depends on the speed of the connection.) The non-Unity voicemail system must support AMIS, which is often an add-on that requires an additional investment.

Bridge Networking

Bridge networking is used to connect a Unity system with an Octel voicemail system. Bridge networking is unique in that it requires an additional server. This is called the Unity bridge server. The bridge server communicates with the Unity server through a TCP/IP connection and with the Octel server across analog lines. The bridge server acts as a translator between the Octel analog protocol and Unity's digital networking protocol. The overall message delivery can experience the same type of delay that is common with AMIS because they both use analog connectivity. Octel networking adds features that are not found in VPIM or AMIS and creates a more feature-rich environment. Bridge net-working is recommended if a company is going to gradually migrate from Octel to Unity.

So which one should you use? The voicemail solution that you choose to integrate with will often dictate the answer. If you have a choice between AMIS and VPIM, most often VPIM is recommended. As mentioned previously, when integrating with Octel, bridge networking should be used. When connecting multiple Unity systems, digital networking is the solution if the Unity systems share the same Active Directory (AD). If they do not share the same AD, the solution is VPIM networking.

Unity Connection Networking

Unity Connection offers two types of networking. The first, digital networking, is used when networking UC systems within a company. The other, VPIM networking, is used to network UC to non-UC voicemail systems and UC systems not within the same company.

Unity Connection digital networking is similar to Unity's digital networking; the big difference is that UC does not use AD. This means that each UC needs to synchronize its directory with the other UC systems on the network. The net effect is the same as it is with Unity, but a little more configuration might be required.

Unity Connection also supports VPIM networking. This is used when networking with a Unity server or other voicemail system. The remote voicemail system must support VPIM. Keep in mind that the remote system will most likely require a license for this feature. VPIM is also used when networking UC systems when digital networking is not an option.

Securing the Environment

With the proliferation of viruses and malicious attacks on computer systems today, it is not just wise, but mandatory, to protect your systems. Many network administrators remember Nimda and Blaster all too well. Even some admins that thought they were fairly well protected got hit. Sometimes it seems that just when one type of attack can be defended against, another begins. To make matters worse, in an IP telephony environment, you need to protect the system not only from computer-related attacks but also from the types of attacks common to voice systems, such as toll fraud. You might as well face it now: There is no silver bullet that completely and forever protects you. But there are steps you can take to make sure that you are not an easy mark. The following sections examine some of the current security concerns that you should be aware of. When possible, solutions are offered. Remember, this is an ongoing battle. The goal of these sections is to make you aware of a few of the security issues and encourage you to be vigilant in protecting your system.

Securing the Operating System

Because Unity uses Windows as its operating system, it is vulnerable to the security issues that exist for Windows. Because Microsoft is undeniably the most commonly installed OS, it is a large target. For various reasons, some people hold grudges against Microsoft and find it fun to attack systems running on a Microsoft OS. Whether they are valid grudges, it is important to protect your systems. What is important is that attacks do occur, and you need to protect your system.

Typically an attack is virus driven. The damage viruses cause can range from something benign to data corruption and destruction. All viruses should be considered dangerous.

For this reason, virus protection software should be installed on all systems. Cisco has qualified the following list of antivirus software for use with Unity 8.0:

■ CA Anti-Virus for the Enterprise version 8.0 and later (formerly called eTrust Antivirus)

■ Computer Associates InoculateIT for Microsoft Windows

■ McAfee

■ ePolicy Orchestrator

■ GroupShield Domino (Unity 7.x and earlier only)

■ NetShield for Microsoft Windows

■ Symantec

■ AntiVirus Corporate Edition

■ Norton AntiVirus for IBM Lotus Notes/Domino (Unity 7.x and earlier only)

■ Norton AntiVirus for Microsoft Exchange

■ Norton AntiVirus for Microsoft Windows

■ Trend Micro

■ ScanMail for Lotus Notes (Unity 7.x and earlier only)

■ ScanMail for Microsoft Exchange

■ ServerProtect for Microsoft Windows

Because Unity uses SQL, keep in mind that in the past, SQL has been the target of attacks. So, attention should be given to this. The best way to secure any SQL installation is to ensure that the latest approved security patches are applied.

Note   *Remember to check that a patch has been tested and approved by Cisco before you apply it.* In some cases, there are special instructions on how to load certain patches. It could even be required that you load only patches available directly from Cisco. Don't assume that all Microsoft patches can be loaded on Unity.

Communications Manager Security Issues

Protecting the system from outside threats is only half the battle. There are also internal threats that exist. Ever since a telephone system has existed, people have tried to exploit it. These exploitations range from illegal wiretapping to toll fraud.

Earlier in this chapter, it was mentioned that a PC can be connected to the back of the phone, allowing both devices to share a single Ethernet port. Although this is an efficient use of ports, if not properly configured, both devices could be using the same VLAN. When both devices are on the same VLAN, it is possible for a PC to capture voice traffic. A tool called Voice Over Misconfigured Internet Telephones (VOMIT) can then reassemble the captured data into a WAV file. The conversation could be played back on a PC. By ensuring that the voice traffic is on a separate VLAN, you help prevent this from occurring, but that alone is not enough. You also need to prevent data and voice networks from communicating with each other as much as possible. It is understood that there are times when the networks might need to send packets to each other, but this traffic should be managed by a firewall to ensure that only the desired traffic is allowed through. Earlier, it was recommended that voice and data traffic be separated on different VLANs so that the voice could be prioritized. Now you see that it can protect not only the quality of the voice but also protect the voice from prying ears.

PC-based phones, such as Cisco IP Communicator, introduce the same problem that having voice and data on the same VLAN produces. Because a PC is being used as phone, the voice traffic is sent on the data VLAN. This allows prying ears on the data network to capture the conversation. For this reason, a properly designed network has voice and data on separate VLANs.

Another often-overlooked area that can be exploited is allowing rogue phones to autoregister. This occurs when autoregistration is used during deployment and not turned off or restricted later. Autoregistration is a useful tool during some deployments. It allows a phone to be plugged into the system and register without having to configure it in Communications Manager first. It is most often used in greenfield deployments. However if autoregistration is not disabled after the initial deployment, rogue phones could register to Communications Manager. This seems like a minor issue until you factor in that if the dial plan has not been secured, a user on a rogue phone could place a call anywhere in the world without detection until the bill arrives.

The administration of Communications Manager should also be considered when securing the voice system. If people get access to Communications Manager administration, they can do anything from changing users' class of control to shutting down gateways, or even the entire system. Security is often a double-edged sword: Too little and anyone can do anything, and too much and no one can do anything. Often, you find that you want to allow limited access to the administration interface. An example might be to allow someone to add users to the Communications Manager directory. You do not want this person to change the dial plan. A Communications Manager add-on, called Multi-Level Access (MLA), enables you to do this by granting limited administration access to individuals. An even higher level of security can be implemented by restricting which physical system can access the Communications Manager through the use of an access list.

The preceding few paragraphs discussed only a few security issues that you need to address. The task of completely securing a Communications Manager environment can seem daunting at times, but all possible efforts must be taken to ensure that the system is protected from both external and internal threats.

Unity Security Issues

Unity offers a new way of looking at message management. It is now possible to store all voicemail, email, and faxes in a single location. In addition, it is possible to retrieve them from nearly anywhere in the world. Of course to do this, there must be a way to access the system. Although this comes as no surprise, remember, at every entry point, there are people trying to exploit that point of entry. Because of the many features that Unity offers, there are many points of entry. By default, Unity enables access through the phone, web browser, and email client. All of these entry points add to the task of securing the system. Securing Unity is not a trivial task, and sufficient attention must be given to this task. The following are just a few examples of areas that must be secured.

Unity uses a third-party message store, and currently this is either Microsoft Exchange or Lotus Notes. Both of these systems are subject to the same types of attacks as any email systems. There are attacks aimed specifically at these systems. Securing these systems requires that you stay current on all security-related patches.

Note *Remember to check that a patch has been tested and approved by Cisco before you apply it.* In some cases, there are special instructions on how to load certain patches. It could even be required that you load only patches available directly from Cisco. When a patch is related to a high-level security issue, Cisco is quick to test and report these patches on Cisco.com. You can find available patches in the software download section of Cisco.com. You can also set up to have alerts emailed to you automatically. Search "Product Alert Tool" at Cisco.com to set this up.

Just as with Communications Manager, administration access has to be secured. By default, the administrator selected when configuring Unity has full administrative access. Often you need to allow others access for limited administrative tasks. You can do this by creating a CoS that enables them only the access that you want them to have.

Unity has the capability to track all administrative access and create reports showing this access. This can prove useful when troubleshooting to determine whether changes were made and who made them. For this reason, it is necessary for every person accessing the administration interface to use individual login credentials. Don't just create one administrative login and allow everyone to use the same one because there is no way to determine who made what changes.

When you create subscribers, you determine which features they can access. A few of these features can affect the security of your system. One of these features is the user's capability to define one-key transfer options that can be performed during his greeting. This enables the outside caller to be transferred to another extension or number by pressing a single key. However, this also opens up the possibility of toll fraud. A subscriber could set up a one-key transfer that transfers the call to a long-distance number, perhaps a friend who lives out of state. This option, of course, would not be announced during the greeting, but the subscriber could dial into his voicemail from home at night and be transferred to his friend's number all on the company's dime. The configuration of such features should be restricted to administrative personnel only. Even then, you might want to take further action to ensure that individuals with the ability to configure this feature do not exploit the privilege. To prevent possible exploitation, you can restrict the numbers to which Unity can transfer these users. Chapter 7, "Unity Predeployment Tasks," discusses how to perform these tasks.

Each subscriber in Unity has two passwords. The first is the phone password. This is the password that is used when accessing Unity through the phone. This password is only numeric because it is entered using the digits on a phone. Unity should be configured to require minimum-length passwords for each subscriber. The longer the minimum length, the harder it is for someone to figure it out. It is important that you don't take Unity phone passwords lightly. Often people don't think that their voicemail password is as important as their email password, but with unified message, if you can access one, you can access the other. The second password subscribers use to access Unity is their AD or NT account password. This password is used when Unity is accessed using a PC, such as when checking messages over the Internet. This password should contain both letters and numbers, and a minimum length of five digits should be used.

Note   All accounts have default passwords. Make sure that these are changed the first time an account is accessed. There are a few default accounts that are created when Unity is installed. Make certain that the default password on these accounts is changed immediately following the installation. On more than one occasion, I have logged in to systems at clients' sites and retrieved messages, unknowingly sent to these accounts, simply by using the default extension and password. This, of course, was done with the full knowledge of the customer and only to show him that his system was not secured by the installer.

This section has touched on only a few security concerns to bring attention to the fact that these are valid concerns that must be addressed. Additional reference material is listed in Appendix A.

Summary

A Cisco IP telephony deployment comprises a number of technologies and platforms. Before beginning to deploy such a solution, much thought must be given to the proper design. It all begins with a reliable, solid infrastructure. A proper infrastructure begins with a redundant physical topology and proper backup power. To allow access to outside systems, gateways are used and methods of Call Admission Control must be implemented.

At the call-processing layer, redundant Communications Managers should be deployed. These systems must run on Cisco-approved hardware called MCSs. Devices such as phones, gateways, and conference bridges register to Communications Manager. When a call is placed or a resource is requested, the request is sent to the Communications Manager to which the device is registered. The Communications Manager uses the configured dial plan to determine how to route the call to the desired location. After the call is complete, Communications Manager ensures that it is properly torn down.

Unity is a unified communications server that enables individuals to have all their voice-mails, emails, and faxes stored in a single location. This enables more efficient access to all messages. Unity has the capability to function as an auto-attendant and have outside callers routed through the system when they make selections from the available menu. In the future, unified communications will enable calls to be routed based on predefined rules that individual users can configure.

Unity Connection is a voicemail system that offers many of the same features as Unity but does not use a third-party message store. This prevents it from offering true unified messaging, but it can still offer comparable feature and, in some cases, features that are not offered by Unity.

The advances being made in IP telephony are exciting. As with most new technologies, there are those who find ways to exploit them. It is critical that sufficient attention be given to securing all IP telephony deployments.

Preparing CUCM for Deployment

To ensure a smooth deployment, certain tasks must be performed in a certain order. In this chapter, you learn what tasks need to be completed before adding devices. As with most things, if you fail to create a solid foundation, you will encounter problems. The topics covered in this chapter give you that firm foundation.

Before adding any devices to the system, ensure that a number of predeployment tasks are accomplished. Because this book assumes that Communications Manager is already installed, most settings discussed in this chapter should already be properly configured.

The goal of this chapter is to help you understand these settings and see how changing them can affect your system. This chapter covers services configuration, enterprise parameters, and device registration tasks. In addition, the chapter includes step-by-step instructions for many of these tasks. It is worth the time to review these settings and make sure that they are configured properly for your system. Although the system might seem to function fine even if some of these tasks are overlooked, it is recommended that all tasks are verified before adding devices.

Configuring Communications Manager for Maximum Performance

Communications Manager is the heart of the call-processing system, and it is important to ensure that it runs at peak performance. A number of processes can run on the Communications Manager, but not all of them are always necessary. The following sections explore the various processes that might run on a Communications Manager and discuss which can be safely disabled to preserve more processing power for other Communications Manager functions.

The following sections look at the services that can be enabled to run on the Communications Manager. There are two types of services: feature and network. For the most part, the average administrator will not need to deal with the network services, so these sections focus on the feature services.

Activating Communications Manager Services

Since the release of Communications Manager 3.3, all Communications Manager services are deactivated by default. Before Communications Manager 3.3, the user determined which services would run by choosing to install them during the installation process. In the current versions of Communications Manager, all services are loaded but none are activated. This section discusses each of these services and explores the proper way to activate them.

Before you can have devices register, you must activate services using the Service Activation screen within the Communications Manager Serviceability interface. You can access this interface by entering **https://[CM_IP Address]/ccmservice**. If you are already logged in to the Communications Manger administration interface, you can access the Serviceability interface by selecting Cisco Unified Serviceability from the Navigation drop-down menu in the upper-right corner. After you are in the Serviceability interface, navigate to **Tools > Service Activation**.

Figure 2-1 shows the Service Activation screen as it appears the first time it is accessed.

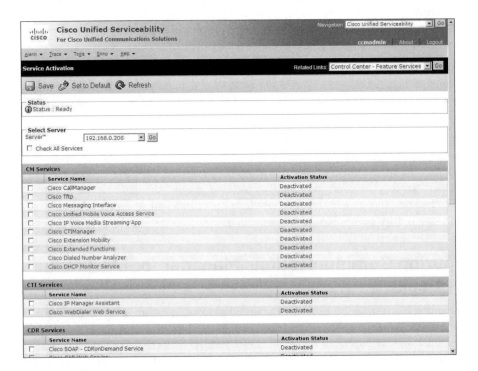

Figure 2-1 *Service Activation Screen*

To activate the Services screen, follow these steps:

Step 1.   Enter **https://[CM_IP Address]/ccmservice** in the address bar of your browser and press **Enter**.

Step 2.   Enter the administrative username and password and click **Login**.

Step 3.   Navigate to **Tools > Service Activation**.

Step 4.   Select the desired server from the Server drop-down list.

Step 5.   Select the check box next to each service that you want to activate and click **Save**.

Note   The Set to Default button is next to the Refresh button. If the Set to Default button is clicked, all the services that are required for the functioning of Communications Manager will be activated. In most cases, you do not activate all the same services on all the servers. Only use this button in a single-server environment. You should not select all services on all the Communications Manager servers because doing so would activate services that might not be needed, thereby consuming CPU cycles that could be used for other functions.

Table 2-1 lists all Communications Manager services, with a brief explanation of their functions and activation recommendations.

After these services are activated, they can be deactivated if desired. To deactivate any of these services, follow these steps.

Step 1.   Enter **https://[**CM_IP Address**]/ccmservice** in the address bar of your browser and press **Enter**.

Step 2.   Enter the administrative username and password and click **Login**.

Step 3.   Navigate to **Tools > Services Activation**.

Step 4.   From the Server drop-down list, select the server on which you want to deactivate service and click **Go**.

Step 5.   Deselect the check box next to each service that you want to deactivate and click **Save**.

After all the services are configured properly on all the servers in the cluster, you can move on to defining Communications Manager Enterprise settings. The next sections explore the various parameters that should be defined before devices are deployed.

Configuring Communications Manager's Enterprise Settings

After services are active, Communications Manager is functioning. However, before devices are added, a few more tasks must be accomplished. The following sections examine the importance of removing Domain Name System (DNS) reliance and the system's enterprise parameters.

Table 2-1   *Communications Manager Services*

Service	Function	Recommendations and Dependencies
Cisco Communications Manager	Provides call-processing, signaling, and call control functions.	In the control center, network services ensure that the Cisco Real-Time Information Serve (RIS) Data Collector service and Database Layer Monitor service are running on the node.
Cisco Trivial File Transfer Protocol (TFTP)	Provides TFTP services for device configuration files. It is also responsible for building the configuration files.	This service should be activated on at least one Communications Manager. This server is responsible for servicing TFTP requests.
Cisco Messaging Interface	Provides Simplified Message Desk Interface (SMDI) connectivity for traditional voicemail systems.	This does not need to be activated if Unity is the voicemail solution.
Cisco Unified Mobile Voice Access Service	Allows Cisco Unified Mobility users to perform the following tasks: • Make calls from a cellular phone as if the call originated from the desk phone. Depending on the device that is used, a user might have to call a local PSTN number owned by the company, enter a PIN, and then establish an outbound toll call through the gateway. Some devices such as the iPhone do not require this. • Turn Cisco Unified Mobility on. • Turn Cisco Unified Mobility off.	For mobile voice access to work, you must activate this service on the first node in the cluster and configure the H.323 gateway to point to the first Voice Extensible Markup Language (VXML) page. In addition, make sure that the Cisco CallManager and the Cisco TFTP services run on one server in the cluster, not necessarily the same server where the Cisco Unified Mobile Voice Access Service runs.

Table 2-1 *Communications Manager Services*

Service	Function	Recommendations and Dependencies
Cisco IP Voice Media Streaming App	Provides service such as Music on Hold (MoH), conferencing, and Media Termination Points (MTP).	You do not need to activate this service on all Communications Managers. Activate it only on Communications Managers that you want to provide these services. This should not be activated in the Publisher.
Cisco Extension Mobility	Used to define time limits for Extension Mobility. Activates the XML service for login function.	This service should be activated on all Communication Mangers in environments for which Extension Mobility is planned.
Cisco Extended Functions	Provides support for Cisco Unified Communications Manager voice-quality features, including Quality Report Tool (QRT). Also enables the callback feature.	The Cisco RIS Data Collector must be running on servers that are running this service. The CTI manager service must be loaded on at least one server.
Cisco Dialed Number Analyzer	Supports Cisco Unified Communications Manager Dialed Number Analyzer.	If you are planning to use Cisco Unified Communications Manager Dialed Number Analyzer, activate this service. This service can consume many resources, so only activate this service on the node with the least amount of call-processing activity or during off-peak hours. It is further recommended that this service only be activated while troubleshooting.
Cisco DHCP Monitor Service	Provides Dynamic Host Configuration Protocol (DHCP) service for phones and monitors IP address changes for IP phones in the database tables.	Activate this service on the Communication Managers that have DHCP server enabled.

Table 2-1   *Communications Manager Services*

Service	Function	Recommendations and Dependencies
Cisco IP Manager Assistant (IPMA)	This is required to enable the IPMA feature. This feature allows managers additional features such as divert and DND.	This service should be active on servers that service these features.
Cisco WebDialer Web Service	Allows users to dial from a web page or desktop application.	Typically, this service is loaded on one server in the cluster.
Cisco SOAP - CDRonDemand Service	Receives Simple Object Access Protocol (SOAP) requests for Call Detail Records (CDR) filename and returns a list of filenames that fit the time duration that is specified in the request.	You can activate the Cisco SOAP - CDRonDemand Service only on the first server.
Cisco CAR Web Service	Loads the user interface for CDR Analysis and Reporting (CAR), a web-based reporting application that generates either CSV or PDF reports by using CDR data.	You can activate the Cisco CAR Web Service only on the first server.
Cisco AXL Web Service	This service allows you to modify database entries and execute stored procedures from client-based applications that use Administrative XML (AXL).	Activate on the first node only. Failing to activate this service causes the inability to update Cisco Unified Communications Manager from client-based applications that use AXL.
Cisco UXL Web Service	This service performs authentication and user authorization checks. The TabSync client in Cisco IP Phone Address Book Synchronizer uses the Cisco UXL Web Service for queries to the Cisco Unified Communications Manager database.	Activate if the Cisco IP Phone Address Book Synchronizer is being used.

Table 2-1 *Communications Manager Services*

Service	Function	Recommendations and Dependencies
Cisco Bulk Provisioning Service	Supports the Bulk Administration Tool (BAT).	You can activate the Cisco Bulk Provisioning Service only on the first node. If you use the BAT to administer phones and users, you must activate this service.
Cisco TAPS Service	This service supports the Cisco Unified Communications Manager Auto-Register Phone Tool, which allows a user to upload a customized configuration on an autoregistered phone after a user responds to Interactive Voice Response (IVR) prompts.	Activate this service on the first node if TAPS is going to be used.
Cisco Serviceability Reporter	Generates a report once daily. The generated reports include statistics on servers, devices, services, call activities, and alerts. These reports can be accessed from the Communications Manager Serviceability Tools menu.	This service is activated on the Publisher. Be careful when running reports, because the service can impact call processing. It is best to run reports after hours.
Cisco CallManager SNMP Service	This service, which implements the CISCO-CCM-MIB, provides SNMP access to provisioning and statistics information that is available for Cisco Unified Communications Manager.	Activate this service on all servers in the cluster if Simple Network Management Protocol (SNMP) is going to be used.
Cisco CTL Provider	If enabled, this changes the security mode from unsecured to mixmode. This service works in concert with the Cisco CTL Client.	This service should be activated on all servers.

Table 2-1   *Communications Manager Services*

Service	Function	Recommendations and Dependencies
Cisco Certificate Authority Proxy Function	Working in conjunction with the CAPF application, the Cisco Certificate Authority Proxy Function (CAPF) service can perform the following tasks, depending on your configuration: • Issue locally significant certificates to supported Cisco Unified IP Phone models. • Using SCEP, request certificates from third-party certificate authorities on behalf of supported Cisco Unified IP Phone models. • Upgrade existing certificates on the phones. • Retrieve phone certificates for troubleshooting. • Delete locally significant certificates on the phone.	Activate on only the first node.
Cisco DirSync	Ensures that the Cisco Unified Communications Manager database stores all user information. If you use an integrated corporate directory, for example, Microsoft Active Directory or Netscape/iPlanet Directory, with Cisco Unified Communications Manager, the Cisco DirSync service migrates the user data to the Cisco Unified Communications Manager database.	Activate on only the first node.

Removing DNS Dependencies

It is recommended that Communications Manager be configured so that the devices that register to it do not have to rely on DNS to resolve the Communications Manager. This affects only devices such as phones and Media Gateway Control Protocol (MGCP) gateways and is accomplished quite easily, as you see in the steps provided later. You might be wondering why it is recommended to remove DNS reliance. Primarily there are three reasons for this. First, it allows devices to be able to register without querying a DNS server. Second, a DNS server failure will not cause devices such as phones to fail registering. Finally, because the device makes a call directly to the IP address of the Communications Manager, it can register faster. This is because an IP address can be resolved at Layer 3 of the Open Systems Interconnection (OSI) model, whereas a DNS request has to go up to Layer 7.

Note   You are removing the DNS reliance from the devices, not DNS from your network. Removing DNS from your network can cause your network to stop functioning properly.

Removing DNS reliance simply requires that you change the name of each Communications Manager server to the IP address. This is done within the web-based Communications Manager Administration tool. Throughout the Communications Manager chapters in this book, this interface is referred to as *CM Administrator* or *CCMAdmin*. To access CM Administrator, point your web browser to https://[CM_IP_address]/ccmadmin. For example, if the IP address of the Communications Manager is 10.3.3.3, the address you enter is **https://10.3.3.3/ccmadmin**. When you are at the login screen, enter an administrator username and password and click **Login**.

Note   Because CM Administrator uses Hypertext Transfer Protocol Secure (HTTPS), you must make sure that you enter HTTPS in the address bar and not HTTP.

To change the names of the servers, follow these steps:

Step 1.   From within CM Administrator, open the System drop-down menu by placing the mouse over **System** at the top of the screen.

Step 2.   Select **Server** from the drop-down menu.

A search criteria screen appears. You can search based on the name or the description of the Communications Manager. You can also leave the search criteria blank, and all servers will be listed. If you want, enter the criteria to narrow the search and click the **Find** button.

Step 3.   Select the first server in the list, and click its name.

A screen similar to that shown in Figure 2-2 appears. In the Host Name/IP Address field, the current name of the server appears. In Figure 2-2, you can see that the name is being changed to 192.168.0.180.

Step 4.   If you use DNS that supports IPv6, enter the IPv6 name in the **IPv6 Name** field. Otherwise, enter the non-link-local IP address.

Step 5.   The **MAC Address** field needs to be populated only if you plan to move the server from time to time. Entering the MAC address aids in helping the other devices identify the server. Enter the MAC address of the server in this field if you plan to move the server.

Step 6.   In the **Description** field, enter a description that will aid in determining the location and function of this server.

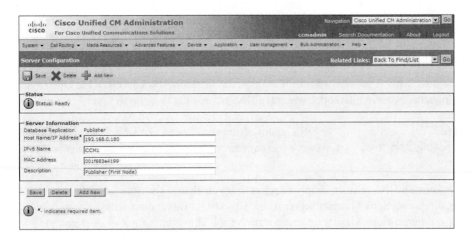

Figure 2-2 *Server Configuration Screen*

Step 7.   Click the **Save** button to save the changes.

Step 8.   Repeat Steps 1–7 for all Communications Managers in the cluster.

Now that the reliance on DNS has been removed, the enterprise parameters should be defined. The next sections discuss the function and proper settings for each of these parameters.

Defining Enterprise Parameters

Enterprise parameters are settings that apply to the entire cluster. There are more than 70 enterprise parameters divided into more than 20 categories. Many of these settings might never need to be changed. The following sections explore the settings that might be of interest to an administrator. In some cases, the recommended setting depends on your environment, and in these cases, an explanation of the setting is offered to help you determine the proper setting for your environment. It is important to understand that although some of these settings can be left alone, others (such as the path entries) should be changed in most environments. Path entries are settings that point to a path that includes the server name. Because it is recommended that the server name be changed to the IP address, any field that points to the old name must be changed to point to the new name (the IP address). One example of such a field is the URL directories path. Because there are such a large number of parameters, an overview of each set will be offered. This will provide a more detailed look at a few sets that might be of interest to the average administrator.

General Parameters

The first category that you find within enterprise parameters has no special designation and is often referred to as general parameters. The majority of these features are left at their default.

The one that might be of interest is the Auto Registration Phone Protocol. This deter-mines what protocol will be used for phones that autoregister. The default value is Skinny Client Control Protocol (SCCP). If you happen to use Session Initiation Protocol (SIP) in your environment and you use autoregistration, you need to change this value to SIP.

The following steps show how to set this field to SIP.

> **Note**   Some of these parameters require that the Communications Manager be restarted before changes will take effect. You will be informed if you change a parameter that requires a restart.

Step 1.   From within CM Administrator, open the System drop-down menu by placing the mouse over **System** at the top of the screen.

Step 2.   Select **Enterprise Parameters** from the drop-down menu.

You are presented with a screen similar to that seen in Figure 2-3.

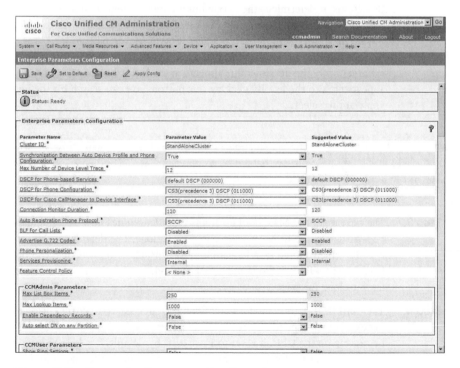

Figure 2-3   *Enterprise Parameters Configuration*

Step 3.   Select the **Auto Registration Phone Protocol** field.

> **Note**   Most field names appear to be hyperlinks. If you click the name of the field, a help screen appears that offers details on the purpose of the field. When you want to change the value of a field, you need to click in the field, not on the name of the field.

Step 4.   Select **SIP** from the drop-down menu that appears.

Step 5.   Click **Save** to save this change.

Communications Manager Administrator Parameters

The second category in enterprise parameters is CM Administrator Parameters. These parameters affect the CM Administrator web-based interface. Because these parameters affect how the system appears, all of them will be reviewed. The following steps show how these parameters are configured and explain the function of each of them:

Step 1.   Navigate to the **Enterprise Parameters** page in CM Administrator.

Step 2.   The first field under the CM Administrator Parameters is labeled **Max List Box Items**. It determines the maximum number of items that a list box can contain. The default value is 250. This setting can be set in the range of 50 to 9999. The larger the number, the longer it takes for the page to load. It is best to leave this value set to default. If the number of items is larger than the value set, only the current value appears in the list. A button labeled "..." appears next to the list. By clicking this button, you can search for the item you want to select.

> **Note**   A list box is the list of items that appears when you click the down arrow at the end of a field. In Figure 2-4, you see that a list box appears when the down arrow is clicked in the Route Partition field.

Step 3.   The next field, the **Max Lookup Items** field determines how many items will be returned to the browser when a lookup is done. The default for this setting is 1000, which should be adequate for most installations. This field can be set from 250 to 99999. Keep in mind that the higher this value is set, the longer it takes to load the page.

Step 4.   The third field in this category, the **Enable Dependency Records**, field determines whether dependency records can be retrieved. Because this feature can be tasking on the CPU, it is set to False (off) by default. It is best to leave this value set to False. However, there are times when this feature can save hours. For example, if you are trying to delete a Calling Search Space (CSS), you can only delete it after you have removed it from all devices to which it is assigned. When you try to remove the CSS, a message displays stating that the CSS cannot be deleted because it is assigned to one or more devices. If dependencies are not enabled, you must manually search to find to which

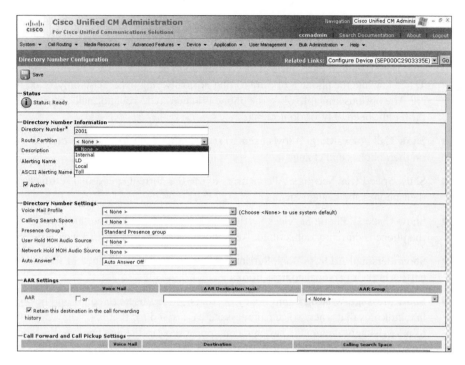

Figure 2-4 *List Box Example*

devices the CSS is assigned. You save time if dependencies are enabled, because you can find out exactly the number and type of devices to which the CSS is assigned. When this feature is needed, it is best to enable it (set the value to True) after hours only and then disable it (set the value to False) when you are finished using it.

Step 5.   The last field in this category is **Auto Select DN on Any Partition**. When this field is set to False and a DN is added that already exists in the database, a partition must be selected. If set to True and a DN that is already in the database is added, it will automatically be in the same partition as the existing DN. The result is a shared line.

CCMUser Parameters

The third enterprise parameters category is called CCMUser Parameters. These settings determine what options are available to a user from the user web pages. The user web pages allow users to change many of their phone settings. Often you might not want the user to change certain settings from the web pages, such as the Message Wait Indication (MWI) policy. Each setting has two valid values: True or False. If an option is set to True, it is available through the user web pages. If it is set to False, it is not available. This section simply explains what action the user can take from the user web page if the option is set to True. If you do not want one or several of these features available from the user web page, set the value to False.

- **Show Ring Settings:** Allows the user to set when and how a line rings, based on the state of the line. This means that if the phone is idle, the user can choose to have the phone ring normally, and when the phone is in use, the user can choose to have it only flash the light. Each line can be configured to act differently. The ring options available while the phone is idle are to ring normally, ring once, flash only, or do nothing. The options available while the phone is in use are to ring normally, ring once, flash only, beep only, or do nothing.

- **Show Call Forwarding:** Allows users to see whether call forwarding is currently set on their phones and change it.

- **Show Speed Dial Settings:** Allows users to see the current speed-dial settings for their phones and change them.

- **Show Cisco IP Phone Services Settings:** Allows users to view the services to which the phone is currently subscribed. Also allows users to subscribe to new services.

- **Show Personal Address Book Settings:** Allows users to view, edit, and add the entries in their personal address books.

- **Show Message Waiting Lamp Policy Settings:** Allows users to edit if and how each line indicates that a new voicemail message has arrived for that line. They can choose to have the light illuminate, have an icon appear next to the line number, both of these options, or have no indication.

- **Show Line Text Label Settings:** Allows users to configure the line text.

- **Show Locale for Phone Settings:** Allows users to set the language on the phone.

- **Show Locale for Web Pages Settings:** Allows users to set the language for the user web pages.

- **Show Change Password Option:** Allows users to change their passwords.

- **Show Change PIN Option:** Allows users to change their PINs.

- **Show Download Plugin Option:** Allows users to download plug-ins.

- **Show Online Guide Option:** Adds a link to the user guide for the type of phone that is associated with the user. The guide is in PDF format. In some cases, the guide might not be available for certain model phones. This is normally the case if the phone model is relatively new.

- **Show Directory:** Allows users to search the directory from the web page.

- **Show Mobility Features Options:** users to access remote destinations and access lists.

- **Show Manager Name in Directory:** Displays the manager's name in the directory find list.

- **Show Extension in Directory:** Displays the extension number in the directory find list.

- **Show LDAP Extension in Directory:** Displays the Lightweight Directory Access Protocol (LDAP) extension in the directory find list.

CDR Parameters

The fourth enterprise parameters category is called CDR Parameters and contains only the CDR File Time Interval parameter. This determines how many minutes of CDR data that each CDR file will contain. The default is 1, which means that each CDR file will contain one minute of data.

Localization Parameters

The fifth category within the enterprise parameters is called Localization Parameters and deals with languages and tones. The language used depends on where the Communications Manager solution is deployed. Just as there are different languages around the world, there are also different tones and cadences for phones. For example, when placing a call in England, the caller hears a double ringback instead of the single ringback that is heard in the United States. The following steps show how to edit these parameters and explains each of them:

Step 1.   Navigate to the **Enterprise Parameters** page in CM Administrator.

Step 2.   The first field under the Localization parameters is the **Default Network Locale** field. This field is used to determine what types of tones and cadences are used by the system. The default is United States. If needed, this parameter may be changed by clicking the down arrow at the end of the field. A list of valid choices display in the drop-down list. Choose the desired language from the list.

Step 3.   The last field in this category is the **Default User Locale** field. This field determines the default language used for the devices in the system. English United States is the default value. If additional languages are installed on the Communications Manager, they display in the drop-down list in this field. Choose the appropriate language for your environment.

Multi-Level Precedence and Pre-Emption (MLPP) Parameters

The sixth category of enterprise parameters is the MLPP Parameters. MLPP adds the ability to grant higher priority to calls. This is useful in many government and military situations where it might be imperative that a call is successful. A call of a higher priority can actually cause a call of a lower priority to be terminated so that the resources can be used to complete the higher-priority call. The MLPP parameters deal with this feature. The following steps include an explanation of each parameter and the recommended settings:

Step 1.   Navigate to the **Enterprise Parameters** page in CM Administrator.

Step 2.   The first field under the MLPP Parameters is the **MLPP Domain Identifier**. MLPP grants higher priority only from calls within the same MLPP domain. For this reason, an MLPP identifier must be chosen. The default value is 0.

Step 3.   The second field in this category, which is called **MLPP Indication Status**, determines whether tones and indications are presented when a precedence call is made. The precedence indication can be a special ringback or a display notification, if the caller's phone supports it, and a special ringer on the called party's side. By default, this parameter is set to MLPP Indication Turned Off. To enable this feature, set this parameter to MLPP Indication Turned On.

Step 4. The next field is **MLPP Preemption Setting.** This parameter determines whether a higher-precedence call preempts a lower-precedence call. The default value of No Preemption Allowed does not allow this to happen. To cause a lower-precedence call to be terminated if a higher-precedence call requires the resources, set this parameter to **Forceful Preemption.**

Step 5. The next field, which is called **Precedence Alternate Party Timeout**, determines how long the system waits before sending a precedence call to the alternative party. The default is 30 seconds. Valid values for this field are 4 to 60. Enter the desired value in the field.

> **Note** This parameter is used when the called party has set an alternate party diversion. This is separate from a standard call forward setting.

Step 6. The last parameter in this category is labeled **Use Standard VM Handling for Precedence Calls** and determines whether precedence calls are forwarded to voicemail in the same manner as all normal calls. It is recommended that precedence calls not be forwarded to voicemail, so the default value is False. For a configuration that forwards precedence calls to voicemail, set the field to **True.** It is recommended that the field be left at **False.**

Security Parameters

The seventh category within enterprise parameters is Security Parameters. These parameters are defined if security is enabled within the cluster and set as default security behavior for phones. There are four fields in this category:

- **Cluster Security Mode:** This is the setting that displays whether the cluster is operating in a nonsecure or mixed-mode fashion. This field is read-only and can only be affected by running the CTL client plug-in. The valid values for this field are 0, which indicates a nonsecure mode, and 1, which indicates a mixed mode.

- **CAPF Phone Port:** This defines a port that listens for Cisco Authority Proxy Function Service (CAPF) requests from a phone for a certificate. The valid values for this field are 1023 through 55556. The default is 3804. Leave this set to 3804 unless the default port is not used.

- **CAPF Operation Expires in (days):** This parameter determines how many days a CAPF operation has to complete. The valid values are 1 to 365. The default is 10.

- **Enable Caching:** Enable credentials can be stored in memory for up to 2 minutes. This can save time for often-accessed credentials.

Prepare Cluster for Roll Back

This category has only one parameter, and it is only used if you are going to roll Communications Manager back to a version earlier than 8.0. If you change this parameter, users lose the use of features such extension mobility but still have basic call functions until the parameter is set to False.

Phone URL Parameters and Secured Phone URL Parameters

The next two categories of enterprise parameters are Phone URL Parameters and Secured Phone URL Parameters. These parameters deal with URLs that phones use for various purposes. One example is the URL for services; this is the address that the phones point to when the Services button is pressed. The difference between the two categories is that the Phone URL Parameters are for the 7940, 7945, 7960, 7965, and 7970 phones, whereas the Secured Phone URL Parameters are for secured models of Cisco phones. The following steps explain each parameter and its recommended configuration:

Step 1. Navigate to the **Enterprise Parameters** page in CM Administrator.

Step 2. The first field under the Phone URL parameters is called **URL Authentication**. This field specifies the URL that certain phones use for authentication proxy services between them and the LDAP directory. This value is set during the installation and in most cases should not be changed. However, if you change the name of the server to the IP address, make sure that you change that portion of the URL. For example, if the URL is http://DTW_CCM/CCMCIP/ authenticate.asp and you have changed the name of the server to its IP address, which is 10.3.3.3, make sure that you change the URL to **http://10.3.3.3/CCMCIP/authenticate.asp.**

Step 3. The next field, which is called **URL Directories**, contains the URL that phones use to access directory functions. This occurs when the Directories button on the phone is pressed. Once again, if you changed the name of the server to the IP address, make sure to change it in this URL.

Step 4. The next field is labeled **URL Idle.** Some Cisco IP Phones have the capability to display information on the screen after the phone is idle for a certain amount of time. This parameter specifies the URL that the phone should call to retrieve this information. A common use for this feature is to display the company's logo on the phone. By default this field is empty. Enter the URL you want to use if you have configured one.

Tip For more information on how to create a graphic that can be used for this purpose, refer to the document titled "Creating Idle URL Using Graphics on Cisco IP Phone" at Cisco.com. The document ID is 42573.

Step 5.   The fourth Phone URL parameter is **URL Idle Time**. This parameter determines how long a phone must be idle before the Idle URL is displayed. The default is 0, which means that the URL is not displayed. Set the desired value in seconds.

Step 6.   The next parameter is **URL Information**. This field specifies the URL that the phone requests when the help function is invoked by pressing the **i** or **?** button on the phone. Make sure that if you change the name of the server to the IP address, you change it in this URL.

Step 7.   The next parameter, which is called **URL Messages**, contains the URL that the phone requests when the Messages button is pressed. By default this field is empty.

Step 8.   The next field, which is labeled **IP Phone Proxy Address**, specifies the address of the proxy server that all phone URL requests use. If this field is blank, the phone tries to make a direct request for URLs. By default this field is empty. If this field is used, the address must contain the server name or IP address and the port number.

Step 9.   The last parameter in this category is **URL Services**. This field contains the URL that the phone requests when the Services button is pressed. Again, if you change the name of the server to the IP address, make sure to change it in this URL.

User Search Parameters

The ninth enterprise parameter category is User Search Parameters. Certain Cisco IP Phones enable the user to search the phone directory from the LCD screen on the phone. This feature is activated by pressing the **Directories** button on the phone. The newer-model phones have an icon that looks like an open book instead of the word *Directories*. This gives the phones a more global look. These two parameters define the breadth of a directory search and its results. These parameters also apply to searches that are made from within the Communications Manager User Options web page.

The first parameter, which is labeled Enable All User Search, determines whether a search, in which the user left all the fields blank, is allowed. By default, the value is True, which means that a search of this nature would attempt to return all the names in the directory. To disable this type of search, set the value to **False**.

The other parameter in this category determines the maximum number of results that a search can return. This parameter is called User Search Limit. The default value is 64, which means that no more than 64 results are returned. The valid values for this parameter range from 1 to 500. Keep in mind that the higher this value is, the longer it can take to return the results. A number higher than 64 can have a negative effect on the performance of the Communications Manager.

CCM Web Services Parameters

The tenth category of enterprise parameters is CCM Web Services Parameters. These parameters limit the number of performance counters and device queries that can be made. If too many requests are made, it can negatively affect performance. Other applications, such as the Voice Health Monitoring and Gateway Statistic Utility, might receive delayed responses. The following are the four parameters with brief descriptions:

- **Allowed Performance Queries Per Minute:** This parameter determines the maximum Architecture for Voice, Video and Integrated Data (AVVID) XML Layer performance counter queries that are allowed per minute. The default value is 50. Valid values for this parameter are 1 to 80.

- **Allowed Device Queries Per Minute:** This parameter determines the maximum AXL device queries that are allowed per minute. The default value is 15. Valid values for this parameter are 1 to 18.

- **Performance Queue Limit:** This parameter determines the size of the queue for performance counter queries. If a query is made and the queue is full, the query is dropped. The default is 100. Valid values for this parameter are 20 to 1000.

- **Maximum Performance Counters Per Session:** This parameter sets the maximum number of performance counters allowed per session.

Trace Parameters

The next set of parameters is the Trace Parameters. The first parameter is called File Close Thread Flag. This parameter is set to False by default. If set to True, it enables separate threads to be used to close trace files. This can improve performance when traces are run.

The last trace parameter is called FileCloseThreadQueueWatermark. This parameter defines how many trace files the separate thread accepts before refusing trace files. The trace file is then closed without the use of a separate thread. The default is 100. The valid values are 0 through 500.

As you can see, there are a number of enterprise parameters. Most of them can be left at the default. But others, such as those that contain the name of the Communications Manager, might need to be changed. In most cases, the integrator makes these changes at the time of installation. It is still a good idea to know the function of each parameter. If one ever needs to be adjusted, you know where to find it, how to change it, and what the impact of the change is.

At this point, the system is almost ready for the attachment and configuration of devices. There are, however, a few more tasks that should be completed before device attachment and configuration. The next sections examine the core tasks that should be accomplished before devices are allowed to register to the system.

User Management Parameters

This category has only one parameter, which is Effective Access Privileges for Overlapping User Groups and Roles. The parameter determines whether the maximum or minimum user privileges will be assigned when a user is a member of multiple groups that contain overlapping rights.

Service Manager TCP Ports Parameters

The TCP ports that the Service Manager uses to send and receive data are defined in the Service Manager TCP Ports Parameters category.

CRS Application Parameters

The two parameters in the CRS Application Parameters category simply define whether the Auto Attendant or IPCC Express is installed. These parameters are read-only and are set by the Customer Response Solutions (CRS) server.

Cluster Domain Configuration

The Cluster Domain Configuration parameters allow you to configure the top-level domain and the fully qualified domain name. For example, the Organization Top Level Domain field for Cisco would be cisco.com. The Cluster Fully Qualified Domain Name parameter for Cisco might be something like cm2.dtw.cisco.com.

Denial-of-Service Protection

The Denial-of-Service Protection parameter should be set to **True** and helps prevent some types of denial of service (DoS) attacks.

TLS Handshake Timer

The Transport Layer Security (TLS) Handshake Timer parameter determines the maximum amount of time (in seconds) that a TLS protocol handshake can be performed. It is recommended that this be left at the default because this value helps prevent DoS attacks.

Cisco Support Use

The two parameters in the Cisco Support Use category are, as you might have guessed, only for use by Cisco technical support.

IPv6 Configuration Modes

There are four parameters in the IPv6 Configuration Modes category. The first one, Enable IPv6, determines whether Communications Manager and the phones are going to participate in an IPv6 environment. The default is False and should only be set to True if your environment is configured to support IPv6.

The next two parameters, IP Addressing Mode Preference for Media and IP Addressing Mode Preference for Signaling Required Field, determine whether IPv4 or IPv6 will be used for media and signaling events. This only applies to dual-stack devices.

The last parameter in this category, Allow Auto-Configuration for Phones, determines whether the phones will be allowed to use stateless autoconfiguration. If set to On, the phone can use advertisements from the router to obtain an address; if set to Off, the phone will use Dynamic Host Configuration Protocol version 6 (DHCPv6).

Cisco Syslog Agent

The Cisco Syslog Agent parameters allow you to define a syslog server that a syslog message can be sent to as well as the severity level of the messages that should be sent. Set the name of the syslog server in the Remote Syslog Server Name field and the severity in the Syslog Severity for Remote Syslog Messages field.

CUCReports Parameters

The Report Socket Connection Timeout parameter defines the maximum amount of time (in seconds) that is allowed while establishing a connection to another server. The Reports Socket Timeout defines the maximum amount of time (in seconds) that is allowed when reading data from another server.

Logical Partitioning Configuration

The last category of parameters is the Logical Partitioning Configuration parameters. Logical partitioning is used to permit or deny calls between the following pairs of VoIP devices:

- VoIP phone and a VoIP gateway
- VoIP gateway and another VoIP gateway
- Intercluster trunk and a VoIP phone
- Intercluster trunk and a VoIP gateway

Certain areas have restrictions on the type of VoIP calls that are permitted. For example, in India, it is illegal to have a call that passes through a PSTN gateway connect directly by using a WAN to a VoIP phone or VoIP PSTN gateway in a different geographic location. Logical partitioning can prevent calls like this from happening.

Logical partitioning works with geolocation settings to determine the location of each device and determine whether the call is allowed. The following four parameters are defined:

- **Enable Logical Partitioning:** This parameter determines whether logical partitioning is enabled. This is used to restrict certain types of features and calls.
- **Default Geolocation:** This parameter determines the default geolocation for all devices. The geolocation settings define up to 17 parameters that define the device's

geographical location. These parameters define the country, city, postal code, and so on. More detail on all 17 parameters can be found in RFC 4119, "GEOPRIV Location Object." This setting can be overridden at the device level.

■ **Logical Partitioning Default Policy:** This parameter determines whether calls between geolocations will be allowed or denied by default.

■ **Logical Partitioning Default Filter:** This parameter can help limit the number of fields that appear in the geolocation configuration window. Geolocation filters must be configured before you can modify this field.

Preparing Communications Manager for Device Registration

When a device registers with Communications Manager, a number of things need to be known about that device, such as the type of device and the IP address and MAC addresses. However, determining other information is also necessary. This includes the particular time zone that the phone is located in and with which Communications Manager the device should register. Instead of defining this information at every device, two components known as device pools and common device configuration are used. Because most often a large number of devices require the same information, the needed information is assigned to a device pool and a common device configuration. Then the device pool and common device configuration are assigned to those devices. This way, instead of defining multiple configuration values for each device, you assign the values once to the device pool and common device configuration.

In the versions of Communications Manager prior to 4.2, there were only device pools. In 4.2, the device pool parameters were spilt into two components, now referred to as device pools and common device configurations. The reason for this change was to add more flexibility for mobility. There are certain parameters that should change if the device moves and others that should stay the same regardless of where the device resides. Parameters that might need to be changed are stored in the device pool, and parameters that will always stay the same, regardless of location, are configured in the common device configuration.

Device Pools

As of Communications Manager 8.0, the device pool contains more than 30 fields. Eight of these fields are required to be configured when creating a new device pool. Although configuring the others is not required, it is recommended. This section briefly explains each field and explores how to configure the fields that are crucial to a proper deployment. The following is a list of fields found in a device pool:

■ **Device Pool Name (Required):** No doubt you can figure out what this is without any description. It is simply the name of the device pool. The name you choose should enable you to easily identify the function of this device pool. For example, you might name the device pool EST-DTW1-DTW2 for a device pool that is used by devices that are in the Eastern time zone and use Communications Manager DTW1 as a primary Communications Manager and Communications Manager DTW2 as a secondary server.

- **Cisco Unified Communications Manager Group (Required):** A Communications Manager group defines which Communications Manager is used as the primary server, which is the secondary server, and which is the tertiary server. The next section discusses how to create these servers.

- **Calling Search Space for Auto-Registration:** When using autoregistration, it is a good idea to restrict where the device can call until its legitimacy is confirmed. This field allows you to specify a calling search space for all devices that autoregister.

- **Adjunct CSS:** This field is used when cross-cluster Extension Mobility is deployed. It is used to ensure that that the country-specific emergency dialing plan is supported.

- **Revert Call Focus Priority:** This determines whether reverted (call returning after being on hold) or incoming calls will be the focus of user action. In other words, if there is an incoming call and a reverted call coming in at the same time, this field will determine which call is answered when the phone goes off hook.

- **Local Route Group:** Local route groups are used to streamline dial plan creation for multisite clusters.

- **Intercompany Media Services Enrolled Group:** IME allows calls outside an organization to be routed across the Internet through dynamic SIP trunks. If IME is deployed in your organization, the appropriate IME enrolled group is required.

- **Date/Time Group (Required):** Because it is possible that devices belonging to the same cluster might be in different time zones, it is necessary to define the correct time zone for each device. The date/time group is used to specify to which time zone a device belongs. The date and time format is also defined by the date/time group. The configuration of date/time groups is covered later in this chapter.

- **Region (Required):** Because VoIP calls can traverse links of different bandwidth, it is often necessary to use a codec that requires less bandwidth to make most efficient use of the link. A codec converts voice signals from their analog form to digital signals that are acceptable to modern digital transmission systems. Some codecs use algorithms that compress the voice stream so that less bandwidth is required. Using regions, you can define what codec one device should use when talking to another device. Further discussion and the configuration of region are covered later in this chapter.

- **Media Resource Group List:** Media resources provide features such as Music on Hold (MoH) and conferencing. A media resource group list defines device access within a media resource.

- **Location:** Locations are used to determine the amount of bandwidth that can be used for VoIP calls. CUCM uses the value in this field in conjunction with the region to determine whether bandwidth is available for a call.

- **Network Locale:** This field determines what locale is used for the devices. The field impacts the tones and cadences used. The default network locale was defined in the enterprise parameters. If a different value is selected here, this value takes precedence. Make sure that you select only a locale that has been loaded in the system; otherwise, the device associated with this device pool fails. If this field is set to None, the enterprise parameter setting is used.

- **Survivable Remote Site Telephony (SRST) Reference (Required):** SRST is a feature that allows phones that are remote to the Communications Manager to continue functioning, even if they cannot communicate with the Communications Manager. This is done by having the phones register with a local router that is acting as an SRST box. The SRST reference is used to define which device the phone should try to register with if it is unable to communicate with the Communications Manager.

  Another use for SRST is when a small office has only a single Communications Manager. Although it is always recommended to have two Communications Managers for redundancy purposes, it is possible to use SRST for redundancy when only one Communications Manager is installed.

- **Connection Monitor Duration:** This setting defines how long a phone, which is in SRST mode, waits to fail back to the Communications Manager after it detects that Communications Manager is back online. This can help prevent the phone from switching back and forth between the SRST server and the Communications Manager when a Communications Manager connection is going up and down (also know as *flapping*).

- **Single Button Barge:** Determines whether barge or cBarge can be invoked by pressing a single button.

- **Join Across Lines:** Determines whether a user can join calls on separate lines together to create an ad hoc conference.

The following parameters relate to device mobility. Device mobility allows a device to assume settings based on physical location. For example, perhaps you work in New York but must relocate to the Chicago office for a month. You can take your phone with you, and when you plug it in to the Chicago network, you would have the same extension but certain settings would change because you are in Chicago. This is accomplished because the device pool can be selected based on the network into which you are plugged. If the device pool that is selected is different than the device's preprogrammed device pool, the system checks the physical location. If the physical location is different, the device is considered to be roaming, and the system assigns the Device Mobility parameters to the device:

- **Physical Location:** This field is used to set the physical location of the device. This is useful when the Device Mobility feature is used. Because device pools can be assigned based on the subnet that a device is in, the correct physical location will be associated to the device automatically when it is moved.

- **Device Mobility Group:** This determines which device mobility group the device belongs to.

Note   If the following parameters are configured here and at the device level, the device level overrides these parameters. If using Device Mobility, it is best to leave these set to the defaults at the device level and set them here.

- Device Mobility Calling Search Space: This Defines the CCS that the device will use when the device is roaming.

- **AAR Calling Search Space:** Automated Alternate Routing (AAR) allows a call to be routed over the PSTN if the WAN is not available. Because a device's CSS might not allow it to place a call using the PSTN, the AAR CSS is used to allow the call to be placed.

- **AAR Group:** This Defines which AAR group the device belongs. This is used to determine how the dialed call must be transformed so that is can be placed over the PSTN.

- **Calling Party Transformation CSS:** Calling party transformation allows you to change the number that is presented as the caller ID. The CSS selected must have access to the calling party transformation pattern that is assigned to the device pool.

- **Called Party Transformation CSS:** Called party transformation allows you to change the number that is dialed. The CSS selected must have access to the called party transformation pattern that is assigned to the device pool.

- **Geolocation:** Some features can require geolocation information. This information is also referred to as a civic address. The geolocation information can be used to determine the logical partition of a device.

- **Geolocation Filter:** There are 17 configurable geolocation fields. Geolocation filters allow you choose which fields are used to create a geolocation identifier.

- **Incoming Calling Party Settings:** These fields allow you to add prefix and strip digits for numbers that are defined as national, international, or subscriber in the Calling Party Number Type field. This field is configured when you create a pattern.

- **Incoming Called Party Settings:** These fields allow you to add prefix and strip digits for numbers that are defined as national, international, or subscriber in the Called Party Number Type field. This field is configured when you create a pattern.

Common Device Configuration

Based on the device's physical location, some of the parameters might need to change. The parameters found in the Common Device Configuration section remain the same regardless of the physical location of the device:

- **Network Hold MOH Audio Source:** There are two kinds of hold: user hold and network hold. A user hold occurs when the Hold button on the phone is pressed. Any other time a call is placed on hold, for example, if the call is being transferred, it is considered a network hold.

  The Network Hold MOH audio source determines what audio stream a caller hears when placed on a network hold.

- **User Hold MOH Audio Source:** The User Hold MOH audio source determines what audio stream a caller hears when placed on a user hold.

- **User Locale:** This parameter determines the language and fonts used for the devices in this device pool. The default user locale, which is set in the enterprise parameters, will be used if this field is set to None.

- **MLPP Indication (Required):** This field determines whether tones and indications are presented when a precedence call is made to or from a device in this device pool. If this field is set to Default, the MLPP Indication setting in the enterprise parameters is used.

- **MLPP Preemption (Required):** This parameter determines whether a higher-precedence call preempts a lower-precedence call. If this field is set to Default, the MLPP Indication setting in the enterprise parameters is used.

- **MLPP Domain:** This field determines which MLPP domain the devices in this device pool belong to. If this field is left blank, the MLPP Domain Identifier defined in the enterprise parameters is used.

  A number of these fields point to other objects that might not have been configured yet. Throughout this book, many of these components are discussed in more detail. From this point on, we are going to focus on the required components that most often need to be defined before devices are deployed.

Creating Communications Manager Groups

A Communications Manager group defines which Communications Managers a given device points to as its primary, secondary, and tertiary Communications Manager. The concept is quite simple. The Communications Manager group contains a list of Communications Managers; the order in which they appear determines their function (that of either a primary, secondary, or tertiary Communications Manager). A Communications Manager can be in more than one group, and its function can be different in each group. For example, Table 2-2 shows two Communications Manager groups. Each group contains the same three servers, but they appear in a different order. The result is that the DTWA Communications Manager is the primary in Group DTWABC, but it is the tertiary in group DTWCBA. The only thing that defines the Communications Manager's function in regard to primary/secondary/tertiary is the order in which they appear in the Communications Manager Group.

Table 2-2 *Two Communications Manager Groups*

Communications Manager Group DTWABC	Communications Manager Group DTWCBA
DTWA	DTWC
DTWB	DTWB
DTWC	DTWA

Creating Communications Manager groups is a simple task, but before creating them, you need to spend some time determining how many Communications Manager groups you need. The number of Communications Managers you have will impact the number of Communications Manager groups you have. For example, if you have only two Communications Managers, you have only two Communications Manager groups at most. However, having six Communications Managers by no means indicates that there will be six Communications Manager groups. When determining the number of Communications Manager groups, keep two goals in mind: redundancy and load balancing. By keeping these goals in mind and using common sense, you can easily figure out the proper number of Communications Manager groups for your environment. For further information on Communications Manager groups and cluster sizes, refer to the Cisco IP Telephony Network Design Guide, which can be found on Cisco.com by searching for "Cisco IP Telephony Network Design Guide."

Communications Manager groups are configured using CM Administrator. The process is quite simple, as you will see in the following steps. Before you start, make sure that all Communications Managers are running and able to communicate with each other. To add Communications Manager groups, follow these steps:

Step 1. From within CM Administrator, open the **System** menu by mousing over System at the top of the window and selecting **Cisco Unified CM Group**.

Step 2. Click the **Add New** link in the upper-left corner of the screen.

The screen will display a figure similar to that shown in Figure 2-5.

Note A default Communications Manager group already exists. If you choose to use the default, make sure that all the desired Communications Managers appear in this group in the desired order. This can be done using the steps listed here as well as by clicking the Find button and then selecting the Default group instead of selecting Add a New Communications Manager Group.

Step 3. Enter the desired name for this Communications Manager group.

Give it a name that it is easily identified. For example, in the example shown in Figure 2-5, the name CMGAB is used to show that Communications Managers DTWA and DTWB belong to that group in that order.

All the available Communications Managers are displayed in the Available Cisco Unified Communications Managers box.

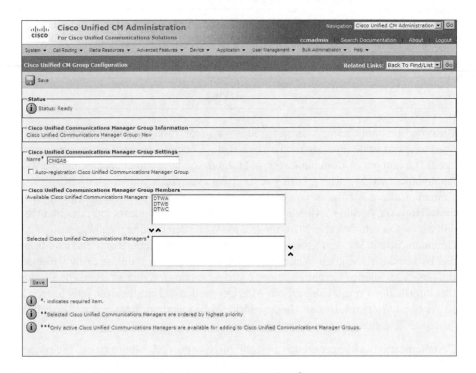

Figure 2-5   *Communications Manager Group Configuration*

Step 4.   Highlight the Communications Manager that you want to act as the primary Communications Manager in this group.

Between the two boxes on the screen are two arrows. To move the selected server, click the arrow that points to the **Selected Cisco Unified Communications Managers** box.

Step 5.   Repeat Step 4 to move the remainder of the desired Communications Managers into the Selected Cisco Unified Communications Managers box.

The order in which the Communications Managers appear in the Selected Cisco Unified Communications Managers box determines whether they are considered primary, secondary, or tertiary. You can change the order in which they appear by highlighting a Communications Manager and clicking the up and down arrows to the right of the box.

Step 6.   After all the Communications Managers have been added and are displayed in the desired order, click the **Save** button.

Use these steps to configure all Communications Manager groups that you need. After that is accomplished, you need to define data/time groups.

Defining Date/Time Groups

Imagine that you have asked someone to call you at 10:00 a.m. and that person calls you at 11:00 a.m. You answer the phone frustrated from the wait, only to find that your friend is calling from a different time zone and thinks she's on time. Just as we need be aware of time zones in our daily lives, we need to make sure that Communications Manager knows the time zone of its registered devices. This is accomplished by configuring a date/time group for each time zone that devices will be in.

The default date/time group, called CMLocal, is created when Communications Manager is installed, and it is set to the zone selected during the installation. If all the devices are in the same time zone, you can use the CMLocal date/time group without adding any others. However, if your devices are in different time zones, you can use these steps to guide you through the process of creating a date/time group for each time zone:

Step 1.   From within CUCM Administrator, open the **System** menu by mousing over System at the top of the window and selecting **Date/Time Group**.

Step 2.   From the screen that displays, either search for an existing date/time group or add a new one. Click the **Add New** link in the upper-left corner of the screen.

A screen similar to that shown in Figure 2-6 appears. All fields on this screen are required. The first field is Group Name.

Step 3.   Give the group a name that is easily identified.

For example, the date/time group that is being created in Figure 2-6 is for the devices that are in Chicago, and Chicago is in the Central time zone, so it has been named Chicago-CST.

Step 4.   In the **Time Zone** field, select the correct time zone from the drop-down list that is displayed when you click the down arrow at the end of the field.

Step 5.   The next field, called **Separator**, is used to define the symbol that is used as a separator when the date is displayed. The valid values for this field are a dash (-), forward slash (/), or dot (.). Choose the desired value from the drop down list.

Step 6.   Choose the desired date format from the **Date Format** drop-down list.

This field determines how the date is presented. The choices are month-day-year, day-month-year, or year-month-day.

Step 7.   Choose the desired time format from the **Time Format** drop-down list.

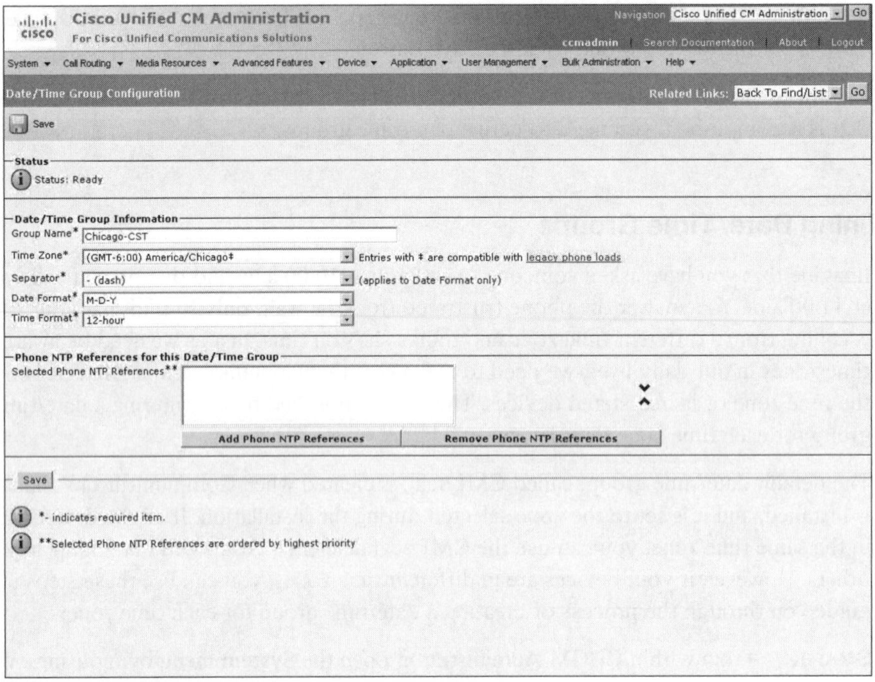

Figure 2-6   *Date/Time Group Configuration*

This field determines whether the time will be displayed in 12-hour or 24-hour format.

Step 8.   Click the **Save** button.

Repeat these steps for each date/time group needed.

Configuring Regions

When calls traverse lower-bandwidth IP links, such as a WAN link between offices, it might be necessary to compress the audio stream so that the link is used efficiently. The compression is accomplished by using a codec that has a lower bandwidth requirement, such as G729, for the call. When using a codec that requires lower bandwidth, the quality of the call is affected. For this reason, it is recommended that these codecs are used only when bandwidth is at a premium. With this in mind, you can understand that the codec used should depend on the call destination, rather than the device placing the call. Regions allow this.

The two most often-used codecs in a Cisco VoIP environment are G.711 and G.729. G.711 requires approximately 80 Kbps when overhead is included. G.729 requires only 24 Kbps including overhead. Because most of the newer-generation Cisco IP Phones support both codecs, G.729 is often used when traversing a WAN link.

By creating and assigning regions, you define which codec is used between regions. Figure 2-7 shows three regions and the codecs that are used when calls are placed within the region and to other regions. As you can see, if someone from Detroit calls another party in Detroit, the G.711 codec is used, but when a party in Detroit calls someone in Chicago, the G.729 codec is used.

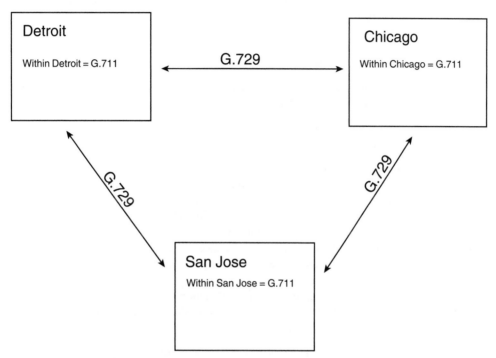

Figure 2-7   *Use of Regions Example*

Note   In newer versions on Communications Manager, you configure the maximum bit rate that is used between regions instead of the codec. The end effect is the same it is just displayed differently. For example if you want to use G.729 between regions you would set the Max Audio Bit Rate to 8 kbps. The bit rate is selected from a drop-down list. Next to the bit rate the codec that aligns with the bit rate displays.

A default region named Default is created during the installation of Communications Manager. If calls in your environment never traverse lower-bandwidth links, additional regions might not be needed. Regions are created from within CM Administrator. You can create the required regions by following these steps:

Step 1.   From within CM Administrator, open the **System** menu by mousing over System at the top of the window and selecting **Region**.

From the displayed screen, you can either search for an existing region or add a new one.

Step 2.   Click the **Add New** link in the upper-left corner of the screen.

Step 3.   On the next screen, enter the name of the region in the **Name** field.

It is recommended that you enter a name that is easily identified. In this example, because the region will be used for devices that are in Detroit, the region is named Detroit.

A figure similar to that shown in Figure 2-8 appears.

At this point, notice that the Max Audio Bit Rate is set to Keep Current Setting. The default for intraregion calls is G.722 if supported; if not, G.711 is used. For inter-region calls G.729 is used by default. Based on these defaults, to have calls over the WAN use G.729, simply create new regions and assign them to device pools. In previous versions of Communications Manager you had to manually set the codec. To change the bit rate/codec, select the desired bit rate from the **Max Audio Bit Rate** dropdown list. For example, in Figure 2-8, the Detroit region is being configured. To change the region used between the Detroit region and the Default region, highlight the Default region in the Regions box and select the desired bit rate from the **Max Audio Bit Rate** drop-down list.

You might want to configure a few more things before creating device pools. One is softkey templates. There is a default softkey template, so if you plan on using just that one, you can move on to creating device pools. Because softkey templates are specific to phones, they are covered in the next chapter with phone button templates. For the purpose of the next section, which covers building device pools, we use the default values available for all other required objects.

Building Device Pools

Now that the device pool's required components have been configured, you can create the device pools. The first thing you have to determine is how many device pools are needed. This is determined by looking at the number of device pool components you have created and how they tie together. Following is a simple example.

Imagine that you have configured two Communications Manager groups, three regions, and two date/time groups, as shown in Table 2-3.

You can tell that because you have three regions, there need to be at least three device pools. If the devices in each region are part of the same date/time groups, and use the

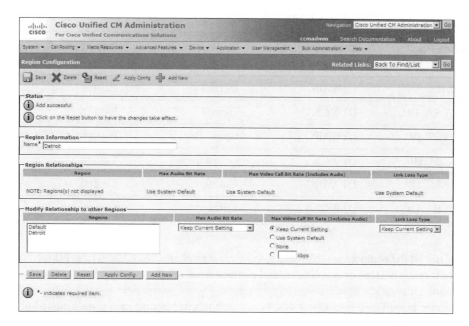

Figure 2-8 *Adding a Region*

same Communications Manager group, only three device pools are needed. However, in this example, you want half the phones in each region to use Communications Manager group DTWABC and the other half to use Communications Manager group DTWCBA, so three device pools won't be enough. It would take six device pools to accomplish this, as shown in Table 2-4.

From this simple example, you can see how the number of device pools could easily grow if not managed properly. So, what is the right number of device pools? There is no definitive answer. That depends on your specific requirements, but make sure that you take the time to properly plan the number of device pools that your environment will require.

Table 2-3 *Determining the Number of Device Pools Needed*

Communications Manager Groups	DTWABC
	DTWCBA
Regions	Detroit Grand Rapids Chicago
Date/time groups	Eastern Central

Table 2-4 *Device Pool Example*

Device Pool	Communications Manager Group	Region	Date/Time Group
DTWABC_DP	DTWABC	Detroit	Eastern
DTWCBA_DP	DTWCBA	Detroit	Eastern
GRRABC_DP	DTWABC	Grand Rapids	Eastern
GRRCBA_DP	DTWCBA	Grand Rapids	Eastern
ORDABC_DP	DTWABC	Chicago	Central
ORDCBA_DP	DTWCBA	Chicago	Central

After all the components that belong in a device pool are created, you have planned out how many device pools you need, and planned what components will belong to each pool, creating the device pools is quite simple. The following steps show how to create a device pool. The steps will not detail each component because each was discussed previously in this chapter.

Step 1. From within CM Administrator, open the **System** menu by mousing over System at the top of the window and selecting **Device Pool**.

From the displayed screen, you can either search for an existing device pool or add a new one.

Step 2. Click the **Add New** link in the upper-right corner of the screen.

A screen similar to that shown in Figure 2-9 appears.

Step 3. In the **Device Pool Name** field, enter the name of the new device pool.

Remember to give the device pool an easily identifiable name.

Step 4. Now simply select the desired object for each of the remaining fields.

If you are uncertain of the function of any object, refer to the earlier section in this chapter that discussed each field. The fields that are marked with an asterisk (*) are required, so you must select a value. The other fields are not required, but it is recommended that a value be set. Many of these values are discussed in more detail in future chapters.

Step 5. After you select an object for all required and desired fields, click the **Save** button.

That's all there is to creating a device pool. Creating a device pool is simple because the pool's only function is to point to other objects. The real work, as you learned in this chapter, is making sure that all the objects contained in the device pool have been created.

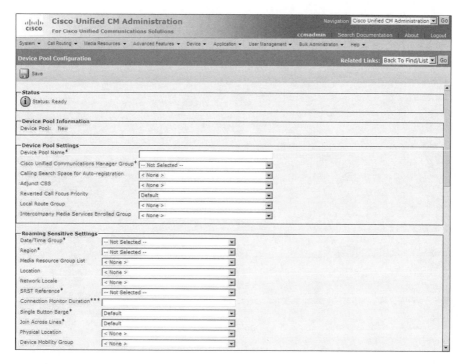

Figure 2-9 *Device Pool Configuration*

Summary

This chapter examined various Communications Manager predeployment tasks. First, the Windows and Communications Manager services that are required were discussed, in addition to those that can be disabled to increase the performance of the server. Next, the DNS requirements and enterprise parameters were covered, and finally the device pools and components of the device pools were explored. At this point, you are ready to start adding devices to the system. The next chapter discusses what tasks must be performed to add phones and gateways and describes the various ways that these devices can be added.

Chapter

Deploying Devices

After all predeployment tasks are completed, devices can be added to the system. This chapter discusses the tasks required to add certain devices to the Communications Manager cluster.

A number of types of devices can be added to the Communications Manager. The devices discussed in this chapter fall into one of two categories: clients or gateways. Other devices, such as gatekeepers, are discussed in future chapters.

You start by looking at clients, more specifically phones. There are a number of different models of Cisco IP Phones, but the task of adding each is similar. Next, gateways are covered. Gateways allow connectivity to another system such as the public switched telephone network (PSTN) or another PBX. In Communications Manager 8.0, there are more than 40 different types of gateways, and although the function of each is similar, the configuration varies. It is not possible to provide a step-by-step guide for the configuration of each gateway, but this chapter includes detailed steps on how to configure the most popular types.

Note In all the steps in this book, I have tried to cover all the parameters that appear on the screen. Because each version of Communications Manager adds fields, all the fields that you see in these steps might not appear on your screen, or additional fields might be present, because of the version of Communications Manager you are running. Regardless of the version you run, the steps in this chapter can help you walk through the process. Not all the parameters must be configured. Some can remain at default, whereas others are not required. The end of the names of required parameters are marked with an asterisk (*). In some cases, you might need to configure only the required parameters for a device to function. It is a good idea, however, to review each parameter so that you can be certain that the device is configured exactly the way you want it.

Adding Clients

Depending on the environment, adding a phone can be as simple as plugging it into a port that has connectivity to the Communications Manager. Although you can configure a Communications Manager to allow phones to be automatically added simply by connecting them to the network, it is not always wise or desired. The following sections explore four ways that phones can be added to the system. Before adding phones to a system, there are a few more components to configure.

You are probably thinking, "Wait a minute; the last chapter discussed predeployment tasks." That's right, it did, but those were the general or global settings that should be configured. These sections look at settings that are specific to phones.

Note   Which came first, the chicken or the egg? This is a question that has plagued the minds of great thinkers from the beginning of time. Okay, maybe it hasn't, but a similar issue sometimes occurs when teaching new technologies. When two separate concepts are interdependent, it might be difficult to grasp either concept until you understand both of them. This being said, you will notice throughout this chapter that new concepts and components are mentioned that are not discussed in detail until later in the book. In these cases, a brief description is offered for each new concept, as is a reference to the chapter that lends greater detail. You might choose to jump ahead to gain a better understanding or just accept the brief description, knowing that more detail is offered later.

Defining Device Settings

Before adding phones, it is recommended, but not required, that some device settings be configured. Configuring the device setting first will most likely save time. These settings include phone button templates, softkey templates, and device defaults. The following section explains the function of each of these and describes how to configure them.

Phone Button Templates

Some Cisco IP Phones have buttons that can be configured for various functions. Although these buttons can be configured to support a number of different functions, the most popular functions are lines and speed dials. When configured as lines, extension numbers can be assigned to the buttons. Each phone must have at least one button configured as a line. When a button is configured as speed dial, administrators or users can assign a speed-dial number to it, and because most Cisco phones have only a few of these buttons (one to eight), the number of speed dials that can be defined in this way is limited. The user can access additional speed dials by using a feature known as abbreviated dial, which is discussed later in this chapter.

In addition to lines and speed-dial functions, these buttons can be configured for other functions, depending on the phone model. Although the majority of phones sold today have configurable buttons, you need to know that not all phones have that capacity.

When you create a new phone button template, it will be quite clear which buttons on certain phones are not configurable.

The exact function that can be assigned to buttons varies depending on the model of the phone. The buttons on most phones can be defined to support a number of features, but the most common are as follows:

- **Line:** Extension number is assigned.

- **Speed dial:** Assigned number is dialed when button is pressed.

- **Service URL:** A phone service is accessible by pressing the button.

- **Privacy:** Makes a call private when Call Barge is enabled.

- **BLF/Speed dial:** In addition to acting as a speed dial, the status of the extension assigned can be monitored.

The other features that can be assigned to buttons are typically assigned to a softkey, so they do not need to be assigned to a button. Softkeys are discussed later in this chapter.

When a phone is added to the system, a phone button template is associated to the phone. The template is used to determine the function that each button will serve. If the phone is added through autoregistration, it uses the template defined under device defaults. Device default settings are discussed later in this chapter. The creation of these templates is fairly simple.

To create phone button templates follow these steps:

Step 1.   From within CCMAdmin, select **Device > Device Settings > Phone Button Template.**

Step 2.   Click the **Add New** link.

Step 3.   On the next page, you must select an existing phone button template to copy. This is because a new phone button template must be based on an existing template. From the drop-down list in the **Phone Button Template** field, select the standard template for the correct model of phone. For example, if you are creating a phone button template for a 7960, select Standard 7960 SCCP.

Step 4.   Click the **Copy** button.

Step 5.   In the **Button Template Name** field, enter a descriptive name and click Save.

Step 6.   A screen similar to that shown in Figure 3-1 displays. At first glance, you might think that you have selected the wrong phone type because it shows 34 buttons instead of the six you were expecting. Because the 7960 can support two 7914 expansion modules, which support 14 buttons apiece, 34 total buttons are possible.

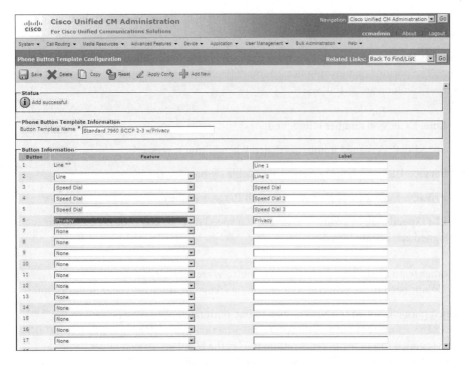

Figure 3-1   *Phone Button Template Configuration*

Note   It is recommended that the button template name identify the configuration of this template. For example, if the template is configured with two lines, three speed dials, and a privacy button, a good name would be "7960 2-3 w/Privacy."

Step 7.   Assign the proper function to each line by selecting the function from the drop-down list next to the button number.

Step 8.   Next to the Feature field is a **Label** field. Enter a descriptive label in this field, such as Speed Dial 2 or Line 3.

Step 9.   Click **Save** to save the new template.

Softkey Template

In addition to the buttons that can be used for lines and speed dials, Cisco IP Phones have buttons that are referred to as softkeys. In Figure 3-2 you can see where softkeys appear on the phone. These buttons (keys) allow the user to access features of the phone such as hold, transfer, conference, as well as many others. The function of each key changes depending on the state of the call. Because there are often more available functions configured than physical softkeys, the last softkey functions as a toggle key, allowing the user to scroll through all the available options. The softkey template allows you to determine what functions are available on the phone and in what order they display. Much like phone button templates, the softkey templates can be associated directly with a phone. However, as you saw in the last chapter, the softkeys templates are also associated with device pools, which are in turn associated with phones. By associating the softkey template to a device pool, you can easily and quickly assign the softkey template to a large number of phones. If different softkey templates are associated with a phone at both the phone level and the device pool, the one at the phone level takes precedence.

Figure 3-2 *Softkeys and Phone Buttons*

The following steps take you through the process of creating a softkey template.

Step 1. From within CCMAdmin, select **Device > Device Settings > Softkey Template**.

Step 2. Click the **Add New** link.

Step 3. On the next page, you must select an existing softkey template for the basis of the new template. Select a template from the drop-down list in the **Create a Softkey Template Based** On field.

Step 4. Click the **Copy** button.

Step 5. On the next screen, enter the name and description for the new template. The description should help identify the features associated with the template.

The Application field lists the applications that are available in this template and cannot be changed on this screen.

Step 6. Click **Save** to add the new template.

Step 7. After the template is added, you must configure it. If you want to add applications that are found on other softkey templates, click the **Add Application** button. If you do not want to add applications from an existing template, skip this and the next step. For example, you would not add an application if you are simply moving or adding standard softkeys to the template.

Step 8. If you selected Add Application in the new window that displays, select the standard softkey template that contains the application you want to add to the new template and click **Save** and then **Close**.

Step 9. In the upper-right area of the screen, you can find the Related Links drop-down list. Make sure that **Configure Softkey Layout** is selected and click **Go**. A screen similar to that found in Figure 3-3 displays. The first field is a drop-down list of all the possible states of a phone. Because the softkeys change depending on the state of the phone, each state must be configured separately. In Figure 3-3, the new template allows access to the callback feature. In this example, the callback softkey must be configured for all states from which it might be accessed, which are On Hook and Ring Out.

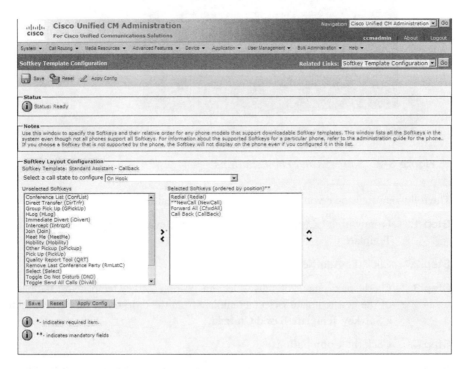

Figure 3-3 *Softkey Layout Configuration*

Step 10. Determine which call state you want to modify and select it from the list. For example, if you wanted to add a softkey that would appear on the phone while you were on a call, you would select **Connected**.

Step 11. The softkey currently assigned displays in the box on the right side of the screen labeled Selected Softkey. The softkeys that can be added display in the box on the left side labeled **Unselected Softkeys**. To add unselected softkeys, click once on the softkey and then click the top arrow of the two arrows that display between the two boxes.

Note   Because there are a limited number of softkeys on the phone, it is common to have more softkeys assigned than buttons on the phone. In this case, the last button becomes a More button that acts as a toggling mechanism to allow users to access the other features. You need to understand that the More button automatically appears on the phone and is not something you configure in the template.

Step 12. To remove a current softkey, click the softkey you want to remove, and click the bottom arrow of the two arrows that display between the boxes.

Step 13. The softkeys display on the phone in the same order that they display in the **Selected Softkeys** box. To change the order in which they display, highlight the desired softkey, and click the up or down arrow that displays on the left side of the Selected Softkey box.

Note   If softkeys are used in more than one call state, for example, the callback softkey is available in the On Hook and Ring Out call states; pay attention to the position of the softkey in each of the call states. It's a good idea to keep the softkey in the same position for each call state if possible. If it is desirable to leave one or more softkey positions unused, the Undefined softkey can be used as a placeholder.

Step 14. After you modify all the desired call states, click **Save**.

Note   When modifying an existing softkey template, you need to reset the devices associated with the templates. To do this, click the **Restart Devices** button on this page. Take care when resetting devices, because resetting causes the phones to be unusable while they reset. This does not affect phones currently on a call. The reset occurs when the phone is idle. It is always recommended that whenever a reset must be performed on a large number of phones, it be done off hours to minimize the impact on the end user.

Device Defaults

When a phone boots, it requests a configuration file from the Communications Manager TFTP server. The file that it requests is associated with the phone's MAC address. If the phone has not previously been registered with a Communications Manager on the system and has not been manually added, no configuration file exists. When autoregistration is being used, a phone uses a default configuration file that defines how it is to attach to the system and register. The Device Defaults settings define the values used.

Three settings are defined under the Device Defaults settings: load information, device pool, and phone template.

Load Information

This is the ID of the firmware load that the device should run. When Communications Manager is shipped, it includes a current version of the firmware loaded for each device. From time to time, the firmware is upgraded to offer additional features or patches. By editing this field, you can specify the ID of the new load. The next time the device boots, it downloads the new firmware load.

Device Pool

This field enables you to define which device pool is used when autoregistration takes place.

Phone Template

This field allows you to define what phone button template devices use when autoregistration takes place.

The following steps show how the device defaults are configured:

Step 1.   From within CCMAdmin, select **Device > Device Settings > Device Defaults**.

Step 2.   A screen similar to that shown in Figure 3-4 displays. Most often, the load information can remain at its default. However, from time to time, new loads need to be deployed. To update the load, you must first locate the name of the device. Enter the new load ID in the **Load Information** field. Make sure that you enter the ID correctly and that the ID is for the correct device. Entering an invalid or incorrect ID in this field can cause the device to fail.

Note   When a new load is to be used, it must first be copied to the TFTP server so that the device can download it.

Step 3.   Next, edit the device pool. To change the default device pool for a device, click the down arrow in the **Device Pool** field associated with the device and select the desired device pool from the displayed list.

Step 4.   The last item that can be selected on this page is the phone button template. To change this item for a device, click the down arrow in the **Phone Template** field associated with the device and select a template from the displayed list.

Adding Phones

When a phone is added to the system, information about the phone is entered into the SQL database. This information defines nearly every aspect of the device. Phones can be added to the system in a number of ways, but the net effect is the same.

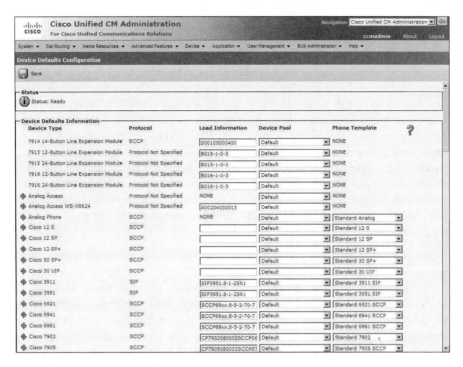

Figure 3-4 *Device Defaults Configuration*

Four methods for adding phones are explored in this chapter, beginning with the method known as autoregistration. Before delving too deeply into this method, take a quick look at all four:

- **Autoregistration:** This allows phones to be plugged into the system and automatically register. An extension is assigned to the phone from a range defined by the administrator.

- **Manual:** All information for the phones is manually entered before the phone is plugged in.

- **Bulk Administration Tool (BAT):** This method is used when installing information for a large number of phones. This is done by entering the information into a comma-separated values (CSV) file and then using BAT to insert the information into the Communications Manager database.

- **Tools for Autoregistration Phone Support (TAPS):** This is similar to BAT, except that the MAC address is not entered in the CSV file. Additional steps are required when the phone is plugged into the network. However, even with the added steps, it is quicker than just using BAT when performing a large installation.

Autoregistration

As the name implies, using this method allows phones to register to the system by merely being plugged into the Communications Manager network. Although this method has the advantage of allowing you to quickly add phones, it has disadvantages as well. When a phone is added by this method, it is assigned an extension number from a range of numbers that you define. It assigns these extensions in a first-come-first-served fashion. For example, if you defined the range to be from 2000 to 2100, the first phone to register would receive the extension 2000, the second 2001, and so on. You can see how this might be undesirable. If you are fortunate enough to be performing a deployment in which you can assign extensions as you want, this might not be a concern. However, in situations such as when you are replacing an existing PBX, you will most likely want to reuse the existing extensions; hence the autoassignment of extensions might not be desirable. Autoregistration can still be used in these environments; you just need to modify the extensions that were automatically assigned.

Rogue phones are another anomaly that can arise when autoregistration is used. If improperly configured, it is possible for a phone to be added to the system without your knowledge. The addition would, of course, have to be made by someone who has a Cisco IP Phone and can plug it into your network. Although this might seem less than likely, it is still important to ensure that the dialing capabilities be restricted for any rogue phones that might find their way onto your system. This is done by defining a Calling Search Space (CSS) for autoregistration in the device pool. CSS defines a device's calling privileges. This concept is discussed in greater detail in Chapter 5, "Configuring Class of Service and Call Admission Control." Choose a CSS that has limited access, perhaps only internal or local access. This, however, also has a drawback. Limiting the CSS of autoregistered phones means that all phones that are added using autoregistration will have a limited CSS. This means that for a phone that was added through autoregistration to have greater calling privileges, the CSS must be changed. Often autoregistration is used during the initial deployment and then turned off.

As you can see, using autoregistration has both benefits and drawbacks. The choice of whether to use it depends on the environment and is ultimately up to you.

If all the previously discussed predeployment tasks have been completed, little additional configuration is required to implement autoregistration. Next, assign an extension range and enable autoregistration at the Communications Manager group. If you choose to use autoregistration, the steps that follow help walk you through these tasks:

Step 1.   From within CCMAdmin, select **System > Cisco Unified CM.**

Step 2.   Enter search criteria in the search field, and click **Find.** You might also leave the search field blank and click Find. This results in all Communications Managers being displayed.

Step 3.   From the list that displays, select the Communications Manager on which you want to enable autoregistration.

Step 4.   A screen similar to that shown in Figure 3-5 displays. Enter the starting extension number in the **Starting Directory Number** field and the ending extension in the **Ending Directory Number** field.

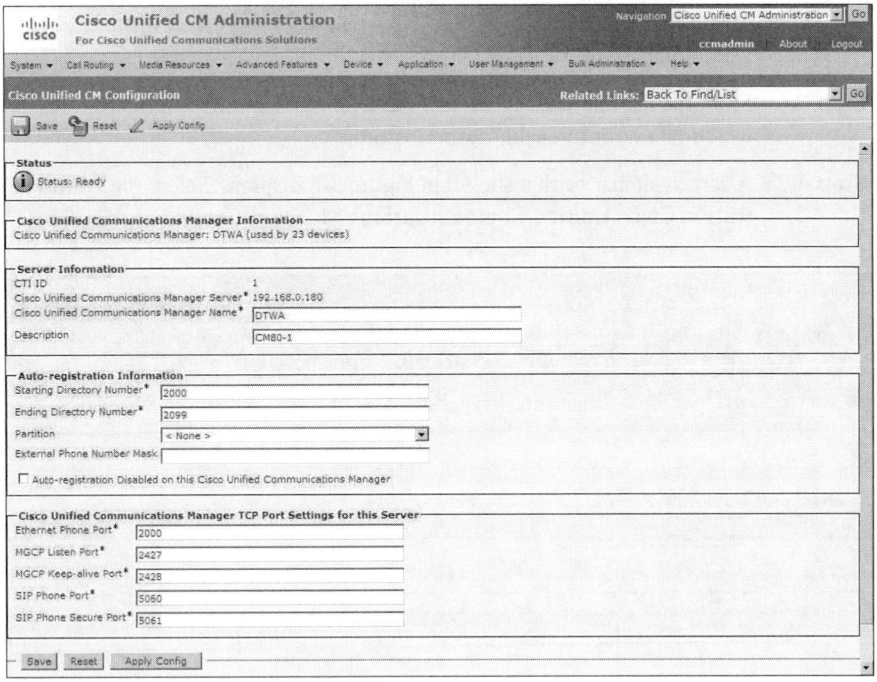

Figure 3-5   *Communications Manager Configuration for Autoregistration*

Step 5.   You should notice that in the Auto-Registration Information section, the **Auto-Registration Disabled** check box is deselected at this point. This check box automatically becomes deselected when you enter a starting and ending extension number. *Do not* select this check box. Selecting this box resets the starting and ending extension numbers.

Step 6.   Click **Save** to save your settings.

Note   In the next section, you select a Communications Manager group for autoregistration. If the Communications Manager group that you select contains more than one Communications Manager, you should enter the starting and ending extension numbers for each of the Communications Managers in the group.

After an extension range is defined, you need to enable autoregistration for the Communications Manager group. The steps that follow show how this is done:

Step 1.   From within CCMAdmin, select **System > Cisco Unified CM Group**.

Step 2.   Enter search criteria in the search field and click **Find**. You can also leave the search field blank and click Find. This results in displaying all Communications Manager Groups.

Step 3.   From the list that displays, select the Communications Manager group on which you want to enable autoregistration.

Step 4.   A screen similar to that shown in Figure 3-6 displays. Select the **Auto-registration Cisco Unified Communications Manager Group** check box.

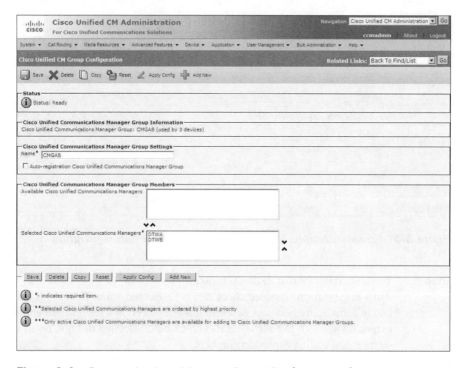

Figure 3-6   *Communications Manager Group Configuration for Autoregistration*

Step 5.   Click **Save** to save your changes.

Note   Only one Communications Manager group can be selected as the autoregistration Communications Manager group. If you select this check box and there is already an existing autoregistration Communications Manager group, a window displays stating, "You have selected this Cisco Communications Manager Group to be the Auto-registration

Cisco Communications Manager Group. The old Auto-registration Cisco Communications Manager Group will be deselected." Only select that check box for the Communications Manager group that is responsible for autoregistration.

Manually Adding Phones

In addition to using autoregistration to add phones, you can manually add them. You often add phones manually for a small number of phones (such as 20). If all the predeployment tasks have been completed, the process to manually add phones is quite simple. This section takes you through the steps of the process.

Manually adding phones has few drawbacks, aside from the fact that it can be somewhat time-consuming. You must enter the MAC address and other information, such as device pool and directory numbers, when you add each phone. Because CCMAdmin is a web-based interface, you must wait for the page to reload when you update information. Although a second or two might not seem that long, when you have to wait for multiple page reloads, it can start to add up. That is just the nature of this type of interface and little can be done about it.

The steps that follow take you through the process of manually adding a phone and explore each field that can be populated for each phone. A brief description is included for any field that has not yet been discussed in this book. The phone used in these steps is a 7960, but the process is similar for most of the more popular Cisco IP Phone models. When you add other phone models, a field might not display. This simply means that the model does not require or support that particular field. Because there are a number of steps to this process, section headings are used to mark the point at which each new set of parameters begins. These same headings display on the configuration screen as well, which should help you keep track of where you are.

Step 1.   From within CCMAdmin, select **Device > Phone**.

Step 2.   Click the **Add New** link.

Step 3.   A new page displays. From the drop-down list, select the type of phone you want to add.

Step 4.   Click **Next**.

Step 5.   Select the desired protocol and click **Next**.

Device Information

Step 6.   A screen similar to that shown in Figure 3-7 should display. The first field that must be entered is the MAC address of the phone. The MAC address can be found on the back of the phone as well as on the box in which the phone was packaged.

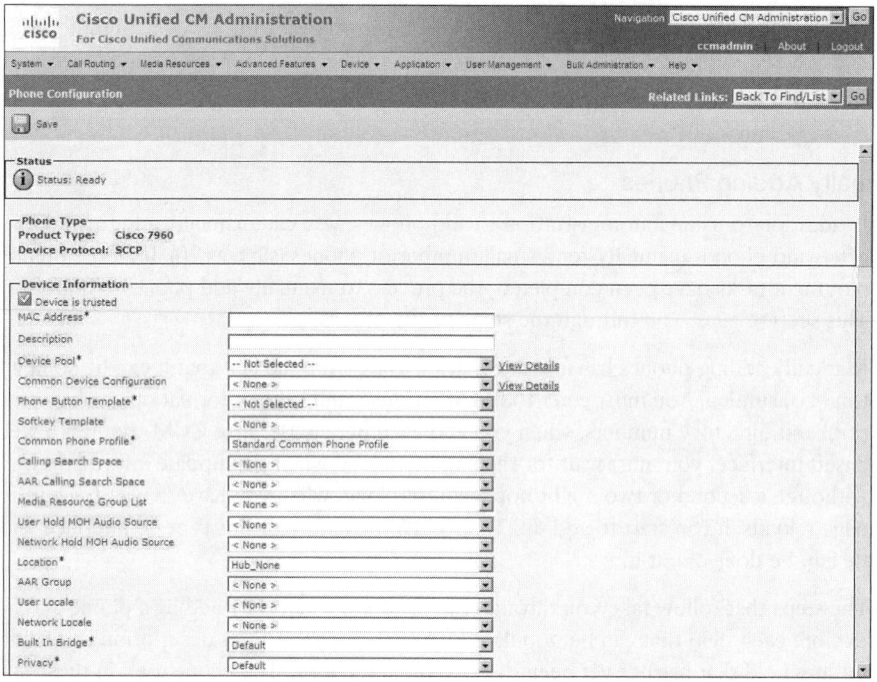

Figure 3-7   *Phone Configuration*

Note   It seems that over the years the numbers on the back of the phone have been getting smaller in type size. Then again, it seems that everything I am reading nowadays is getting smaller, so maybe it's not the phone. If you find the same to be true, you can also get the MAC address to display on the LCD of the phone. The method for this differs among the various models. On the 7960 and 7940, press the Settings and then the 3 keys on the keypad. Of course, power must first be supplied to the phone.

Step 7.   The next field is the **Description** field. Enter a description that will help you quickly identify the phone later.

Note   If you do not enter anything in the Description field, a default description, which is the MAC address preceded by SEP, is entered automatically. SEP stands for Selsius Ethernet Phone. Selsius was the name of the company that made Communications Manager before Cisco purchased the company and the product. A description I like to apply uses the following format: Last name, First name Extension number (for example, Smith, John 2012). This format allows you to search by name and easily see the extension number from the search page.

Step 8.   From the **Device Pool** drop-down list, select the device pool that the phone will use.

> **Note**   Although there are a number of required fields, most of them contain default values. The device pool, MAC address, phone button template, and device security profile (on certain models) are the only required fields that do not contain default values. You can add a Skinny Client Control Protocol (SCCP) phone without configuring any other parameters. This is useful if you need to quickly add phones and you are certain that the default system values, and those set in the device pool, are adequate for this phone.

Step 9.   From the **Common Device Configuration** drop-down list, select the common device configuration that the phone will use.

Step 10.   In the next field, a phone button template is selected for this phone. From the drop-down list in the **Phone Button Template** field, select the desired template.

> **Note**   Not all the templates will display in this field, only those that apply to the model of phone you are adding.

Step 11.   From the drop-down list in the **Softkey Template** field, select a softkey template for the phone.

Step 12.   The **Common Phone Profile** field contains user-specific service and feature attributes such as Do Not Disturb (DND) options, phone personalization information, and product-specific configuration information. Often the default profile is adequate. Select the appropriate profile from the drop-down list.

Step 13.   The CSS determines the destinations that can be dialed from the phone. CSSs are discussed in Chapter 5. Choose a CSS from the **Calling Search Space** drop-down list. If this field is left at None, the dial privileges of the phone could be limited.

Step 14.   Automated Alternate Routing (AAR) is used to provide an alternate route if a call fails because of insufficient bandwidth. The AAR CSS can be used to limit the paths a call can use when it is rerouted. ARR is covered in Chapter 6, "Configuring CUCM Features and Services." Select an AAR CSS from the **AAR Calling Search Space** drop-down list.

Step 15.   The next field is Media Resource Group List. It determines the accessibility of media resources to the phone. Media resources are discussed in further detail in Chapter 5. From the **Media Resource Group** List drop-down list, select the desired group. If no media resource group list is chosen, the list defined in the device pool is used.

Step 16.   The next two fields allow you to configure what audio source is heard when a call is placed on hold. The first field, which is labeled **User Hold Audio Source**, determines what is heard when the call is placed on hold by pressing the Hold button. The second, **Network Hold Audio Source**, determines what audio is heard when the call is placed on hold by pressing the Transfer, Call Park, or Conference button. Select the desired audio source from the drop-down list for each field. If no audio source is chosen, the source defined in the enterprise parameters is used.

Step 17.   Information entered in the **Location** field is used to prevent WAN links from becoming oversubscribed in centralized deployments. These locations are discussed more in Chapter 5. If you have defined locations, select the appropriate one for this phone from the drop-down list.

Step 18.   The **AAR Group** field determines the appropriate association of this device with an AAR group. An AAR group defines the prefix that is assigned when a call fails because of insufficient bandwidth. AAR is discussed in further detail in Chapter 6. Select an AAR group if AAR is being used. If this field is set to None, the AAR group associated with the device pool or line is used.

Step 19.   The **User Locale** field determines the language and fonts used for the phone. The default user locale, which is set in the enterprise parameters, is used if this field is left set to None. If the phone needs to use a different locale than is defined by its device pools, or the enterprise parameters, select the proper one from the drop-down list.

Step 20.   The **Network Locale** field determines what locale is used for the phone. This impacts the tones and cadences used. The default network locale was defined in the enterprise parameters. If a different value is selected here, this value takes precedence. If this field is set to None, the enterprise parameter setting is used. If this phone needs to use a different locale than is defined by its device pools or the enterprise parameters, select the proper locale from the drop-down list.

Step 21.   The **Built-In Bridge** field is used to enable and disable the built-in bridge. This bridge can be used when the Barge feature is invoked. Select the desired state of the built-in bridge from the drop-down list.

Note   Barge is a feature that allows a phone to join an active call on another phone if the two phones have a shared line.

Step 22.   The **Privacy** field is used to determine whether the phone can enable privacy for calls on a shared line. Select the desired state for this field from the drop-down list.

Step 23. Device Mobility allows a device to use different settings for the following parameters based on the physical location of the device:

- Cisco Unified Communications Manager Group

- Roaming Device Pool

- Location

- Region

- Network Locale

- AAR Group

- AAR Calling Search Space

- Device Calling Search Space

- Media Resource Group List

- Survivable Remote Site Telephony (SRST)

The **Device Mobility Mode** determines whether device mobility is enabled on this device. Set this field to On to enable device mobility and Off to disable it. If left at Default, the mode is based on the service parameter device mobility setting.

Step 24. Using the **Owner User ID** drop-down list, assign a user ID to this device. The ID will be recorded in the Call Detail Records (CDR).

Step 25. **Phone Load Name** is the name of the firmware load that the device should be running. When Communication Manager is shipped, it includes a current version of the firmware loaded for each device. From time to time, the firmware is upgraded to offer additional features or patches. By editing this field, you can specify the name of the new load. The next time the device boots, it downloads the new firmware load. This field allows the load to be changed on one phone so that it can be tested. To change the load on all phones, the load information should be updated in the Device Defaults settings.

Step 26. The **Single Button Barge** field determines whether a Barge or cBarge can be initiated using a single button. Set this field to Barge to configure it for single-button barge or to cBarge to configure single-button cbarge. If left at Default, the service parameter setting is used.

Step 27. The **Join Across Lines** fields determine whether this feature is enabled. To enable the feature, set this field to **On**. To disable this feature, set this field to **Off**. The service parameter setting is used if the field is set to **Default**.

Step 28. The **Use Trusted Relay Point** field determines whether a relay point such as a Media Termination Point (MTP) or a transcoder must be labeled trusted to be used by this device. This field is typically changed only in virtualized environments.

Step 29.   The **BLF Audible Alerts Setting (Phone Idle)** field determines whether an audible alert is played for the BLF DN when there is no current call. When set to **On**, an alert is played. When set to **Off**, an alert is not played. The service parameters setting is used when set to **Default**.

Step 30.   The **BLF Audible Alerts Setting (Phone Busy)** field determines whether an audible alert is played for the BLF when there is an active call on the BLF DN. When set to **On**, an alert is played. When set to **Off**, an alert is not played. The service parameters setting is used when set to **Default**.

Step 31.   The **Always Use Prime Line** field determines which line is activated when the phone is taken off hook. If this field is set to **Off**, whichever line is ringing will be used when the phone goes off hook. When set to **On**, the primary line will always be used even if an incoming call is ringing another line of the phone. To answer any line other than the primary line, the user must manually select the line. The service parameter setting is used when this field is set to **Default**.

Step 32.   If **Always Use Prime Line for Voice Messages** is set to **On**, the voicemail account associated with the primary line is dialed when the Messages button is pressed. If set to **Off**, the account associated with the line that has voice-mail will be dialed. If set to **Default**, the service parameter setting is used.

Step 33.   Calling party transformation enables you to change the caller ID. Select a **Calling Party Transformation CSS** that contains the called party transformation pattern that is assigned to the device. You can also leave this set to **None** and use the Calling Party Transformation CSS assigned to the device pool by selecting the **Use Device Pool Calling Party Transformation CSS** check box.

Step 34.   The geolocation information can be used to determine the logical partition of a device. If you are using features that depend on geolocation, select the desired geolocation from the drop-down list.

Step 35.   If the **Retry Video Call as Audio** check box is selected, a video call will try to connect as an audio call if it cannot connect as a video call.

Step 36.   If the **Ignore Presentation Indicators (internal calls only)** check box is select-ed, internal caller ID restrictions are ignored. This means that if an internal call is configured to block caller ID, the caller ID will still show up on the device.

Step 37.   Select the **Allow Control of Device from CTI** check box to enable computer telephony integration (CTI) control.

Step 38.   The **Logged into Hunt Group** check box allows an administrator to log the device out of a hunt group by deselecting this box.

Step 39.   The **Remote Device** check box causes Communications Manager to allocate a buffer for the phone that allows SCCP messages to be bundled. This should only be selected if the device is a remote device and is experiencing delayed connect times.

Step 40. If the **Protected Device** check box is selected, a two-second tone is played when a call is encrypted. This tone informs the callers that the call is "protected."

Step 41. A feature known as Private Line Auto Ringdown (PLAR) allows a call to be placed by simply picking up the handset. **Hot Line Device** is an extension of PLAR. If this check box is selected, the device can connect only with other Hot Line devices.

Note   If Hot line Device is enabled, a custom softkey template without supplementary services must be created and assigned to this device.

Protocol-Specific Information

Step 42. The next two fields, **Packet Capture Mode** and **Packet Capture Duration**, are for troubleshooting purposes only and should not be configured when adding a new phone.

Step 43. Presence is a feature that allows a user to monitor the status of another party's line. The **Presence Group** that a device belongs to determines what lines it is allowed to monitor. Select the Presence group this device should belong to. If no Presence group is selected, the device can monitor all devices that are not in a Presence group.

Step 44. The next field is labeled **Device Security Profile**. This field defines Certificate Authority Proxy Function (CAPF) information such as authentication mode and key size. A security profile must be selected. If you choose to not enable security on a phone, the nonsecure profile can be selected.

Step 45. The **SUBSCRIBE Calling Search Space** determines which partitions the device can access when invoking a presence request. Select a CSS that includes the partitions assigned to the lines the device can monitor.

Step 46. The **Unattended Port** check box is used to indicate that the device has unattended ports. This is normally implemented if the port is used to send calls to an application such as a voicemail server. In most cases, this box should be left deselected.

Step 47. The **Require DTMF Reception** field is often required for remote phones. This is often needed for remote phones connected through a SIP trunk because it allows dual-tone multifrequency (DTMF) signals to be received out of band.

Step 48. RFC 2833, "RTP Payload for DTMF Digits, Telephony Tones and Telephony Signals," deals with DTMF relay. To disable this feature, select the **RFC2833 Disabled** check box. In most cases, this box should be left deselected.

Certificate Authority Proxy Function (CAPF) Information

Step 49.   The next set of parameters deals with CAPF. These settings are used to configure certificate-specific information. Certificates are used to help prevent the tampering of call signaling and media streams. For more information on CAPF, refer to the Cisco IP Phone Authentication and Encryption for Cisco Communications Manager guide at Cisco.com. This guide can be found by searching for "Cisco IP Phone Authentication and Encryption" at Cisco.com. If CAPF is not being used, these fields do not need to be configured. The **Certificate Operation** field is used to install, upgrade, or delete a certificate. The available options are

- **No Pending Operation:** Displays when a certificate operation is currently inactive.

- **Install/Upgrade:** Select this when you want to install or upgrade a certificate.

- **Delete:** When selected, the current certificate will be deleted.

- **Troubleshoot:** Allows certificate information to be viewed in a CAPF trace file.

Step 50.   The **Authentication Mode** field determines the method that will be used by the phone to authenticate with CAPF. Choose one of the following:

- By Authentication String

- By Null String

- By Existing Certificate (Precedence to LSC)

- By Existing Certificate (Precedence to MIC)

Step 51.   The **Authentication String** is used only when By Authentication String is chosen in the previous step. Enter the string you want to use. It must be between 4 to 10 digits.

Step 52.   The **Key Size** field determines the key size for the certificate. The valid choices are 512, 1024, and 2048. Select the desired value.

Step 53.   The **Operation Completes By** field specifies when the install, upgrade, or delete must be complete. Enter the desired date and time in this field.

Step 54.   The **Certificate Operation Status** field displays the progress of the certificate operation. Nothing is entered in this field; it is read-only.

Expansion Module Information

Step 55.   The fields labeled **Module 1** and **Module 2** are used when expansion modules (7914, 7915, or 7916) are used with the phone being added. If the phone has expansion modules, select the modules from the drop-down list.

Step 56. The **Module 1 Load Name** and **Module 2 Load Name** fields are used to define which firmware load ID the expansion modules use. In most cases, these fields should be left blank. When left blank, the load ID specified on the Device Defaults Configuration page is used. If the need ever arises to set a specific phone to a specific load ID, the load ID should be entered in this field.

Cisco IP Phone—External Data Locations

Step 57. The next set of fields is used to define data locations for the phone. This information is used to determine where the phone should search for certain data, such as help screens and phone services. In most cases, these fields can be left blank and the system defaults will be used. Table 3-2 lists these fields and a brief description of each. If values other than the system defaults need to be used by this phone, enter them in the appropriate fields. Any values entered in these fields will be used for the device and will override the values found on the Enterprise Parameters page.

Note   The fields labeled Secure are similar to those listed in Table 3-2. The only difference is that they point to a secure server. Secured servers might be desired if you want this transmitted data to be encrypted.

Table 3-1   *Cisco IP Phone—External Data Locations Parameters*

Parameter	Description
Information	The URL the phone uses when the (i) is pressed on the phone.
Directory	The location of the directory the phone uses.
Messages	The URL that is used when the Messages button is pressed. Because you normally want a number to be dialed when this button is pressed, this field should be left blank.
Services	The URL where services can be found.
Authentication Server	URL of the authentication server for requests made to the phone web server.
Proxy Server	The proxy server used by the phone.
Idle	The URL that is displayed on the phone after the idle timer expires.
Idle Timer	The amount of time in seconds that the phone must remain idle before the idle URL is displayed.

Extension Information

Step 58. Extension mobility allows users to log in to phones and have that phone take on the characteristics such as extension number, speed dials, and so on of their phone. If extension mobility is used on this device, select the **Enable Extension Mobility** check box.

Step 59. The **Log Out Profile** field determines what device profile will be assigned to this phone when a user logs out of extension mobility. Select the desired profile from the drop-down list.

Step 60. The **Log In Time** field displays the time the user logged in to the device using extension mobility.

Step 61. The **Log Out Time** field displays the time a user logged off of the device using extension mobility.

Multilevel Precedence and Preemption Information

Step 62. The next three fields define Multilevel Precedence and Preemption (MLPP) characteristics of the phone. If these fields are left blank or set to default, the values set in the device pool are used. If MLPP is not being used, these fields can be left blank. The first MLPP field is the **MLPP Domain**. MLPP grants only higher priority from calls within the same MLPP domain. For this reason, an MLPP domain is needed.

Step 63. The second field in this category, which is called **MLPP Indication**, determines whether tones and indications are presented when a precedence call is made. The precedence indication can be a special ringback or a display if the caller's phone supports it, and a special ringer on the called party's side.

Step 64. The third MLPP field is **MLPP Preemption**. This parameter determines whether a higher-precedence call preempts a lower-precedence call. The value of Disabled does not allow this to happen. To cause a lower-precedence call to be terminated if a higher-precedence call requires the resources, set this parameter to Forceful.

Do Not Disturb

Step 65. The **Do Not Disturb** check box allows an administrator to enable DND on this device. To enable it, select the check box.

Step 66. From the **DND Option** drop-down list, you can select how the phone will behave when DND is enabled and an incoming call arrives. When Ringer Off is selected, the phone will not ring, but the caller information is displayed on the phone. When Call Reject is selected, caller information is not displayed, and based on the DND Incoming Call Alert (see the next parameter), a beep can be played or the light can flash. The DND Option set in the Common Phone Profile is used when Use Common Phone Profile Setting is selected.

Step 67. The **DND Incoming Call Alert** works in concert with DND Option. This parameter determines whether the phone beeps or the light flashes when the

DND Option is set to **Call Reject** or **Ringer Off**. When this setting is set to **None**, the setting in the Common Phone Profile is used. To turn the flash and beep off, set this to **Disable**. To have a beep played, set this parameter to **Beep Only**. When set to **Flash Only**, the light on the phone will flash.

Secure Shell Information

Step 68.   Certain phones support Secure Shell (SSH). This is normally used by Cisco TAC when troubleshooting an issue. Unless instructed by TAC, you should leave the **Secure Shell User** and **Secure Shell Password** fields empty.

Product-Specific Information

Step 69.   The last set of fields, labeled Product Specific Configuration, are specific to the model of phone you are configuring. To see an explanation of each of these fields, consult the online help.

Step 70.   After all settings have been defined, click the **Save** button at the top of the screen.

Add a Line to a Phone

After a phone is added, a line must be configured for it. The following steps illustrate the process of adding a line to a phone. Because there are a number of steps to this process, section headings are used to mark the point at which a new set of parameters begins.

Step 1.   If you are adding a new phone and have used the steps in the preceding section, you should see a screen similar to that shown in Figure 3-8. To add a line to an existing phone, follow Steps 2 though 4 to reach this screen. If you are already at this screen, skip to Step 5.

Step 2.   From within CCMAdmin, select **Device > Phone**.

Step 3.   Enter search criteria in the search field to limit the results and click the **Find** button.

Step 4.   From the list that is generated, select the phone to which you want to add a line.

Step 5.   On the left side of the Phone Configuration screen, the available lines are listed. Choose a line that has the label **Add new DN**.

Note   If all lines have an extension number already assigned, you cannot add any additional lines to this device. If the phone button template assigned to this phone has some of the buttons defined as speed dial, you might add more lines by changing the phone button template.

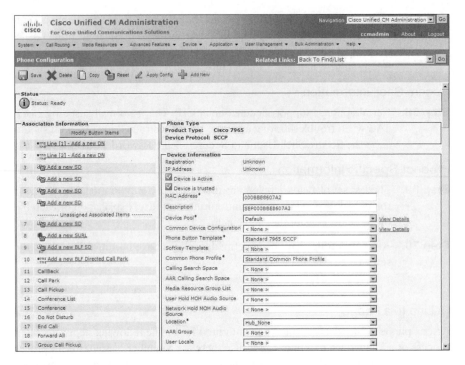

Figure 3-8 *Directory Number Configuration*

Directory Number

Step 6. The first and only field you must complete is the **Directory Number**. Enter the extension number in this field.

Step 7. The **Route Partition** field defines the partition to which this directory number is assigned. The partition is used to determine the devices that can call this extension. Partitions are discussed in more detail in Chapter 5.

Step 8. The next field is the **Description** field. Enter a description that can help you quickly identify the line later.

Step 9. In the **Alerting Name** field, enter the name that should be displayed on the caller's phone while the called party's phone is ringing.

Step 10. The **ASCII Alerting Name** field is used on devices that do not support Unicode characters.

Step 11. Select the **Allow Control of Device from CTI** check box to enable CTI control of this line.

Step 12. The **Associated Devices** box lists all the devices that this line is assigned to. To remove the line from a listed device, highlight the device in the Associated Devices box and click the down arrow that is between the **Associated Devices** box and the **Dissociated Devices** box. The device should now appear in the Dissociated Devices box. Click **Save** and the line is removed from the selected device.

> **Note** The Allow Control of Device from CTI and Associated Devices fields do not appear on the screen until the DN has been saved.

Directory Number Settings

Step 13. The **Voice Mail Profile** field determines which voicemail profile the directory number uses. The voicemail profile defines the number that is dialed when the Messages button on the phone is pressed. Voicemail profiles are discussed in further detail in Chapter 5. Select the voicemail profile from the drop-down list.

Step 14. The next field allows a CSS to be assigned as the line level. This determines what destinations can be reached when calling from this line. Select **Calling Search Space** from the drop-down list.

> **Note** It is important to understand what happens when a CSS is assigned to the line and the device. In short, the two CSSs are combined; however, there is a little more to it. For a detailed explanation, refer to Chapter 5.

Step 15. The Presence group that a line belongs to determines what devices are allowed to monitor this line. Select the **Presence Group** this device should belong to.

Step 16. The next two fields allow you to configure what audio source is heard when a call is placed on hold. The first, which is labeled **User Hold Audio Source**, determines what is heard when the call is placed on hold by pressing the Hold button. The second, **Network Hold Audio Source**, determines what audio is heard when the call is placed on hold by pressing the **Transfer**, **Call Park**, or **Conference** button. Select the desired audio source from the drop-down list for each field. If no audio source is chosen, the source defined at the device level is used, and if None is chosen, the source set in the device pool is used.

Step 17. The **Auto Answer** field determines whether the line automatically answers incoming calls without the handset being lifted. This parameter can be set to auto-answer using the speakerphone or headset. If you want the line to auto-answer, select either Auto Answer with Headset or Auto Answer with Speakerphone from the drop-down list. If auto-answer is not desired on the line, leave this field set to Auto Answer Off.

AAR Settings

Step 18.   Automated Alternate Routing (AAR) is used to provide an alternate route if a call fails because of insufficient bandwidth. To have inbound calls that fail to reach this line because of insufficient bandwidth sent to voicemail, select the check box under Voice Mail. If you do not choose to send the calls to voicemail, you must choose an AAR group and you might need to configure the AAR destination mask. By default, AAR uses the external phone number mask to determine the fully qualified number of the destination. If you do not want to use the external phone number mask, enter the correct mask in the **AAR Destination Mask** field. The **AAR Group** field determines the AAR group with which the device is associated. An AAR group defines the prefix that is assigned when a call fails because of insufficient bandwidth. Select the appropriate AAR group from the drop-down list.

Call Forward and Pickup Settings

Step 19.   The next ten fields deal with call forwarding. These fields determine the forwarding destination, which depends on the reason for the forward. Table 3-2 provides ten forwarding types and associated actions.

You can configure each type of "forward" to forward calls to voicemail or a specific extension. To forward to voicemail, select the **Voice Mail** check box. To accomplish this, a voicemail profile must be defined for the line. To for-

Table 3-2   *Forward Types*

Forward Type	Forward Action
Forward All	Forwards all incoming calls
Forward Busy Internal	Forwards calls from internal callers when the line is busy
Forward Busy External	Forwards calls from external callers when the line is busy
Forward No Answer Internal	Forwards calls from internal callers that are not answered
Forward No Answer External	Forwards calls from external callers that are not answered
Forward No Coverage Internal	Forwards calls from internal callers when a line group has no coverage
Forward No Coverage External	Forwards calls from external callers when a line group has no coverage
Forward on CTI Failure	Forwards calls when a CTI route point or CTI port fails
Forward Unregistered Internal	Forwards calls from internal callers when the line is not registered
Forward Unregistered External	Forwards calls from external callers when the line is not registered

ward calls to another extension, enter the extension number in the **Destination** field. When a destination is entered into any of the internal forwards, the number is automatically entered into the corresponding external forward. If you want the external calls to be forwarded to a different destination, simply enter the desired destination in the appropriate external forward field. A calling search space can be applied to each forward type, which limits the destinations to which a call can be forwarded. This is useful when you want to restrict a line from forwarding calls to numbers that are long distance, but still want long-distance calls to be placed from the line. The CSS selected must contain the partition of the number in the destination field. Enter the appropriate destinations and calling search spaces for each forward type.

Step 20. In the **No Answer Ring Duration** field, enter the number of seconds that the line will ring before forwarding to the Forward No Answer destination. If this field is left blank, the value configured in the Communications Manager service parameter is used.

Step 21. The **Call Pickup Group** field determines which call pickup group this directory number belongs to. Call pickup groups allow a user to redirect an incoming call on another phone to the user's phone. Select the desired call pickup group from the drop-down list. Call pickup groups are covered in more detail in Chapter 6.

Park Monitoring

Step 22. The **Park Monitoring Forward No Retrieve Destination External** field determines where external calls are forwarded to when they are placed on park and not retrieved. To send them to voicemail, select the check box below Voice Mail. To send them to an alternative number, enter that number in the destination field. If the parker's CSS does not have rights to dial the alternate destination, you need to select a CSS from the Calling Search Space drop-down list.

Step 23. The **Park Monitoring Forward No Retrieve Destination Internal** field determines where internal calls are forwarded to when they are placed on park and not retrieved. To send them to voicemail, select the check box below Voice Mail. To send them to an alternative number, enter that number in the destination field. If the parker's CSS does not have rights to dial the alternate destination, you need to select a CSS from the Calling Search Space drop-down list.

Step 24. The **Park Monitoring Reversion Timer** field determines how many seconds a call can be parked before Communications Manager sends an alert to the parker phone. If left blank, the value set in the service parameters is used. The default is 60 seconds.

MLPP Alternate Party Settings

Step 25. The next set of parameters deals with MLPP alternative party settings. These settings allow you to configure an alternate destination for precedence calls that are not answered on this line or the forwarded number assigned to this line. If MLPP is not being used, these parameters can be left empty. In the first field, which is labeled **Target (Destination)**, enter the number to which unanswered precedence calls should be forwarded.

Step 26. In the **MLPP Calling Search Space** field, select the appropriate search space from the drop-down list. This calling search space limits the destinations to which precedence calls can be forwarded.

Step 27. In the **MLPP No Answer Ring Duration** field, enter the number of seconds that the phone will ring when it receives a precedence call before forwarding to the Forward No Answer destination if unanswered.

Line Settings for all Devices

Step 28. The **Hold Reversion Ring Duration** field determines how many seconds a call can be on hold before Communications Manager rings the phone that placed the call on hold. The call will ring until it is answered or the maximum hold duration expires. Enter the desired amount of seconds in this field. If left blank, the value set in the service parameters is used.

Step 29. The **Hold Reversion Notification Interval** field determines the intervals at which the holding parties receive an alert reminding them that a call is on hold. Enter the desired amount of seconds in this field. If left blank, the value set in the service parameters is used.

Step 30. The **Party Entrance Tone** field determines whether a tone is played when a new caller joins a call. When this parameter is set to **Default**, the value set in the service parameters is used. To ensure that a tone is played, set this to **On**. To ensure that no tone is played, set this to **Off**.

Line Settings for this Device

Step 31. The set of parameters under Line Settings for this Device define caller ID, Message Waiting Indicator (MWI), and ring settings. The first two fields, labeled **Display (Internal Call ID)**, are used to configure which caller ID is displayed when calls placed to other internal callers are connected. Enter up to 30 characters in this field. Both letters and numbers are allowed. If this field is left blank, the line's directory number will be used.

Note There two fields for the Internal Caller ID. The second, which is labeled ASCII Display, is used for devices that do not support Unicode character display. This is also true for the next two fields, which are labeled Line Text Label.

Step 32. The next two fields, which are labeled **Line Text Label**, are used to define how the line displays on the phone. If you want the extension number to display next to the line button, leave this field blank. To display a label other than the directory number next to the line button, enter that label in this field.

Step 33. The **External Phone Number Mask** field can be used to modify the external caller ID for calls placed from this line. An example mask might be

408370XXXX. The extension number is used to fill in the XXXX portion. In this example, if the directory number is 1401, the external phone mask would cause the external caller ID number to be 4083701401. The external phone mask on the first line creates the fully qualified directory number that is displayed above the first extension on certain IP phones. The configuration also makes the fully qualified number appear on the top bar of the phone's display. The external phone number mask is also used with AAR. Masks are explored in further detail in Chapter 4, "Implementing a Route Plan."

Step 34. The **Visual Message Waiting Indicator Policy** field determines whether the light on the phone is turned on when a new message is left for this extension. In most cases, this value should be left at Use System Policy. The available choices are as follows:

- **Light and Prompt:** The light turns on and the envelope icon next to the line displays.

- **Prompt Only:** Only the envelope icon next to the line displays.

- **Light Only:** Only the light is turned on.

- **None:** No indication is used.

- **Use System Policy:** Uses the setting selected in CCM services parameters.

Step 35. The **Audible Message Indicator Policy** field determines whether a stutter dial tone is heard when a message is waiting. Select Off to disable this. Select On to enable this.

Step 36. The next two settings determine whether the phone rings when incoming calls are being received on this directory number. In most cases, this value should be left at Use System Default. The available choices are as follows:

- **Disable:** Phone does not ring.

- **Flash Only:** The light flashes. No ring.

- **Ring Once:** Rings once and then stops.

- **Ring:** Normal ringing.

- **Beep Only:** A beep is played (only valid for the Phone Active setting).

- **Use System Policy:** Uses the setting selected under services parameters.

Step 37. Select the desired value for **Ring Setting (Phone Idle)** and **Ring Setting (Phone Active)**.

Step 38. The **Call Pickup Group Audio Alert Setting (Phone Idle)** parameter determines whether members of a call pickup group will hear a tone while their phone is on hook and a call comes in to another member of the call pickup group. To ensure that an alert is not sent, set this parameter to **Disable**. To have a short ring sent, set the parameter to **Ring Once**. To use the service parameters settings, set the parameter to **Use System Default**.

Step 39. The **Call Pickup Group Audio Alert Setting (Phone Active)** parameter determines whether members of a call pickup group will hear a tone while they are on a call and a call comes in to another member of their call pickup group. To ensure that an alert is sent, set the parameter to **Disable**. To have a short ring sent, set the parameter to **Ring Once**. To use the service parameters settings, set the parameter to **Use System Default**.

Step 40. The **Monitoring Calling Search Space** field is used when silent monitoring is used. A supervisor must have a CSS that can access the lines that are to be monitored.

Multiple Call / Call Waiting Settings

Step 41. The next field, which is labeled **Maximum Number of Calls**, determines how many active calls can be on the line. The maximum is 200 active calls per phone. Enter the maximum number of calls in this field. The default of 4 should be adequate for most phones.

Step 42. The field labeled **Busy Trigger** determines how many active calls are required before the line is considered busy. The default is 2. This means that if the maximum number of calls on the line is 4 and the busy trigger is 2, the third call will receive a busy indication. However, two more calls could be placed from this phone because the maximum number of calls is four.

Forwarded Call Information Display

Step 43. The **Forwarded Call Information Display** section determines what information is sent when a call is forwarded. Select the information to be sent by selecting the check box next to each desired field.

Users Associated with Line

Step 44. To associate an end user to a line, click the **Associate End Users** button. When the new window appears, click Find. Check the box next to the user you want to associate to the line, and click the **Add Selected** button.

Step 45. Click the **Save** button to complete the configuration of this line.

That's all there is to it! It is a simple task after you are familiar with all the parameters that need to be configured. However, if you are new to Communications Manager, a number of these parameters might seem confusing. Rest assured that these parameters will be explained in greater detail throughout the remainder of this book.

Using BAT to Add Devices

Imagine having to add more than a hundred phones and you must choose between adding them manually or using autoregistration. At first glance, you would most likely choose to add them using autoregistration. Normally, this would be a good choice;

however, you discover that each phone needs to have a specific directory number. To make things more complicated, a number of the phones need to use different phone button templates. You could still use autoregistration, but after the phones were added, you would have to change the directory numbers and phone button templates of each phone. It would be more efficient to add these phones and not have to go back and modify each one. This is where a utility called Bulk Administration Tool (BAT) comes in. BAT allows you to prepopulate Communications Manager with all the information for the phones before they are connected to the system. By adding the phones' information, a configuration file is created that the phones download from the TFTP server when it boots up.

Note Although this section portrays only BAT as a tool to add phones, it can be used to add gateways, client matter codes, forced authentication codes, pickup groups, and other information to the Communications Manager database. It can also be used to update device information and export information.

BAT adds devices to Communications Manager by importing a comma-separated values (CSV) file that contains the required information about the phones. The CSV file contains a number of fields that must be populated. The easiest way to create this CSV file is to use an Excel template that is included with BAT. The template is an Excel XTL file that is used to generate the CSV files. It offers an easy, well-formatted interface to add all the required and optional information.

Activating the BAT Service

In early versions of Communications Manager, BAT had to be installed before it could be used, but now it is installed by default and accessible from Communications Manager Administration. However, the Cisco Bulk Provisioning Service must be activated before you can use BAT. To activate the service, follow these steps:

Step 1.   Enter **https://[CM_IP Address]/ccmservice** in the address bar of your browser and press Enter.

Step 2.   Enter the administrative username and password and click **Login**.

Step 3.   Navigate to **Tools > Service Activation**.

Step 4.   Select the desired server from the Server drop-down list.

Step 5.   Select the check box next to the **Cisco Bulk Provisioning Service** and click **Save**.

Step 6.   A window will appear informing you that activating or deactivating service can take a while. Click **OK** and wait for the page to refresh.

BAT CSV and Template Overview

After the service is activated, CSV files and templates must be created. The order in which you create these is not too important. However, it is necessary that both are created before the next steps can be performed. To create a CSV file, it is recommended that you use the Excel template that was mentioned previously. The Excel template is stored on the Communications Manager server. You need to download the template to your PC before you can use it. To do this, follow these steps:

Step 1.   From within Communications Manager Administrator, select **Bulk Administration > Upload/Download Files**.

Step 2.   Click **Find**.

Step 3.   Select the check box next to the file named bat.xlt and click **Download Selected**.

Step 4.   Save the file in a location of your choosing using a descriptive name such as 7960BAT.xls.

The number of available fields in the template depends on the model of the phone you are importing. For example, the 7960 can contain more than 30 fields. The top row displays what information should be entered into the field and whether it is a required field. The fields include, but are not limited to, information such as the user's name, MAC address of the phone, directory numbers, and speed-dial numbers. When you first open the template, it displays only a few fields. The template then enables you to add other fields as you want. This feature enables you to avoid dealing with unneeded fields. After the information is added to the template, a CSV file is created and must be uploaded to the Communications Manager server. The necessary steps are presented later in this section.

It might appear that the hardest part of creating the CSV file is the entry of all the information. However, it is often more difficult to acquire the information that must be entered into the template. Make sure that you take the proper amount of time beforehand to ensure that you have obtained all the required information. The best way to get this information is to perform station reviews. A station review is a formal process that is used to record information about each phone that is to be added to the system. The information acquired during this process includes the number of lines (and directory numbers assigned to each), number of speeds, required features (conference calls, voicemail, and so on), and the type of calls that can be placed by the phone (local, national, international, and so on). This, of course, is only a sample of the information that is gathered during the station review process. It is important that you gather as much information as possible during station reviews. After this information is collected, you can create the CSV files.

In addition to the CSV file that is created, templates within the BAT application must also be created. These templates define the characteristics of the phones that you are going to add. These templates contain parameters for things such as phone type, phone button template, softkey templates, calling search spaces, number of lines, and partitions, just to name a few. After these templates are configured, they are used in concert with the CSV file that has been created to insert phones into the system. Because these templates contain many parameters, it might be necessary to create a number of templates depending upon your environment. For each set of phones that require different settings on any parameter defined within a template, a new template must be created. Now look at a simple example so that you can see how easily the number of these templates can grow.

Consider that you have 70 7940s and 50 7960s to deploy. Right off the bat (no pun intended), you know that you need at least two templates because there are two types of phones. For this example, assume that half the 7940s are going to be two-line phones and the other half are going to be one-line phones. This means that at least two templates are needed for the 7940s alone. As for the 7960s, assume that through the station review process, you determine that you need two-, three-, and four-line phones, which means that at least three templates are needed for the 7960s. If all the phones with the same number of lines do not differ in any other way, five templates in all are needed. However, just to make things interesting, consider that half of the three-line phones and half of the four-line phones require different calling search spaces. This adds the need for two more templates, bringing the total to seven. You can see how minor changes can cause the number of required templates to grow quite quickly. It is important to understand that because each template is used with a CSV file, you need to create the same number of CSV files as there are templates.

Note Make sure that you take time to determine the number of templates that will be needed. Sometimes after determining how many templates are needed, you might feel it is not worth the effort. I can remember an installation of 3000 phones that required more than 230 templates. Although this was a large number of templates, days if not weeks of time were saved on that deployment by creating the templates and CSV files. Keep in mind that this is an extreme example. Another deployment of 300 phones required only one template.

Before you can determine how many templates you need, you must be familiar with all the parameters that are set in the BAT templates. Each model of phone has unique parameters, but there are also a number of parameters that are common among all models. The following is an example of some of the parameters that can be defined in the template for most models of phones:

- Protocol
- Device Pool
- Calling Search Space
- AAR Calling Search Space
- User and Network Hold Audio Source
- Location
- User Locale
- Network Locale

- Phone Button Template
- Phone Load Name
- External Data Locations
- Multilevel Precedence and Preemption Information
- Number of Lines

By taking the number of different models of phone that will be deployed and determining how many of the parameters defined in the template will be different among like models, you can determine approximately how many templates and CSV files that must be created.

Note After you have set up a template, you can often reuse it with only minor modifications.

Now that you have a good overview of what is required for BAT to work, take a look at the steps required to add phones to the system using BAT.

After BAT is installed, you can begin the process of creating the CSV files and the templates. Before creating the templates and CSV files, you should have conducted a detailed analysis of the phones that are to be deployed. Based on the disparity of the phones in your system, you should have a good idea of how many templates and CSV files you need. The analysis should also have supplied the information that will be needed to create the templates and files.

You can create either the template or the CSV file first. In the steps that follow, the creation of the CSV file is described first.

Note It's a good idea to use same naming convention for both the template and the CSV file that will be used together. This way, when you are selecting the CSV file, it is easy to determine which file goes with which template.

Creating a CSV File for BAT

Follow these steps to create the CSV file:

Step 1. Open the BAT template in Excel. You might get a security warning about macros. Macros must be enabled for this template to function properly, so you might need to change Excel's settings to allow this.

Step 2. Select the **Phones** tab. A template similar to that shown in Figure 3-9 displays. As you can see, by default, only two fields display in the template.

Step 3. Click the **Create File Format** button to add fields.

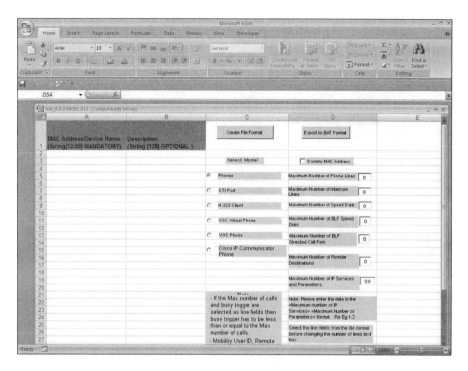

Figure 3-9 *Excel BAT Template*

Step 4. A screen similar to that shown in Figure 3-10 should display. Select the device, line, and intercom fields that you want to add to the template by highlighting the field in the box on the left side and clicking the double arrows (**>>**).

Step 5. To remove the device, line, and intercom fields from the template, highlight the field in the box on the right side and click the double arrows (**<<**).

Step 6. After you move all the desired fields to the box on the right side, click the **Create** button. When asked whether you want to overwrite the existing CSV format, click **Yes**.

Step 7. Proceed to the far right of the template, and in the appropriately labeled fields (refer to Figure 3-8), enter the number of lines and speed dials these phones will have. Then click another field so that the new values will register. When you enter information in these fields, the template adds the appropriate fields.

Step 8. At this point, the template is ready for the data to be entered.

Step 9. After all the data is entered, click the **Export to BAT Format** button, which is located at the upper-right portion of the template.

Step 10. You are prompted for a place to store this file. BAT creates a default location and filename. An example is C:\XlsDataFiles\Phones-02102010135805. BAT

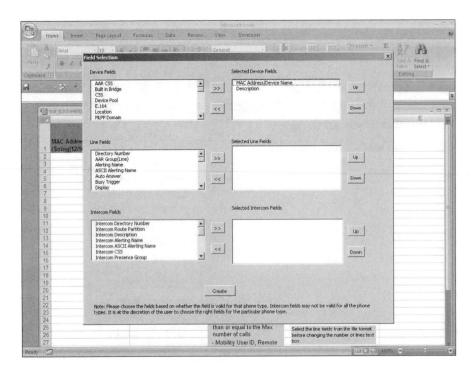

Figure 3-10   *Excel BAT Template File Format*

always selects c:\XlsDataFiles as the default file location. The filename is based in part on the tab you have selected to export, such as Phones, PhoneUsers, and UserDeviceProfiles, followed by a hyphen. The second part of the filename is the date and time that the file was exported. Note that in the preceding example, 02102010135815 represents February 10, 2010 at 1:58 p.m. and 15 seconds. If you prefer a different file location or name, you can change it before clicking **OK**.

After the CSV file is created, you need to upload it to the Communications Manager server. The following steps illustrate how to upload a file to the Communications Manager server:

Step 1.   From within Communications Manager Administrator, select **Bulk Administration > Upload/Download Files.**

Step 2.   Click the **Add New** link.

Step 3.   A window similar to the one shown in Figure 3-11 will appear. Click **Browse**, and select the CSV file you created.

Step 4.   Select the type of data in the CSV file from the **Select The Target** drop-down list. For example, if the CSV contained the information for phones that you added, select **Phones**.

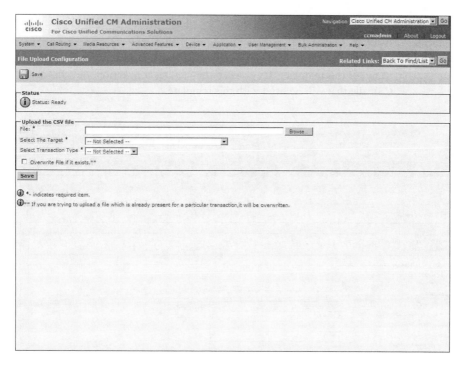

Figure 3-11 *File Upload*

Step 5.   Select the type of transaction that you want to complete, such as **Insert Phones**.

Note   If a file of the same name already exists, you need to select the **Overwrite File** check box.

Step 6.   Click **Save** and the file is uploaded.

Adding Phones Using BAT

The process of inserting phones using BAT is actually a four-stage process, and each stage has its own set of steps. The first stage of adding phones in BAT is creating the templates. A template is used to define the settings for devices added by BAT. The following steps walk you through this process. A 7965 template is created in this example.

Step 1.   From within Communications Manager Administrator, select **Bulk Administration > Phones > Phone Template**.

Step 2.   Click the **Add New** link.

Step 3.   Select the model of the phone you are adding and click **Next**.

Step 4.   Now select the proper protocol and click **Next.**

Step 5.   A screen similar to that shown in Figure 3-12 displays. On this screen, you define the parameters for this template. In the Template Name field, enter a name for this template. Try to keep the naming convention the same as for the CSV file that will be used with this template.

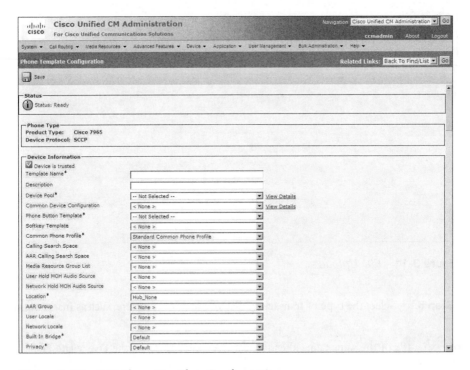

Figure 3-12   *BAT Phone Template Configuration*

Step 6.   The remainder of this page contains all the parameters that can be configured for the device. Because all these parameters are covered earlier in this chapter, they are not discussed in this section. If necessary, refer to Steps 7–70 in the "Manually Adding Phones" section, earlier in this chapter, for details of each parameter. Enter the appropriate information in each field.

Step 7.   After the parameters have been configured, click the **Save** button at the top of the screen. When the save is complete, a window similar to the one shown in Figure 3-13 appears.

Step 8.   After the template is inserted, line details need to be configured. Click **Line[1] - Add a New DN.**

Step 9.   A screen similar to that shown in Figure 3-14 displays. This screen is used to define all the parameters for this line. A name must be assigned to each line template. Because all the remaining parameters are covered earlier in this chapter, they are not discussed in this section. If necessary, refer to Steps 6–44 in the "Add a Line to a Phone" section, earlier in this chapter, for details on each parameter. Enter the appropriate information in each field and click **Save**.

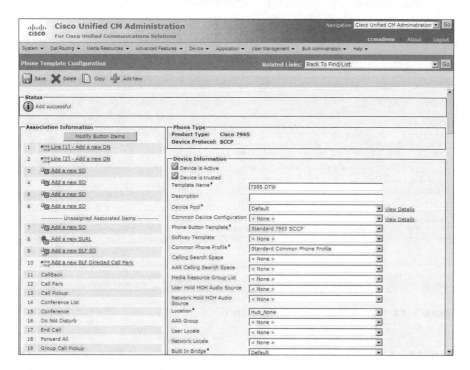

Figure 3-13   *Phone Template*

Step 10. To configure additional lines, select **Configure Device** from the Related Links drop-down menu and click **Go**. Now repeat Steps 8 through 9 for each additional line.

Step 11. When configuring templates for certain models of phones, you can also add speed dial and services to the template. To add speed dials to the template, click one of the lines labeled **Add a New SD** or select **Add/Update Speed Dials** from the Related Links drop-down menu and click **Go**.

Step 12. A screen displays that allows you to add two types of speed dials. The first type is associated with a button on the phones. The user accesses the second type by pressing the two-digit speed-dial number (which has the number he wants to reach assigned to it) and by pressing the **AbbrDial** softkey. Enter the desired speed dials and click **Save**. After you have entered all speed dials, click **Close**.

Step 13. To add services to the template, select **Subscribe/Unsubscribe Services** from the Related Links drop-down menu and click **Go**. Services are cover in more detail in Chapter 6.

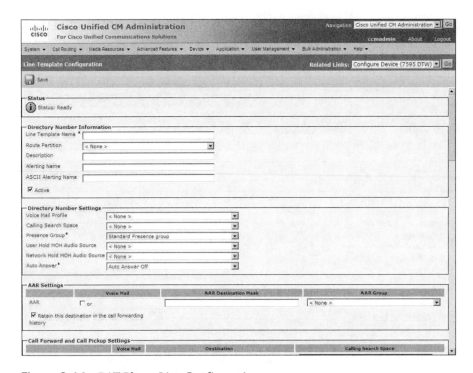

Figure 3-14   *BAT Phone Line Configuration*

Step 14.   A window displays that allows you to select the available services. Select the desired service and click **Next**. Enter any additional information that the service might require and click **Subscribe**.

Step 15.   After all services have been added, the template is complete. Click the **Save** button and close the window.

Step 16.   Now click the **Save** button on the Phone Template configuration screen.

Now that the template and CSV file are created, it is time to validate that the information in the CSV file will align with the template that was created. For example, if the CSV file has two directory numbers defined but the template has only one, the validation process will alert you. The following steps show you how to validate the data.

Step 1.   From within Communications Manager Administrator, select **Bulk Administration > Phones > Validate Phones**.

Step 2.   Make sure that the **Validate Phones Specific Details** radio button is selected. From the File Name drop-down list, select the CSV file that you created using the Excel template. Only the CSV file uploaded will display in this list.

Step 3.   Select the corresponding template that you created from the **Phone Template Name** drop-down list.

> **Note** The Validate Phone All Details radio button and corresponding File Name field are used to validate from an exported phones file that was generated by using the All Details option.

Step 4. Click the **Submit** button, and the validation request will be sent to the job scheduler.

After the job is submitted, you will want to check to confirm the completion and review the results. The following steps illustrate this process:

Step 1. From within Communications Manager Administrator, select **Bulk Administration > Job Scheduler**.

Step 2. Click **Find**.

Step 3. A list of jobs will appear. If the one you are interested in is complete (check the status column), click the job ID and the results of the validation will appear.

If everything was configured properly, the report should show that no errors were found. If errors were found, click the name in the Log File Name column to review the log. When you have determined why it failed, correct the problem and repeat the validation process.

These last steps examine how to insert the phones into the Communications Manager database:

Step 1. From within Communications Manager Administrator, select **Bulk Administration > Phones > Insert Phones**.

Step 2. Make sure that the **Insert Phones Specific Details** radio button is selected. From the File Name drop-down list, select the CSV file that you created using the Excel template. Only the uploaded CSV file will display in this list.

Step 3. Select the corresponding template that you created from the **Phone Template Name** drop-down list.

Step 4. Leave the **Create Dummy MAC Address** check box deselected. Dummy MAC addresses are with Tool for Auto-Registered Phones Support (TAPS), which is discussed later in this chapter.

> **Note** The Insert Phone All Details radio button and corresponding File Name fields are used to insert from an exported phones file that was generated by using the All Details option.

Step 5. The next section is Override Options. If you are inserting phones that are already in the database, you might need to select the override option so that the new data is inserted. Select the check boxes associated with the data you want to overwrite.

Step 6.   In the Job Information section, enter a descriptive name for this transaction and then select the Run Immediately radio button. This will cause the job to run as soon as you click the Submit button. If you want to wait and run the job later, select the **Run Later** radio button.

Step 7.   Click **Submit**, and the job will be submitted to the scheduler.

After the job is submitted, you will want to confirm the completion and check the results. The following steps describe this process:

Step 1.   From within Communications Manager Administrator, **select Bulk Administration > Job Scheduler.**

Step 2.   Click **Find.**

Step 3.   A list of jobs will appear. If the one you are interested in is complete (check the status column), click the job ID, and the results of this transaction will appear.

If everything was done properly, the report should show that no errors were found. If errors were found, click the name in the Log File Name column to review the log. When you have determined why it failed, correct the problem and repeat the process.

Adding Phones Using TAPS

A more advanced method of adding phones, called Tool for Auto-registered Phone Support (TAPS), is also available. This tool allows you to prepopulate Communications Manager's database with all the information about the phones, except for the MAC address. After the information is entered, the phones are plugged into the system and autoregistered. Because the MAC addresses have not been entered into the system, the TFTP server cannot deliver a configuration file to the phone based on the MAC address. This causes a default configuration to be issued and the phone to be registered with basic configuration. After the phone is registered, a predetermined number is dialed that routes the call to an Interactive Voice Response (IVR) server. The IVR server asks what language you would like to use and the extension number that should be assigned to the phone. After this is completed, the MAC address of the phone is associated with the configuration that matches the extension number entered, and a configuration file is created. The phone gets this file from the TFTP server when it reboots.

Integrators often use this method of adding phones during large deployments. Because this method allows the integrator to populate the system without having to add MAC addresses, the deployment of the phones is simpler. Integrators don't have to make sure that a certain phone with a certain MAC address is plugged into a certain jack. The integrator need only be concerned that the proper model is placed in each location. Previous to the introduction of this tool, the MAC addresses had to be entered before the phones were deployed, and this required the integrator to label the box of each phone with the extension number for which it was configured. This also meant that no information could be added to the system until the phones were in hand.

The detailed steps for TAPS are outside the scope of this book, but further information can be found in the Cisco Bulk Administration Tool documentation on the Cisco website. You can find the latest copy of this by searching for "bulk administration tool guide" at Cisco.com.

Adding Gateways

After phones are configured, calls can be placed to other phones within the cluster. Although this is useful, it has its limitations. Imagine if the phone system were allowed to reach only other phones within the cluster. Most likely, not many of these systems would be sold. Therefore, you need to consider how to allow calls outside the cluster. This is accomplished by configuring gateways that connect the cluster to other systems. The function of a gateway is to allow connectivity between dissimilar systems, that is, to allow your phone system to make calls to other phone systems.

In most cases, the first system you should connect to your system is the public switched telephone network (PSTN). This allows callers on your system to call nearly any other phone in the world. In addition to connecting to the PSTN, you might also want to connect your system to other systems in your company and bypass the PSTN. In either case, the steps are similar.

The following sections explore six types of gateways. The main difference in these gateways is the protocol that they use to communicate with the Communications Manager. Their functions are the same: to provide connectivity to another system.

Table 3-3 describes the six types of gateways and gives a brief description of each.

Adding H.323 Gateways

The first type of gateway to be discussed is an H.323 gateway. H.323 is best described as a suite of protocols. It is also often referred to as an umbrella under which a number of other protocols exist. The specifics of what H.323 is and how it works are far beyond the scope of this book. This section focuses on the process of configuring an H.323 gateway.

The configuration steps required for an H.323 gateway are somewhat more advanced than those for other types of gateways. This is because much of the configuration has to be done using the command-line interface (CLI) of the gateway itself. For example, when configuring a Media Gateway Control Protocol (MGCP) gateway, only a few commands must be entered in the CLI, and Communications Manager handles all the call routing. An H.323 gateway does not depend on the Communications Manager for call routing; it contains a dial plan of its own. This means that the dial plan must be entered using the CLI, which increases the difficulty of configuring an H.323 gateway. To properly configure an H.323 gateway, you must have a high level of experience in configuring IOS devices for VoIP deployments. Because it is not possible to provide you with all the required knowledge to configure the CLI portion of an H.323 gateway in a book of this size, we focus on the steps required in CCMAdmin. The CLI configuration varies in each environment and can sometimes become quite complex. For more information on the CLI configuration for an H.323 gateway, refer to the Cisco IOS Voice, Video, and Fax Configuration Guide, which can be found at Cisco.com by searching "Cisco IOS Voice, Video, and Fax Configuration Guide."

Table 3-3   *Gateway Descriptions*

Gateway	Connectivity	Requires Own Dial Plan Configuration?	Amount of Configuration Required
H.323	Used to connect to the PSTN	Yes	Requires a significant amount of configuration on the gateway
MGCP	Used to connect to the PSTN	No	Requires minimal configuration on the gateway
Non-IOS MGCP	Used to connect to the PSTN	No	Requires almost no configuration on the gateway itself
SCCP	Used to connect to the analog port gateways	No	Requires minimal configuration on the gateway
Intercluster Trunk	Connects Communications Manager clusters together	No	All configuration is done on the Communications Manager
SIP	Connects Communications Manager to SIP trunks and devices	Yes	Requires some configuration on the gateway

After the entire CLI configuration of the gateway is completed, it can be configured in Communications Manager. There are a number of Cisco devices that can be configured as H.323 gateways. Because the list of supported devices is always evolving, it is best to check the Cisco website to see what gateways currently support H.323. You can find a list of supported gateways by searching "Understanding Voice Gateways" at Cisco.com. You can further refine the search by including the Communications Manager version with this search. For example, by searching "Understanding Voice Gateways 4.1(2)," the first result is a link to the correct page. Because there are a variety of devices that can be configured as an H.323 gateway, it is impossible to include a step-by-step guide on how to configure each of them. Because the configurations are similar, you should be able to use the following steps to configure a Cisco 3620 as an H.323 gateway and install the H.323 gateway you choose.

The following steps are required to configure a Cisco 3825 as an H.323 gateway. Because there are a number of steps to this process, section headings are used to mark the point at which each new set of parameters begins. These same headings display on the configuration screen as well, which should help you keep track of where you are.

Step 1. From within CCMAdmin, select **Device > Gateway**.

Step 2. Click the **Add New** link.

Step 3. Select H.323 Gateway from the **Gateway Type** drop-down list and click **Next**.

Device Information

Step 4. The Gateway Configuration screen, as shown in Figure 3-15, displays. Enter the DNS name or IP address of the gateway in the **Device Name** field.

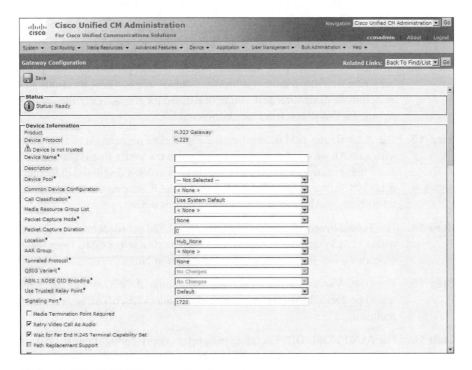

Figure 3-15 *H.323 Gateway Configuration*

Step 5. In the **Description** field, enter a description that will help make this device easily identifiable.

Step 6. From the **Device Pool** drop-down list, select the desired Communications Manager group for this gateway.

Step 7.   From the **Common Device Configuration** drop-down list, select the common device configuration (CDC) the gateway will use. If you have not configured a CDC, leave this set to <none>.

Step 8.   From the **Call Classification** drop-down list, select whether incoming calls on this device should be considered OnNet or OffNet. This parameter is used to determine whether calls can be transferred and forwarded to help prevent fraud.

Step 9.   The next field is **Media Resource Group List**. This determines the accessibility of media resources to the phone. Media resources are discussed in further detail in Chapter 6. From the Media Resource Group List drop-down list, select the desired group. If no media resource group list is chosen, the one defined in the device pool is used.

Step 10.   The **Packet Capture Mode** parameter is only used during troubleshooting and is beyond the scope of this book. Leave this set to None.

Step 11.   The **Packet Capture Duration** parameter is also only used for troubleshooting and is beyond the scope of this book. Leave this set to 0.

Step 12.   Information entered in the **Location** field is used to prevent WAN links from becoming oversubscribed in centralized deployments. These locations are discussed more in Chapter 5. If you have defined locations, select the appropriate one for this phone from the drop-down list.

Step 13.   The **AAR Group** field determines the appropriate association of this device with an AAR group. An AAR group provides the prefix that is assigned when a call fails because of insufficient bandwidth. AAR is discussed in further detail in Chapter 6. Select an AAR group if AAR is being used. If this field is set to None, AAR is, in effect, disabled on this device.

Step 14.   The **Tunnel Protocol** parameter allows non-H.323 protocol information to be within H.323 signaling information. To enable this, select QSIG from the drop-down list. In most cases, this can be left at None.

Step 15.   The **QSIG Variant** parameter is only configurable if QSIG is selected as the tunnel protocol. Leave this parameter alone unless Cisco TAC instructs you to change it.

Step 16.   The **ASN.1 ROSE OID** Encoding parameter is only configurable if QSIG is selected as the tunnel protocol and is beyond the scope of this book.

Step 17.   The **Use Trusted Relay Point** field determines whether a relay point such as a Media Termination Point (MTP) or a transcoder must be labeled trusted to be used by this device. This field is typically changed only in virtualized environments.

Step 18.   The **Signaling Port** field defines the H.225 signaling that the gateway uses. The default of 1720 can be used in most cases.

Step 19. The **Media Termination Point Required** check box needs to be selected if the H.323 device does not support features such as hold and transfers. This is the case with H.323 version 1 gateways. These gateways cannot support such features because H.323v1 does not have the capability to modify a channel, which means that it cannot transfer a call or place a call on hold. That would require modifying the channel.

Step 20. If the **Retry Video Calls as Audio** check box is selected, Communications Manager sets up a voice call if a video call fails to set up.

Step 21. When the **Wait for Far End H.245 Terminal Capability Set** check box is selected, Communications Manager expects to receive the far end's capabilities before sending its own.

Step 22. **Path Replacement Support** is used in conjunction with QSIG tunneling and is automatically selected when QSIG is selected as the tunnel protocol. Leave this set at the default.

Step 23. If **Transmit UTF-8 for Calling Party Name** is left deselected, the user locale setting in the device pool will be used to determine whether Unicode information is sent and translated. Typically, this can be left at the default.

Step 24. If you want to allow both secure and nonsecure calls on this gateway, you must select the **SRTP Allowed** check box. If this is not selected, only nonsecure calls are allowed.

Step 25. If the **H.235 Pass Through Allowed** check box is selected, the shared-secret key will be able to pass through a Communications Manager, allowing H.323 endpoints to set up a secure connection.

Step 26. If this gateway is used to connect to the PSTN, make sure that the **PSTN Access** check box is selected.

Step 27. The only MLPP setting that can be configured is the **MLPP Domain**. Enter the domain in this field. If left blank, the settings found in enterprise parameters are used.

Call Routing Information—Inbound Calls

Step 28. The next set of fields deals with inbound calls. The **Significant Digits** field determines the number of digits of an incoming dialed number that Communications Manager uses. Communications Manager counts from right to left, so if the number entered in this field is 4 and the digits received are 8105559090, 810555 would be removed and only 9090 would be used to determine the destination of this call.

Step 29. A Calling Search Space (CSS) determines the accessibility and destination of an inbound call to the gateway CSS, as discussed in Chapter 5. Choose a CSS from the **Calling Search Space** drop-down list. If this field is left at None, the dial privileges of this device could be limited.

Step 30. The Automated Alternate Routing (AAR) is used to provide an alternate route if a call fails because of insufficient bandwidth. The AAR CSS can be used to limit the paths a call can use when it is rerouted. Select an AAR CSS from the **AAR Calling Search Space** drop-down list.

Step 31. The **Prefix DN** field defines what digits will be added to the front of the incoming destination number. This is applied to the number after Communications Manager truncates the number based on the Significant Digits setting.

Step 32. If your voicemail system supports redirecting number IE, select the **Redirecting Number IE Delivery–Inbound** check box. Otherwise, leave this box deselected.

Step 33. Select the **Enable Inbound FastStart** check box if you want to support H.323 FastStart. H.323 FastStart requires only two message exchanges to open logical channels, whereas normal setup requires 12. However, if FastStart is selected, both ends must support and be configured for FastStart.

Call Routing Information—Outbound Calls

Step 34. The next set of fields examines outbound calls. The **Calling Party Selection** field determines what number is sent to outbound calls. The Calling Party Selection choices are as follows:

- **Originator:** The directory number of the device that placed the call

- **First Redirect Number:** The directory number of the first device to forward the call

- **Last Redirect Number:** The directory number of the last device to forward the call

- **First Redirect Number (External):** The external directory number of the first device to forward the call

- **Last Redirect Number (External):** The external directory number of the last device to forward the call

Select the desired value for this field.

Step 35. The **Calling Party Presentation** field determines whether Communications Manager sends caller ID information. To send caller ID information, select Allowed from the drop-down list. To block caller ID, select Restricted from the drop-down list.

Step 36. Cisco recommends that the next four fields remain set to the default of Cisco CallManager:

- Called party IE number type unknown

- Calling party IE number type unknown

- Called Numbering Plan

- Calling Numbering Plan

These fields deal with dial plan issues and should be changed only when advised to do so by Cisco or an experienced dial plan expert. The need to change these usually occurs when installing Communications Manager internationally.

Step 37. The **Caller ID DN** field is used to determine what caller ID is sent out this gateway. A mask or a complete number can be entered in this field. For example, if the mask 55536XX is entered in this field, Communications Manager sends 55536 and the last two digits of the directory number (DN) that is placing the call.

Step 38. If the **Display IE Delivery** check box is selected, the calling and called party name information is included in messages.

Step 39. The **Redirecting Number IE Delivery–Outbound** check box should be selected when integrating with a voicemail system that supports redirecting number IE. Otherwise, leave it deselected.

Step 40. Select the **Enable Outbound FastStart** check box if you want to support H.323 FastStart. H.323 FastStart requires only two message exchanges to open logical channels, whereas normal setup requires 12. However, if FastStart is selected, both ends must support and be configured for FastStart.

Step 41. If FastStart Outbound is enabled, you must select a codec to be used for FastStart. Select the desired codec from the **Codec for Outbound FastStart** drop-down list.

Step 42. Called party transformation allows you to change the number that is dialed. The CSS selected must have access to the calling party transformation pattern that is assigned to the device. You can also leave this set to None and use the Called Party Transformation CSS assigned to the device pool by selecting the **Use Device Pool Called Party Transformation CSS** check box.

Step 43. Calling party transformation allows you to change the caller ID. Select a **Calling Party Transformation CSS** that contains the called party transformation pattern that is assigned to the device. You can also leave this set to None and use the Calling Party Transformation CSS assigned to the device pool by selecting the Use Device Pool Calling Party Transformation CSS check box.

Geolocation

Step 44. Some features might require geolocation information. This information is also referred to as a civic address. The geolocation information can be used to determine the logical partition of a device. If you are using the geolocation feature, select the appropriate geolocation from the **Geolocation** drop-down list.

Step 45.   There are 17 configurable geolocation fields. Geolocation filters allow you choose which fields are used to create a geolocation identifier. If you are using the geolocation feature, select the appropriate geolocation filter from the **Geolocation Filter** drop-down list.

Intercompany Media Engine

Step 46.   **E.164 Transformation Profiles** are used when Intercompany Media Engine (IME) is used. IME allows different companies to automatically learn routes that allow calls to travel across the Internet instead of the PSTN.

Incoming Calling/Called Party Settings

Step 47.   The Incoming Calling Party settings and Incoming Called Party settings are used to globalize numbers. Each calling and called party number has a number type assigned to it. The incoming calling/called part settings are based on the number type assigned. There are four number types: national, international, unknown, and subscriber. There are four settings for each of these number types:

- **Prefix:** Digits entered are added to the beginning of the number after the number of strip digits specified are removed.

- **Strip Digits:** The number of digits that should be stripped from the number before the prefix is applied.

- **Calling Search Space:** The CSS that is used after transformation has occurred.

- **Use Device Pool CSS:** When this check box is selected, the device pool CSS is used.

If your environment requires the manipulation of incoming called and calling numbers, configure the appropriate settings for each of these fields.

Step 48.   Click Save.

Adding MGCP Gateways

Cisco recommends that you use a Media Gateway Control Protocol (MGCP) gateway whenever possible. MGCP is a protocol that, as its name implies, is used to control gateways. Unlike H.323, MGCP does not handle the routing of calls; it depends on Communications Manager for this. Therefore, very little needs to be configured at the CLI.

MGCP gateways that are used in a Cisco Communications Manager solution are separated into two categories: Internetworking Operating System (IOS) and non-IOS MGCP gateways. The difference is whether the device that is acting as the gateway is running IOS or not. For example, a 3825, which runs IOS, is considered an IOS gateway, whereas a

Catalyst 6500 running native IOS is considered a non-IOS gateway. The following section focuses on IOS MGCP Gateways. Non-IOS gateways are discussed in a later section.

Adding IOS MCGP Gateways

As with an H.323 gateway, some configuration must be done from the CLI of the gateway. Figure 3-16 shows a sample of the commands that previously had to be entered in the CLI to configure the gateway to communicate through MGCP. As you can see, the CLI configuration is quite simple. At present, it is even easier now that the MGCP gateway can be configured to download its configuration from the Communications Manger. Only two commands are required to configure this. They are

- ccm-manager config server 10.1.1.1

- ccm-manager config

```
mgcp
mgcp call-agent 172.10.10.1
mgcp dtmf-relay  codec all mode out-of-band
mgcp sdp simple
!
ccm-manager  switchback graceful
ccm-manager  redundant-host 172.10.10.10
ccm-manager mgcp
!
voice-port 1/1/1
!
dial-peer voice 4 pots
 application MGCPAPP
 port 1/1/1
```

Figure 3-16 *MGCP Gateway CLI Configuration Example*

An MGCP gateway does not require as much configuration on the gateway device because it relies on Communications Manager for all call routing functions. For this reason, it is recommended that an MGCP gateway be used whenever possible.

For more information on the CLI configuration for an MCGP gateway, refer to the Cisco IOS Voice, Video, and Fax Configuration Guide, which can be found at Cisco.com by searching for "Cisco IOS Voice, Video, and Fax Configuration Guide."

After the CLI configuration is completed, the MGCP gateway must be configured in CCMAdmin. There are a number of Cisco routers that can act as MGCP gateways, and it is not possible to include a step-by-step guide for each type in this section. However, because their configuration is similar, you should be able to use the following steps that show how to configure a Cisco 3825 as an MGCP gateway. You can use these steps as a guide to help you install the MGCP gateway you are using.

The following steps are required to configure a Cisco 3825 as an MGCP gateway. Because there are a number of steps to this process, section headings are used to mark the point at which each new set of parameters begins. These same headings display on the configuration screen as well, which should help you keep track of where you are.

Step 1.   From within CCMAdmin, select **Device > Gateway**.

Step 2.   Click the **Add New** link.

Step 3.   On the next page, select the desired gateway from the **Gateway Type** drop-down list. In this example, the 3825 is selected. Click **Next**.

Step 4.   Select MCGP from the **Protocol** drop-down list and click **Next**.

Step 5.   A page similar to that shown in Figure 3-17 displays. In the first field, enter the DNS name of the gateway in the **Domain Name** field, if DNS is configured to resolve this name. If DNS is not used, enter the host name of the gateway. It is important to note that if an IP domain name is configured on the router, it must be included in the Domain Name field. For example, if the host name is MGCPGateway and the IP domain name is configured as cisco.com, the Domain Name field should read MGCPGateway.cisco.com. The name is case-sensitive. The gateway will not register to Communications Manager if the name is not entered correctly.

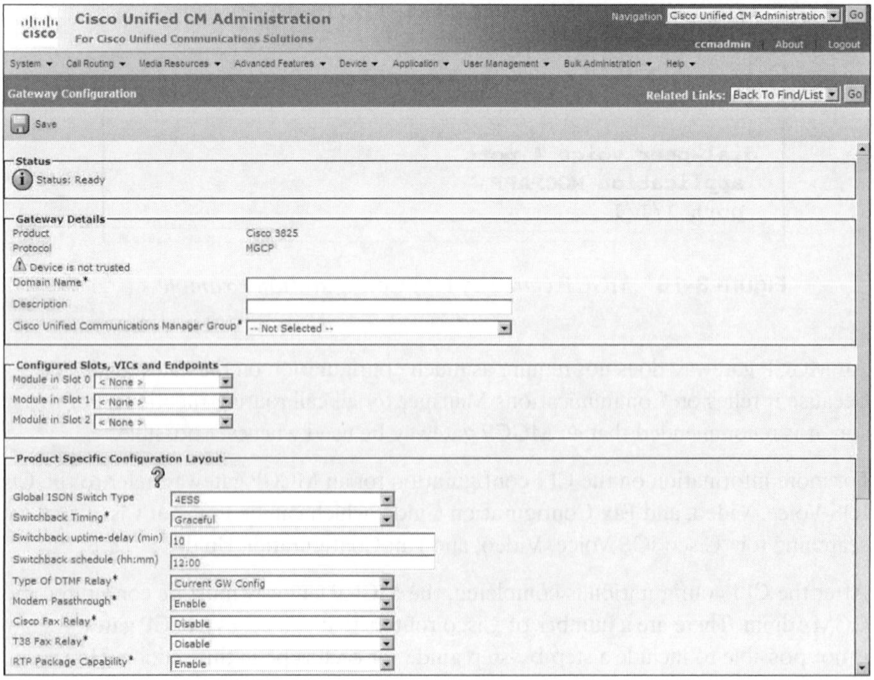

Figure 3-17   *MGCP Gateway Configuration*

Step 6. In the **Description** field, enter a description that will help make this device easily identifiable.

Step 7. From the **Cisco Unified Communications Manager Group** drop-down list, select the desired Communications Manager group for this gateway.

Installed Voice Cards

Step 8. The next set of fields defines what type of voice ports are installed in the gateway. This example assumes that two FXS and two FXO ports are installed. Select the voice module(s) from the drop-down list next to each slot. For this example, the NW-4VWIC-MBRD is selected.

Step 9. Click the **Save** button. New fields display next to each configured slot. From the Subunit drop-down list, select the device that is installed in this slot. In this example, VIC-2FXS was selected for subunit 0 and a VIC-2FXO was selected for subunit 1.

Step 10. Click the **Save** button. Endpoint identifiers display next to each configured subunit, as seen in Figure 3-18.

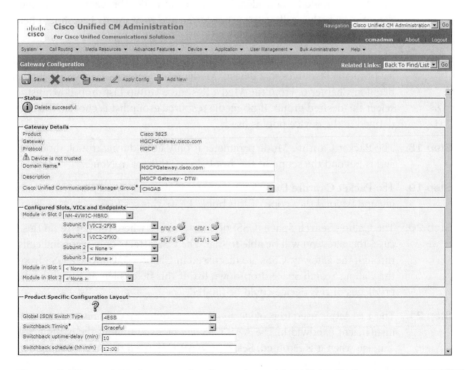

Figure 3-18 *MCGP Gateway Configuration with Endpoints*

Gateway Information

Step 11.   The endpoint identifiers must be configured. Select an endpoint to display the Endpoint Configuration page. In this example, the 0/0/0 FXS port is used. Select the 0/0/0 port by clicking the icon that looks like a phone jack with a question mark in the upper-right corner. Depending on the type of port selected, the fields you work with can differ.

Step 12.   On the next screen, select the port type from the drop-down list and click **Next**. In this example, POTS is selected.

Step 13.   A description for this endpoint is prepopulated in the **Description** field. You can modify it if you like.

Step 14.   From the **Device Pool** drop-down list, select the device pool that this endpoint will use.

Step 15.   From the **Common Device Configuration** drop-down list, select the common device configuration the device will use.

Step 16.   From the **Call Classification** drop-down list, select whether incoming calls on this device should be considered OnNet or OffNet. This parameter is used to determine whether calls can be transferred and forwarded. This should help prevent fraud.

Step 17.   The next field is the **Media Resource Group List.** It determines the accessibility of media resources to a device. Media resources are discussed in further detail in Chapter 6. From the Media Resource Group List drop-down list, select the desired group. If no media resource group list is chosen, the one defined in the device pool is used.

Step 18.   The **Packet Capture Mode** parameter is only used during troubleshooting and is beyond the scope of this book. Leave this set to None.

Step 19.   The **Packet Capture Duration** parameter is also only used for troubleshooting and beyond the scope of this book. Leave this set to 0.

Step 20.   The **Calling Search Space** (CSS) field determines where the device (in this case, the gateway) will be able to dial. The CSS affects only incoming calls through the gateway. CSSs are discussed in Chapter 5. Choose a CSS from the Calling Search Space drop-down list. If this field is left at None, the dial privileges of this device could be limited.

Step 21.   The z (AAR) is used to provide an alternate route if a call fails because of insufficient bandwidth. The AAR CSS can be used to limit the paths a call can use when it is rerouted. Select an AAR CSS from the **AAR Calling Search Space** drop-down list.

Step 22.   In centralized deployments, locations are used to prevent WAN links from becoming oversubscribed. These are discussed more in Chapter 5. If you have defined locations, select the appropriate one for the phone from the **Location** drop-down list.

Step 23. The **AAR Group** field determines the appropriate association of the device with an AAR group. An AAR group provides the prefix that is assigned when a call fails because of insufficient bandwidth. AAR is discussed in further detail in Chapter 6. If AAR is being used, select an AAR group. If this field is set to None, AAR is, in effect, disabled on this endpoint.

Step 24. The **Network Locale** field determines what locale is used for this endpoint. This impacts the tones and cadences used. The default network locale was defined in the enterprise parameters. If a different value is selected here, this value takes precedence. If this field is set to None, the enterprise parameter setting is used. If the phone requires a different locale than is defined by its device pools, or the enterprise parameters, select the proper one from the drop-down list.

Step 25. Some features might require geolocation information. This information is also referred to as a civic address. The geolocation information can be used to determine the logical partition of a device. If you are using the geolocation feature, select the appropriate geolocation from the **Geolocation** drop-down list.

Step 26. If **Transmit UTF-8 for Calling Party Name** is left deselected, the user locale setting in the device pool will be used to determine whether Unicode information is sent and translated. Typically, this can be left at the default.

Step 27. Calling party transformation allows you to change the caller ID. Select a **Calling Party Transformation CSS** that contains the called party transformation pattern that is assigned to the device. You can also leave this set to None and use the Calling Party Transformation CSS assigned to the device pool by selecting the Use Device Pool Calling Party Transformation CSS check box.

Step 28. **Hot Line Device** is an extension of PLAR. If this check box is selected, the device is restricted to connect only with other hot line devices.

Multilevel Precedence and Preemption (MLPP) Information

Step 29. The next three fields define the Multilevel Precedence and Preemption (MLPP) characteristics of the endpoint. The only field that applies to the device in this example is the **MLPP Domain**. MLPP grants higher priority only from calls with the same MLPP domain. For this reason, an MLPP domain is needed if MLPP is being used.

Port Information

Step 30. The **Port Direction** parameter determines whether this port is to be used for inbound or outbound calls. Select Inbound to set the port for inbound calls only. Select Outbound for outgoing calls only. To allow inbound and outbound calls, select Bothways.

Step 31. The **Prefix DN** field defines what digits will be added to the front of an incoming destination number. This is applied to the number after Communications Manager truncates the number based on the Num Digits setting.

Step 32. The **Num Digits** field determines the number of digits of an incoming dialed number that Communications Manager will use. Communications Manager counts from right to left, so if the number entered in this field is 4 and the digits received are 8105559090, 810555 would be removed and only 9090 would be used to determine the destination of this call.

Step 33. The **Expected Digits** field defines how many digits are expected on inbound calls. This field is rarely used and can be left at the default of 0 in most cases.

Step 34. The last field, which is the **SMDI Port Number**, is used only when integrating with a traditional voicemail system. The port number should be set to the same port number as on the voicemail system.

Step 35. The **Unattended Port** check box is used to indicate that the device has unattended ports. This is normally applied if the port is used to send calls to an application such as a voicemail server. In most cases, this box should be left deselected.

Step 36. Click **Save**. The endpoints now display on the left side of the page. After you have configured all the endpoints, directory numbers can be assigned.

Step 37. To add a directory number to an endpoint, click the **Add a new DN** link on the left side of the screen.

Step 38. The Directory Number Configuration page displays, which is just like the page used when adding a line to a phone. For detailed information on how to configure this page, refer to Steps 6–44 in the "Add a Line to a Phone" section, earlier in this chapter.

Step 39. Navigate to the Gateway Configuration page. To do this, select the **Configure Device** option from the Related Links drop-down list and click **Go**. Now, select **Back to MGCP Configuration** from the Related Links drop-down list and click **Go**.

Step 40. Configure the remaining ports by following the previous steps.

Step 41. After all configurations are completed, return to the Gateway Configuration page and click the **Reset** button.

Step 42. A window will appear from which you need to click **Reset**. When the status changes to *Reset request was sent successfully*, click **Close**.

Adding Non-IOS MGCP Gateways

As mentioned in the previous section, some non-IOS devices can be configured as MGCP gateways. Just as with the IOS MGCP gateway, these devices do not handle call-routing tasks. They depend on Communications Manager to handle all call-routing needs. Unlike the IOS MGCP gateway, there is virtually no configuration required on the gateway itself.

The most widely used non-IOS gateways are the Catalyst 6000 T1/E1 blades. The T1 blades are Cisco 6608s and have eight T1 ports. These ports must be configured in the

Catalyst switch with the appropriate IP configuration, including the TFTP server address and VLAN information. To complete the configuration of the T1 port in CCMAdmin, you need to know the MAC address of the port.

While the 6608 is no longer sold it is still in use in some environments so the following configuration steps have been provided. These steps take you through the configuration of a single T1 port of a 6608 as a non-IOS MGCP gateway. Because there are a number of steps to this process, section headings are used to mark the point at which each new set of parameters begins. These same headings also display on the configuration screen, which should help you keep track of where you are.

Step 1.   From within CCMAdmin, select **Device > Gateway**.

Step 2.   Click the **Add New** link.

Step 3.   On the next page, select the desired gateway from the Gateway Type drop-down list. In this example, the Cisco Catalyst 6000 T1 VoIP Gateway is selected. Click **Next**.

Step 4.   Select either Digital Access PRI or Digital Access T1 from the Protocol drop-down list and click **Next**. In this example the Digital Access PRI is used.

Device Information

Step 5.   The Gateway Configuration page displays. Enter the MAC address of the T1 port in the **MAC Address** field. The MAC address can be found by using the **show port** command at the CLI of the Catalyst 6000.

Step 6.   In the **Description** field, enter a description that will help make this device easily identifiable.

Step 7.   From the **Device Pool** drop-down list, select the device pool that this gateway or device will use.

Step 8.   From the **Common Device Configuration** drop-down list, select the common device configuration to be used by the gateway.

Step 9.   From the **Call Classification** drop-down list, select whether incoming calls on this device should be considered OnNet or OffNet. This parameter is used to determine whether calls can be transferred and forwarded. This should help prevent fraud.

Step 10.   From the **Network Locale** drop-down list, select the locale for this gateway. If it remains set to None, the locale selected in the device pool is used.

Step 11.   The next field is **Media Resource Group List**. It determines the accessibility of media resources to a device. Media resources are discussed in further detail in Chapter 6. From the Media Resource Group List drop-down list, select the desired group. If no media resource group list is chosen, the one defined in the device pool is used.

Step 12.   Locations are used to prevent WAN links from becoming oversubscribed in centralized deployments. These are discussed more in Chapter 5. If you have

defined locations, select the appropriate one for this device from the
Locations drop-down list.

Step 13. The **AAR Group** field determines the appropriate association of this device
with an AAR group. An AAR group defines the prefix that is assigned when a
call fails because of insufficient bandwidth. AAR is discussed in further detail
in Chapter 6. If AAR is being used, select an AAR group. If this field is set to
None, AAR is disabled on this gateway.

Step 14. The next field defines which firmware load ID the gateway uses. In most
cases, this field should be left blank. When left blank, the load ID specified
on the device defaults configuration page is used for this gateway. If the need
ever arises to set a specific gateway to a specific load ID, the load ID should
be entered in this field.

Step 15. The **Use Trusted Relay Point** field determines whether a relay point such as a
Media Termination Point (MTP) or a transcoder must be labeled as trusted to
be used by this device. This field is typically changed only in virtualized
environments.

Step 16. If **Transmit UTF-8 for Calling Party Name** is left deselected, the user locale
setting in the device pool will be used to determine whether Unicode information is sent and translated. Usually this can be left at the default.

Step 17. If this gateway is used to connect to the PSTN, make sure that the **PSTN
Access** check box is selected.

Multilevel Precedence and Preemption (MLPP) Information

Step 18. The next three fields define the Multilevel Precedence and Preemption
(MLPP) characteristics of this gateway. If these fields are left blank or set to
default, the values set in the device pool are used. The first MLPP field is the
MLPP Domain. MLPP grants higher priority only from calls with the same
MLPP domain. For this reason, an MLPP domain is needed.

Step 19. The second field in this category, which is called **MLPP Indication**, determines whether tones and indications will be presented when a precedence call
is made. If the is field set to Off, no precedence indication is presented. If this
field is set to On, indication is used for a precedence call.

Step 20. The third MLPP field is **MLPP Preemption**. This parameter determines
whether a higher-precedence call preempts a lower-precedence call. The value
of Disabled does not allow this to happen. To cause a lower-precedence call
to be terminated if a higher-precedence call requires the resources, set this
parameter to Forceful.

Interface Information

Step 21. The next set of fields defines characteristics of the interface. The first of these
fields, labeled **PRI Protocol Type**, defines the protocol used. The value placed
in this field depends on the type of equipment the T1 is connected to on the

other side. Your T1 provider should be able to supply this information. Select the appropriate protocol from the drop-down list.

Step 22.   The **QSIG Variant** parameter is only configurable if PRI ISO QSIG T1 is selected as the PRI protocol type. Leave this parameter alone unless Cisco TAC instructs you to change it.

Step 23.   The **ASN.1 ROSE OID Encoding** parameter is only configurable if PRI ISO QSIG T1 is selected as the PRI protocol type. It is beyond the scope of this book.

Step 24.   The **Protocol Side** field determines whether the T1 connects to a network device or a user device. The easiest explanation is that one side must be User and the other side Network. If connecting to the phone company's central office (CO), you will most likely choose User. Select the appropriate protocol side from the drop-down list.

Step 25.   The **Channel Selection Order** field determines in what order the ports are used, either starting at the first, which is referred to as TOP_DOWN, or starting at the last, which is referred to as BOTTOM_UP. Select the desired value from the drop-down list.

Step 26.   The next field, which is labeled **Channel IE Type**, determines the channel selection method. The selection in this field depends on the connection on the other side.

Step 27.   The **PCM Type** field determines the type of encoding format that is being used. For the United States, Japan, Taiwan, and Hong Kong, select "μ-law" (mu-law). In the rest of the world, select "a-law."

Step 28.   The **Delay for First Restart (1/8 sec ticks)** field determines how long this port waits before restarting when instructed. This allows you to stagger the restart times when a large number of PRIs are installed.

Step 29.   The next field, labeled **Delay Between Restarts (1/8 sec ticks)**, determines the length of time between restarts of the PRI when PRI RESTART is sent.

Step 30.   The **Inhibit Restarts at PRI Initialization** check box determines whether a RESTART message is sent when the D-channel successfully connects. The default is to leave this box selected, which does not cause a RESTART message to be sent.

Step 31.   When the **Enable Status Poll** check box is selected, the Change B-Channel Maintenance Status is enabled, which allows individual B-Channels to be taken out of service. The default is to leave this box deselected.

Step 32.   The **Unattended Port** check box is used to indicate that the device has unattended ports. This is normally used if the port is used to send calls to an application such as a voicemail server. In most cases, this box should be left deselected.

Call Routing Information—Inbound Calls

Step 33. The next set of fields deals with inbound calls. The **Significant Digits** field determines the number of digits of an incoming dialed number that will be used by Communications Manager. Communications Manager counts from right to left, so if the number entered in this field is 4 and the digits received are 8105559090, 810555 will be removed and only 9090 will be used to determine the destination of this call.

Step 34. A **Calling Search Space** (CSS) determines the accessible destinations of inbound calls to the gateway. CSS is discussed in Chapter 5. Choose a CSS from the Calling Search Space drop-down list. If this field is left at None, the dial privileges of the calls coming in to the gateway could be limited.

Step 35. Automated Alternate Routing (AAR) is used to provide an alternate route if a call fails because of insufficient bandwidth. The AAR CSS can be used to limit the paths a call can use when it is rerouted. Select an AAR CSS from the **AAR Calling Search Space** drop-down list.

Step 36. The **Prefix DN** field defines what digits are added to the front of an incoming destination number. This is applied to the number, after Communications Manager truncates the number, based on the Significant Digits setting.

Call Routing Information—Outbound Calls

Step 37. The next set of fields deals with outbound calls. The **Calling Line ID Presentation** field determines whether Communications Manager sends caller ID information. To send caller ID information, select Allowed from the drop-down list. To block caller ID, select Restricted from the drop-down list.

Step 38. The **Calling Party Selection** field determines what number is sent to outbound calls. The choices are

- **Originator:** The directory number of the device that placed the call

- **First Redirect Number:** The directory number of the first device to forward the call

- **Last Redirect Number:** The directory number of the last device to forward the call

- **First Redirect Number (External):** The number of the first device to forward the call using the external phone mask

- **Last Redirect Number (External):** The number of the last device to forward the call using the external phone mask

Select the desired value for this field.

Step 39. Cisco recommends that the following four fields remain set to the default of Cisco CallManager:

- Called party IE number type unknown

- Calling party IE number type unknown

- Called Numbering Plan

- Calling Numbering Plan

These fields deal with dial plan issues and should be changed only when advised to do so by Cisco or an experienced dial plan expert. The need to change these usually occurs when installing Communications Manager internationally.

Step 40. The next field, which is labeled **Number of Digits to Strip**, determines how many digits should be stripped for outbound calls. For example, if this value is set to 2 and the number 995551001 is dialed, the 99 is stripped before the call is sent.

Step 41. The **Caller ID DN** field is used to determine what caller ID is sent out this gateway. A mask or a complete number can be entered in this field. For example, if the mask 55536XX is entered in this field, Communications Manager sends 55536 and the last two digits of the calling number.

Step 42. The **SMDI Base Port** field is used only when integrating with a traditional voicemail system. Enter the first T1 port being used for voicemail functions.

Step 43. Called party transformation allows you to change the number that is dialed. The **Called Party Transformation CSS** selected must have access to the calling party transformation pattern assigned to the device. You can also leave this set to None and use the Called Party Transformation CSS assigned to the device pool by selecting the **Use Device Pool Called Party Transformation CSS** check box.

Step 44. Calling party transformation allows you to change the caller ID. Select a **Calling Party Transformation CSS** that contains the called party transformation pattern that is assigned to the device. You can also leave this set to **None** and use the Calling Party Transformation CSS assigned to the device pool by selecting **the Use Device Pool Calling Party Transformation CSS** check box.

PRI Protocol Type–Specific Information

Step 45. The PRI Protocol Type Specific Information fields determine what information elements are sent in messages. For most installations, this field can remain at the default.

UUIE Configuration

Step 46. The **Passing Precedence Level Through UUIE** check box determines whether the MLPP precedence is sent through the use of the User-to-User Information Element (UUIE). This is only configurable if the PRI protocol type is 4ESS. To enable this, select the check box and set the security access level.

Intercompany Media Engine

Step 47.   **E.164 transformation profiles** are used when Intercompany Media Engine (IME) is used. IME allows different companies to automatically learn routes, which allow calls to travel across the Internet instead of the PSTN.

Incoming Calling Party Settings

Step 48.   The Incoming Calling Party Settings are used to globalize numbers. Each calling and called party numbers has a number type assigned to it. The incoming calling party settings are based on the number type assigned. There are four number types: national, international, unknown, and subscriber. There are four settings for each of these number types:

- **Prefix:** The digits entered are added to the beginning of the number after the number of strip digits specified are removed.

- **Strip Digits:** This is the number of digits that should be stripped from the number before the prefix is applied.

- **Calling Search Space:** The CSS that is used after transformation has occurred.

- **Use Device Pool CSS:** When this check box is selected, the device pool CSS is used.

If your environment requires the manipulation of incoming calling numbers, configure the appropriate settings for each of these fields.

Product-Specific Configuration

Step 49.   The last set of fields, which is labeled Product Specific Configuration, is specific to the gateway you are configuring. To see an explanation of each of these fields, click the **i** icon located to the right of the category title. The information needed to determine the settings of these fields comes from the T1 carrier. Enter the information provided by your carrier in the appropriate fields. Tables 3-4 through 3-7 list these fields and supply a brief description of each field.

Step 50.   After the required and desired parameters have been entered, click the Insert button at the top of the page. After the gateway is added, an alert window informs you that the gateway needs to be reset. Click the **OK** button.

Geolocation Configuration

Step 51.   Some features might require geolocation information. This information is also referred to as a civic address. The geolocation information can be used to determine the logical partition of a device. If you are using the geolocation feature, select the appropriate geolocation from the **Geolocation** drop-down list.

Step 52.   Geolocation filters allow you choose which fields are used to create a geolocation identifier. If you are using the geolocation feature, select the appropriate geolocation filter from the **Geolocation Filter** drop-down list.

Step 53.   Click Save.

Table 3-4 *Product-Specific Configuration Detail*

Parameter	Description
Clock Reference	This parameter specifies the location from which the master clock is derived. Required field. Default: Network
TX-Level CSU	This parameter determines the transmit value based on the distance between the gateway and repeater. Default: 0dB
FDL Channel	This determines what type of Facility Data Link (FDL) is supported. Default: ATT 54016
Framing	This parameter specifies the multiframe format of the span. Required field. Default: ESF
Audio Signal Adjustment into IP Network	This parameter specifies the gain or loss applied to the received audio signal relative to the port application type. Required field. Default: NoDbPadding
Audio Signal Adjustment from IP Network	This parameter specifies the gain or loss applied to the transmitted audio signal relative to the port application type. Required field. Default: NoDbPadding
Yellow Alarm	This parameter determines how a remote alarm is coded. Default: Bit2
Zero Suppression	This parameter specifies how the T1 or E1 span electrically codes binary 1s and 0s on the wire (line coding selection). Required field. Default: B8ZS
Digit On Duration (50–500 ms)	This parameter specifies the duration in milliseconds of dual-tone multifrequency (DTMF) digits generated by the gateway. Valid durations range from 50 to 500 ms. Required field. Default: 100 Minimum: 50 Maximum: 500

Table 3-4 *Product-Specific Configuration Detail*

Parameter	Description
Interdigit Duration (50–500 ms)	This parameter specifies the duration to pause between digits when sequences of DTMF digits are generated by the gateway. This parameter is in milliseconds. Valid durations range from 50 to 500 ms. Required field. Default: 100 Minimum: 50 Maximum: 500
SNMP Community String	This parameter specifies the community string to be used for accessing the Simple Network Management Protocol (SNMP) agent for this interface. Default: public
Disable SNMP Set Operations	This parameter specifies whether all SNMP set operations are disabled. Required field. Default: false
Debug Port Enable	This parameter specifies whether the developer (debug) port should be enabled. Required field. Default: true
Hold Tone Silence Duration	This parameter specifies, in milliseconds, the intertone (off) duration of the hold tone. If this value is set to 0, the default duration of 10 seconds is used. Required field. Default: 0 Minimum: 0 Maximum: 65535
Port Used for Voice Calls	This parameter should be selected if this port is used for voice calls. If this port is used only for fax or modem calls, do not select this option. Required field. Default: true
Port Used for Modem Calls	This parameter should be selected if this port is used for modem calls. If this port is used only for fax or voice calls, do not select this option. Required field. Default: true

Table 3-4   *Product-Specific Configuration Detail*

Parameter	Description
Port Used for Fax Calls	This parameter should be selected if this port is used for fax calls. If this port is used only for voice or modem calls, do not select this option. Required field. Default: true

Table 3-5   *Product-Specific Configuration Detail for Fax and Modem Parameters*

Parameter	Description
Fax Relay Enable	This parameter specifies whether Cisco fax relay encoding should be negotiated when a fax tone is detected. Required field. Default: true
Fax Error Correction Mode Override	This parameter specifies whether error correction mode (ECM) should be disabled for fax transmissions using Cisco fax relay. Required field. Default: true
Maximum Fax Rate	This parameter specifies the maximum fax rate to negotiate. This parameter applies only to fax transmissions using Cisco fax relay. Required field. Default: 14400bps
Fax Payload Size	This parameter specifies the fax payload size. The default is 20 bytes. Required field. Default: 20 Minimum: 20 Maximum: 48
Non-Standard Facilities Country Code	This parameter specifies the nonstandard facilities country code. A value of 65535 will leave this field unused. This parameter applies only to fax transmissions using Cisco fax relay. Required field. Default: 65535 Minimum: 0 Maximum: 65535

Table 3-5   *Product-Specific Configuration Detail for Fax and Modem Parameters*

Parameter	Description
Non-Standard Facilities Vendor Code	This parameter specifies the nonstandard facilities vendor code. A value of 65535 will leave this field unused. This parameter applies only to fax transmissions using Cisco fax relay. Required field. Default: 65535 Minimum: 0 Maximum: 65535
Fax/Modem Packet Redundancy	This parameter specifies whether packet redundancy (RFC 2198) should be enabled for modem calls and fax calls not using Cisco fax relay. Required field. Default: false
Named Service Event (NSE) Type	This parameter specifies the NSE type to be used for peer-to-peer messaging. Required field. Default: Non-IOS Gateways

Table 3-6   *Product-Specific Configuration Detail for Playout Delay Parameters*

Parameter	Description
Initial Playout Delay	This parameter specifies the initial delay introduced by the jitter buffer in milliseconds. Required field. Default: 40 Minimum: 20 Maximum: 150
Minimum Playout Delay	This parameter specifies the minimum delay introduced by the jitter buffer in milliseconds. Required field. Default: 20 Minimum: 20 Maximum: 150
Maximum Playout Delay	This parameter specifies the maximum delay introduced by the jitter buffer in milliseconds. Required field. Default: 150 Minimum: 20 Maximum: 150

Table 3-7   *Product-Specific Configuration Detail for Echo Canceller Configuration*

Parameter	Description
Echo TailLength (ms)	This parameter defines the tail length duration (in ms) to be used by the echo canceller. Supported values are 24, 32, 48, and 64 ms. Required field. Default: 32ms
Minimum Echo Return Loss (ERL) (db)	This parameter defines the minimum ERL value that can be handled by the echo canceller. Available options are 0db, 3db, and 6db. Required field. Default: 6db

Adding Intercluster Trunks

The last type of gateway to be covered is known as an intercluster trunk (ICT). This type of gateway is configured to allow calls to be placed between Communications Manager clusters across some type of IP connectivity. Intercluster trunks are normally used to connect clusters, within the same organization, together across an exiting WAN link, thus utilizing the WAN link for both data and voice.

The concept is simple. In each cluster, a gateway is configured that points to the IP address(es) of the Communications Manager in the other cluster. It can be confusing at first because unlike other types of gateways, there is no real gateway "device" used. The easiest way to think of it is that an intercluster trunk is a process that runs on the Communications Manager cluster.

The following steps show how to configure an intercluster trunk and explain the various settings. Because there are a number of steps to this process, section headings are used to mark the point at which each new set of parameters begins. These same headings display on the configuration screen as well, which should help you keep track of where you are.

Step 1.   From within CCMAdmin, select **Device > Trunk**.

Step 2.   Click the **Add New** link and then click **Next**.

Step 3.   On the next page, select Inter-Cluster Trunk (Non-Gatekeeper Controlled) from the **Trunk Type** drop-down list.

Note   Typically nongatekeeper-controlled intercluster trunks are used only when bandwidth is not an issue. Gatekeepers and gatekeeper-controlled intercluster trunks are discussed in Chapter 5. The configuration of intercluster trunks is very similar for both types.

Step 4.   The **Device Protocol** field can be left at Inter-Cluster Trunk. No other option is available. Click the Next button.

Device Information

Step 5.   The Trunk Configuration screen, as shown in Figure 3-19, displays. Enter a functional name for the device in the **Device Name** field.

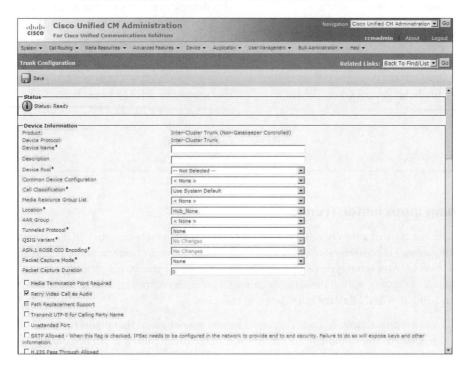

Figure 3-19   *Trunk Configuration*

Step 6.   In the **Description** field, enter a description that makes this device easily identifiable.

Step 7.   From the **Device Pool** drop-down list, select the desired device pool for this gateway.

Step 8.   From the **Common Device Configuration** drop-down list, select the common device configuration the phone will use.

Step 9.   From the **Call Classification** drop-down list, select whether incoming calls on this device should be considered OnNet or OffNet. This parameter is used to determine whether calls can be transferred and forwarded. This should help prevent fraud.

Step 10.   The next field is the **Media Resource Group List**. It determines the accessibility of media resources to a device. These are discussed further in Chapter 6.

Step 11.   Information entered in the **Location** field is used to prevent WAN links from becoming oversubscribed in centralized deployments. These are discussed more in Chapter 5. If you have defined locations, select the appropriate one for this device from the drop-down list.

Step 12. The **AAR Group** field determines the appropriate association of this device with an AAR group. An AAR group provides the prefix that is assigned when a call fails because of insufficient bandwidth. AAR is discussed in further detail in Chapter 6. Select an AAR group if AAR is being used. If this field is set to None, AAR is, in effect, disabled on this device.

Step 13. The **Tunneled Protocol** drop-down list allows you to select Q Signaling (QSIG), which enables intercluster trunk (ICT) to transport non-H.323 protocol information by tunneling it through H.323. Leave this set to **None**, unless you know that this type of tunneling is required.

Step 14. The **QSIG Variant** parameter is only configurable if QSIG is selected as the tunnel protocol. Leave this parameter alone unless Cisco TAC instructs you to change it.

Step 15. The **ASN.1 ROSE OID Encoding** parameter is only configurable if QSIG is selected as the tunnel protocol. This is beyond the scope of this book.

Step 16. The next two fields, **Packet Capture Mode** and **Packet Capture Duration**, are for troubleshooting purposes only and should not be configured when adding a new phone.

Step 17. The **Media Termination Point Required** check box needs to be selected if the H.323 device does not support features such as hold and transfers.

Step 18. If the **Retry Video Call as Audio** check box is selected, Communications Manager sets up a voice call if a video calls fails to set up.

Step 19. The **Path Replacement Support** check box is automatically selected if you select QSIG from the Tunneled Protocol drop-down list. Otherwise it is left deselected.

Step 20. If the **Transmit UTF-8 for Calling Party Name** check box is left deselected, the user locale setting in the device pool will be used to determine whether Unicode information is sent and translated. Typically, this can be left at the default.

Step 21. The **Unattended Port** check box is used to indicate that the device has unattended ports. This is normally used if the port is used to send calls to an application such as a voicemail server. In most cases, this box should be left deselected.

Step 22. If you want to allow both secure and nonsecure calls on this gateway, you must select the **SRTP Allowed** check box. If this is not selected, only nonsecure calls are allowed.

Step 23. If the **H.235 Pass Through Allowed** check box is selected, the shared-secret key will be able to pass through a Communications Manager, allowing H.323 endpoints to set up a secure connection.

Step 24. Service Advertisement Framework (SAF) is a network service that allows clusters to exchange information and build dynamic route plans. To allow SAF information to be sent across this trunk, you must select the **Enable SAF** check box.

Step 25. The **Use Trusted Relay Point** field determines whether a relay point such as a Media Termination Point (MTP) or a transcoder must be labeled as trusted to be used by this device. This field is typically changed only in virtualized environments.

Step 26. If this gateway is used to connect to the PSTN, make sure that the **PSTN Access** check box is selected.

Intercompany Media Engine

Step 27. E.164 transformation profiles are used when Intercompany Media Engine (IME) is used. IME allows different companies to automatically learn routes, which allows calls to travel across the Internet instead of the PSTN.

Incoming Calling/Called Party Settings

Step 28. The Incoming Calling Party Settings and Incoming Called Party Settings are used to globalize numbers. Each calling and called party numbers has a number type assigned to it. The incoming calling/called part settings are based on the number type assigned. There are four number types: national, international, unknown, and subscriber. There are four settings for each of these number types:

- **Prefix:** The digits entered are added to the beginning of the number after the number of strip digits specified are removed.

- **Strip Digits:** This is the number of digits that should be stripped from the number before the prefix is applied.

- **Calling Search Space:** This is the CSS that is used after transformation has occurred.

- **Use Device Pool CSS:** When this check box is selected, the device pool CSS is used.

If your environment requires the manipulation of incoming called and calling numbers, configure the appropriate settings for each of these fields.

Multilevel Precedence and Preemption (MLPP) Information

Step 29. The next two fields define the Multilevel Precedence and Preemption (MLPP) characteristics of this gateway. If these fields are left blank or set to default, the values set in the device pool are used. The first MLPP field is the **MLPP Domain.** MLPP grants higher priority only from calls with the same MLPP domain. For this reason, an MLPP domain is needed.

Step 30. The second field is called **MLPP Indication.** It determines whether tones and indications will be presented when a precedence call is made. If the is field set to Off, no precedence indication is presented. If this field is set to On, indication is used for a precedence call.

Call Routing Information—Inbound Calls

Step 31. The next set of fields relates to inbound calls. The **Significant Digits** field determines the number of digits of an incoming dialed number that Communications Manager uses. Communications Manager counts from right to left, so if the number entered in this field is 4 and the digits received are 8105559090, 810555 would be removed and only 9090 would be used to determine the destination of this call.

Step 32. A Calling Search Space (CSS) determines the accessible destinations of inbound calls to the gateway CSS as discussed in Chapter 5. Choose a CSS from the **Calling Search Space** drop-down list. If this field is left at **None**, the dialing privileges of this gateway could be limited.

Step 33. Automated Alternate Routing (AAR) is used to provide an alternate route if a call fails because of insufficient bandwidth. The AAR CSS can be used to limit the paths a call can use when it is rerouted. Select an AAR CSS from the **AAR Calling Search Space** drop-down list.

Step 34. The **Prefix DN** field defines what digits are added to the front of an incoming destination number. This is applied to the number, after Communications Manager truncates the number, based on the Significant Digits setting.

Step 35. The **Redirecting Number IE Delivery–Inbound** check box should be used if your voicemail system supports redirecting number IE. Otherwise, leave this box deselected.

Step 36. If the **Enable Inbound FastStart** check box is selected, FastStart will be used. H.323 FastStart requires only two message exchanges to open logical channels, whereas normal setup requires 12. However, if FastStart is selected, both ends must support and be configured for FastStart.

Call Routing Information—Outbound Calls

Step 37. Called party transformation allows you to change the number that is dialed. The **Called Party Transformation CSS** selected must have access to the calling party transformation pattern assigned to the device. You can also leave this set to None and use the Called Party Transformation CSS assigned to the device pool by selecting the **Use Device Pool Called Party Transformation CSS** check box.

Step 38. Calling party transformation allows you to change the caller ID. Select a **Calling Party Transformation CSS** that contains the called party transformation pattern that is assigned to the device. You can also leave this set to None and use the Calling Party Transformation CSS assigned to the device pool by selecting the **Use Device Pool Calling Party Transformation CSS** check box.

Step 39. The **Calling Party Selection** field determines what number is sent for out-bound calls. The choices are

- **Originator:** The directory number of the device that placed the call

- **First Redirect Number:** The directory number of the first device to redirect the call

- **Last Redirect Number:** The directory number of the last device to redirect the call

- **First Redirect Number (External):** The external directory number of the first device to redirect the call

- **Last Redirect Number (External):** The external directory number of the last device to redirect the call

Select the desired value for this field.

Step 40. The **Calling Line ID Presentation** field determines whether Communications Manager sends caller ID information. To send caller ID information, select Allowed from the drop-down list. To block caller ID, select Restricted from the drop-down list.

Step 41. Cisco recommends that the next four fields remain set to the default of Cisco CallManager. The four fields are

- Called party IE number type unknown

- Calling party IE number type unknown

- Called Numbering Plan

- Calling Numbering Plan

These fields deal with dial plan issues and should be changed only when advised to do so by Cisco or an experienced dial plan expert. The need to change these usually occurs when installing Communications Manager internationally.

Step 42. The **Caller ID DN** field is used to determine what caller ID is sent out this gateway. A mask or a complete number can be entered in this field. For example, if the mask 55536XX is entered in this field, Communications Manager sends 55536 and the last two digits of the calling number.

Step 43. If the **Display IE Delivery** check box is selected, the calling and called party name information is included in messages.

Step 44. The **Redirecting Number IE Delivery–Outbound** check box should be selected when integrating with a voicemail system that supports redirecting number IE. Otherwise, leave it deselected.

Step 45. If the **Enable Outbound FastStart** check box is selected, FastStart will be used. H.323 FastStart requires only two message exchanges to open logical channels, whereas normal setup requires 12. If FastStart is selected, both ends must support and be configured for FastStart.

Step 46. If the check box is selected, you must select the codec that is to be used. This is selected from the **Codec for Outbound FastStart** drop-down list.

Remote Cisco Communications Manager Information

Step 47. In the next three fields, the IP addresses of the Communications Manager in the destination cluster are entered. Enter the IP addresses of the remote Communications Manager group. Enter the remote primary Communications Manager IP address in the Server 1 field, the remote backup Communications Manager IP address in the Server 2 field and, if remote tertiary Communications Manager exists, enter its IP address in the Server 3 field. If there are more than three Communications Managers in the remote cluster, additional intercluster trunks might need to be configured.

UUIE Configuration

Step 48. The **Passing Precedence Level Through UUIE** check box determines whether the MLPP precedence is sent through the use of the User-to-User Information Element (UUIE). To enable this, select the check box and set the security access level.

Geolocation Configuration

Step 49. Some features might require geolocation information. This information is also referred to as a civic address. The geolocation information can be used to determine the logical partition of a device. If you are using the geolocation feature, select the appropriate geolocation from the **Geolocation** drop-down list.

Step 50. Geolocation filters allow you choose which fields are used to create a geolocation identifier. If you are using the geolocation feature, select the appropriate geolocation filter from the **Geolocation Filter** drop-down list.

Step 51. Click **Save**.

Summary

This chapter covered all the required tasks needed to add phones and gateways to a Communications Manager system. Four methods to add phones to the system were discussed: manual registration, autoregistration, BAT, and TAPS.

After phones were added, the addition of four types of gateways was discussed. A description and an installation example of H.323, MGCP, non-MGCP, and intercluster trunk gateways were provided.

The chapter should help you feel comfortable with the task of adding phones and gateways. Because it is not possible to include step-by-step instructions for every possible type of phone and gateway in this book, the examples given were based on widely deployed models. These instructions should serve as a good guide to help you deploy most other models as well.

Now that the phones and gateways are deployed, a dial plan is needed. A dial plan is used to determine how calls are routed. The next chapter explores dial plans.

Implementing a Route Plan

After phones and gateways have been added to the cluster, a dial plan must be created to allow calls to reach destinations outside the cluster. As soon as the first directory number is entered in Communications Manager, the creation of a dial plan begins. By default, calls that are placed to destinations within the same cluster can be successfully routed. This is because all directory numbers that are registered to the Communications Manager cluster become part of that cluster's dial plan. However, for Communications Manager to route a call to a destination that is outside its cluster, additional information must be programmed that will make up Communications Manager's external dial plan. Although directory numbers do belong to the dial plan, it is common to refer to the external dial plan as "the dial plan."

A dial plan has five components: a numbering plan, path selection, digit manipulation, class of service, and call coverage. This chapter focuses on the first three, which are often referred to as a route plan. It is not uncommon for a route plan to be called a dial plan, but it is important to understand that there is more to a dial plan then just the route plan components. Chapter 5, "Configuring Class of Service and Call Admission Control," focuses on class of service. Call coverage is covered in Chapter 12, "Maximizing CUCM and Unity/Connection."

A dial plan can become quite complex, and many unforeseen issues can arise, so you should outline the plan on paper before any devices are deployed. Someone that has proven experience in this field should create the dial plan. After the dial plan is created on paper, configuring it in the Communications Manager can begin. If you are new to dial plans, seek out an individual with dial plan experience for assistance.

Before discussing how to configure a dial plan, take a closer look at the components that are required to make a call. The next section provides an overview of the flow of a typical call.

Note   Because the components within a route plan have to be created in the opposite order of the call flow, it is recommended that you read the entire chapter before trying to implement any of the specific tasks covered. This can help you achieve a higher understanding of each component and its role in the call flow process.

Understanding Call Flow

A call begins when someone picks up the handset and dials a number. Although this seems rather simple, much more is happening than the entry of numbers on one end and the magical ringing of the phone on the other end. For the purposes of this chapter, you are only concerned with how the call is routed within the cluster. After the call is handed off to a device outside the cluster, the Communications Manager has no control on the path that the call takes.

Before examining an example call flow, you need to be familiar with a dial plan's required components. The following is a list of components that are used to make up a route plan, along with a brief description of each. Later, sections of the chapter supply more detail on each component:

■   **Route pattern:** Patterns are made up of numbers, wildcards, and special characters. Wildcards allow a single pattern to match multiple dialed numbers. The most popular wildcard is the "X." This wildcard matches any single digit 0–9. For example, a pattern of 91248XXXXXXX matches any dialed number that begins with 91248 and is followed by seven more digits, such as 912485554123. Wildcards are covered in detail later in this chapter.

■   **Device:** This is a gateway that connects the Communications Manager system to another system such as the public switched telephone network (PSTN). In some documentation, this is also referred to as a route group device.

■   **Route group:** This is an ordered list of gateways to which a call can be sent. The call is sent to the first device in the group, and if the call is unable to use that gateway for any reason, the route group sends the call to the next device in its list.

■   **Route list:** This prioritized list of route groups is used to determine to which route groups an outbound call is sent. The call is sent to the first route group in the list. If that route group refuses the call for any reason, the route list sends the call to the next route group in its list.

The following steps outline what happens within the cluster when a call is placed to a destination outside the cluster. For example, assume that the call is being placed to the pizza parlor down the street.

Step 1.   The caller dials the phone number of the pizza parlor.

Step 2.   Communications Manager looks at those digits and finds a pattern that matches it. If it finds multiple patterns that match, it uses the closest (the one with the fewest possible matches).

Step 3.   The pattern that the dialed number matches points to a route list that in turn points to one or more route groups.

Step 4.   The route list sends the call to the first route group in its list.

Step 5.   The route group points to one or more gateways (or trunks) and sends the call to the first gateway in the group.

Step 6.   If the gateway cannot handle the call, the route group sends the call to the next gateway in its list if one is available.

Step 7.   If no other gateway exists in the group or if the last gateway in the group cannot route the call, the call is returned to the route list and the route list sends the call to the next route group in the list.

Step 8.   The next route group sends the call to the first gateway in the group.

Step 9.   After the call reaches a gateway that can handle the call, the call is sent out of the system using that gateway.

Step 10.   If no gateway is available, the call fails.

Figure 4-1 offers an example of the preceding steps. This simple example shows that the processing of a single call can be quite complicated. For calls to be delivered to the proper destination, each of the components discussed in this example, such as patterns, route list, route groups, and gateways, must be configured in Communications Manager. This section has offered a broad overview of these components. The following sections build on what you have learned here, they offer more detail on each component, and they explain how each component is configured.

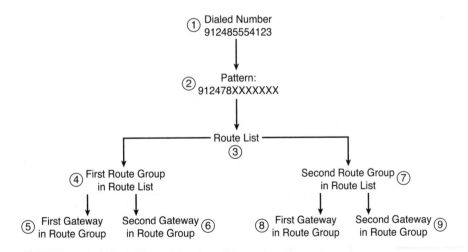

Figure 4-1   *Call Flow*

Note The flow of the call starts at the pattern and ends at the gateway. However, the creation of the required components is in the opposite order. When a route group points to a gateway, the gateway in which it's pointed to must exist. Therefore, the gateway must be configured first, followed by the route group, then the route list, and last but not least, the pattern. Because gateway configuration is discussed in the last chapter, you look at the route groups and lists first.

Understanding Route Groups and Route Lists

The job of a route group is to send the call to the gateway or gateways to which it points. The route group sends the call to the first gateway in the group, and if that gateway cannot handle the call, the route group sends the call to the next gateway in the group. This process is repeated until a gateway in the list is identified that is able to handle the call, or there are no more gateways in the group. If the route group is unable to find an available gateway, the call is returned to the route list.

The job of a route list is to send the call to a route group, which in turn sends the call to a gateway. In the example shown in Figure 4-2, the call is first routed across the WAN. If that path is unable to accommodate the call, it is routed to the PSTN. As you can see, depending on which path the call takes, a different number of digits need to be sent. If the call is sent across the intercluster trunk (ICT), only five digits are needed, assuming that the remote cluster is using five-digit directory numbers. However, if the call goes across the PSTN, 11 digits are needed. To accomplish this, digit manipulation must take place. Digit manipulation occurs when a called (dialed) or calling (caller ID) number is changed. In this case, the digit translation strips the required number of digits from the called number so that the call can be routed across the chosen path. Because the path the call takes is not known until it reaches the route group, the digit manipulation should take place there.

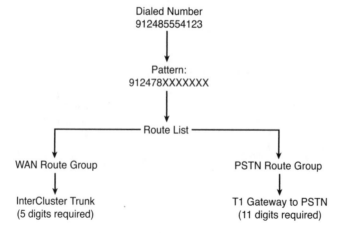

Figure 4-2 *Digit Manipulation Required*

Digit manipulation can be accomplished in a number of ways. Each of the various methods used for digit manipulation is covered in this chapter, as are examples of when each type might be used. First look at what type of digit manipulation can take place at the route group level.

After the call is sent to a route group and an available gateway is found, six types of digit manipulation can be performed. Three affect the calling number (caller ID), and three affect the called party number. Digit manipulation can be performed by applying a mask to digits. Communications Manager applies the mask to digits by right-justifying both the digits and the mask, placing the mask directly under the digits, so to speak. Where there are Xs in the mask, Communications Manager will pass the digits. Where there are numbers in the mask, Communications Manager will replace the digits with the number in the mask. For example, a mask of 612555X2XX applied to the digits 4321 would look like this:

```
      4321 - Digits
612555X2XX - Mask


6125554221 - End Result
```

The following is a list of the six methods of digit manipulation and a brief explanation for each:

- **Calling party's external phone mask:** If configured under the directory number, this mask changes the caller ID information. When adding a route group to a route list, you can choose to enable or disable this mask. For example, this mask can be used to send a phone's Direct Inward Dial (DID) number for caller ID. If you apply an external phone mask of 408370XXXX to a 4-digit extension number and you choose to enable this mask, Communications Manager can pass the DID number for caller ID. For example:

  ```
        4112 - Extension number
  408370XXXX - External Phone Mask


  4083704112 - Caller ID
  ```

  With this type of mask, Communications Manager passes the actual fully qualified directory number as caller ID.

- **Calling party transformation mask:** Sometimes it is not desirable to pass the phone's DID number as caller ID, or the phone DN is not a DID number. The calling party transformation mask can be used to further manipulate digits passed for caller ID. It can also be used to pass a DID number for caller ID if the external phone mask is not used. The actual digits supplied depend on whether the external phone number mask is applied. If the external phone mask is not used, the calling party transformation mask is applied to the extension number as follows:

```
        4112 - Extension Number
 408370XXXX - Calling Party Transformation Mask

 4083704112 - End Result
```

If the external phone mask is used, the calling party transformation mask is applied to the end result of the external phone mask transformation as follows:

```
 4083704112 - Result of external phone mask transformation
 4083701200 - Calling party transformation mask

 4083701200 - End result (perhaps the company's main number)
```

As you can see, transformation masks are powerful tools.

- **Prefix digits:** These digits prepend the calling party number to which they are applied. An example might be to use 40837 as prefix digits in a 5-digit internal dial plan. For example, if the extension number is 58321, Communications Manager adds 40837 in front of 58321, which results in 4083758321.

- **Discard digits:** This determines whether any dialed digits are discarded. Discard digits are often used to remove the 9 from the front of outbound calls. The specific options of this field are covered later in this chapter.

- **Called party transformation mask:** This mask changes the called number (dialed digits). This could be used in an environment that requires callers to dial only five digits to reach a phone through an ICT. However, if the ICT cannot accommodate the call, it is routed to the PSTN. The PSTN needs the full phone number, so a transformation mask is used. A mask of 1408370XXXX could be used in this example. This mask tells Communications Manager to apply 1408370XXXX to the dialed number of 58321 as follows:

```
      58321 - Dialed number
 1408370XXXX - Called party transformation mask

 14083708321 - Digits passed to the PSTN
```

The assumption in this example is that 14083708321 is the called party's phone number.

- **Prefix digits:** These digits are added to the front of a called number (dial digits). An example might be 140837. This mask tells Communications Manager to place 140837 in front of the extension. For example, if the extension number is 58321, Communications Manager adds 140837 in front of 58321, which results in 14083758321.

Even though digit manipulation can be done at the group level, it is applied to the group at the route list level. This might sound confusing at first, but it makes more sense after you have seen it applied. This is examined in the section "Creating a Route List," later in this chapter.

Now that you understand the task of the route list and the route groups, take a look at how they are created. Because they must be created in the opposite order of the call flow, the route groups must be created first.

Creating Route Groups

Because route groups point to gateways, the gateways must be configured before creating route groups. For information on gateway configuration, refer to Chapter 3, "Deploying Devices." The steps presented in this section assume that gateways already exist and that you have a written dial plan, which you can refer to while configuring the route groups.

The following steps show how to create a route group that can point to multiple gateways:

Step 1.   From within CCMAdmin, select **Route Plan > Route/Hunt > Route Group**.

> **Note**   In earlier versions of Communications Manager, the path to reach route groups is slightly different, such as **Route Plan > Route Group**.

Step 2.   Click the **Add New** link.

A screen similar to that shown in Figure 4-3 displays.

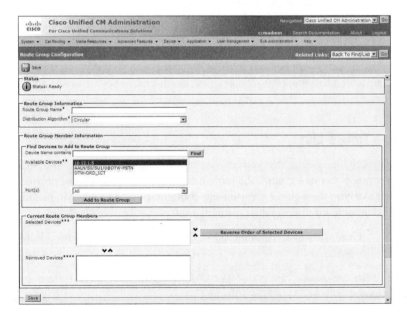

Figure 4-3   *Route Group Configuration*

Step 3.   Enter a descriptive name in the **Route Group Name** field.

Step 4. From the **Distribution Algorithm** drop-down box, choose how Communications Manager will distribute the calls. If you want Communications Manager to send the call to the first available gateway in the list, choose **Top Down.** When Circular is chosen, the calls are load balanced across multiple gateways.

Step 5. From the **Available Devices** box, highlight the gateway that you want to add to this route group. If there are many gateways, you can limit the ones that appear in this box by entering search criteria in the Device Name Contains field.

Step 6. Certain gateways allow you to choose which ports on the gateway you want to use for this route group. In the **Port**(s) field, select the ports on this gateway that should be added to this route group. If the gateway you are configuring does not allow the selection of ports, leave this field set to the default.

Step 7. Click the **Add to Route Group** button. Repeat Steps 5 through 7 for gateways that you want to add to this group.

Step 8. After you have selected all the desired gateways, they appear in the **Selected Devices** box. The order in which they appear in this box determines the order in which calls are distributed. To change the order, highlight the gateway you want to move and click the up or down arrow to the right of the box.

Step 9. You can remove a gateway from the route group by highlighting the gateway and clicking the down arrow below the **Selected Devices** box. The gateway then appears in the Removed Devices box.

Step 10. Click the **Save** button to complete the configuration of this route group.

After the route group is created, it must be added to a route list. As mentioned previously, digit manipulation can be done at the route group level, but is configured when route groups are added to a route list. The next section discusses how to create and configure route lists.

Creating a Route List

Before proceeding, ensure that you have created all required route groups. Because a route list points to route groups, the route groups must exist. The steps provided in this section guide you through the creation and configuration of a route list, in addition to configuring route-group-level digit manipulation.

Step 1. From within CCMAdmin, select **Call Routing > Route/Hunt > Route List.**

Note   In earlier versions of Communications Manager, the path to reach route groups is slightly different, such as **Route Plan > Route List.**

Step 2. Click the **Add New** link.

A screen similar to that shown in Figure 4-4 displays.

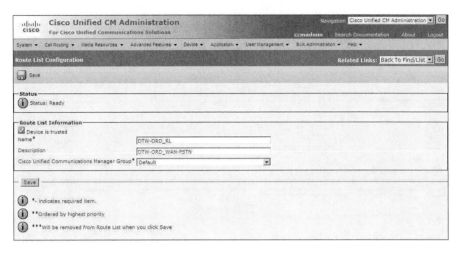

Figure 4-4 *Route List Configuration*

Step 3.   Enter a descriptive name in the **Route List Name** field.

Step 4.   In the **Description** field, enter a description that helps to easily identify this route list.

Step 5.   From the **Cisco Unified Communications Manager Group** drop-down list, select the Communications Manager group that will be used to determine to which Communications Manager this route list will register.

Step 6.   Click the **Save** button.

Step 7.   A screen similar to that shown in Figure 4-5 displays. Notice that below the Communications Manager group is a check box labeled **Enable this Route list**. By default, this is selected, which means that the route group is active. If during testing or troubleshooting you need to disable this route group, deselect this check box. For now, leave it at the default.

Step 8.   To add a route group to this list, click the **Add Route Group** button.

A screen similar to that shown in Figure 4-6 displays.

Step 9.   From the **Route Group** drop-down menu, select the desired route group.

Step 10. This is the point at which you can configure digit manipulation. If you want to affect caller ID information, configure the three fields found under the Calling Party Transformations heading. These fields are discussed earlier in this chapter. The first field is labeled **Use Calling Party's External Phone Number Mask**. This field determines whether the mask configured on the directory number is used for calls that are routed through this route group.

Step 11. In the **Calling Party Transform Mask** field, enter any mask that you want to affect the caller ID.

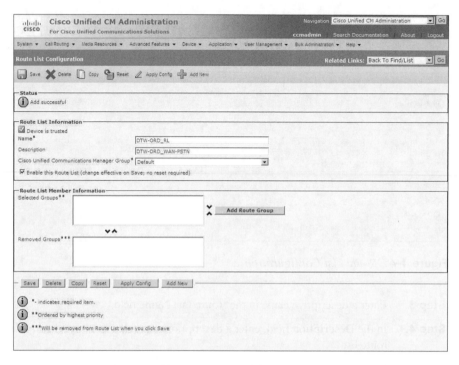

Figure 4-5   *Route List Configuration—Adding Route Groups*

Step 12.   In the **Prefix Digits (Outgoing Calls)** field, enter any digits that you want to have added to the front of the caller ID.

Step 13.   By default, the **Calling Party Number Type** and the **Calling Party Number Plan** fields are set to Cisco Unified Communications Manager. Only an individual that has extensive knowledge and experience using the dialing plans such as the North American Numbering Plan (NANP) or the European dialing plan should change this field. In many cases, these can be left to the default, but some service providers might require these values to be set based on the type of call being made. Check with your service provider to see whether this is required in your environment.

Step 14.   The fields under the **Called Party Transformations** heading affect the dialed number. This is where you can manipulate the number sent to the gateway. An example of how this might be used was shown in Figure 4-2. When the call goes across the WAN, only five digits are needed, but if the WAN cannot handle the call and it is sent to the PSTN, 11 digits are needed for the PSTN to properly route the call. From the Discard Digits drop-down list, select the digit discard instructions that should apply to calls that are sent out this gateway. A discard instruction determines which digits are removed from the dialed digits before the call is sent out the gateway. There are more than 30 different discard instructions for this field. However, most of them are combinations of one another. Table 4-1 lists the seven core discard instructions.

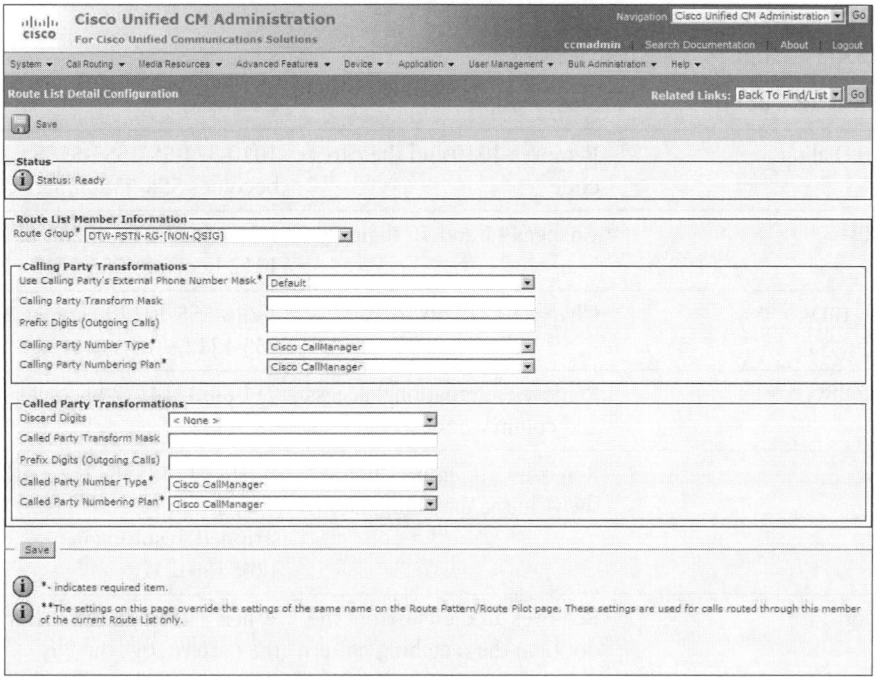

Figure 4-6 *Adding Route Groups to the Route List*

Note   If the @ wildcard is not used, the only valid discard digit instructions are PreDot and None.

Note   These instructions are combined to create more than 30 instructions that you will find in the list. Here's an example. The discard instruction PreDot 10-10-Dialing removes any number before the dot in the pattern, the 10-10, and carrier code. When the number 910103215835551212 is dialed, it matches the 9.@ pattern. The PreDot instruction causes the 9 to be removed. The 10-10 and carrier code of 321 are removed because of the 10-10 Dialing instruction. The final result is 5835551212. Applying what you learned here, you can quite easily determine what effect the other discard instruction will have on a dialed number.

Note   Some of the discard instructions depend on the pattern that is matched when the number is dialed. The following examples make reference to these patterns, and the next section explains these patterns in more detail. So, if you are unfamiliar with patterns shown in these examples, fear not—you will find explanations for them very soon.

Table 4-1   *Digit Discard Instructions*

Discard Instruction	Description	Example
10-10-Dialing	Removes 1010 and the carrier code	1010-321-585-555-5555 becomes 585-555-5555.
11/10D->7D	Changes 11 and 10 digits to 7	1-246-555-1212 or 246-555-1212 becomes 555-1212.
11D->10D	Changes 11 digits to 10	1-246-555-1212 becomes 246-555-1212.
Intl TollBypass	Removes international access and country codes	011-64-3214322 becomes 3214322.
PreAt	Removes all numbers before the @ in the matching pattern	When 912485551212 matches the pattern 9@, the 9 is stripped, resulting in 12485551212.
PreDot	Removes all digits before the dot (.) in the matching pattern	When 912485551212 matches the pattern 9.@, the 9 is stripped, resulting in 12485551212.
Trailing-#	Removes the # from the end of the dialed digits	12465551212# becomes 12465551212.

Step 15.   In the **Called Party Transform Mask** field, enter the mask that you want to use for calls going out this gateway.

Step 16.   In the **Prefix Digits (Outgoing Calls)** field, enter any digits that you want to add to the front of the dialed number before the call is sent out the gateway.

Note   Because a number of transformations can be applied, it is important to understand the progression in which the transformations take place. The order for calling party transforms is external phone mask first, followed by calling party transform mask, and finally prefix digits. The order for called party transforms is discard instructions, followed by called party transform mask, and finally prefix digits.

Step 17.   By default, the **Called Party Number Type** and **Called Party Number Plan** fields are set to Cisco Unified Communications Manager. Only an individual that has extensive knowledge and experience using the dialing plans such as the NANP or the European dialing plan should change this field. It is recommended that this field be left at the default.

Step 18. Click the **Save** button.

Step 19. An informational window displays stating that the route group has been added and that the route list must be reset for the changes to take effect. Click **OK**.

Step 20. The page shown in Figure 4-5 redisplays with the addition of the route group that you just added. Repeat Steps 8 through 16 for any additional route groups that you want to enter.

Step 21. After all route groups are added, they display in the **Selected Groups** box. The order in which they display in this box determines the order in which calls are distributed. To change the order, highlight the route group you want to move and click the up or down arrow to the right of the box.

Step 22. You can remove a route group from the route list by highlighting the route group and clicking the down arrow below the Selected Groups box. This route group displays in the **Removed Groups** box.

Step 23. Click the **Save** button to complete the configuration of this route list.

Step 24. Depending on the version of Communications Manager, the route list might need resetting before the change takes effect. Some versions of Communications Manager include a note that states "change effective on update; no reset required." If a message appears stating that a reset is required, click **OK** and you will be returned to the Route List Configuration page. From this page, click the **Reset** button.

Step 25. You need to complete the reset by clicking the **Reset** button in the Device Reset window that appears. Close the Device Reset window.

After all route groups and route lists are created, patterns need to be configured so that when someone dials a number, there is something to match it against and route it to the proper route list.

Understanding Route Patterns

When dialed digits are sent to the Communications Manager, the Communications Manager must be able to match those digits with a pattern. A pattern is simply a set of numbers or wildcards that Communications Manager matches against a dialed number. If there is no pattern configured in Communications Manager that matches the dialed digits, the call fails. You have already seen some examples of patterns in previous sections. However, this section supplies more detail and the configuration process on patterns. Now that you know that every dialed number must have a matching pattern configured in Communications Manager, you might think that it is impossible to enter a pattern for every number that might ever be dialed. If not for wildcards, you would be correct.

Patterns are made up of numbers, wildcards, and special characters. Wildcards allow a single pattern to match multiple dialed numbers. The most popular wildcard is the "X." This wildcard matches any single digit of 0 through 9. You could use it, for example, if you want to configure a pattern that matches the five-digit extensions of another cluster. Perhaps the extension range of the other cluster is 52000 through 52999. In this case, a pattern of 52XXX can be used because it matches all numbers within this range.

The "X" is only one of a number of useful wildcards. Table 4-2 list all the wildcards that can be used.

Note   You can extend the power of patterns by using multiple wildcards in the same pattern. This can also lead to unexpected behavior. For example, the pattern 532X? results in matching nearly any dialed number that begins with 532. Take time to test the patterns that you create to make sure that they behave as expected.

Table 4-2   *Pattern Wildcards*

Pattern	Definition	Example
X	This wildcard matches any single digit 0–9.	52XXX matches 52000 through 52999.
@	The "at" sign matches any number in NANP. A simple way to think of this pattern is that it matches any number that can be dialed from a phone in North America.	9.@ matches a number that can be dialed from North America and is proceeded by a 9.
!	The exclamation point (!) matches one or more digits.	55! matches any number that begins with a 55. The possible matches that result from using the (!) are almost limitless.
[ ]	The digits found within the bracket represent a range of numbers that a single digit can match.	55[2-5] matches 552, 553, 554, and 555.
[^]	The digits found within brackets that include a caret (^) represent a range of numbers that are to be excluded when matching a single digit.	55[^2-5] matches 550, 551, 556, 557, 558, 559, 55*, and 55#.
+	The plus sign (+) matches one or more instances of the preceding character or range in the pattern.	91X+ matches all numbers in the range 910 through 9199999999999999999999.

In addition to wildcards, there are other characters that can be part of a pattern. These are sometimes referred to as special characters and are listed as follows:

Table 4-2 *Pattern Wildcards*

Pattern	Definition	Example
?	The question mark (?) matches zero or more instances of the preceding character in the pattern.	57?2 matches 572, 5772, 5772, 577772, and 5777772. In short, it matches any pattern that begins with a 5 followed by any number of 7s that is followed by a 2 as the last number.
.	The dot (.) is used with digit manipulation. It is used to determine what digits are to be stripped.	If the discard instruction of PreDot is used with the pattern 9.@, the 9 is stripped because it is in front of (pre) the dot (.). If the number 912485551212 is dialed, the 9 is stripped leaving, 12485551212.
*	The asterisk (*) is a valid digit that can be dialed from a phone, so it can be part of a pattern. It is important to realize that this is not a wildcard. The asterisk is used as a wildcard in many applications, but not when it is part of a Communications Manager pattern.	543* matches only 543*.
#	The octothorpe (#), which is often referred to as the pound sign or hash mark, is also a valid digit that can be dialed. However, it is most often used to signify that the caller has finished dialing. The octothorpe should only be used as the last digit of a pattern. Discard instructions can be used with this pattern to remove the (#) before sending the call out.	542342# matches only 542342# and routes the call as soon as the (#) is pressed. This is useful when the (!) is used in a pattern. Typically the (#) is used after the (!) in a pattern.

Now that you know what a pattern does and what characters can be used to make up a pattern, you can create some. The following section takes you through the steps that are required to add a basic route pattern, and to point that pattern to a route list.

Creating Basic Route Patterns

Before creating any route patterns, route lists should be created. This is because route patterns point to route lists and can't point to something that doesn't exist. The following steps show how to create a route pattern and point the route pattern to a route list. For example, you can create a route pattern that matches all 11-digit calls and uses 9 as the PSTN access code.

A number of route patterns are needed to create an efficient dial plan. The exact number of route patterns needed varies. There are many things to consider when creating dial plans. One example is the number of digits that must be dialed for each type of call.

> **Note**   While configuring a route pattern, keep in mind that, as with many components that are configured in Communications Manager, not all parameters need to be configured. In some cases, you might need to configure only a few parameters. To allow you to fully understand the purpose of each, these steps cover each parameter.

Step 1.   From within CCMAdmin, select **Call Routing > Route/Hunt > Route Pattern**.

Step 2.   Click the **Add New** link. A screen similar to that shown in Figure 4-7 displays. Enter the route pattern in the Route Pattern field. In this example, you want to match 11 digits; this includes the 9 that is used as a PSTN access code. The route pattern is 9[2-9]XX[2-9]XXXXXX. The [2-9] is used instead of an X because in the NANP area codes and exchanges, you should never start with a 1 or 0.

Step 3.   The **Route Partition** field determines what devices can access this route pattern. Partitions are discussed in more detail in Chapter 5. Select the desired partition from the Partition drop-down list.

Step 4.   In the **Description** field, enter a description that helps identify the purpose of this route pattern.

Step 5.   In the **Numbering Plan** field, choose the appropriate numbering plan.

Step 6.   From the **Route Filter** drop-down list, select the route filter that is to be applied to this route pattern. Route filters are used to limit what digits match the route pattern. These are explained in more detail in Chapter 5.

> **Note**   The Numbering Plan and Route Filter fields are only configurable if the pattern has an @ in it, such as 9.@.

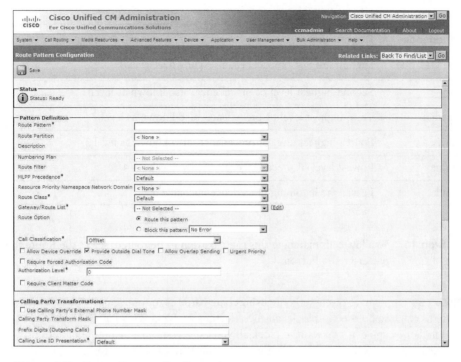

Figure 4-7 *Route Pattern Configuration*

Step 7. Determine the precedence level to be assigned to this route pattern from the **MLPP Precedence** drop-down list (MLPP stands for Multilevel Precedence and Preemption). Table 4-3 shows the available options.

Step 8. The **Resource Priority Namespace Network Domain** field is used in environments that utilize Voice over Secured IP (VoSIP) using SIP trunks. If your organization is utilizing this, select the appropriate domain from the drop-down list.

Step 9. The **Route Class** parameter should be left at the default. This is usually used only when the class route of an inbound T1-CAS needs to be translated to a CM route class.

Step 10. From the **Gateway/Route List** drop-down list, select the route list to which calls matching this route pattern are sent.

Note Typically a route list is selected here; however, there might be times that you want to send a call directly to a gateway. This usually occurs when troubleshooting route plan issues.

Table 4-3 *MLPP Precedence Levels*

Precedence	Description
Flash Override	Highest level of precedence, also known as level 0
Flash	Second-highest level of precedence, also known as level 1
Immediate	Third-highest level of precedence, also known as level 2
Priority	Fourth-highest level of precedence, also known as level 3
Routine	Lowest level of precedence, also known as level 4
Default	Leaves the incoming precedence unchanged

Step 11. To allow calls matching this route pattern to be routed, select the **Route this pattern** radio button.

> **Note** So far, we have discussed only using route patterns to route calls. However, route patterns can also be used to block calls by selecting the **Block This Pattern** radio button. For example, if you want to block all 900 calls, you can add a route pattern of 91900[2-9]XXXXXX and then select the Block This Pattern radio button.

Step 12. From the **Call Classification** drop-down list, select whether incoming calls on this device should be considered OnNet or OffNet. This parameter is used to determine whether calls can be transferred and forwarded. This is to help prevent fraud.

Step 13. The **Allow Device Override** check box allows the call classification setting configured on the gateway or trunk to be used. It is recommended that this be left deselected.

Step 14. To have a secondary dial tone played after the first digit is dialed, select the **Provide Outside Dial Tone** check box.

> **Note** One caveat to the Provide Outside Dial Tone option is that dial tone is provided only when all possible matching patterns have this option selected. This can result in a dial tone being provided after multiple digits have been dialed.

Step 15. If the device you connect to requires that each digit is sent to it one at a time, select the **Allow Overlap Sending** check box. While this is sometimes used in Europe, in most cases, this box can be left deselected.

Step 16. To route a call as soon as it matches this route pattern, select the **Urgent Priority** check box. Typically, a call is not routed if there are other patterns that might also match, for example, if there is a 911 route pattern and a 91XXXXXXXXXX route pattern. When a caller dials 911, Communications Manager matches the 911 route pattern but could also match the 91XXXXXXXXXX route pattern. If Urgent Priority is not selected, Communications Manager waits for the interdigit timeout to expire (15 seconds by default) before routing the call. You can see how this is undesirable in many cases. By selecting **Urgent Priority**, you ensure that Communications Manager does not wait for any other digits to be dialed and instead routes the call immediately.

Step 17. In some versions of Communications Manager, you have the ability to choose the **Require Forced Authorization Codes** (FAC) and **Client Matter Codes** (CMC) fields. FAC forces the user to dial a code to be able to place the call. CMC allows the user to enter a code so that the call can later be billed back to a client. If you are implementing these features, select the appropriate check boxes. If you are implementing FAC, enter an authorization level. FAC and CMC are discussed in greater detail in Chapter 6, "Configuring CUCM Features and Services."

Step 18. If you want to affect caller ID information, configure the fields found under the Calling Party Transformations heading. These fields are discussed earlier in this chapter. The first field is labeled **Use Calling Party's External Phone Number Mask**. It determines whether the mask configured on the directory number is used for calls that are routed through this route group.

Step 19. In the **Calling Party Transform Mask** field, enter any mask that you want to affect the caller ID.

Step 20. In the **Prefix Digits (Outgoing Calls)** field, enter any digits that you want to have added to the front of the caller ID.

Step 21. The **Calling Line ID Presentation** field determines whether caller ID information is to be blocked for outbound calls that match this route pattern. To block caller ID, select Restricted from the drop-down list. To allow caller ID, select Allowed from the drop-down list.

Step 22. The **Calling Name Presentation** field determines whether caller name information is to be blocked for outbound calls that match this route pattern. To block calling name ID, select Restricted from the drop-down list. To allow calling name ID, select Allowed from the drop-down list.

Step 23. By default, the **Calling Party Number Type** and the **Calling Party Number Plan** fields are set to Cisco Unified Communications Manager. Only an individual that has extensive knowledge and experience using the dialing plans such as the NANP or the European dialing plan should change this field. It is recommended that this field be left at the default.

Step 24. The **Connected Line ID Presentation** field determines whether the connected (destination) party's ID information should display on the calling party's phone. To block the connected party's ID, select **Restricted** from the drop-down list. To allow the connected party's ID, select **Allowed** from the drop-down list.

Step 25. The **Connected Name Presentation** field determines whether the connected party's name information is displayed on the calling party's phone. To block the connected party's name, select **Restricted** from the drop-down list. To allow the connected party's name, select **Allowed** from the drop-down list.

Step 26. From the **Discard Digits** drop-down list, select the digit discard instruction that should be applied to calls that match this route pattern. These instructions are explained earlier in this chapter. Refer to Table 4-1 for additional information.

Step 27. In the **Called Party Transform Mask** field, enter the mask that you want to use for calls that match this route pattern. If no mask will be used, leave this field empty.

Step 28. In the **Prefix Digits (Outgoing Calls)** field, enter any digits that you want to have added to the front of a dialed number before it is sent to the route list.

Step 29. By default, the **Called Party Number Type** and the **Called Party Number Plan** fields are set to Cisco Unified Communications Manager. Only an individual that has extensive knowledge and experience using the dialing plans such as the NANP or the European dialing plan should change this field. It is recommended that this field be left at the default.

Step 30. ISDN network service can be invoked by configuring the ISDN Network-Specific Facilities Information Element fields. To do this, first select the appropriate protocol from the **Network Service Protocol** drop-down list. Your carrier provides this information.

Step 31. Enter the carrier code in the **Carrier Identification Code** field. Your carrier provides this information if required.

Step 32. Based on the protocol used, various services can be selected and configured using the last three fields, which are **Network Service, Service Parameter Name**, and **Service Parameter Value**. These are rarely used and are left blank in most cases.

Step 33. Click the **Save** button at the top of the screen to save this route pattern.

Now that you know how to add route patterns, move on and take a look at what a basic route plan might look like.

Using Pattern Wildcards to Create a Basic Dial Plan

Many factors have to be taken into consideration when implementing a route plan, such as types of calls that will be allowed, the path that each type of call will take, and the dialing characteristics of your local carrier. To help explain these factors in more detail, take a look at a mock company. This illustration touches on the different factors to consider and offers a sample route plan for the company.

Figure 4-8 shows an overview of what must be accomplished for this company.

Dialing Rules for Chicago
• Calls to San Jose use 7 as a leading digit followed by an extension number.
• Most 10-digit calls and all 7-digit calls are local.
• Toll charges apply to area codes 249 and 348.
• All long-distance calls are allowed.
• International calls are allowed.
• 900 numbers are to be blocked.
• 911 calls are to be given priority.
• Must dial 9 to access the PSTN.

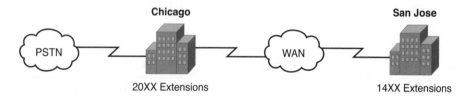

Figure 4-8   *Example Company Overview*

The goal is to create a route plan for the Chicago office that satisfies the following dialing rules:

■   To reach the San Jose office, callers should dial 7 followed by the extension number.

■   All calls routed to the PSTN should be preceded by a 9.

■   The user should be able to dial all local calls.

■   Ten-digit calls that are not local should be allowed. These numbers require a pattern different from the one that matches ten-digit calls that are local. This is done so that when calling search spaces and partitions are added, these calls can be restricted.

■   Long-distance calls should be allowed.

■   International calls should be allowed.

■   900 calls should be blocked.

■   911 calls should be routed immediately.

At first glance, you might think that the 9.@ pattern can accomplish these goals. However, it will not because it does not allow calls to the San Jose office and it does not block 900 calls. So, as you can see, a single pattern will not suffice. Using the 9.@ could allow calls that you had not intended. 9.@ matches any number that can be dialed from

North America as long as a 9 is dialed first. The @ wildcard is equal to adding hundreds of patterns. Because you often want to restrict the destinations that can be reached from certain devices, it is sometimes desirable to use patterns more specific than 9.@.

Now look at the requirements one at a time to determine what patterns need to be created. Table 4-4 lists the goals and the patterns needed to accomplish this goal.

This example offers you a small sample of the types of patterns that need to be created for an efficient and effective dial plan. This is only an example and should by no means be interpreted as a recommended dial plan. Remember that dial plans vary based on the environment. It is up to you to design a proper route plan from scratch and thoroughly test it before using it in a production environment. Chapter 5 builds on this example to show how to restrict certain devices from dialing certain numbers.

> **Note**   There is a 911 and a 9911 pattern. This is done to ensure that all attempts to reach emergency services are successful. It is not possible to know whether people dialing 911 will know or remember that they must first dial a 9 and then 911. By having both patterns, the call will be successful regardless of which pattern is used.

Table 4-4   *Example Dial Plan*

Goal	Pattern	Notes
To reach the San Jose office, callers should be able to dial 7 followed by the extension number.	7.14XX	PreDot Discard
All calls routed to the PSTN should be preceded by a 9.	—	Add 9. to the front of all patterns that point to the PSTN.
Ensure that local calls can be dialed.	9.[2-9]XXXXXX 9.773[2-9]XXXXXX 9.847[2-9]XXXXXX	PreDot Discard PreDot Discard
Allow nonlocal 10-digit calls that use a pattern different from that used for 10-digit calls that are local.	9.249[2-9]XXXXXX 9.348[2-9]XXXXXX	PreDot Discard PreDot Discard
Allow long-distance calls.	9.1[2-9]XX[2-9]XXXXXX	PreDot Discard
Allow international calls.	9.011! 9.011!#	PreDot Discard PreDot Trailing-# Discard
Block 900 calls.	9.1900[2-9]XXXXXX	Block Pattern
Route 911 calls immediately.	911 9.911	Urgent Priority PreDot Discard and Urgent Priority

Now that you understand what a route plan is and how to create one, move on and take a look at some additional components that can be used when creating complex dial plans.

Advanced Route Plan Components and Behavior

The following sections examine the function and configuration steps for three additional components that are found in dial plans:

- Route filter

- Translation pattern

- Computer Telephony Integration (CTI) route points

These components are used when creating a more complex dial plan.

You start with a brief overview of each component and then see a more detailed exploration of the configuration of each. The first component is a route filter. Route filters are applied to route patterns to limit the matches of the pattern. As mentioned before, the @ wildcard is equal to hundreds of different patterns. Route filters allow you to reduce the number of patterns that match the @. For example, you can create a pattern of 9.@ and apply a route filter that disallows 900 numbers from matching this pattern. The next section takes a look at how these are configured.

The next component that is discussed is the translation pattern. Translation patterns allow a dialed number to be changed to another number. This is another place that digit manipulation can be accomplished. You might wonder why you would need another place for digit manipulation because it can be done at both the route group and the route pattern. There are times when digit manipulation might need to be done before matching a route pattern and for incoming calls. Translation patterns allow the manipulation of both the dialed number and the caller ID of the calling party. In addition, translation patterns can be used to grant a different Calling Search Space and MLPP precedence. In the "Creating Translation Patterns" section, later in this chapter, these are explored in greater detail.

The last route plan component examined in this chapter is CTI route points. CTI route points are used to route calls to external service or devices. For example, CTI route points are used to direct calls to a Cisco IP Interactive Voice Response (IVR) system and the Cisco Personal Assistant system. After a CTI route point is created, a device or service registers with it and Communications Manager learns its IP address. All calls that match the CTI route point are then sent to the registered IP address. More discussion and configuration examples are offered in the "Creating CTI Route Points" section, later in this chapter.

Creating Route Filters

Route filters can make the @ wildcard much more manageable. It is often tempting to just add the @ pattern to your route plan to make sure that all calls are allowed to be placed, and if your company is unconcerned with who is calling where, you might get away with this. However, most companies today want to make sure that their resources are not being misused. By applying route filters to route patterns, you can limit which calls match the pattern. Route filters allow you to use the @ and still ensure that only intended types of calls are successful. Route filters are only used with route patterns that contain the @.

Note   It is important to ensure that calls that should not be placed cannot be placed. "When in doubt, don't let it out." This simply means that it is better for a route plan to be too restrictive than too liberal. If callers can place calls that normally get placed, they will be sure to let you know. However, if they discover they can place calls that they normally cannot place, don't expect them to tell you. This being said, remember above all else, that you *must* ensure that certain types of calls, such as emergency services, can be placed from *all* phones.

To make route filters work, you create one or more mandatory conditions for the filter to allow the call to match the pattern. Figure 4-9 shows how a filter can affect which calls match a pattern. As you see, the pattern used in this example is 9.@, and the condition in the filter is that the area code matches 248. All the dialed digits match the pattern, but only 912485559093 match the filter conditions. You might think that the 92485559090 should match because the area code is 248, but if it is not preceded by a 1, it is considered a local area code and does not meet the conditions of the filter. There is a condition that can be set on a route filter matching local area codes, but it is not included in this example.

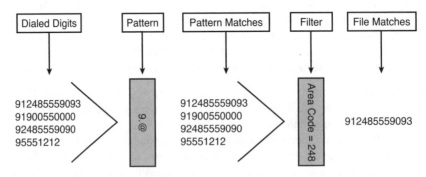

Figure 4-9   *Route Filter Example*

Now create a route filter and apply it to a pattern. The following steps show how to create a route filter:

Step 1.   From within CCMAdmin, select **Call Routing > Route Filter**.

Step 2.   Click the **Add New** link.

Step 3.   Select the appropriate numbering plan from the **Numbering Plan** drop-down list and click Next.

Step 4.   A page similar to that shown in Figure 4-10 displays. In the **Route Filter Name** field, enter a descriptive name for this filter. For example, if this filter is going to match an area code of 248, you might want to name it **AC248**. Whatever naming convention you choose, make sure that it helps you recognize the function of the route filter.

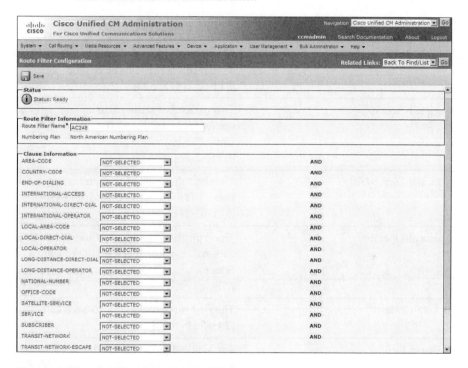

Figure 4-10   *Configuring a Route Filter*

Step 5.   Choose what conditions must be met.

Table 4-5 lists each tag and gives a brief description. The example in the description shows the portion of the number to which the tag is referring in bold.

Step 6.   To enable any of these tags, you have to select an operator from the drop-down list to the right of the tag. The available operators are

- **NOT-SELECTED:** Ignores this tag.

- **EXISTS:** Requires that this portion of the number exist.

- **DOES-NOT-EXIST:** Requires that this portion of the number does not exist.

- **==:** Requires that this portion of the number match the value entered in the box that appears to the right of this operator. The value box does not appear unless this operator is selected.

Table 4-5   *Route Filter Tags*

Tag	Description
Area-Code	Three digits that follow the 1 when dialing 11-digit numbers. [1-**248**-555-9093]
Country-Code	Each country has a one-, two-, or three-digit country code. [011-**63**-2-475983#]
End-of-Dialing	Character used to signify the end of a dialing string. This is the # in the NANP. [011-**62**-2-475983#]
International-Access	Two digits that signify that an international number is being dialed. 01 is used in the United States. [**011**-62-2-475983#]
International-Direct-Dial	The digit that follows the International-Access code. 1 is used in the United States. [011-**62**-2-475983#]
International-Operator	The digit that is used when accessing the international operator. 0 is used in the United States. [00]
Local-Area-Code	The first three digits of a 10-digit call. [**248**-555-9093]
Local-Direct-Dial	The single-digit code dialed when dialing a local call directly. 1 is used in the NANP. [**1**-555-9093]
End-of-Dialing	Character used to signify the end of a dialing string. This is the # in the NANP. [011-**62**-2-475983#]
Local-Operator	The digits used to reach the operator. 0 is used in the NANP. [**0**]
Long-Distance-Direct-Dial	The single-digit code dialed when dialing a long-distance call directly. 1 is used in the NANP. [xxx]

Table 4-5   *Route Filter Tags*

Tag	Description
Long-Distance-Operator	One- or two-digit code that requests operator assistance for the call. [xxx]
National-Number	The nation-specific portion of an international call. [xxx]
Office-Code	The first three digits of a 7-digit call. [**555**-9093]
Satellite-Service	Single digit used to access satellites for international calls. [xxx]
Service	Three-digit codes used for services. [**911**]
Subscriber	The last four digits of a 7-digit number. [555-**9093**]
Transit-Network	The 4-digit carrier code. [101**0321**-1-248-555-9093]
Transit-Network-Escape	The 3-digit code entered before the carrier code [**101**0321-1-248-555-9093]

Step 7.   Select the operator for each tag that you want to enable, and enter the value for any tag you select (==) as the operator.

Step 8.   Click the **Save** button.

Figure 4-11 shows what a page looks like for a filter that matches on a number that does not include a country or area code and has 248 as the local area code. The filter would allow the number 248-555-9093 through, but not 1-248-555-9093.

Now that the route filter is created, it must be applied to a route pattern. Typically route filters are applied when the route pattern is created. The steps for creating a route pattern showed how to apply a route filter. The following steps show how to add a route filter to a route pattern that already exists:

Step 1.   From within CCMAdmin, select **Calling Plan > Route/Hunt > Route Pattern.**

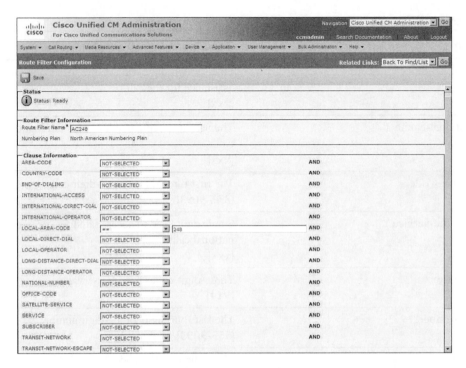

Figure 4-11 *Route Filter Configuration Example*

Step 2. Search for the route pattern that you want to add to the route filter. You can search by pattern, description, or partition by selecting one of these from the first drop-down list. In the next drop-down list, select the search match operator and enter the search criteria in the field to the left of the Find button. Click the **Find** button. Leaving the search criteria empty results in returning all route patterns. You can use the drop-down list to the left of Items Per Page to select how many results you want to have returned on a page.

Note It is important to remember that route filters only work with patterns that include the @ wildcard.

Step 3. From the results that display, select the route pattern that you want to add to the route filter.

Step 4. The next page that appears shows the properties of the route pattern you selected. From the **Route Filter** drop-down list, select the route filter that you want to apply to this pattern.

Step 5. Click the **Save** button to save the changes.

As you can see, route filters have a significant effect on the route patterns to which they are applied. Make sure that after you have created and applied route filters to route patterns, the pattern behaves as you expect. The Dialed Number Analyzer is a good tool for verifying the results. This tool can be found on, and installed from, the Install Plugins page. The Dialed Number Analyzer allows you to enter an origination and destination number, and shows you how the call will be handled based on the current dial plan. For more information on this tool, refer to the Dialed Number Analyzer guide, which can be found at Cisco.com by searching for "Dialed Number Analyzer."

Creating Translation Patterns

At times, digit manipulation might be necessary other than at the route pattern or route group level. This is where translation patterns can be used. Translation patterns allow called and calling digit manipulation to be performed. Translation patterns can also change the calling search space and MLPP precedence of a call.

The issues that you can address by using translation patterns are limited only by your imagination. Often, I come across interesting problems that are resolved using translation patterns. The change in extension numbers represents one of the more common issues that translation patterns can resolve. Often when a company moves, it is forced to get a new range of DID numbers from the phone company. More times than not, the new range is completely different than the old range. When the last few digits of a person's DID is also his or her extension number (which is normal), the person ends up with a new extension number after the move. Employees are used to dialing the old extensions, which are no longer valid, so the call fails. By creating a translation pattern that matches the old extension and transforms it to the new extension, you can reduce the frustration of the users while they get used to the new extension range.

Now take a closer look at how this would work. Assume that the old extension range was 5000–5999, but the new DID range is 7000–7999. The only part of the extension number that changes is the first digit, so a translation pattern of 5XXX is created that changes 5XXX to 7XXX. When a user dials 5050, it matches the 5XXX translation pattern and changes the called number to 7050. Because 7050 is the new extension, the call is extended to the phone.

Another use for a translation pattern is to change the calling search space of a call. An example of this is used with Cisco Personal Assistant (PA). PA has the capability to intercept calls on behalf of a PA user and route the call based on rules that the user creates. This is done by creating a CTI route point that matches the extension of all PA users' phones. The phones are then placed in a partition to which only the PA has access. This works wonderfully until the PA is not functioning. At this point, all calls to the PA users' phones fail. By creating a translation pattern that also matches the PA users' phones and assigning a calling search space that has access to the PA users' phones, calls are allowed directly to the phone if the PA fails. More complete information on the configuration can be found in the PA installation guide, but the previous summary gives you an idea of how a translation pattern can help resolve this issue by granting a call in the required calling search space.

The following steps show how to create and configure a translation pattern:

Step 1. From within CCMAdmin, select **Call Routing** > **Translation Pattern**.

Step 2. Click the **Add New** link.

Step 3. A screen similar to that shown in Figure 4-12 displays. In the **Translation Pattern** field, enter the pattern that you want to match. For example, if you are trying to match all calls to the extensions from 2000 to 2999, enter **2XXX**.

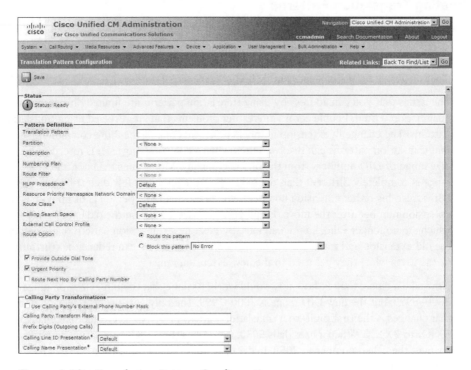

Figure 4-12 *Translation Pattern Configuration*

Step 4. The **Partition** field determines what devices can access this pattern. Partitions are a grouping of patterns and are discussed in more detail in Chapter 5. Select the desired partition from the drop-down Partition list.

Step 5. In the **Description** field, enter a description that helps identify the purpose of this pattern.

Step 6. In the **Numbering Plan** field, choose the appropriate numbering plan.

Step 7. From the **Route Filter** drop-down list, select the route filter that is to be applied to this pattern. Route filters are used to limit what digits match the pattern and are only used when the pattern contains the @.

Step 8. Determine the precedence level that will be assigned to this pattern from the **MLPP Precedence** drop-down list. Refer to Table 4-3, earlier in this chapter, for the available options.

Step 9. The **Resource Priority Namespace Network Domain** field is used in environments that utilize Voice over Secured IP (VoSIP) using SIP trunks. If your organization is utilizing this, select the appropriate domain from the drop-down list.

Step 10. From the **Calling Search Space** drop-down list, select the calling search space that the translation pattern searches for the newly created number.

Step 11. In certain version of Communications Manager, you can use an adjunct route server to make routing decisions. If you are using this feature, select the desired profile from the **External Call Control Profile** drop-down list.

Step 12. To allow calls to be routed that match this pattern, select the **Route This Pattern** radio button. To disallow calls that match this pattern, select the **Block This Pattern** radio button. When you select the button that blocks the pattern, you must select a reason from the drop-down list to the right of the radio button.

Step 13. To provide a secondary dial tone, select the **Provide Outside Dial Tone** check box.

Step 14. To route a call as soon as it matches this route pattern, select the **Urgent Priority** check box. Typically, a call is not routed if there are other patterns that might also match, for example, if there is a 911 route pattern and a 91XXXXXXXXXX route pattern. When a caller dials 911, Communications Manager matches the 911 route pattern, but could also match the 91XXXXXXXXXX route pattern. If Urgent Priority is not selected, Communications Manager waits for the interdigit timeout to expire (15 seconds by default) before routing the call. You can see how this is undesirable in many cases. By selecting Urgent Priority, you ensure that CallManager does not wait for any other digits to be dialed and instead routes the call immediately.

Note In earlier versions of Communications Manager, the Urgent Priority box cannot be deselected. This means that as soon as a pattern matches a translation pattern, the call is sent through the translation pattern. Communications Manager does not wait for additional digits even if other possible matches exist.

Step 15. If call screening that is based on the calling party number is being used between clusters, you should select the **Route Next Hop by Calling Party Number** check box. However, in most cases, you can leave this box deselected.

Step 16. The **Use Calling Party's External Phone Number Mask** field determines whether the mask configured on the directory number is used for calls that are routed through this route group.

Step 17. In the **Calling Party Transform Mask** field, enter any mask that you want to affect the caller ID.

Note This is where most people make mistakes. Often administrators enter the pattern here to which they want the number changed. This is incorrect. This field affects caller ID, not the number dialed. To affect a change on the dialed number, change the called party transform mask. This is a common mistake because the Called Party Transform Mask field cannot be seen on the screen unless you scroll down.

Step 18. In the **Prefix Digits (Outgoing Calls)** field, enter any digits that you want to have added to the front of the caller ID.

Step 19. The **Calling Line ID Presentation** field determines whether caller ID information is to be blocked for outbound calls that match this pattern. To block caller ID, select Restricted from the drop-down list. To allow caller ID, select Allowed from the drop-down list.

Step 20. The **Calling Name Presentation** field determines whether caller name information is to be blocked for outbound calls that match this pattern. To block calling name ID, select Restricted from the drop-down list. To allow calling name ID, select **Allowed** from the drop-down list.

Step 21. By default, the **Calling Party Number Type** and the **Calling Party Number Plan** fields are set to Cisco Unified Communications Manager. Only an individual that has extensive knowledge and experience using the dialing plans such as the NANP or the European dialing plan should change this field. It is recommended that this field be left at the default.

Step 22. The **Connected Line ID Presentation** field determines whether the connected party's ID information is to be displayed on the calling party's phone. To block the connected party's ID, select Restricted from the drop-down list. To allow the connected party's ID, select **Allowed** from the drop-down list.

Step 23. The **Connected Name Presentation** field determines whether the connected party's name information is displayed on the calling party's phone. To block a connected party's name, select **Restricted** from the drop-down list. To allow a connected party's name, select **Allowed** from the drop-down list.

Step 24. The next set of fields determines whether digit manipulation is performed on the dial digits. From the **Discard Digits** drop-down list, select the digit discard instruction that should be applied to calls that match this pattern. These instructions are explained earlier in Table 4-1.

Step 25. In the **Called Party Transform Mask** field, enter the mask you want to use for calls that match this pattern. This field determines how the dialed digits will be transformed.

Step 26. In the **Prefix Digits (Outgoing Calls)** field, enter any digits that you want to have added to the front of the dialed number before it is sent to the route list.

Step 27. By default, the **Called Party Number Type** and the **Called Party Number Plan** fields are set to Cisco Unified Communications Manager. Only an individual that has extensive knowledge and experience using the dialing plans such as the NANP or the European dialing plan should change this field. It is recommended that this field be left at the default.

Step 28. Click the **Save** button at the top of the page to add this translation pattern.

At this point, you should feel comfortable with translation patterns and understand how to create them. When trying to create custom solutions, make sure that you keep translation patterns in mind because they can be used in a limitless number of ways.

Creating CTI Route Points

The last route plan component that is covered in this chapter is CTI route points. CTI route points can be viewed as virtual ports that allow connectivity to other services and devices. CTI route points are also sometimes used as "dummy" phones when you have a DID that is associated with a voice mailbox, but not assigned to a physical phone. A CTI route point can be created to match the DID number. This number is then configured to forward all calls directly to the voicemail system.

The creation and configuration of CTI route points are similar to those of a phone. The following steps show how to create and configure a CTI route point:

Step 1. From within CCMAdmin, select **Device > CTI Route Point**.

Step 2. Click **Add New** link.

Step 3. A screen similar to that shown in Figure 4-13 displays. The first field that must be configured is the device name for this route point. Use a name that helps identify the function of this route point. For example, if this route point is to be used for a contact center system, a name such as "CC_Route_Point" would be a good choice.

Step 4. The next field is the **Description** field. Enter a description that helps you quickly identify the CTI route point.

Step 5. From the **Device Pool** drop-down list, select the device pool that this CTI route point will use.

Step 6. From the **Common Device Configuration** drop-down list, select the common device configuration that the CTI route point will use.

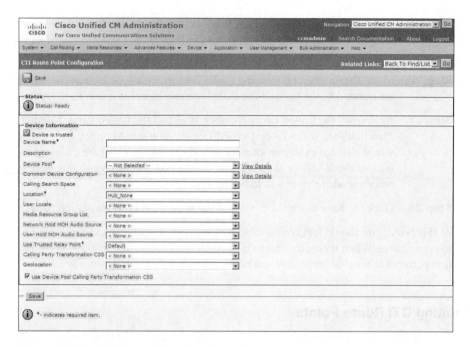

Figure 4-13   *CTI Route Point Configuration*

Step 7.   A **Calling Search Space** (CSS) determines what destination the CTI route point will be able to reach. CSS is discussed in Chapter 5. Choose a CSS from the Calling Search Space drop-down list. If this field is left at None, the dial privileges of this CTI route point could be limited.

Step 8.   **Locations** are used to prevent WAN links from becoming oversubscribed in centralized deployments. These are discussed more in Chapter 5. If you have defined locations, select the appropriate one for this CTI route point from the Location drop-down list.

Step 9.   The **User Locale** field determines the language and fonts used for the CTI route point. The default user locale, which is set in the enterprise parameters, is used if this field is left at None. If this CTI route point needs to use a different locale than is defined by its device pools or the enterprise parameters, select the proper one from the drop-down list.

Step 10.   The **Media Resource Group List** field determines to which media resources this CTI route point will have access. Media resources are discussed in further detail in Chapter 6. From the Media Resource Group List drop-down list, select the desired group. If no media resource group list is chosen, the one defined in the device pool is used.

Step 11.   The next two fields allow you to configure what audio source is heard when a call is placed on hold. The first of the two, which is labeled **User Hold Audio Source**, determines what is heard when the call is placed on hold by the application. The **Network Hold Audio Source** field determines what audio is heard when the call is placed on hold by pressing the Transfer, Call Park, or Conference button. Select the desired audio source from the drop-down list for each field. If no audio source is chosen, the one defined in the device pool is used.

Step 12. The **Use Trusted Relay Point** field determines whether a relay point such as a Media Termination Point (MTP) or a transcoder must be labeled *trusted* to be used by this device. This field is typically changed only in virtualized environments.

Step 13. Calling party transformation allows you to change the caller ID. Select a **Calling Party Transformation CSS** that contains the calling party transformation pattern assigned to the device. You can also leave this set to None and use the Calling Party Transformation CSS assigned to the device pool by selecting the Use Device Pool Calling Party Transformation CSS check box.

Step 14. The geolocation information can be used to determine the logical partition of a device. If you use features that depend on geolocation, select the desired geolocation from the drop-down list.

Step 15. Click the **Save** button to create the CTI route point.

Adding a Line to a CTI Route Point

Follow these steps to add a line to a CTI route point:

Step 1. If you are adding a new CTI route point and have used the previous steps, click Line [1] - **Add a New DN**. You should see a screen similar to that shown in Figure 4-14. To add a line to an existing CTI route point, follow Steps 2 through 5 to reach this screen. If you are already at this screen, skip to Step 6.

Step 2. From within CCMAdmin, select **Device > CTI Route Point**.

Step 3. Enter search criteria in the search field to limit the results and click the **Find** button.

Step 4. Select the CTI route point to which you want to add a line from the list that is generated.

Step 5. At the bottom of the CTI Route Point Configuration screen, the available lines are listed. Choose a line that has the label **Add New DN**.

Directory Number Information

Step 6. The first and only field that you must complete is the **Directory Number** field. Enter the extension number in this field.

Step 7. The **Route Partition** field defines the partition to which this directory number is assigned. The partition is used to determine what devices can call this extension. Partitions are discussed in more detail in Chapter 5.

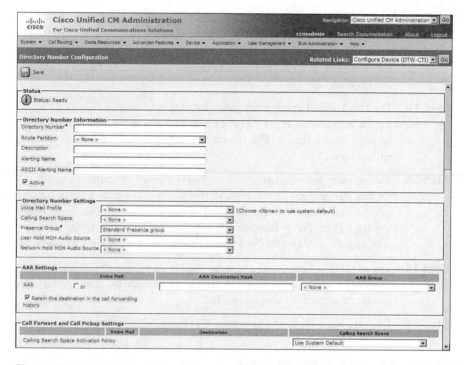

Figure 4-14   *CTI Route Point Directory Number Configuration*

Step 8.   In the **Description** field, enter a description that will help you quickly identify the line later.

Step 9.   In the **Alerting Name** field, enter the name that should be displayed on the caller's phone while it is ringing.

Step 10.   The **ASCII Alerting Name** field is the used on devices that do not support Unicode characters.

Step 11.   The **Associated Devices** box lists all the devices to which this line is assigned. To remove the line from a listed device, highlight the device in the Associated Devices box and click the down arrow that is between the Associated Device box and the Dissociate Devices box. The device should not appear in the **Dissociate Devices** box. Click **Save** and the line is removed from the selected device.

Directory Number Settings

Step 12.   The **Voice Mail Profile** field determines which voicemail profile the directory number will use. The voicemail profile defines the number that is dialed when the Messages button on the phone is pressed. Voicemail profiles are discussed in further detail in Chapter 5. Select the voicemail profile from the drop-down list.

Step 13. The next field allows a **Calling Search Space** (CSS) to be assigned as the line level. This determines what destinations can be reached when calling from this line. Select the Calling Search Space from the drop-down list.

Note It is important to understand what happens when a CSS is assigned to the line and the device. In short, the two CSSs are combined; however, there is a little more to it. For a detailed explanation, refer to Chapter 5.

Step 14. The presence group to which a line belongs determines which lines are allowed to monitor. Select the **presence group** to which this device should belong.

Step 15. The next two fields allow you to configure what audio source is heard when a call is placed on hold. The first of the two, which is labeled **User Hold Audio Source**, determines what is heard when the call is placed on hold by pressing the Hold button. The second field, **Network Hold Audio Source**, determines what audio is heard when the call is placed on hold by pressing the Transfer, Call Park, or Conference button. Select the desired audio source from the drop-down list for each field. If no audio source is chosen, the source defined at the device level is used, and if None is chosen, the source set in the device pool is used.

AAR Settings

Step 16. Automated Alternate Routing (AAR) is used to provide an alternate route if a call fails because of insufficient location bandwidth. To have failed calls reach this line because of insufficient bandwidth sent to voicemail, select the check box under Voice Mail. If you do not choose to send the calls to voicemail, you must choose an AAR group and you might need to configure the AAR destination mask. By default, AAR uses the external phone number mask to determine the fully qualified number of the destination. If you do not want to use the external phone number mask, enter the correct mask in the **AAR Destination Mask** field. The **AAR Group** field determines the AAR group with which the device is associated. An AAR group defines the prefix that is assigned when a call fails because of insufficient bandwidth. Select the appropriate **AAR group** from the drop-down list.

Call Forward and Pickup Settings

Step 17. The next seven fields deal with call forwarding. These fields determine the forwarding destination, which depends on the reason for the forward. Table 4-6 lists the ten types of forwards.

You can configure each type of "forward" to forward calls to voicemail or a specific extension.

Table 4-6 *Forward Types*

Forward Type	Forward Action
Forward All	Forwards all incoming calls
Forward Busy Internal	Forwards calls from internal callers when the line is busy
Forward Busy External	Forwards calls from external callers when the line is busy
Forward No Answer Internal	Forwards calls from internal callers that are not answered
Forward No Answer External	Forwards calls from external callers that are not answered
Forward No Coverage Internal	Forwards calls from internal callers when the application that controls the directory number fails
Forward No Coverage External	Forwards calls from external callers when the application that controls the directory number fails
Forward on CTI Failure	Forwards calls when a CTI route point or CTI port fails
Forward Unregistered Internal	Forwards calls from internal callers when the line is not registered
Forward Unregistered External	Forwards calls from external callers when the line is not registered

To forward to voicemail, select the Voice Mail box. For this to work, a voicemail profile must be defined for the line.

To forward calls to another extension, enter the extension number in the Destination field. When a destination is entered into any of the internal forwards, the number is automatically entered into the corresponding external forward.

If you want the external calls to be forwarded to a different destination, simply enter the desired destination in the appropriate external forward field. A calling search space can be applied to each forward type, which limits the destinations to which a call can be forwarded. This is useful when you want to restrict a line from forwarding calls to numbers that are long distance, but still want long-distance calls to be placed from the line. Enter the appropriate destinations and calling search spaces for each forward type.

Step 18. In the **No Answer Ring Duration** field, enter the number of seconds that the line will ring before forwarding to the Forward No Answer destination. If this field is left blank, the value configured in Communications Manager service parameters is used. The default value is 12 seconds.

Step 19. The **Call Pickup Group** field determines to which call pickup group this directory number belongs. Call pickup groups allow a user to redirect an incoming call on another phone to the user's phone. Select the desired call pickup group from the drop-down list. Call pickup groups are covered in more detail in Chapter 6.

Park Monitoring

Step 20. The **Park Monitoring Forward No Retrieve Destination External** field determines where external calls are forwarded to when they are placed on park and not retrieved. To send them to voicemail, select the check box below Voice Mail. To send them to an alternate number, enter that number in the Destination field. If the parker's CSS does not have rights to dial the alternate destination, you need to select a CSS from the Calling Search Space drop-down list.

Step 21. The **Park Monitoring Forward No Retrieve Destination Internal** field determines where internal calls are forwarded to when they are placed on park and not retrieved. To send them to voicemail, select the check box below Voice Mail. To send them to an alternative number, enter that number in the Destination field. If the parker's CSS does not have rights to dial the alternate destination, you need to select a CSS from the Calling Search Space drop-down list.

Step 22. The **Park Monitoring Reversion Timer** field determines how many seconds a call can be parked before CM sends an alert to the parked phone. If left blank, the value set in the service parameters is used. The default is 60 seconds.

MLPP Alternate Party Settings

Step 23. The next set of parameters deals with MLPP alternate party settings. These settings allow you to configure an alternate destination for precedence calls that are not answered on this line or the forwarded number assigned to this line. If MLPP is not being used, these parameters can be left empty. In the first field, which is labeled **Target (Destination)**, enter the number to which unanswered precedence calls should be forwarded.

Step 24. In the **MLPP Alternate Party Calling Search Space** field, select the appropriate search space from the drop-down list. This calling search space limits the destinations to which precedence calls can be forwarded.

Step 25. In the **MLPP No Answer Ring Duration** field, enter the number of seconds that the phone will ring when it receives a precedence call before forwarding to the Forward No Answer destination if unanswered.

Line Settings for All Devices

Step 26. The **Hold Reversion Ring Duration** field determines how many seconds a call can be on hold before CM rings the phone that placed the call on hold. The call will ring until it is answered or the maximum hold duration expires. Enter the desired amount of seconds in this field. If left blank, the value set in the service parameters is used.

Step 27. The **Hold Reversion Notification Interval** field determines the intervals at which the holding party will receive an alert reminding him or her that a call is on hold. Enter the desired amount of seconds in this field. If left blank, the value set in the service parameters is used.

Step 28. The **Party Entrance Tone** field determines which tone is played when a new caller joins a call. When this parameter is set to Default, the value set in the service parameters is used. To ensure that a tone is played, set this to On. To ensure that no tone is played, set this to Off.

Line Settings for This Device

Step 29. The next two fields, labeled **Display (Internal Call ID)**, are used to configure which caller ID is displayed when calls are placed to other internal callers. Enter up to 30 characters in this field. Both letters and numbers are allowed. If this field is left blank, the line's directory number will be used.

Note There two fields for the internal caller ID. The second, which is labeled ASCII Display, is used for devices that do not support Unicode character display. This is also true for the next two fields labeled Line Text Label.

Step 30. The **External Phone Number Mask** field can be used to modify the external caller ID for calls placed from this line. An example mask might be **408370XXXX**. The extension number is used to fill in the XXXX portion. In this example, if the directory number is 1401, the external phone mask would cause the external caller ID number to be 4083701401. The external phone mask on the first line creates the fully qualified directory number that is displayed above the first extension on certain IP phones.

Multiple Call / Call-Waiting Settings

Step 31. The next field, which is labeled **Maximum Number of Calls**, determines how many active calls can be on the line. The maximum is 10,000 active calls per phone. Enter the maximum number of calls in this field.

Step 32.   The **Busy Trigger** field determines how many active calls are required before the line is considered busy. The default is two. This means that if the maximum number of calls on the line is four and the busy trigger is two, the third inbound call will receive a busy indication. The user can place additional outbound calls up to the maximum number of four.

Forwarded Call Information Display

Step 33.   The Forwarded Call Information Display section determines what information is sent when a call is forwarded. Select the information to be sent by selecting the check box next to each desired field.

Step 34.   Click the **Save** button at the top of the screen to add this line.

The number of CTI route points you need depends on their individual requirements and number of applications needed for connection. Refer to the specific application installation guide when configuring CTI route points to ensure that you set all the parameters correctly.

Summary

This chapter has covered the tasks required to implement a basic dial plan. The call flow was explored to give the reader a good overview of the components that make up a dial plan. After that, each individual component was discussed, including route groups, route lists and route patterns, and step-by-step configurations. Additional components that are used in more advanced dial plans, such as route filters, translation patterns, and CTI route points, were also covered. After completing this chapter, you should feel comfortable with how a basic route plan works and how to configure one. The next chapter covers components that can be added to a route plan to restrict certain devices from placing calls to certain destinations, and discusses ways to ensure that WAN links are not over-subscribed, which in turn helps maintain good voice quality.

Configuring Class of Service and Call Admission Control

Now that you have created a basic dial plan, it is time to build on that and create a more complete dial plan. Often you want to allow and disallow access to certain destinations. For example, you might want only a certain group of callers to dial international numbers. This is done by creating a telephony class of service (CoS). In addition, if there are calls traversing limited-bandwidth links, some type of Call Admission Control (CAC) should be deployed to help ensure voice quality. This chapter examines the various concepts associated with CoS and CAC and describes how to configure the required components for each.

Rights and Restrictions

After the dial plan is created and users can place calls to destinations outside the cluster, you might think that you are all set and can sit back and relax. Not quite. After the system is configured to enable calls to be placed outside of the system, you need to start working on how to prevent certain calls from being placed. This chapter touches on how you can use route patterns to block certain destinations, and now you need to move beyond that and discuss how certain destinations can be reachable by some devices, but not by others. To accomplish this, you need to configure Calling Search Spaces (CSS) and partitions. The following sections explain what these are and how they work.

Understanding Call Search Spaces and Partitions

Of all the concepts within a Communications Manager environment, it is believed that the CSS and partitions cause the most confusion. This is rather odd because they are not complex. Simply put, the partition assigned to the destination affects what devices can reach it, and the CSS determines which destinations can be reached. Locks and key rings are good analogies. Think of the partition as a lock and the CSS as the key ring. To place a call to a destination, you must have a key that matches the device's lock. The key ring contains all the keys and therefore determines which destinations you can reach.

Of course, there is more to it than just locks and keys, but by using this analogy, you begin to understand how they work. You take a closer look at this analogy. Figure 5-1 shows five phones. The first four phones have partitions (locks). It is important to point out that the partitions (locks) are not assigned to devices, but rather to patterns and directory numbers (DN). For this example, assume that each phone has only a single line and that the partition (lock) is assigned to that line. Below each phone is a CSS (key ring) that shows to which partitions (locks) the phone has access. CSS (key rings) can be assigned to the device or the line. In this example, assume that they are assigned to the device.

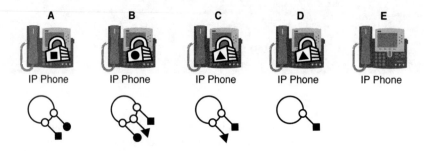

Figure 5-1   *Calling Search Spaces and Partitions Analogy*

The locks in this figure have different-shaped keyholes, which means that to open a lock, you must have a key ring that has the correct-shape key. Keeping in mind that the locks represent partitions and that the key rings represent CSS, answer the following questions:

- What phones can phone A reach?

- What phones can phone D reach?

- What phone can reach all other phones?

- What phones can reach phone E?

- What phones can phone E reach?

The answers to these questions are as follows:

Q. What phones can phone A reach?

A. To determine what phones phone A can reach, you need to look at its CSS (key ring). Phone A has a circular key and a square key on its key ring, which means that it can call itself and phone B. However, because phone E has no lock (partition) assigned to it, any phone can reach it, just as a door with no lock can be opened by anyone.

Q. What phones can phone D reach?

A. Because phone D has only a square key, it can dial phone A and, of course, phone E because it has no lock (partition).

Q. What phone can reach all other phones?

A. Because phone B has a key ring (CSS) that contains all the keys, it can reach all the devices.

Q. What phones can reach phone E?

A. Because phone E has no lock (partition), all phones can reach it.

Q. What phones can phone E reach?

A. Because phone E has no keys, it can only reach devices that have no locks. In this example, phone E can only dial itself.

Figure 5-1, along with these questions and answers, should help you begin to understand how partitions and CSS work. Of course, as with any simple concept, it has the potential to become more complicated as the number of CSS and partitions grows. This is where some people begin to become confused, because of an inaccurate base understanding of the concepts. Now look at some of the more interesting aspects of CSS and partitions.

The first misconception that should be dispelled is this: If two devices have the same partition, they can call each other. Having the same partition alone is not enough. Going back to the lock and key ring analogy, if two people have the same locks, keyed the same way on their houses, but they have no keys, can they access each other's houses? Of course they can't, and they cannot even access their own houses. This demonstrates that a device's partition (lock) has no effect on where the device can call. However, if two devices that have the same partition also have a CSS that enables them access to their partitions, they can dial each other.

The next important point is the order of CSS. As demonstrated in the earlier example, CSS can enable access to more than one partition. Now, imagine that a device has a CSS that enables it to match two devices with the same number, but in different partitions. Figure 5-2 offers an example of this situation.

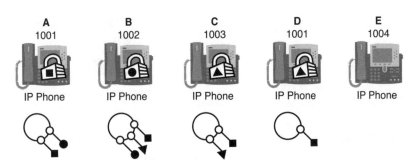

Figure 5-2 *CSS Matches Multiple Destinations*

In this example, phones A and D have the same extension of 1001. Phones B and C can reach both phones because their CSS enables access to both the square and triangle partition. So the question is, which phone rings when phone C dials 1001? Often people answer this question with, "It takes the closer match." Because 1001 matches 1001 exactly, both phones are the closest matches. Others assume that both phones ring because phone C has access to both partitions. What actually happens is that when a search for a match is conducted, multiple closest matches are found. Because there are multiple closest matches, the order in which objects appear in the CSS comes into play. When you create a CSS, you prioritize the order in which partitions should be searched. This order determines which partition is used if there are two closest matches. In the example, Figure 5-2 shows that the order of the keys for phone C is square followed by triangle, meaning that when phone C dials 1001, it would first match the 1001 that has the square partition, which is phone A.

To add a little more complexity to this, it is possible to have a CSS on both the device and the line. For example, the phone can have a CSS that grants access to the square partition, and a line on the phone can have a CSS that grants access to the triangle partition. In such a case, the line CSS takes priority. Figure 5-3 shows an example of this. This example moves away from the locks and keys analogy to focus more on the actual terms.

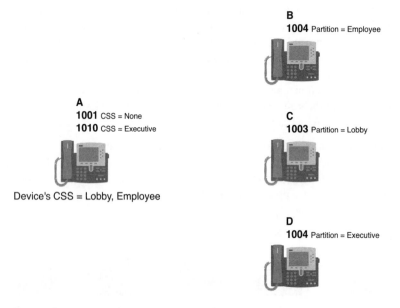

Figure 5-3   *Line/Device CSS Example*

In Figure 5-3, phone A has two lines, 1001 and 1010. 1001 has no CSS, and line 1010 has a CSS that grants access to devices in the executive partition. Phone A also has a CSS at the device level, which enables access to devices in the lobby and employee partitions. Because the 1001 line does not have a CSS of its own, it has access only to devices that can be reached using the device's CSS. Because line 1010 has a CSS of its own, it has access to devices that can be reached using its CSS and the device's CSS. This means that when dialing from line 1001, only devices in the lobby and employee partitions are accessible; but when dialing from line 1010, devices in the lobby, employee, and exec partitions are accessible.

Now, take a look at the other three phones. Phone B has the extension of 1004, and that line is in the employee partition. Phone C has the extension of 1003, and that line is in the lobby partition. Phone D has the extension of 1004, and that line is in the exec partition.

Using what you have learned, answer the following three questions:

- What is the result if 1004 is dialed from line 1001?

- What is the result if 1004 is dialed from line 1010?

- Can line 1010 reach line 1003?

The answers to these questions are as follows:

Q. What is the result if 1004 is dialed from line 1001?

A. Because line 1001 has no CSS of its own, it relies solely on the device's CSS. The device's CSS has access to the employee and lobby partitions, so line 1001 can reach only the 1004 on phone B because it is in the employee partition.

Q. What is the result if 1004 is dialed from line 1010?

A. Because line 1010 has a CSS, it has access to all devices to which the line and device's CSS grants access. Because it can reach phones B and D and both of them match 1004, the line's CSS takes priority and phone D rings.

Q. Can line 1010 reach line 1003?

A. Line 1010 can reach any device to which the line and/or the device's CSS grants access. Because the device's CSS has access to the lobby partition, which is the partition that 1003 is in, it can reach it.

At this point, you should have a good idea of how partitions and CSS work. We now take a look at a real-world, practical example of how CSS and partitions can be used.

The BGD Company has deployed a Communications Manager solution and has configured the route patterns that are shown in Table 5-1. As you can see, the route patterns enable callers to reach anywhere they need to dial with the exception of 1-900 numbers, which are blocked. The problem is that these patterns also enable some callers to make unauthorized calls that the company disapproves of. For example, if a person's job does not require the placement of international calls, the dial plan should not enable the employee's phone to place them.

In this example, BGD has decided that it actually has four classes of users. The first class, the executives, can make any calls they want, other than 1-900 calls. The second class, the administrative assistants, are not allowed to make 1-900 calls or international calls. The third class, standard users, can only reach internal extensions, local numbers, and emergency services. The fourth class, lobby phones, for example, can only make calls internally and to emergency services. To accomplish this, partitions and CSS must be configured and assigned to patterns and devices.

Table 5-1   *BGD's Route Patterns*

Pattern	Notes	Matches
9.[2-9]XXXXXX	PreDot Discard	Local 7- and 10-digit calls
9.810[2-9]XXXXXX	PreDot Discard	
9.810586XXXX	PreDot Discard	10-digit calls that are not
9.810587XXXX	PreDot Discard	local
9.1[2-9]XX[2-9]XXXXXX	PreDot Discard	Long-distance calls
9.011!	PreDot Discard	International calls
9.011!#	PreDot Trailing-# Discard	
9.1900[2-9]XXXXXX	Block Pattern	1-900 numbers
911	Urgent Priority	Emergency service calls
9.911	PreDot Discard and Urgent Priority	

When creating partitions, a common practice is to name them so that the name describes to what the partition is assigned. For example, a partition that is going to be assigned to a pattern that matches a local number can be called Local PT.

> **Tip**   The PT at the end of the name helps identify this object as a partition. Because it is possible to have partitions and CSS with the same name, it is recommended that you add a PT to the end of partition names and CSS to the end of CSS names.

In this example, five types of calls are allowed: internal, local, long-distance, international, and emergency. The following is the list of partitions that are needed, and to which patterns they are assigned:

- **Internal_PT:** Patterns that match internal numbers

- **Local_PT:** Patterns that match local numbers

- **LD_PT:** Patterns that match long-distance numbers

- **International_PT:** Patterns that match international numbers

- **Emergency_PT:** Patterns that match emergency service numbers

After the partitions are created, CSS are needed. Because BGD has defined four classes of users, four CSS are needed. Just as with partitions, it is recommended that CSS are named so that the name helps identify to which partitions the CSS have access. Table 5-2 shows the CSS and the partitions to which each has access and that are needed for BGD.

Now that partitions and CSS are defined, take a look at what each is assigned to. First, examine the partitions. You need to understand that partitions are assigned to patterns of DNs, not devices. This means that if you want to prevent a device from making long-distance calls, you assign a partition to the patterns that match long-distance numbers, and make sure that the device's CSS does not have access to the partition. Table 5-3 shows the five partitions that have been created and the patterns to which each is assigned.

Table 5-2 *CSS and Associated Partitions*

CSS	Partitions
Internal_CSS	Internal_PT Emergency_PT
Internal_Local_LD_CSS	Internal_PT Local_PT Emergency_PT
Internal_CSS	Internal_PT Local_PT LD_PT Emergency_PT
Unlimited_CSS	Internal_PT Local_PT LD_PT International_PT Emergency_PT

Table 5-3 *Partitions and Patterns*

Partitions	Patterns
Internal_PT	DNs of the phones
Local_PT	9.[2-9]XXXXXX 9.810[2-9]XXXXXX
LD_PT	9.810586XXXX 9.810587XXXX 9.1[2-9]XX[2-9]XXXXXX
International_PT	9.011! 9.011!#
Emergency_PT	911 9.911

You might notice that the 9.1900[2-9]XXXXXX pattern has not been assigned to a partition but will still work. Remember, if a pattern does not have a partition explicitly assigned, it falls into the null partition, and all devices have access to the null partition. Because the 9.1900[2-9]XXXXXX pattern is set up so that it blocks all calls that match it, you want all devices to have access to it so that no one can place these types of calls. However, it is recommended to apply partitions to all patterns to ensure that no calls can be placed by phones that do not have the proper CSS. With this is mind, the Internal_PT partition can be applied to the 9.1900[2-9]XXXXXX pattern because all devices can reach that partition.

Now look at how the CSS should be assigned. Remember that CSS can be assigned at both the device and line. For this example, they are assigned at the device level only. Table 5-4 shows the CSS and the types of device to which each is assigned.

Table 5-4 *CSS and Assigned Devices*

CSS	Devices
Unlimited_CSS	Executive phones
Internal_Local_LD_CSS	Administrative assistant phones
Internal_Local_CSS	Standard users
Internal_CSS	Lobby phones

Now that you understand which CSS and partitions are needed for BGD, and where each is applied, take a look at the big picture. Table 5-5 shows which CSS is assigned to each of the four different classes of phones. Under the CSS heading is a list of the partitions that can be accessed. Under the partitions is a list of patterns. Using this table, it is easy to see what destinations various phones can reach.

Table 5-5 *CSS Assigned to Phones and the Patterns They Can Reach*

Device	CSS>Partition>Patterns
Executive phones	Unlimited_CSS
	Internal_PT
	All Internal Phones
	Local_PT
	9.[2-9]XXXXXX
	9.810[2-9]XXXXXX
	LD_PT
	9.810586XXXX
	9.810587XXXX
	9.1[2-9]XX[2-9]XXXXXX
	International_PT
	9.011!
	9.011!#
	Emergency_PT
	911
	9.911

Table 5-5   *CSS Assigned to Phones and the Patterns They Can Reach*

Device	CSS>Partition>Patterns
Administrative assistant phones	Internal_Local_LD_CSS Internal_PT
	All Internal Phones
	Local_PT
	9.[2-9]XXXXXX
	9.810[2-9]XXXXXX
	LD_PT
	9.810586XXXX
	9.810587XXXX
	9.1[2-9]XX[2-9]XXXXXX
	Emergency_PT
	911
	9.911
Standard user phones	Internal_Local_CSS Internal_PT
	All Internal Phones
	Local_PT
	9.[2-9]XXXXXX
	9.810[2-9]XXXXXX
	Emergency_PT
	911
	9.911
Lobby phones	Internal_CSS Internal_PT
	All Internal Phones
	Emergency_PT
	911
	9.911

Up to this point, only the assigning of CSS to phones and lines has been discussed. CSS are assigned to devices, which include gateways. A CSS is assigned to a gateway so that inbound calls can reach internal destinations. In the example of BGD, all the internal phones are placed in the Internal_PT partition. If the gateways do not have access to this partition, no incoming calls are allowed. So you can see that not only must phones have CSS, but gateways require them as well. In the case of BGD, the Internal_CSS can be assigned to the gateways, which would grant outside calls access to all internal phones.

> **Note**   CSS and partitions are only locally significant. This means, for all intents and purposes, that after a call leaves the local system, the CSS and partitions no longer exist.

In the BGD example, all internal phones were in the Internal_PT partition, meaning that because all devices had a CSS that granted access to the Internal_PT partition, all phones could be reached. In some cases, this is undesirable. Sometimes there are certain numbers that should be reached only by certain devices. An example often used is that of an executive's phone. Often it is desired that only the executive's assistant be able to reach the executive. To accomplish this, the executive's phone is placed in a separate partition, to which only the assistant's phone has access.

Now that you have a good idea of what CSS and partitions are, move on to discussing how they are created and configured.

Creating Calling Search Spaces and Partitions

Creating CSS and partitions is much easier than understanding and properly applying them. Before you move on to the process of creating them, you should make sure that you have taken the time to determine the different classes of users your environment has, and what destinations each user will be allowed to call. After you have done this, create a list of the partitions that are required. Next, create a CSS that defines what partitions are accessible. After you have created this, you can begin to create the partitions and CSS. Because CSS are created by choosing partitions to which they will have access, the partitions must be created first. The following steps show how to create partitions:

Step 1.   From within CCMAdmin, select **Call Routing > Class of Control > Partition**.

Step 2.   Click the **Add New** link.

Step 3. A screen displays that offers an area in which you can enter the name of the partition followed by a description. You must place a comma (,) between the name and description. If you do not enter a description, the name of the partition will be used as the description. You can create up to 75 partitions at a time on this screen by placing each on a new line. Figure 5-4 shows an example of adding five partitions at one time.

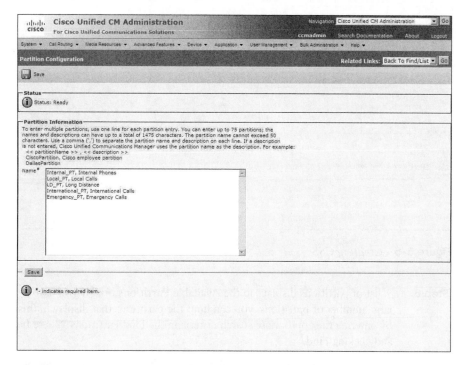

Figure 5-4 *Creating Partition Configurations*

Step 4. After you enter all the desired partitions, click **Save**.

As you can see, the creation of partitions is a simple task. Now that partitions are added, you can start to create CSS by working through the following steps:

Step 1. From within CCMAdmin, select **Call Routing > Class of Control > Calling Search Space**.

Step 2. Click the **Add New** link.

Step 3. A screen similar to that shown in Figure 5-5 displays.

Step 4. Enter a name in the **Calling Search Space Name** field. Remember that the name should help identify the purpose of this CSS.

Step 5. Enter a description in the **Description** field.

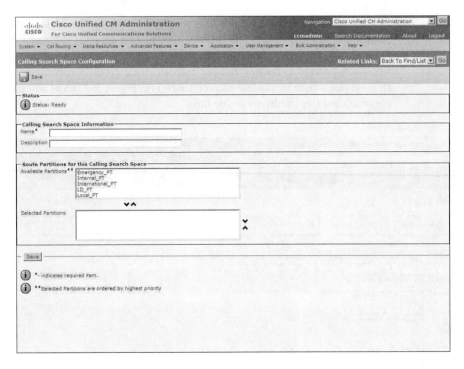

Figure 5-5 *Creating CSS*

Step 6. A list of partitions displays in the **Available Partitions** box. If you have a large number of partitions, you can limit the partitions that display in this list by entering the appropriate search criteria in the Find Partitions Where fields and clicking **Find**.

Step 7. Highlight the first partition to which you want the CSS to have access, and click the Down Arrow below this box. This causes that partition to display in the **Selected Partitions** box.

Step 8. Repeat Step 7 for each partition to which you want the CSS to have access. These should be added in the order you want to have them searched.

Step 9. After all the partitions have been added, you can change the order in which they display. Remember, the order in which they display determines which partition is used if multiple partitions within the same CSS contain exact matches for a dialed number. To change the order, highlight the partition you want to move, and click the Up or Down Arrow to the right of the box. Figure 5-6 shows what the screen looks like when adding the Internal_Local_CSS, which was used in the previous example.

Step 10. After all desired partitions are listed in the correct order in the Selected Partitions box, click **Save**.

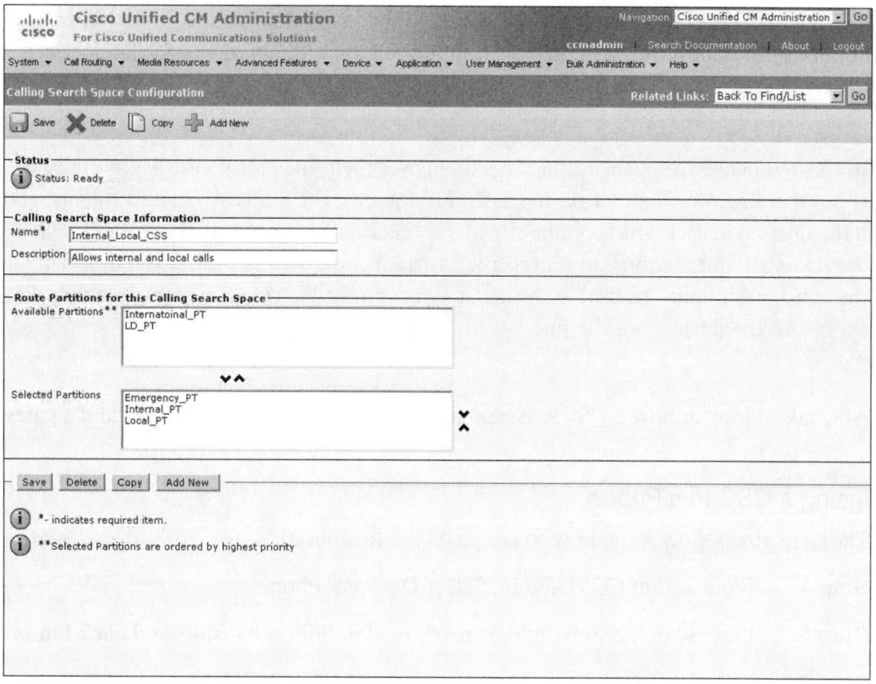

Figure 5-6   *Example CSS*

You need to repeat these steps to add all the CSS that your environment requires. After all the partitions and CSS are added, it is time to apply them. Adding partitions and CSS have absolutely no effect on call processing until they are applied to patterns and devices.

Applying Calling Search Spaces and Partitions

You are now ready to start applying the partitions and CSS to devices and patterns. After a partition is added to a pattern, only devices that have the correct CSS can reach that pattern. For this reason, you might want to assign CSS to the devices before assigning partitions. Assigning partitions before assigning CSS is similar to putting a lock on a door and not giving anyone a key. Until the keys are handed out, no one can get in.

Note   When adding partitions and CSS to a system, it is best to apply them during non-production times. After they are added, thorough testing should be done. If it is not possible to add them off-hours, be certain to apply CSS before applying partitions. A good tool that can be used to verify the results is called the Dialed Number Analyzer. This tool can be installed from the Install Plugins page. This tool enables you to enter an origination and destination number and shows you how the call will be handled, based on the current dial plan. For more information on this tool, refer to the Dialed Number Analyzer guide, which can be found at Cisco.com by searching for Dialed Number Analyzer.

CSS are applied to devices and lines. When applied to both, the line's CSS has priority but does not nullify the devices. This means a line that has its own CSS has access to partitions that both the line's CSS and the device's CSS allow.

> **Note** Often people want their assistants to answer their lines for them. To do this, you must put the directory number on the assistant's phone. The CSS assigned to the line stays with the line, no matter which phone the line is on. This means that if the boss's line has the rights to call international numbers, the assistant can do so as well, if the boss's line is on the assistant's phone. To deal with this, it is recommended that the more generous CSS be applied to the device, not the line.

Now take a look at how a CSS is assigned to a phone, a line on the phone, and a gateway.

Assigning a CSS to a Phone

The steps that follow show how to assign a CSS to a phone:

Step 1. From within CCMAdmin, Select **Device > Phone**.

Step 2. Enter search criteria in the search field to limit the results and click **Find**.

Step 3. Select the phone to which you want to assign a CSS from the list that is generated.

Step 4. The Phone Configuration screen displays. To assign a CSS to the phone, select a CSS from the **Calling Search Space** drop-down list, as shown in Figure 5-7.

Step 5. Click **Save**.

Step 6. A window displays to inform you that you must click the **Apply Config** button for the change to take affect. Click **OK**.

Step 7. Click **Apply Config**.

Step 8. A window displays to warn you that when you apply the configuration, the device might go through a restart. Click **OK**.

Assigning a CSS to a Line

The steps that follow show how to assign a CSS to a line on a phone:

Step 1. From within CCMAdmin, select **Device > Phone**.

Step 2. Enter search criteria in the search field to limit the results and click **Find**.

Step 3. Select the phone that contains the desired line from the list of phones that is generated.

Step 4. Click the desired line on the left side of the screen.

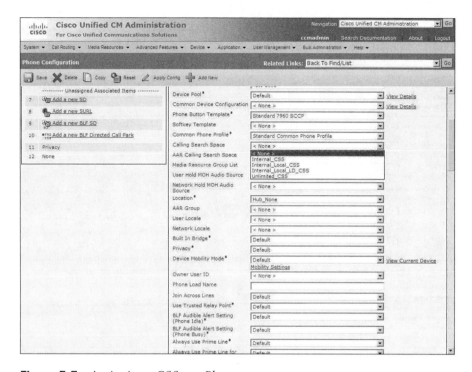

Figure 5-7 *Assigning a CSS to a Phone*

Step 5. On the Directory Number Configuration page, select the desired CSS from the **Calling Search Space** drop-down list, as shown in Figure 5-8.

Step 6. Click **Save**.

Note When you make a change to the directory number configuration and click Update, the line will be reset on all the phones that appear on this line. If a caller is currently on a call, the line resets after the call is ended.

Assigning a CSS to a Gateway or Trunk

The steps that follow show how to assign a CSS to a gateway or a trunk. Because the steps are so similar for both components, they have been combined.

Step 1. From within CCMAdmin, select **Device > Gateway or Device > Trunk**.

Step 2. Enter search criteria in the search field to limit the results, and click **Find**.

Step 3. From the list that is generated, select the gateway/trunk to which you want to assign a CSS.

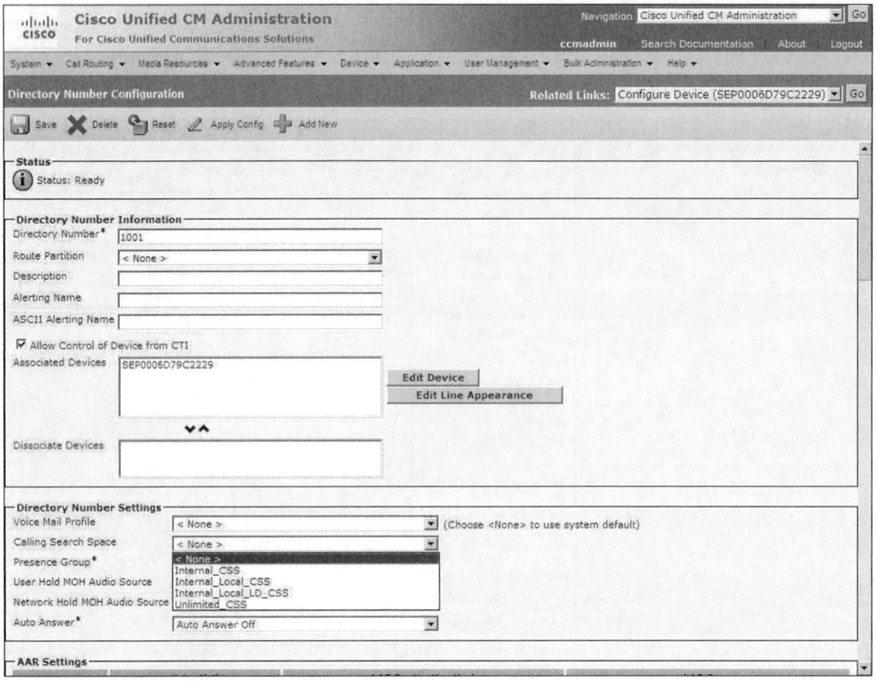

Figure 5-8   *Assigning a CSS to a Line*

Note   When configuring CSS for Session Initiation Protocol (SIP) trunks, additional CSSs are configured. In the Inbound Call section, select the desired AAR CSS from the AAR Calling Search Space drop-down list. Under the Outbound Calls section, select the desired CSS from the Called Party Transformation CSS and Calling Party Transformation CSS drop-down lists. Under the SIP Information section, there are additional CSSs that should be configured. These included the Rerouting Calling Search Space, Out-Of-Dialog Refer Calling Search Space, and SUBSCRIBE Calling Search Space.

Step 4.   Select the CSS from the **Calling Search Space** drop-down list.

Note   For some gateways such as Media Gateway Control Protocol (MGCP), you need to navigate to the subunit configuration page to assign a CSS.

Step 5.   Click **Save**.

Step 6.   A window displays informing you that you must click **Apply Config** for the change to take affect. Click **OK**.

Step 7.   Click **Apply Config**.

Step 8.   A window displays warning you that when you apply the configuration, the device might go through a restart. Click **OK**.

Now that you have assigned CSS, you can assign partitions. Partitions are assigned to patterns of directory numbers. Examples of how to assign them to CSS and partitions follow.

Assigning a Partition to a Line (Directory Number)

The following steps show how to assign a partition to a line:

Step 1.   From within CCMAdmin, select **Device > Phone**.

Step 2.   Enter search criteria in the search field to limit the results and click **Find**.

Step 3.   Select the phone that contains the desired line from the list of phones that is generated.

Step 4.   Click the desired line on the left side of the screen.

Step 5.   On the Directory Number Configuration page, select the desired partition from the **Route Partition** drop-down list, as shown in Figure 5-9.

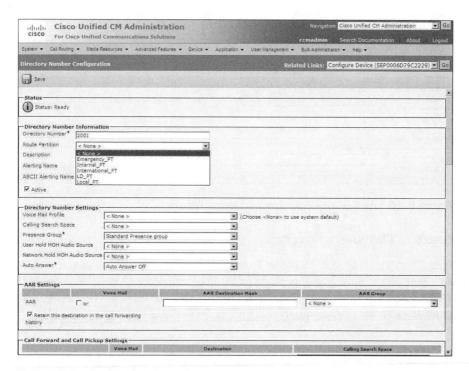

Figure 5-9   *Assigning a Partition to a Line*

Step 6.   Click **Save**.

Assigning a Partition to a Pattern

Step 1.   From within CCMAdmin, select **Call Routing** > **Route/Hunt** > **Route Pattern**.

Step 2.   To limit the results, enter search criteria in the search field and click **Find**.

Step 3.   Select the route pattern from the list that displays.

Step 4.   Select the partition from the **Route Partition** drop-down list, as shown in Figure 5-10.

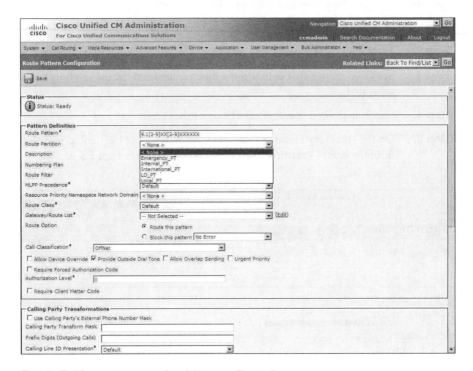

Figure 5-10   *Assigning a Partition to a Route Pattern*

Step 5.   Click **Save**.

> **Note**   Two alert windows can appear. If you have not assigned authorization codes to this pattern, an alert will inform you of this. You can click OK. The other alert informs you that any update to a route pattern automatically resets the route list or gateway; click OK.

After the partitions are applied, you can begin testing the system to ensure that allowed calls can be placed, and those that are not allowed cannot be placed.

Adding CSS and partitions after the system is in place can require a lot of work. Remember that you can use the the Bulk Admin Tool (BAT) to quickly apply or change a CSS or partition on a large number of objects.

Implementing Call Admission Control

After you have set up your system to allow calls to be placed to outside destinations and have applied CSS and partitions to restrict access, you need to configure the system to ensure the quality of the calls. Although there are many things that can affect the quality of the call, this book deals only with things that can be configured directly in Communications Manager. The following sections discuss what must be configured to ensure that the Voice over Internet Protocol (VoIP) link is not over subscribed.

When calls are placed between sites using an IP link as the transport, the quality of the call can be affected if more calls are allowed than what the link can support. To prevent this, some type of Call Admission Control must be deployed. How this is accomplished depends on the environment. If the calls are being sent across intercluster trunks, a gatekeeper is required. If calls are being placed to remote sites that are part of the same cluster, locations are used. If both types of calls are taking place, both solutions must be deployed.

Locations are objects that are configured within Communications Manager. A location for each site is created that contains available bandwidth for calls. A closer look at the configuration of locations is offered later in this chapter. Before looking at locations, gatekeepers are examined.

Configuring CAC for a Distributed Deployment

A gatekeeper is a process that runs on a Cisco IOS router. It keeps track of the active calls between clusters and determines whether a call can be placed across an intercluster trunk. In most cases, only one gatekeeper is needed because each can support more than a 100 sites. It is recommended, however, to have a redundant gatekeeper. This can be accomplished by having a second router running Hot Standby Routing Protocol (HSRP) or by implementing gatekeeper clustering. The only requirement for the physical location of a gatekeeper is that all clusters must reach it through an IP path.

When a call is placed across a gatekeeper-controlled H.225 or intercluster trunk, the Communications Manager on the originating side asks the gatekeeper whether the call can be placed. If there is enough bandwidth, the gatekeeper grants admission. If admission is granted, call setup begins, and the Communications Manager on the other side of the call must request admission. If the gatekeeper determines that there is enough bandwidth, admission is granted and the call setup is complete.

A gatekeeper grants admission based upon availability of configured bandwidth. The gatekeeper is configured with the amount of bandwidth that can be used for calls. Each time a call is placed, the gatekeeper removes a certain amount from the available bandwidth. When the call is over, it returns the bandwidth to the available pool.

The amount of bandwidth required for each call depends on which codec is being used. The gatekeeper has the preconfigured amount of bandwidth that each codec requires, and this number cannot be changed. This figure might not be the actual bandwidth the call needs, but is used to ensure that enough bandwidth is available. A gatekeeper running IOS 12.2(2)XA or later assumes that 128 kbps is needed for G7.11 calls and 16 kbps is required for G.729 calls. Although it might seem odd that the gatekeeper might request more or less bandwidth than it needs, it isn't a problem because the amount of available bandwidth is a setting that you configure in the gatekeeper. The gatekeeper does not have the ability to monitor the link and decide whether there is available bandwidth. It relies totally on the number that is configured. It is best to determine the amount of calls you want to allow on the link and the codec that will be used. Then simply multiply the amount of bandwidth the gatekeeper uses for that codec by the number of calls. The result is the amount of bandwidth that should be configured. For example, if the gatekeeper is running IOS version 12.2(2)XA or later and you want to allow ten calls all using the G.729 codec, the formula is 10 x 16 (10 calls x 16 kbps), which means that 160 kbps will be needed.

The gatekeeper can also be configured to provide the destination IP address to which the call should be sent. This feature is sometimes referred to as an *anonymous device*. An anonymous device is preferred in many environments, especially those with multiple intercluster trunks. When more than two clusters are connected, an intercluster trunk must be created between each cluster if an anonymous device is not used. Figure 5-11 shows that when connecting four clusters, 12 intercluster trunks are required.

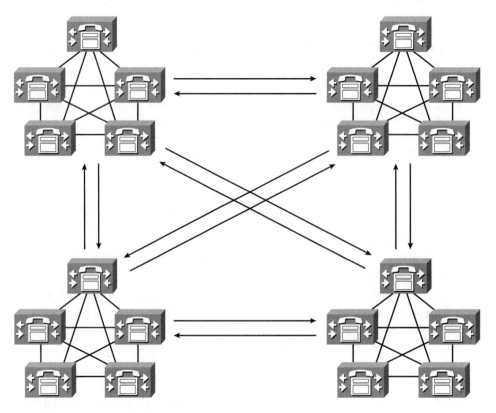

Figure 5-11 *Intercluster Trunks*

The formula used to determine how many intercluster trunks are required is N x (N−1). That is the number of clusters times the number of clusters minus 1. In Figure 5-11, there are four clusters. This means that the total number of intercluster trunks is 4 x (4−1) or 4 x 3, which equals 12. As the number of clusters increases so does the number of required trunks. For example, with four clusters, 12 intercluster trunks are needed, but with eight clusters, 56 intercluster trunks are needed. This is where an anonymous device becomes extremely useful. Instead of creating all the intercluster trunks, just one gatekeeper-controlled intercluster trunk is created, and all calls destined to any of the other clusters are sent to this trunk. When the gatekeeper responds to an admission request, it also provides the IP address of the destination.

Because the gatekeeper is going to provide destination information, it must know the destination IP address. This is part of the configuration that must be done on the gatekeeper itself. The bandwidth allowed for calls must also be configured in the gatekeeper to give you an idea of what needs to be configured. The following example shows a partial configuration:

```
gatekeeper
zone local DTW bgd.com 10.10.12.28
zone prefix DTW 4...
gw-type-prefix 1#* default-technology
bandwidth total zone DTW 256
no shutdown
```

A complete explanation of this configuration can be found in the article "Configuring H.323 Gatekeepers and Proxies" on Cisco.com. However, to give you an idea of what this configuration is achieving, the third command, "zone prefix DTW 4...," denotes that calls in the 4000 range can be handled by the DTW gatekeeper. The fifth command, "bandwidth total zone DTW 256," means that the total amount of bandwidth available for calls to and from DTW is 256 kbps.

Warning   The gatekeeper should be configured only by an individual who is extremely knowledgeable of IOS configurations and commands and who thoroughly understands VoIP technologies. Because the gatekeeper might also be serving other routing functions, incorrect configuration could negatively affect the network as a whole.

Configuring a Gatekeeper

In addition to the required configuration on the gatekeeper itself, the gatekeeper must also be configured in the Communications Manager. Adding a gatekeeper in Communications Manager is quite simple. The following steps show how this is done:

Step 1.   From within CCMAdmin, select **Device > Gatekeeper**.

Step 2.   Click the **Add New** link.

Step 3.   A screen similar to that shown in Figure 5-12 displays. Enter the IP address of the gatekeeper in the **Host Name/IP Address** field.

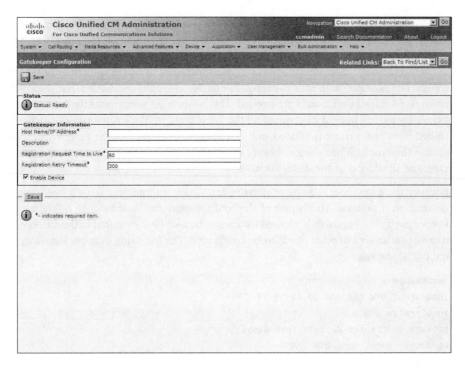

Figure 5-12   *Gatekeeper Configuration*

Step 4.   In the **Description** field, enter a description that helps to identify this gate-keeper.

Step 5.   The **Registration Request Time to Live** field should be left at the default. Change this field only if the Cisco Technical Assistance Center (TAC) tells you to do so. This field determines how often the Communications Manager must send a registration keepalive to the gatekeeper.

Step 6.   The **Registration Retry Timeout** field should be left at the default. Change this field only if TAC tells you to do so. This value determines how long Communications Manager waits before trying to register after a registration attempt fails.

Step 7.   Typically, the **Enable Device** check box should be left selected. This allows the gatekeeper to register with Communications Manager. When you need to gracefully unregister the gatekeeper, deselect this box.

Step 8.   Click **Save**.

After a gatekeeper is configured, you must create a gatekeeper-controlled intercluster trunk so that the calls placed across the intercluster trunk request admission from the gatekeeper. This also allows you to take advantage of the anonymous device features if the gatekeeper is configured to provide call-routing information. Creating a gatekeeper-controlled intercluster trunk is similar to creating a nongatekeeper-controlled intercluster trunk.

Configuring a Gatekeeper-Controlled Trunk

The steps required to configure a gatekeeper-controlled H.225 trunk and a gatekeeper-controlled intercluster trunk are similar. The following steps show how to configure a gatekeeper-controlled intercluster trunk and explain its various settings:

Step 1.   From within CCMAdmin, select **Device > Trunk**

Step 2.   Click the **Add New** link.

Step 3.   On the next page, select Inter-Cluster Trunk (Gatekeeper Controlled) from the **Trunk Type** drop-down list.

Step 4.   The Device Protocol field can be left at Inter-Cluster Trunk. No other option is available. Click the **Next** button.

Step 5.   The Trunk Configuration screen, as shown in Figure 5-13, displays. Enter a functional name for the gateway in the **Device Name** field.

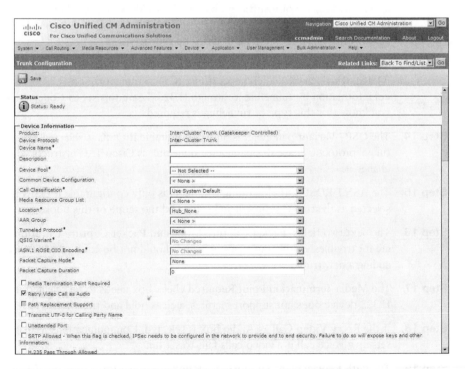

Figure 5-13   *Trunk Configuration*

Step 6.   In the **Description** field, enter a description that makes this device easily identifiable.

Step 7.   From the **Device Pool** drop-down list, select the desired device pool for this gateway.

Step 8.   From the **Common Device Configuration** drop-down list, select the common device configuration that the trunk will use.

Step 9.   From the **Call Classification** drop-down list, select whether incoming calls on this device should be considered OnNet or OffNet. This parameter is used to determine whether calls can be transferred and forwarded. This is to help prevent fraud.

Step 10.   The next field is the **Media Resource Group List**. It determines the accessibility of media resources to a device. These are discussed further in Chapter 6, "Configuring CUCM Features and Services."

Step 11.   Information entered in the **Location** field is used to prevent WAN links from becoming oversubscribed in centralized deployments. If you have defined locations, select the appropriate one for this device from the drop-down list.

Step 12.   The **AAR Group** field determines the appropriate association of this device with an AAR group. An AAR group provides the prefix that is assigned when a call fails because of insufficient bandwidth. AAR is discussed in further detail in Chapter 6. Select an AAR group if AAR is being used. If this field is set to None, AAR is, in effect, disabled on this device.

Step 13.   The **Tunneled Protocol** drop-down list allows you to select Q Signaling (QSIG), which enables intercluster trunk (ICT) to transport non-H.323 protocol information by tunneling it through H.323. Leave this set to None, unless you know that this type of tunneling is required.

Step 14.   The **QSIG Variant** parameter is only configurable if QSIG is selected as the tunnel protocol. Leave this parameter alone unless Cisco TAC instructs you to change it.

Step 15.   The **ASN.1 ROSE OID Encoding** parameter is only configurable if QSIG is selected as the tunnel protocol and is beyond the scope of this book.

Step 16.   The next two fields, **Packet Capture Mode** and **Packet Capture Duration**, are for troubleshooting purposes only and should not be configured when adding a new trunk.

Step 17.   The **Media Termination Point Required** check box needs to be selected if the H.323 device does not support features such as hold and transfers.

Step 18.   If the **Retry Video Call as Audio box** is selected, Communications Manager sets up a voice call if a video calls fails to set up.

Step 19.   The **Path Replacement Support** check box is automatically selected if you select QSIG from the Tunneled Protocol drop-down list. Otherwise it is left deselected.

Step 20. If the **Transmit UTF-8 for Calling Party Name** check box is left deselected, the user locale setting in the device pool will be used to determine whether Unicode information is sent and translated. Typically this can be left at the default.

Step 21. The **Unattended Port** check box is used to indicate that the device has unattended ports. This is normally used if the port is used to send calls to an application such as a voicemail server. In most cases, this box should be left deselected.

Step 22. If you want to allow both secure and nonsecure calls on this gateway, you must select the **SRTP Allowed** check box. If this is not selected, only nonsecure calls are allowed.

Step 23. If the **H.235 Pass Through Allowed** check box is selected, the shared-secret key can pass through a CM, allowing H.323 endpoints to set up a secure connection.

Step 24. The **Use Trusted Relay Point** field determines whether a relay point such as a Media Termination Point (MTP) or a transcoder must be labeled *trusted* to be used by this device. This field is typically only changed in virtualized environments.

Step 25. If the **Cisco Intercompany Media Engine** feature is being used and calls through this trunk might reach the PSTN, make sure the that PSTN Access check box is selected.

Intercompany Media Engine

Step 26. E.164 transformation profiles are used when Intercompany Media Engine (IME) is used. IME enables different companies to automatically learn routes, which enables calls to travel across the Internet instead of the PSTN.

Incoming Calling/Called Party Settings

Step 27. The **Incoming Calling Party Settings** and **Incoming Called Party Settings** are used to globalize numbers. Each calling and called party number has a number type assigned to it. The incoming calling/called part settings are based on the number type assigned. There are four number types: national, international, unknown, and subscriber. The four settings for each of these number types are

- **Prefix:** Digit enters are added to the beginning of the number after the specified number of strip digits are removed.

- **Strip Digits:** This is the number of digits that should be stripped from the number before the prefix is applied.

- **Calling Search Space:** This is the CSS that is used after transformation has occurred.

■ **Use Device Pool CSS:** When this box is selected, the device pool CSS is used.

If your environment requires the manipulation of incoming called and calling numbers, configure the appropriate settings for each of these fields.

Step 28. The next two fields define the Multilevel Precedence and Preemption (MLPP) characteristics of this gateway. If these fields are left blank or set to default, the values set in the device pool are used. The first MLPP field is the **MLPP Domain.** MLPP grants higher priority only from calls with the same MLPP domain. If MLPP is used, an MLPP domain is needed; otherwise, this field can be left at None.

Step 29. The second field in this category, **MLPP Indication,** determines whether tones and indications will be presented when a precedence call is made. If the is field set to Off, no precedence indication is presented. If this field is set to On, indication is used for a precedence call.

Call Routing Information—Inbound Calls

Step 30. The next set of fields refers to inbound calls. The **Significant Digits** field determines the number of digits of an incoming dialed number that Communications Manager uses. Communications Manager counts from right to left. So if the number entered in this field is 4 and the digits received are 8105559090, 810555 would be removed. Only 9090 would be used to determine the destination of this call.

Step 31. A Calling Search Space (CSS) determines the accessible destinations of inbound calls. Choose a CSS from the **Calling Search Space** drop-down list. If this field is left at None, the dialing privileges of this gateway could be limited.

Step 32. Automated Alternate Routing (AAR) is used to provide an alternate route if a call fails because of insufficient bandwidth. The AAR CSS can be used to limit the paths a call can use when it is rerouted. Select an AAR CSS from the **AAR Calling Search Space** drop-down list.

Step 33. The **Prefix DN** field defines what digits are added to the front of an incoming destination number. This is applied to the number, after Communications Manager truncates the number, based on the Significant Digits setting.

Step 34. The **Redirecting Number IE Delivery–Inbound** check box should be selected if your voicemail system supports redirecting number IE. Otherwise, leave this box deselected.

Step 35. If the **Enable Inbound FastStart** check box is selected, FastStart will be used. H.323 FastStart requires only two message exchanges to open logical channels, whereas normal setup requires 12. However, if FastStart is selected, both ends must support and be configured for FastStart.

Call Routing Information—Outbound Calls

Step 36. Called party transformation enables you to change the number that is dialed. Select the **Called Party Transformation CSS** that contains the called party transformation patterns that should be applied to calls routed through the trunk. You can also leave this set to None and use the Called Party Transformation CSS assigned to the device pool by selecting the **Use Device Pool Called Party Transformation CSS** check box.

Step 37. Calling party transformation enables you to change the caller ID. Select a **Calling Party Transformation CSS** that contains the calling party transformation pattern that is assigned to the device. You can also leave this set to None and use the Calling Party Transformation CSS assigned to the device pool by selecting the Use Device Pool Calling Party Transformation CSS check box.

Step 38. The **Calling Party Selection** field determines what number is sent for outbound calls. The choices are

- **Originator:** The directory number of the device that placed the call.

- **First Redirect Number:** The directory number of the first device to redirect the call.

- **Last Redirect Number:** The directory number of the last device to redirect the call.

- **First Redirect Number (External):** The external directory number of the first device to redirect the call.

- **Last Redirect Number (External):** The external directory number of the last device to redirect the call. Select the desired value for this field.

Step 39. The **Calling Line ID Presentation** field determines whether Communications Manager sends caller ID information. To send caller ID information, select Allowed from the drop-down list. To block caller ID, select Restricted from the drop-down list.

Step 40. Cisco recommends that the next four fields remain set to the default of Cisco CallManager. The four fields are

- Called party IE number type unknown

- Calling party IE number type unknown

- Called Numbering Plan

- Calling Numbering Plan

These fields deal with dial plan issues and should be changed only when advised to do so by Cisco or an experienced dial plan expert. The need to change these usually occurs when installing Communications Manager internationally.

Step 41.   The **Caller ID DN** field is used to determine what caller ID is sent out of this gateway. A mask or a complete number can be entered in this field. For example, if the mask 55536XX is entered in this field, Communications Manager sends 55536 and the last two digits of the calling number.

Step 42.   If the **Display IE Delivery** check box is selected, the calling and called party name information is included in messages.

Step 43.   The **Redirecting Number IE Delivery-Outbound** check box should be selected when integrating with a voicemail system that supports redirecting number IE. Otherwise, leave it deselected.

Step 44.   If the **Enable Outbound FastStart** check box is selected, FastStart will be used. H.323 FastStart requires only two message exchanges to open logical channels, whereas normal setup requires 12. However, if FastStart is selected, both ends must support and be configured for FastStart.

Step 45.   If the Enable Outbound FastStart check box is selected, you must select the codec that is to be used. This is selected from the **Codec for Outbound FastStart** drop-down list.

Gatekeeper Information

Step 46.   From the **Gatekeeper Name** drop-down list, select the desired gatekeeper.

Step 47.   The **Terminal Type** field specifies the type of devices this trunk controls. Choose Gateway for normal trunks.

Step 48.   The **Technology Prefix** field enables you to assign a prefix that matches the prefix in the gatekeeper. By assigning a matching prefix, you can avoid having to add the IP address of each Communications Manager in the gatekeeper on the gw-type-prefix line. It is recommended that you use 1#* in both this field and the gatekeeper configuration. The value entered in this field must exactly match what is configured in the gatekeeper.

Step 49.   The **Zone** field determines which zone this Communications Manager registers with on the gatekeeper. If this field is left blank, the gatekeeper's zone subnet command is used to determine to what zone the Communications Manager registers. If you enter a zone name in this field, it must match exactly with what is configured in the gatekeeper (this includes capitalization).

Geolocation Configuration

Step 50.   The geolocation information can be used to determine the logical partition of a device. If you are using the geolocation feature, select the appropriate geolocation from the **Geolocation** drop-down list.

Step 51.   There are 17 configurable geolocation fields. Geolocation filters enable you to choose which fields are used to create a geolocation identifier. If you use the geolocation feature, select the appropriate geolocation filter from the **Geolocation Filter** drop-down list.

Step 52.   Click **Save**.

After the gatekeeper-controlled intercluster trunk is configured, you can add it to a route group. Then configure a pattern that matches calls that should be routed over this trunk. The pattern should point to a route list that contains the route group of which this trunk is a member.

Configuring CAC for a Centralized Deployment

To accomplish CAC for environments that have remote sites, locations are configured in Communications Manager. Locations define the amount of bandwidth that can be used to place calls to and from the remote sites. After locations are configured, they must be assigned to devices such as phones, trunks, and gateways. You can accomplish this by assigning them to a device pool. This process enables the phones, trunks, and gateways' device pool to determine the location. When a call is placed across the IP WAN, Communications Manager uses the location information to determine whether there is enough available bandwidth for the call. By deducting available bandwidth for each call that is active on the WAN, Communications Manager can determine availability. When using locations, Communications Manager assumes that the following bandwidth is required for each codec:

- A G.711 call uses 80 kbps.

- A G.722 call uses 80 kbps.

- A G.723 call uses 24 kbps.

- A G.728 call uses 16 kbps.

- A G.729 call uses 24 kbps.

- A GSM call uses 29 kbps.

- A wideband call uses 272 kbps.

To better understand locations, now look at the steps required to create and apply them.

Creating Locations

The following steps show how to create a location:

Step 1.   From within CCMAdmin, select **System > Location**.

Step 2.   Click the **Add New** link.

Step 3.   A screen similar to that shown in Figure 5-14 displays. Enter the name of the location in the **Name** field.

Step 4.   In the **Audio Bandwidth** field, enter the amount of bandwidth available for voice calls to and from this location. If you select the **Unlimited** radio button, no limit is placed on voice calls. To determine the value to enter here, take the bandwidth that Communications Manager used for each call based on the

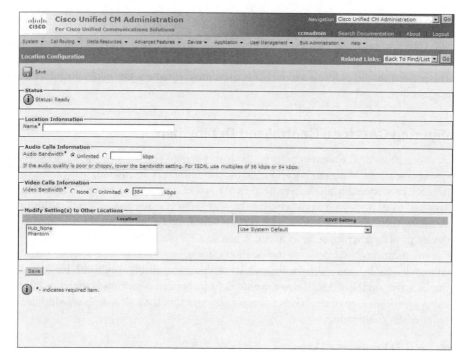

Figure 5-14 *Location Configuration*

codec that is being employed, and multiply it by the number of calls that you know can safely traverse the link. For example, if you use G.729 and you know that ten calls can traverse the link, multiply 24 kbps by 10. This tells you that 240 should be entered in this field. The bandwidth that Communications Manager assumes for each codec is listed earlier in this section.

Step 5. In the **Video Bandwidth** field, enter the amount of bandwidth available for video calls to and from this location. If you select the **Unlimited** radio button, no limit is placed on video calls. You can also select the **None** radio button, which prohibits video calls.

Note Video bandwidth is in increments of the video codec. If video codec is 384 and two video calls are allowed, the bandwidth should be set to 768.

Step 6. Resource Reservation Protocol (RSVP) can be used to reserve bandwidth for calls. The RSVP settings can be determined by highlighting a location in the Modify Setting(s) to Other Locations section and selecting the desired RSVP setting from the **RSVP Setting** drop-down list.

Step 7. Click the **Save**. The location has been added when the status line reads Insert Completed.

Assigning a Location to Devices

After locations are added, you must assign them to devices. As stated earlier, it is recommended that the location information be assigned to the device pool. The following steps show how to assign a location to a device pool:

Step 1.   From within CCMAdmin, navigate to **System > Device Pool**.

Step 2.   To limit the results, enter search criteria in the search field, and click **Find**.

Step 3.   Select the device pool to which you want to assign a location from the list that is generated.

Step 4.   Select a location from the **Location** drop-down list.

Step 5.   Click **Save**.

Step 6.   The device pool must be reset. Click **Reset**.

Step 7.   A new window will appear; click **Reset** in the new window.

Step 8.   Close the Device Reset window.

If you want to assign the location at the device level, follow these steps. The steps to add a location to a phone, trunk, or gateway are all similar. The following steps can be used to add a location to any of these devices:

Step 1.   The path you select from within CCMAdmin depends on which type of device you are assigning a location. To assign a location to a phone, select **Device > Phone**. To assign a location to an ICT, select **Device > Trunk**. To assign a location to a gateway, select **Device > Gateway**.

Step 2.   To limit the results, enter search criteria in the search field, and click **Find**.

Step 3.   Select the device to which you want to assign a location from the list that is generated.

Step 4.   If configuring an MGCP gateway, select the endpoint to which you want to assign a location. If you are not configuring an MGCP gateway, skip this step.

Step 5.   The Device Configuration screen displays. Select a location from the **Location** drop-down list, as shown in Figure 5-15. Figure 5-15 shows a phone configuration screen, but the screen should be similar regardless of the device that you are configuring.

Step 6.   Click **Save**.

Step 7.   A window displays informing you that you must click the **Apply Config** button for the change to take affect. Click **OK**.

Step 8.   Click **Apply Config**.

Step 9.   A window displays warning you that when you apply the configuration, the device might go through a restart. Click **OK**.

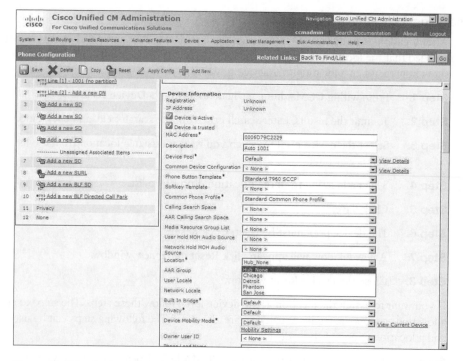

Figure 5-15   *Assigning a Location to a Device*

That's all there is to it. Unlike gatekeeper, no additional configuration is required outside of Communications Manager. Communications Manager handles all the CAC functions itself when locations are used for remote sites.

Special Services Configuration

There are certain types of calls that should always be given priority and availability to be dialed from all phones. The first call of this type is 911. When a 911 call is placed, it is important that the call gets through. Not only is it necessary to make the call possible, but you also need to ensure that it goes to the right destination. The following sections discuss some of the issues that can arise with these services.

Special Services Overview

Depending on your local service, various special services might be available. For example, the following is a list of special service numbers that are commonly available in North America. Check with your local phone company to see which of these are valid in your area.

- **311:** Nonemergency police services

- **411:** Directory assistance

- **511:** Travel information

- **611:** Phone equipment repair

- **711:** Telecommunications Device for the Deaf (TDD) operator

- **911:** Emergency

After you determine which services are available, you must configure route patterns that will match these calls. The most important of these calls is 911. Because in an emergency, a person might not think to dial 9 before dialing 911; patterns should be created that enable the call to go out regardless of whether 9 is dialed first. This means that two patterns need to be created, 911 and 9.911. PreDot discard instructions must be applied to the 9.911 pattern so that only 911 is sent out the public switched telephone network (PSTN).

When there are remote locations, things become a little more complicated. Imagine that you have an office in San Jose and a remote office in San Francisco. When callers dial 911 from San Francisco, the call must be routed to the local emergency service, not the service in San Jose. Although this seems obvious, it is sometimes overlooked. To accomplish this, multiple 911 and 9.911 patterns must be created. Partitions and CSS are used to allow phones in each location to match only the pattern that routes the call to the correct location.

For all other special services, the 9.X11 pattern should be sufficient. Once again, be sure to create patterns for each remote location so that the call is routed to the local PSTN.

Another concern when dealing with 911 calls is that some local legislation requires that more detailed location information be sent than just the street address. These laws normally apply to buildings that are over a certain size. Typically the floor and room number are required in addition to the street address. This requirement is referred to as an E911 or enhanced 911. Imagine that someone dialed 911 from a 20-story building and all that was sent was the street address. This would make it difficult to determine which floor, let alone which office, it came from. The solution is to have a database that contains the detailed address information for each phone number in your company. This database is typically maintained by an outside company and is accessible by the emergency service.

Another issue that arises with Communications Manager is that because a phone can be moved so easily, the information in the database can become outdated rather quickly. In addition to this, a feature known as extension mobility makes the Communications Manager system even more nomadic. To deal with these issues, Cisco offers an Emergency Responder product. This product ensures that the correct detailed information is sent when a 911 call is placed. For more details on this product, refer to the "Cisco Emergency Responder Administration Guide" on Cisco.com.

Configuring Special Services Route Patterns

To ensure that special services numbers are accessible, you must create route patterns for them. As mentioned previously, it is recommended that you create at least three patterns for each location. The first two are for 911 services and should be 911 and 9.911. If your location does not use a leading 9 for PSTN access, the first 9 in the 9.911 pattern should be replaced with whatever number is used for PSTN access. The third pattern is 9.X11. This pattern will match all other special services numbers.

The 9.911 and 911 patterns should be marked Urgent Priority so that as soon as the number is dialed, it is sent. If this pattern is not marked Urgent Priority, delays could occur before the call is sent, and this should never happen.

As often happens, one solution creates another problem. I have heard people say that they do not use the 911 pattern because people often dial it by mistake. What happens is that a person dials 9 for an outside line, then presses one to begin a long distance call, and then mistakenly presses one again. This, of course, matches 911 and routes the call to emergency services. It is *never* recommended that you not include the 911 pattern. Although people misdialing 911 is problematic, it is gravely problematic if 911 cannot be dialed during an emergency. I have heard of many ways people have fixed this problem, but I would not recommend any of them because they all result in either the failure or delay of the call.

An overview of the tasks required to create patterns to allow access to special services numbers follows. Refer to Chapter 4, "Implementing a Route Plan," for detailed steps on how to create route patterns.

Step 1.   Create a 911 route pattern.

Step 2.   Assign a partition to this pattern that all phones in the location can dial. If there are remote locations, a separate pattern must be created and placed in a partition that only phones in that location can reach. This pattern must then point to a route list that will send the call out the local PSTN. Figure 5-16 shows an example of this.

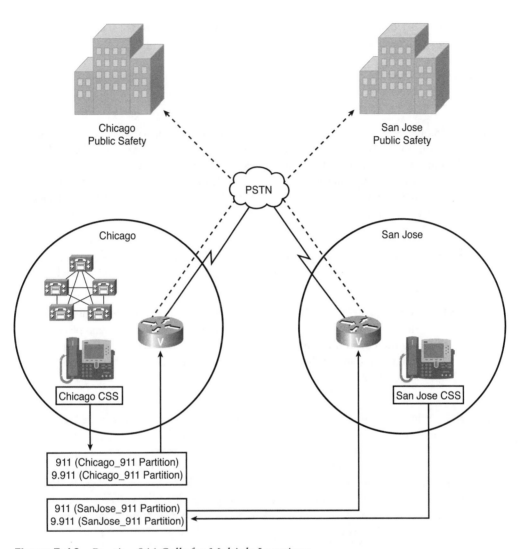

Figure 5-16   *Routing 911 Calls for Multiple Locations*

Warning   When configuring 911 patterns in environments that include remote locations, it is imperative that you create a route plan that will send the call to the proper 911 operator. For example, if the Communications Manager cluster is in Chicago and a remote location is in San Jose, you must make certain that when a user in San Jose dials 911, the call reaches the San Jose 911 operator, not the Chicago 911 operator. The responsibility to ensure that this works properly is solely upon you. If you are uncertain how to properly implement this, you should seek additional help from an individual with proven experience in this field.

Step 3. Select a gateway or route list that will send this pattern out the local PSTN gateway.

Step 4. Select the Urgent Priority and OffNet Pattern (and Outside Dial Tone) check boxes.

Note Although it is not necessary to provide an outside dial tone for this pattern, if you do not, the outside dial tone will not be played for any number that begins with 9, until enough digits are dialed so that the number does not match 911. That means, in most cases, when dialing a long-distance number, the outside dial tone is not heard until three digits are dialed. For this reason, it is recommended that you select the OffNet Pattern (and Outside Dial Tone) check box.

Step 5. Create a 9.911 route pattern. If your location does not use a leading 9 for PSTN access, the first 9 in the 9.911 pattern should be replaced with whatever number is used for PSTN access.

Step 6. Assign a partition to this pattern that all phones in the location can dial. If there are remote locations, a separate pattern must be created and placed in a partition that only phones in that location can reach. The pattern must then point to a route list that will send the call out the local PSTN. Figure 5-16 shows an example of this.

Warning When configuring 9.911 patterns in environments that include remote locations, it is imperative that you properly create a route plan that will send the call to the proper 911 operator. For example, if the Communications Manager cluster is in Chicago and a remote location is in San Jose, you must make certain that when a user in San Jose dials 9.911, the call reaches the San Jose 911 operator, not the Chicago 911 operator. The responsibility to ensure that this works properly is solely upon you. If you are uncertain as to how to properly implement this, you should seek additional help from an individual with proven experience in this field.

Warning Special emergency call routing considerations must be made when deploying device mobility or extension mobility. Since device mobility and extension mobility allow the user to change physical locations you must ensure that the call will be routed based on the physical location of the user. The techniques used to ensure this are beyond the scope of this book. If you are unsure as to how this should be configured you should enlist the assistance of a experienced Cisco voice engineer. The responsibility to ensure all call routing, which includes emergency call routing, works properly is solely upon you.

Step 7.   Select a gateway or route list that will send the pattern out the local PSTN gateway.

Step 8.   Select the Urgent Priority and OffNet Pattern (and Outside Dial Tone) check boxes.

Step 9.   Set the discard digits to PreDot.

Step 10.   Create a 9.X11 route pattern.

Step 11.   Assign a partition to the pattern that all phones in the location can dial. If there are remote locations, a separate pattern must be created and placed in a partition that only phones in that location can reach. The pattern must then point to a route list that can send the call out the local PSTN.

Step 12.   Select a gateway or route list that will send the pattern out the local PSTN gateway.

Step 13.   Set the discard digits to PreDot.

Step 14.   Select the OffNet Pattern (and Outside Dial Tone) check box.

It is essential that after you have created patterns for these services, you make test calls to ensure that the call is routed properly. The steps provided previously are only general practices; additional configuration might be required. There is no guarantee that the previous steps will work in each situation. It is your responsibility to make sure that you test these services thoroughly before the system goes live.

Summary

This chapter explored how certain calls can be restricted by applying CSS and partitions to devices and patterns. Because it is often required that different devices have access to various destinations, the steps for creating and applying CSS and partitions are provided.

When deploying VoIP solutions, ensuring the quality of the call is essential. To accomplish this, CAC was discussed. Detailed steps were provided that show how to configure a gatekeeper that provides CAC for calls between clusters. Steps were also included to show how to configure locations for CAC, for calls to and from remote sites.

Finally, special services, such as 911, were discussed in this chapter. An overview of the required steps for the proper configuration of these services was given.

Chapter 6

Configuring CUCM Features and Services

Communications Manager provides a number of features that users have come to expect, and each new version of Communications Manager adds new features. Many features add needed functionality, such as conference calls, whereas others simply help to make the phone system more enjoyable, such as Music On Hold (MoH). Years ago, Communications Manager was not as feature rich as other traditional systems. Lately Communications Manager has begun to provide features that go beyond those offered by traditional systems. This chapter examines a wide range of features and the configuration tasks required to implement them.

Configuring Features

You start by looking at some of the basic features that are most often implemented. These are features that offer users extended functionality and are found on most modern phone systems.

As one might expect, all these features are configured in CCMAdmin. Each of the following six sections introduce you to a feature, explain its function, and show you how to configure these features.

Many of the features available to the users do not require any additional configuration. Because configuration is not required, these features are not discussed in detail in this chapter. The features that do not require configuration include Hold, Call Waiting, Mute, Transfer, On-Hook Dialing, and Redial.

Creating Call Pickup Groups

Call pickup groups enable people to answer a line that is ringing on another phone from their phone. For example, if extension 1005 is ringing, the call can be answered from a phone that does not have 1005 as an extension. This can occur two ways. The first is called call pickup, which enables a call to be picked up from another phone if both phones are in the same pickup group. The second type of call pickup is called group call pickup, which enables a call to be picked up from another phone if both phones are not in the same pickup group. To help clarify this, Figure 6-1 shows three phones. Phones A and B are in the same call pickup group, whereas phone C is in a separate call pickup group.

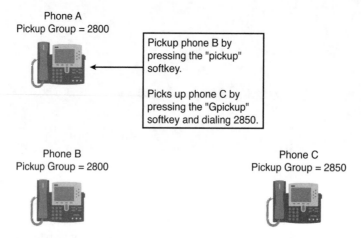

Figure 6-1   *Call Pickup Example*

If phone B is ringing, the call can be answered from phone A by going off-hook and pressing the pickup softkey. After the softkey is pressed, phone A will start ringing, and the call can be answered. However, if phone C is ringing and a user wants to answer the call from phone A, the user would have to go off-hook, press the Gpickup softkey, and enter phone C's group pickup number. After this is done, Phone A starts to ring and the call can be answered.

There are a couple of things to be aware of when deploying the call pickup feature. First, a phone must be a member of a call pickup group to use this feature. If a phone has not been assigned to a call pickup group, that phone cannot answer another phone's incoming call. Second, for a user to answer a call ringing on a phone that is not in the same call pickup group, the user must know the extension number. In addition, if the call pickup number has a partition assigned to it, the phone or line must have a Calling Search Space (CSS) with access to that partition.

To implement the call pickup feature, call pickup groups must be created and then assigned to the phones. The following steps show how to perform both of these tasks.

Add a Call Pickup Number

Follow these steps to add a call pickup number:

Step 1.   From within CCMAdmin, select **Call Routing > Call Pickup Group**.

Step 2.   Click the **Add New** link.

Step 3.   A screen similar to that shown in Figure 6-2 displays. Enter a name in the **Call Pickup Group Name** field. Make sure that it is descriptive because the same name is used when assigning a pickup group to a line.

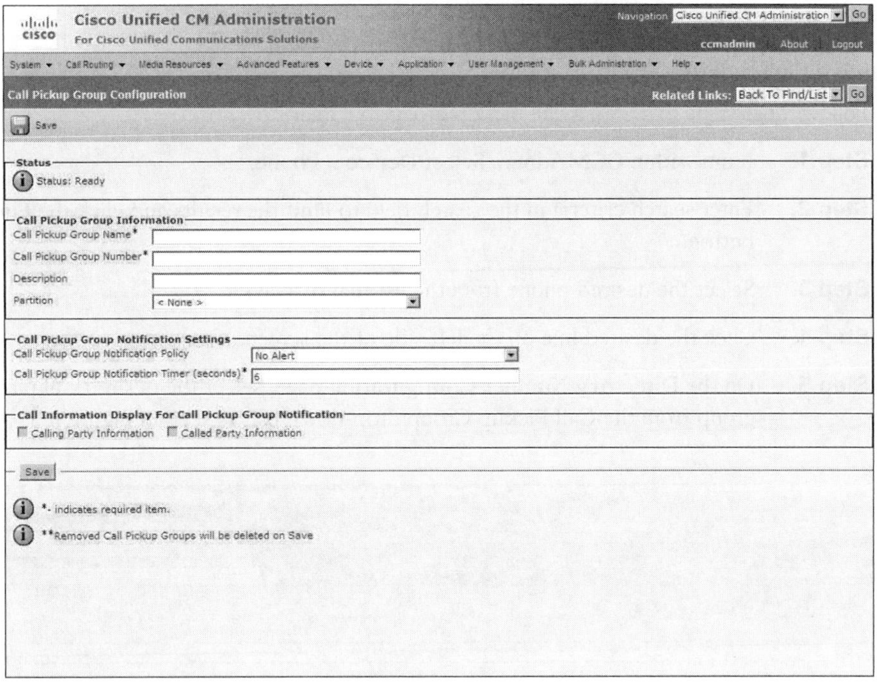

Figure 6-2   *Call Pickup Group Configuration.*

Step 4.   In the **Call Pickup Group Number** field, enter the desired number. This number must be unique, in that it is not assigned to any other function or device.

Step 5.   Enter a description that helps identify the purpose of this call pickup group in the **Description** field.

Step 6.   If you want to assign a partition to this call pickup group, select one from the **Partition** drop-down list.

An alert can be sent to all the phones in a group if any phone in the group does not answer an incoming call after a specified period of time. If you do not want this configured, skip to Step 10.

Step 7.   To enable call pickup group notification, select the type of alert you want to have sent from the **Call Pickup Group Notification Policy** drop-down list.

Step 8.   Next, in the **Call Pickup Group Notification Timer** field, enter the number of seconds that should pass before the alert is sent.

Step 9.   To include the calling and/or called party information in the visible alert, select the appropriate check boxes in the **Call Information Display for Call Pickup Group Notification** area.

Step 10.   Click the **Save** button to add this call pickup group.

Assign a Call Pickup Group to a Line

Follow these steps to assign a call pickup group to a line:

Step 1.   From within CCMAdmin, Select **Device > Phone**.

Step 2.   Enter search criteria in the search field to limit the results and click the **Find** button.

Step 3.   Select the desired phone from the list that displays.

Step 4.   Click the desired line on the left side of the screen.

Step 5.   On the **Directory Number Configuration** page, select the desired call pickup group from the Call Pickup Group drop-down list, as seen in Figure 6-3.

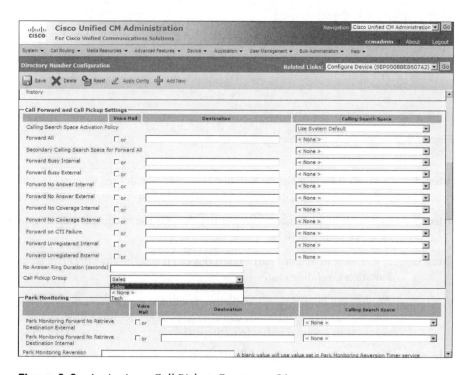

Figure 6-3   *Assigning a Call Pickup Group to a Line*

Step 6.   Click **Save** at the top of the screen.

After call pickup groups are created and assigned to lines, this feature can be used. A common mistake that users make when trying to use this feature is that they press the pickup softkey without going off-hook. This softkey is not available until the phone is off-hook. After off-hook, the pickup softkey can be pressed and the call starts to ring on the phone.

> **Note** Because call pickup groups are assigned to lines, a different call pickup group can be assigned to line 1, then to line 2, and so on. One variation that is successful for some customers is having different pickup groups assigned to different lines instead of using group call pickup (the Gpickup softkey). This way, the user need only remember which line belongs to which pickup group instead of having to memorize the pickup group number.

Creating Meet-Me Patterns

Communications Manager supports two types of conference calls. The first is called an ad hoc conference call. An ad hoc conference call is the type that takes place when two people who are having a phone conversation decide to conference in another person. One of the active callers initiates the conference call by pressing the Conference button, which is the softkey labeled Confrn on the phone, and calling the third party.

The other type of conference call is called a meet-me. A meet-me conference call is scheduled ahead of time, and all participants are told to call a certain number to join the conference.

Both types of conference calls require some type of conference resources, which are referred to as conference bridges. Communications Manager supports two types of conference bridges: hardware and software. When Communications Manager is installed, a software conference bridge is installed on Communications Manager when the Cisco IP Voice Media Streaming Application is activated. Configuring hardware conference bridges is discussed later in this chapter.

Ad hoc conference calls require no configuration if a conference bridge is available. By default, the Conference button is available on each of the standard softkey templates. By pressing this key, an ad hoc conference can be established. You can limit the number of participants allowed in a conference with the use of settings in the Communications Manager services parameters.

Meet-me conferences require more configuration than just having a conference bridge available. A meet-me pattern must also be created. This is the number that participants will use for the call. Each active meet-me conference requires a unique number. This means that the meet-me patterns you create will determine the maximum amount of meet-me conferences that can take place at one time.

Meet-me patterns enable the use of wildcards, which means that you can create one pattern that will result in multiple meet-me numbers. For example, if the pattern 523X is used, it defines ten numbers as meet-me conference numbers, 5230 through 5239.

Creating meet-me patterns is accomplished through CCMAdmin. The following steps take you through this process:

Step 1.   From within CCMAdmin, select **Call Routing > Meet-Me Number/Pattern**.

Step 2.   Click the **Add New** link.

Step 3.   A screen similar that shown in Figure 6-4 displays. In the **Directory Number** or Pattern field, enter the number or pattern that you want to use as a meet-me number.

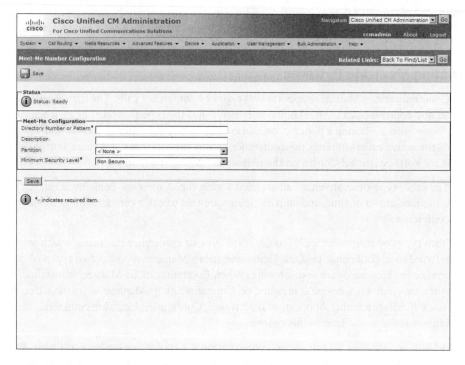

Figure 6-4   *Creating a Meet-Me Pattern*

Step 4.   In the **Description** field, enter a description that helps identify the purpose of the meet-me pattern.

Step 5.   To allow only certain people to join a conference, assign partitions to the pattern. This prevents callers who do not have access to this partition from establishing or joining a conference using this number. This ensures that unauthorized callers can not accidentally join a conference call. If you want to restrict the callers who can reach this meet-me number, select the desired partition from the **Partition** drop-down list. To allow all devices access to this meet-me number, select None for the partition.

Step 6. The Minimum Security Level field determines whether nonsecured phones are able to join the conference. Select one of the following options from the **Minimum Security Level** drop-down list:

- **Authenticated:** Prevents nonsecure phones

- **Encrypted:** Prevents authenticated and nonsecure phones

- **Non Secure:** Allows all phones

Step 7. Click the **Save** button to create the meet-me number.

After the meet-me numbers are created, users can start to use this feature. To initiate a meet-me conference, the Meet-Me button must be pressed. All standard softkey templates include the Meet-Me softkey. Limiting access to specific meet-me numbers by using a partition was discussed previously. One way to restrict a device from initiating meet-me conferences is by assigning it a softkey template that does not have a Meet-Me softkey. Phones without a Meet-Me softkey can still join a meet-me conference by simply dialing the meet-me number after the meet-me conference is active.

Note The most common error made with meet-me conference calls is when the user presses the Meet-Me button when attempting to join an active conference call. Make sure that users understand that the Meet-Me button is only used to initiate conference calls.

Creating Call Park Numbers

Calls can be placed on hold by pressing the Hold button; however, the call can only be picked up from the same line. This means that when a call is placed on hold, it can only be retrieved from a phone with the same directory number from which it was placed on hold. Often, a call placed on hold needs to be retrieved on a different phone. To accomplish this, the Call Park feature is used.

Call Park places the call on hold and parks it on a virtual directory number. By dialing that number, you can retrieve the call from a different phone. A common use for Call Park is to have an attendant or operator park the call and then announce the call using an overhead paging system.

For Call Park to work, call park numbers must be configured. As with meet-me numbers, wildcards are allowed. This means that a single pattern can result in multiple call park numbers.

Call Park patterns are created through CCMAdmin. The following steps take you through this process.

Step 1. From within CCMAdmin, select **Call Routing > Call Park**.

Step 2. Click the **Add New** link.

Step 3. A screen similar to that shown in Figure 6-5 displays. In the **Call Park Number/Range** field, enter the number or pattern that you want to use as a call park number.

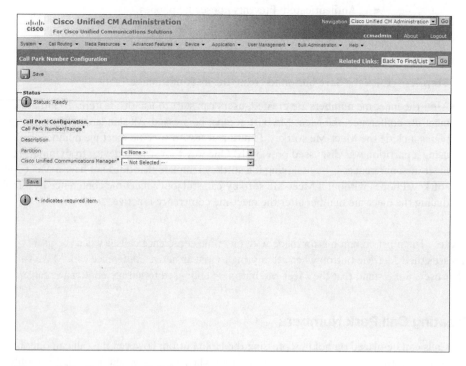

Figure 6-5 *Creating a Call Park Pattern*

Step 4. In the **Description** field, enter a description that helps identify the purpose of the call park pattern.

Step 5. To restrict the retrieval of a parked call, a partition can be assigned to the call park number. Only devices that have access to the assigned partition can then retrieve the parked call. To restrict access to this call park number, select the desired partition from the **Partition** drop-down list. To allow all devices access to this call park number, select None for the partition.

Step 6. From the **Cisco Unified Communications Manager** drop-down list, select the pattern in Communications Manager that registers with the call park.

Note For a call to be parked, call park numbers must be configured for phones that are registered to the Communications Managers. For this reason, it is recommended that all Communications Managers employ this process. This means that you must also configure call park numbers for backup Communications Managers, so that the Call Park feature is available if the primary Communications Manager fails.

Step 7.   Click the **Save** button to create the call park number.

After call park numbers are created, the feature is available for use. It is important that users understand how this feature works. This feature is activated when the Park softkey is pressed. The call is then automatically parked. The phone displays the number at which the call is parked. Often users think that they choose the location of the parked call, but actually Communications Manager chooses the number automatically based on the available call park numbers. This means that the person parking the call must look at the phone display to see the number where the call is parked. By default, a call only stays "parked" for 60 seconds before it reverts to the phone that originated the park. This value can be modified through the call park reversion timer found in the Communications Manager Service parameters.

Creating Directed Call Park Numbers

Often users prefer to select the number that the call will be parked on. For this reason, more recent versions of Communications Manager have added the Directed Call Park feature. To use this feature, the user transfers a call to the directed call park number by pressing the Transfer softkey and the directed call park number that they want the call parked at.

It is important to understand that directed call park numbers are different than call park numbers and must be configured separately.

Directed call park patterns are created through CCMAdmin. The following steps take you through this process:

Step 1.   From within CCMAdmin, select **Call Routing > Call Directed Park**.

Step 2.   Click the **Add New** link.

Step 3.   A screen similar to that shown in Figure 6-6 displays. In the **Number** field, enter the number or pattern that you want to use as a call park number.

Step 4.   In the **Description** field, enter a description that helps identify the purpose of this call park pattern.

Step 5.   To restrict who can retrieve a parked call, a partition can be assigned to the call park number. Only devices that have access to the assigned partition can then retrieve the parked call. To restrict access to this call park number, select the desired partition from the **Partition** drop-down list. To allow all devices access to this call park number, select None for the partition.

Step 6.   In the **Reversion Number** field, enter the extension that the parked call should be forwarded to if it is not retrieved.

Step 7.   Select a Calling Search Space (CSS) from the **Reversion Calling Search Space** drop-down list. Make sure to select a CSS that has access to the partition that the reverted number is in.

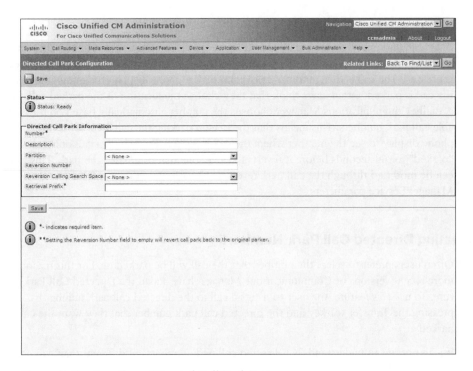

Figure 6-6   *Creating a Directed Call Park Pattern*

Step 8.   The **Retrieval Prefix** field is required so that Communications Manager knows that the user is trying to retrieve a directed call park and not a standard call park. When retrieving a call that was parked using Directed Call Park, the user enters this prefix first, followed by the number at which the call was parked. Enter the desired prefix in the Retrieval Prefix field.

Step 9.   Click the **Save** button.

Creating Intercoms

In earlier versions of Communications Manager a true intercom function was not available. There was a work around for it which used speed dials and the auto-answer function of certain phones. In more recent versions, a true intercom feature has been added. It allows a user to press a button that is configured as an intercom. When pressed, a one way audio stream is setup to another phone. The user at the phone can then accept the call and a two way stream is setup.

There are basically four sets required to setup an intercom. These steps are

■   Create intercom partitions

■   Verify the automatically created intercom CSS

- Create intercom numbers

- Assign intercom numbers

Creating Intercom Partitions

Intercom partitions are similar to standard partitions. They are assigned to intercom directory numbers. The calling intercom line must have an intercom CSS that allows access to the intercom partition assigned to the destination intercom directory number. Creation of intercom partitions is very similar to the creation of standard partitions. The following steps show how to create intercom partitions:

Step 1. From within CCMAdmin, select **Call Routing > Intercom > Intercom Route Partition.**

Step 2. Click the **Add New** link.

Step 3. A screen displays that offers an area in which you can enter the name of the partition followed by a description. You must place a comma (,) between the name and description. If you do not enter a description, the name of the partition will be used as the description. You can create up to 75 partitions at a time on this screen by placing each on a new line.

Step 4. After you have entered all the desired partitions, click the **Save** button.

Intercom Calling Search Spaces

An intercom CSS is similar to a standard CSS. It determines which intercom partitions an intercom directory number has access to. When you create an intercom partition, an intercom CSS is automatically created. The name that is assigned to it is the same as the partition's name with "_GEN" added to the end. For example, if you create an intercom partition and name it Sales_Intercom, an intercom CSS named Sales_Intercom_GEN is created.

> **Note**   Automatically generated calling search spaces can be modified, this may be required if an intercom directory number needs to dial multiple intercom numbers.

Creating Intercom Numbers

Intercom DNs are similar to directory numbers as they are assigned to phone buttons. They differ in the fact that normally they are not used to place calls to any destination other than other intercom directory numbers. Intercom DN may be created two ways. The first is to simply add it when you assign it to a phone. The other is to create them under the call routing menu. The second way allows you to create multiple intercoms at once which can save time since the parameters only have to be configured once. The following steps show how to configure a range of intercom DNs

Step 1. From within CCMAdmin, select **Call Routing > Intercom>Intercom Directory Number.**

Step 2.   Click the **Add New** link.

Step 3.   To create a range on intercom DNs, enter a starting directory number in the **Intercom Directory Number** field and then an ending number in the next field to the right. By doing this you are able to add multiple intercom DNs at once.

> **Note**   You can create a single intercom number by entering the same DN in both fields.

Step 4.   The **Route Partition** field defines the intercom partition to which this intercom directory number is assigned. The partition is used to determine the intercoms DNs that can reach this intercom. Select the desired partition. Partitions are discussed in more detail in Chapter 5.

Step 5.   The next field is the **Description** field. Enter a description that will help you quickly identify the intercom DN later.

Step 6.   In the **Alerting Name** field, enter the name that should be displayed on the caller's phone when this number is dialed and the phone is ringing.

Step 7.   The **ASCII Alerting Name** field is used on devices that do not support Unicode characters.

Step 8.   The next field allows a CSS to be assigned to the intercom DN. This determines what intercom DNs can be reached when calling from this line. Select **Calling Search Space** from the drop-down list.

Step 9.   The Presence group that an intercom DN belongs to determines what devices are allowed to monitor this DN. Select the **Presence Group** this DN should belong to.

Step 10.   The **Auto Answer** field determines whether the speakerphone or headset is used when the intercom uses auto answered. This field is typically set to Auto Answer with Speakerphone.

Step 11.   The **Default Activated Device** field defines the device that this intercom DN is active on. If you are creating a range of intercom DNs leave this field blank and configure it when you assign the intercom DN to a phone. If you are creating a single intercom DN select the desired device from the drop-down list.

Step 12.   Click **Save**.

Once the intercom DNs are created they must be assigned to phones.

Assigning an Intercom DN to a Phone

The steps required to add an intercom DN to a phone are similar to those used to assign a DN to a phone but there are fewer parameters that must be configured. The following steps show how to do this.

Step 1.   From within CCMAdmin, Select **Device > Phone**.

Step 2.   Enter search criteria in the search field to limit the results and click the **Find** button.

Step 3.   Select the desired phone from the list that displays.

Step 4.   Click the **Add a new Intercom** on the left side of the screen.

Note   If none of the buttons are configured as an intercom button, you need to create a new phone button template that has an intercom button and assign it to the phone.

Step 5.   Enter the desired intercom DN in the **Intercom Directory Number** field.

Step 6.   The **Route Partition** field defines the intercom partition to which this intercom directory number is assigned. The partition is used to determine the intercoms DNs that can reach this intercom. If an intercom DN that has already been created is assigned, the partition that was defined when it was created it is automatically assigned. Partitions are discussed in more detail in Chapter 5, "Configuring Class of Service and Call Admission Control."

Step 7.   The next field is the **Description** field. Enter a description that will help you quickly identify the intercom DN later.

Step 8.   In the **Alerting Name** field, enter the name that should be displayed on the caller's phone when this number is dialed and the phone is ringing.

Step 9.   The **ASCII Alerting Name** field is used on devices that do not support Unicode characters.

Step 10.   The next three fields, calling search space, presence group and auto-answered are automatically populated using the parameters that were assigned to the intercom DN when it was created. In most cased these fields should not need to be changed.

Step 11.   The **Default Activated Device** field defines the device that this intercom DN is active on. Select the device this DN is assigned to from the drop-down list.

Step 12.   The next two fields, labeled **Display (Internal Call ID)** and **ASCII Display (Internal Call ID)**, are used to configure what caller ID is displayed when calls to other internal callers are connected. Enter up to 30 characters in this field. Both letters and numbers are allowed.

Step 13.   The next two fields, which are labeled **Line Text Label** and **ASCII Line Text Label**, are used to define how the line displays on the phone. Enter that label in this field that you want displayed for this intercom DN.

Step 14.   In the **Speed Dial** field enter the number that is automatically dialed when the intercom button is pressed. This is used when configuring an intercom that is only used between two phones, such as an executive and assistant. If this field is left blank the intercom line can be used to call multiple intercom numbers.

Step 15.   The **External Phone Number Mask** can be set to the main number of the phone.

Step 16.   The **Forwarded Call Information Display** section determines what information is sent when a call is forwarded. Select the information to be sent by selecting the check box next to each desired field.

Step 17.   Click **Save**.

Creating Forced Authorization Codes

Earlier in this book, you learned how CSS and partitions are used to allow and restrict calls from being placed to certain destinations. The problem with CSS and partitions is that they are based on the device from which the call is being placed, not from the person who is making the call. In new versions of Communications Manager, you can use forced authorization codes (FAC) to allow calls to be placed based on a code that is entered. This means that the call is permitted or prohibited based on who is calling and not the device from which they are calling.

It works this way: When a call is placed that requires an authorization code, a double beep or prompt is heard that alerts the caller to enter the code. After the code is entered, the call is completed.

Enabling FACs requires that FACs exist and that the route patterns that are to be restricted are configured to require a FAC. The following steps show how to accomplish both of these tasks.

Create a Forced Authorization Code

Follow these steps to create a FAC:

Step 1.   From within CCMAdmin, select **Call Routing > Forced Authorization Codes**.

Step 2.   Click the **Add New** link.

Step 3.   A screen similar to that shown in Figure 6-7 displays. In the **Authorization Code Name** field, enter a name for this code. Choose a name that helps identify the code. This name displays in authorization code reports that can be produced.

Step 4.   In the **Authorization Code** field, enter a numeric code. This is the code a caller will have to enter to place calls that require authorization.

Step 5.   In the **Authorization Level** field, enter a numeric value between 0 and 255. This value determines the authorization level of this code. For the code to allow a call, the value in this field must be equal to or greater than the value assigned to the pattern.

Step 6.   Click the **Save** button to add this code. After the code is created, the status line displays "Add successful."

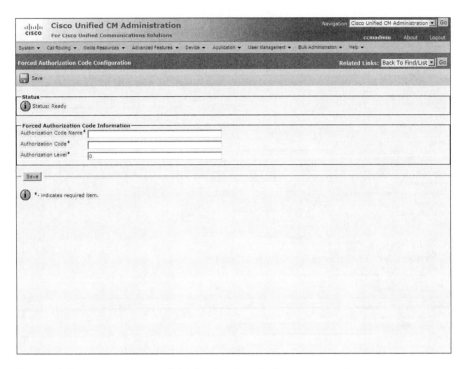

Figure 6-7   *Creating Forced Authorization Codes*

Assign a Forced Authorization Code to a Route Pattern

Follow these steps to assign a FAC to a route pattern:

Step 1.   From within CCMAdmin, select **Call Routing > Route/Hunt > Route Pattern**.

Step 2.   Enter search criteria in the search field to limit the results, and click the **Find** button.

Step 3.   From the list that displays, select the route pattern to which you want to add a FAC.

Step 4.   A screen similar to that shown in Figure 6-8 displays. Select the **Require Forced Authorization Code** check box, and enter a numeric value in the Authorization Level field. This value is used to determine which FACs have permission to use this pattern. A FAC must have a value equal to or greater than this value to be granted access.

Step 5.   Click the **Save** button to apply the FAC to this pattern.

Step 6.   Repeat these steps for all other route patterns on which you want to enable a FAC.

After completing these two tasks, FAC is enabled. Make sure that you take the time to properly plan the implementation of FAC. If it is not properly implemented, it can cause

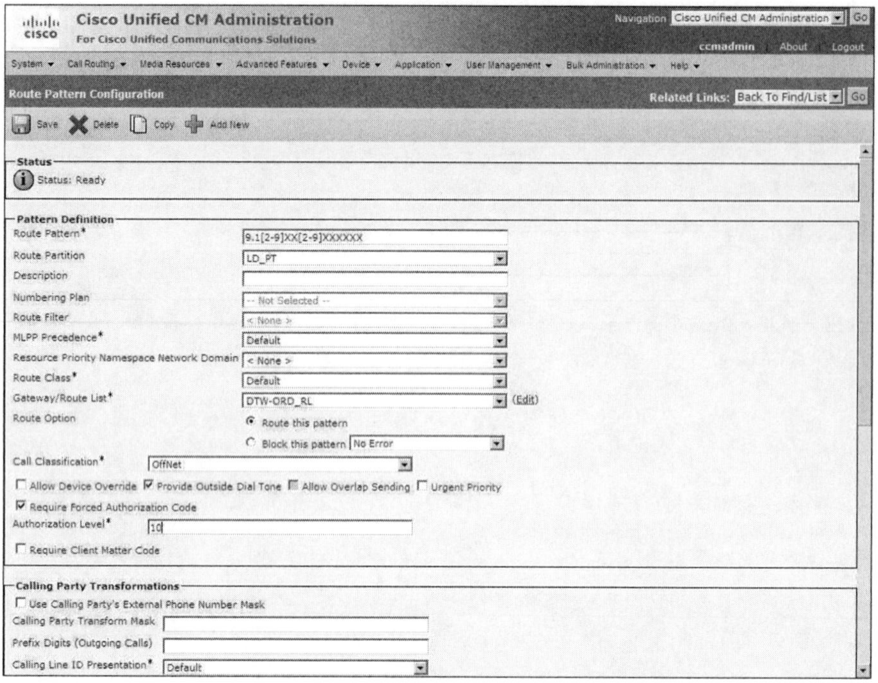

Figure 6-8 *Require a Forced Authorization Code for a Route Pattern*

adverse effects. Make certain that FAC is never applied to a pattern that allows access to emergency services such as 911.

Configuring Client Matter Codes

Another commonly requested feature is client matter codes (CMC). This enables a caller to enter a client code while placing a call so that the call is associated with a client. Companies that bill customers for time spent on projects, such as lawyer firms, require this feature.

The process to enable CMCs is similar to that of configuring FACs. First, CMCs must be created and then route patterns need to be configured to require CMCs. The following steps walk you through both processes.

Create a Client Matter Code

Follow these steps to create a CMC:

Step 1. From within CCMAdmin, select **Call Routing** > **Client Matter Code**.

Step 2. Click the **Add New** link.

Step 3.   A screen similar to that shown in Figure 6-9 displays. In the **Client Matter Code** field, enter the desired code.

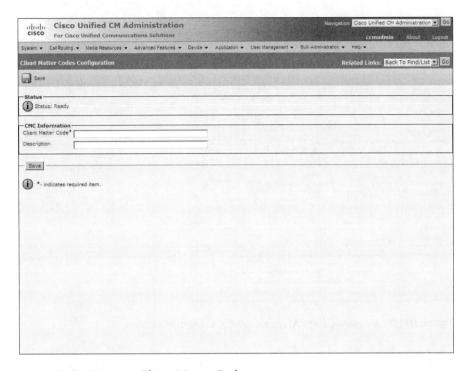

Figure 6-9   *Creating Client Matter Codes*

Step 4.   In the **Description** field, enter a description that identifies the client or project associated with the code.

Step 5.   Click the **Save** button to add this code. After the code is created, the status line displays "Add successful."

Assign a Client Matter Code to a Route Pattern

Follow these steps to assign a CMC to a route pattern:

Step 1.   From within CCMAdmin, select **Call Routing > Route/Hunt > Route Pattern**.

Step 2.   Enter search criteria in the search field to limit the results, and click the **Find** button.

Step 3.   From the list that displays, select the route pattern to which you want to add a CMC.

Step 4.   A screen similar to that shown in Figure 6-10 displays. Select the **Require Client Matter Code** check box.

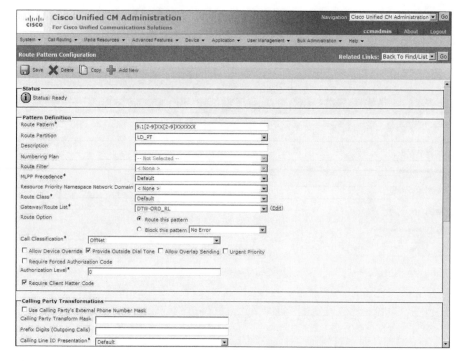

Figure 6-10 *Require Client Matter Codes on a Route Pattern*

Step 5. Click the **Save** button to apply the CMC requirement to this pattern.

Step 6. Repeat these steps for all other route patterns on which you want to require a CMC.

After these two tasks are completed, CMC is enabled. Make certain that CMC is never applied to a pattern that enables access to emergency services such as 911.

Configuring Voice Ports and Profiles

Another feature—voicemail—is covered in great detail in the second half of this book. To integrate with a voicemail system, a number of feature configurations must be completed. The voicemail feature menu has five different submenus. This section examines the function of each of these and describes how each is configured.

Table 6-1 lists the five voicemail submenu items with a brief explanation of each.

The first thing that must be configured is the voicemail ports. Voicemail ports can be created manually or by using the wizard. It is recommended that you use the wizard because it walks you through the process. The wizard enables you to add ports for a new voice-

Table 6-1   *Voicemail Submenu Items*

Item	Description
Cisco Voice Mail Port	A virtual port that enables communications between Communications Manager and Unity
Cisco Voice Mail Port Wizard	A wizard for creating voicemail ports
Message Waiting	Directory numbers for MWI activation
Voice Mail Pilot	A directory number that defines voicemail pilot numbers
Voice Mail Profile	A profile that defines voicemail parameters for devices

mail server, add ports for an existing voicemail server, or delete ports. The following steps walk you through adding ports of a new voicemail server:

Step 1.   From within CCMAdmin, select **Advanced Features > Voice Mail > Cisco Voice Mail Port Wizard**. Select the **Create a New Cisco Voice Mail Server** radio button, and add ports to it and click **Next**.

Step 2.   On the next page, enter the voicemail port name in the **Add Ports to a New Cisco Voice Mail Server Using This Name** field. In most cases, you can leave it at CiscoUM1. This field needs to be changed only if CiscoUM1 is already being used for another voicemail integration. Click **Next**.

Step 3.   In the next field, from the drop-down list, select the number of voicemail ports you want to create. Click **Next**.

Step 4.   A screen similar to that shown in Figure 6-11 displays. In the **Description** field, enter a description that helps identify the purpose of these voicemail ports.

Step 5.   From the **Device Pool** drop-down list, select the desired device pool to be used by the voicemail ports.

Step 6.   A CSS determines where the voicemail port can dial. Choose a CSS from the **Calling Search Space** drop-down list. If this field is left at None, the dial privileges of this voicemail port could be limited. This can affect message notification and call transfers.

Step 7.   Automated Alternate Routing (AAR) is used to provide an alternative route if a call fails because of insufficient bandwidth. The AAR CSS can be used to limit the paths a call will use when it is rerouted. Select an AAR CSS from the **AAR Calling Search Space** drop-down list.

Step 8.   Locations are used to help WAN links from becoming oversubscribed in centralized deployments. Select the appropriate one for these voicemail ports from the **Location** drop-down list.

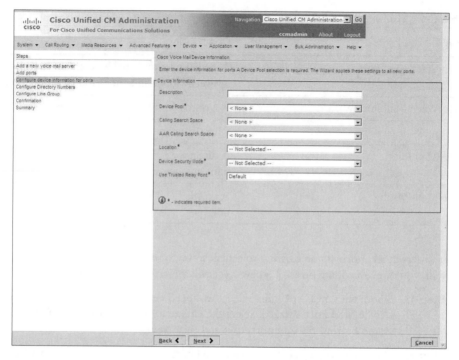

Figure 6-11   *Voice Mail Port Wizard Device Configuration*

Step 9.   From the **Device Security Mode** drop-down list, select a security mode for the ports. If authentication using a mutual certificate is desired, select Authenticated Voice Mail Port. To have the audio stream encrypted, select **Encrypted Voice Mail Port**. To configure the port without security, select **Non Secure Voice Mail Port**.

Step 10.   The Use **Trusted Relay Point** drop-down list enables you to enable or disable this requirement. In most cases, it can be left at the default.

Step 11.   Click **Next**.

Step 12.   A screen similar to that shown in Figure 6-12 displays. In the **Beginning Directory Number** field, enter the directory number to be assigned to the first voicemail port. Each additional port is assigned the next consecutive number.

Note   On the previous configuration page, the parameters for the device were configured. In this section, you configure the parameters for the line. This is the reason why you see some of the same fields as those on the previous configuration page.

Step 13.   Select the desired partition for the voicemail port line from the **Partition** drop-down list.

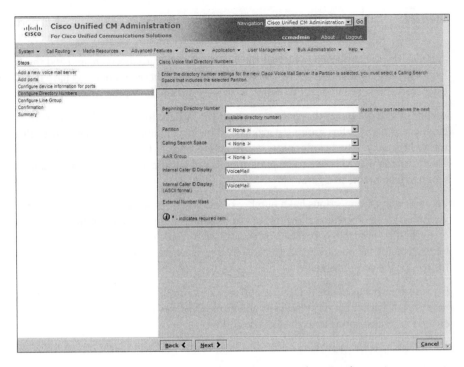

Figure 6-12 *Voice Mail Port Wizard Directory Number Configuration*

Step 14. Select the desired CSS for the line from the **Calling Search Space** drop-down list.

Step 15. Select the AAR group for the line from the **AAR Group** drop-down list.

Step 16. In the **Internal Display** field, enter the name that is displayed on a phone when connected to voicemail.

Step 17. In the **Internal Display** field (ASCII format), enter the name that is displayed on a phone when connected to voicemail.

Step 18. In the **External Number Mask** field, enter the mask that should be applied to the voicemail port line number when it places outside calls.

Step 19. Click **Next**.

Step 20. You are now asked whether these lines should be assigned to a line group. Think of a line group as a group of lines through which a call can be forwarded. If the first line doesn't answer, it is sent to the next number, and so on. In most new installations, choose **Yes, Add Directory Numbers to a New Line Group**. Click **Next**.

Step 21. Enter a name that helps identify this line group, perhaps **VoiceMailLG**. Click **Next**.

Step 22.   A summary screen displays listing the configuration of the voicemail ports. If all the information is correct, click **Finish**.

A screen displays informing you that the voicemail ports have been created and that a hunt list and a hunt pilot must be created now. Because these components have not been discussed yet, take a moment to define what they are and how they work.

A hunt pilot is a number that points to a hunt list. A hunt list is a list that points to one or more line groups. A line group is a group of directory numbers through which a call can travel. These combined components create hunt groups in Communications Manager. The flow is similar to how a route pattern points to a route list, which points to a route group, which points to a gateway.

Because Unity Connections has a number of ports on which a call can enter, a hunt group has to be created to allow the call to try the first number and, if unavailable, move on to the first available port. The Voicemail Port Wizard first creates the lines. Next, the wizard creates the line group. Unfortunately, this is where the wizard ends and you begin the rest of the setup manually.

Because the voicemail line and line group are configured, the hunt list must be created next. Just as with route patterns, lists, and groups and devices, these components must be created in a flow opposite to the call travel flow.

The following steps show how to create a hunt list:

Step 1.   From within CCMAdmin, select **Call Routing > Route/Hunt > Hunt List**.

Step 2.   Click the **Add New** link.

Step 3.   On the screen that displays, enter the name of the hunt list in the **Hunt List Name** field.

Step 4.   In the **Description** field, enter a description that helps identify this hunt list, such as VoiceMailHL.

Step 5.   Select the Communications Manager group that this hunt group will use from the **Cisco Unified Communications Manager Group** drop-down list.

Step 6.   Click the **Save** button.

Step 7.   From the screen similar to that shown in Figure 6-13, the **Enable This Hunt List** check box is selected by default. Typically, this is left at the default. If you want to disable this hunt group, deselect this box.

Step 8.   Because you plan on using this hunt list for voicemail, select the **For Voice Mail Usage** check box.

Step 9.   Click the **Add Line Group** button. A new screen displays. Select the desired line group from the Line Group drop-down list. Click **Save**.

Step 10.   An informational window displays telling you that the hunt list must be reset before changes will take effect. Click **OK**.

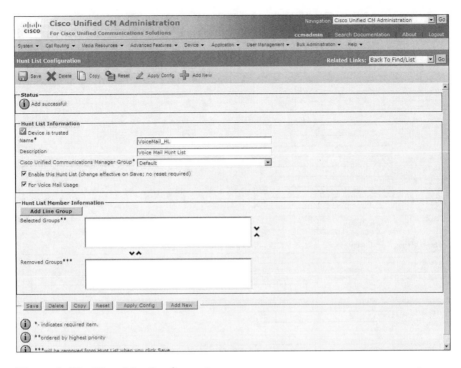

Figure 6-13 *Hunt List Configuration*

Step 11. The Hunt List Configuration screen returns. Click the **Reset** button. An informational window informs you that calls to this hunt list will be refused while the list is being reset. Click **Reset**.

Step 12. The informational window reappears. The status should read "Reset request was successfully sent." Click **Close**.

Now that the hunt list is configured, a hunt pilot needs to be created. The hunt pilot is the number that users will dial to reach the voicemail system. The steps that follow demonstrate how to complete this process:

Step 1. From within CCMAdmin, select **Call Routing > Route/Hunt > Hunt Pilot**.

Step 2. Click the **Add New** link.

Step 3. A screen similar to that shown in Figure 6-14 displays. Enter the route pattern in the **Hunt Pilot** field.

Step 4. The **Route Partition** field determines what devices can access the hunt pilot. Select the desired partition from the Route Partition drop-down list.

Step 5. Enter a description that helps identify the purpose of the hunt pilot in the **Description** field.

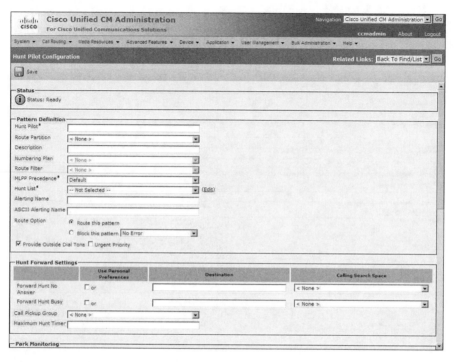

Figure 6-14 *Hunt Pilot Configuration*

Step 6.   Because you are configuring an internal extension, the Numbering Plan and Route Filter drop-down lists will not be accessible.

Step 7.   Determine the precedence level that will be assigned to the hunt pilot by selecting it from the **MLPP Precedence** drop-down list.

Step 8.   From the **Hunt List** drop-down list, select the appropriate hunt list to determine which calls are sent to the hunt pilot.

Step 9.   In the **Alerting Name** field, enter the name that should be displayed on the caller's phone while the hunt group is ringing.

Step 10.   The **ASCII Alerting Name** field is the used on devices that do not support Unicode characters.

Step 11.   Select the **Route This Pattern** radio button.

Step 12.   To have a secondary dial tone played after the first digit is dialed, select the **Provide Outside Dial Tone** check box. In most cases, this box should be deselected.

Step 13.   To route a call as soon as it matches this route pattern, select the **Urgent Priority** check box. In most cases, this box should be deselected.

Step 14. The next two fields determine where a call is sent if the call is unanswered or if all ports are busy. The fields are **Forward Hunt No Answer** and **Forward Hunt Busy.** Enter the appropriate destination number in the Destination field. If desired, a separate CSS can be defined for forwarded calls.

Step 15. Call pickup groups allow a user to redirect an incoming call on another phone to the user's phone. Pickup groups should not be added to voicemail hunt pilots.

Step 16. In the **Maximum Hunt Timer** field, enter the maximum number of seconds that a call is allowed to remain in the hunt group before being classified as unanswered.

Step 17. The **Park Monitoring Forward No Retrieve Destination** field determines where calls are forwarded to when they are placed on park and not retrieved. To send them to an alternative number, enter that number in the Destination field. Because Park should not be configured for voicemail components, these fields should be left at the default.

Note In most cases, the remaining fields can be left at the default. The following steps can help you understand the purpose of each field.

Step 18. If you want to affect caller ID information, configure the fields located under the Calling Party Transformation heading. These fields are discussed earlier in this chapter. Use **Calling Party's External Phone Number Mask** is the first field.

Step 19. In the **Calling Party Transform Mask** field, enter any mask that you want to affect the caller ID.

Step 20. In the **Prefix Digits (Outgoing Calls)** field, enter any digits that you want to have added to the front of the caller ID.

Step 21. The **Calling Line ID Presentation** field determines whether caller ID information is to be blocked for outbound calls from the hunt pilot. To block caller ID, select **Restricted** from the drop-down list. To allow caller ID, select **Allowed** from the drop-down list.

Step 22. The **Calling Name Presentation** field determines whether caller name information is blocked for outbound calls from the hunt pilot. To block calling name ID, select **Restricted** from the drop-own list. To allow calling ID name, select **Allowed** from the drop-down list.

Step 23. Cisco recommends that the following two fields remain set to the default of Cisco CallManager:

   ■ Calling Party Number Type

   ■ Calling Party Numbering Plan

Step 24. The **Connected Line ID Presentation** field determines whether the connected party's ID information is displayed on the calling party's phone. To block the connected party's ID, select **Restricted** from the drop-down list. To allow the connected party's ID, select **Allowed** from the drop-down list.

Step 25. The **Connected Name Presentation** field determines whether the connected party's name information is displayed on the calling party's phone. To block the connected party's name, select **Restricted** from the drop-down list. To allow the connected party's name, select **Allowed** from the drop-down list.

Step 26. From the **Discard Digits** drop-down list, select the digit discard instruction that is applied to calls that match this route pattern.

Step 27. In the **Called Party Transform Mask** field, enter the mask that you want to use for calls that match this route pattern.

Step 28. In the **Prefix Digits (Outgoing Calls)** field, enter any digits that you want to have added to the dialed number before it is sent to the route list.

Step 29. Cisco recommends that the following two fields remain set to the default of Cisco CallManager:

- Called Party Number Type
- Called Party Numbering Plan

Step 30. The AAR Group field is responsible for determining the device associated with the AAR group. An AAR group provides the prefix that is assigned when a call fails because of insufficient bandwidth. Select an AAR group if AAR is being used. If this field is set to **None**, AAR is, in effect, disabled on this device.

Step 31. AAR uses the external phone number mask to determine the fully qualified number of the destination. Assign a mask that will expand the hunt pilot number into a fully qualified number.

Step 32. Click the **Save** button.

A hunt pilot is now configured that points to a hunt list, which routes the call to the line group of the voicemail port lines.

By dialing the hunt pilot number, users can access Unity. This is, of course, assuming that Unity is running and properly integrated with Communications Manager. The Unity side of the integration is covered in the Unity portion of this book.

Now the Message Waiting Indicator (MWI) settings must be configured so that the MWI on the phone will activate when a new message is received. The MWI setting is simply a directory number that is configured to act as either MWI on or MWI off. The following steps show how to create MWI directory numbers in Communications Manager:

Step 1. From within CCMAdmin, select **Advanced Features** > **Voice Mail** > **Message Waiting**.

Step 2.   On the next page, select the **Add New** link.

Step 3.   A screen similar to that shown in Figure 6-15 displays. In the **Message Waiting Number** field, enter the directory number that you want to apply to activate MWI on or MWI off.

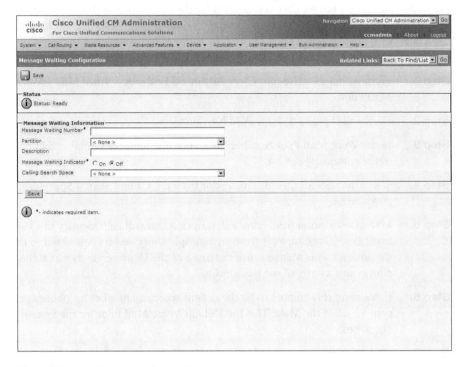

Figure 6-15   *MWI Configuration*

Step 4.   If you want to assign a partition to the MWI number, select the desired one from the **Partition** drop-down list. To allow unrestricted access to this number, select **None**.

Step 5.   In the **Description** field, enter a description that helps identify the purpose of the MWI number.

Step 6.   Select either the On or Off radio button to define whether the number will be used to turn MWI on or off.

Step 7.   Assign a CSS that has access to all the phones on which the MWI will activate the MWI. Select the appropriate CSS from the **Calling Search Space** drop-down list.

Step 8.   Click **Save** to create this MWI number.

After you create an MWI on and off number, you can test them by dialing each number from a Cisco IP Phone. When the MWI on number is dialed, the light should come on. When the MWI off number is dialed, the light should go off.

Now a voicemail pilot must be created. A voicemail pilot is used to determine the number dialed when users press the Messages button on their phones. This number is normally the same as the hunt pilot number you defined for the voicemail hunt list. After the voicemail pilot number is created, it is assigned to a voicemail profile. Voicemail profiles are associated with lines on phones and are used to define voicemail-related attributes. Voicemail profiles will be discussed shortly, but first, we create a voicemail pilot:

Step 1.   From within CCMAdmin, select **Advanced Features > Voice Mail > Voice Mail Pilot.**

Step 2.   On the next page, click the **Add New** link.

Step 3.   In the **Voice Mail Pilot Number** field, enter the hunt pilot number that points to the voicemail hunt list.

Step 4.   Select the CSS for this voicemail pilot from the **Calling Search Space** drop-down menu.

Step 5.   In the **Description** field, enter a description that will help identify this voicemail pilot. For example, if there are multiple Unity servers connected to this Communications Manager, use the name of the Unity server to which this pilot points as part of the description.

Step 6.   If you want this number to be the default voicemail number for phones on the system, select the **Make This the Default Voice Mail Pilot** for the System check box.

Step 7.   Click the **Save** button to add the voicemail pilot.

The last thing that must be configured is a voicemail profile. Voicemail profiles are assigned to lines and determine what voicemail pilot the line uses. A voicemail profile also applies a voice mailbox mask, if one is defined. A voice mailbox mask is used to change the extension number that is sent to Unity. This might be necessary if the extension number in Unity is different than the one assigned to the phone. However, some similarity is needed. For example, if the extension on the phone is 2001 and the extension in Unity is 52001, a mask of 5XXXX could be used. This mask changes 2001 to 52001.

To create a voicemail profile, follow these steps:

Step 1.   From within CCMAdmin, select **Advanced Features > Voice Mail > Voice Mail Profile.**

Step 2.   On the next page, click the **Add New** link.

Step 3.   In the **Voice Mail Profile** Name field, enter a name for this voicemail profile.

Step 4.   In the **Description** field, enter a description that helps identify this voicemail profile. For example, if there are multiple Unity servers connected to this

Communications Manager, use the name of the Unity server to which this profile points as part of the description.

Step 5. Select the voicemail pilot from the **Voice Mail Pilot** drop-down list.

Step 6. In the **Voice Mail Box Mask** field, enter a mask if it is necessary to change the extension number that is sent to Unity.

Step 7. If you want this profile to be the default voicemail profile for phones on the system, select the **Make This the Default Voice Mail Profile** for the System check box.

Step 8. Click the **Save** button to add the voicemail pilot.

All the configuration required within Communications Manager for a Unity integration should now be complete. By default, all the phones on the system will use the default voicemail profile that is defined as shown in Step 7 of the previous steps.

Creating Users

Some Communications Manager features require that users be defined on Communications Manager. By default, the users added to Communications Manager used to be stored in a Lightweight Directory Access Protocol (LDAP) directory on Communications Manager. As of Communications Manager 5.0, the user is stored in the Informix database.

Some of the features covered later in this chapter require that users be created, so we now take a look at how this is done. This section demonstrates the primary principles of how to create a user. Later in the chapter, advanced user configuration is discussed. This section is also limited to covering how to add a user when using DC Directory, which is installed on the Communications Manager, not AD or Netscape.

The following steps show how to create a user on Communications Manager:

Step 1. From within CCMAdmin, select **User Management > End User**.

Step 2. Click the **Add New** link.

Step 3. A screen similar to that shown in Figure 6-16 displays.

Step 4. In the **User ID** field, enter a username. This name is used when the user logs in to Communications Manager's user web pages. After the user is added, this field cannot be changed.

Note If extension mobility is going to be used, you might want to make the user ID all numeric. Extension mobility can be configured to accept only digits for user IDs. This accelerates the login process for the users so that they don't have to spell out user IDs.

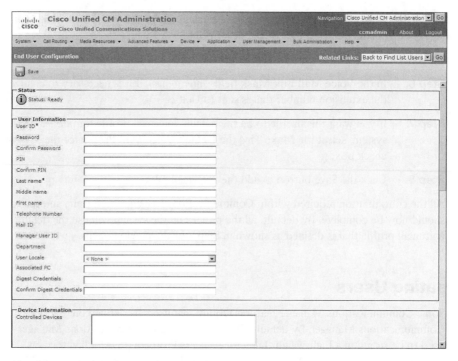

Figure 6-16   *User Configuration*

Step 5. Enter the password for the user in the **User Password** field and confirm it in the Confirm Password field. The user password is the same one that is used when the user logs in to the user web pages.

Step 6. Enter a PIN in the **PIN** field and confirm it by entering it again in the Confirm PIN field. The PIN can only be numeric and is used to log in to services on the phone.

Step 7. Enter the first and last name in the appropriate fields.

Step 8. Enter the telephone number of the user in the **Telephone Number** field.

Step 9. Enter the user email address.

Step 10. Enter the manager of the user in the **Manager User ID** field. The user you enter in this field must already exist in the directory.

Step 11. In the **Department** field, enter the name of the department in which the user works.

Step 12. Select the locale for the user from the **User Locale** drop-down list. This information is used for features such as extension mobility.

Step 13. When a Cisco softphone is used on a PC, the IP address or the host name of the PC must be enter in the **Associated PC** field.

Step 14. When using third-party SIP phones, digest credentials are required. This is an alphanumeric string that is used for authentication purposes. If this user is using a SIP phone, enter the appropriate credentials in the **Digest Credential** field.

Step 15. Enter the digest credentials again in the **Confirm Digest Credential** field.

Step 16. The Controlled Devices box lists the devices that are associated to the user. To associate a device to the user, click the **Device Association** button. The Device Association button only appears after the user is saved. Click the **Find** button. Select the check box next to the device that you want to associate and click the **Save Selected/Changes** button. Now select **Back to User** from the Related Links drop-down list and click Go to return to the User Configuration page.

Step 17. In the Extension Mobility section, a list of available extension mobility profiles are listed in the Available Profile box. To assign a profile to the user, highlight the desired profile in the **Available Profile** box, and click the down arrow below the Available Profile box. This causes the profile to appear in the Controlled Profile box.

Step 18. From the **Default Profile** drop-down list, select the extension mobility profile that should be used as the default profile for this user.

Step 19. The presence group that a device belongs to determines the lines that are allowed to be monitored. Select the presence group that the user should belong to.

Step 20. The **SUBSCRIBE Calling Search Space** field determines which partitions this device can access when invoking a presence request. Select a CSS that includes the partitions assigned to the lines that this user can monitor.

Step 21. To allow control of the device from CTI applications, select the **Allow Control of Device from CTI** check box.

Step 22. As of CM 8.0, extension mobility can be configured to work across multiple clusters. To allow a user to use this feature, the **Enable Extension Mobility Cross Cluster** check box must be selected.

Step 23. Because multiple phones and extensions can be assigned to a single user, you can define the user's primary extension by selecting it from the **Primary Extension** drop-down list.

Step 24. To enable Mobile Connect, select the **Enable Mobility** check box.

Step 25. If you select the Enable Mobility check box, you must select a primary device that will be associated to this user from **Primary User Device** drop-down list.

Step 26. To allow voice access to Mobile Connect, select the **Enable Mobile Voice Access** check box.

Step 27.   The **Maximum Wait Time for Desk Pickup** value determines how much time is allowed for a desk phone to be answered when a call is transferred from the user's cell phone. This value is set in milliseconds.

Step 28.   The **Remote Destination Limit** value determines the maximum number of devices that a user can send calls to through Mobile Connect.

Step 29.   A remote destination profile defines parameters such as calling search space, MoH audio source, and the device pool that should be used with Mobile Connect. Select the desired profile from the **Remote Profile Destination** drop-down list.

Step 30.   Click the **Save** button to add this user.

After users are added, the user can log in to Communications Manager's user web pages and change items, such as passwords and PINs. The user web pages also enable users to subscribe to phone services, configure speed dials, and configure other features on the phone, but this can only be done after a device is associated with the user. The following steps demonstrate how to associate a device to a user.

Step 1.   From within CCMAdmin, select **User Management > End User**.

Step 2.   Enter the user's last name in the Search field, and click **Find**.

Step 3.   From the displayed list, select the user you want to associate to the profile.

Step 4.   Click the **Device Association** link.

Step 5.   Enter search criteria to limit the results returned, and click **Find**.

Step 6.   A list of devices displays. Select the check box next to the device(s) that you want to associate with this user and click **Save Selected/Changes**.

Configuring Advanced Services

In addition to the standard features that users expect a phone system to offer, Communications Manager offers a number of advanced features. The first part of the following sections explores a number of Communications Manager features that offer additional flexibility. These features enable users to do things such as log in to phones other than their own and have those phones take on all the attributes of their own phones, including directory numbers. There are a number of other features that can be configured that are accessible from a Cisco IP Phone by pressing the Services button. These sections examine a few of these.

The second part of the following sections looks at media resources, which are required for many standard features, such as conferencing and MoH. A number of media resources are automatically installed when certain services are activated, such as the software conference bridge that was discussed earlier in this chapter. A closer look at these and hardware media resources is offered later in these sections.

Implementing Advanced Features

All users expect a phone to enable them to place a call on hold, transfer a call, and possibly initiate a conference call from time to time. These types of features are considered standard on most systems. But how about being able to look up stock quotes or check the status of an airline flight on the display of your phone? Although many would not consider this a standard feature, it is just one of the many advanced features that can be performed on many Cisco IP Phones. As cool and useful as some of these features are, not all phones need them, so they can be made available only to certain phones if you want. However, before any of these features can be used, they must first be configured on the Communications Manager. Now take a look at some of these features and the configuration that each requires.

Configuring IP Phone Services

Most Cisco IP Phones have the capability to run services. These services enable them to perform functions that range from checking the weather to serving as a time clock. The services available are too numerous to mention. Each service is an XML script that the phone downloads from a server. If you have programming experience, you can choose to create your own services or purchase services from a variety of companies that sell prepackaged phone services.

Before any phone can use a service, the system administrator must make the service available by configuring it on the Communications Manager. The steps required to configure the services are similar for all services, but many services require specific parameters. Each service includes instructions that are unique for that particular service.

To give you an idea of how these services are configured on Communications Manager, the following steps take you through the process of adding a typical service:

Step 1.   From within CCMAdmin, select **Device > Device Settings > Phone Services**.

Step 2.   On the next page, click the **Add New** link.

Step 3.   A screen similar to that shown in Figure 6-17 displays. In the **Service Name** field, enter a descriptive name. This field determines the name of the service. The name displays on the phone under Services.

Step 4.   In the **ASCII Service Name** field, enter the service name to be displayed on devices that do not support Unicode characters.

Step 5.   In the **Service Description** field, enter a description for the service. In this example, use Personal Address Book.

Step 6.   In the **Service URL** field, enter the location of the service. In this example, use "http://*x.x.x.x*/ccmpd/xmlExample.asp," where *x.x.x.x* is the IP address of the Communications Manager and the quotes are not used. Before entering the URL, you can always check to make sure that it is correct by entering the URL in your browser address box and pressing Enter. A good URL gives you a line-by-line display of the code; a bad URL gives you the following message: "This page cannot be displayed."

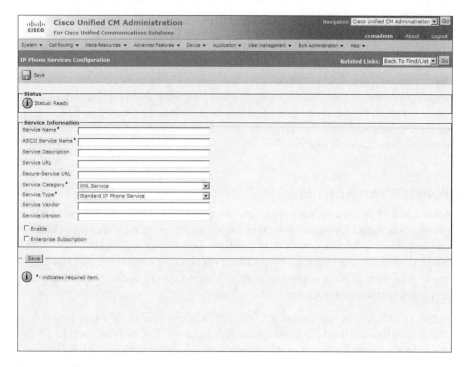

Figure 6-17   *IP Phone Service Configuration*

Step 7.   The **Secure-Service URL** is similar to the service URL. However, when using a secure-service URL, the connection between the server and the endpoint will be encrypted.

Note   The URL might be case-sensitive, so be sure to enter it exactly as the installation notes state.

Step 8.   Cisco supports XML and Java for phone services. Depending on the type of phones you are using, Java might not be supported. Select the service category (XML or Java) from the drop-down list.

Step 9.   The **Service Type** value determines whether the service will be associated with the Services, Directories, or Messages button on the phone. Typically, **Standard IP Phone Services** should be selected.

Step 10.   The **Service Vendor** field allows you to define the vendor of this service. This field is required when using Cisco-signed Java MIDlets.

Step 11.   You can enter the version of the server in the **Service Version** field, but it is not mandatory.

Step 12.   Select the **Enable** check box.

Step 13.   If you want the service to be available to all devices without having to subscribe to it, select the **Enterprise Subscription** check box. This field cannot be modified after the service is configured, so be sure to set it properly.

Step 14.   Click **Save**.

Some services can require additional information to be entered. Make sure that you consult the configuration documentation for a service prior to adding it.

Extension Mobility

Extension mobility is another feature of Communications Manager. This allows users to log in to other phones and have those phones take on all the attributes of their own phones or user profiles. A user device profile includes all the required phone attributes, including extension numbers. This can be useful in environments where users are often working in different locations.

A number of items must be configured to implement extension mobility, and because certain tasks depend on the completion of other tasks, the order in which these tasks are done is important. First, you need to make sure that the Extension Mobility service is activated. The following steps walk you through this process:

Step 1.   Enter **https://[*CM_IP Address*]/ccmservice** in the address bar of your browser and press Enter.

Step 2.   Enter the administrative username and password and click **Login**.

Step 3.   Navigate to **Tools > Service Activation**.

Step 4.   Select the desired server from the Server drop-down list.

Step 5.   Select the **Cisco Extension Mobility Service** check box and click **Save**.

Now it is necessary to configure the extension mobility service parameters. To configure the extension mobility services on the Communications Manager, follow these steps:

Step 1.   From within CCMAdmin, select **System > Service Parameters**.

Step 2.   Select the Communications Manager name from the Server drop-down list.

Step 3.   Select **Cisco Extension Mobility** from the Service drop-down list.

Step 4.   A screen similar to that shown in Figure 6-18 displays. The **Enforce Intra-cluster Maximum Login Time** field determines whether the value in the Maximum Login Time field is enforced. If set to True, phones automatically log out when the time entered in the Intra-cluster Maximum Login Time field has expired. If you do not want to log out phones after this time has expired, select **False**.

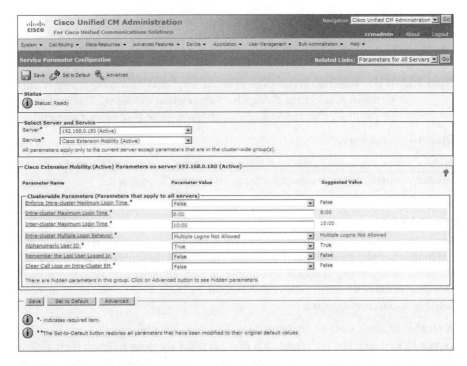

Figure 6-18   *Extension Mobility Service Parameters*

Step 5.   In the **Intra-cluster Maximum Login Time** field, enter the amount of time after which phones will automatically log out when logged in locally. This value is used only if the Enforce Intra-cluster Maximum Login Time field is set to **True**.

Step 6.   In the **Inter-cluster Maximum Login Time** field, enter the amount of time after which phones will automatically log out when logged in remotely.

Step 7.   From the **Intra-cluster Multiple Login Behavior** drop-down list, choose whether multiple logins will be permitted and how. The choices are

- **Multiple Logins Allowed:** A user can log in to multiple devices at the same time.

- **Multiple Logins Not Allowed:** A user can log in to only one device at a time.

- **Auto Logout:** If a user who is already logged in to one device logs in to another device, he or she will be automatically logged out of the first device.

Step 8.   The **Alphanumeric User ID** drop-down list defines whether user IDs will contain letters and numbers or numbers only. Selecting **True** means that the ID contains letters and numbers, and False means that the ID contains only numbers.

Step 9.   The **Remember the Last User Logged** In field determines whether the phone will remember the ID of the last user who logged in. For security reasons, it is recommended that this be set to False.

Step 10.   The **Clear Call Logs on Intra-Cluster EM** value determines whether missed, placed, and received call history is removed from the phone when a user logs in or out. To have the information cleared, set this value to True.

Step 11.   If you have changed any of the values on this page, click **Save**.

We now look at the steps required to add the extension mobility IP phone service:

Step 1.   From within CCMAdmin, select **Device > Device Settings > Phone Services**.

Step 2.   On the next page, click the **Add New** link.

Step 3.   Enter **Extension Mobility** in the Service Name field.

Step 4.   Enter **Extension Mobility** in the ASCII Service Name field.

Step 5.   Enter **Extension Mobility Service** in the Service Description field.

Step 6.   Enter **http://*x.x.x.x*:8080/emapp/EMAppServlet?device=#DEVICENAME#**, where *x.x.x.x* is the IP address of the Communications Manager.

Step 7.   Select **XML Service** from the Service Category drop-down list.

Step 8.   In the **Service Type** field, select **Standard IP Phone Service**.

Step 9.   Enter **Cisco** in the Service Vendor field.

Step 10.   Enter the version of extension mobility in the **Service Version** field.

Step 11.   Select the **Enable** check box.

Step 12.   If you want this service to be available to all devices without having to subscribe to it, select the **Enterprise Subscription** check box. This field cannot be modified, after the service is configured, so be sure to set it properly.

Step 13.   Click **Save**.

After these tasks are completed, user device profiles must be created for users who will be using extension mobility. In most cases, the user device profile should have the same attributes as the user's phone. The following steps show how to create a user device profile:

Step 1.   From within CCMAdmin, select **Device > Device Settings > Device Profile**.

Step 2.   On the next page, click the **Add New** link.

Step 3.   From the **Device Profile Type** drop-down list, select the type of phone on which this profile is based and click **Next**.

Step 4.   Select the protocol that the device will use from the **Device Protocol** drop-down list and click **Next**.

Step 5.   A screen similar to that shown in Figure 6-19 displays. In the **Device Profile Name** field, enter a name for this profile.

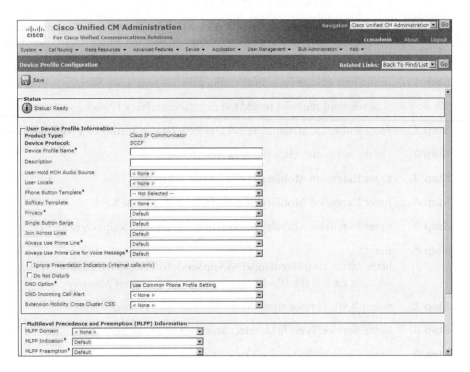

Figure 6-19   *Device Profile Configuration*

Step 6.   In the **Description** field, enter a description that helps identify this profile.

Step 7.   From the **User Hold MoH Audio Source** field, select the audio source to be played when a call is placed on hold by pressing the Hold button.

Step 8.   The **User Locale** field determines the language and fonts used for the phone. The default user locale, which is set in the enterprise parameters, is used if this field is left set to **None**. If this phone needs to use a different locale than is defined by its device pools or the enterprise parameters, select the proper one from the drop-down list.

Step 9.   From the drop-down list in the **Phone Button Template** field, select the desired template for this profile.

Step 10.   From the drop-down list in the **Softkey Template** field, select a softkey template for the phone.

Step 11.   The **Privacy** field is used to determine whether the device can enable privacy for calls on a shared line. Select the desired state for this field from the drop-down list.

Step 12. The **Single Button Barge** field determines whether a barge or cbarge can be initiated using a single button. Set this field to **Barge** to configure it for single-button barge or cBarge to configure single-button cbarge. If left at **Default**, the service parameter setting is used.

Step 13. The **Join Across Lines** field determines whether this feature is enabled. To enable this feature, set this field to **On**. To disable this feature, set this field to Off. The service parameter setting is used if the field is set to **Default**.

Step 14. The **Always Use Prime Line** field determines which line is activated when the device is taken off-hook. If this field is set to **Off**, whichever line is ringing will be used when the phone goes off-hook. When set to **On**, the primary line will always be used, even if an incoming call is ringing another line of the phone. To answer any line other than the primary line, the user must manually select the line. The service parameter setting is used when this field is set to **Default**.

Step 15. If the **Always Use Prime Line for Voice Message** field is set to **On**, the voicemail account associated to the primary line is dialed when the Messages button is pressed. If set to **Off**, the account associated to the line that has voicemail will be dialed. If set to **Default**, the service parameter setting is used.

Step 16. If the **Ignore Presentation Indicators (internal calls only)** check box is selected, internal caller ID restrictions are ignored. This means that if an internal call is configured to block caller ID, the caller ID will still show up on this device.

Step 17. The **Do Not Disturb** check box enables an administrator to enable DND on this device. To enable it, select the check box.

Step 18. From the **DND Option** drop-down list, you can select how the device will behave when DND is enabled and an incoming call arrives. When **Ringer Off** is selected, the device will not ring, but caller information will display on the phone. When **Call Reject** is selected, caller information is not displayed and, based on the DND Incoming Call Alert (see next parameter) setting, a beep might be played or the light might flash.

Step 19. The **DND Incoming Call Alert** field works in concert with DND Option. This parameter determines whether the device will beep or the light will flash when the DND option is set to **Call Reject** or **Ringer Off**. When this setting is set to **None**, the setting in the common phone profile is used. To turn the flash and beep off, set this to **Disable**. To have a beep played, set this parameter to **Beep Only**. When set to **Flash Only**, the light on the phone will flash.

Step 20. From the **Extension Mobility Cross Cluster CSS** drop-down list, select the CSS that is to be used with this profile through the Extension Mobility Cross Cluster feature.

Step 21. The next two fields, **Module 1** and **Module 2**, are used when expansion modules (7914, 7915, or 7916) are used with this profile. If this profile is going to use expansion modules, select the modules from the drop-down list.

Step 22.   The next three fields define MultiLevel Precedence and Preemption (MLPP) characteristics of this phone. If these fields are left blank or set to default, the values set in the device pool are used. The first MLPP field is the **MLPP Domain.** MLPP only grants higher priority from calls with the same MLPP domain. For this reason, an MLPP domain is needed.

Step 23.   The **MLPP Indication** field determines whether tones and indications are presented when a precedence call is made. The precedence indication can be a special ringback or a display, if the caller's phone supports it, and a special ringer on the called party's side.

Step 24.   The **MLPP Preemption** field determines whether a higher-precedence call preempts a lower-precedence call. The value of Disabled does not permit this to happen. To cause a lower-precedence call to be terminated if a higher-precedence call requires the resources, set this parameter to Forceful.

Step 25.   In the **Login User ID** field, enter the user ID of the user associated to the profile. If the user device profile is used as a logout profile, specify the login user ID that is associated with the phone. After the user logs out from this user device profile, the phone will automatically log in to this login user ID.

Step 26.   Click the **Save** button to add this profile.

Step 27.   Now you must add lines to this profile. Select the first **Add a New DN** link on the left side of the screen. There might be more than one link with this label.

Step 28.   A screen that enables you to configure the parameters for the line displays. In the **Directory Number** field, enter the extension number to be used for this line.

Step 29.   The remaining settings on this page are the same as those found on the directory line configuration of a phone. Because you should already be familiar with those settings, individual steps are not included for each. However, if you want to review the individual steps, refer to the "Adding a Line to a Phone" section in Chapter 3, "Deploying Devices."

Step 30.   After you complete filling in the remaining fields, click **Save** to add the line. A message displays stating that the changes have been made and that any device using this profile must log out and log back in before the changes will take effect. Click **OK.**

Step 31.   Click the **Configure Device Profile (name)** link and add additional lines as needed.

Note   If the Enterprise Subscription check box were selected when the Extension Mobility service was configured, the service is available to all devices, so the next four steps are not required.

Step 32.   After all lines are configured, you must add the extension mobility service to this profile. Select **Subscribe/Unsubscribe Services** from the Related Links drop-down menu and click **Go.**

Step 33.   A screen similar to that shown in Figure 6-20 displays. Select Extension Mobility from the **Select a Service** drop-down list. Click **Next.**

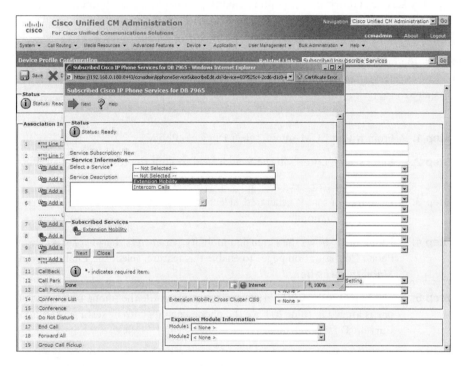

Figure 6-20   *Add Extension Mobility Service to a Profile*

Step 34.   Click the **Subscribe** button.

Step 35.   After the window refreshes, close it.

Now the profile must be associated with a user as shown in the steps that follow. These steps assume that the user already exists in the directory.

Step 1.   From within CCMAdmin, select **User Management > End User.**

Step 2.   Enter the user's last name in the Search field and click **Find.**

Step 3.   From the list that displays, select the user that you want to associate with the profile.

Step 4.   In the Extension Mobility section make sure that the **Allow Control of Device from CTI** check box is selected. If it isn't, select the box and click **Save.**

Step 5. Highlight the desired profile from the **Available Profiles** box, and click the down arrow below that box to move the profile to the Controlled Profiles box.

Step 6. Click **Save**.

After device profiles are configured and associated with a user, extension mobility must be enabled on the phones. This requires that the phone is subscribed to the extension mobility service and that the extension mobility parameters are configured on the phone. The following steps show how to complete the tasks:

Note If the Enterprise Subscription check box were selected when the Extension Mobility service was configured, the service is available to all devices, so these steps are not required.

Step 1. From within CCMAdmin, select **Device > Phone**.

Step 2. Enter search criteria in the Search field to limit the results and click the **Find** button.

Step 3. From the list that is generated, select the phone that you want to subscribe to the extension mobility service.

Step 4. Figure 6-21 shows the extension mobility parameters that display on the Phone Configuration page. To enable this feature, select the **Enable Extension Mobility** check box.

Step 5. The **Log Out Profile** field determines what profile the phone uses when no one is logged in to it. To have the phone keep its current settings, select **Use Current Device Settings**.

Step 6. Click **Save** to save the changes. A message displays stating that you must click the **Apply Config** button before the changes take effect. Click **OK**.

Step 7. Click **Apply Config**. A window appears to inform you to save changes before applying the configuration. Click **OK**.

Step 8. Select **Subscribe/Unsubscribe** Services from the Related Links drop-down menu and click **Go**.

Step 9. A screen similar to that shown when adding the extension mobility server to a device profile displays. Select Extension Mobility from the **Select a Service** drop-down list. Click **Next**.

Step 10. Click the **Subscribe** button.

Step 11. After the window refreshes, close it.

At this point, users should be able to start to use the extension mobility feature.

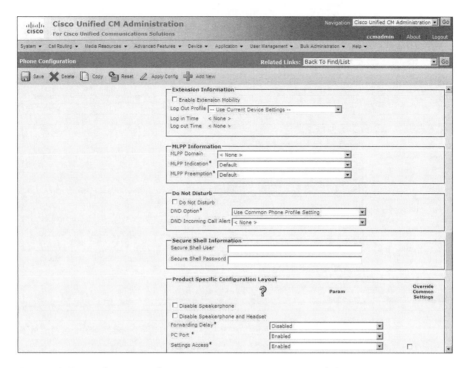

Figure 6-21   *Phone Configuration Page—Extension Mobility*

Creating and Managing Media Resources

To function, some of the features that are available on Communications Manager require *media resources*. These resources can be processes that run on the Communications Manager or separate hardware devices. The following sections explore various media resources and describe how each is configured. A few of these are created automatically when certain Communications Manager services are activated, such as annunciators, MoH servers, software Media Termination Points (MTP), and software conference bridges. For these types, these sections focus more on the function than the creation because these media resources are automatically created.

Configuring an MOH Server

MoH requires an MoH server. This is a service that runs on Communications Manager and is created when the IP Voice Media Streaming Application is activated. This service provides the resources needed to play an audio source while a call is on hold. Because this resource is automatically created, detailed configuration steps are not provided here. However, certain parameters that are unique to this service are explained. Figure 6-22 shows the configuration screen for an MoH server. Navigate to **Media Resources > Music On Hold Server**, click **Find**, and select the desired MoH server to reach this page.

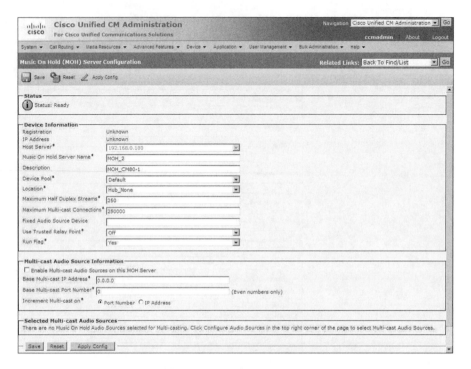

Figure 6-22   *Music on Hold Server Configuration*

The following parameters are unique to the MoH server:

- **Maximum Half Duplex Streams:** Determines the number of devices to which the server can provide a unicast audio stream at one time.

- **Maximum Multicast Connections:** Defines the maximum number of devices to which the server can provide a multicast music audio stream at one time.

- **Fixed Audio Source Device:** Enables you to use a live audio source for MoH if a sound card is installed in the Communications Manager that is acting as the MoH server.

- **Run Flag:** When set to **No**, the MoH server does not provide music on hold. Set this field to **Yes** to have the MoH server provide music.

- **Base Multicast IP Address:** The base address that multicast uses if multicast is enabled. To enable multicast, the **Enable Multi-cast Audio Sources** on this MOH Server check box must be selected, and the MoH server must be assigned to a multi-cast media resource group. Media resource groups are discussed later in this section.

- **Base Multicast Port Number:** Determines the base port number that the multicast stream uses.

The multicast stream can increase, based on port number or IP address. This is configured by choosing the appropriate radio button on this page.

Additional audio files can be added to the MoH server. After they are added, devices can be configured to play different audio sources. Adding new audio sources is fairly simple. The audio file must be in WAV format. The following steps take you through the process of adding an audio source file:

Step 1. The file must first be uploaded to the Communications Manager that is functioning as the MoH server. From within CCMAdmin, navigate to **Media Resources > Music on Hold Audio Source Files**.

Step 2. Click the **Add New** link.

Step 3. Click the **Upload File** button.

Step 4. An Explorer window opens, enabling you to select the WAV file on your PC.

Step 5. After the name of the desired file appears in the Upload File field, click **Upload File**.

Step 6. After the file is uploaded, you are returned to the Upload File window. Click **Close**.

Step 7. Up to 51 audio sources can be configured. Using the MOH Audio Stream Number drop-down list, select the number that determines where this audio source displays in the list of audio sources.

Step 8. From the **MOH Audio Source File** drop-down list, select the desired audio source. After you select a file, the detail of the file displays in the MOH Audio Source File status box.

Step 9. Enter a name in the **MOH Audio Source Name** field that helps identify this audio source later.

Step 10. To ensure that the audio source repeats when it reaches the end, select the **Play Continuously** check box.

Step 11. If you have enabled multicast for the MOH server, the **Allow Multicast** check box must be selected for audio sources that you want to use as a multicast stream.

Step 12. Click the **Save** button to add this audio source.

The audio source is now available to be added to a device. Throughout this book, you have seen that an MoH audio source file can be placed at the line level, the device level, or the device pool level. If an audio source is not specified on any of these levels, the default level defined on the Cisco Communications Manager service parameters configuration page is used. The steps that follow illustrate how to assign the user hold and network hold audio source fields at the device level for a phone.

Assign an MOH Audio Source to a Phone

The steps that follow show how to assign an MoH audio source to a phone:

Step 1. From within CCMAdmin, select **Device > Phone**.

Step 2. Enter search criteria in the Search field to limit the results, and click the **Find** button.

Step 3. From the list that is generated, select the phone to which you want to assign an MoH audio source.

Step 4. The phone configuration screen displays. To assign a user hold audio source to the phone, select an audio source from the **User Hold Audio Source** drop-down list.

Step 5. To assign a network hold audio source to the phone, select an audio source from the **Network Hold Audio Source** drop-down list.

Step 6. Click **Save**.

Step 7. A window displays informing you that you must click the Apply Config button for the change to take effect. Click **OK**.

Step 8. Click the **Apply Config** button.

Step 9. A window displays informing you to save the configuration before continuing. Click **OK**.

After all audio sources are added, assign them as desired. In most cases, audio source files can be added at the device-pool level. If there is a need to have phones within the same device pool use different audio sources, you can configure the audio sources at the device level, which will override the device pool settings.

It is important to understand that a device's audio source determines what the held party hears when a call is placed on hold. A device's audio source does not determine what that device hears when it is placed on hold. To determine what outside callers hear, configure the audio sources on the PSTN gateway.

Creating Conference Bridges

As discussed earlier, Communications Manager has the ability to accommodate conference calls. To do this, a conference bridge is required. Conference bridges come in two types: hardware and software.

The software bridge runs on the Communications Manager and is created during the installation of Communications Manger. Because the software conference bridge is a process that runs on Communications Manager, it takes available CPU cycles away from other functions of the Communications Manager. To avoid this, hardware conference bridges are recommended.

Hardware conference bridges run on a number of Cisco devices. These devices have digital signal processors (DSP) that can be used for conferencing purposes. The devices that support hardware conference bridges are continuing to expand. It is recommended that you check Cisco.com for the most current list of hardware. The Cisco ISR 2800 with a DSP farm is an example of the type of equipment that can serve as a conference bridge.

Depending on the hardware that is being used, the configuration of a conference bridge varies slightly. The main difference is the first field you need configure. It will either be a MAC address or the name of the device. To give you an idea of the design process, the following steps show how to configure a Cisco IOS Enhanced Conference Bridge. It is important to understand that there is additional configuration required on the device that functions as the conference bridge. This configuration is beyond the scope of this book, but you can find more information by searching "configuring enhanced conferencing and transcoding for voice gateway routers" at Cisco.com.

Step 1. From within CCMAdmin, select **Media Resource > Conference Bridge**.

Step 2. On the next page, click the **Add New** link.

Step 3. From the **Conference Bridge Type** drop-down list, select Cisco IOS Enhanced Conference Bridge.

Six different types of conference bridges can be configured. Table 6-2 provides a brief explanation of each bridge and examples of the type of hardware required.

Step 4. Enter the name of the bridge as it is specified in the device's configuration. To find the name, you must access the CLI of the device that is functioning as the bridge. The **associate profile** command contains the name.

Step 5. In the **Description** field, enter a description that helps identify the purpose of the conference bridge. In the description, you might want to include on which Catalyst it is installed.

Step 6. From the **Device Pool** drop-down list, select the device pool for the conference bridge.

Step 7. From the **Common Device Configuration** drop-down list, select the common device configuration that the device will use.

Step 8. From the **Location** drop-down list, select a location for this conference bridge if one is required.

Step 9. From the **Device Security Mode** drop-down list, select **Non Secure Conference Bridge** or **Encrypted Conference Bridge**. This setting must match what is configured on the device functioning as the bridge.

Step 10. The **Use Trusted Relay Point** field determines whether a relay point such as a Media Termination Point (MTP) or a transcoder must be labeled *trusted* to be used by this device. This field is typically changed only in virtualized environments.

Table 6-2   *Conference Bridges*

Bridge Type	Feature	Hardware
Cisco Conference Bridge (WS-SVC-CMM)	Up to 32 conference resources per ACT port adapter. Codecs supported are G7.11 and G7.29.	WS-SVC-CMM-ACT
Cisco Conference Bridge Hardware	Up to 32 conference resources depending on codec. Codecs supported are G7.11, G7.29, G7.23, GSM FR, and GSM EFR.	WS-X6608-T1 (EoS) WS-X6608-E1 (EoS)
Cisco Conference Bridge Software	Up to 64 ad hoc or 128 meet-me conference resources. Supports G7.11 codec.	Runs on Communications Manager. The Cisco IP Voice Media Streaming App must be activated.
Cisco IOS Conference Bridge	Total supported number of participants per conference is six. Codecs supported are G7.11 and G7.29.	NM-HDV NM-HDV-FARM
Cisco IOS Enhanced Conference Bridge	Total supported number of participants per conference is eight. Codecs supported are G7.11, G7.29.	NM-HD NM-HD-2V NM-HD-1V/2V/2VE
Cisco Video Conference Bridge (IPVC-35xx)	The number of conferencing resources varies based on hardware and the type of conferencing. Supports a wide variety of audio and video codecs.	IP/VC 3511 IP/VC 3540

Step 11.   Click the **Save** to add this bridge.

After the conference bridge is created, it is available for use. Sometimes it might be necessary to reset the T1 port on the Catalyst 6000 for it to register to Communications Manager before the bridge can be used.

Configuring MTPs

Media Termination Points (MTP) are typically thought of as a software process that runs on the Communications Manager. Although MTPs can also be hardware devices, this section focuses on the function and configuration tasks for software MTPs. Hardware MTPs are discussed in the next section.

MTPs serve two different functions. First, they provide what are called supplementary services for calls coming from an H.323 (version 1) gateway. Supplementary services are features such as hold, transfer, conferencing, and park. Each of these features requires that the connection be modified, and H.323 (version 1) does not have the ability to modify connections. So, the MTPs serve as a termination point between the endpoint and the gateway. This allows modification of the connection to take place between the MTP and the endpoint while the connection between the MTP and the gateway remains intact.

MTPs can also be required for Session Initiation Protocol (SIP) calls. SIP sends dual-tone multifrequency (DTMF) tones in-band, whereas Skinny Client Control Protocol (SCCP) uses out-of-band. This means that DTMF tones need to be translated between the two. MTPs can provide this function.

Software MTPs are created during the installation of Communications Manager. No other configuration is needed except to change the MTP's device pool. To change the MTP's device pool, follow these steps:

Step 1.   From within CCMAdmin, select **Media Resources > Media Termination Point**.

Step 2.   On the next page, enter search criteria to limit the results and click **Find**.

Step 3.   Select the MTP from the list that displays.

Step 4.   Select the desired device pool from the **Device Pool** drop-down list.

Step 5.   Click **Save**. A message displays stating that the change will take effect when the streaming is idle. Click **OK**.

The activation of the Cisco IP Voice Media Streaming Application service initiates the creation of MTPs. Therefore, nothing else needs to be executed other than assigning MTPs to media resource groups and lists, which will be discussed later in this chapter.

Creating Transcoders

Transcoders are hardware devices that convert calls from one codec to another. This needs to be done when a call is placed between two devices that cannot communicate using the same codec. For example, if a device that could only use G.729 called a device that could only use G.711, a transcoder is necessary to convert the codec for the call to take place. Here is a real-world example. A phone in a remote branch, which is configured to use G.729 when placing calls across the WAN, wants to participate in a conference call that originated on the other side of the WAN, and a software conference bridge is being used. Because software conference bridges support only G.711 and the remote branch can only support G.729 across the WAN, a transcoder is needed to convert G.729 to G.711 and vice versa.

Transcoders can run on a number of Cisco devices. These devices have digital signal processors (DSP) that can be used for transcoding purposes. The devices that support hardware transcoding continue to expand. It is recommended that you check Cisco.com for the most current list of hardware. The Cisco 2821 with an NM-HDV2 is an example of the wide range of equipment that can serve as transcoders.

Depending on the hardware that is being used, the configuration of a transcoder will vary. The main difference is the first field that you need configure. It will either be a MAC address or the name of the device. To give you an idea of the configuration process, the following steps illustrate how to configure a Cisco 2821XM with an NM-HDV2 as a transcoder:

Step 1.   From within CCMAdmin, select **Media Resource > Transcoder**.

Step 2.   On the next page, click the **Add New** link.

Step 3.   From the **Transcoder Type** drop-down list, select Cisco Conference Enhanced IOS Media Termination Point.

  Four different types of transcoders can be configured. Table 6-3 provides a brief explanation of each with examples of the type of hardware required.

Step 4.   In the **Description** field, enter a description that helps identify the purpose of the conference bridge. In that description, you might want to include on which Catalyst it is installed.

Table 6-3   *Transcoders*

Transcoder Type	Feature	Hardware
Cisco Media Termination Point (WS-SVC-CMM)	Transcodes G.711, G.729, and G.723	WS-SVC-CMM-ACT
Cisco Media Termination Point Hardware	Transcodes G.711, G.729, G.723, GSM FR, and GSM EFR	WS-X6608-T1 WS-X6608-E1
Cisco IOS Media Termination Point	Transcodes G.711 and G.729	NM-HDV
Cisco IOS Enhanced Media Termination Point	Transcodes G.711 and G.729	NM-HD NM-HDV2 NM-HD-1V/2V/2VE

Step 5. Enter name of the IOS device in which the transcoding resource is installed in the **Device Name** field.

Step 6. From the **Device Pool** drop-down list, select the device pool for the conference bridge.

Step 7. From the **Common Device Configuration** drop-down list, select the common device configuration that the device will use.

Step 8. The **Special Load** field enables you to enter special load information. In most cases, this field is left blank.

Step 9. The **Use Trusted Relay Point** field determines whether a relay point such as a Media Termination Point (MTP) or a transcoder must be labeled *trusted* to be used by this device. This field is typically changed only in virtualized environments.

Step 10. Click the **Insert** button to add the transcoder.

After the transcoder is created, it is available for use. Later in this chapter, you see how to assign transcoders to media resource groups and lists.

Configuring Annunciators

Annunciator is a process that runs on a Communications Manager that plays recorded announcements to devices. These announcements are triggered by specific events. An example is when a user dials a number that is not valid. In the past, the user would receive a reorder tone, which sounds like a fast busy signal. With the annunciator, a message plays that states "Your call cannot be completed as dialed. Please consult your directory and call again or ask your operator for assistance. This is a recording."

The annunciator is also used to play other messages to inform the caller of events, such as service disruption or the MLPP causing a call to fail.

An annunciator is created during the installation of Communications Manger. No other configuration is needed other than to change the device pool. To change the device pool of an annunciator, follow these steps.

Step 1. From within CCMAdmin, select **Media Resources > Annunciator**.

Step 2. On the next page, enter search criteria to limit the results and click **Find**.

Step 3. Select the **Annunciator** from the list that displays.

Step 4. Select the desired device pool from the **Device Pool** drop-down list.

Step 5. Click **Save**.

Step 7. Click the **Apply Config** button.

Step 9. A window displays informing you to save the configuration before continuing. Click **OK**.

Because an annunciator is created when the Cisco IP Voice Media Streaming Application service is activated, the only other configuration that you might want to make is to add the annunciator to a media resource group. Media resource groups and lists are discussed next.

Media Resource Management

After all the media resources are configured, they can be used. To make the most effective use of the resources, Communications Manager allows you to manage how resources are used and what devices are allowed to use them. In addition, media resource management permits the resource to be shared throughout the cluster.

Media resource management is accomplished by creating media resource groups (MRG) and media resource group lists (MRGL). Media resource groups contain various media resources. A media resource group list contains one or more media resource groups. A device is then assigned to a media resource group list that determines the accessibility of the device to media resource groups. The order in which the groups display in the list determines which group is queried first for a requested resource. Resources that are assigned to an MRG are shared in a round-robin fashion, with the exception of conference bridges. Consequently, the first conference resource listed in an MRG wouldn't necessarily be the one that is used. In the case of conference resources, Communications Manager checks each conference bridge in the MRG to see how many resources are available and selects the bridge with the greatest number available, which gives the user the greatest chance of successfully adding the number of audio streams to the conference. The order in which the media resources appear in the group determines the order in which requested resources are used. Figure 6-23 shows an example of this.

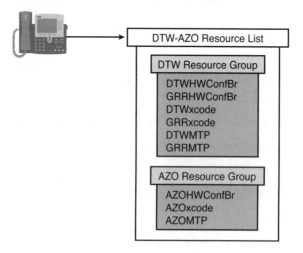

Figure 6-23 *Media Resource Group List Example*

In this example, the phone is assigned the DTW-AZO resource list. When the phone needs a conference bridge resource, all conferences in the MRG are queried to see which one has the most available resources. When all resources are available on all conference bridges, the first one is used. In this example, it would be the DTWHWConfBr because it is the first one listed in the first group. If all the conference resources in the first group were unavailable, the AZOHWConfBr would be used because it is in the second group. In the event that a device requests a resource that is not in any of its resource groups, an attempt is made to use a resource allocated to the default group. Any device that is not associated with a specific group is part of the default group.

Creation and configuration of media resource groups and lists are very similar to those of route groups and lists. We now take a look at how a media resource group is configured.

The following steps explain how to create a media resource group:

Step 1. From within CCMAdmin, select **Media Resources > Media Resource Group**.

Step 2. Click the **Add New** link.

Step 3. A screen similar to that shown in Figure 6-24 displays. In the **Name** field, enter a name for this group.

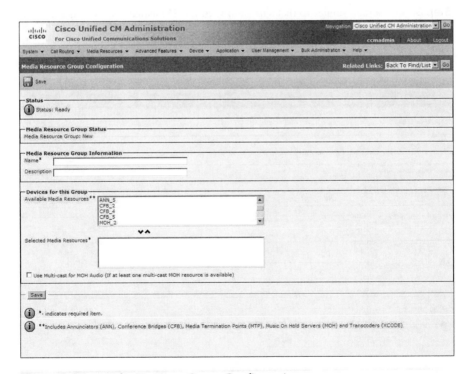

Figure 6-24 *Media Resource Group Configuration*

Step 4. In the **Description** field, enter a description that helps identify this group.

Step 5. From the **Available Media Resources** box, select the resource that you want to add to this group. Click the down arrow below this box.

Note You can select more than one resource at a time by holding down the **Ctrl** key when selecting them.

Step 6. The selected resources now display in the **Selected Media Resources** box. You can remove a resource by selecting it and clicking the up arrow.

Step 7. After all the desired resources are in the Selected Media Resources box, click the **Save** button to add this group.

Now the groups need to be assigned to a media resource list. The following steps illustrate how to assign an MRG to an MRGL.

Step 1. From within CCMAdmin, select **Media Resources > Media Resource Group List**.

Step 2. Click the **Add New** link.

Step 3. A screen similar to that shown in Figure 6-25 displays. Enter a descriptive name in the **Name** field.

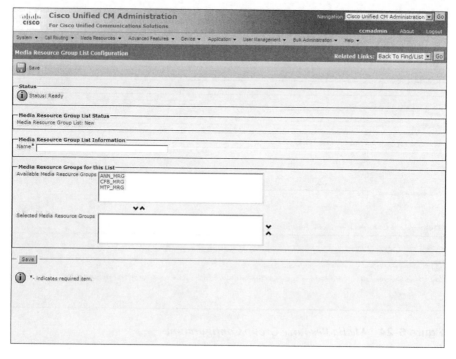

Figure 6-25 *Media Resource Group List Configuration*

Step 4.   From the **Available Media Resource Groups** box, select the groups that you want to add to this list. Click the down arrow below this box.

Note   You can select more than one group at a time by holding down the Ctrl key when selecting them.

Step 5.   The selected resources now display in the Selected Media Resource Groups box. You can change the order in which a group displays in the list by highlighting the name and clicking the up and down arrows located to the right of the Selected Media Resource Groups box. You can also remove a group by selecting it and clicking the Up Arrow located above the box.

Step 6.   After all the desired groups are in the Selected Media Resource Groups box, click the **Save** button to add this group.

After the resource lists are created, you must assign them to devices. This can be done at the device level or at the device pool level. If a media resource list is not assigned to a device, the device will use the one assigned to its device pool.

The following steps show how to assign a media resource group list to a phone and a device pool.

Assign a Media Resource Group List to a Phone

Follow these steps to assign an MRGL to a phone:

Step 1.   From within CCMAdmin, select **Device > Phone**.

Step 2.   Enter search criteria in the Search field to limit the results, and click the **Find** button.

Step 3.   From the list that is generated, select the phone to which you want to assign a media resource group list.

Step 4.   The phone configuration screen displays. Select a media resource group list from the **Media Resource Group List** drop-down list.

Step 5.   Click the **Save** button.

Step 6.   A window displays informing you that you must click the Apply Config button for the change to take effect. Click **OK**.

Step 7.   Click the **Apply Config** button.

Step 8.   A window displays informing you to save the configuration before continuing. Click **OK**.

Assign a Media Resource Group List to a Device Pool

Follow these steps to assign an MRGL to a device pool:

Step 1. From within CCMAdmin, select **System > Device Pool**.

Step 2. To limit the results, enter search criteria in the Search field and click the **Find** button.

Step 3. From the list that is generated, select the device pool to which you want to assign a media resource group list.

Step 4. The device pool configuration screen displays. Select a media resource group list from the **Media Resource Group List** drop-down list.

Step 5. Click the **Save** button.

In most cases, it is recommended to assign the media resource group list at the device pool level. This makes it easier to manage and advantageous if you are using extension mobility. If a device requires a unique media resource, it should be assigned at the device level.

Configuring Remote Site Failover

When deploying Communications Manager with remote sites, it is necessary to deploy some type of remote site redundancy in the event that the link with the central site is lost. Every time a phone places a call, it must be able to talk to Communications Manager. No call can be placed if the phone is unable to communicate with a Communications Manager. As mentioned earlier in this book, as soon as the phone goes off-hook, it sends a request to Communications Manager. If the primary Communications Manager fails, the secondary can respond to all requests. What happens in a remote environment when the link to the Communications Manager fails? Because the phone can't reach the Communications Manager, the phone doesn't know to provide dial tone. The solution is to deploy a Survivable Remote Site Telephony (SRST) solution at the remote site.

Another issue that can occur with remote sites is that the link can be operating properly but all the available bandwidth is in use and additional calls cannot be sent across this link. So, when a phone on the remote site tries to call a phone at the central site, the call is rejected because of insufficient bandwidth. This means that until bandwidth is available, the only way to reach the central site is by sending the call over a different path such as the public switched telephone network (PSTN). This requires the caller to hang up and dial a number that will use the PSTN instead of the WAN link. The solution for this issue is to configure AAR groups.

The following sections examine how SRST and AAR work and how each is configured.

SRST Overview

SRST is a service that can run on a number of Cisco devices such as the 1861, 2821, and 3925, just to name a few. The SRST device is located at the remote site and is typically the same device that is used for the remote site PSTN gateway.

When phones cannot communicate with any of the Communications Managers at the central site, they register with the SRST device. The device then accepts and responds to SCCP requests. All calls that are not destined for devices at the remote site are then routed out to the PSTN.

Because the SRST device is responsible for routing calls, it must have some type of route plan programmed in it, just like a normal H.323 gateway.

The majority of the configuration is done on the SRST device itself. This part of the configuration requires some IOS telephony programming experience.

Configuring SRST

The configuration of an SRST solution occurs in two places. The first is on the SRST device, and the second is in the Communications Manager. First take a look at a sample of the configuration on the SRST device itself:

```
access-code fxo 9
default-destination pattern 2002
dialplan-pattern 1 547....
ip source-address 10.1.1.2 port 2000
keepalive 30
max-ephones 24
max-dn 48
transfer-pattern 5472...
voicemail 5479100
```

Table 6-4 provides nine commands and definitions for the configuration process.

In addition to these commands, further dial plan and port configuration are required. It is recommended that only those familiar with IOS devices and telephony configuration of such devices perform this portion of the configuration.

After the SRST device is configured, you must configure Communications Manager so that phones can use this service. If the SRST device is the phone's default gateway at the remote site, fewer configurations are required. However, if the SRST device is not the default gateway for the phone, an SRST reference must be created.

An SRST reference is used to instruct the phone to register with the appropriate device if it cannot communicate with a Communications Manager. The following steps show how to create an SRST reference. If the SRST device is the phone's default gateway, skip to the "Assign an SRST Reference to a Device Pool" section, later in this chapter.

Table 6-4 *Configuring SRST*

Command	Description
access-code fxo 9	Signifies that when a 9 is the first digit, the call is routed out an FXO port.
default-destination pattern 2002	Causes all inbound calls that do not match a registered directory number to be routed to extension 2002.
dialplan-pattern 1 547 . . .	For inbound calls (calls to an IP phone in a Cisco SRST system) where the calling party number matches the dial-plan pattern, the call is considered a local call and has a distinctive ring that identifies the call as internal. Any calling party number that does not match the dial-plan pattern is considered an external call and has a distinctive ring that is different from the internal ringing. For outbound calls, the **dialplan-pattern** command converts the calling party's extension number to an E.164 calling party number. Outbound calls that do not use an E.164 number and go through a Primary Rate Interface (PRI) connection to the PSTN, can be rejected by the PRI link as the calling party identifier.
ip source-address 10.1.1.2 port 2000	Specifies the IP address of the interface that services all SCCP requests.
keepalive 30	Defines the keepalive interval in seconds.
max-ephones 24	Determines the maximum number of phones that are allowed to register to this device.
max-dn 48	Determines the maximum number of directory numbers that are allowed to register to this device.
transfer-pattern 5472 . . .	Determines to what numbers calls can be transferred. In this case, calls can only be transferred to seven-digit numbers that begin with 5472. IP phone directory numbers that have registered to SRST can also be transferred without additional configuration.
voice mail 5479100	Defines the number that is dialed when users press the Voicemail button on their phones.

Creating an SRST Reference to a Device Pool

Follow these steps to create an SRST reference to a device pool:

Step 1.   From within CCMAdmin, select **System > SRST**.

Step 2.   Click the **Add New** link.

Step 3.   A screen similar to that shown in Figure 6-26 displays. In the **Name** field, enter a name for this SRST reference.

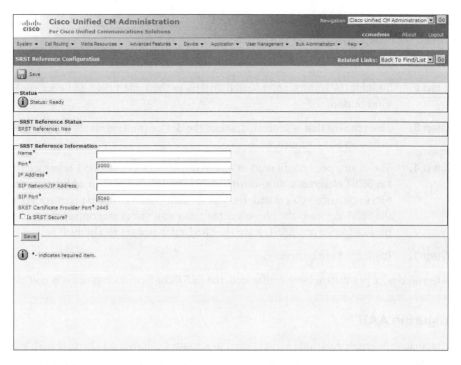

Figure 6-26   *SRST Reference Configuration*

Step 4.   Enter the port number that is used for SCCP in the Port field. In most cases, this should be left at 2000.

Step 5.   In the **IP Address** field, enter the IP address in the interface of the SRST device that is going to service SCCP requests.

Step 6.   In the **SIP Network/IP Address** field, enter the server that SIP phones will register to when SRST is active.

Step 7.   In the **SIP Port field**, enter the SIP port of the SRST gateway. This is typically 5060.

Step 8.   If the SRST device contains a self-signed or certificate-authority-issued certificate, select the **Is SRST Secure?** check box.

Step 9.   Click **Save** to add this SRST reference.

After you configure all the necessary SRST references, you must define which references will be used by which devices. This is done by assigning an SRST reference to the device pools. The following steps show how this is accomplished.

Assign an SRST Reference to a Device Pool

Follow these steps to assign an SRST reference to a device pool:

Step 1.   From within CCMAdmin, select **System > Device Pool**.

Step 2.   To limit the results, enter search criteria in the search field and click the **Find** button.

Step 3.   From the list that is generated, select the device pool on which you want to define an SRST reference.

Step 4.   The device pool configuration screen displays. Select an SRST reference from the **SRST Reference** drop-down list. You will notice that, in addition to the SRST reference you created, the Use Default Gateway option is provided. If the SRST device is the phone's default gateway, select this option. To prohibit phones from using SRST, leave the SRST reference set to Disable.

Step 5.   Click the **Save** button.

After all device pools have been configured, the SRST configuration process is complete.

Configuring AAR

Automated Alternate Routing (AAR) is used to reroute a call over an alternate path when the call fails because of lack of bandwidth. This is accomplished by creating AAR groups that define a prefix that should be assigned to a number if the call fails because of inadequate bandwidth. Figure 6-27 shows an example.

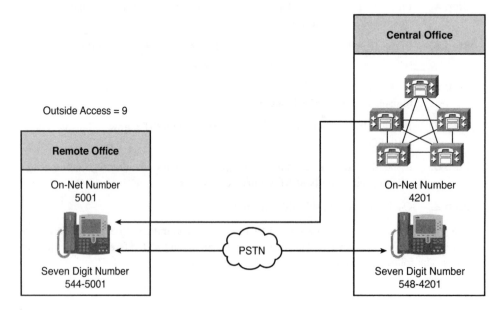

Figure 6-27   *AAR Group Example*

The user at the remote office only needs to dial 4201 to reach the phone in the central office. If there is enough bandwidth, the call will be successful. However, if there is insufficient bandwidth, the call needs to be rerouted over the PSTN. Because 9 is used as the outside access code, the number that needs to be dialed to reach extension 4201 through the PSTN is 95484201. With AAR properly configured, the dialed digits of 4201 are automatically changed to 95484201 and the call is sent out the PSTN.

Note   If an external phone number mask is assigned (for example, 612548XXXX), the prefix digits are added to the end result of the mask's transformation. Hence, in this example, 916125484201 would be the end result.

To configure AAR, you simply need to create AAR groups and assign them to directory numbers.

Creating an AAR Group

The following steps show how to create an AAR group:

Step 1.   From within CCMAdmin, select **Call Routing > AAR Group**.

Step 2.   Click the **Add New** link.

Step 3.   Enter a name for the AAR group in the **Name** field and click **Save**.

Step 4.   A screen like that shown in Figure 6-28 displays. Because this is the first group, there is only one field to populate. In the **Dial Prefix** field, enter the digits that will be added to the beginning of the dialed number when a device from within this group dials another device within the same group.

Step 5.   Click **Save**.

Step 6.   To see how the configuration changes when more than one group exists, create another group by clicking the **Add New** link.

Step 7.   Enter a name for the ARR group in the **Name** field and click Insert.

Step 8.   A screen similar to that shown in Figure 6-29 displays. In the **Dial Prefix** field, enter the digits that will be added to the beginning of the dialed number when a device from within this group dials another device within this group.

Step 9.   On this screen, there are additional fields that do not exist when only one AAR group is created. In the **Dial Prefix (From <AAR GROUP NAME>)** field, enter the digits that will be added to the beginning of the dialed number when a device from within this group dials a device within the other group.

Step 10.   In the **Dial Prefix (To <AAR GROUP NAME>)** field, enter the digits that will be added to the beginning of the dialed number when a device in the other group dials a device within this group.

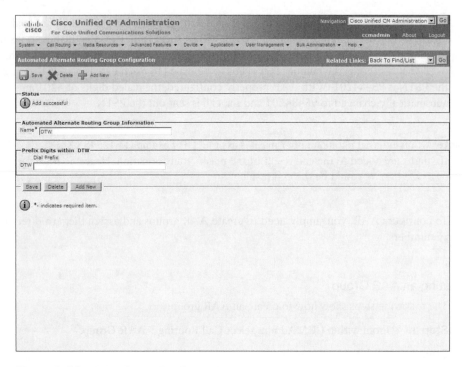

Figure 6-28   *AAR Group Configuration*

Step 11.   Click **Save**.

Now the AAR groups must be assigned to lines.

Assign an AAR Group to a Line

The following steps show how to assign an AAR group to a line on a phone:

Step 1.   From within CCMAdmin, select **Device > Phone**.

Step 2.   Enter search criteria in the Search field to limit the results, and click the **Find** button.

Step 3.   Select the desired phone from the list that displays.

Step 4.   Click the desired line on the left side of the screen.

Step 5.   On the Directory Number Configuration page, select the desired AAR group from the **AAR Group** drop-down list, as shown in Figure 6-30.

Step 6.   Click the **Save** button.

Note   When you make a change to the directory number configuration and click **Save**, the phone might reset. If a caller is currently on a call, the phone will reset after the call is ended.

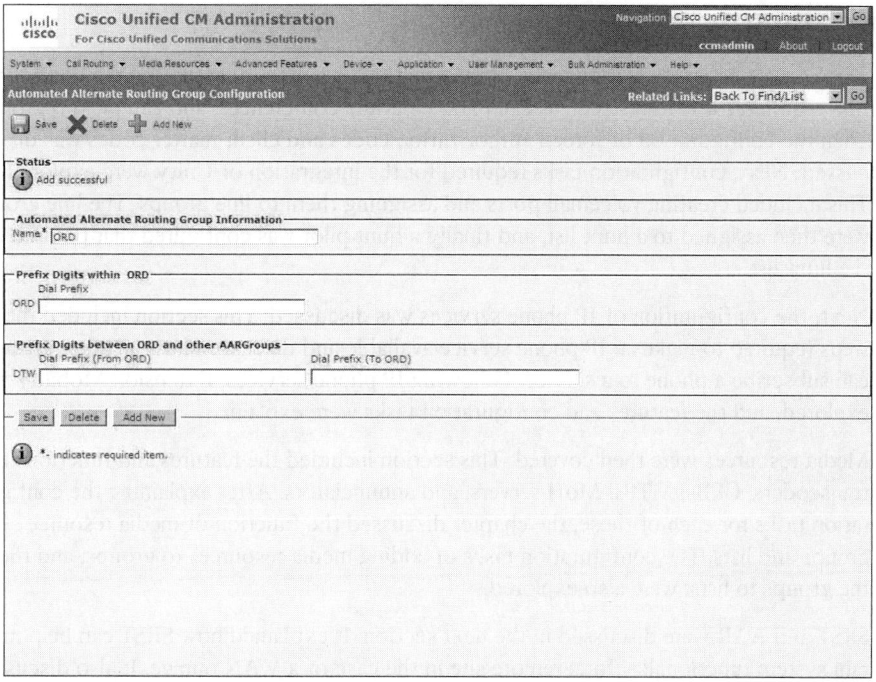

Figure 6-29 *AAR Group Configuration (Multiple Groups)*

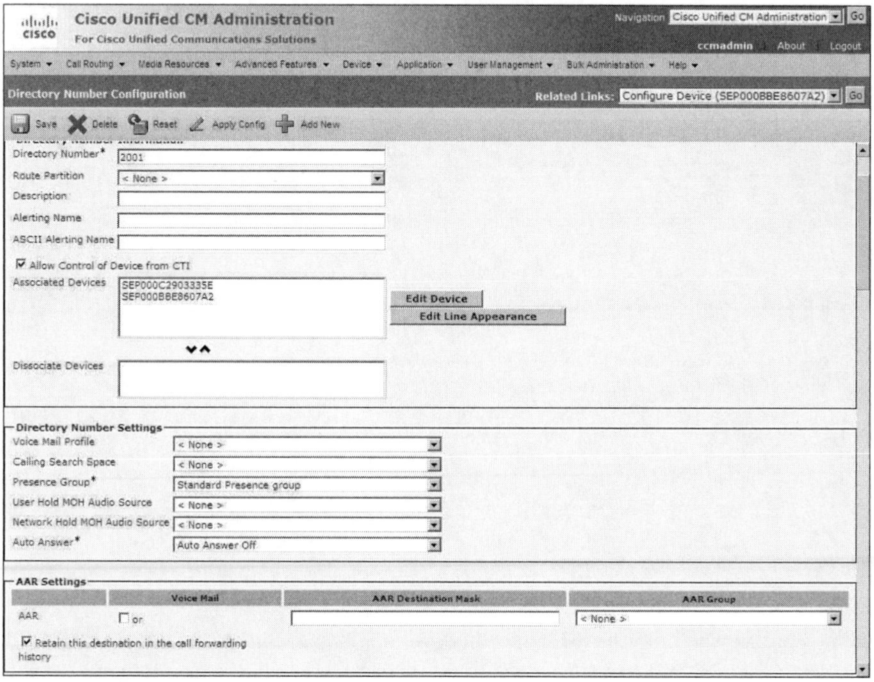

Figure 6-30 *Assigning an AAR Group to a Line*

Summary

This chapter covered an abundance of information. It began by exploring the configuration required for features such as call park, meet-me conferences, and call pickup groups. Then the configuration of forced authorization codes and client matter codes was discussed. Next, configuration tasks required for the integration of Unity were explored. This included creating voicemail ports and assigning them to line groups. The line groups were then assigned to a hunt list, and finally a hunt pilot was configured that pointed to the hunt list.

Next, the configuration of IP phone services was discussed. This section included the steps required to make an IP phone service available and discussed how an administrator can subscribe a phone to a service. Following IP phone services, Extension Mobility was explored, and the features and configuration tasks were explained.

Media resources were then covered. This section included the features and functions of transcoders, CFBs, MTPs, MoH servers, and annunciators. After explaining the configuration tasks for each of these, the chapter discussed the function of media resource groups and lists. The configuration tasks of adding media resources to groups, and then the groups to lists, were also explored.

SRST and AAR were discussed in the next section. It explained how SRST can help maintain system functionality for a remote site in the case of a WAN outage. It also discussed how AAR can allow a call to successfully be routed over an alternate path if the call is rejected because of bandwidth limitations.

Chapter 7

Unity Predeployment Tasks

One of the most widely deployed phone system add-ons is voicemail. For a number of years, Unity was the voicemail solution of choice for Communications Manager. However, over the last few years, a new Cisco voicemail solution has become quite popular. The new product is called Unity Connection. Because both platforms integrate well with Communications Manager, both are covered in the following chapters. There are many similarities between these products. They are so comparable that much of what one learns about one product can be directly applied to the other. Whenever possible, the chapters are written so that they are applicable regardless of which product you are using.

Although Unity and Unity Connection are similar, they are not identical. They offer different features. Because both have the word *Unity* in their name, it can sometimes cause confusion when discussing either product. For clarification the following terms are used throughout the messaging section of this book to help you clearly identify which product is being discussed:

- **Unity:** Used when the topic applies only to Unity

- **Unity Connection:** Used when the topic only applies to Unity Connection

- **Unity/Connection:** Used when the topic applies to both products

For the majority of tasks that an administrator performs on a day-today basis, the main difference is the look and feel of the administrative interface. Because the interfaces are not identical, step-by-step instructions for both interfaces are offered.

If your solution is going to be effective, proper configuration is essential. The first step to proper configuration is verifying that the integration is correct and that all predeployment tasks have been completed. This chapter includes step-by-step instructions for completing predeployment tasks, such as verifying integration, defining system parameters, and creating templates, distribution lists, and class of service (CoS). First you look at the administrative interface to see how these tasks are accomplished within Unity.

Accessing and Navigating Unity Administrator

Most of the configurations discussed throughout the messaging portion of this book are accomplished through a web-based administration interface. Because this is the main administration interface, it is used for most administration tasks, so it is important that you become familiar with it. This section introduces you to the Unity administrative interface (Unity Administrator). The Unity Connection interface is reviewed in the next section.

To access Unity Administrator, open Internet Explorer (6.0 or higher) and enter the server's name followed by **/sa/web.** If the server's name is DTWUNITY, for example, you enter **DTWUNITY/sa/web** in the address bar of Internet Explorer. Unlike when using CM, you should not be prompted for a username and password. You are authenticated based on your Window's Active Directory (AD) credentials. If you are logged in as a user who does not have an associated Unity subscriber with administrative rights, you will not have access to this interface. You need to log in to the network as a user that has Unity administrative rights.

Unity Administrator is often referred to as System Administrator (SA). The term *SA* has been used for this interface for a number of years, whereas the *UA* term is relatively new. For this reason, the term *SA* will be used throughout this book.

Note It is important to understand that administrative rights for Unity are not associated with Windows rights. Having administrator rights for Windows does not automatically give you administrative rights for Unity. To access SA, your Windows account must have an associated Unity subscriber that has Unity administrative rights. During the installation, an administrator was selected. Use this account for now, and how to add administrative rights to subscribers is discussed later.

After you log in to SA, you see an interface similar to that shown in Figure 7-1. In Figure 7-1, each section of this interface is labeled. The section labeled 1 is referred to as the navigation panel. This panel is used to access the various configuration screens. The section labeled 2 is referred to as the title strip, which contains icons that enable you to perform functions such as adding, deleting, and saving. The section labeled 3 is referred to as the page body. This is where the majority of the actual work is performed. From the page body, you enter the specific configuration information for the object on which you are working.

The following example should help you to better understand how this interface works; it is an example of changing the extension number that is associated with a subscriber. Each step includes a screen shot of the SA.

Note Although a screen shot is provided here for almost every configuration task, it is not the general practice in this book. Step-by-step screen shots are important in this chapter to introduce you to the interface. However, throughout the rest of the book, screen

shots are provided to help reinforce the topic being discussed and do not illustrate each
step as they do in this example.

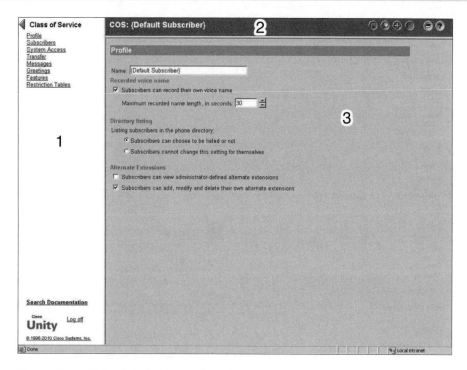

Figure 7-1   *Unity Administrator Interface*

Step 1.   Log on to SA by entering the server's name followed by **/Web/SA**. Figure 7-2
shows the main SA screen. Note that there is no title strip in this figure.

Note   If you are accessing SA using the Unity server's keyboard and screen, there is an
icon on the desktop that is labeled System Administrator. Clicking this icon should open
the System Administrator interface.

Step 2.   From the navigation panel, click the **Subscribers** link, which is shown in
Figure 7-2.

Step 3.   Figure 7-3 shows that the title strip displays and the page body changes after
you select the of the object you want to configure. Also note that the navigation panel changes and presents you with all the configuration options for that
type of object. By looking in the navigation panel, you are in a Subscriber
configuration, and by looking at the heading in the page body, you are in the
profile portion of the Subscriber configuration. For simplicity's sake, this

screen is referred to as the **Subscribers > Profile** page. You see many references of this type of syntax (called navigation syntax) throughout this portion of the book, so be sure that you are comfortable with this concept.

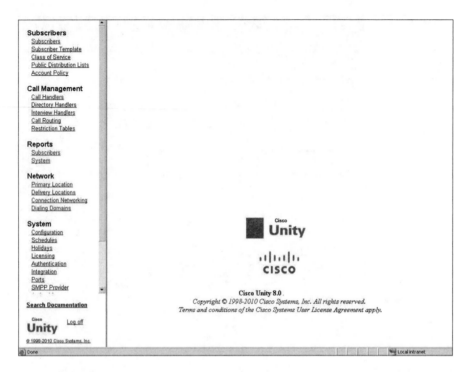

Figure 7-2 *SA Main Screen*

Note   In future step-by-step tasks, navigation syntax will be used to help you quickly understand at exactly which screen you should be. For example, if the navigation syntax were **Call Handlers > Call Transfer**, you would click **Call Handlers** from the main navigation menu and then select **Call Transfer**.

Step 4.   In the page body, the extension is 4321. Figure 7-4 illustrates this. To change the extension, simply change the number that displays in the **Extension** field to 4123. Although colors do not show in the screen captures of this book, you can see the colors on the screen if you follow these steps on a live system. The icon that looks like a floppy disk will change colors. Before you change the extension it is grayed out; when the extension number is changed, it is blue. The disk displaying in blue signifies that changes have been made but not saved. The disk displaying in gray indicates that there is no new information that needs to be saved. In the title strip, that there is an asterisk next to the subscriber's name. This is another indication of unsaved data. Click the **Disk** icon to save the change.

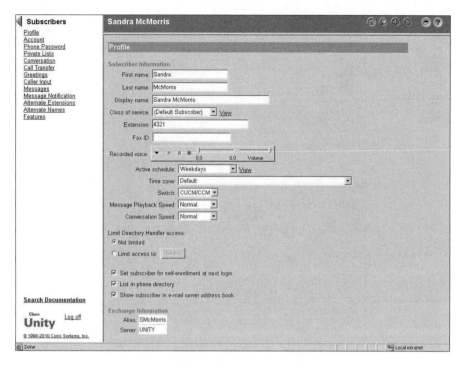

Figure 7-3 *Subscribers > Profile*

This example was fairly simple. Other Unity tasks will be more detailed. The goal of this example is to introduce you to the SA interface and some of the syntax that is used in the step-by-step tasks.

Before moving on, look at the other icons that display in the title strip. In addition to the disk, there is a blue magnifying glass, a blue plus sign, a red X, a book framed by a yellow button, and a question mark framed by another yellow button. In addition, an icon of a running man displays when you run reports. A brief explanation of each follows:

- **Disk (Save icon):** Displays in blue if there is unsaved data. Clicking this icon saves any unsaved data.

- **Magnifying glass (Find icon):** Used to find items. Clicking this icon opens a search criteria window.

- **Plus sign (Add icon):** Used to add a new object.

- **X (Delete icon):** Used to delete the current object.

- **Book (Help icon):** Opens an online documentation window.

- **Question mark (Field Help):** Displays a question mark next to each field. Clicking a question mark opens a help window that explains that field.

- **Running man (displays when reports are running)** (Run icon): Clicking the icon causes the selected report to be queued.

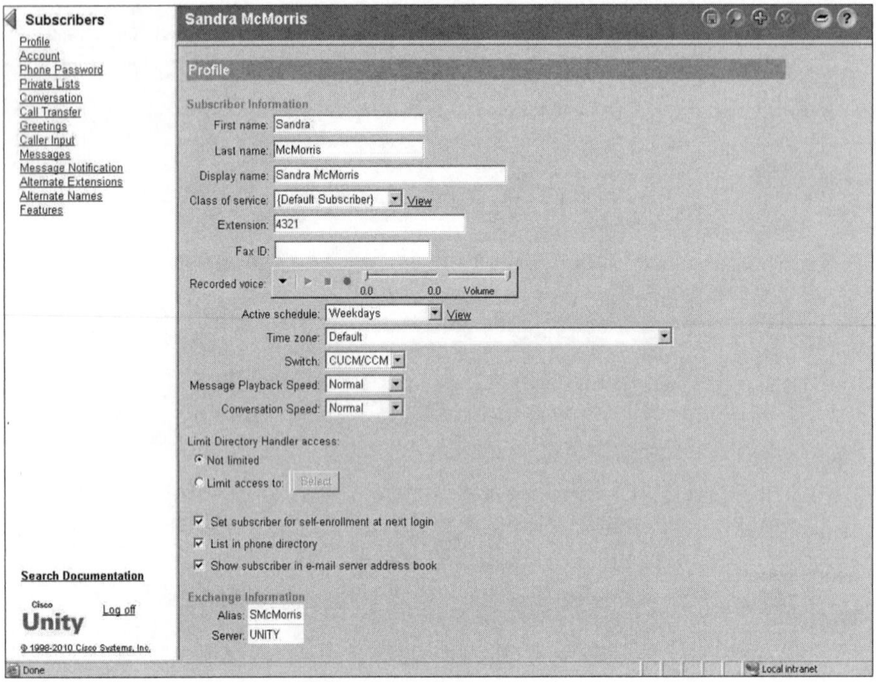

Figure 7-4 *Unity Subscriber Screen*

Note   These icons are sometimes referred to as *sweet tarts*.

In the earlier example, you were introduced to navigation syntax. Now look at one more example to make sure that you are comfortable with the concept.

The navigation syntax for this example is **Subscribers > Class of Service > Transfer**. Figure 7-5 shows the main navigation menu. **Class of Service** is under the **Subscribers** heading. After selecting **Class of Service**, the menu in the navigation panel changes to display a list of the configuration screens that deal with class of service. From this list, select **Transfer**, as shown in Figure 7-6. To return to the main navigation menu, click the blue arrow located in the upper-left corner of the navigation panel.

Now that you are familiar with the SA interface and the syntax that will be used in this portion of the book, first look at the tasks that need to be accomplished to ensure a properly configured system.

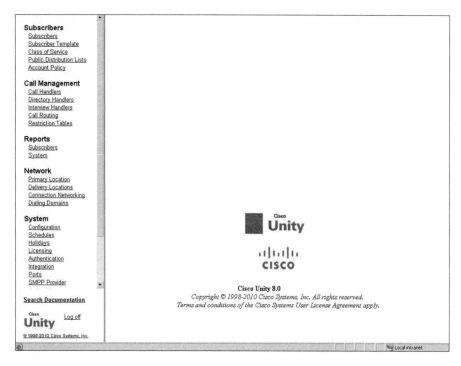

Figure 7-5   *Unity Main Screen*

Accessing and Navigating Unity Connection Administrator

The Unity Connection administrative interface is accessed by entering the IP address of the Unity Connection server followed by "/cuadmin" in the address bar of a browser. For example, if the server's IP address is 10.1.1.10, you would enter **https://10.1.1.10/cuadmin**. You will be presented with a login screen. In this book, this interface is called CUAdmin. Enter the username and password for the CUAdmin page and click **Login**. A screen similar to the one shown in Figure 7-7 appears. Unlike Unity, Unity Connection does not require integration to Microsoft AD. For this reason, you need to log in to CUAdmin even if you are already logged in to AD.

Note   Unity Connection supports the following browsers:

* Microsoft Internet Explorer (IE) 7 when running in Microsoft Windows XP SP3

* Microsoft Internet Explorer (IE) 8 when running in Microsoft Windows XP SP3 or Microsoft Vista SP2

* Firefox 3.x when running in Microsoft Windows XP SP3, Microsoft Vista SP2, or Safari 4.x when running on Apple MAC OS X

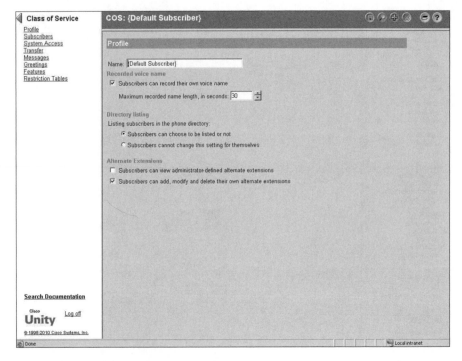

Figure 7-6   *Unity Submenu Screen*

The layout of this interface is fairly intuitive. The left side of the screen is the navigation panel, and the right side is where the configuration information is entered. After you select an item from the navigation panel, the configuration page appears, as seen in Figure 7-8. To become familiar with this interface, use the following steps to change the voicemail password for a user.

Step 1.   To change the password of a user, you need to navigate to the user search screen. Figure 7-8 shows the navigation panel fully expanded. This enables you to examine the subchoices under each main heading. For example, the first main heading you see is **Users**. Clicking only the main heading expands and collapses the subchoices. To navigate to a configuration page, click the subchoice. In this case, you want to select the subchoice **Users** under the main **Users** heading. To make this easier throughout the rest of the text, navigation syntax will be used. Using navigation syntax, this step is simplified to "From the menu on the left, select **Users > Users**."

Step 2.   The users are listed as seen in Figure 7-8. If the users you are looking for are not displayed in the list, you can search by alias, extension, first name, last name, or display name. Enter the search criteria and click **Find**.

Step 3.   Select the user from the list that appears by clicking the alias. A screen similar to the one shown in Figure 7-9 appears.

Figure 7-7   *Unity Connection Administrator*

Step 4.   There are drop-down menus at the top of the screen. Mouse over **Edit** and a list similar to that seen in Figure 7-10 appears; select **Change Password**.

Step 5.   Enter the new password in the **Password** field, as seen in Figure 7-11.

Step 6.   Enter the password again in the **Confirm Password** field.

Step 7.   Click **Save**.

In this example, you were introduced to navigation syntax. Now look at one more example to make sure that you are comfortable with the concept.

The navigation syntax for this example is **Call Management > Call Routing > Direct Routing Rules**. Figure 7-12 shows the main navigation menu.

Now that you have a good understanding of how to navigate the interfaces for both Unity and Unity Connection, look at what needs to be configured before you start to add users. The rest of this chapter is split in two parts: Unity and Unity Connection. This enables you to jump directly to the portion that is of most interest to you.

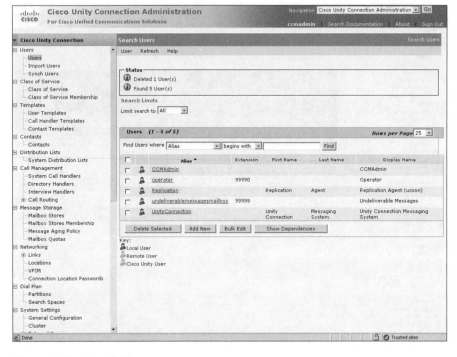

Figure 7-8   *Search Users*

Unity Integration Verification

Before Unity can be integrated with any system, you need to ensure that the all required PBX configuration is completed. The configuration tasks required on the PBX are based on the type of PBX with which you are integrating. This book only addresses the configuration tasks required when integrating with a Cisco solution. If you are integrating with a traditional PBX, you need to refer to the installation guides and release notes available at Cisco.com. A list of all integration guides can be found by searching "unity configuration guides" at Cisco.com.

At one time, more than 150 PBXs were supported and approved to work with Unity. That number has been drastically reduced. The main reason that Cisco acquired Activoice, the original developer of Unity, was so that Cisco could offer a feature-rich unified messaging solution that would integrate well with Communications Manager. This does not mean that Cisco removed all support for traditional PBXs. There are times when Communications Manager will be integrated with an existing PBX. By allowing Unity to integrate with both Communications Manager and the existing PBX, Unity becomes a much more attractive solution to some customers. Cisco has since added support for other Voice over IP (VoIP) solutions, such as Session Initialization Protocol (SIP). The following sections discuss tasks that should be completed to ensure that the Cisco IP-based solution with which Unity will integrate is configured properly.

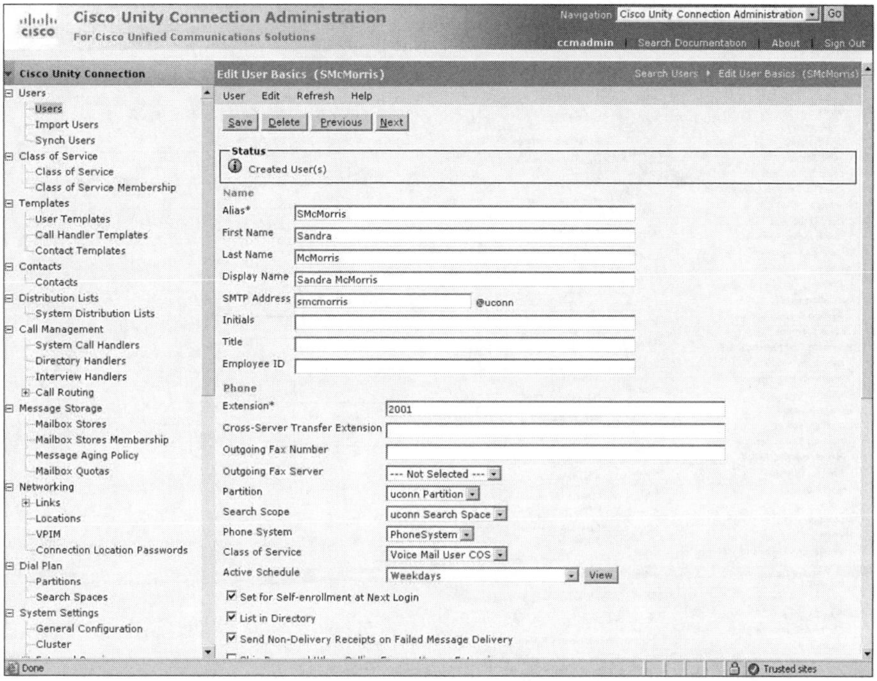

Figure 7-9   *Edit User Basics*

Communications Manager Integration

In this book, it is expected that most Unity installations will be configured to operate with Communications Manager. Before Unity can communicate with Communications Manager, certain tasks must be accomplished on the Communications Manager and the Unity systems. In Chapter 6, "Configuring CUCM Features and Services," the Communications Manager side of the voicemail configuration was discussed. If necessary, refer back to that chapter to review the configuration of the required components. Because the actual configuration steps have already been discussed, the following sections will focus on how to verify whether all required configuration has been completed.

Voicemail Port Configuration

Unity communicates with PBXs through a port. With traditional PBXs, the ports are most often analog lines. To enable this communication, a voice board is installed in the Unity server. The voice board usually has either four or 12 analog ports, which connect back to analog ports on the PBX. As of Unity 8.0, voice boards are no longer supported, and integration with a PBX is accomplished by using PMIG or TIMG, which is discussed later. When Unity is integrated with Communications Manager, analog lines are not used. Instead, virtual ports are configured on the Communications Manager. The only physical connectivity between the Unity server and the Communications Manager is Ethernet.

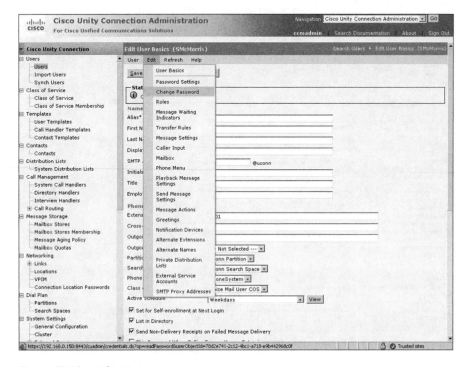

Figure 7-10 *Edit Menu*

When these ports are configured in Unity, a name and a Directory Number (DN) are assigned to them. The DN is significant only to the Communications Manager. Unity does not need to know what the DN is because Unity is concerned only with the name assigned to the port. Typically, the name looks something like Cisco-UM-VI1. This naming convention is only a suggestion; any name can be used.

The Unity Telephony Integration Manager (UTIM) is used to configure the voicemail port names in Unity. The UTIM verifies that Unity can communicate with the port after you enter the name. If you are not sure of the name of the voicemail port, you can find it by using the Communications Manager configuration interface, as outlined in the steps that follow:

Step 1.   Log on to the CCMADMIN interface.

Step 2.   Select **Advanced Feature > Voice-mail > Cisco Voice-mail Port**.

Step 3.   Click the **Find** button. On the left side of the screen, all the voicemail ports display. You are concerned with the prefix portion of the name. That is the portion that displays before the number. For example, if the name were CiscoUM-VI1, the prefix would be CiscoUM-VI.

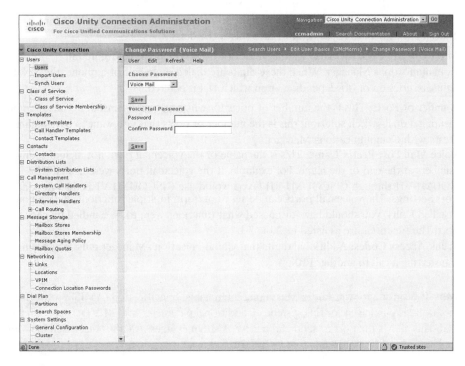

Figure 7-11 *Change Password*

Unity Telephony Integration Manager (Communications Manager)

The current integration settings can be found in the Unity's SA interface but can only be changed using UTIM. To view the integration settings, open SA and click Integration. This can be found under the System heading on the left side. If there are multiple switch types, you can view the desired integration by clicking the appropriate integration in the list on the left side of the integration page.

The configuration for the integration is accomplished using UTIM. When configuring UTIM, enter information about the Communications Manager with which you are integrating Unity. The following checklist provides information necessary before applying UTIM:

✓ **Integration Name:** This name is used to identify the integration. If the name is changed, make sure that you use a name that makes it easy to identify the integration.

✓ **Communications Manager Cluster Name:** This name is used for reference only. Choose a name that helps to easily identify the cluster.

✓ **Communications Manager IP Addresses:** Unity needs to know the IP addresses of both the primary and secondary Communications Managers with which it will be communicating.

✓ **TCP Port:** This is the TCP port number that Unity will use for connecting to Communications Manager. The default value is 2000. Leave it at the default.

✓ **Starting RTP Audio Port:** This is the first IP port number that is used for Real-time Transport Protocol (RTP) sessions. Leave this at the default.

✓ **MWI On/Off DNs:** Message Waiting Indicator (MWI) DNs are configured in Communications Manager. When these digits are dialed on behalf of a phone, the MWI lights, or goes on or off depending upon which DN is entered.

✓ **Number of Ports:** This is the number of ports for which you are licensed. If you are implementing a dual-switch solution, this is the number of ports that you want to have communicate with Communications Manager.

✓ **Voice Mail Port Prefix Name:** This is the name of the voicemail port, not including any numbers at the end of the name. For example, if the voicemail ports were named CIS-COUM1-VI1 through CISCOUM1-VI12, you would use CISCOUM1-VI as the prefix name.

✓ **Port Settings:** The voicemail ports can be set to perform multiple functions. Before you installed Unity, you should have discussed what functions were to be handled by each port. The functions are as listed in Table 7-1.

✓ **Trunk Access Codes:** Additional digits that Communications Manager must dial when transferring a call to another PBX.

Note   If licensing for the Audio Messaging Interchange Specification (AMIS) protocol networking is purchased for this system, an additional parameter of AMIS Delivery can be listed. This allows the port to send and receive AMIS messages. AMIS is discussed in more detail in Chapter 10, "Implementing Unity Networking."

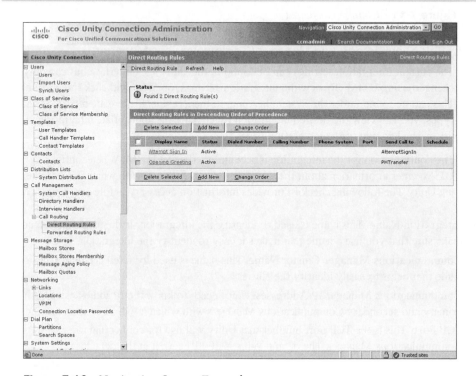

Figure 7-12 *Navigation Syntax Example*

Table 7-1 *Voicemail Port Settings*

Parameter	Description
Description	Enables the port to be used by Unity
Answer Calls	Enables the port to answer incoming calls
Message Notification	Enables the port to make outgoing calls for message notification purposes
Dialout MWI	Enables the port to be used to send MWIs
Telephony Record and Playback (TRAP) Connection	Enables the port to be used for recording and playing messages when a subscriber is using the web or an email client

UTIM is part of the installation process. If the Unity server is already loaded, this information should already be configured. You can check and change the integration information by running UTIM. To run UTIM, follow these steps:

Step 1. On the Unity Server, choose **Start > Programs > Unity > Manage Integrations.**

Step 2. To show the Communications Manager clusters, from the UTIM window, click the **CUCM/CCM**, which displays in the left column.

Step 3. Select the name of the Communications Manager cluster that you want to manage by clicking its name.

Note If more than one Communications Manager cluster displays, make certain that you select the correct one. If configured properly, the name assigned to each cluster enables you to determine which one you want to access. If the name does not help you identify the cluster, you need to identify it by the IP address.

Step 4. A screen similar to Figure 7-13 displays. There are four tabs along the upper right portion of the screen labeled Servers, MWI, Ports, and Advanced.

Step 5. Click the **Servers** tab to make certain that the server parameters are brought to the front. From this screen, you can change the display name of the cluster, the voicemail port device name prefix, and the cluster security mode. To change any of these settings, simply enter the desired value. If you want to change the IP address in the CM, TCP port, or TLS number, highlight the address of the server that you want to change and click the **Modify** button. Enter the new information and click OK.

Step 6. Click the **MWI** tab to change the MWI values.

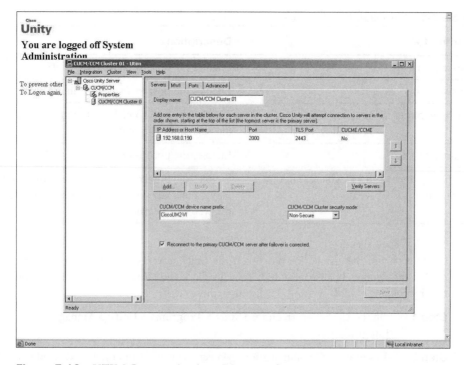

Figure 7-13   *UTIM Communications Manager Screen*

Step 7.   To change the functions that each voicemail port is allowed to perform, click the **Ports** tab and set each port. You can refer to Table 7-1 for an explanation of each function.

Step 8.   If you need to change the starting RTP port number, select the **Advanced** tab and set a starting number. Leave this value at the default.

Step 9.   After you have changed all the values you want, click **Save**. When you save, you are prompted to restart Unity. Restarting Unity causes active calls to drop, so it is best to do this after hours. A restart is required for the changes to take effect.

Step 10.   You can close the UTIM by clicking the **X** in the upper-right corner.

After you have verified that the information is correct, Communications Manager and Unity should be able to communicate. The simplest way to check this is to dial the DN assigned to the first voicemail port. If you are dialing from a subscriber's phone, you should be asked to enter a password; otherwise, you should hear the opening greeting.

SIP Integration

Since the release of Unity 4.0, SIP integration has been supported. SIP is an open standard protocol that is used for call setup. SIP provides the same function in a SIP integration as Skinny Client Control Protocol (SCCP) does in a Communications Manager integration. The configuration required on the SIP proxy server is outside the scope of this book. The next section describes the general configuration steps required on the SIP proxy server. For more detailed information refer to "Cisco SIP Integration Guide for Unity," which can be found at Cisco.com. Currently Unity is supported with SIP when using a Cisco SIP proxy server. The configuration steps that follow are based upon the assumption that the Cisco SIP proxy server is being used.

SIP Configuration

If you are integrating with a SIP solution, it is assumed that you have a solid understanding of SIP components and how the protocol works. With this understanding in mind, now look at an overview of the steps required on the SIP server side.

Of course, before you can integrate Unity into a SIP solution, you must have a fully installed and functioning SIP solution. This includes the installation and setup of a Cisco SIP proxy server.

After the server is installed, the phones need to be configured so that calls are forwarded to the Unity system when the called party is on the phone or does not answer. You will set up the phone to forward to the SIP address of the Unity system. The format of this address is the same as all SIP addresses: host@server. The host portion of the address will be the line number used for Unity.

On the SIP gateway, you need to configure an application session. This is accomplished by configuring a VoIP dial-peer using the **application session** command.

On the SIP gateway, it is required that you disable the SIP media inactivity timer. This is done by issuing the following command at the gateway configuration prompt:

```
no timer receive-rtcp
```

Finally, you need to configure a VoIP dial peer on the gateway that enables a dual-tone multifrequency (DTMF) relay. The commands to employ this are issued at the start of the configuration prompt and are as follows:

```
Dial-peer voice <dial peer number> voip
Session target ipv4:<ip_address)
Session protocol sipv2Dtmf-relay rtp-ntme
```

After you have made certain that all the SIP server configuration tasks are completed, you need to configure the Unity portion of the integration.

Table 7-2   *Voicemail Port Settings*

Parameter	Description
Enabled	Enables the port to be used by Unity
Answer Calls	Enables the port to answer incoming calls
Message Notification	Enables the port to make outgoing calls for message notification purposes
TRAP Connection	Enables the port to be used for recording and playing messages when a subscriber is using the web or an email client

Unity Telephony Integration Manager (SIP)

Just as with Communications Manager integration, UTIM is used to configure the integration parameters for a SIP integration. Before you run UTIM, you need to make sure that you have the information that will be entered in UTIM. The following checklist provides the information necessary before applying UTIM:

✓ **Integration Name:** This name is used to identify the integration. If this name is changed, make sure that you use a name that makes it easy to identify the integration.

✓ **Cluster Name:** This name is used for reference only. Choose a name that helps to easily identify the server. This is also referred to as the Display Name.

✓ **IP Addresses:** Unity needs to know the IP addresses of both the primary and secondary SIP proxy server with which it will be communicating.

✓ **Number of Ports:** These are the number of ports that will be used between the SIP server and Unity. This can be the same number of ports for which the system is licensed, unless you are using Unity in a dual-switch integration environment.

✓ **Contact Line Number:** This is the number that is associated with Unity. Unity registers this name with the SIP proxy server.

✓ **Unity Port:** This is the TCP port number that Unity uses to connect to the SIP server. Leave it at the default. Only change this number if you know that a different port is being used for SIP in your environment.

✓ **Preferred Codec:** This is the codec that Unity first tries to use when placing outgoing calls.

✓ **Authentication Name and Password:** If SIP proxy authentication is being used, this is the username and password that Unity uses.

✓ **Port Settings:** The voicemail ports can be set to perform multiple functions. Before you installed Unity, you should have decided what functions were being handled by each port. The functions are as listed in Table 7-2.

✓ **Trunk Access Codes:** Additional digits must be dialed when transferring a call to another PBX.

Note   If licensing for AMIS networking is purchased for this system, an additional parameter of AMIS Delivery can be listed. This enables the port to send and receive AMIS messages. AMIS is discussed in more detail in Chapter 10.

When you have all the information available, you can configure the SIP parameters for an existing integration or create a new integration using UTIM.

To add a new SIP integration, follow these steps:

Step 1. On the Unity Server, choose **Start > Programs > Unity > Manage Integrations**.

Step 2. From the UTIM interface, select **Integration > New**.

Step 3. The Welcome to the Telephony Integration Setup Wizard window displays. Select **SIP** as the phone system type. Click **Next**.

Step 4. On the following screen, enter an integration name and a cluster name. The integration name should be something that helps you easily identify which phone system goes with this integration. The cluster name helps identify the specific SIP server in this integration. The cluster name appears as the display name when modifying this integration. After you have entered this information, click **Next**.

Step 5. On the next screen, enter the IP addresses for the primary and secondary SIP proxy server, and the port that will be used. Click **Next**.

Step 6. The next screen requests the number of ports that you want to configure for this integration. If you are integrating only with a single SIP system, you should enter the total number of ports you have purchased. If you are integrating with multiple PBX systems, enter only the number of ports that you have decided to give to the SIP portion of the integration. Click **Next**.

Step 7. The following screen enables you to enter the Contact Line Name, Unity SIP Port, Preferred Codec, and Preferred Transport Protocol. After entering this information, click **Next**.

Step 8. On the next screen, you must enter the username and password for SIP authentication, if you are using it. If you are not applying authentication, deselect the check box and click **Next**.

Step 9. If you have other integrations, the following screen requests the access code to be used to send calls to the other systems. Click **Next** after entering this information.

Step 10. The next screen allows you to reassign subscribers to this integration. If you want to reassign subscribers to this integration, select the desired subscribers and click **Next**.

Step 11. The following screen allows you to reassign all handlers to this integration. If you want to reassign call handlers to this integration, select the desired call handlers and click **Next**.

Step 12. The final screen shows a summary of what you have chosen. Click **Finish** to complete the configuration.

Step 13. You are now prompted to allow Unity to restart. Restarting Unity causes active calls to drop, so it is best done after hours. A restart is required for the changes to take effect.

To change an existing integration, follow these steps:

Step 1.   On the Unity Server, choose **Start > Programs > Unity > Manage Integrations**.

Step 2.   From the UTIM window, click the SIP integration that will display in the left column to show the SIP clusters.

Step 3.   Click the name of the SIP cluster that you want to manage.

Step 4.   A screen similar to that shown in Figure 7-14 displays. Notice that there are four tabs along the upper portion of the screen: Servers, SIP Info, Ports, and Advanced.

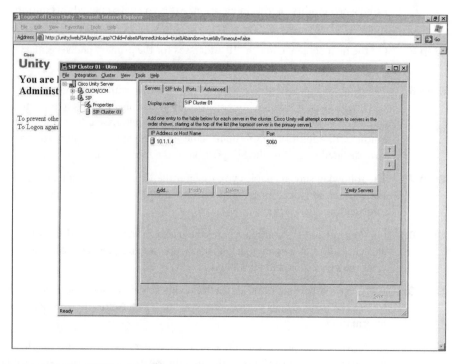

Figure 7-14   *UTIM SIP Screen*

Step 5.   Click the **Servers** tab to make certain that the server parameters are brought to the front. From this screen, you can change the display name of the cluster. To change the IP address or TCP port number, highlight the address of the server that you want to change and click the **Modify** button. Enter the new information and click **OK**.

Step 6.   You can change the Contact Line Name, SIP Port, Preferred Codec, and Preferred Transport Protocol by clicking the SIP Info tabs and changing the values. You can also change the SIP authentication settings from this screen.

Step 7. To change the functions that each voicemail port is allowed to perform, click the **Ports** tab, and set each port as you desire. You can refer to Table 7-2 for an explanation of each function.

Step 8. The **Advanced** tab enables you to change RTP, DTMF timing, and disconnect tone trim. It is recommended that these be left at the default.

Step 9. After all changes are made, click the **Save** button. After changes are saved, you are prompted to restart Unity, which will cause active calls to drop. It is best if this is done after hours. A restart is required for the changes to take effect.

Step 10. You can close the UTIM by clicking the **X** in the upper-right corner.

After you have verified that the information is correct, Unity should be able to communicate within the SIP environments. The simplest way to check this is to dial the DN assigned to the voicemail port. If you are dialing from a subscriber's phone, you should be asked to enter a password; otherwise, you should hear the opening greeting.

PIMG/TIMG Integration

In the past, voice boards were used to integrate with traditional PBXs. Since the release of Unity 8.0, voice boards are no longer supported. To integrate with many traditional PBXs, a PBX IP Media Gateway (PIMG) or T1 IP Media Gateway (TIMG) device must be used. These devices have analog or digital ports (depending on the PBX they are connecting to) and an Ethernet port. The analog or digital port is used to connect to the PBX. The device converts the signal from the PBX to SIP and sends the SIP signal out the Ethernet port to the Unity server.

PIMG/TIMG Configuration

The PIMG/TIMG integration is similar to the Communications Manager and SIP integrations. In some ways, it is even a little simpler.

Unity Telephony Integration Manager (PIMG/TIMG)

Just as with a Communications Manager and SIP integration, UTIM is used to configure the integration parameters for PIMG/TIMG integration. Before you run UTIM, you need to make sure that you have the information that will be entered in UTIM. The following checklist provides the information necessary before applying UTIM:

✓ **Integration Name:** This name is used to identify the integration. If this name is changed, make sure that you use a name that makes it easy to identify the integration.

✓ **PIMG type:** You must select the model of PIMG that you are using from the drop-down list.

✓ **SIP Port:** This is the SIP TCP port number of the PIMG unit. It should always be 5060.

✓ **Number of Phone Lines:** These are the number of ports that will be used between the PIMG and PBX. This can be the same number of ports for which the system is licensed, unless you are using Unity in a dual-switch integration environment.

✓ **Contact Line Name:** This is the number (name) that is used to contact Unity. It is also the name that will be registered to the PIMG device.

✓ **Display Name:** This name is used for reference only. Choose a name that helps to easily identify the server.

✓ **IP Addresses:** Unity needs to know the IP address of the PIMG device.

✓ **Unity SIP Port:** This is the TCP port number on the Unity server. Leave it at the default. Only change this number if you know that a different port is being used for SIP in your environment.

✓ **Preferred Codec:** This is the codec that Unity first tries to use when placing outgoing calls.

✓ **Trunk Access Codes:** Additional digits must be dialed when transferring a call to another PBX.

When you have all the information available, you can configure the SIP parameters for an existing integration or create a new integration using UTIM.

To add a new SIP integration, follow these steps:

Step 1.   On the Unity Server, choose **Start > Programs > Unity > Manage Integrations.**

Step 2.   From the UTIM interface, select **Integration > New.**

Step 3.   The Welcome to the Telephony Integration Setup Wizard window displays. Select **Circuit-Switched via PIMG (including TIMG)** as the phone system type. Click **Next.**

Step 4.   On the following screen, enter an integration name. The integration name should be something that helps you easily identify which phone system goes with this integration. Click **Next.**

Step 5.   On the next screen, click **Next** and enter the display name, PIMG type, IP address of the PIMG device, SIP port, and the number of phone lines connected. After this information is entered, click **OK.**

Step 6.   The following screen shows a summary of the information that you just entered. Click **Next.**

Step 7.   If Simplified Message Desk Interface (SMDI) will be employed for this integration, select **Yes.** This PIMG unit is the serial master. If you are not using SMDI, click **Next.**

Step 8.   The following screen allows you to enter the Contact Line Name, Unity SIP Port, and Preferred Codec. After entering this information, click **Next.**

Step 9.   If you have other integrations, the following screen requests the necessary access code to send calls to the other systems. Click **Next** after entering this information.

Step 10. The next screen allows you to reassign subscribers to this integration. If you want to do so, select the desired subscribers and click **Next.**

Step 11. The following screen allows you to reassign all handlers to this integration. If you want to do so, select the desired call handlers and click **Next.**

Step 12. The final screen shows a summary of what you have chosen. Click **Finish** to complete the configuration.

Step 13.   You are now prompted to allow Unity to restart. Restarting Unity causes active calls to drop, so it is best done after hours. A restart is required for the changes to take effect.

To change an existing integration, follow these steps:

Step 1.   On the Unity Server, choose **Start > Programs > Unity > Manage Integrations.**

Step 2.   From the UTIM window, click the PIMG integration that will display in the left column.

Step 3.   Click the name of the PIMG that you want to manage.

Step 4.   Notice that there are four tabs along the upper portion of the screen that appear: PIMG, SIP Info, Ports, and Advanced.

Step 5.   Click the **PIMG** tab to make certain that the PIMG parameters are brought to the front. From this screen, you can change the display name, the PIMG type, the IP address, and the SIP port number used. To change any of these settings, simply enter the desired value.

Step 6.   You can change the Contact Line Name, Unity SIP Port, and Preferred Codec by clicking the **SIP Info** tab and changing the values.

Step 7.   To change the functions that each voicemail port is allowed to perform, click the **Ports** tab and set each port as you desire. You can refer to Table 7-2 for an explanation of each function.

Step 8.   The **Advanced** tab allows you to change RTP, DTMF timing, and disconnect tone trim. It is recommended that these be left at the default.

Step 9.   After all changes are made, click the **Save** button. After changes are saved, you are prompted to restart Unity, which will cause active calls to drop. It is best if this is done after hours. A restart is required for the changes to take effect.

Step 10.   You can close the UTIM by clicking the **X** in the upper-right corner.

After you have verified that the information is correct, Unity should be able to communicate with the PIMG device. The simplest way to check this is to dial the DN assigned to the voicemail port. If you are dialing from a subscriber's phone, you should be asked to enter a password; otherwise, you should hear the opening greeting.

Defining Unity System Configuration

Although it is possible to begin adding users now, you should first make sure that the system settings are appropriate for your environment. Many technicians are often tempted to accept system defaults and assume that they can go back and fix them later. In most cases, you can go back and change any setting you need, but it is more efficient and less time consuming if you had set things up properly at the beginning.

Note   I once had a student who had a configuration issue that could have been avoided if the integrator had spent 2 minutes changing a few parameters before adding users. The integrator was not familiar with the system and assumed that, if necessary, the parameters could be changed later. To compound matters, the integrator then told the student how to fix the problem but not the easy way. The problem could have been fixed in about 5 minutes but instead took 3 days. The integrator was not invited to bid on any more projects. The old saying applies to such situations: An ounce of prevention is worth a pound of cure. The issue in this case was that the template used was not configured to have the user's phone ring when someone dialed the extension from within the auto-attendant.

The following sections cover topics associated with system settings, such as schedules, languages, recording, and port settings. Because these settings affect all subscribers on the system, they can be thought of as global settings. If you log on to SA, you see the settings that are listed under the System heading in the navigation panel on the left side of the screen. The topics covered in these sections include configuration, schedules, holidays, authentication, and ports. You might notice that licensing and integration also display under the System heading in SA. However, these are informational only and not configurable from the SA. They are not covered in the section.

Note   In some more recent versions of Unity, Short Message Peer-to-Peer (SMPP) support was added. This feature enables you to send message notifications to Short Message Service (SMS) devices, such as cell phones. More details on this feature can be found by searching "Setting Up Client SMS Applications" at Cisco.com.

Creating Schedules and Holidays

Just because something is first in a list doesn't mean it is the first thing you do. You have probably noticed that we have started the configuration process on the last five major headings in the navigation panel. The navigation menu was designed more for ease of use than as an ordered list of tasks. So, just as we did not begin at the first major area, we are not going to begin at the first area under System. Because you define a default schedule in the Configuration area, it would only make sense to have the schedules defined first. After defining schedules, adding holidays is discussed.

Schedules are assigned to subscribers, and call handlers and are used to define what hours Unity should consider opened and closed. Unity has the capability to play up to five different greetings. Two of these greetings depend on the schedule. The Standard greeting plays during open hours, and the Closed greeting plays during closed hours.

A default schedule is defined and is assigned to all subscribers and call handlers when they are created. After an object is created, you can assign a different schedule to it. A total of 64 schedules can be defined.

Schedules are configured at the **System > Schedules** level of SA. Step-by-step instructions on how to perform the following schedule-related tasks are as follows:

- Viewing/changing an existing schedule

- Adding a new schedule

- Selecting a default schedule

- Deleting a schedule

View and Change a Schedule

To view and change existing schedules, use the steps that follow:

Step 1.   From within SA, select **System > Schedules**.

Step 2.   From the title strip, select the **Find** icon (magnifying glass). A list of schedules displays.

Step 3.   Highlight the desired schedule and click **View**.

Note   The main part of the schedule screen is a grid that represents the seven days of the week, divided into half-hour increments. Check marks indicate the open hours.

Step 4.   To modify the schedules, place check marks on the half hours that you want to be considered open. Remove the check marks from times to be considered closed.

Note   You can copy the open and closed hours of one day to another day, and to all weekdays and weekends by using the Copy Day's Schedule function at the bottom of the screen. Select the source day from the first drop-down list and the destination day(s) from the second drop-down list; then click Copy Day's Schedule.

Step 5.   At the top of the screen, there is a check box labeled **Observe Holidays**. If this box is selected, this schedule is treated as if all hours are closed on holidays that are created in Unity.

Step 6.   After all changes are made, click the **Save** icon in the title strip. The changes do not take effect until you have saved them.

Add a Schedule

To add a new schedule, similar steps are performed. The following are the required steps:

Step 1.   From within SA, select **System > Schedules**.

Step 2.   From the title strip, select the **Add** icon (blue plus sign). An **Add a Schedule** window displays.

Step 3.   Enter the name of the new schedule. You can choose to base the new schedule on an existing one. Doing this causes the new schedule to have the same open and closed hours as an existing one. Choose whether the new schedule should be based on an existing one or not and click the **Add** button.

Step 4.   The new schedule displays.

Note   The main part of the schedule screen is a grid that represents the seven days of the week, divided into half-hour increments. Check marks indicate the open hours.

To modify the schedules, place check marks on the half hours that you want to be considered open. Remove the check marks if you want that time to be considered closed.

Note   You can copy the open and closed hours of one day to another day, all weekdays, or weekends by using the Copy Day's Schedule function at the bottom of the screen. Select the source day from the first drop-down list and the destination day(s) from the second drop-down list; then click Copy Day's Schedule.

Step 5.   At the top of the screen, there is a check box labeled **Observe Holidays**. If this box is selected, this schedule is treated as if all hours are closed on holidays that are created in Unity.

Step 6.   After all changes are made, click the **Save** icon in the title strip. The changes do not take effect until you have saved them.

Define a Default Schedule

The default system schedule that is selected during installation is the Weekdays schedule. The default schedule is changed at the **System > Configuration > Settings** level of SA. All the settings at this level are discussed in the next section. This section deals only with the default schedule portion of this level. To change the default schedule, follow these steps:

Step 1.   From within SA, select **System > Configuration> Settings**.

Step 2.   The first field on this screen is **Default Schedule**. Select the schedule from the drop-down list.

Step 3.   Click the **Save** icon.

To remove a schedule from Unity, follow these steps:

Step 1.   From within SA select, **System > Schedules.**

Step 2.   From the title strip, click the **Find** icon (magnifying glass). A list of schedules displays.

Step 3.   Highlight the desired schedule, and click **View.**

Step 4.   The selected schedule displays on the screen. Click the delete icon (red **X**) from the title strip.

Step 5.   You are prompted to determine to which schedule you want to reassign all objects that are currently using this schedule. Select a schedule from the drop-down list and click **Delete.**

Now that you have the schedules defined, the next logical thing to configure is the holiday schedule. Holidays are configured so that Unity knows which days the company will be closed. Unity plays the closed greeting the entire day on holidays.

Add a Holiday

To add holidays, follow these steps:

Step 1.   From within SA, select **System > Holidays.**

Step 2.   The current list of holidays displays on the screen.

Step 3.   To add a new holiday, click the **Add** icon (the plus sign).

Step 4.   An **Add a Holiday** window displays. Select the date from the drop-down list and click **Add.**

Step 5.   Repeat Steps 3 and 4 for each holiday that you want to add.

Note   Keep in mind that you do not have to save these additions. Saving is required only when an object is changed. When an object is added, it is immediately written.

You have the option of copying holidays that were defined for one year to another year. This can be a great timesaver, but you need to make sure that the holidays you are copying are on the same date in the year to which you are copying them. To copy holidays from one year to another, simply click the appropriately labeled button. This causes all the holidays from the earlier year to be copied. Remember to remove or change any incorrect dates.

Modify or Delete a Holiday

To change or delete a holiday, follow these steps:

Step 1.   From within SA, select **System > Holidays.**

Step 2.   The current list of holidays displays.

Step 3.   Click the holiday that you want to change or delete. The fields in the **Edit Holiday For** field should now show the date you selected.

Step 4.   To change the holiday's date, edit the fields in the **Edit Holiday For** area and click the **Save** icon.

Step 5.   To delete this holiday, click the **Delete** icon. You are prompted to confirm the deletion. Click **OK.**

Now that you have all the schedules and holidays configured, system settings should be completed. The next section discusses a number of global system settings that should be defined before the system is put into production.

Defining Configuration Settings

Configuration settings are general Unity settings that define schedules, security, languages, and a number of other things. All of these settings will be configured using the SA interface. This section is divided into subsections so that you can easily follow the settings shown here in the order in which they are presented in SA. If you go to the **System > Configuration** level in SA, you see the eight selections that will be discussed in this section. Table 7-3 lists these topics and provides a brief description of each.

All the settings discussed throughout this section are configured under the **System > Configuration** level of the Unity Administrator pages.

Settings

The first configuration level under **System > Configuration** is Settings. From this level, you configure items that deal with general settings within Unity. The following steps walk you through the Settings screen. Figure 7-15 shows the screen that contains most of the fields that will be discussed in these steps.

Step 1.   From within SA, select **System > Configuration > Settings.**

Step 2.   Select the schedule that you want to use as the default schedule from the drop-down list.

Step 3.   If you want time to be expressed in 24-hour format (1900 hours instead of 7:00 p.m.), select the **Use 24-Hour Time Format for Conversations and Schedules** check box.

Step 4.   Next there is a box labeled **Enable Spelled Name Search.** Typically you want other subscribers to spell by name, so this box should be selected. If you want to allow them to dial only by extension, deselect this box.

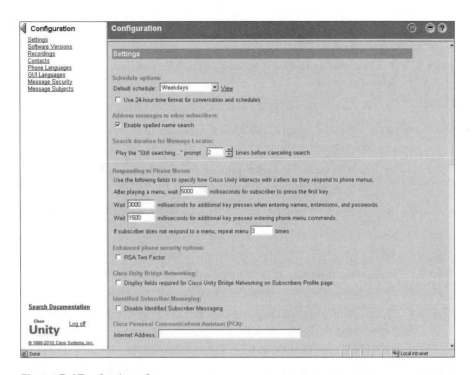

Figure 7-15 *Settings Screen*

Table 7-3 *SA Configuration Settings Selections*

Topic	Description
Settings	General settings such as schedules, log files, and RSA settings
Software Versions	List of the version number of each Unity process
Recordings	Time limits for silence and clip length
Contacts	Name and number of those responsible for the system
Phone Languages	Phones languages that are available and loaded
GUI Languages	Languages available and loaded for the Unity Administrator pages
Message Security	Determines whether messages will be encrypted
Message Subjects	Defines the formatting for message subject heading

Step 5.   In the **Message Locator** field, enter the number of times you want the "still searching" prompt to play when the user is using message locator.

Step 6.   The **Responding to Phone Menus** fields define how long Unity waits for the following actions:

- Milliseconds that Unity waits for the user to enter the first digit

- Milliseconds that Unity waits for the user to enter additional digits when entering names or extensions

- Milliseconds that Unity waits for the user to enter additional digits when entering phone menu commands

- The number of times that Unity replays the menu if the user does not respond

Enter the desired values if each field.

Step 7.   If you have implemented an RSA server for use with Unity, select the **RSA Two Factor** check box. Typically this check box is deselected.

Step 8.   The check box labeled **Display Fields Required for Cisco Unity Bridge Networking on Subscribers Profile Page** is only used if you are using a bridge server to integrate with an Octel system. Typically this box is left deselected.

Step 9.   If you want messages that are left by a subscriber to include the subscriber's name or ID, leave the **Disable Identified Subscriber Messaging** check box selected. If this box is selected, the subscriber leaving the message will have to log in to be identified.

Step 10.   Enter the URL used to access the Cisco Personal Communications Assistant (CPCA) pages in the Internet Address field. Unity includes this address in an email message notification. If CPCA is not being used, leave this field blank.

Step 11.   Set the number of days that you want to keep log files in the **Cleanup Interval Portion of the Files Cleanup** field for each type of log.

The Settings screen contains four more areas. Three of these areas are not configurable and are used to initiate replication or to view information. The last area enables you to configure substitute objects. Figure 7-16 shows these areas.

The first area is titled Replicate Cisco Unity Directory Objects. You can force a replication between AD and Unity to occur from here. When you click the Changed Objects or the All Objects button, Unity replicates with AD immediately. The button that you select determines whether you want to force a complete replication or only look for changed objects. This action should be performed only during off hours.

The next area is titled Cisco Unity Computer Settings. This area displays the computer name of the Unity server and the domain to which it belongs.

The third area on this screen is titled Disk Usage. This area displays the number and size of the logical hard drives in the Unity server.

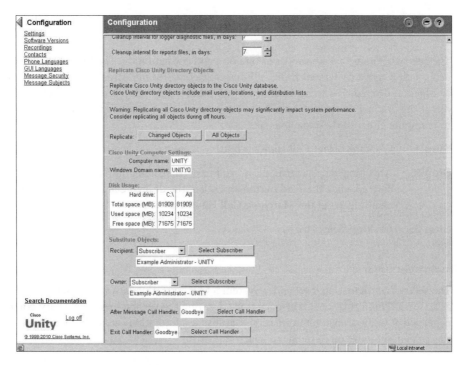

Figure 7-16 *Settings Screen (Cont'd)*

The final area is titled Substitute Objects and contains four configurable parameters: Recipient, Owner, After Message Call Handler, and Exit Call Handler.

The Recipient parameter is used to define where messages should be delivered when they are left to a call handler or interview handler whose original recipient has been deleted. The Owner parameter is used to define which subscriber or public distribution list will become the owner of an object if the object's current owner is deleted.

The Recipient and Owner parameters are configured in the same way, so the following steps show how to configure either:

Step 1.   Select either **Subscriber** or **Public Distribution List** from the **Recipient** drop-down list.

Step 2.   The button next to this field is labeled either **Select Subscriber** or **Select Distribution List** based on whether **Subscriber** or **Public Distribution List** was selected. Click this button.

Step 3.   If you are choosing a subscriber, a window displays that allows you to enter search criteria. After they are entered, click the **Find** button and select the desired subscriber from the results listed in the **Matching Subscribers** box. If you are choosing a public distribution list, a window displays containing the lists. Select the desired public distribution list.

Step 4.   After you have selected the subscriber or distribution list, click the **Select** button.

The last two parameters are similar in function and configuration. The first of the two deals with where a call is sent if the subscriber selected for the After Message Action of an object is deleted. The second defines where a call is sent when it exits a directory handler if the original destination object has been deleted. The following steps can be used to configure either of these parameters:

Step 1.   Click the **Select Call Handler** button.

Step 2.   A window displays that allows you to enter search criteria. After they are entered, click the **Find** button and select the desired call handler from the results listed in the **Matching Call Handlers** box.

Step 3.   Click the **Select** button.

Software Versions

The second configuration level under **System > Configuration** is Software Settings. This area is strictly informational. The page is used to find the version of several Unity components and Windows version information. Because configuration cannot be performed on this screen, we move on to the next area.

Recordings

The third configuration level under **System > Configuration** is Recordings. The Recordings page deals with time limits for silence and clip length settings. Figure 7-17 shows this screen and all its settings.

To set these configurations, follow these steps:

Step 1.   From within SA select, **System > Configuration > Recordings**.

Step 2.   Select the amount of time you want to have clipped off the end of a recording when the octothorpe (#) is pressed in the field labeled **Allowed Time for Recording, in Milliseconds**. This is performed so that the tone produced when the octothorpe (#) is pressed is not included in the messages. This value normally does not need to be changed unless the tone is being heard in messages or the ends of messages are being clipped off.

Note   The octothorpe is referred to by different names in different countries. For example, it is called the pound sign in the United States and the hash in England.

Note   The next value, labeled **Allowed Time for Short Recording, in Seconds**, cannot be changed. This value determines the permitted length of a message before Unity considers it a long message. This is statically set to 10. In Step 5, you see how the value is used.

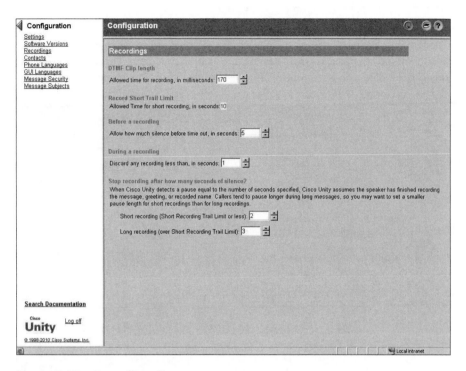

Figure 7-17 *Recordings Screen*

Step 3. Determine how long Unity will wait for someone to start talking by entering a value in the box labeled **Allow How Much Silence Before Time Out, in Seconds.** If the caller leaving a message does not begin talking within the amount of time set here, Unity assumes that the caller is not going to leave a message.

Step 4. The field labeled **Discard Any Recording Less Than, in Seconds** is used to prevent Unity from recording hang-ups. Typically, a value of 1 is sufficient for this field. Enter the desired value.

Step 5. The last two fields on this page determine how many seconds of silence Unity allows in a message. Two different values are set here. The first one, labeled **Short Recording,** is the value used during the first ten seconds of the message. As discussed in the note following Step 2, a short recording is defined as 10. The second value, labeled **Long Recording,** is used when the message that is being recorded is longer than 10 seconds. Typically, these values can be left at the default.

Step 6. Click the **Save** icon at the top of the page.

Contacts

The fourth configuration level under **System** > **Configuration** is Contacts. In the Contacts area, administration and support contact information is entered. This information helps others determine who is responsible for the system. Figure 7-18 shows this screen.

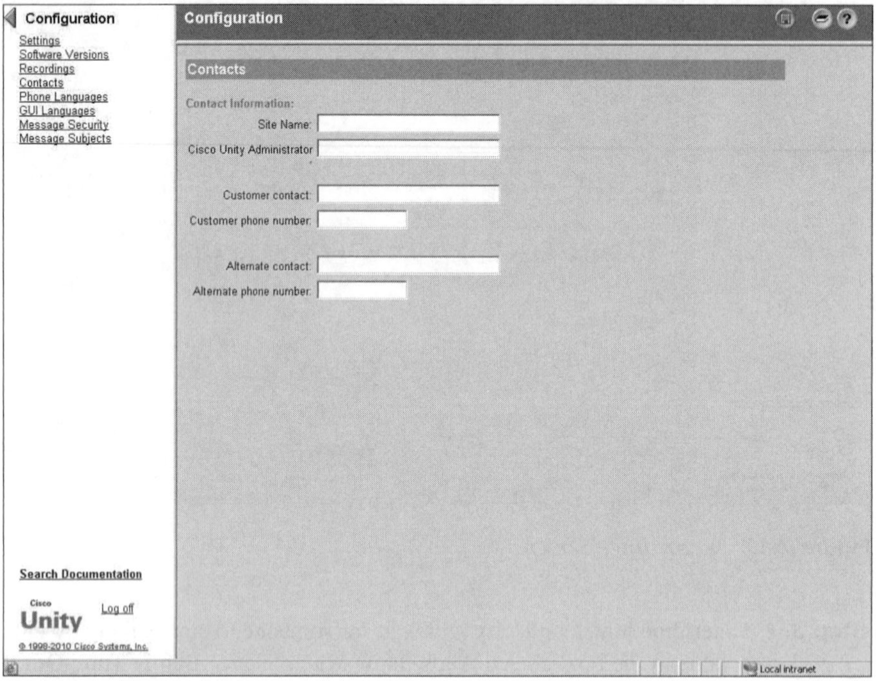

Figure 7-18 *Contacts Screen*

To enter this information, go to **System** > **Configuration** > **Contacts** in SA and enter the appropriate names and numbers. When you are finished, click the **Save** icon.

Phone Languages

The fifth configuration level under **System** > **Configuration** is Phone Languages. This is where you determine the phone languages that will be active on the Unity system. The phone language is the language that the Unity system employs when talking to a caller. One of the languages loaded must match the Windows operating system locale that was selected during the Windows install. Figure 7-19 shows this screen.

To configure the Phone Language settings, follow these steps:

Step 1. From within SA, select **System** > **Configuration** > **Phone Languages**.

Step 2. The number of languages for which the system is licensed, and the number loaded, display at the top of the page under the heading **License Counts**. If the system is licensed for more than one language, add any of the languages listed in the field labeled **Available**. Highlight the desired language and click the **->** arrow. The language should now display in the loaded field.

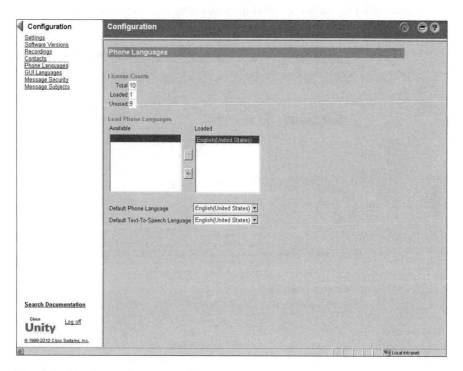

Figure 7-19 *Phone Languages Screen*

Note Only languages that were chosen during the installation display are available. To add languages that do not display in the list, you must run the Cisco Unity Installation and Configuration Assistant (CUICA). Because running CUICA causes some downtime, it should be run during a planned off-hours period.

Step 3. From the drop-down list labeled **Default Phone Language**, select the language that you want Unity to employ by default for all objects.

Step 4. From the drop-down list labeled **Default Text-To-Speech Language**, select the language that you want Unity to use by default when reading emails to subscribers over the phone.

GUI Languages

The sixth configuration level under **System > Configuration is GUI Languages.** This is the language in which the SA will be displayed. Figure 7-20 shows this screen.

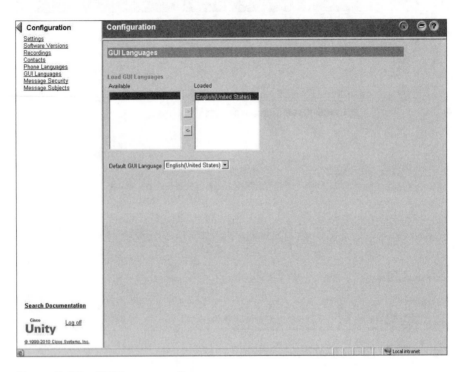

Figure 7-20 *GUI Languages Screen*

To access this configuration screen, go to **System > Configuration > GUI Languages** from within SA. You can move any language that displays in the **Available** list over to the **Loaded** list by highlighting the desired language and clicking the -> arrow.

Message Security

The next setting is Message Security. Here you can define whether messages should be encrypted. You have the choice to encrypt all messages, no messages, or only messages marked private. You can also enable message aging. If enabled, encrypted messages will automatically be unavailable after the specified time.

Message Subjects

The Message Subjects settings determine how the subject line of a message will appear. In most cases, these can be left at the default. However, you can change them if you desire.

Configuring Authentication Settings

Now examine the next area of the system, the authentication settings. This encompasses the authentication settings used when a subscriber logs in to CPCA. If you have chosen to employ anonymous authentication for SA, these settings apply to SA and Status Monitor logins as well. The configuration of these settings, which is outlined in the steps that follow, is fairly simple:

Step 1. From within SA, select **System > Authentication**.

Step 2. The screen shown in Figure 7-21 displays. The first configuration on this screen determines whether the users' logon names are stored on their local PC and, if so, the length of time stored. To have the logon name stored, select the **Remember Logons For** check box and enter the number of days that you want it to be stored in the box to the right of the label. If you do not want the logon name stored on the client, make sure that this box is deselected. For security reasons, it is recommended that you do not have the login names stored on the client.

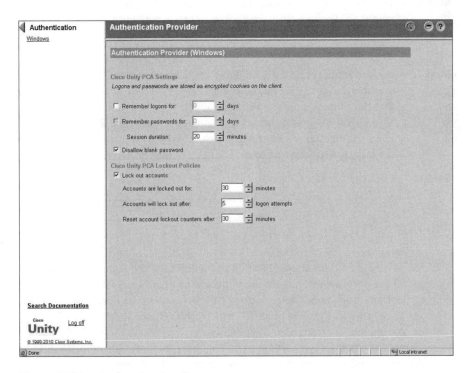

Figure 7-21 *Authentication Screen*

Step 3. If you chose to have the logon name stored, the next field will be available for configuration. This field determines whether the users' passwords are stored on their local PC and, if so, the length of time stored. To have the password stored, select the **Remember Passwords For** check box, and enter the number of days you want to have it stored in the box to the right of the label. If you do not want to have the password stored on the client, make sure that this box is deselected. For security reasons, it is recommended that you do not have the passwords stored on the client.

Step 4.   The **Session Duration** field allows you to set how long a subscriber remains logged in to the interface if no activity has taken place. In other words, if the session is idle for the amount of minutes entered in this field, the subscriber is automatically logged out. The default is 20 minutes, and in most cases, this should be adequate.

Step 5.   The third configuration field on this page determines whether blank passwords are allowed. To allow blank passwords, deselect the **Disallow Blank Password** check box. Select this box if you do not want to permit blank passwords. For security reasons, it is recommended that this field be checked so that blank passwords cannot be used.

Step 6.   The next check box is used to enable lockout polices. If you want to limit the number of times users can enter the incorrect password, this box should be selected. If this box is left deselected, users can enter incorrect passwords an unlimited number of times.

Step 7.   If lockout polices are enabled, limits must be set. Enter the number of minutes that a user will be locked out in the box labeled **Accounts Are Locked Out For**. Enter the number of times that users can enter incorrect passwords before they are locked out in the box labeled **Accounts Will Lock Out After**. Enter the number of minutes in which Unity will reset the login attempts in the box labeled **Reset Account Lockout Counters After**.

Step 8.   Click the **Save** icon.

Configuring Ports

Ports is the last area of system configuration in this section. As discussed previously, voicemail ports are used for communication between Unity and Communications Manager. These ports are created on Communications Manager. As shown earlier in this chapter, the Unity portion of configuration of these ports can be done using UTIM. However, these ports can also be modified from within SA. Regardless of how these ports are configured, the results are the same. Figure 7-22 shows the **System > Ports** screen. From this interface, you can properly configure the ports according to their desired purpose. Table 7-4 lists the functions a port can be configured to perform.

Note   If licensing for AMIS networking is purchased for this system, an additional parameter of AMIS Delivery can be listed. This allows the port to send and receive AMIS messages. AMIS is discussed in more detail in Chapter 10.

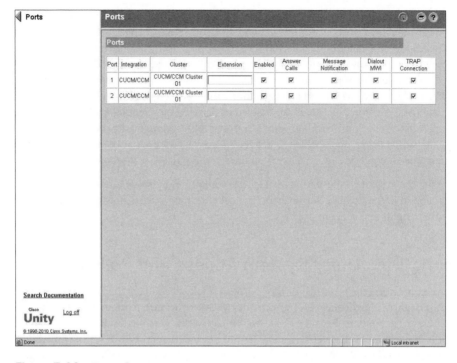

Figure 7-22 *Ports Screen*

Table 7-4 *Voicemail Port Settings*

Parameter	Description
Extension	Should contain the extension number that is configured in Communications Manager for this port
Enabled	Enables the port to be used by Unity
Answer Calls	Enables the port to answer incoming calls
Message Notification	Enables the port to make outgoing calls for message notification purposes
Dialout MWI	Enables the port to be used to send MWI notifications
TRAP Connection	Enables the port to be used for recording and playing messages when a subscriber is using the web or an email client

Before you start to configure the port, decide what functions are needed and which ports will provide these functions. While making these decisions, keep in mind that outbound calls are sent from the higher-numbered ports and incoming calls are answered on the lower-numbered ports. With this in mind, it makes sense to configure the higher-numbered ports for functions such as MWI and message notification. This leaves the lower-numbered ports available to answer incoming calls. It is recommended that approximately 75 percent of the ports should be configured to answer calls, whereas 25 percent should be configured for MWI and message notification. As you can see in Figure 7-22, other than the extensions, all values are enabled or disabled by selecting and deselecting the appropriate check box. To configure the ports, locate **System > Ports** in SA, enter the extension number, and enable the desired function(s) for each port. Although it is not required to configure the extension number in these fields, it is recommended.

After the system configuration settings are completed, there are a few more tasks to attend to before loading subscribers. The next sections discuss how to configure system access rights and account policies.

Configuring Unity System Access and Policies

Andrew Grove, the chairman of Intel, wrote a book called *Only the Paranoid Survive*. Although this might seem like an extreme title, there is much truth to it, especially when it comes to computers. Because Unity has the capability to access both voicemail and email, it is important to secure your system. Part of the securing process is setting up account polices and class of service (CoS). Account policies allow you to define parameters for subscribers' phone passwords. These parameters can prevent subscribers from using passwords that could easily be compromised. CoS defines the rights a subscriber has within the system, including the accessibility to Unity and the features they can use. Because these settings affect subscribers, it is best to configure them before adding subscribers.

Defining Account Polices

Account policies are basically about securing the subscribers' access to Unity. The link to Account Policy is located under the major heading of Subscribers. Two things are configured here: password restrictions and phone lockout policies.

We examine the configuration of password restrictions first. Password requirements are set here, including when a password expires, the required length of a password, and whether the password must be unique when changed. In Figure 7-23, you can see the settings for this screen.

To configure phone password restrictions, follow these steps:

Step 1.   From within SA, select **Subscribers > Account Policy > Phone Password Restrictions.**

Step 2.   Set the length of time for which passwords are valid. Click the **Days Until Password Expires** radio button and enter the number of days for which the password will be valid. This determines how often subscribers have to change their passwords. If you have decided to allow the users to never have to change their passwords, click the **Password Never Expires** radio button. It is recommended that you set passwords to expire.

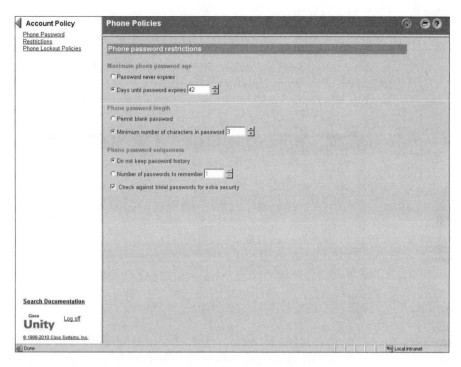

Figure 7-23   *Phone Password Restrictions Screen*

Step 3.   Click the labeled **Minimum Number of Characters in Password** radio button and enter the desired number in the corresponding field. If you want to permit blank passwords, click the **Permit Blank Password** radio button instead. It is recommended that a password be required and that it be at least eight digits.

Step 4.   Click the **Number of Passwords to Remember** radio button. In the corresponding field, enter the number of previously used passwords that you want Unity to keep in its history. The subscriber cannot use any previous password if it is still in Unity's history. If you do not want Unity to keep a history, click the **Do Not Keep Password History** radio button. This allows a subscriber to reuse the same password when the password expires. It is recommended that Unity keep at least three passwords in history.

Step 5.   The last thing to configure is whether Unity should check against trivial passwords. Any of the following are considered trivial passwords:

- Password with all the same digits

- Consecutive digits

- The subscriber's extension

Select the **Check Against Trivial Passwords for Extra Security** check box if you want this feature to be active. It is recommended that this be selected.

Step 6.   Click the **Save** icon.

The second area of configuration at this level is Phone Lockout Polices. These settings determine how many times a subscriber can enter the incorrect phone password before being locked out. The length of time a subscriber will be locked out of the account is also configured here. The steps that follow describe how to configure the settings that are shown in Figure 7-24:

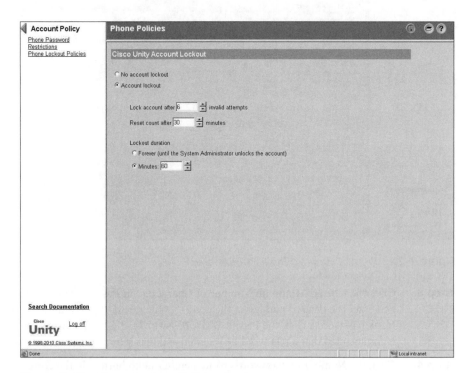

Figure 7-24   *Phone Lockout Policies Screen*

Step 1.   From within SA, select **Subscribers > Account Policy > Phone Lockout Polices.**

Step 2.   Check the **Account Lockout** radio button.

Step 3.   Enter the number of times that a subscriber can enter the incorrect password in the **Lock Account After (Field) Invalid Attempts** field. If the **No Account Lockout** radio button labeled is checked, the account never locks regardless of how many times invalid passwords are entered. For security reasons, it is recommended that the **Lock Account After (Field) Invalid Attempts** radio button be selected.

Step 4.   Enter the number of minutes Unity waits before resetting the attempts counter in the **Reset Count After (Field) Minutes** field.

Step 5.   The last thing to configure on this screen is how long the account will be locked out if a subscriber exceeds the maximum invalid attempts. If you want the account to be locked until a system administrator unlocks it, click the **Forever** radio button. You can also choose to have the account locked for a specified amount of time by clicking the **Minutes** radio button and entering the number of minutes in the corresponding field.

Step 6.   Click the **Save** Icon.

Now that account policies have been defined, CoS needs to be addressed.

Configuring Class of Service

Each subscriber in the system has an associated CoS that is basically a list of rights and restrictions. The CoS defines how subscribers are allowed to access the system and how they can use the system after they have accessed it. Because subscribers are assigned to a CoS when it is created, it is best to have all CoSs composed before adding users.

The CoS in Unity components fit into eight categories. Navigate to **Subscribers > Class of Service** in SA; the eight categories display as submenus under the Class of Service heading. Table 7-5 provides each submenu and a brief description of each of the categories.

Before you configure CoS, it is best to record how many CoSs you need and how each will be configured. Typically, there are at least two CoSs: one for administrators and one for basic users. Unity has two default CoSs, so if you need only two, you can simply edit the defaults.

It is a good idea to leave the Default Administrator CoS alone. This is the CoS that allows administrative access. If you need a limited-administrative-access CoS, it is best to create a new one.

The following tasks must be performed to add and edit a CoS. Each task is followed by step-by-step instructions.

Adding a CoS

Step 1.   From within SA, select **Subscribers > Class of Service > Profile**.

Step 2.   Click the **Add** icon (plus sign) in the title strip.

Step 3.   A window displays, as shown in Figure 7-25, prompting you for a CoS name. From this screen, you can also choose to create the new CoS based on an existing one. This is useful if you need a new CoS that is similar to an existing one. Enter a name and select the CoS that you want to use as a base, or select **New CoS**.

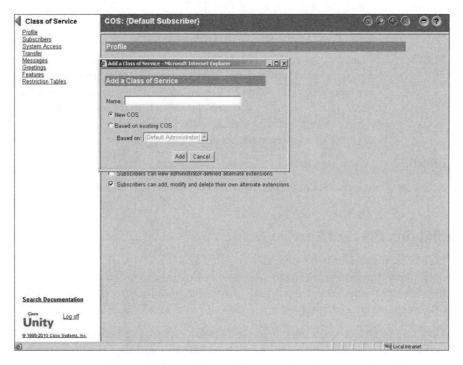

Figure 7-25   *Adding a CoS*

Step 4.   Click **Add** and the new CoS is added. You are not required to save it. The saving action is required only when an object is modified, not when it is created.

Modifying a CoS

Modifying a CoS might require the configuration of all eight CoS categories or perhaps only one. For this reason, we will examine the configuration of each of these categories separately. However, before you can modify a CoS, you must first find it.

Finding a CoS to Modify

To find the CoS that you want to modify, follow these steps:

Step 1.   From within SA, select **Subscribers > Class of Service > Profile**.

Step 2.   Click the **Find** icon. A list of CoSs displays.

Step 3.   Select the CoS that you want to modify and click **View**.

Modifying a CoS Profile

Now that the CoS has been found, the first configuration area is the CoS profile. The following steps are required to modify the profile of a CoS:

Step 1.   From within SA, select **Subscribers > Class of Service > Profile**.

Table 7-5   *CoS Components*

Category	Description
Profile	Defines the name of the CoS and subscriber's name setting and directory listing.
Subscribers	Enables assignment of subscribers to CoS.
System Access	Defines the level of administrative access for a subscriber.
Transfer	Specifies whether a subscriber can use Unity's holding and screening features.
Messages	Defines the message length and other message-related settings.
Greetings	Defines the greeting length.
Licensed Features	Defines which licensed features the sub scriber has.
Restriction Tables	Defines locations to which Unity can make calls on behalf of a subscriber. Restriction tables would be used, for example, for message notification.

Step 2.   As you can see in Figure 7-26, the first field is the name of the CoS. If you want to change it, enter the new name.

The next two settings determine whether a subscriber is allowed to add or modify alternate extensions. Alternate extensions are used to associate a phone number other than the subscriber's extension to a subscriber's mailbox. This is typically used to associate a subscriber's cell phone number to the mailbox. When subscribers call from their cell phones, they are prompted to log in.

Step 3.   To allow the subscriber to view alternate extensions that are defined by the administrator, select the **Subscribers Can View Administrator-Defined Alternate Extensions** radio button. To allow subscribers to add and manage their own alternate extensions, select the **Subscribers Can Add, Modify and Delete Their Own Alternate Extensions** radio button.

Step 4.   Click the **Save** icon.

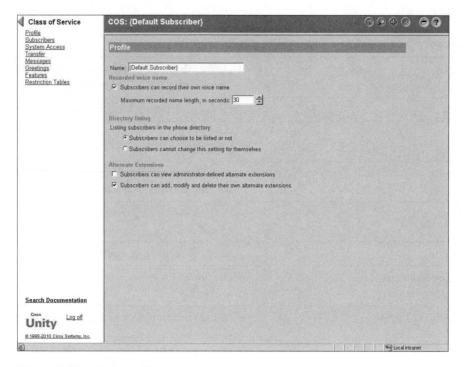

Figure 7-26   *CoS Profile*

Modifying CoS Subscribers

You can also modify which subscribers are assigned to a CoS. During the creation process, a subscriber is assigned to a CoS. The CoS that subscribers are assigned to is determined by the subscriber template that is used. If, for any reason, you need to move a subscriber to a different CoS, follow these steps:

Step 1.   From within SA, select **Subscribers > Class of Service > Subscribers**. The screen shown is Figure 7-27 displays.

Step 2.   As you can see, three actions can be performed. You can view the subscribers in this CoS, move (reassign) subscribers to a different CoS, or add (assign) subscribers to this CoS. Click the radio button associated with the action that you want to perform.

Step 3.   To view subscribers in this CoS, click the **View** radio button and click the **Find** button. You can enter search criteria in the field in front of **Find** to narrow your search. A list of subscribers that match the criteria is displayed.

Step 4.   To move a subscriber from the current CoS to another CoS, click the **Reassign** radio button. Figure 7-28 shows a screen that is slightly different than Figure 7-27. Enter search criteria in the field in front of the **Find** button and click **Find**. From the list that displays, select the subscriber who you want to move. Now, from the drop-down list next to the **Reassign** button, select the CoS to which you want to move him. Click **Reassign**.

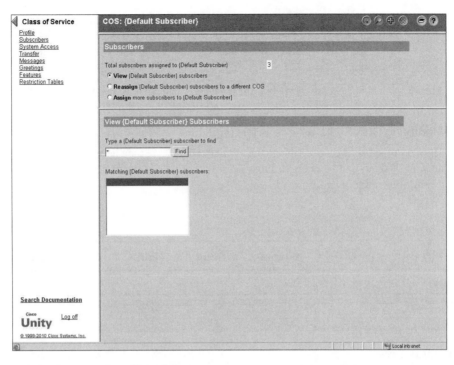

Figure 7-27   *CoS - Subscribers (View)*

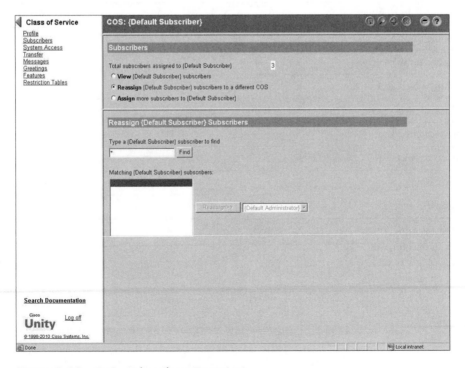

Figure 7-28   *CoS - Subscribers (Reassign)*

Step 5.   To move a subscriber to the current CoS, click the **Assign** radio button. Enter search criteria in the field in front of the **Find** button and click **Find**. From the list that displays, select the subscriber who you want to add. Click **Assign**.

Step 6.   It is not necessary to save these changes, as they are saved automatically.

Modifying CoS System Access Settings

The CoS of subscribers determines the administrative level they have on the system. A number of rights can be granted. Table 7-6 shows these rights and describes what access can be assigned to them.

Table 7-6   *CoS Subscriber Rights*

	Enable	Read	Edit	Add	Delete
UA access	X				
CoS access		X	X	X	X
Directory handlers access		X	X	X	X
Subscribers access		X	X	X	X
Unlock accounts	X				
Public distribution lists		X	X	X	X
Schedules/holidays	X				
Restriction tables access	X				
Routing tables access	X				
Call handlers access	X				
Status monitor access	X				
Reports access	X				
Network access	X				
Diagnostic access	X				
Technician functions access (configuration, licensing, ports, and switch pages)	X				

Figure 7-29 illustrates these fields as they display on the screen.

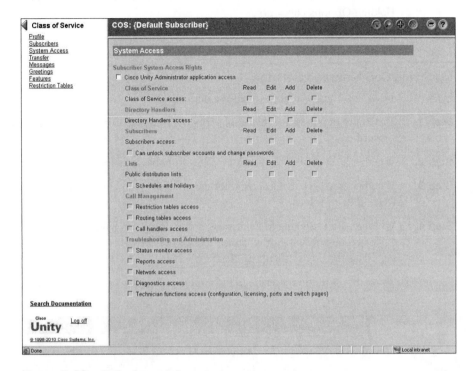

Figure 7-29   *CoS - System Access*

To assign system access rights to a CoS, follow these steps:

Step 1.   From within SA, select **Subscribers > Class of Service > System Access.**

Step 2.   Select the **Cisco Unity Administrator Application Access** check box.

Step 3.   Select the appropriate boxes to assign the rights that you want this CoS to have.

Step 4.   Click the **Save** icon.

Modifying CoS Transfer Settings

A CoS can define whether a subscriber can use the call-screening and -holding options. To configure these options, follow these steps:

Step 1.   From within SA, select **Subscribers > Class of Service > Transfer.**

Step 2.   To allow subscribers to determine whether Unity announces who is calling before they accept the call, select the **Subscribers Can Change Call Screening Options** check box.

Step 3.   To allow subscribers to configure Unity to place an incoming call on hold when they are already on the phone, select the **Subscribers Can Change Call Holding Options** check box.

Step 4.   Click the **Save** icon.

Modifying CoS Message Settings

In the CoS message setting area, four things are defined:

Step 1.   The length of a message that a subscriber with this CoS can leave for another subscriber.

Step 2.   Whether a subscriber can send messages to public distribution lists.

Step 3.   Whether messages that a subscriber deletes from the phone are moved to the Deleted Items folder.

Step 4.   Whether, after listening to a message, a subscriber can have Unity dial the extension number of another subscriber or outside caller who left the message. This feature is called Live Reply.

Figure 7-30 shows the configuration screen for these settings.

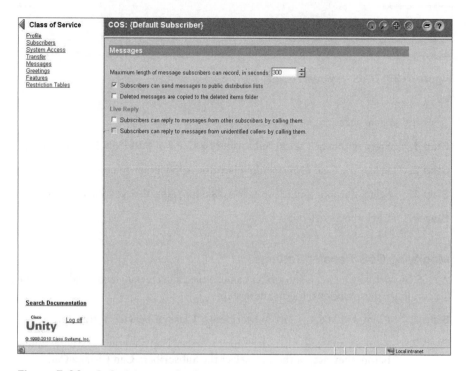

Figure 7-30   *CoS - Message Settings*

To configure these settings, follow these steps:

Step 1. From within SA, select **Subscribers > Class of Service > Messages.**

Step 2. In the **Maximum Length of Message Subscribers Can Record, in Seconds** field, enter the maximum length in seconds of a message from a subscriber with this class of service, to another subscriber.

Step 3. Select the **Subscribers Can Send Messages to Public Distribution Lists** check box if you want to allow subscribers with the CoS to send messages to distribution lists.

Step 4. Select the **Deleted Messages Are Copied to the Deleted Items Folder** check box to allow messages that are deleted from the phone to be stored in the Deleted Items folder. Keep in mind that enabling this can have a negative impact on disk space.

Step 5. To allow subscribers to use the Live Reply feature to reach other subscribers, select the **Subscribers Can Reply to Messages from Other Subscribers by Calling Them** check box.

Step 6. To allow subscribers to use the Live Reply feature to reach unidentified callers, such as an outside caller, select the **Subscribers Can Reply to Messages from Unidentified Callers by Calling Them** check box.

Step 7. Click the **Save** icon.

Modifying CoS Greetings Settings

The greetings configuration for CoS defines the maximum length of a greeting. To configure the settings, follow these steps:

Step 1. From within SA, select **Subscribers > Class of Service > Greetings.**

Step 2. Set the maximum number of seconds that you want for a subscriber's greeting in the **Maximum Greeting Length, in Seconds** field.

Step 3. You can configure a message that callers must listen to before they can leave a message. This recording plays after the subscriber's greeting. Select the **Play Recording Only for Unidentified Callers** radio button to create a recording that is heard only by outside callers, or select the **Play Recording to All Callers** radio button to record a message that all callers hear.

Step 4. Use the **Click to Record** button to record a message. Your phone should ring and you can use it to record the message. If your phone doesn't ring, make sure that you have the phone selected as the recording device. You can confirm this by clicking the down arrow next to the word *Recording* and select **Recording Devices** from the drop-down menu. More information on the record functions can be found later in this chapter in the "Creating Public Distribution Lists" section.

Step 5. Click the **Save** icon.

Modifying CoS Features Settings

The features to which a subscriber has access are, in part, determined by the features configured in the CoS to which they are assigned.

The features that can be assigned to a subscriber are determined by the license that was purchased. The following is a list of the features that you might be able to assign through the CoS:

- **FaxMail:** Fax management through the phone

- **Text-to-Speech:** Emails to be heard over the phone

- **Unity Assistant:** Subscriber's settings managed through the web

- **Unity Inbox:** Voicemail retrieved through the web

To configure these settings, follow these steps:

Step 1.   From within SA, select **Subscribers > Class of Service > Features**. The screen shown in Figure 7-31 displays.

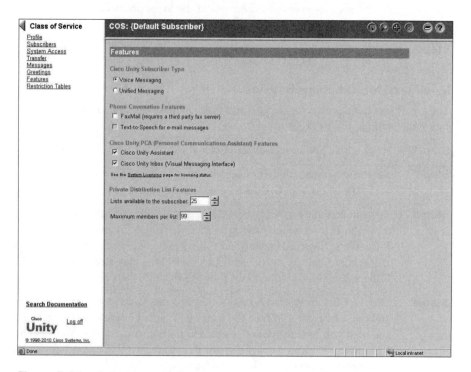

Figure 7-31   *CoS - Licensed Features*

Step 2. Select either **Voice Messaging** or **Unified Messaging** for the type of subscriber. A voice-messaging subscriber is someone who uses Unity exclusively for voicemail. A unified-messaging subscriber is someone who can access a single mailbox for voicemail, email, and faxes.

Step 3. Select the check boxes of the features that you want subscribers of this CoS to have.

Step 4. Two settings determine the size and quantity of personal distribution lists available to a subscriber. Enter the maximum number of lists that a subscriber can have in the **Lists Available to the Subscriber** field. Enter the maximum number of members that each list can contain in the **Maximum Members per List** field.

Step 5. Click the **Save** icon.

The last area to be configured in CoS is Restriction Tables. Because restriction tables deal with call management, they are covered in Chapter 9, "Call Management."

Now that the CoS has been configured, we are almost ready to begin the process of adding subscribers, which is covered in Chapter 8, "User/Subscriber Reference." Before moving on, one last topic needs to be discussed—public distribution lists.

Creating and Managing Unity Public Distribution Lists

The final material discussed in this section is public distribution lists (PDL). PDLs allow a single message to be sent to a group of people. Although subscribers can be added to PDLs manually, it is more efficient to add them during subscriber creation. This can be accomplished because the template that is used during subscriber creation can contain the PDLs to which the subscriber is assigned. PDLs can contain both subscribers and other PDLs. For example, you might have three groups, one for Detroit sales, one for New York sales, and one for Chicago sales. Each of these groups will contain subscribers from the associated location. You could then create a PDL called USSales and simply add the three sales PDLs, instead of having to add each subscriber again.

Creating Public Distribution Lists

To create and configure PDLs, follow these steps:

Step 1. From within SA, select **Subscribers > Public Distribution Lists > Profile**. The screen shown in Figure 7-32 displays.

Step 2. To add a new PDL, click the **Add** icon (plus sign). Enter the name of the PDL in the window that displays. You can choose to create a completely new PDL, base it on an existing list, or import an Exchange group. Choose the appropriate option for this group and click **Add**.

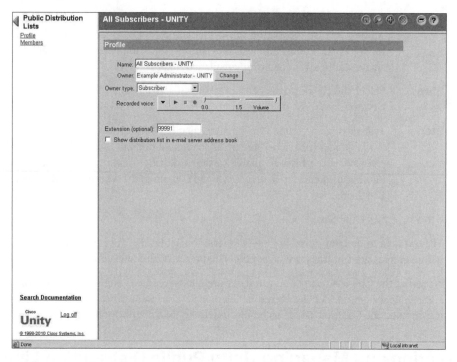

Figure 7-32 *Public Distribution Lists*

Step 3.   On the Profile screen, as shown in Figure 7-26, notice that the name and owner fields are populated. Each PDL must have an owner. By default, the owner will be the subscriber that created the PDL.

Step 4.   You can record a name for this PDL by clicking the **Record** button on the media master control panel. The panel that has VCR-like buttons is the media master, and the **Record** button is the round (red) button. The recorded name is played back when a subscriber dials the PDL by name.

Note   It is a good idea to become familiar with the media master interface because you will be using it within SA when recording messages for objects, such as call handlers and subscribers. The first time that you click the **Play** or **Record** button on the media master panel, the **Phone Record and Playback Settings** window displays. This window prompts you for the extension number of the phone that you will use for recording and the name of the Unity server. This displays only the first time that you use this interface from a particular PC.

Figure 7-32 illustrates the four buttons on this control panel. The first is an arrow that points down. When this button is clicked, you are presented with a menu that offers the following eight options:

- **Paste:** Enables you to paste audio that is on the clipboard into the current recording

- **Paste from File:** Enables you to paste an audio file into the current recording

- **Copy:** Enables you to copy the current recording to the clipboard

- **Copy to File:** Enables you to copy the current recording to a file

- **Playback Devices:** Enables you to choose to use either a phone or the sound card of the PC for playback

- **Record Devices:** Enables you to choose to use either a phone or the sound card of the PC for recording

- **Options:** Enables you to change the name of the server and the extension that you entered when the Phone Record and Playback Settings box appeared, the first time you used the media master on the PC

- **About:** Displays version details for the media master

Note   The next button is the **Play** button (an arrow that points to the right). This arrow is blue if there is a recording already present for the object. To listen to the recording, click the **Play** button. The phone should ring, and the recording is played when the phone is answered.

The third button is the **Stop** button (square). To stop the recording, click this button.

The final button is the **Record** button (red circle). To record a message, click the **Record** button. The phone should ring. Answer the phone and record the message after the beep. In some cases an informational window displays in SA asking whether you want to over-write the current recording before you can record the message.

Take a few minutes to get use to this interface, because you will find yourself using it often within SA.

Step 5.   You can assign an extension by entering the desired extension number in the **Extension** field. An extension is not required but is recommended. If a new extension is not assigned, a subscriber can only send a message by using the phone to dial the PDL by name.

Step 6.   If you want the PDL to display in the email address book, select the **Show Distribution List in E-mail Server Address Book** check box.

Step 7.   Click the **Save** icon.

Managing PDL Members

As mentioned earlier, the easiest way to add a subscriber to a PDL is at the point of creation. You can also add or make changes afterward manually from within SA. To view, add, or remove members from PDLs, follow these steps:

Step 1.   Navigate to **Subscribers > Public Distribution Lists > Members** of the PDL that you want to manage. The screen shown in Figure 7-33 should display.

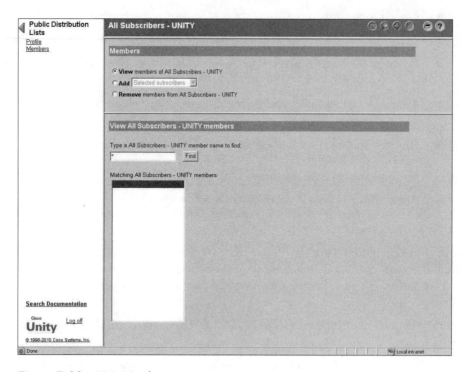

Figure 7-33   *PDL Members*

Step 2.   You have the option of viewing, adding, or removing members from the PDL. Select an action by clicking the appropriate radio button at the top of the screen. If you choose to add members, you must select either **Selected Subscriber** or **Public Distribution Lists** from the drop-down list.

Step 3.   Enter the search criteria for the subscriber (or public distribution list) that you want to manage in the field to the left of the **Find** button and click **Find**. If you are simply viewing, the PDL list displays. If you are adding or removing, a list displays with either an **Add to List** button or a **Remove** button. Select the subscriber that you want to manage and click the **Add** or **Remove** button.

Step 4.   Click **Save**.

The settings that are configured in this chapter affect the entire system. Now that the system is set up, you must conduct tests to ensure that the configurations you made are going to deliver the results you are anticipating. Take the time to test that the various settings you configured, such as schedules, holidays, and port functions, to name a few, are configured properly.

Unity Connection Integration Verification

In most environments, Unity Connection is integrated with CM. However, CM is not the only system that can integrate with Unity Connection. When integrating with CM, it can use SCCP or SIP. To integrate with other phone systems, SIP is used. When integrating with a Communications Manager Express system, it can use SIP straight through because CME understands SIP. However, to integrate with many traditional PBXs, a PIMG or TIMG device must be used. These devices have analog or digital ports (depending on the PBX it is connecting to) and an Ethernet port. The analog or digital port is used to connect to the PBX. The device converts the signal from the PBX to SIP and sends the SIP signal out the Ethernet port to the Unity Connection server.

This book focuses on the Communications Manager integration. Because the focus of this book is administration, it is assumed that Unity Connection is already integrated with CM. But we take a few minutes to explore the Unity Connection integration settings.

Communications Manager Integration

In this book, it is expected that most Unity Connection installations will be configured to operate with Communications Manager. Before Unity Connection can communicate with Communications Manager, certain tasks must be accomplished on the Communications Manager and the Unity systems. In Chapter 6, the Communications Manager side of the voicemail configuration was discussed. You might need to refer back to Chapter 6 to see how to configure the required components. Because the actual configuration steps have already been discussed, this section focuses on the process that verifies that all required configuration has been completed.

The integration settings can be viewed from within the CUAdmin web page. Under the Telephony Integration heading you find Phone System, Port Group, Port, and Trunk. This is where you locate all the integration settings. The following steps take you through the process of verifying the integration settings:

Step 1.   From within CUAdmin, navigate to **Telephony Integrations > Phone System.**

Step 2.   A list of the phones systems that are integrated with Unity Connection appears, as seen in figure 7-34. The name of the default integration is **PhoneSystem.** If you do not see that name, it means that someone changed the name of the default integration or deleted it and created a new one. Click the name of your phone system.

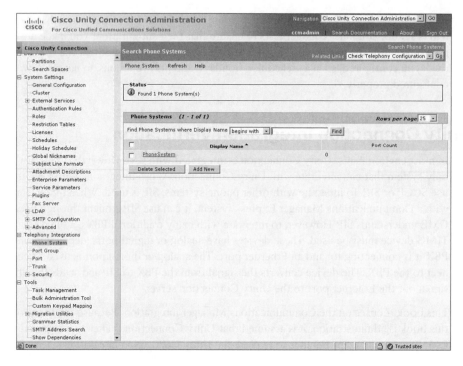

Figure 7-34 *Phone Systems*

Step 3. The phone system basic information page appears. From this page, you can change the parameters listed in Table 7-7.

Step 4. Each phone system must have a port group associated with it. Navigate to **Telephony Integrations > Port Group** to see a list of the port groups configured in your system. You will notice that next to the name of the port group is the name of the affiliated phone system.

Step 5. Select a port group from the list (you can have only one port group in your list). The parameters on this page vary based on the type of integration you have.

Table 7-8 lists the parameters found in an SCCP integration.

Step 6. As the name implies, port groups consist of ports. Navigate to **Telephony Integrations > Port** to see a list of the ports configured on your system. You will notice that next to the name of the port is the name of the affiliated phone system.

Step 7. Select a port from the list. Depending on the type of integration, the parameters on this page can vary slightly. Table 7-9 lists those found with an SCCP integration.

Table 7-7 *Phone System Parameters*

Parameter	Description
Phone System	
Phone System Name	Descriptive name for the phone system.
Default TRAP Phone System	This check box determines whether this will be the default Telephone Record and Playback (TRAP) system. It is always selected if it is the only phone system.
Message Waiting Indicators	
Send Message Counts	If selected, Unity Connection sends a message count when a new message arrives, even if the MWI is already lit. When deselected, Unity Connection will not send the message count when a new message arrives if the MWI is already lit. *Default: Not selected*
Use Same Port for Enabling and Disabling MWIs	If selected, the MWI off request is sent using the same port that the MWI on request used. *Default: Not selected*
Force All MWIs Off for This Phone System	When selected, all MWIs for this system will be turned off when the Synchronize All MWIs on This Phone System Run button is clicked. *Default: Not selected*
Synchronize All MWIs on This Phone System	When the Run button is clicked, all the MWIs for the system are synchronized.
Call Loop Detection by Using DTMF	
Enable for Supervised Transfers	When this box is selected, Unity Connection uses DTMF to detect and reject calls transferred using supervised transfer. This helps prevent the message prompt from being recorded, which can occur during a call loop. *Default: Not selected*
Enable for Forwarded Message Notification Calls (by Using DTMF)	When this box is selected, Unity Connection uses DTMF to detect and reject message notifications that are forwarded from a remote device such as a cell phone. This helps prevent false new message call notifications, which can occur during a call loop. *Default: Not selected*
DTMF Tone to Use	Determines the DTMF tone to be used for loop detection. *Default: A*
Guard Time	Determines the length of time that DTMF is played when DTMF is used for loop detection. *Default: 2500 milliseconds*

Table 7-7 *Phone System Parameters*

Parameter	Description
Call Loop Detection by Using Extension	
Enable for Forwarded Message Notification Calls (by Using Extension)	When selected, Unity Connection checks the extension to determine whether a message notification is being forward to it from a remote device such as a cell phone. It helps prevent false new message call notifications, which can occur during a call loop.
Phone View Settings	
Enable Phone View	If selected, Phone View is enabled on this phone system. *Default: Not selected*
CTI Phone Access User Name	The name of the application user that is associated to user phones must be entered for Phone View to function.
CTI Phone Access Password	The password of the CTI Phone Access user must be entered for Phone View to function.
Enable Outgoing Calls	Allows Unity Connection to use this phone system for outgoing calls such as message notifications. *Default: Selected*
Disable All Outgoing Calls Immediately	When selected, Unity Connection cannot use this phone system to place outgoing calls. *Default: Not selected*
Disable All Outgoing Calls Between	When selected, outgoing calls are disabled based on the times entered. *Default:* Not selected

Defining Unity Connection System Configuration

After the system is installed and the integration is complete, you need to start adding users. Unity Connection includes a number of default objects that can be used so that you can begin adding users immediately. It is recommended that you take some time to evaluate how your system is going to be utilized before you jump in and start adding users. When you have a good understanding of the types of users you have and the manner in which the system will be used, you might determine that some of the default settings aren't appropriate for your environment.

The following sections discuss systemwide settings. These are settings that affect the system and its users as a whole.

Table 7-8 *SCCP Port Group Parameters*

Parameter	Description
Display Name	A descriptive name for the port group.
Integration Method	Displays the type of integration (SCCP, SIP, and PIMG).
Device Name Prefix	The prefix used for the voicemail ports created in CM.
Reset Status	Displays whether the port group needs to be reset.
Enable Message Waiting Indicators	When selected, the ports of this port group can be used to send MWI requests. *Default: Selected*
MWI On Extension	The extension number configured in Communications Manager for MWI On.
MWI Off Extension	The extension number configured in Communications Manager for MWI Off.
Delay Between Requests	The number of milliseconds between MWI requests. *Default: 0*
Maximum Concurrent Requests	The maximum number of MWI requests that can be sent at the same time. *Default: 0*
Retries After Successful Attempt	The number of times that the MWI request should be resent after a success is reported to ensure success. *Default: 0*
Retry Interval After Successful Attempt	The number of milliseconds between MWI retries after a success is reported. *Default: 5*

Defining General Configuration

The first area to configure is the General Configuration settings. These are settings that define things such as time zone, language, recording settings, and default search parameters. The following steps show how to configure the general configuration settings:

Step 1.   From within CUAdmin, navigate to **System Settings > General Configuration**. The screen shown in Figure 7-35 appears.

Step 2.   The first field is the **Time Zone** field. You cannot change this from CUAdmin. It can only be changed from the CLI. Because the CLI is not used by most administrators, it is not covered in this book.

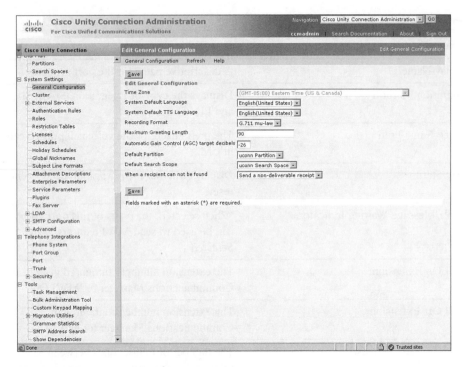

Figure 7-35   *General Configuration*

Step 3.   From the **System Default Language** drop-down list, make sure that the desired language is selected. This is the language that system prompts are played in.

Step 4.   From the **System Default TTS Language** drop-down list, be sure that the desired TTS language is selected. This determines what language Text-to-Speech (TTS) uses if there is no TTS for the language configured for the calling phone.

Step 5.   From the **Recording Format** drop-down list, select the codec that you want to use for recorded messages. The default is G.711 Mu-law. The other available choices are PCM-linear, G.711 a-law, G.729a, G.726, and GSM 06.10.

Step 6.   In the **Maximum Greeting Length** field, enter the maximum number of seconds that a record greeting should exist for a call handler. The default is 90 and the maximum is 1200.

Step 7.   The **Target Decibel Level for Recordings and Messages** field determines the volume established when audio normalization is used. The default is –26. If the volume of messages and recordings is too low, set this value higher. If messages and recordings are too loud, adjust the setting lower. Keep in mind that you are working with negative numbers, so –40 is actually lower than –29.

Table 7-9 *SCCP Port Parameters*

Parameter	Description
Enable	Enables the port to be used by Unity. *Default: Selected*
Port Name	Displays the name of the voicemail port.
Restart Button	Restarts the port when clicked.
Phone System	Displays the name of the phone system that uses this port.
Port Group	Displays the name of the port group that the port belongs to.
Server	The name of the Unity Connection server that controls this port.
Answer Calls	Enables the port to answer incoming calls. *Default: Selected*
Perform Message Notification	Enables the port to make outgoing calls for message notification purposes. *Default: Selected*
Send MWI Requests	When selected, allows this port to be used to send MWI requests. *Default: Selected*
Allow TRAP Connections	When selected, allows the port to be used for recording and playing messages when a subscriber is using the web or an email client. *Default: Selected*
Outgoing Hunt Order	Determines the place in the hunt order for this port.
Security Mode	Used to determine the security mode. *Default: Nonsecure*
SCCP Device Name	Displays the name of the device as configured in CM.
Certificate	When clicked, the certificate for this port is displayed.

Step 8.   From the **Default Partition** drop-down list, select the partition that is to be assigned to objects when they are first created.

Step 9.   From the **Default Search Scope** drop-down list, select the search scope that is to be assigned to objects when they are first created.

Note Partitions and search scopes are similar to partitions and calling search spaces in CM. They are covered in more detail in the "Configuring Unity Connection System Access and Policies" section, later in this chapter.

Step 10. The **When a Recipient Cannot Be Found** field determines what Unity Connection executes with a Simple Mail Transfer Protocol (SMTP) message that is addressed to an invalid address. By default, Unity Connection sends a Non-Deliverable Receipt (NDR). You can also choose to have the message sent to a smart host so that it can try to deliver it.

> **Note** A smart host is a mail relay server that aides in the delivery of email. It can be used as a central mail server, which helps reduce the administration in larger environments.

Step 11. If you changed any settings on this page, click **Save**.

Now that general configuration settings are complete, we move on to defining mailbox quotas. Unlike Unity, Unity Connection uses an on-box message store so that quotas are configured within Unity Connection. Unity uses Exchange as its message store, so quotas are configured on the Exchange store if you are using Unity. The next section discusses how to set system-wide mailbox quotas.

Defining Mailbox Quotas

How many times have you heard, "I'm sorry, but the mailbox of the party you are calling is full . . . *click*"? Don't you just love that? This section examines how to configure mailbox quotas so that others can hear that message. Well, actually it's to keep your system's drive from filling up.

Unity Connection enables you to set three quota levels. When users connects to the first level, they are warned that the mailbox is almost full. When they tie into the second level, they are prevented from sending voicemails. When they hit the third level, the mailbox is truly full and messages cannot be sent or received. Unity Connection enables you to configure systemwide quotas, but you can override these quotas at the user configuration level. The following steps illustrate the configuration process for systemwide mailbox quotas.

Step 1. From within CUAdmin, navigate to **Message Storage > Mailbox Quotas**. The screen shown in Figure 7-36 appears.

Step 2. Check the **Custom** radio button that is to the right of **Warning Quota** and enter the number of megabytes allowed for message storage before a warning message is played. The default is 12.

> **Note** G.729 requires 60 KB of disk space for every minute of speech. This means that the default of 12 MB will allow about 200 minutes of messages. G.711 requires approximately a half a megabyte per minute of recorded speech, meaning that the default setting of 12 MB will allow about 25 minutes of messages.

Step 3. Click the **Custom** radio button located to the right of **Send Quota** and enter the number of megabytes allowed for message storage before a user can no longer send messages. The default is 13.

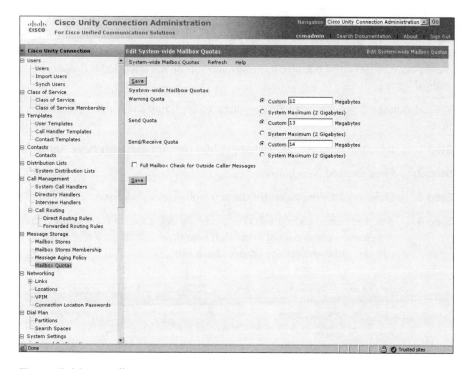

Figure 7-36   *Mailbox Quotas*

Step 4.   Click the **Custom** radio button positioned to the right of **Send/Receive Quota** and enter the number of megabytes allowed for message storage before a user can no longer send or receive messages. The default is 14.

Step 5.   By default, the **Full Mailbox Check for Outside Caller Messages** check box is not selected. When deselected, Unity Connection does not verify whether the mailbox is full. This means that the caller can leave a message even if the mailbox is full. To make sure that this doesn't occur, select the box. This setting only affects outside callers.

Step 6.   Click **Save** to save the settings.

In addition to setting the mailbox size, you can set messaging aging policies that determine how long messages can stay on the system. The next section discusses how to create and configure message policies.

Configuring Message Aging Policy

Now that mailbox quotas are set, we define message-aging polices. Message-aging policies determine how Unity Connection will acknowledge messages based on their age. This can help keep mailboxes clean, but if misconfigured, this can also cause messages to be deleted without ever being heard.

Two message policies are preconfigured on Unity Connection; the Default System Policy and the Do Not Age Messages Policy. Default System Policy is a fairly conservative rule. It permanently deletes deleted messages after 15 days. The Do Not Age Messages Policy is even more conservative because it doesn't accomplish anything and it is not even enabled by default.

You can edit these policies or create new ones. To configure a new policy, follow these steps:

Step 1.   From within CUAdmin, navigate to **Message Storage > Message Aging Policy**.

Step 2.   Click the **Add New** button.

Step 3.   Enter a descriptive name for the new policy, and click **Save**.

Step 4.   A screen similar to figure 7-37 appears. By default, a message-aging policy is not enabled when it is fist created. It cannot be edited until it is enabled. To edit this policy, select the **Enable** check box.

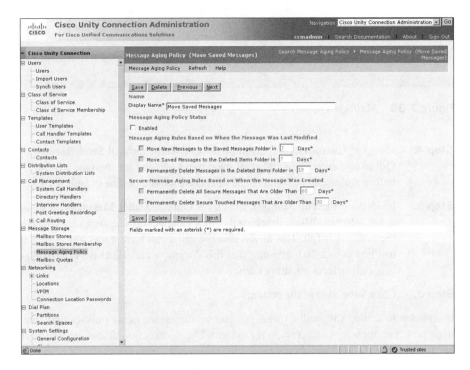

Figure 7-37   *Message-Aging Policy*

Step 5.   The three options in the **Message Aging Rules Based on When the Message Was Last Modified** section are similar. They define how many days Unity Connection waits before taking the specified action. For example, **Move New Messages to the Saved Messages Folder in ___ Days** determines how many days after a new message arrives that it is automatically moved to the Saved

Messages folder. By default, the only one of these options that is enabled is the last one, which permanently deletes deleted messages. To enable an option, select the check box and enter the desired number of days. To disable an option, deselect the check box.

Warning   Take care when enabling these options because it could result in messages being deleted without ever being heard. For example, if this were configured to move new messages to the Saved folder after 5 days and then move saved messages to the Deleted folder after 5 days, a user that did not have phone access for 2 weeks would have unheard messages in the Deleted folder. It only gets worse if the option to permanently delete deleted messages is enabled.

Step 6.   The next section, **Secure Message Aging Rules Based on When the Message Was Created**, determines how secure messages are handled. The only difference between the two options is that the first one, **Permanently Delete Secure Touched Messages That Are Older Than __ Days**, only applies to messages that the user has "touched" by an action such as saving, opening, or deleting. The second option, **Permanently Delete All Secure Messages That Are Older Than __ Days**, takes action regardless of whether the message had been "touched." To enable an option, select the check box and enter the desired number of days. To disable an option, deselect the check box.

Step 7.   Click **Save** to save the settings.

Now that you have message-aging policies configured, it's time to move on to the settings that determine the hours of operation. The next sections discuss how to create schedules and holidays.

Creating Schedules and Holidays

You want to confirm that when people calls your company, they hear a message that is accurate and informative. For example, if you call on a Saturday, you don't want to hear the standard greeting that tells you to please wait for your call to be answered if the company is actually closed. You want to be informed that the company is closed and to notify you when it will reopen. To have Unity Connection play a different greeting based on hours of operation, you must configure schedules and holidays.

View and Change a Schedule

To view and change existing schedules, use the following steps:

Step 1.   From within CUAdmin, navigate to **System Settings > Schedules**.

Step 2.   Select the schedule that you want to edit from the list that appears.

Step 3.   A screen similar to that shown in Figure 7-38 appears. The grid offers a graphical representation of the open hours. The solid boxes with a plus sign in them signify open hours. Above the grid in the **Schedule Details** section, you see a summary of the open hours. In this example, the open hours are 8:00 a.m. to 5:00 p.m.

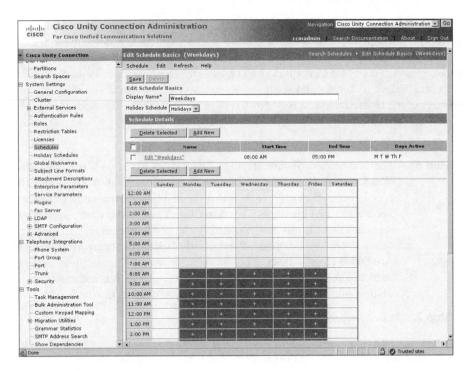

Figure 7-38 *Schedules*

Step 4.   You can either add additional hours to be open or edit the current hours. To edit the current hours, click the **Edit** button. A screen similar to Figure 7-39 appears.

Step 5.   Enter a descriptive name in the **Name** field.

Step 6.   Using the drop-down lists, select the desired start and end times. If you want the end time to be midnight, you can simply select the **End of Day** check box.

Step 7.   Select the check box next to the days of the weeks that you want these open hours to be assigned to.

Step 8.   Click **Save** to save the settings.

Step 9.   To verify that the new hours are in the schedule, navigate to **System Settings > Schedules**.

Step 10. If you want to add additional open hours to this schedule, click the **Add New** button in the **Schedule Details** section, as shown previously in Figure 7-38. Now repeat Steps 5–8.

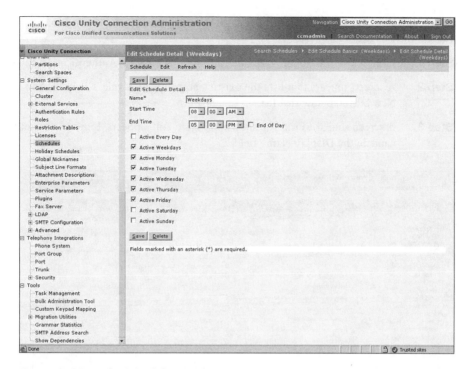

Figure 7-39   *Edit Schedule Details*

Now that system settings are configured, it's time to look at system access and policies. The next section discusses system access and policies.

Configuring Unity Connection System Access and Policies

Before you put your system into production, make sure that it is configured as you intended and used only by those you intended. Just as with any computer system today, make sure that it is secure. Because different types of people will be accessing it for different purposes, you need to configure access for a few types of permissions. For example, you need to define what users are allowed to access the administrative interface, but you also need to determine how many times a user can enter an invalid password before she is locked out. The following sections discuss the various types of permissions that you should be concerned with and describe how to configure them.

Configuring Authentication Rules

Authentication rules deal with passwords and login attempts. They define the characteristics of a password and describe how Unity Connection deals with failed login attempts. Unity Connection comes with two default authentication rules. They can be edits, or you can create additional rules. The following steps show how to create a new rule as well as explain the aspects of each setting:

Step 1.   From within CUAdmin, navigate to **System Settings > Authentication Rules**.

Step 2.   A screen appears that lists the existing authentication rule. Click the **Add New** button below that list.

Step 3.   A screen similar to the one shown in Figure 7-40 appears. Enter a descriptive name in the **Display Name** field.

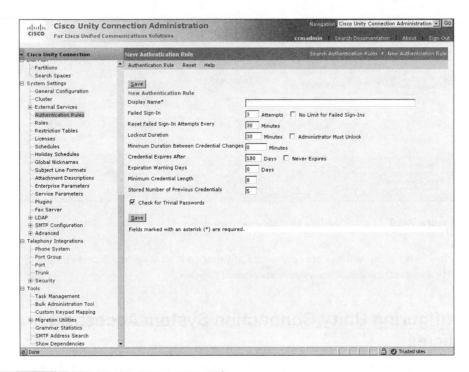

Figure 7-40   *New Authentication Rule*

Step 4.   In the **Failed Sign-In** field, enter the maximum number of times that a user is permitted to enter an incorrect password. If you do not want to set a limit, select the **No Limit for Failed Sign-Ins** check box.

Step 5.   The **Reset Failed Sign-In Attempts Every** field determine how many minutes must pass before Unity Connection resets the failed sign-in counter. For example, if the failed sign-in field is set to 5 and the user enters the wrong password four times and then waits the time specified in this field, Unity Connection will act as if there were no failed sign-ins. Enter the desired number of minutes in the field.

Step 6.   The **Lockout Duration** field determines the length of time that an account stays locked when the failed sign-in attempts have been exceeded. Enter the desired number of minutes in this field. If you want the account to be locked until an administrator unlocks it, select the **Administrator Must Unlock** check box.

Step 7.   The **Minimum Duration Between Credential Changes** field determines how many minutes expire between password changes. The default setting is 1440 minutes, which means that a user must wait one day since the last time he changed his password before he can change it again. Enter the desired number of minutes.

Step 8.   The **Credential Expires After** field determines when a password expires. The default is 180, which means that users must change their passwords approximately twice a year. Enter the desired number of days. If you do not want passwords to expire, select the **Never Expires** check box.

Step 9.   The **Expiration Warning Days** field determines when a user will be warned that her password is about to expire. Enter the number of days prior to the expiration date that you want the warning played. If you enter 0, the user will not be warned.

Step 10.   The **Minimum Credential Length** field determines the minimum length for a password. Enter a value between 1 and 64. The default is 6.

Step 11.   The **Stored Number of Previous Credentials** field determines how many previous passwords Unity Connection will store and prevents you from using the password again. Enter the desired number. The default is 5.

Step 12.   If the **Check for Trivial Passwords** box is selected, Unity Connection will not allow a user to create passwords considered to be trivial. Unity Connection considers the following trivial:

- Digits all the same
- Consecutive digits
- Primary extension

Step 13.   Click **Save** to save the settings.

Keep in mind that users can log in from phones and from a web page. For this reason, you want to configure authentication rules for each type of log in.

Just as you restrict access to the system by defining password characteristics, you need to restrict user capability after users are logged in. The next section discusses how to configure restriction tables to help prevent misuse of certain features.

Configuring Restriction Tables

Certain features, such as faxing and call transfers, require UC to be able to make out-bound calls. Because users configure what numbers UC should dial for these various functions, you need to be able to restrict what numbers can be configured. If restrictions are not in place, it could result in unexpected toll charges or toll fraud.

To set these restrictions, you must create restriction tables and assign them to a class of service (CoS). Each user is assigned to a CoS; hence the restriction table assigned to the CoS affects the user.

UC is preconfigured with five restriction tables, which in most cases are sufficient in North America. But, there might be a time that you need to create or change one. The following steps show how to change the Default Transfer restriction table.

Step 1.   From within CUAdmin, navigate to **System Settings > Restriction Tables**.

Step 2.   Select **Default Transfer** (or the restriction table that you want to modify) for the list. A screen similar to the one shown in Figure 7-41 appears.

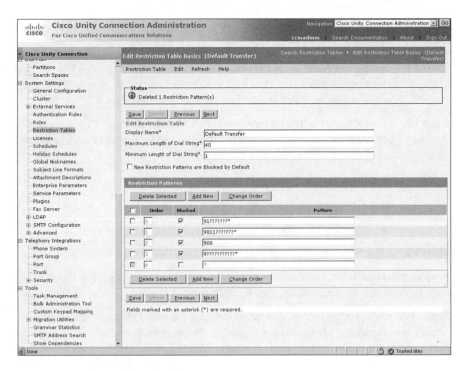

Figure 7-41   *Restriction Table*

Step 3.   The **Display Name** field should contain a descriptive name.

Step 4.   In the **Maximum Length of Dial String** field, enter the maximum number of digits allowed in a single dial string. If a user enters a string larger than this number, it is rejected before it is even checked against the patterns defined in the table.

Step 5. In the **Minimum Length of Dial String** field, enter the minimum number of digits permitted in a single dial string.

Step 6. When you create a new pattern, you can set it to be blocked or allowed. To set all new patterns to be blocked, select the **New Restriction Patterns Are Blocked by Default** check box.

Step 7. The **Restriction Patterns** section of this page is where you configure the patterns that will be blocked and allowed. The wildcards used for the restriction table are different than those used in CM. A ? matches a single digit, and a * matches any digit and any number of digits. For example, the first pattern in Figure 7-41 is 91???????*. This pattern matches a pattern that starts with a 91 and is followed by at least seven digits. To modify an existing pattern, simply edit the **Pattern** field.

Note New patterns are positioned at the top of the list and, by default, are allowed. Because the pattern of * is entered automatically, when you add a new pattern, you need to be careful. If you accidentally save this pattern at the top position, you have, in effect, allowed nearly any pattern to be entered by a user.

Step 8. To add a new pattern, click the **Add New** button below the pattern. A new pattern appears at the top of the list. Edit this pattern and select the **Block** check box. If you are creating a pattern that you want to allow, do not select the **Block** check box.

Step 9. You can also delete patterns by selecting the check box to the far left of the pattern and then clicking the **Delete Selected** button.

Step 10. To change the order of the patterns, click the **Change Order** button. All the patterns appear in a box in their current order. Highlight the pattern that you want to move and use the up and down arrow below the box to move it. After you are done rearranging the patterns, click the **Save** button.

Step 11. If you did not change the order of the patterns, click the **Save** button to save the changes. If you did change the order, your changes were saved when you clicked **Save** in this step.

Because restriction tables are assigned to a CoS, they should be configured before the CoS. After they are configured, you can move on to configuring classes of service. The next section covers how to create various CoSs.

Configuring CoS

UC offers many features, and you might not want to allow all of your users full entry, or you might want to control what level of access they have to them. To do this, you must create various classes of service. This section will walk you through the steps to create a new class of service and offer explanations for each setting. The following steps illustrate this process:

Step 1.   From within CUAdmin, navigate to **Class of Service > Class of Service**.

Step 2.   A list of currently configured classes of service appears. Click the **Add New** button located under the list.

Step 3.   A screen similar to the one shown in Figure 7-42 appears. Enter a descriptive name in the **Display Name** field.

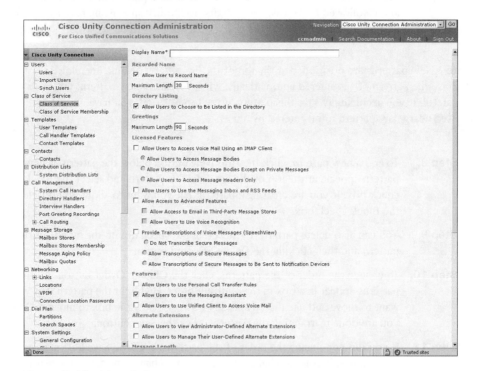

Figure 7-42   *New CoS*

Step 4.   The **Allow User to Record Name** check box determines whether a user is allowed to record his own name. If this box is selected, the user will be prompted to record a name during the first-time enrollment process. To permit users to record their name, ensure that the box is selected. If you do not want users to record a name, make sure that the check box is not selected.

Step 5.   In the **Maximum Length** field below the **Allow User to Record Name** field, enter the maximum number of seconds desired for recording a name.

Step 6. The **Allow Users to Choose to Be Listed in the Directory** check box determines whether users are permitted to decide whether they want to be listed in the directory. Typically, you want to make sure that this box is not selected.

Step 7. In the **Maximum Length** field under the **Greetings** heading, enter the maximum number of seconds desired for a user's greeting. The default is 90.

Step 8. UC allows a user to access voicemail from his email client. One option is to configure it as an IMAP client. To permit user access, select the **Allow Users to Access Voicemail Using an IMAP Client** check box. Under this setting, you can define the type and portions of the message that you allow them to retrieve. If you enable this feature, you must select one of the access settings. The choices are

- **Allow Users to Access Message Bodies:** Enables full access to all voicemails.

- **Allow Users to Access Message Bodies Except on Private Messages:** Enables full access to all emails except those marked private.

- **Allow Users to Access Message Headers Only:** Enables the user to see that there is a new voicemail, but not download the message.

Step 9. Users can check voicemail from a web page called UC Messaging Inbox. To enable this feature, you must select the **Allow Users to Use the Messaging Inbox and RSS Feeds** check box.

Step 10. The **Allow Access to Advanced Features** check box determines whether the user will be able to access email stored on Exchange and have entry to voice recognition services. To enable these features, select this check box and the check boxes below for the features that you desire.

Step 11. UC has the ability to send messages to a third-party transcription service. To enable this feature for users, select the **Provide Transcriptions of Voice Messages (SpeechView)** check box. You must also define whether secure messages will be allowed to be transcribed. If this feature is enabled, you must also select one of the following options:

- **Do Not Transcribe Secure Messages:** Secure message will not be sent to the transcription service.

- **Allow Transcriptions of Secure Messages:** Secure message will be sent to the transcription service, but users will not receive these transcriptions on their notification devices.

- **Allow Transcriptions of Secure Messages to Be Sent to Notification Devices:** Secure message will be sent to the transcription service, and users will receive these transcriptions on their notification devices.

Step 12. The next three check boxes determine the features that are accessible to the user. Select the box for each feature that you want users to have in this class of service The available features are

- **Allow Users to Use Personal Call Transfer Rules:** Personal call transfer rules allow a user to define how a call is handled based on the call information and other factors such as time of day.

- **Allow Users to Use the Messaging Assistant:** The Messaging Assistant is a web-based interface that allows users to configure the settings for their voicemail.

- **Allow Users to Use Unified Client to Access Voicemail:** This permits users to access voicemail using the Cisco Unified Personal Communicator.

Step 13. Multiple extensions can be assigned to a single user. This is accomplished by defining alternate extensions. You can choose to allow users to view and/or assign their own alternate extensions. Select the **Allow Users to View Administrator-Defined Alternate Extensions** check box to permit access to the alternate extensions that an administrator has assigned to their accounts. To allow users to personally assign extensions, select the **Allow Users to Manage Their User-Defined Alternate Extensions** check box.

Step 14. The **Maximum Length** field located under the **Message Length** heading determines the maximum length of a message left by the user to another user in the system. Enter the desired number of seconds in the field.

Step 15. The next four check boxes determine message options for the user. Select the desired options. The available options are

- **Allow Users to Send Messages to System Distribution Lists:** Enables users to send messages to distributions lists.

- **Delete Messages Without Saving to Deleted Items Folder:** When selected, messages are deleted immediately and not saved to the Deleted Items folder.

- **Users Can Reply to Messages from Other Users by Calling Them:** Enables a user to press 4-4 while listening to a message and respond to the sender of the message if the sender is another UC user. This is often referred to as Live Reply.

- **Users Can Reply to Messages from Unidentified Callers by Calling Them:** Enables a user to press 4-4 while listening to a message and call the sender of the message if the sender is not a UC user. This is often referred to as Live Reply.

Step 16. The **Require Secure Messaging** field determines what messages are marked as secure. Select the desired setting from the drop-down list. The available settings are

- **Always:** All messages are marked secure.

- **Never:** No messages are marked secure.

- **Ask:** Only marked secure when user selects the secure option from the special delivery options.

- **Private:** Mark private messages secure.

Step 17. The two fields located under **Private Distribution List** determine the maximum number of private lists per user and the maximum number of members per list. Enter the maximum number of lists a user can have in the **Maximum List per User** field, and enter the maximum number of members per list in the **Maximum Members per List** field.

Step 18. The **Allow Users to Change Call Screening Options** check box determines whether the user can enable call screening. It is recommended that this rarely be used because it can affect call-processing performance.

Step 19. The **Allow Users to Change Call Holding Options** check box determines whether callers can change call-holding options. If enabled, use Message Assistant to configure this.

Step 20. Restriction tables determine what type of calls UC is allowed to place. The configuration details were covered in the previous section. Select a restrictions table for each of the three types of calls that UC can place. They are

- **Outcalling:** Restricts the number that a user can enter for UC to use for record and playback functions

- **Transfer:** Restricts the number that a user can enter for UC to use for transfer functions

- **Fax:** Restricts the number that a user can enter for UC to use for fax functions.

Step 21. Click **Save** to save the settings.

The CoS defines what types of functions and features a user has access to, but it does not define any administrative access. Administrative access is determined by the roles that are assigned to a user.

Understanding Roles

Roles determine the administrative level that's accessible to a user. There are eight predefined roles. They cannot be edited, and additional roles cannot be added. Each role permits access to functions that common types of administrators need. Table 7-10 lists the roles and their functions.

For a closer look at the exact privileges a role offers, navigate to **System Settings > Roles**. Select the role that you are interested from the list that appears. A screen similar to that shown in Figure 7-43 appears. The allowable applications are listed in detail under

Table 7-10 *Predefined Roles*

Role	Function
Audio Text Administrator	Administers call handlers, directory handlers, and interview handlers
Greeting Administrator	Manages call handler recorded greetings through the phone
Help Desk Administrator	Resets user passwords and unlocks user accounts, views user settings
Mailbox Access Delegate Account	Access to all messages through messaging APIs
Remote Administrator	Administers the database using remote management tools
System Administrator	Access to all connection administrative functions, reports, and tools for server and users
Technician	Access to functions that enable management of system and phone system integration settings, viewing of all system and user settings, running all reports and diagnostic tools
User Administrator	Access to all user administration functions, user reports, and user administration tools

the Role Privileges heading. You can also see which users are assigned to this role by clicking the Role Assignments button.

Now that you are familiar with the use and function of roles, there is only one more access-related component. Now move on to learn about partitions and search scopes.

Defining the Dial Plan

This section examines the configuration of partitions and search spaces. They are similar to the partitions and calling search spaces that are employed in CM. Within UC, they can be used to restrict a user's accessibility to objects. This is beneficial in a multitenant environment.

Because these are nearly identical to partitions and call search spaces within CM, not much time is spent covering the details of how they work. If you need to refresh your memory, refer to Chapter 5, "Configuring Class of Service and Call Admission Control." The main difference is that calling search spaces are simply referred to as search spaces in UC.

As you recall, partitions are assigned to prevent or permit accessibility to objects. A search space is a list of partitions. The search space assigned to a user determines his or her level of access.

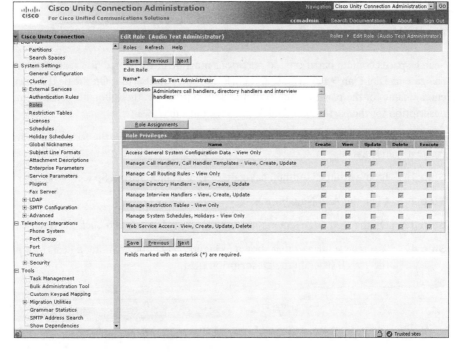

Figure 7-43 *Role Assignments*

Partitions are assigned to the following:

- Users with mailboxes (primary extension)
- User alternate extensions
- Contacts (including VPIM contacts)
- System call handlers
- Directory handlers
- Interview handlers
- System distribution lists
- VPIM locations

Search spaces are assigned to the following:

- Users with mailboxes
- Routing rules (both direct and forwarded)
- Phone directory handlers
- System call handlers

- Voice-enabled directory handlers

- VPIM locations

Search spaces contain partitions, so partitions must be created first. To create a partition, navigate to **Dial Plan > Partitions**, and click the **Add New** button. On the next screen, enter a name for the partition and click the **Save** button. On the following screen, enter a description for the partition and click the **Save** button.

After you have created all the partitions, create search spaces. Use the following steps to create a search space:

Step 1. From within CUAdmin, navigate to **Dial Plan > Search Space**.

Step 2. Click the **Add New** button.

Step 3. On the next page, enter a name for the search space and click the **Save** button.

Step 4. A screen similar to that shown in Figure 7-44 appears. Enter a description for the search space in the **Description** field.

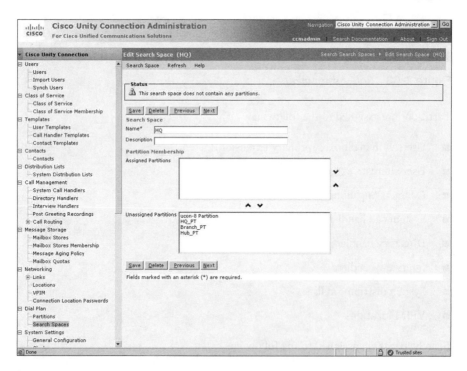

Figure 7-44 *Search Spaces Configuration*

Step 5. In the **Unassigned Partition** box, highlight the partition that you want to assign to this search space and click the Up Arrow directly above the **Unassigned Partition** box.

Step 6.   The partition selected should now appear in the **Assigned Partition** box. Repeat Step 5 until all the desired partitions are listed in the **Assigned Partition** box.

Step 7.   After all the partitions have been added, you can change the order in which they display. Remember, the order in which they display determines which partition is searched first. To change the order, highlight the partition that you want to move and click the Up or Down Arrow to the right of the box.

Note   You can remove a partition from a search space by highlighting it and clicking the Down aArrow below the **Assigned Partition** box. The selected partition should now appear in the **Unassigned Partition** box.

Step 8.   Click **Save** to save the settings.

After the partitions and search spaces are created, they can be assigned to various objects. You will see how they are assigned Chapters 8 and 9 as we explore the objects that might require them.

Summary

That's all there is to it. Well, not really. There is much more, but these steps complete the chapter. All the hard work you have done up to now is about to pay off. In this chapter, you first learned how to verify a proper integration with Communications Manager for Unity and Unity Connection. Then system configuration settings such as schedules, holidays, and languages were discussed. In addition, authentication and port settings were examined. This chapter also discussed the configuration of account policies and class of service (CoS) settings. The next chapter examines the process of adding subscribers and users.

Chapter 8

User/Subscriber Reference

After a proper integration between Unity and Communications Manager is achieved and the predeployment tasks discussed in the previous chapter are completed, users can be added. Unity refers to users as subscribers, whereas Unity Connection refers to them simply as users. To keep things simple, this chapter uses the term *users* as a general term that refers to both Unity subscribers and Unity Connection users. In this chapter, the different types of users are examined, and the proper usage for each is discussed. Next you explore the process for adding, importing, and managing users. Within the Managing Users section, various administrative tasks are discussed, ranging from learning how to reset a subscriber password to granting a user administrative access. Each task includes step-by-step instructions.

Note Throughout this chapter, the term *subscriber* is used when referring to a Unity user. The term *user* is used when discussing Unity Connection users. When the subject matter is referring to both Unity subscribers and Unity Connection users, the term *user* is used.

In Chapter 1, "CUCM and Unity Connection Overview," you learned about the various types of users. This chapter discusses how to create and manage users.

Defining Various Types of Subscribers

Even though you are already familiar with the different types of subscribers, we take a minute to briefly review the different types of subscribers.

Exchange

The Exchange subscriber is the most common subscriber found in a Unity deployment. As the name implies, this type of subscriber uses Exchange for its message store. Exchange subscribers can be either voicemail-only or unified messaging subscribers. Voicemail-only subscribers use the Exchange server as a place to store only their voice-mail messages. They are not able to retrieve their email through Unity or their voicemail through a PC. The unified messaging subscribers have both their email and voicemail stored on the same Exchange server and can access both types of messages from a phone or a PC.

These types of users can have many different ways to access Unity, such as through the Internet or over a phone. The user's CoS determines exactly what entry points he can use.

Networked Subscribers

In addition to the Exchange subscriber, there is also a Network subscriber that is created only if some type of Unity networking is deployed. Because these users are directly related to Unity networking, they are discussed in Chapter 10: "Implementing Unity Networking."

Unity Connection Users

Unity Connection has two types of users, one with a mailbox and one without. You might wonder why you would ever create a user on a voicemail system that doesn't have a mailbox. It is recommended for administrative purposes. In other words, do not use your normal voicemail user login information for administrative tasks. There are also objects that are called contacts that are similar to a network user in Unity. A contact is simply a pointer to another system. These are created so that people that have a voicemail account on a different system can appear in the directory and have messages forwarded to them.

Creating Users

The actual process of creating a single user is, at the surface, a simple task. However, when examined closely, you see that each user has well over 50 individual settings. It is logical to assume that this process is so simple because it requires only a few pieces of information and a few keystrokes. To ensure that the user is properly configured, it requires much more work. Each time a user is added, every setting must be given a value. So, creating a user requires the configuration of more than 50 settings, but at the same time, a user can be created with just a few keystrokes. How is this possible? The creation of a user is based on what is known as a template. The values configured in the template are applied to the newly created user. The next section discusses the use and creation of user templates.

Exploring Templates

When you create or import users, a large number of them have similar attributes. Templates automatically enable you to assign the same settings to each user during the creation process. The use of a template is not optional. Each time you add a user, a template must be chosen.

Before creating templates, plan how each user will use the system. Templates enable you to configure everything from the user's time zone to what happens to a call if a caller presses 4 while listening to the greeting. Because of their configuration, it is possible to find yourself creating many templates. Be careful not to get carried away. Remember, the templates are used to help assign settings to a group of users that are going to have similar, but not necessarily identical, attributes. In most cases, the template you create should apply to at least five users. If you find that you are creating a large number of templates and applying each of them to a small number of users, you might want to rethink your deployment strategy. Although each user has unique settings, there will be a large number of settings that are the same for the majority of users.

When determining how many templates you need, it is a good idea to try to organize users into groups. These groups should begin at a very general level. The members in these groups require the same type of features and access to Unity/Connection. Assume that you are implementing unified messaging, but only some of the users need to retrieve their email from the phone. From this, we can assume that there are at least three types of users. One group, which is needed in all environments, is the administrator group. The other two types of users are those that need access to text-to-speech and those that don't. There might be a requirement for additional groups, but this lets you determine the different templates you might need.

Refer to the following list of questions that should be considered when determining the necessary number of templates. They are directly related to the various settings that should be configured in the templates. In addition to answering these questions, it is recommended that you walk through the process of creating a test template to become familiar with the settings that are configured.

Step 1.   How many CoSs are there?

Typically you will need at least one template for each CoS you have created.

Step 2.   How many schedules are there?

Step 3.   Are all users in the same time zone?

Step 4.   Are all users on the same phone switch?

Step 5.   Are multiple mailstores (Exchange servers) being used?

Step 6.   Will there be call accounting for outbound calls?

Step 7.   How many billable departments are there?

The system can create a report of each outbound call that it places and associate it with a billing ID.

Step 8.   Will all users have the same password restrictions?

Step 9.   Will users be allowed to control their own conversation flow? If not, how many base flows are needed?

This deals with things such as menu styles, time format, and message playback order.

Step 10.   Will all phones ring when dialed from within the system?

This refers to what happens when a user's extension is dialed from within the system. Typically, you want the phone to ring, but in some cases, you might want the call to go directly to voicemail or a different extension.

Step 11.   Will all phones ring the same number of times when transferred?

Step 12.   What greetings are enabled by default?

A user can have multiple greetings. You need to determine which greeting is enabled by default and whether the same greetings are enabled for all users.

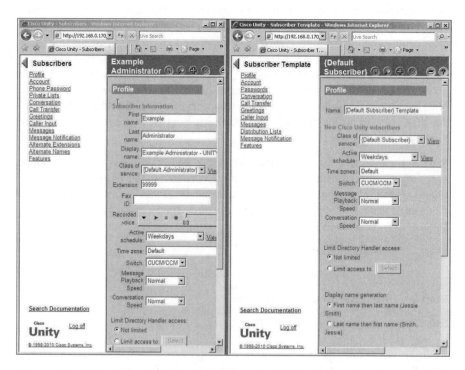

Figure 8-1   *Subscriber and Subscriber Template Submenus*

Step 13.   While listening to a greeting, what options will a caller have? Will this be the same for all phones?

While listening to a greeting, the caller can be given a list of options such as "To skip this message, press <option number>" or "To reach an operator, press <option number>."

Step 14. How long can messages be? Will the length be the same for all phones?

Step 15. How many distribution lists are there?

Step 16. Will message notification be used? How many groups will require this?

This is not necessarily a complete list of the questions you need to ask, but it gives you a good idea of the types of information you need to gather. After you have assembled this type of information, you are ready to start creating templates. Because the creation of Unity templates is somewhat different than that of Unity Connection templates, the details are discussed separately in the following two sections. The first section discusses how to create Unity templates and describe how to use them to create Unity subscribers. The second section focuses on these same tasks for Unity Connection.

Creating Unity Subscriber Templates

Before moving on to the actual process of creating subscriber templates, it is important that you understand that these templates are significant only at the point of creation. This means that the setting of a template affects the subscriber only when the subscriber is first created. If you create 50 users using a template, changes that you make to that template after the subscribers are created do not affect the subscriber's settings. If you need to change certain settings on a large number of subscribers, use the Bulk edit utility. This utility is discussed in Chapter 11, "Exploring Unity/Connection Tools."

Figure 8-1 displays a split screen that shows the submenu for a subscriber and the submenu for a subscriber template. This figure shows that the submenus are similar.

There are more than 50 configurable settings for each subscriber, so there must be at least that many settings for each subscriber template. It is important to understand the effect of each setting. Table 8-1 provides an overview of the types of settings that each submenu contains.

Table 8-1 *Subscriber Template Submenus*

Submenu	Description
Profile	General settings, such as schedules and time zones, are set in this area. Information relating to the subscribers' names is also set here, such as how their Windows domain usernames are generated.
Account	This area enables you to set a billing ID for subscribers and determine whether the subscriber's account will be available for use as soon as it is created or whether an administrator will have to unlock it first.
Passwords	This area enables you to configure default passwords and expiration settings.

Table 8-1 *Subscriber Template Submenus*

Submenu	Description
Conversation	The Conversation area enables you to configure how the Unity system interacts with a subscriber. This includes things such as volume, menu style, time format, message playback order, and many other settings. If you allow the subscribers access to Cisco Personal Communication Assistant (CPCA), subscribers can change most of these settings themselves.
Call Transfer	This area determines what action is taken when a subscriber's extension is dialed from within Unity. Most of the time, this occurs when an outside caller dials the extension from the auto-attendant.
Greetings	The Greetings area configures which greetings are enabled, what action is allowed during the greeting, and what action is taken after the greeting.
Caller Input	During a greeting, a caller has a number of choices, such as to skip the greeting by pressing # or to reach an operator by pressing 0. The caller input settings determine what happens if a digit is pressed while the greeting is being played.
Messages	The settings in this area determine how long messages can be, whether callers can edit messages, and the actions taken after taking a message. The extension to use for the Message Waiting Indicator (MWI) is also configured here.
Distribution Lists	The distribution lists to which the subscriber belongs are configured here.
Message Notification	The devices used to notify a subscriber of a new message are configured in this area.
Features	The features such as broadcast messages, message locator, and message security are configured in this area.

Note The conversation settings are important to the success of the system because they allow control over the settings to make the new system more acceptable to the end user. I was once asked to deliver some end-user training for a company whose employees were frustrated with the system. As it turned out, 90 percent of their concerns related to the conversation settings. After they learned to configure these settings themselves, the majority of the issues were resolved.

Two user templates are created during the installation process. These are the default administrator and the default subscriber templates. As their names imply, they each have settings that are commonly found in administrative-level subscribers and standard subscribers.

Note   Although you can use the default templates to create subscribers, it is best to confirm the context of the default template's settings first. Do not assume that the default settings are the best settings for your deployment.

At this point, you should have an idea of the different templates that you need. I'll go through the process of creating and managing a template so that you fully understand all the settings that must be configured. I begin by adding a new template. The following are the steps required to add a new subscriber template:

Step 1.   From within SA, select **Subscribers > Subscriber Template**.

Step 2.   Click the **Add** icon in the title strip.

Step 3.   A window such as the one in Figure 8-2 displays. Enter the name for the new subscriber template.

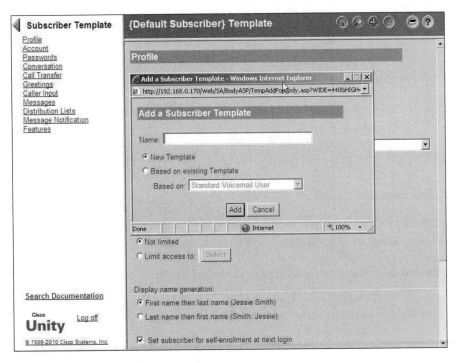

Figure 8-2   *Subscribers > Subscriber Template (Adding)*

Step 4.   If there is an existing template similar to the one you are creating, click the **Based on Existing Template** radio button and choose the existing template from the drop-down list. Otherwise, click the **New Template** radio button and click **Add**.

The creation of a template is the easy part. Now you need to configure the settings within each submenu. As Figure 8-1 shows, there are 11 submenus under Subscriber Templates. The configuration of settings in each submenu follows.

Configuring Subscriber Template Profile Settings

We start by configuring the template's Profile settings. Figure 8-3 illustrates the Subscriber Template Profile page, and the following steps describe the configuration process:

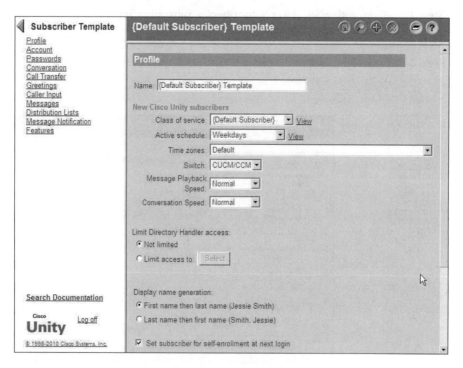

Figure 8-3   *Subscribers > Subscriber Template > Profile*

Step 1.   From the previous steps, click **Profile** from the list on the left side of the screen and move on to the next step. Otherwise, from within SA, select **Subscribers > Subscriber Template**. If the name of the template you want to manage does not display in the title strip, click the **Find** icon, and select the desired subscriber template. After the template is active, click **Profile** from the list on the left side of the screen.

Step 2.   The name of the template displays in the **Name** field on this screen. This name is chosen when the template is created. You can change it here if you want.

Step 3.   Select the desired **Class of Service**, **Active Schedule**, and **Time Zones** from the appropriate drop-down lists.

Step 4.   In a dual-switch integration, choose the phone system that the subscriber's phone is on in the **Switch** field. This field displays only with a dual-switch integration.

Step 5.   The **Message Playback Speed** setting enables you to speed up or slow down the speed at which voicemail is played back. Select the desired setting from the drop-down list.

Step 6.   The **Conversation Speed** setting permits you to speed up or slow down the speed at which Unity's prompts are played to the subscribers. Select the desired setting from the drop-down list.

Step 7.   By default, subscribers have access to all directory handlers. This enables subscribers to address messages and add users to private distribution lists through the phone. To restrict subscribers to access only certain directory handlers, select the **Limit Access To** radio button. Now click **Select**. A window appears from which you can select the directory handlers to which the subscribers will have access. In many cases, this can be left set to **Not Limited**.

Step 8.   Under the **Display Name Generation** heading, choose either **First Name Then Last Name** or **Last Name Then First Name**. This setting should be similar to the existing names in Exchange.

Step 9.   To force subscribers to record a name and greeting and change their passwords on the next login, select the **Set Subscriber for Self-Enrollment at Next Login** check box. Subscribers can choose to be listed in the directory during the self-enrollment process, if the subscribers' CoS allows this option.

Step 10.   To list subscribers in the auto-attendant directory, select the **List in Phone Directory** check box.

Step 11.   Select the **Show Subscriber in E-mail Server Address Book** check box if you want the subscriber's address to display in the Outlook address book. If this box is deselected, other subscribers cannot use the Outlook address book to address messages to the subscriber. When an Exchange server has two accounts for each user, one for email and one for voicemail, it is a good idea to deselect this box. This prevents an email user from mistakenly sending email to a voicemail inbox.

Step 12.   Finally, you need to choose how to generate the Exchange alias. Use this when creating subscribers who do not already have AD accounts. An Exchange and AD account is created when the subscriber is added, and the alias generated is based on this selection. If there are existing Exchange accounts, make sure that the format you choose matches the format of the existing Exchange aliases.

Step 13.   Click the **Save** icon in the title strip.

Configuring Subscriber Template Account Settings

Next, configure account information for the template:

Step 1.   If you are continuing from the previous steps, click **Account** from the list on the left side of the screen and continue to the next step. Otherwise, from within SA, select **Subscribers > Subscriber Template**. If the name of the template you want to manage does not appear in the title strip, click the **Find** icon and select the desired subscriber template. After the template is active, click **Account** from the list on the left side of the screen.

Step 2.   The Cisco Unity **TUI Access Status** check box enables you to lock the account at the point of creation. You might want the account to be locked at the point of creation so that the account cannot be used before the deployment is completed. Decide whether you want the accounts you create, using this template, to be locked upon creation and select the check box accordingly.

Step 3.   The other setting for account information is a billing ID. A billing ID determines which subscriber or department is billed for outbound calls placed by Unity. A billing ID is assigned to an individual mailbox or a group of mailboxes. If you want to assign the same billing ID for all subscribers using this template, enter it here. If you plan to have different billing IDs for each user or not use them at all, leave this field blank.

Step 4.   Click the **Save** icon in the title strip.

Configuring Subscriber Template Passwords Settings

The Subscriber Template Passwords page enables you to define password-specific settings. From this page, you can set default passwords and phone password settings. Figure 8-4 illustrates how the settings are configured.

To configure these settings, follow these steps:

Step 1.   From the previous steps, click **Passwords** from the list on the left side of the screen and move on to the next step. Otherwise, from within SA, select **Subscribers > Subscriber Template**. If the name of the template you want to manage does not display in the title strip, click the **Find** icon, and select the desired subscriber template. After the template is active, click **Passwords** from the list on the left side of the screen.

Step 2.   Under the **Phone Password Settings** heading, there are three settings. These settings determine whether the subscribers are able to change their passwords, whether subscribers must change their passwords on the next login, and whether the password will expire. If you do not want the users to be able to change their passwords, select the **User Cannot Change Password** check box.

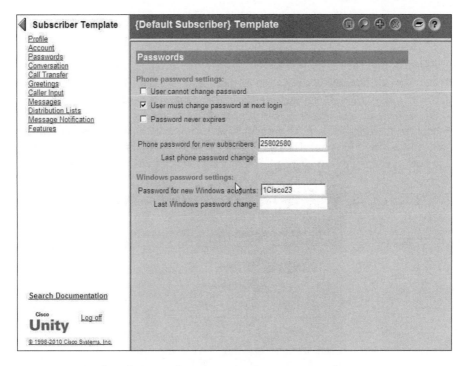

Figure 8-4   *Subscribers > Subscriber Template > Passwords*

Step 3.   You want to force subscribers to change their passwords on their first login. select the **User Must Change Password at Next Login** check box to do so.

Step 4.   To enhance security, it is a good idea to force subscribers to change their passwords on a regular basis. However, a password can be set to never expire. If you choose to configure the phone's password so that it never expires, select the **Password Never Expires** check box. If this box is left deselected, the password expires based on the setting you make in Account Policy. Although you can set a password never to expire, this is not recommended.

Step 5.   The subscribers' default passwords are determined by the passwords set in the template. In the **Phone Password for New Subscribers** field, enter the desired default phone password.

Step 6.   The next field is not configurable. The **Last Phone Password Change** field displays the date on which the phone password was last changed.

Step 7.   When new Exchange subscribers who do not have existing Windows domain accounts are added, Windows domain accounts are created for them. In the **Password for New Windows Accounts** field, enter the Exchange password you want to have assigned this account.

Step 8.   The final field on this screen in not configurable. The **Last Windows Password Change** field displays the date the last time the Windows password was changed.

Step 9.   Click the **Save** icon in the title strip.

Configuring Subscriber Template Conversation

The Subscriber Template Conversation settings enables you to configure how Unity interacts with a subscriber. This page has more configurable settings than any other page in Unity, so there is more configuration. It is important to understand how these affect a subscriber's settings because the settings have a significant impact on the subscriber's satisfaction with the system. The following steps explain what effect the settings have and how to configure them. Figure 8-5 shows the fields covered in Steps 1–8.

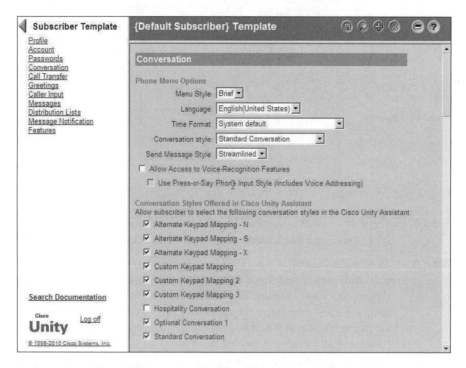

Figure 8-5   *Subscribers > Subscriber Template > Conversation*

Step 1.   From the previous steps, click **Conversation** from the list on the left side of the screen and proceed to the next step. Otherwise, from within SA, select **Subscribers > Subscriber Template**. If the name of the template you want to manage does not display in the title strip, click the **Find** icon and select the desired subscriber template. After the template is active, click **Conversation** from the list on the left side of the screen.

Step 2. The first setting determines whether the subscriber hears full or brief menus. It is a good idea to set the menus to full for users who are new to the system because full menus explain more than brief menus. After users are familiar with the menus, you might want to change to a brief menu. Choose the desired menu style from the **Menu Style** drop-down list.

Step 3. If multiple languages are installed, you can select the language from the **Language** drop-down list. This determines the language for the subscriber conversation.

Step 4. Select a time format different from the system default by selecting 12-hour or 24-hour format from the **Time Format** drop-down list. If you leave this field set to **System Default**, the format selected under **Setting > Configuration** is used.

Step 5. The **Conversation Styles** fields determine which touch tones you use to do things such as save and delete messages. If you are migrating from another voicemail system, it is a good idea to become familiar with these conversations and pick the one closest to previous voicemail system conversations. There are a number of options to choose from. The **Standard Conversation** is a good choice for locations where users are unfamiliar with a certain voicemail menu format. The **Optional Conversation 1** is a good choice if users are familiar with an Octel-like menu system. The **Hospitality Conversation** is only used when Unity's Hospitality and Property Management System is deployed.

Step 6. From the **Send Message Style** drop-down list, you can select **Standard** or **Streamline**. The Streamline option enables the subscriber to send messages and select sending options using fewer keystrokes than the Standard style. Select the desired style from the **Send Message Style** drop-down list.

Step 7. To allow subscribers to use Unity's voice recognition, select the **Allow Access to Voice-Recognition Features** check box. If this is enabled, you can also select the **Use Press-or-Say Phone Input Style** check box to permit a user to say a number in response to a prompt instead of having to press the number on the keypad.

Step 8. Unity offers a number of additional conversation styles that sound similar to other voicemail systems. This enables users to apply the same keys to perform actions such as delete, save, and so on, as they did on their previous system. Users can select the conversation style from within Unity Assistant. The conversations they can select from are determined by which are selected in the **Conversation Styles Offered in Cisco Unity Assistant** section. Select the check box of each conversation you would like to make available.

The next three sets of settings deal with phone menu responses, exit actions, and message addressing and sending. Figure 8-6 shows the fields covered in Steps 9–16.

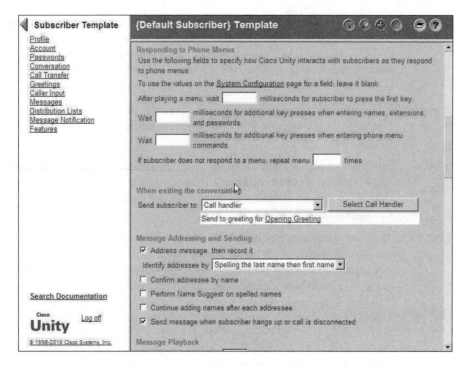

Figure 8-6   *Subscribers>Subscriber Template>Conversation (Continues)*

Step 9.   There are four values that require configuration in the **Responding to Phone Menus** section. The first three values deal with timing:

- Milliseconds to wait for subscriber to press the first key

- Milliseconds to wait for additional key presses when entering names, extensions, and passwords

- Milliseconds to wait for additional key presses when entering phone menu commands

The fourth value determines the number of times the menu will repeat if the subscriber does nothing. These values can be left blank if you want to use the ones you configured under the System Configuration. If you want values that are different than those configured in System Configuration, enter the desired values in each field.

Step 10.   Under the **When Exiting the Conversation** heading, you can configure where subscribers are sent when they end the subscriber conversation. A number of choices are available from the drop-down list; normally this is configured to send the subscriber to a call handler or hang up. Select the destination from the **Send Subscriber To** drop-down list. If **Call Handler** is selected, click the **Select Call Handler** button to choose the desired call handler.

Step 11.   To have subscribers prompted to address a message before being allowed to record it, select the **Address Message and Then Record It** check box. To allow subscribers to record a message and then address it, deselect this box.

Step 12.   To configure how a subscriber is prompted to address messages to other subscribers, select one of the available choices from the **Identify Addressee By** drop-down list: **Spelling the Last Name Then First Name, Spelling the First Name Then Last Name,** or **Enter the Extension.**

Step 13.   To have Unity confirm the name of each addressee as it is added, select the **Confirm Addressee by Name** check box. If deselected, this feature is disabled.

Step 14.   If the **Perform Name Suggest on Spelled Names** check box is selected, Unity will search for name matches after each key is pressed (starts searching after the second key). If it finds a single match, it plays the name of the match. When it finds between two and six matches, it states how many matches have been found. If the box is deselected, this feature is disabled.

Step 15.   To allow subscribers to enter addresses one after the other, select the **Continue Adding Names After Each Addressee** check box. After the user is done entering the addresses, she presses 2 to send the message. If this box is not selected, the user must press 1 after each address to enter another one.

Step 16.   When the **Send Message When Subscriber Hangs Up or Call Is Disconnected** check box is selected, Unity automatically sends the message when the call disconnects. If this box is not selected, the subscriber must press # for the message to be sent.

The next group of settings to configure in the conversation area deal with the messages playback option. Figures 8-7, 8-8, and 8-9 show the fields that are covered in these steps.

Step 17.   When a subscriber is listening to messages, he can fast-forward and rewind the message. The amount of time that is applied to these functions is defined by the value entered in the **Fast-Forward Messages By** and **Rewind Messages By** fields. The default is 5 seconds and is adequate in most cases. To change this value, simply enter the new value in the appropriate field.

Step 18.   If the **Confirm Deletions of New and Saved Messages** check box is selected, a subscriber will be prompted to confirm each time that she attempts to delete a message. If you have a user that frequently deletes messages by mistake, this might be a feature you should turn on.

Step 19.   The **Mark a Message as Saved Upon Hangup or Disconnection** field determines how Unity will mark messages that are being listened to when the call is disconnected. If the box is selected, the message is marked read. If left deselected, the message is marked as new.

Step 20.   To have Unity play the extension number of the subscriber that sent a message along with the subscriber's recorded name, select the **Announce**

Sender's Extension for Messages from Subscribers check box. In most cases, this box is left deselected.

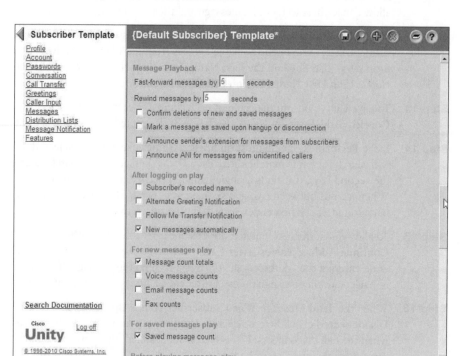

Figure 8-7   *Subscribers > Subscriber Template > Conversation (Continues)*

Step 21.   To have Unity play the Automatic Number Identification (ANI) of an unidentified caller that sent a message, select the **Announce ANI for Messages from Unidentified Callers** check box.

Step 22.   To have the recorded name of the subscriber played when he logs in to Unity, select the **Subscriber's Recorded Name** check box.

Step 23.   An alternate greeting is used when a subscriber is out of the office for a long period of time, such as vacation. It is important that the subscriber remember to turn this greeting off when he or she returns. Configure Unity to inform the subscriber whether the alternate greeting is enabled when he logs in by selecting the **Alternate Greeting Notification** check box. Starting with Unity 4.04, when a subscriber enables the alternate greeting, he can automatically schedule a time for the alternate greeting to be disabled.

Step 24.   Unity offers a follow-me feature. This feature is used to have calls sent to a number other than users' desk phones. It is similar to a call-forward feature. When enabled, Unity will not send the call to the SB's desk phone. To have the SB notified when this feature is on, select the **Follow Me Transfer Notification** check box. If an SB leaves this feature on, she is notified the next time she checks her voicemail. She is then offered the option of turning it off or leaving it on.

Step 25. To have Unity start playing new messages as soon as the SB logs in, select the **New Messages Automatically** check box. This prevents the SB from having to press a key before new messages are played.

Step 26. To configure Unity to inform the subscriber of the total number of new messages and of the message count, select the box next to each type of message count you want the subscriber to hear. The choices are **Message Count Totals**, **Voice Message Counts**, **Email Message Counts**, and **Fax Counts**. It is best to offer only the message counts for the messages the subscriber is likely to retrieve using the phone. For example, if the subscriber retrieves only voicemail using the phone, only **Voice Message Counts** is chosen.

Step 27. To announce the number of saved messages to the subscriber, select the **Saved Message Count** check box.

Step 28. Figure 8-8 shows the next set of fields. To allow subscribers to determine the types of messages they want to hear, select the **Message Type Menu** check box. When this option is enabled, the subscriber hears the following message: "Press 1 to hear voice messages, press 2 to hear emails, press 3 to hear faxes, press 4 to hear receipts."

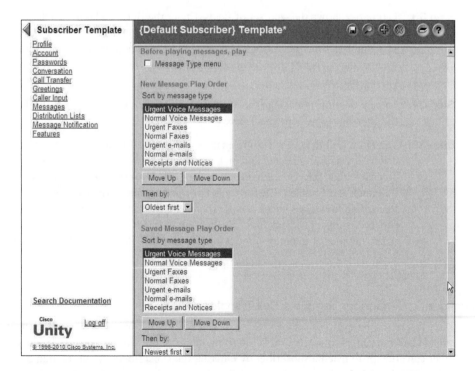

Figure 8-8 *Subscribers > Subscriber Template > Conversation (Continues)*

Step 29. The order in which new messages are played can be modified. Under the **New Message Play Order** heading is a list of the various types of messages. The messages are played as they appear from top to bottom. To change the order, highlight the type of message you want to move, and then click the **Move Up** or **Move Down** button. Repeat this process with all the message types until they are in the desired order.

Step 30. When playing new messages, the default behavior of Unity is to play the oldest message first. To play the newest message first, choose **Newest First** from the **Then By** drop-down list. In most cases, it is best to leave this setting at **Oldest First**.

Step 31. The order in which saved messages are played can be modified. Under the **Saved Message Play Order** heading is a list of the various types of messages. The messages are played as they appear from top to bottom. To change the order, highlight the type of message you want to move, and then click the **Move Up** or **Move Down** button. Repeat this process with all the message types until they are in the desired order.

Step 32. When playing saved messages, the default behavior of Unity is to play the newest message first. To play the oldest message first, choose **Oldest First** from the **Then By** drop-down list. In most cases, it is best to leave this setting at **Newest First**.

Step 33. Figure 8-9 shows the next set of fields. Under the **Before Playing Each Message, Play** heading you can choose to play the sender's information, message number, time the message was sent, and message duration. To configure what is played, select the box next to each type of information that you want to have played.

Step 34. To play the time a message was sent after a message is played, select the **Time the Message Was Sent** check box.

Step 35. The Drop Call Recovery feature enables an SB to call Unity back when the call has been disconnected and pick up where he was when the call dropped. To enable this, select the **Enable DCR for Calls Dropped During Message Playback** and **Enable DCR for Calls Dropped While Addressing or Recording Messages** check boxes. You can also modify the time in which a subscriber must call back in for this feature to be invoked by entering the desire number of minutes in the **After Disconnect, Recover Calls For** fields.

Step 36. Click the **Save** icon in the title strip.

Configuring Subscriber Template Call Transfer

The subscribers' template call transfer settings determine what happens to a call when an outside caller attempts to reach a subscriber's phone from the auto-attendant. An outside caller can attempt to reach a subscriber by entering the subscriber's extension number or by using Unity's dial-by-name feature. When Unity finds a match for either the extension number or the name, it looks at the subscriber's call transfer settings to determine where to send the call. One would think that Unity would send the call to the PBX so that the call could be delivered to the phone. Although this is the most common action, it is not always desired. A number of circumstances can dictate that the call not be sent to the phone.

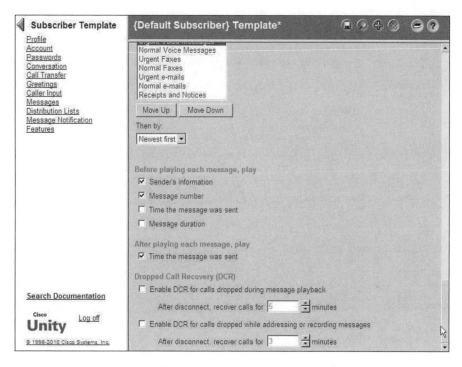

Figure 8-9   *Subscribers > Subscriber Template > Conversation (Continued).*

If the call is sent to the phone, it can be transferred to the PBX in one of two ways, Released to Switch and Supervised Transfer.

A **Released to Switch** transfer enables Unity to send the call to the PBX and is then finished with that call. If the called party does not answer or the phone is busy, it is the responsibility of the PBX to forward the call back to Unity. You might think that if the PBX sent the call back to Unity, Unity would just loop the call back to the PBX because the call transfer settings dictate it. The reason it does not loop is because the call transfer settings do not affect calls that are forwarded to Unity from the PBX. If the transfer settings were applied to every call, unanswered and busy calls would loop forever.

The second type of transfer is called **Supervised Transfer.** On a supervised transfer, Unity holds open the port used to transfer the call and tries to determine whether the call is answered. When Unity determines that the call is answered, Unity releases the call and the port is closed. If Unity determines that the call is busy or is not answered within the number of rings defined for this transfer, Unity pulls the call back and plays the subscriber's greeting. Because Unity maintains control of the call during a supervised transfer, additional features can be implemented, such as holding options and call screening.

Figure 8-10 shows the Call Transfer Setting page. The following steps describe how to configure the various settings and discuss the effect they have on transferred calls.

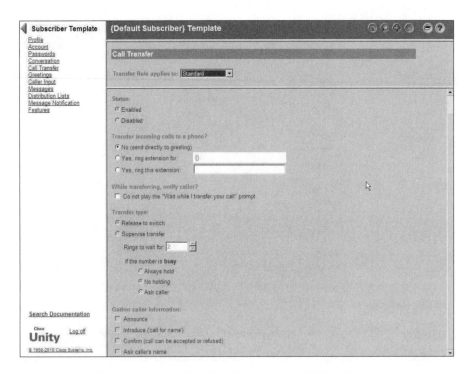

Figure 8-10   *Subscribers > Subscriber Template > Call Transfer.*

Step 1.   From the previous steps, click **Call Transfer** from the list on the left side of the screen and proceed to the next step. Otherwise, from within SA, select **Subscribers > Subscriber Template**. If the name of the template you want to manage does not appear in the title strip, click the **Find** icon and select the desired subscriber template. After the template is active, click **Call Transfer** from the list on the left side of the screen.

Step 2.   Calls can be handled differently during open hours and closed hours. A call can also be handled differently if the follow-me feature is enabled. Because of this, it might be necessary to configure transfer settings for both situations. To accomplish this, use the **Transfer Rule Applies To** drop-down list to select the schedule or follow feature that you want to configure. Table 8-2 illustrates the six types of transfer rules that can be configured.

Step 3.   To enable the type of call transfer that you select in Step 2, select the **Enable** radio button.

Table 8-2 *Transfer Rules*

Type	Description
Standard	This transfer rule applies during open hours. It also applies at all hours if no other transfer rule is enabled.
Closed	If enabled, the Closed transfer rule applies during closed hours.
Alternate	If the enabled, it supersedes the other transfer rules and is applied all hours on all days.
Follow-Me Here	It is used with the follow-me feature.
Follow-Me Home	It is used with the follow-me feature.
Follow-Me Mobile	It is used with the follow-me feature.

Step 4. To configure whether, and to which phone, a call will be sent, select the **Yes, Ring Extension For** radio button. If you do not want the phone to ring and for the call to be sent straight to the subscriber's greeting, select the **No (Send Directly to Subscriber's Greeting)** radio button. The call can also be sent to an extension other than the one associated with the subscriber by selecting the **Yes, Ring This Extension** radio button. Set the transfer setting to send the call to the subscriber's extension. If **No (Send Directly to Subscriber's Greeting)** is selected, the remaining steps in this section do not apply.

Step 5. By default, Unity plays a prompt to the caller informing her that the call is being transferred. To disable this prompt, select the **Do Not Play the "Wait While I Transfer Your Call" Prompt** check box.

Step 6. If the call is transferred to an extension, the type of transfer must be selected under the **Transfer Type** heading. If holding and screening options are desired, select the **Supervise Transfer** radio button. If these features are not needed, select the **Release to Switch** radio button. If **Release to Switch** is selected, the remaining steps in this section do not apply.

Step 7. Unity has the capability to queue calls for subscribers if they are on the phone when a call is transferred from Unity. You must choose one of three options for Unity to know whether the subscriber's extension is busy. The choices are

- **Always hold:** Informs the caller that the extension is busy and places the caller on hold

- **No holding:** Prompts the caller to leave a message or dial another extension

- **Ask caller:** Informs the caller that the extension is busy and offers the choice of holding, leaving a message, or dialing another extension

Select the desired action by clicking the associated radio button.

Note   When implementing the option to allow the caller to hold, remember that this will hold a port open while the caller is on hold. If this option is offered to a number of sub- scribers, it could adversely affect Unity's ability to handle incoming calls.

Step 8.   Unity has the capability to gather caller information for screening purposes on a supervised transfer. There are four options under the **Gather Caller Information** heading. These options are as follows:

- **Announce:** Unity announces "transferring call" when the subscriber answers the call.

- **Introduce:** Unity announces whom the call is for when the subscriber answers the phone. This feature is used when more than one person receives calls on the same phone.

- **Confirm:** Unity asks the subscriber to press 1 to accept the call or press 2 to send the call to voicemail.

- **Ask caller's name:** Unity asks the callers to record their names and plays the recorded names to the subscriber when the phone is answered.

Select the options you want to enable by selecting the radio button next to each option.

Step 9.   Click the **Save** icon in the title strip.

Configuring Subscriber Template Greetings

The Greetings setting of the template enables you to define what greetings are enabled and how they are configured. A subscriber can use up to five greetings, each played under different circumstances. Table 8-3 lists these greetings and the function of each.

Table 8-3   *Greetings*

Greeting	Function
Standard	Plays during open hours unless overridden by another greeting. If the Closed greeting is not enabled, Standard plays after hours.
Closed	Plays during closed hours as defined in the schedule associated with the sub- scriber.
Busy	Plays when the call is transferred to Unity because the subscriber's extension was busy.
Internal	Plays when the caller is another subscriber on the system.
Alternate	When enabled, overrides all other greetings. This greeting plays all hours, all days until disabled.

Figure 8-11 shows the Subscriber Template Greetings configuration screen. The following steps discuss the effects of these settings and describe how to configure them.

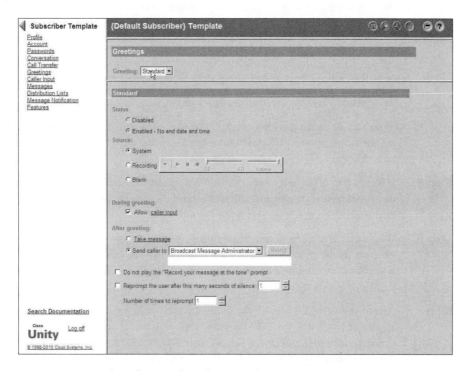

Figure 8-11   *Subscribers>Subscriber Template>Greetings*

Step 1.   After applying the previous steps, click **Greetings** from the list on the left side of the screen and proceed to the next step. Otherwise, from within SA, select **Subscribers > Subscriber Template.** If the name of the template you want to manage does not appear in the title strip, click the **Find** icon, and select the desired subscriber template. After the template is active, click **Greetings** from the list on the left side of the screen.

Step 2.   From this screen, you can enable and configure each of the five greetings. From the **Greeting** drop-down list, select the greeting you want to configure. Start with the Standard greeting.

Step 3.   Under the **Status** heading, the greeting can be enabled or disabled. If the greeting is disabled, it will not be used. The Standard greeting is enabled by default and cannot be disabled. If you are configuring a greeting other than the standard greeting, select the **Enabled** radio button to enable this type of greeting.

Step 4.   Under the **Source** heading, the source of the message is chosen. The three choices for the source are as follows:

- **System:** Plays the prerecorded greeting "Sorry, <subscriber's name> is not available." If the subscriber has not yet recorded a name, the greeting "Sorry, the subscriber at extension <subscriber's extension number> is not available" is played.

- **Recording:** Plays the greeting that the subscriber recorded.

- **Blank:** Plays no greeting and goes directly to the after-greeting action.

Typically, **Recording** is chosen for this setting so that the subscribers can create their own greetings. Select the desired source by clicking the appropriate radio button.

Step 5.   If **Recording** is chosen, you can use the media master control panel (the VCR-like panel next to the record label) to record a greeting. This interface also enables you to copy, cut, and paste the recording.

Step 6.   To allow callers to try to reach another extension or select options during a greeting, select the **Allow Caller Input** check box. Notice that *caller input* is underlined; this is a link to the Caller Input page. The Caller Input page is covered later in this section.

Step 7.   After the greeting is played, the caller has the opportunity to leave a message. To enable this, click the **Take Message** radio button. If you want a different action to take place, click the **Send Caller To** radio button and select the desired destination. Table 8-4 lists the destination options and actions from the drop-down list.

When choosing to send the call to a call handler, directory handler, interview handler, or another subscriber, you have to specify the specific handler or subscriber. A **Select Type_of_Object_You_Selected** button becomes available to the right of the type of object you select.

For example, if you select the option to send the call to a subscriber, choose the **Select Subscriber** button. When you click this button, a search criteria window displays. Enter the appropriate criteria and click **Find**. Select the desired object from the list. If a subscriber or call handler is selected, you must also select whether the call should be sent to the greeting or the phone extension. To send the call to the extension, select **Attempt Transfer For** from the **Conversation** drop-down list. To send the call to the subscriber's greeting, select **Send to Greeting For** from the **Conversation** drop-down list.

Note   Because you have to choose to send the call to the greeting, or attempt to transfer it, has caused many administrators hours of frustration and troubleshooting. Make sure that if you want the phone of the subscriber to whom the call is transferred to ring, you must select **Attempt Transfer For**.

Table 8-4 *Send Caller To Destinations*

Destination	Action
Broadcast Message Administrator	Sends the call to a conversation for sending broadcast messages.
CVM Mailbox Reset	Sends the call to a conversation that allows the caller to reset the mailbox. This is only available when the Community Voice-mail (CVM) package is being used.
Call Handler	Sends the call to the selected call handler.
Caller System Transfer	Sends the callers to a prompt that allows them to enter another extension to which they would like to be transferred.
Directory Handler	Sends the call to the directory handler you select.
Greetings Administrator	Sends the call to a conversation that allows them to manage the greetings of call handlers that they own.
Hang Up	Disconnects the call.
Hotel Checked Out	This option works in concert with Cisco Unity's Hospitality and Property Management Integration. It allows guests to archive their messages when checking out.
Interview Handler	Sends the call to the interview handler you select.
Sign-in	Sends the call to subscriber sign-in.
In Archived Mailbox	Enables subscribers to access messages on the Cisco Unity server by entering their old Cisco Unity primary extension.
Subscriber	Sends the call to another subscriber's greeting or extension depending upon how it is configured.
Subscriber System Transfer	Enables callers to transfer to another extension after they log in with subscriber credentials. They can then transfer to any number that their restriction table allows.

Step 8.   By default, Unity plays a prompt after the subscriber greeting that instructs the caller to leave a message after the tone. Because many subscribers include

these instructions in their greeting, you might want to disable this prompt. You can do so by selecting the **Do Not Play the "Record Your Message at the Tone" Prompt** check box.

Step 9.   If callers remain silent after being offered the opportunity to leave a message, they can be reprompted. To have a caller reprompted, select the **Reprompt the User After This Many Seconds of Silence** check box and enter the number of seconds to wait for the caller to begin speaking. Then enter the number of times you want the caller to be reprompted; the maximum is 100.

Step 10. Click the **Save** icon in the title strip.

Configuring Subscriber Template Caller Input

When callers reach a greeting, a list of options is made available to them. Often the caller is given the option to dial another extension or reach an operator by pressing a certain digit. Adding options to a spoken greeting isn't enough; these options must also be configured under the Caller Input section of the template.

The following steps show how to configure the Caller Input settings, which are shown in Figure 8-12.

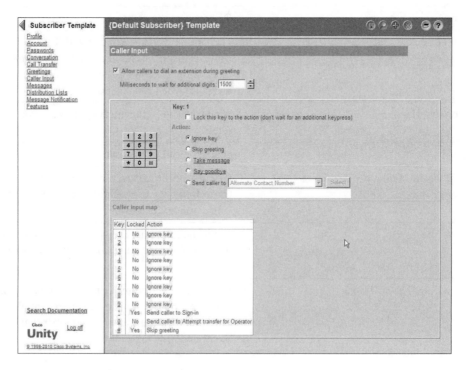

Figure 8-12   *Subscribers> Subscriber Template > Caller Input.*

Step 1.   After applying the previous steps, click **Caller Input** from the list on the left side of the screen and move on to the next step. Otherwise, from within SA, select **Subscribers > Subscriber Template**. If the name of the template you want to manage does not appear in the title strip, click the **Find** icon and select the desired subscriber template. After the template is active, click **Caller Input** from the list on the left side of the screen.

Step 2.   The first setting that must be configured determines whether callers are able to reach a different extension when listening to a subscriber's greeting. This is commonly allowed because callers might rather try to reach someone else instead of leave a message. To allow a caller to enter another extension while listening to a greeting, select the **Allow Callers to Dial an Extension During Greeting** box check.

Step 3.   If the option to allow callers to dial another extension during the greeting is enabled, an interdigit timeout must also be configured. The **Milliseconds to Wait for Additional Digits** setting is the amount of time Unity waits before deciding that the caller has finished pressing digits. The default value is 1500 milliseconds, which is a second and a half. Typically, this value is adequate. If, during a greeting, callers are transferred or receive error messages from Unity before they are finished dialing an extension, increase this value.

Step 4.   From the dial pad on the screen, you can configure the action that is taken when a digit is pressed. A button can be configured for five types of actions. Table 8-5 provides descriptions and actions for caller input.

- **Ignore key:** No action is taken when digit is pressed.

- **Skip greeting:** The greeting is skipped and Unity proceeds to the after-greeting action.

- **Take message:** The caller can press this key to cause Unity to take a message.

- **Say goodbye:** Unity plays a good-bye message and disconnects the call.

- **Send caller to:** This option allows various destinations for the caller. Table 8-5 provides descriptions and actions for caller input.

Step 5.   Click the digit you want to configure, and then select the action by clicking the appropriate radio button.

As with the Greetings settings, when choosing to send the call to a call handler, directory handler, interview handler, or another subscriber, you have to designate the specific handler or subscriber.

Step 6.   If the **Lock This Key to the Action (Don't Wait for an Additional Keypress)** check box is selected, an extension that begins with this digit cannot be entered. Unity then transfers the call to the destination assigned to that key without waiting to see whether the caller is going to enter other digits. Only enable this field on digits that are not leading digits for any extensions.

Step 7.   After you have all the digits configured, click the **Save** icon in the title strip.

Table 8-5   *Caller Input Actions*

Action	Description
Alternate Contact Number	Sends the call to the number that you specify in the **Number to Dial** field.
Broadcast Message Administrator	Sends the call to a conversation for sending broadcast messages.
CVM Mailbox Reset	Enables the caller to reset the mailbox (available with Community Voice-mail package).
Call Handler	Sends the call to the selected call handler.
Caller System Transfer	Enables the caller to transfer to another extension after he logs in with subscriber credentials. He can then transfer to any number that his restriction table allows.
Directory Handler	Sends the call to the directory handler you select.
Easy Sign-In	Sends the call to a login process that asks for the password for this mailbox.
Greetings Administrator	Sends the call to a conversation that allows users to manage the greetings of call handlers that they own.
Hang Up	Disconnects the call.
Hotel Checked Out	This option works in concert with Cisco Unity's Hospitality and Property Management Integration. It enables guests to archive their messages when checking out.
Interview Handler	Sends the call to the interview handler you select.
Sign-In	Sends the call to the subscriber sign-in.
Sign-In Archived Mailbox	Enables subscribers to access messages on the Cisco Unity server by entering their old Cisco Unity primary extension.
Subscriber	Sends the call to another subscriber's greeting or extension, depending upon how it is configured.

Table 8-5 *Caller Input Actions*

Action	Description
Subscriber System Transfer	Enables callers to transfer to another extension after they log in with subscriber credentials. They can then transfer to any number that their restriction table allows.

Configuring Subscriber Template Messages Settings

The Subscriber Template Messages section enables you to configure caller message-specific attributes, such as message length, post-message options, caller options, and MWI settings.

Figure 8-13 shows the various settings that are configured from this screen. The following steps illustrate how to configure these settings and describe the effect on each setting.

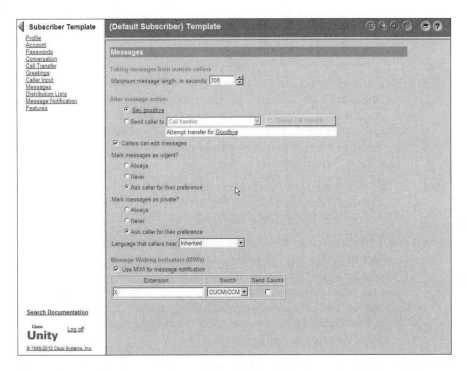

Figure 8-13 *Subscribers > Subscriber Template > Messages*

Step 1. From the previous steps, click **Messages** from the list on the left side of the screen and proceed to the next step. Otherwise, from within SA, select **Subscribers > Subscriber Template**. If the name of the template you want to manage does not appear in the title strip, click the **Find** icon, and select the desired subscriber template. After the template is active, click **Messages** from the list on the left side of the screen.

Step 2.   To set the maximum length of a message that an outside caller can leave, enter the value in seconds in the **Maximum Message Length, in Seconds** box. This setting applies only to messages left from outside callers. The limit for subscribers is set by the subscriber's CoS.

Step 3.   After the message is recorded, select either the **Say Goodbye** or the **Send Caller To** radio button. When choosing **Send Caller To**, the destination must be chosen. The destinations are the same as those under the **Send Caller To** drop-down list in the caller input section.

Step 4.   If you want to let callers listen to, change, or delete the message they leave, the select the **Callers Can Edit Message** check box.

Step 5.   Allow the caller to label a message urgent by selecting the **Ask Caller for Their Preference** radio button under the **Mark Messages as Urgent** heading. To mark a message always urgent without asking the caller, select the **Always** radio button, or to never mark the message urgent, select the **Never** radio button.

Step 6.   Callers can be given the option to mark a message private. When messages are marked private, they can be encrypted based on the message security settings. To always have a message marked private, select the **Always** radio button in the **Mark Messages as Private** section. To never have a message marked private, select the **Never** radio button. To allow the caller to decide whether he wants to have the message marked private, select the **Ask Caller for Their Preference** radio button.

Step 7.   Select the language in which Unity plays its prompt from the **Language That Callers Hear** drop-down list. When this field is set to **Inherited**, it uses the language used by the parent call handler.

Step 8.   Under the **Message Waiting Indicators (MWIs)** heading, enable MWI by selecting the **Use MWI for Message Notification** check box. Entering an X in the **Extension** box causes the extension associated with the subscriber to be activated. If you place an extension number in this field, that extension's MWI is activated when users created from the template receive a voicemail. If the **Send Count** check box is selected, the message count appears on the screen of phones that support this feature.

Step 9.   If you do not want to use MWI, simply deselect the **Use MWI for Message Notification** check box.

Step 10. Click the **Save** icon in the title strip.

Configuring Subscriber Template Distribution Lists Settings

The most efficient way to add subscribers to a public distribution list is by adding them through the subscriber template. The following steps show how this is done:

Step 1. From the previous steps, click **Distribution Lists** from the list on the left side of the screen and proceed to the next step. Otherwise, from within SA, select **Subscribers > Subscriber Template**. If the name of the template you want to manage does not appear in the title strip, click the **Find** icon and select the desired subscriber template. After the template is active, click **Distribution Lists** from the list on the left side of the screen.

Step 2. Figure 8-14 shows that the available **Public Distribution Lists** are displayed on the left side of the screen and the **New Subscribers Added To** lists are on the right side. To move a list from one column to the other, highlight the desired list and select either the **>>** button or the **<<** button.

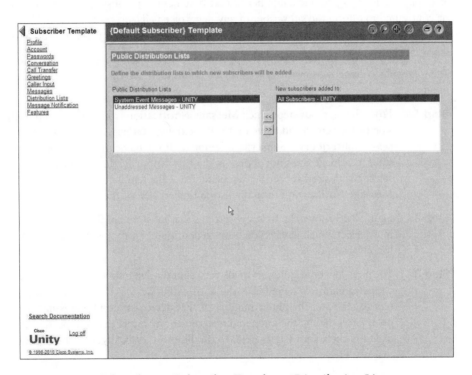

Figure 8-14 *Subscribers > Subscriber Template > Distribution Lists*

Step 3. Click the **Save** icon in the title strip.

Configuring Subscriber Template Message Notification Settings

Message notification allows a subscriber to be informed through a pager, phone, or other external device when a new message arrives. This type of notification is very useful for subscribers who are seldom in the office, such as outside salespeople or service technicians.

It might seem odd that you can set up message notification in the subscriber template. After all, you will not want to send a message to the same pager when any subscriber, who was created using this template, receives a new message. However, the subscriber template is an excellent place to create the same type of flow and generic notification settings for a large number of subscribers. After the subscribers are added, you can have them fill in the details such as the specific phone numbers using Cisco Personal Communications Assistant (CPCA).

More than a dozen devices can be configured for message notification. This includes eight phones, four pagers, and a number of text-based devices. Message notification can be configured to inform the subscriber of any new voicemails, faxes, and emails. The settings on this screen determine what type of message triggers a notification and what device(s) are notified.

The following steps show how these settings are configured and discuss the effect they produce:

Step 1.   From the previous steps, click **Message Notification** from the list on the left side of the screen and move on to the next step. Otherwise, from within SA, select **Subscribers > Subscriber Template**. If the name of the template you want to manage does not appear in the title strip, click the **Find** icon, and select the desired subscriber template. After the template is active, click **Message Notification** from the list on the left side of the screen.

Step 2.   Figure 8-15 shows the first few settings that must be configured. First you must select which device you want to configure. From the **Device** drop-down list, choose a device.

Step 3.   The next few configuration fields vary slightly depending on whether you choose a phone or an email as the notification device. If you choose a phone or a pager, enter the phone number of that device in the **Phone Number** field. After dialing the phone number, enter any digits that still need to be dialed in the **Extra Digits** field. Extra digits are typically needed for pagers that use PINs.

If you choose a device that will use an email address as the delivery mechanism, such as a text pager or Text for Visual Messaging Interface (VMI), enter the email address in the **To** field. Then enter the pilot number for Unity in the **From** field. Some cell phones will act as pagers and can call back the number that is in the **From** field. Figure 8-16 shows these fields.

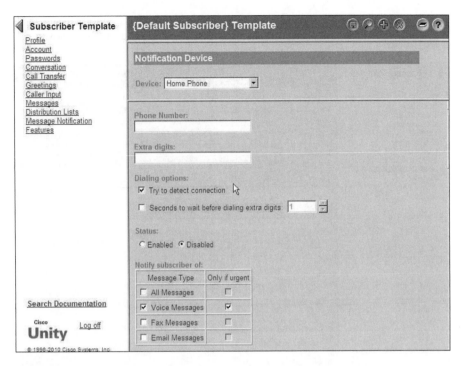

Figure 8-15 *Subscribers > Subscriber Template > Message Notification (Phone or Pager).*

Note   VMI is the old name for CPCA Inbox, which enables a subscriber to check messages from a web page.

Step 4.   When a phone is chosen as the notification device, you can set it so that the extra digits are not sent until a connection is detected, as seen in Figure 8-15. To enable this option, select the **Try to Detect Connection** check box. If you want it to wait a specified number of seconds, instead of trying to detect a connection, select the **Seconds to Wait Before Dialing Extra Digits** check box, and enter the number of seconds to wait in the box to the right of that field. You can use the **Seconds to Wait** option if Unity is having trouble detecting a connection because of various factors, such as poor line quality. In some cases you might need to use both the **Try to Detect a Connection** and **Seconds to Wait** options. It might be necessary to set the parameters and then test these settings a few times before getting them to work properly with different paging companies.

Step 5.   When a device that uses an email address is selected, enter the text that you want to appear in the notification in the **Text** field, as seen in Figure 8-16. A message count can be included in this notification by selecting the **Include**

Voice-mail, E-mail, and Fax Counts check box. Caller information can also be included by selecting the Include Caller Information check box.

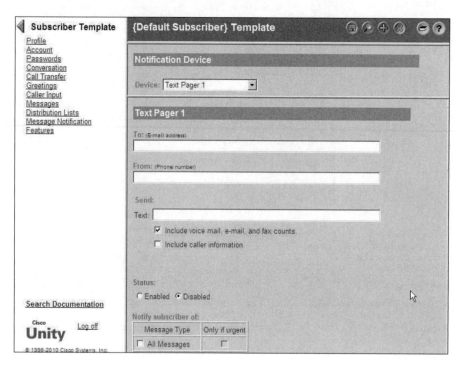

Figure 8-16 *Subscribers > Subscriber Template > Message Notification (E-Mail Device)*

Step 6. To enable this device to be used for message notification, you must select the **Enabled** radio button. It is not enough to simply configure the device—you must ensure that the **Enable** button is selected.

Step 7. Under the **Notify Subscriber Of** heading, select the types of messages of which the subscriber should be notified. As shown in Figure 8-16, you can select all messages or only one type, such as voicemail. You can further narrow it down by selecting only urgent messages.

Step 8. The next area of the screen, shown in Figure 8-17, is a grid that represents the days of the week, with each day broken into half-hour segments. This grid is used to define at what hours of the day notifications are sent out. The boxes that have a check mark represent the time of day that notifications will be sent. Edit the schedule as needed.

Note   You can copy the open/closed hours of one day to another day, and to all weekdays or weekends, by using the **Copy Day's Schedule** field under the grid. Select the

Source Day from the first drop-down list and the **Destination Day(s)** from the second drop-down list. Then click **Copy Day's Schedule**, as shown in Figure 8-17.

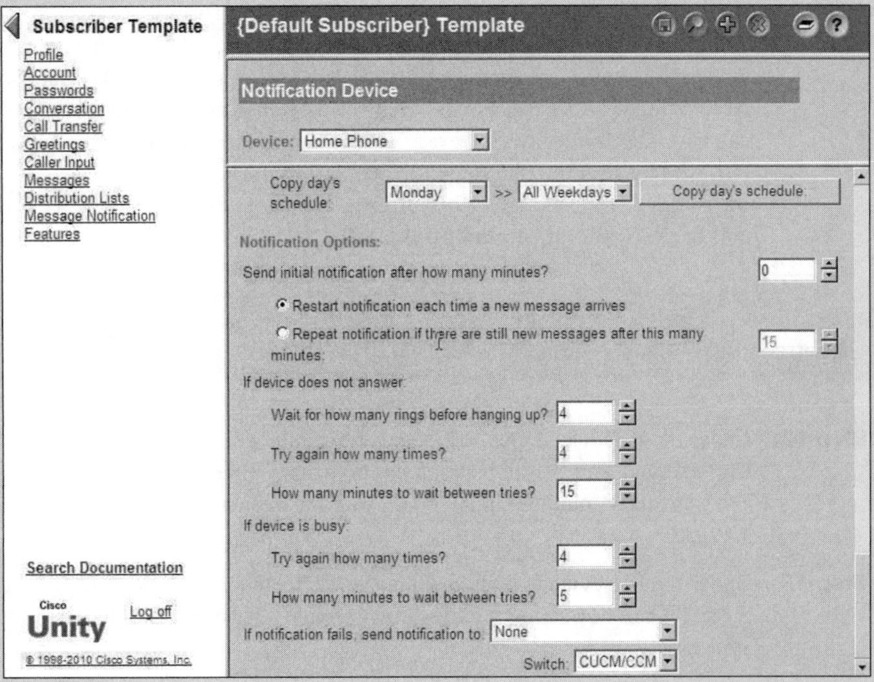

Figure 8-17   *Subscribers > Subscriber Template > Message Notification*

Step 9.   The notification can be configured to be sent immediately or to wait a specified number of minutes. If cascading notification is being deployed, some devices are configured to wait for a certain number of minutes before being notified. The term *cascading notification* means that notification is sent, and if the message has not been retrieved after a specified number of minutes, a different device is notified. If, after an additional amount of time, the message is still not retrieved, another device is notified. An example of cascading flow might look something like this:

1.   First notification is sent to your pager.

2.   You don't retrieve the message.

3.   Ten minutes later, a notification is sent to your cell phone.

4.   You don't retrieve the message.

5.   Ten minutes later a notification is sent to your boss's pager.

6.   You're busted!

Step 10.   Enter the number of minutes that Unity should wait before notifying this device in the **Send Initial Notification After How Many Minutes** field. Unity only sends the notification if the message has not been retrieved after this amount of time.

Step 11.   To have Unity send another notification to this device only when a new message arrives, select the **Restart Notification Each Time a New Message Arrives** radio button. To invoke what some refer to as the "nag factor," you can have the device notified every couple of minutes until the message is retrieved by selecting the **Repeat Notification if There Are Still New Messages After This Many Minutes** radio button. Enter the number of minutes in the field to the right of this label.

Note   If the device you are configuring is a text pager or Text for VMI, none of the following settings display. Simply click the **Save** icon in the title strip to complete this task.

Step 12.   Under the **If Device Does Not Answer** heading, enter the number of rings Unity should wait before hanging up, how many times Unity should try again, and how many minutes Unity should wait between attempts in the appropriate fields.

Step 13.   Under the **If Device Is Busy** heading, enter the number of times Unity should try again and how many minutes Unity should wait between attempts in the appropriate fields.

Step 14.   If the notification fails, you can specify another device to be informed by selecting the device from the **If Notification Fails, Send Notification To** drop-down list.

Step 15.   Click the **Save** icon in the title strip.

Configuring Subscriber Feature Settings

The Features configuration page allows you to enable and configure certain features for SBs. This area deals with broadcast messages, message locator, and message encryption. You might notice that this area does not include all features that Unity offers. I refer to the features in this section as the enhanced messaging features. The following steps offer more details on each feature and show how to configure them:

Step 1.   From the previous steps, click **Features** from the list on the left side of the screen and proceed to the next step. Otherwise, from within SA, select **Subscribers > Subscriber Template**. If the name of the template you want to manage does not appear in the title strip, click the **Find** icon and select the desired subscriber template. After the template is active, click **Features** from the list on the left side of the screen. A screen similar to Figure 8-18 appears.

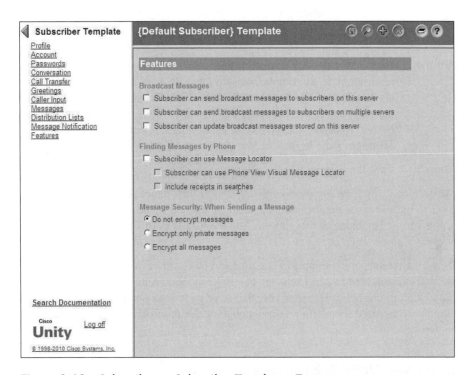

Figure 8-18   *Subscribers > Subscriber Template > Features*

Step 2.   Broadcast messages are messages that are sent to all users on the Unity server. These messages do not cause the MWI to light and are played before other messages. The user cannot skip them. They can be configured to expire automatically. Because these messages affect everyone on the system, you want to limit their accessibility. To grant rights to send broadcast messages only to users on this Unity server, select the **Subscriber Can Send Broadcast Messages to Subscribers on This Server** check box. To allow subscribers to send them to users on all Unity servers that are networked together, select the **Subscriber Can Send Broadcast Messages to Subscribers on Multiple Servers** check box. If you want to allow SBs to modify broadcast messages, select the **Subscriber Can Update Broadcast Messages Stored on This Server** check box.

Step 3.   Message locator allows SBs to search their voicemails when calling in to Unity. When this feature is enabled, the SB can search by extension, subscriber name, or outside caller phone number. Because this feature can be processor intensive, take care when determining how many SBs have access to it. To enable this feature, select the **Subscribers Can Use Message Locator** check box. To allow the results of a search to appear on the screen of a Cisco IP Phone, select the **Subscriber Can Use Phone View Visual Message Locator** check box. By default, message locator does not search non-delivery receipts (NDR) or return (read and delivery) receipts. To include these in the search, select the **Include Receipts in Searches** check box.

Step 4.   Unity has the ability to encrypt messages so that only the intended recipient can listen to it. By default this is disabled. To leave it disabled, ensure that the **Do Not Encrypt Messages** radio button is selected. To encrypt only messages marked as private, select the **Encrypt Only Private Messages** radio button. To enable encryption for all messages, select the **Encrypt All Messages** radio button.

Step 5.   Click the **Save** icon in the title strip.

At this point, you have completed creating a subscriber template. Make sure to take some time to figure out the number of templates you will need, based on the information discussed at the beginning of this chapter. Add the templates to Unity using the preceding steps as a guide.

Now that the subscriber templates are created, you can start to add subscribers. The next section explains how to add Exchange-based subscribers. A lot of configuration is necessary to get to this point. However, the success of your deployment rests heavily upon an accurately prepared foundation. Okay, enough of this foundation stuff; now start adding subscribers!

Creating New Unity Subscribers

Now that you have the subscriber templates constructed, the process of creating a user is fairly simple. To create a subscriber, enter a few pieces of information and click **Add**, and the user is created. Because subscriber creation is based on one of the templates you created, all the additional settings will be populated. There are times when you want to change the settings of a subscriber; the process for making the most common changes comes later in this chapter in the "Managing Users" section.

This section focuses on the creation of Exchange-based subscribers. The next section discusses the import process for existing Exchange subscribers.

The following steps illustrate how to add a new Exchange-based subscriber to Unity:

Step 1.   From within SA, select **Subscribers > Subscribers**.

Step 2.   Click the **Add** icon (plus sign) in the title strip.

Step 3.   A window like that shown in Figure 8-19 displays. Select the **New Subscriber** radio button and select **Exchange** from the drop-down list to the right of the label.

Note   If you have more than one Exchange server, click the **Select** button, which appears next to the name of the default Exchange server near the bottom of the page. A search criteria window opens. Click the **Find** button and select the Exchange server from the list provided. The reason you perform this step first is that if you fill in the other fields and then select a different Exchange server, all the information you entered disappears and you need to reenter it.

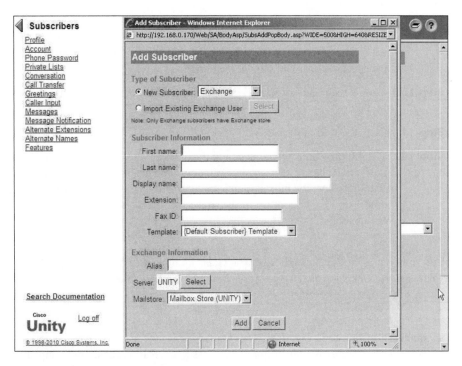

Figure 8-19   *Add Subscriber Window*

Step 4.   Enter the first and last name of the new subscriber in the fields labeled as such. The display name is automatically generated. This is the name that is displayed in Exchange and the SA. If needed, you can edit this.

Step 5.   An extension number must be assigned to every subscriber, and this should be the extension number that is assigned to the subscriber's phone. Enter the subscriber's extension number in the **Extension** field. In rare cases, the extension number in Unity is different than the actual extension assigned to the subscriber's phone, but this should be avoided. All extensions in Unity must be unique—that is, each extension can only be assigned to one subscriber.

Step 6.   In the **Fax ID** field, enter the number that a caller dials to send a fax to this subscriber.

Step 7.   Select the subscriber template that is used during the creation of this subscriber from the **Template** drop-down list.

Step 8.   The Exchange alias is automatically populated based on the settings you select on the Subscriber Template Profile screen, but this can be edited if needed. One of the options available was not to populate the **Exchange Alias** field automatically. If the aforementioned was selected, this field must be manually configured.

Step 9. As mentioned in the note at the beginning of these steps, you should have already chosen the desired Exchange server. Be aware that selecting a different Exchange server at this point will cause all the information entered on this page to disappear and require reentering.

Step 10. If more than one mailstore is available, select the one you want from the **Mailstore** drop-down list.

Step 11. Click the **Add** button.

Step 12. The information is processing, and it can take up to 15 seconds. During this time, an Exchange mailbox and Windows domain account is being created. The Unity-specific information is being added to the SQL database. After the user is created, you return to the subscriber profile screen of the newly created subscriber.

> **Note** You do not have to click the Save icon when adding a user. That is because you only have to save when you are changing something. Whenever something new is added, it is written to the database automatically.

So, that is all there is to it. The subscriber you added is now ready for use. As you can see, adding a subscriber is a much simpler process than creating subscriber templates. Because you use a template during the creation process, the majority of the subscriber settings are automatically configured, which shows the value of the subscriber template. However, there are three types of subscriber configurations that are not configured using the subscriber template. These are private lists, alternate extensions, and alternate names. These settings are not part of the subscriber template because they are unique for each subscriber.

Private lists are lists of other subscribers with whom a subscriber can communicate when sending voicemail. Instead of having to add each subscriber as a recipient, the subscriber can select a private list as the recipient, and the voicemail will be sent to everyone in the list. Subscribers are encouraged to create their own private lists, but these lists can be created and managed using SA.

Alternate extensions are used for multiple purposes. When an alternate extension is added to a subscriber, Unity treats all calls to or from that extension as if they are to or from the subscriber's primary extension. Think of it as a way to associate multiple extensions to one mailbox. Imagine that a subscriber has multiple extensions on the system. When someone calls the subscriber and the call is not answered, the caller is forwarded to the same mailbox regardless of which of the subscriber's extensions the caller dialed. This feature is also used to allow subscribers easy message access when calling from an outside phone. When calling from the outside, a subscriber must press the asterisk (*) key and enter an extension number and password. By adding the phone number of phones that are commonly used to access voicemail, such as a cell phone, this process is simplified. Because Unity recognizes the incoming caller ID as an alternate extension, the subscriber is simply being prompted for a password, just as if calling from an office phone.

Alternate names enable you to enter additional names that a subscriber can go by such as nicknames, shortened names (Bob instead of Robert), or a maiden name. These names are included in a search when voice recognition is used.

Configuring private lists, alternate extensions, and alternate names are covered in the "Managing Users" section of this chapter.

Importing Unity Subscribers

When integrating Unity with an existing Exchange server, you can import the users from the existing mailstore. This can be done one at a time or in bulk by using the Unity Bulk Import Wizard. When importing a large number of users, use the Bulk Import Wizard. When importing only one or two users, SA can be used.

The following steps illustrate how to import a single Exchange user. The steps for importing a Domino user are very similar:

Step 1.   From within SA, select **Subscribers > Subscribers**.

Step 2.   Click the **Add** icon.

Step 3.   Select the **Import Existing Exchange User** radio button.

Step 4.   Click the **Select** button. A search criteria window displays like that shown in Figure 8-20.

Step 5.   Select the **Exchange** radio button.

Step 6.   Ensure that the user's domain is in the **Domain** field.

Step 7.   You can search for the user by alias, first name, or last name. Select one of these choices from the **Find By** drop-down list and enter the search criteria in the next field. Click **Find**.

Step 8.   A list of users that match the search displays. Click the first name of the user you want to import. An **Add Subscriber** window like that shown in Figure 8-21 displays.

Step 9.   Only the **Extension, Fax ID**, and **Template** fields are edited on this screen. All other fields are populated using the information imported from the mailstore account. Enter the extension number in the **Extension** field. If the subscriber has a fax extension, enter it and select the subscriber template you want to use from the **Template** drop-down list.

Step 10. Click **Add**.

As mentioned previously, subscribers can be added using the Bulk Import Wizard. This utility can import users from an existing mailstore or from a CSV file. When importing from a CSV file, Unity adds Exchange mailboxes and Windows domain accounts for the imported users if these accounts do not already exist. Because the accounts already exist when importing from an Exchange server, there is no need for Unity to create these.

When importing from a Domino server, only Unity subscribers are created; no AD accounts are automatically created for these subscribers.

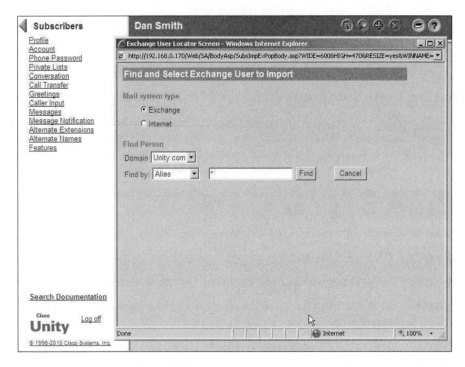

Figure 8-20   *Exchange User Search Screen*

The Import utility functions in much the same way, regardless from which source you are importing. The following steps are required when importing from a CSV file:

Step 1.   Create a CSV file. There are more than 40 values that can be entered in the CSV file for each subscriber. Of these fields, only three are required: **FIRST_NAME**, **LAST_NAME**, and **DTMF_ACCESS_ID**. The remaining fields are populated with the settings defined in the subscriber template you choose during the import.

Step 2.   Using the start menu on the Unity server, choose **Start > Programs > Unity > Cisco Unity Bulk Import.**

Step 3.   The Import Wizard starts. Click **Next.**

Step 4.   You are asked whether you want to import the users from a CSV file or AD. Choose **CSV** and click **Next.**

Step 5.   You can accept the default for the log files location and click **Next.**

Step 6.   The next page asks you to select what type of subscriber you are importing. In most cases, you will choose either **Unified Messaging** or **Voice-mail Only.** Choose the desired type of subscriber and click **Next.**

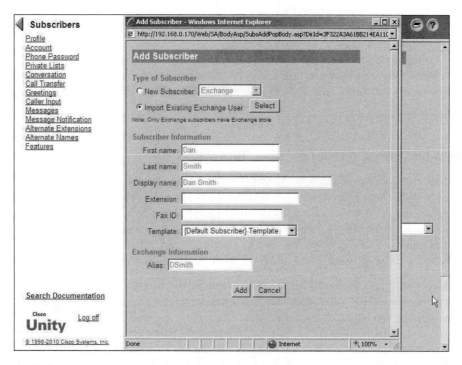

Figure 8-21   *Importing an Exchange User*

Step 7.   On the following screen, accept the default to create new mailboxes and Windows account. Click **Next**.

Step 8.   Choose a template to apply for the users you will import. Select the appropriate subscriber template and click **Next**.

Step 9.   Choose a domain and container in which to create the new users. Click **Browse**, highlight the appropriate container, and click **OK**. You will return to the previous window; click **Next**.

Step 10.   Select your server in the next window. Make sure that you have highlighted your server before continuing. Click **Next**.

Step 11.   Select the CSV file you want to use. Click **Browse**. Locate the CSV file and click **Next**.

Step 12.   The data is examined and you are presented with a summary of findings. Click **Next**.

Step 13.   Select the box of each subscriber you want to import. You can also click **Select All**. Click **Next**.

Step 14.   Confirm that you want to import the data that is shown in the summary screen. Click **Next**.

Step 15. When the import is complete, you see a final summary screen. You can view the output and error log from this screen. Click **Finish**.

Now that the subscribers are added, your system is ready for basic voicemail use. Users can now configure their personal settings, such as passwords and greetings, by dialing the voicemail pilot number and going through subscriber self-enrollment.

Next you examine how these same tasks are accomplished within Unity Connection.

Creating Unity Connection User Templates

Now that you understand how to create Unity user templates, you need to explore how to configure user templates for Unity Connection. Many of the tasks are similar, so those of you that have read the Unity section might feel that you have read some of this already. Each section is purposefully not dependent on the previous one. This is done so that you can go directly to the section you are interested in and retrieve the information without having to bounce back and forth across multiple sections or chapters.

Before moving on to the actual process of creating user templates, it is important that you understand that these templates are significant only at the point of creation. This means that the setting of a template affects the user only when the user is first created. If you create 50 users using a template, changes you make to that template after the users are created do not affect the user's settings. If you need to change certain settings on a large number of users, use the Bulk edit mode. This utility is discussed in Chapter 11.

There are more than 80 configurable settings for each user, so there must be at least that many settings for each user template. It is important to understand the effect of each setting. Figure 8-22 shows the Edit drop-down list that displays each configurable category of a user template.

Table 8-6 lists the types of settings that each section contains.

Note The Phone Menu, Playback Message and Send Message settings are important to the success of the system, because allowing control over the settings makes the new system more acceptable to the end user. I was once asked to deliver some end-user training for a company whose employees were very frustrated with the system. As it turned out, 90 percent of their concerns related to the Phone Menu, Playback Message and Send Message settings. After they learned to configure these settings themselves, the majority of the issues were resolved.

Two user templates are created during the installation process. These are the administrator template and the voicemail user template. As their names imply, they each have settings that are commonly found in administrative-level users and voicemail users.

Note Although you can use the default voicemail user template to create users, it is best to confirm the template's settings first. Do not assume that the default settings are the best settings for your deployment.

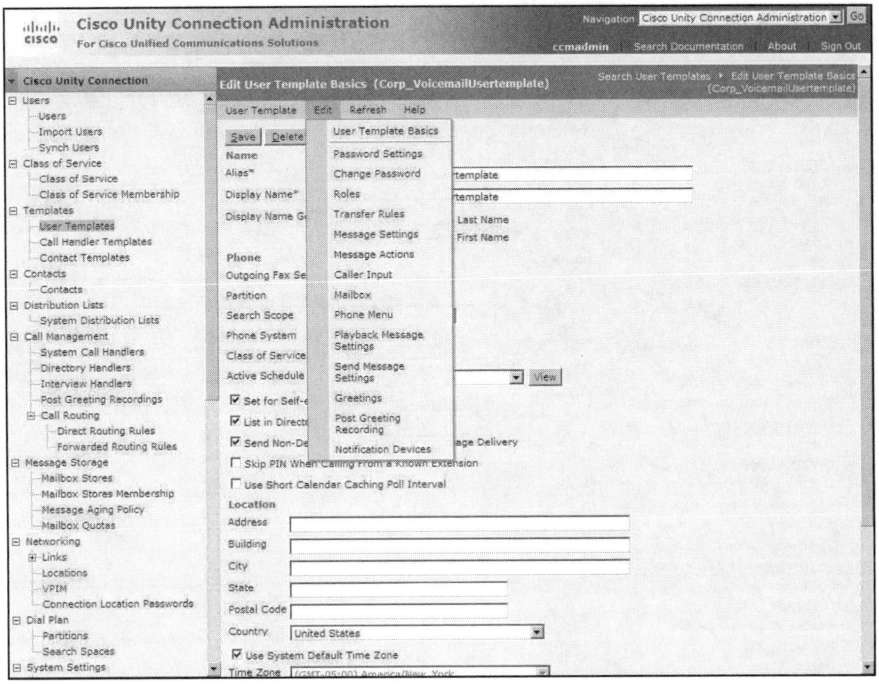

Figure 8-22 *User Template*

At this point, you should have an idea of the different templates you need. We go through the process of creating and managing a template so that you fully understand all the settings that must be configured. We begin by adding a new template. The following steps are required to add a new user template when creating users with mailboxes:

Step 1. From within Unity Connection Administrator (UCA), select **Templates > User Templates**.

Step 2. Click the **Add New** button.

Step 3. A window similar to Figure 8-23 displays. To create a template for a standard type of user, select **User Template With Mailbox** from the **User Template Type** drop-down list.

Note You would select **User Template Without Mailbox** from the **User Template Type** drop-down list when creating a template that will be used to create administrative users.

Step 4. From the **Based on Template** drop-down list, select the existing template that you want to use as a starting point for creating the new template.

Step 5. Enter a unique name for the template in the **Alias** field.

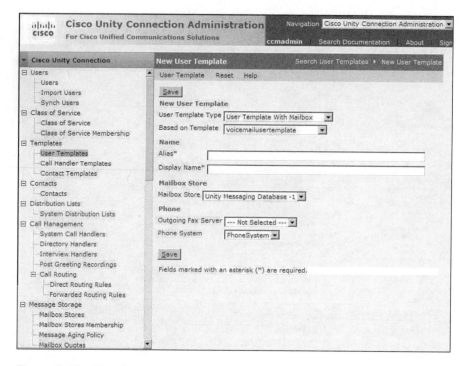

Figure 8-23   *Templates > User Templates (Adding)*

Step 6.   Enter a description name in the **Display Name** field.

Note   Often in a single Unity Connection server environment, you only need to configure the first four fields.

Step 7.   From the **Mailbox Store** drop-down list, select the mailbox store that the mailboxes are created on for users created using this template.

Step 8.   If you are implementing the fax feature of Unity Connection, you can select the fax server from the **Outgoing Fax Server** drop-down list.

Step 9.   From the **Phone System** drop-down list, select the phone system to be associated with users.

Step 10.   Click **Save**.

The creation of a template is the easy part. Now you need to configure the settings within each submenu. As Figure 8-22 shows, there are 13 submenus under User Templates. The configuration of settings in each submenu follows. We start by configuring the template's basic settings. Figure 8-24 shows the User Templates Basic page, and the following steps describe how to configure these settings:

Table 8-6 *User Template Categories*

Category	Description
User Template Basics	General settings, such as schedules, location, class of service, and time zones are set in this area.
Password Settings	This area enables you to determine whether the user's account will be available for use as soon as it is created or whether an administrator will have to unlock it first. It also defines whether users have the ability to change their own password and whether it expires automatically.
Change Password	This area enables you to configure default passwords.
Roles	This area enables you to define what roles are assigned to users created using this template.
Transfer Rules	This area determines what action is taken when a user's extension is dialed from within Unity. Most of the time, this occurs when an outside caller dials the extension from the auto-attendant.
Message Settings	The settings in this area determine the length permitted for messages, whether callers can edit messages, and post-message actions.
Message Actions	Determines what Unity Connection does with each type of message. There are four types that can be configured: Voicemail, Email, Fax, and Delivery Receipt.
Caller Input	Provides a number of choices, such as to skip the greeting by pressing # or to reach an operator by pressing 0. The Caller Input settings determine what happens if a digit is pressed while the greeting is being played.
Mailbox	Defines the size of a user's mailbox.

Table 8-6   *User Template Categories*

Category	Description
Phone Menu, Playback Message Settings, Send Message Settings	These settings enable you to configure how the system interacts with a user. This includes things such as volume, menu style, time format, message playback order, and many other settings. If you allow the users access to the web-based Cisco Unity Connection Assistant, users can change most of these settings themselves.
Greetings	The Greetings area configures which greetings are enabled, what action is allowed during the greeting, and what action is taken after the greeting.
Post Greeting Recording	This area enables you to determine whether an additional greeting is played after the user's greeting and, if so, which greeting to play.
Notification Devices	The devices used to notify a user of a new message are configured in this area.

Configuring User Template Basics Settings

The following steps describe how to configure the settings on the User Templates Basic page:

Step 1.   From the previous steps, select **User Template Basic** from the drop-down **Edit** menu. Otherwise, from within UCA, select **Templates > User Templates**. Select the template you want to manage from the list that appears. After the template is active, select **User Template Basic** from the drop-down **Edit** menu.

Step 2.   The **Alias** and **Display Name** fields were defined when the template was created. You can change them now, but in most cases, they are left alone.

Step 3.   The **Display Name Generation** selection determines how the display name is formatted. Select either **First Name, Then Last Name** or **Last Name, Then First Name**.

Step 4.   The **Outgoing Fax Server** field was defined when the template was created. You can change it now, but in most cases, it is left alone.

Step 5.   From the **Partition** drop-down list, select the partition that the primary extension of the user is associated with.

Step 6.   From the **Search Space** drop-down list, select the search space that is associated to objects created using this template.

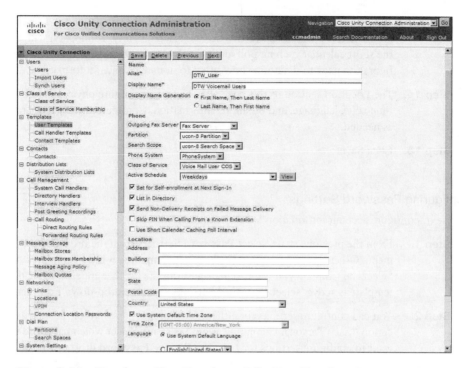

Figure 8-24 *Templates>User Templates>Edit>User Templates Basics.*

Step 7.   The **Phone System** field is defined when the template is created. You can change it now, but in most cases, it is left alone.

Step 8.   Select the desired **Class of Service** and **Active Schedule** from the appropriate drop-down lists.

Step 9.   To assure that users record their name and greeting and change their passwords on the next login, select the **Set User for Self-Enrollment at Next Login** check box. Users can choose to be listed in the directory during the self-enrollment process if the users' CoS allows this option.

Step 10.   To list users in the auto-attendant directory, select the **List in Phone Directory** check box.

Step 11.   If a message is not successfully delivered, Unity Connection can send a notice to the sender. To enable this select the **Send Non-Delivery Receipts on Failed Message Delivery** checkbox. To disable this feature, deselect the check box.

Step 12.   To allow a user to automatically log in to voicemail when calling from the extension that is associated to his mailbox, select the **Skip PIN When Calling from a Known Extension** check box. When this is enabled, the user will not need to enter a password.

Step 13. The **Use Short Calendar Caching Poll Interval** field is only used if calendar integration is enabled. When this box is selected, Unity Connection will use the short calendar caching poll interval value set in the external services configuration page to determine how often to update calendar information.

Step 14. The **Location** section of this page allows you to configure physical address, time zone, language, and billing ID information. Configure these parameters as needed.

Step 15. Click **Save**.

Configuring Password Settings

Next, configure account information for the template:

Step 1. From the previous steps, select **Password Settings** from the drop-down **Edit** menu. Otherwise, from within UCA, select **Templates > User Templates**. Select the template you want to manage from the list that appears. After the template is active, select **Password Settings** from the drop-down **Edit** menu.

Step 2. You can configure settings for either the voicemail password or the web application (Cisco Personal Communication Assistant). Select which password you want to configure settings for from the **Choose Password** drop-down list.

Step 3. The **Locked by Administrator** check box allows you to lock the account at the point of creation. You might want the account to be locked so that the account cannot be used before the deployment is complete. Decide whether you want the accounts you create using this template to be locked upon creation and select the check box accordingly.

Step 4. To prevent the user from being able to change her password, select the **User Cannot Change** check box. In most cases, you want users to be able to change their passwords, so this is left deselected.

Step 5. Typically, you want newly created users to change their password on their first login, so the **User Must Change at Next Sign-In** box should be selected.

Step 6. To override the password expiration settings, you can select the **Does Not Expire** check box. This will prevent the password from expiring. It is recommended that users be required to change passwords, so in most cases, this box is left deselected.

Step 7. From the **Authentication Rule** drop-down list, select the authentication rule that you want to assign to this template.

Step 8. Click **Save**.

Configuring Template Passwords

The User Template Change Password page enables you to define the default password for this template.

To configure these settings, follow these steps:

Step 1.   From the previous steps, select **Change Password** from the drop-down **Edit** menu. Otherwise, from within UCA, select **Templates > User Templates**. Select the template you want to manage from the list that appears. After the template is active, select **Change Password** from the drop-down **Edit** menu.

Step 2.   You can configure the voicemail or the web application (Cisco Personal Communication Assistant) password. Select which password you want to configure settings for from the **Choose Password** drop-down list.

Step 3.   Enter the password you want to have assigned to users that are created using this template in both the **Password** and **Confirm Password** fields.

Step 4.   Click **Save**.

Configuring Roles

Roles define the administrator rights of a user. This was discussed in more detail in the previous chapter. The following steps illustrate to the process of assigning roles to a template:

Step 1.   From the previous steps, select **Roles** from the drop-down **Edit** menu. Otherwise, from within UCA, select **Templates > User Templates**. Select the template you want to manage from the list that appears. After the template is active, select **Roles** from the drop-down **Edit** menu.

Step 2.   Select the desired roles from the **Available Roles** box, and click the Up Arrow above that box to move them to the **Assigned Roles** box.

Step 3.   Click **Save**.

Configuring User Template Transfer Rules

The template transfer rules determine the outcome of a call when an outside caller attempts to reach a user's phone from the auto-attendant. An outside caller can attempt to reach a user by entering the user's extension number, using Unity Connection's dial-by-name feature or by speaking the name if voice recognition is used. When Unity Connection finds a match for either the extension number or the name, it looks at the user's transfer rules settings to determine where to send the call. One would think that Unity Connection would send the call to the CM so that the call could be delivered to the phone. Although this is the most common action, it is not always desired. A number of circumstances can dictate that the call not be sent to the phone.

If the call is sent to the phone, it can be transferred to the Communications Manager in one of two ways. The first is called **Release to Switch**. In this type of transfer, Unity

Connection sends the call to the Communications Manager and is finished with that call. If the called party does not answer or the phone is busy, it is the responsibility of the Communications Manager to forward the call back to Unity Connection. You might think that if the Communications Manager sent the call back to Unity Connection, Unity Connection would just loop the call back to the Communications Manager because the call transfer settings dictate it. The reason it does not loop is because the transfer rules do not affect calls that are forwarded to Unity Connection from the Communications Manager. If the transfer rules were applied to every call, unanswered and busy calls would loop forever.

The second type of transfer is called **Supervised Transfer.** On a supervised transfer, Unity Connection holds open the port used to transfer the call and tries to determine whether the call is answered. When Unity Connection establishes that the call is answered, Unity Connection releases the call and the port is closed. If Unity Connection decides that the call is busy or unanswered within the number of rings defined for this transfer, Unity Connection pulls the call back and plays the user's greeting. Because Unity Connection maintains control of the call during a supervised transfer, additional features can be implemented, such as holding options and call screening.

Figure 8-25 shows the standard Transfer Rule page. The steps that follow describe how to configure the various settings and discuss the effect they have on transferred calls:

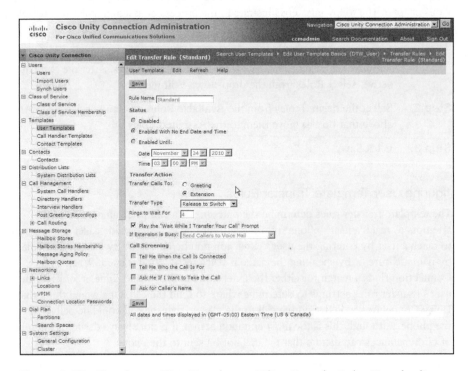

Figure 8-25   *Templates > User Templates > Edit > Transfer Rules (Standard).*

Step 1.   From the previous steps, select **Transfer Rules** from the drop-down **Edit** menu. Otherwise, from within UCA, select **Templates > User Templates**. Select the template you want to manage from the list that appears. After the template is active, select **Transfer Rules** from the drop-down **Edit** menu.

Step 2.   There are three rules that can be configured:

- **Standard rule:** Determines how the transfer is handled during open hours.

- **Closed rule:** If enabled, determines how the transfer is handled during closed hours.

- **Alternate rule:** If enabled, will override the Standard and Closed rule and the transfer will be handled according to its settings.

Select the transfer rule you want to configure.

Step 3.   The **Rule Name** field is static and cannot be changed.

Step 4.   The **Status** section determines whether the rule is enabled. The Standard rule cannot be disabled. If you are configuring one of the other rules, you must enable it for it to take effect. You can select **Enable with No End Date and Time** to have it always enabled. If you want to have it enabled until a specific time and date, select **Enable Until** and end the desired date and time.

Step 5.   In the **Transfer Action** section, select **Extension** to have the call transferred to the user's extension. If you do not want the call to be sent to the user's phone, select **Greeting** and the call will be transferred directly to the greeting.

Step 6.   If the call is transferred to an extension, the type of transfer must be selected under the **Transfer Type** heading. If holding and screening options are desired, select the **Supervise Transfer** radio button. If these features are not needed, select the **Release to Switch** radio button. If **Release to Switch** is selected, the remaining steps in this section do not apply.

Step 7.   In the **Rings to Wait** field, enter the number of rings that Unity Connection should wait before sending the call to the user's voicemail greeting.

Step 8.   Unity Connection can let the caller know that it is going to transfer the call. To enable this feature, select the **Play the "Wait While I Transfer Your Call" Prompt** check box.

Step 9.   Unity Connection has the capability to queue calls for users if they are on the phone when a call is transferred from Unity Connection. You must choose one of three options for Unity Connection to use if the user's extension is busy. The choices are

- **Send the Caller to Voicemail:** If selected, the call is not placed on hold but sent directly to voicemail.

- **Put Callers on Hold Without Asking:** If selected, the caller is placed on hold. The third choice,

- **Ask Callers to Hold:** If selected, informs the caller that the extension is busy and offers the choice of holding.

Select the desired action by clicking the associated radio button.

Note   When implementing the option to allow the caller to hold, remember that this will hold a port open while the caller is on hold. If this option is offered to a number of subscribers, it could adversely affect Unity Connection's capability to handle incoming calls.

Step 10.   Unity Connection has the capability to gather caller information for screening purposes on a supervised transfer. There are four options under the **Call Screen** heading. These options are as follows:

- **Tell Me When the Call Is Connected :** Unity Connection announces "transferring call" to the user when the user answers the call.

- **Tell Me Who the Call Is For:** Unity Connection announces whom the call is for when the user answers the phone. This feature is used when multiple users receive calls on the same phone.

- **Ask Me If I Want to Take the Call:** Unity Connection asks the user to press 1 to accept the call or press 2 to send the call to voicemail.

- **Ask for Caller's Name:** Unity Connection asks the caller to record his name and plays the recorded name to the user when the phone is answered.

Select the options you want to enable by selecting the radio button next to each option.

Step 11.   Click **Save.**

Configuring User Template Messages Settings

The User Template Messages section enables you to configure caller message-specific attributes, such as message length, post-message actions, and caller options.

Figure 8-26 shows the various settings that are configured from this screen. The following steps illustrate the configuration process of these settings and describe the effect of each setting:

Step 1.   From the previous steps, select **Message Settings** from the drop-down **Edit** menu. Otherwise, from within UCA, select **Templates > User Templates.** Select the template you want to manage from the list that appears. After the template is active, select **Message Settings** from the drop-down **Edit** menu.

Step 2.   To set the maximum length of a message that an outside caller can leave, enter the value in seconds in the **Maximum Message Length, in Seconds** box. This setting applies only to messages left from outside callers. The limit for users is set by the user's CoS.

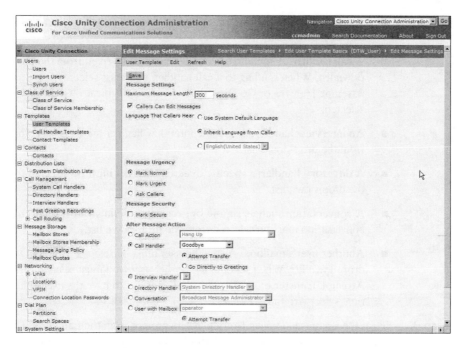

Figure 8-26 *Templates > User Templates > Edit > Message Settings*

Step 3. If you want to let callers listen to and change or delete the message they leave, select the **Callers Can Edit Message** check box.

Step 4. The **Language** setting defines what language is used to play the system. When **Inherit Language from Caller** is selected, the language that was set by the handler or rule that transferred the call is used. If it is set to **Use System Default Language**, the system default language is used. To specify a particular language, choose the radio button next to the drop-down list of languages. If only one language is installed on this system, the drop-down box is not available.

Step 5. Allow the caller to label a message urgent by selecting the **Ask Caller** radio button under the **Message Urgency** heading. To mark a message always urgent without confirmation from the caller, select the **Mark Urgent** radio button or, to never mark the message urgent, select the **Mark Normal** radio button.

Step 6. To have messages that are left by outside or unknown callers marked secure, select the **Mark Secure** check box.

Step 7. After the message is recorded, the call can be sent to a number of destinations. Typically, the call is sent to the goodbye call handler, but you can pick from any of the following:

- **A call action such as hang-up:** A specific action must be selected from the drop-down list.

- **A call handler:** A specific call handler must be selected from the drop-down list. When sending to a call handler, you must select either **Attempt Transfer** or **Go Directly to Greeting.** Typically, **Greeting** is selected.

- **An interview handler:** A specific interview handler must be selected from the drop-down list.

- **A directory handler:** a specific directory handler must be selected from the drop-down list.

- **A conversation such as sign-in or greetings administrator:** A specific conversation must be selected from the drop-down list.

- **Another user's mailbox:** A specific user must be selected from the drop-down list. When sending to another user, you must select either **Attempt Transfer** or **Go Directly to Greeting.** To have the user's phone ring, select **Attempt Transfer.**

Step 8.   Select the language in which Unity plays its prompt from the **Language That Callers Hear** drop-down list. When this field is set to **Inherited,** it uses the language used by the parent call handler.

Step 9.   Click **Save.**

Configuring User Template Message Actions

The Message Actions section determines what Unity Connection does with a message when it receives it. You would assume that it accepts the message and then delivers it to the proper mailbox. However, there are times when you might not want this to occur. Unity Connection can be configured to handle four different types of messages: voicemail, email, fax, and delivery receipts. Different message actions can be applied to each type. The actions that can be applied are

- **Accept the Message:** Accepts and delivers the message to the user's mailbox

- **Reject the Message:** Rejects the message and attempts to send a non-delivery receipt to the sender

- **Relay the Message:** Forwards the message to the address specified in the **Relay Address** field

- **Accept and Relay the Message:** Accepts and delivers the message to the user's mailbox and forwards a copy of the message to the address specified in the **Relay Address** field

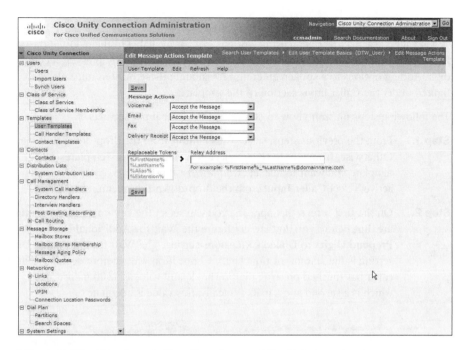

Figure 8-27 *Templates > User Templates > Edit > Message Settings.*

Figure 8-27 shows the various settings that are configured from this screen. The following steps illustrate the configuration process of these settings and describe the effect on each setting:

Step 1.   From the previous steps, select **Message Actions** from the drop-down **Edit** menu. Otherwise, from within UCA, select **Templates > User Templates**. Select the template you want to manage from the list that appears. After the template is active, select **Message Actions** from the drop-down **Edit** menu.

Step 2.   In the **Message Actions** section, select the desired action for each type of message.

Step 3.   Replaceable tokens are used when the message is configured to be relayed. To configure this, select the desired token and press the arrow that points to the relay address. For example, if the domain for the relay address is cisco.com and the email name is the same as the alias defined in Unity Connection, the relay address would be %Alias%@cisco.com. The result for a user with the alias of djones would be djones@cisco.com.

Step 4.   Click **Save**.

Configuring User Template Caller Input

When callers reach a greeting, a list of options is made available to them. Often the caller is given the option to dial another extension or reach an operator by pressing a certain digit. Adding options to a spoken greeting isn't enough; these options must also be configured under the Caller Input section of the template.

The following steps illustrate how to configure the Caller Input settings:

Step 1. From the previous steps, select **Caller Input** from the drop-down **Edit** menu. Otherwise, from within UCA, select **Templates > User Templates**. Select the template you want to manage from the list that appears. After the template is active, select **Caller Input** from the drop-down **Edit** menu.

Step 2. On the first screen that appears, you can select the key you want to configure. But before you do that, configure the **Wait for Additional Digits, Prepend Digits to Dialed Extensions** setting. The **Wait for Additional Digits** setting is the amount of time Unity Connection waits before deciding that the caller has finished pressing digits. The default value is 1500 milliseconds, which is a second and a half. Typically, this value is adequate.

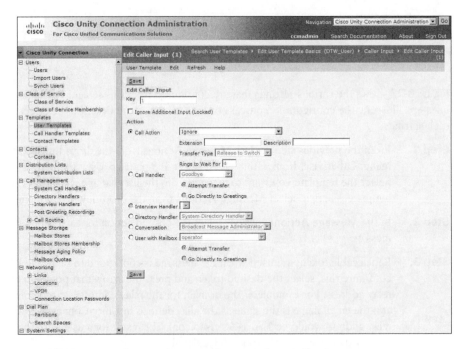

Figure 8-28   *Templates > User Templates > Edit > Caller Input.*

Step 3. The **Prepend Digits** setting determines whether any digits are prepended to the extension a caller enters. This is useful if your callers are used to entering four digits but the actual extension number is seven digits. For example, the caller can enter 3322, but the full extension that the call needs to be transferred to is 5423322. By entering 542 in the **Digits to Prepend** field and selecting the **Enable** check box, the call would be transferred to 5423322.

Step 4.   Now you can start configuring the Caller Input section and keys. Select the key you want to configure. A screen similar to that shown in Figure 8-28 appears.

Step 5.   The **Key** field is static and simply displays the number of the key you are configuring.

Step 6.   The next field determines whether the key is locked. If the **Ignore Additional Input (Locked)** check box is selected, an extension that begins with this digit cannot be entered. Unity Connection transfers the call to the destination assigned to that key without waiting to see whether the caller is going to enter other digits. Only enable this field on digits that are not leading digits for any extensions.

Step 7.   The **Action** section determines where the call is sent when the key is pressed. Choose from the following:

- **A call action such as a hang-up:** A specific action must be selected from the drop-down list.

- **A call handler:** A specific call handler must be selected from the drop-down list. When sending to a call handler, you must select either **Attempt Transfer** or **Go Directly to Greeting**. Typically, **Greeting** is selected.

- **An interview handler:** A specific interview handler must be selected from the drop-down list.

- **A directory handler:** A specific directory handler must be selected from the drop-down list.

- **A conversation such as sign-in or greetings administrator :** A specific conversation must be selected from the drop-down list.

- **Another user's mailbox:** A specific user must be selected from the drop-down list. When sending to another user, you must select either **Attempt Transfer** or **Go Directly to Greeting**. To have the user's phone ring, select **Attempt Transfer**.

Step 8.   Click **Save**. Return to the Caller Input page to select other keys to configure.

Configuring User Template Mailbox Settings

The Mailbox Settings section enables you to configure aging and mailbox size limits. As you might recall, mailbox size limits can be configured as a system setting. If you choose to define limits here, the system's limits will not be available for users created using this template.

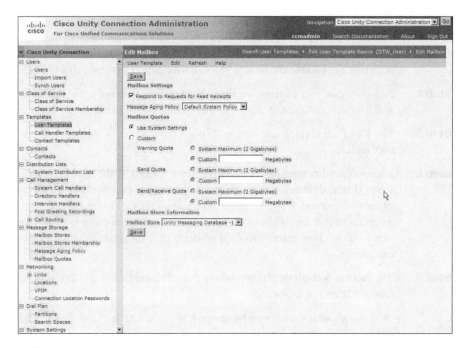

Figure 8-29   *Templates > User Templates > Edit > Mailbox.*

Figure 8-29 shows the settings that are configured from this screen. The following steps illustrate the configuration process for these settings and describe the effect of each setting:

Step 1.   From the previous steps, select **Mailbox** from the drop-down **Edit** menu. Otherwise, from within UCA, select **Templates > User Templates**. Select the template you want to manage from the list that appears. After the template is active, select **Mailbox** from the drop-down **Edit** menu.

Step 2.   User can request *read receipts* so that they are notified when a message has been retrieved. To have the receipts sent, select the **Respond to Requests for Read Receipts** check box. To prevent these receipts from being sent, deselect this box.

Step 3.   From the **Message Aging Policy** drop-down list, select the desired policy.

Step 4.   When **Use System Settings** under the **Mailbox Quotas** heading is selected, the mailbox limits are set by the system settings. To set customs limits, select **Custom** and set the limits as you desire.

Note   When calculating the size for the mailbox quota, it is helpful to understand the number of minutes of voice that can be stored per megabyte. When using G.711, approximately 2 minutes of recorded voice can be stored per megabyte of space. When using G.729, approximately 17 minutes of recorded voice can be stored per megabyte of space.

Step 5. From the **Mailbox Store** drop-down list, select the mailbox store the user's mailbox should be created on.

Step 6. Click **Save**.

Configuring User Template Phone Menu

The User Template Phone Menu settings enable you to configure conversation parameters such as volume, speed, and whether brief or full menus are played. From this page, you can also configure menu timeout settings and set up what the user hears when he logs in and out. Figure 8-30 illustrates most of the settings on this page. The following steps explain the effect of the settings and describe the configuration process:

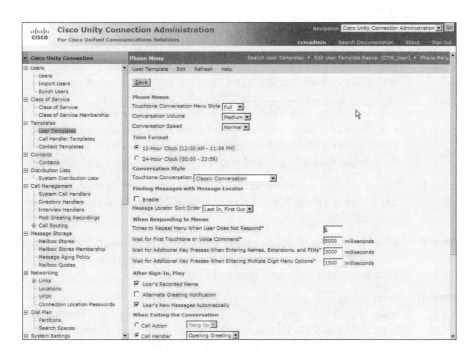

Figure 8-30 *Templates > User Templates > Edit> Phone Menu.*

Step 1. From the previous steps, select **Phone Menu** from the drop-down **Edit** menu. Otherwise, from within UCA, select **Templates > User Templates**. Select the template you want to manage from the list that appears. After the template is active, select **Phone Menu** from the drop-down **Edit** menu.

Step 2. The first setting determines whether the user hears full or brief menus. It is recommended that you set the menus to full for users who are unaccustomed to the system because full menus explain more than brief menus. After users are familiar with the menus, you might want to change to a brief menu. Choose the desired menu style from the **Menu Style** drop-down list.

Step 3.   Select the volume at which the Unity Connection conversation is played from the **Conversation Volume** drop-down list. The choices are Quieter, Medium, and Louder. Medium should be adequate for most users.

Step 4.   The **Conversation Speed** setting enables you to speed up or slow down the speed at which voicemail is played back. Select the desired setting from the drop-down list.

Step 5.   Select a time format by selecting 12-hour or 24-hour format below the **Time Format** heading.

Step 6.   The **Touchtone Conversation** field determines which touch tones you would use to save and delete messages. If you are migrating from another voicemail system, it is a good idea to become familiar with these conversations and choose the one most similar to previous voicemail system conversations. Use the classic conversation if you are uncertain which conversation to use.

Step 7.   The **Message Locator** field allows users to search their voicemails when calling in to Unity Connection. When this feature is enabled, the users can search by extension, username, or outside caller phone number. Because this feature can be processor intensive, take care when determining how many users have access to it. To enable this feature, select the **Enable** check box under the **Finding Messages with Message Locator** heading. If enabled, select the order in which the message should be checked from the **Message Locator Sort Order** list.

Step 8.   Enter the number of times the menu should repeat if the user does not respond to the menu in the **Times to Repeat Menu When User Does Not Respond** field.

Step 9.   Enter the number of milliseconds Unity Connection waits before determining the user is not going to respond by entering the desire value in the **Wait for First Touchtone or Voice Command** field.

Step 10.   Enter the number of milliseconds Unity Connection waits before it determines whether the user is finished pressing touch tones when entering names, extensions, and PINs by entering the desired value in the **Wait for Additional Key Presses When Entering Names, Extensions, and PINs** field.

Step 11.   Enter the number of milliseconds Unity Connection waits before it determines whether the user has completed pressing touch tones when entering multiple digit menu options by entering the desired value in the **Wait for Additional Key Presses When Entering Multiple Digit Menu Options** field.

Step 12.   When users log in to the system, they can be greeted by hearing their recorded names so that they know they are logged in to the correct account. To enable this greeting, select the **User's Recorded Name** check box.

Step 13.   An alternate greeting is used when a user is out of the office for a long period of time, such as vacation. It is important that the user remember to turn this greeting off when he returns. Configure Unity Connection to inform the user whether the alternate greeting is enabled when he logs in by selecting the **Alternate Greeting Notification** check box.

Step 14. If the **User's New Messages Automatically** check box is selected, users are taken directly to new messages after login.

Step 15. Under the **When Exiting the Conversation** heading, you can configure where users are sent when they end the user conversation. A number of choices are available. Typically, you set this to send the caller to the opening greeting call handler or the hang-up call action. However, you can choose from the following:

- **A call action such as a hang-up:** A specific action must be selected from the drop-down list.

- **A call handler:** A specific call handler must be selected from the drop-down list. When sending to a call handler, you must select either **Attempt Transfer** or **Go Directly to Greeting**. Typically, **Greeting** is selected.

- **An interview handler:** A specific interview handler must be selected from the drop-down list.

- **A directory handler:** A specific directory handler must be selected from the drop-down list.

- **A conversation such as sign-in or greetings administrator:** A specific conversation must be selected from the drop-down list.

- **Another user's mailbox:** A specific user must be selected from the drop-down list. When sending to another user, you must select either **Attempt Transfer** or **Go Directly to Greeting**. To have the user's phone ring, select **Attempt Transfer**.

Step 16. Click **Save**.

Configuring User Template Playback Message Settings

The playback message settings determine the order in which messages will be played and the information that is included during playback. The setting in this area has a large impact on creating a positive user experience. It is important that you take time to consider the impact these settings will have on the users before you configure them. If you grant access to Unity Connection Messaging Assistant, users can change most of these fields from that interface.

Figures 8-31 and 8-32 show the settings that are configured in this area. The following steps illustrate the configuration process of these settings:

Step 1. From the previous steps, select **Playback Message Settings** from the drop-down **Edit** menu. Otherwise, from within UCA, select **Templates > User Templates**. Select the template you want to manage from the list that appears. After the template is active, select **Playback Message Settings** from the drop-down **Edit** menu.

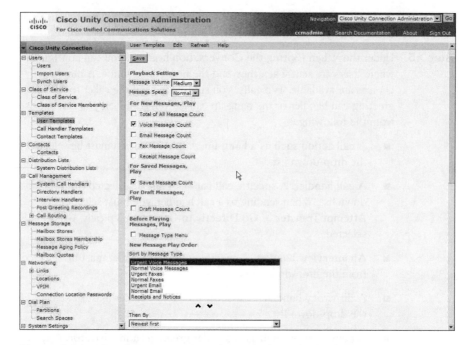

Figure 8-31   *Templates > User Templates > Edit > Playback Message Settings.*

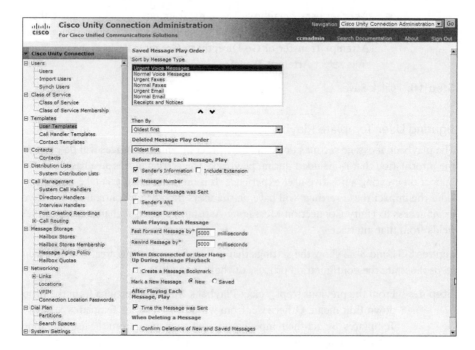

Figure 8-32   *Templates > User Templates > Edit > Playback Message Settings (Continued)*

Step 2.   From the **Message Volume** drop-down list, select the volume that messages should be played back at.

Step 3.   From the **Message Speed** drop-down list, select the speed that messages should be played back at.

Step 4.   To configure Unity Connection to inform the user of the total number of new messages and of the message count, select the check box next to each type of message count you want the user to hear. The choices are

- **Total of All Message Count**

- **Voice Message Count**

- **Email Message Count**

- **Fax Message Count**

- **Receipt Message Count**

It is best to offer only the message counts for the messages the user is likely to retrieve using the phone. For example, if the user retrieves only voicemail using the phone, only **Voice Message Counts** is chosen.

Step 5.   To announce the number of saved messages to the user, select the **Saved Message Count** check box.

Step 6.   To announce the number of draft messages to the user, select the **Draft Message Count** check box.

Step 7.   To allow users to determine the types of messages they want to hear, select the **Message Type Menu** check box. When this option is enabled, the user hears the following message: "Press 1 to hear voice messages, press 2 to hear emails, press 3 to hear faxes, press 4 to hear receipts."

Step 8.   Users can configure the order in which new messages are played. Under the **New Message Play Order** heading is a list of the various types of messages. The messages are played as they appear from top to bottom. To change the order, highlight the type of message you want to move, and then click the Up or Down Arrows below the box. Repeat this process with all the message types until they are in the desired order.

Step 9.   When playing new messages, the default behavior of Unity Connection is to play the oldest message first. To play the newest message first, choose **Newest First** from the **Then By** drop-down list. In most cases, it is best to leave this setting at **Oldest First**.

Step 10.   Users can configure the order in which saved messages are played. Under the **Saved Message Play Order** heading is a list of the various types of messages. The messages are played as they appear from top to bottom. To change the order, highlight the type of message you want to move, and then click the up or down arrows below the box. Do this with all the message types until they are in the desired order.

Step 11. When playing saved messages, the default behavior of Unity Connection is to play the newest message first. To play the oldest message first, choose **Oldest First** from the **Then By** drop-down list. In most cases, it is best to leave this setting at **Newest First**.

Step 12. When playing deleted messages, the default behavior of Unity Connection is to play the oldest message first. To play the newest message first, choose **Newest First** from the drop-down list below the **Deleted Message Play Order** heading.

Step 13. Under the **Before Playing Each Message, Play** heading, you can choose to play the sender's information, message number, time the message was sent, Automatic Number Identification (ANI), and message duration. To configure what is played, select the check box next to each piece of information that you want to have played.

Step 14. When a subscriber is listening to messages, he can fast-forward and rewind the message. The amount of time that is applied to these functions is defined by the value entered in the **Fast-Forward Messages By** and **Rewind Messages By** fields. The default is 5000 milliseconds (5 seconds) and is adequate in most cases. To change these values, simply enter the new value in the appropriate field.

Step 15. If the **Create a Message Bookmark** check box is selected, Unity Connection will set a bookmark at the point of the message the user was at if the caller gets disconnected. If the caller dials back in shortly after the disconnection, she can pick up where she left off.

Step 16. By default, when a call is disconnected in the middle of a user listening to a message, the message is left marked as new. To change this so that the message is marked as saved, select the **Saved** radio button near the **Mark a New Message** heading.

Step 17. To play the time a message was sent after a message is played, select the **Time the Message Was Sent** check box.

Step 18. To require that the user confirm the deletion of messages, select the **Confirm Deletions of New and Saved Messages** check box. This is useful if you have users that often delete messages by mistake.

Step 19. Click **Save.**

Configuring User Template Send Message Settings

The send message settings define how the user interacts with Unity Connection when sending messages. It also determines whether the user can send broadcast messages. This is another area that can impact whether the user has a positive experience and therefore a positive attitude toward Unity Connection.

Figure 8-33 shows the settings that are configured in this area. The following steps illustrate how to configure these settings:

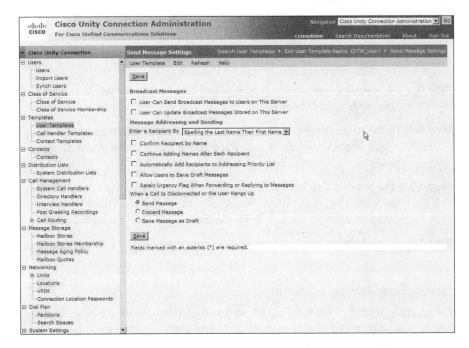

Figure 8-33   *Templates > User Templates > Edit > Send Message Settings.*

Step 1.   From the previous steps, select **Send Message Settings** from the drop-down **Edit** menu. Otherwise, from within UCA, select **Templates > User Templates**. Select the template you want to manage from the list that appears. After the template is active, select **Send Message Settings** from the drop-down **Edit** menu.

Step 2.   To allow a user to send broadcast messages, select the **User Can Send Broadcast Messages to Users on This Server** check box.

Step 3.   To allow a user to update broadcast messages, select the **User Can Update Broadcast Messages Stored on This Server** check box.

Step 4.   The **Enter a Recipient By** drop-down list determines the user's search options for sending messages. You can select to search by first then last name, last then first name, or extension. In most cases, you should select **Entering the Extension** from this list.

Step 5.   To have Unity Connection play the name of the addressee, select the **Confirm Recipient by Name** check box. Typically, this is left deselected.

Step 6.   To allow a user to enter multiple addresses, select the **Continue Adding Names After Each Recipient** check box. If this box is not selected, the user must press **1** after each address to enter another one.

Step 7.   If the **Automatically Add Recipients to Addressing Priority List** check box is selected, Unity Connection will acknowledge the addresses that the user chose. This allows Unity Connection to initially offer those addresses as a possible match.

Step 8.   To permit a user to save a message as a draft, select the **Allow Users to Save Draft Messages** check box.

Step 9.   If the **Retain Urgency Flag When Forwarding or Replying to Messages** check box is selected, the urgency marking will stay with the message when it is replied to or forwarded.

Step 10.   The **When a Call Is Disconnected** or the **User Hangs Up** selections determine whether a message is sent, discarded, or saved as a draft if the call is disconnected before the user sends the message. Select the desired action.

Step 11.   Click **Save**.

Configuring User Template Greetings

The greetings setting of the template allows you to define what greetings are enabled and how they are configured. A user can play up to five greetings, each played under different circumstances. Table 8-7 lists these greetings and the function of each.

Table 8-7   *Greetings*

Greeting	Function
Standard	Plays during open hours unless overridden by another greeting. If the Closed greeting is not enabled, Standard plays after hours.
Closed	Plays during closed hours as defined in the schedule associated with the user.
Busy	Plays when the call is transferred to Unity because the user's extension was busy.
Internal	Plays when the caller is another user on the system.
Alternate	When enabled, overrides all other greetings. This greeting plays all hours, all days until disabled.
Error	Plays when a caller presses an invalid key.
Holiday	Plays on dates defined as holidays.

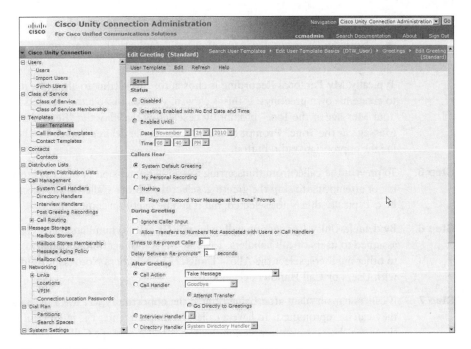

Figure 8-34   *Templates > User Templates > Edit > Greetings.*

Figure 8-34 shows the User Templates Greeting configuration screen. The following steps discuss the effects of these settings and describe how to configure them:

Step 1.   From the previous steps, select **Greetings** from the drop-down **Edit** menu. Otherwise, from within UCA, select **Templates > User Templates**. Select the template you want to manage from the list that appears. After the template is active, select **Greetings** from the drop-down **Edit** menu.

Step 2.   A list of greetings appears. Select the greeting you want to configure.

Step 3.   The **Status** section determines whether the greeting is enabled. The Standard greeting is always enabled and cannot be disabled. If you are configuring one of the other greetings, you must enable it for it to take effect. You can select **Enable with No End Date and Time** to have it always enabled. If you want to have it enabled until a specific time and date, select **Enable Until** and enter the desired date and time.

Step 4.   Under the **Callers Hear** heading, the source of the message is chosen. The three choices for the source are as follows:

   ■ **System Default Greeting:** Plays the prerecorded greeting "Sorry, <user's name> is not available." If the user has not yet recorded a name, the greeting "Sorry, the user at extension <user's extension number> is not available" is played.

- **My Personal Recording:** Plays the greeting that the user recorded.

- **Nothing:** Does not play a greeting and defaults to the after-greeting action.

Typically, **My Personal Recording** is chosen for this setting to allow the user to create his own greetings. If this is chosen, you can disable the "Record Your Message at the Tone" prompt by deselecting the **Play the "Record Your Message at the Tone" Prompt** check box. Select the desired source by clicking the appropriate radio button.

Step 5.   To prevent the caller from transferring to another extension during the greeting or attempting to skip the greeting, select the **Ignore Caller Input** check box. Typically this is not selected, but it can be useful in some situations.

Step 6.   By default, Unity Connection will only transfer calls to numbers that are assigned to users or call handlers. To allow Unity Connection to transfer calls to other numbers, select the **Allow Transfers to Numbers Not Associated with Users or Call Handlers** check box.

Step 7.   If callers remain silent after being offered the opportunity to leave a message, they can be reprompted. To have a caller reprompted, enter the number of times she should be reprompted in the **Times to Re-prompt Caller** field.

Step 8.   Enter the number of seconds Unity Connection should wait between playing the prompt again in the **Delay Between Re-prompts** field.

Step 9.   After the greeting is played, the caller has the opportunity to leave a message. To enable, click the **Call Action** radio button and select **Take Massage** from the drop-down list. Table 8-8 provides additional options.

Step 10. If more than one language is installed, greetings can be recorded in multiple languages. To record a greeting, select the language from the **Select Language** drop-down list and click the **Play/Record** button. A recording panel opens. Click the red button on the panel. Enter your extension when prompted. When the phone rings, answer it and record the greeting. Typically, you would not record a greeting when creating a template.

Step 11. Click **Save**.

Configuring User Template Post-Greeting Recording

Unity Connection enables you to configure a greeting to be played after the user's greeting. You can also select whether all callers hear the recording or just unidentified callers. To configure the post-greeting settings, follow these steps:

Step 1.   From the previous steps, select **Post Greeting Recording** from the drop-down **Edit** menu. Otherwise, from within UCA, select **Templates > User Templates**. Select the template you want to manage from the list that appears. After the template is active, choose **Post Greeting Recording** from the drop-down **Edit** menu.

Table 8-8 *Call Action*

Action	Description
Call action such as hang-up	A specific action must be selected from the drop-down list.
Call handler	A specific call handler must be selected from the drop-down list. When sending to a call handler, you must select either **Attempt Transfer** or **Go Directly to Greeting**. Typically, **Greeting** is selected.
Interview handler	A specific interview handler must be selected from the drop-down list.
Directory handler	A specific directory handler must be selected from the drop-down list.
Conversation such as sign-in or greetings administrator	A specific conversation must be selected from the drop-down list.
Another user's mailbox	A specific user must be selected from the drop-down list. When sending to another user, you must select either **Attempt Transfer** or **Go Directly to Greeting**. If you prefer to have the user's phone ring, select **Attempt Transfer**.

Step 2.   If you do not want Unity Connection to play a post-greeting recording, simply select the **Do Not Play Recording** radio button and click **Save**. If you do want a post-greeting recording to play, proceed to Step 3.

Step 3.   To have the post-greeting recording played for all callers, select the **Play Recording to All Callers** radio button. If you want to play the recording specifically for unidentified callers, click the **Play Recording Only to Unidentified Callers** radio button.

Step 4.   Select the desired greeting from the **Post Greeting Recording Selection** drop-down list. Post-greeting recordings must be created before they can be selected here.

Step 5.   Click **Save**.

Configuring User Template Message Notification Settings

Message notification allows a user to be advised through a pager, phone, or other external device when a new message arrives. This type of notification is useful for users who are seldom in the office, such as outside salespeople or service technicians.

It might seem odd that you can set up message notification in the user template. After all, you will not want to send a message to the same pager when any user who was created using this template receives a new message. However, the user template is an excellent place to create the same type of flow and generic notification settings for a large number of users. After the users are added, you can have them fill in the details such as the specific phone numbers using CPCA.

There are five devices that can be configured for message notification. This includes three phones, one pager, and an STMP (email) address. Message notification can be configured to notify the user of any new voicemails or faxes. The settings on this screen determine what type of message triggers a notification and what devices are notified.

The following steps illustrate how these settings are configured and describe the effect they produce:

Step 1. From the previous steps, select **Notification Devices** from the drop-down **Edit** menu. Otherwise, from within UCA, select **Templates > User Templates**. Select the template you want to manage from the list that appears. After the template is active, select **Notification Devices** from the drop-down **Edit** menu.

Step 2. A page appears that lists the five devices that can be configured. Select the device you want to configure.

Step 3. Figure 8-35 illustrates the required settings that must be configured. The **Enabled** check box must be selected for this device to receive notifications.

Step 4. The **Display Name** field is used to identify the device. In most cases, the existing display names are acceptable, but you can change them if you desire.

Step 5. The notification can be configured to be sent immediately or to wait a specified number of minutes. If cascading notification is being deployed, some devices are configured to wait for a certain number of minutes before being notified. The term *cascading notification* means that notification is sent, and if the message has not been retrieved after a specified number of minutes, a different device is notified. If, after an additional amount of time, the message is still not retrieved, another device is notified. An example of cascading flow might look something like this:

   1. First notification is sent to your pager.

   2. You don't retrieve the message.

   3. Ten minutes later, a notification is sent to your cell phone.

   4. You don't retrieve the message.

   5. Ten minutes later, a notification is sent to your boss's phone.

   6. You're busted!

Step 6. Enter the number of minutes that Unity Connection should wait before notifying this device in the **Delay Before First Notification Attempt** field. Unity

Connection only sends the notification if the message has not been retrieved after appropriated time.

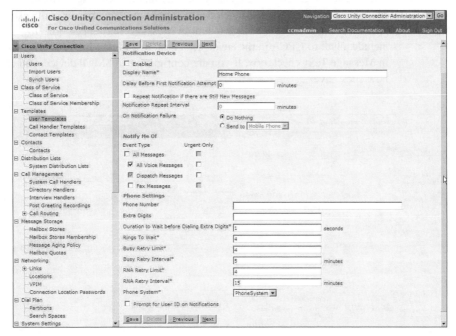

Figure 8-35   *Templates > User Templates > Edit > Notification Devices (Phones and Pager).*

Step 7.   To invoke what some refer to as the "nag factor," you can have the device notified at specified intervals until the message is retrieved. Select the **Repeat Notification if There Are Still New Messages** check box, and then enter the number of minutes in the **Notification Repeat Interval** field.

Step 8.   The **On Notification Fail** setting enables you to specify another device to be notified if the notification fails. To do this, select the **Send To** radio button and select the device from the drop-down list. If you do not want to have another device notified, select the **Do Nothing** radio button.

Step 9.   Under the **Notify Me Of** heading, select the types of messages of which the user should be notified. As shown in Figure 8-35, you can select all messages or only one type, such as voicemail. You can further narrow it down by selecting only urgent messages.

Step 10.   The rest of the fields vary depending on whether you choose a phone or email as the notification device. Figure 8-36 shows the fields that are available if you choose SMTP as the delivery mechanism. You have the option to send transcriptions. You can choose to send them for all voicemails or only those marked urgent. Because you are configuring a template, you would not enter information in the **To, From, Message Header, Message Text,** or **Message**

Footer fields. In most cases, the values for these fields vary based on the specific user. To have information like caller name, caller ID, urgency marking, and time message left in the email, select the **Include Message Information in Message Text** check box. To include the number of new messages the user has, select the **Include Message Count in Message Text** check box. To include a link to CPCA in the email, select the **Include a Link to Cisco PCA in Message Text** check box. If you are configuring an SMTP device, you can now click **Save**.

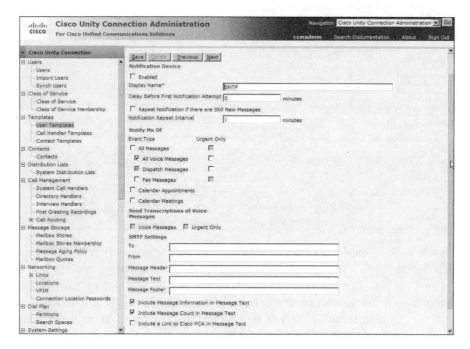

Figure 8-36   *Templates> User Templates > Edit > Notification Devices (Email).*

Step 11.   If you choose a phone or a pager, you have a number of options to choose from. Table 8-9 lists the available fields.

Step 12.   Click **Save**.

At this point, you have completed creating a user template. Be sure to analyze the number of templates required based on the information discussed at the beginning of this chapter. Add the templates to Unity Connection using the preceding steps as a guide.

Now that the user templates are created, you can start to add users. The next section explains the process of adding users to the template. A lot of configuration is required to accomplish this task. However, the success of your deployment rests heavily upon a properly prepared foundation. Okay, enough of this foundation stuff; let's start adding users!

Table 8-9 *Phone or Pager Notification Fields*

Field	Description
Phone Number	The number to dial when sending notifications. This field is normally left blank when configuring templates.
Extra Digits	Digits that are sent after the call is connected. This can be used when sending a notification to a pager. This field is normally left blank when configuring templates.
Duration to Wait Before Dialing Extra Digits	The number of seconds to wait before sending the extra digits.
Ring to Wait	The number of rings to wait before determining whether the call is going to be answered. This should be set lower than the number of rings that an answering machine or service (voicemail) waits before answering a call. This prohibits the notification from being answered by the service.
Busy Retry Limit	The number of times that the notification will be attempted when the device is busy.
Busy Retry Interval	The length of time between the notification retry when the device is busy.
RNA Retry Limit	The number of times that the notification will be tried when the device does not answer.
RNA Retry Interval	The length of time between the notification retries when the device does not answer.
Phone System	The phone system that is used for this notification device.
Prompt for User ID on Notification	If selected, the user will have to enter his ID (extension number) and PIN to retrieve the messages. Even if this is not selected, the user will only be required to enter his PIN.

Creating New Unity Connection Users

Now that you have the user templates created, the process of creating a user is fairly simple. To create a user, enter a few pieces of information and click **Save**, and the process is complete. Because user creation is based on one of the templates you created, all the additional settings will be populated. On occasion you might opt to change the settings of a user. The process for implementing the most common changes comes later in this chapter in the "Managing Users" section.

This section focuses on the creation of users with mailboxes. The next section discusses how to import existing users.

The following steps show how to add a new Exchange-based user to Unity:

Step 1.   From within UCA, select **Users > Users**.

Step 2.   Click the **Add New** button.

Step 3.   A window such as that shown in Figure 8-37 displays. Select **User with Mailbox** from the **User Type** drop-down list.

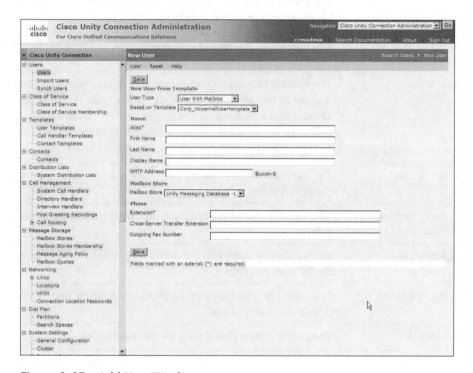

Figure 8-37 *Add User Window*

Step 4.   Select the template this user should be based on from the **Based on Template** drop-down list.

Step 5.   Enter an alias for the user in the **Alias** field. The alias is the ID a user will use to log in to the system from a web page. The alias must be unique.

Step 6.   Enter the first and last name of the new user in the fields labeled as such.

Step 7.   The display name is used by the voice recognition server when callers speak the name of the person they are trying to reach. It is also used to play the name of the user if the user has not recorded a name. The display name is automatically generated based on the settings you define in the template. You can change it if you desire by entering the specified name in the **Displayed Name** field.

Step 8. The **SMTP Address** field is optional. This is used to identify a user that is using an SMTP client. If you do not enter anything, the display name is used to create the address.

Step 9. If more than one mail store exists in your environment, select the mail store from the **Mailbox Store** drop-down list to be used for this user.

Step 10. An extension number must be assigned to every user, and this should be the extension number that is assigned to the user's phone. Enter the user's extension number in the **Extension** field. In rare cases, the extension number in Unity Connection is different than the actual extension assigned to the user's phone, but this should be avoided. All extensions in Unity Connection must be unique—that is, each extension can only be assigned to one user.

Step 11. A cross-server transfer occurs when a call is transferred to a user on a different Unity Connection server. If the cross-server transfer fails, the call is sent to the extension number entered in the **Cross-Server Transfer Extension** field. Enter the desire extension in this field.

Step 12. In the **Outgoing Fax Number** field, enter the number that provides a user with access to send faxes for printing purposes.

Step 13. Click the **Save** button.

Step 14. After the user is added to the database, you will be returned to the **Edit User Basics** screen.

So, that is all there is to it. The user you added is now ready for use. As you can see, adding a user is a much simpler process than creating user templates. Because you use a template during the creation process, the majority of the user settings are automatically configured, which shows the value of the user template. However, there are five types of user configurations that are not configured using the user template:

■ Private lists

■ Alternate extensions

■ Alternate names

■ External service account

■ SMTP proxy addresses

These settings are not part of the user template because they are unique for each user.

Private lists are lists of multiple users with whom a user can communicate when sending voicemail. Instead of having to add each user as a recipient, the user can select a private list as the recipient, and the voicemail will be sent to everyone in the list. Users manage their own private lists.

Alternate extensions are used for multiple purposes. When an alternate extension is added to a user, Unity Connection regards all calls to or from that extension as if they are to or from the user's primary extension. Consider it as a way to associate multiple extensions to one mailbox. Imagine that a user has multiple extensions on the system. When someone calls the user and the call is not answered, the caller is forwarded to the same mailbox regardless of which of the user's extensions the caller dialed. This feature is also used to allow users easy message access when calling from an outside phone. When calling from the outside, a user must press the asterisk (*) key and enter an extension number and password. By adding the phone number of phones that are commonly used to access voicemail, such as a cell phone, this process is simplified. Because Unity recognizes the incoming caller ID as an alternate extension, the user is simply being prompted for a password just as if calling from an office phone.

Alternate names allow you to enter additional names that a subscriber can be referred to, such as nicknames, shortened names (Bob instead of Robert), or a maiden name. These names are included in a search when voice recognition is used.

External service accounts are used to allow integration with email, calendar, and conference services. The external service accounts must be configured by the system engineer before they can be assigned to users.

SMTP proxy addresses are required when a user is going to use an IMAP client to send and receive messages. The SMTP proxy address should be the same as the user's corporate email address.

Configuring private lists, alternate extensions, alternate names, external service accounts and SMTP proxy addresses are covered in the "Managing Users" section, later in this chapter.

Importing Unity Connection Users

When integrating Unity Connection with CM, you can import users from CM. You can also channel users from a Lightweight Directory Access Protocol (LDAP) server. Some configuration is required to properly integrate to a Communications Manager or LDAP server. While the integration steps are beyond the scope of this book, the steps for the actual importing process are covered.

The following steps show how to import a CM user. The process of importing an LDAP user are similar:

Step 1.   From within UCA, select **Users > Import Users**.

Step 2.   Select the Communications Manager server from the **Find End Users In** drop-down list.

Step 3.   From the drop-down list located next to the **Where** heading, select the field you want to search. You can search by extension, first name, last name, or alias. If alias is selected, the search is based on the user ID in CM.

Step 4.   In the next drop-down list, select how you want the search to match the criteria you enter. The choices are **Begins With, Contains**, and **Is Exactly**.

Step 5.   Enter the search string in the list field and click **Find**.

Step 6.   Select the check box next to each user you want to import.

Step 7.   Click the **Import Selected** button. Optionally, you can click the **Import All** button if you want to select all the users that appear on the page.

Step 8.   After the users are imported, a summary of the import process will appear below the **Status** heading at the top of the page.

As mentioned previously, users can be added using the Bulk Administration Tool. This utility can import users from a CSV file.

The following steps are required when importing users from a CSV file:

Step 1.   Create a CSV file. There are more than 80 values that can be entered in the CSV file for each user. Of these fields, only three are required: **Alias**, **Template Alias**, and **Extension**. Many of the remaining fields are populated with the settings defined in the user template you choose during the import.

Step 2.   From within UCA navigate to **Tools > Bulk Administration Tool**. A screen similar to that shown in Figure 8-38 should appear.

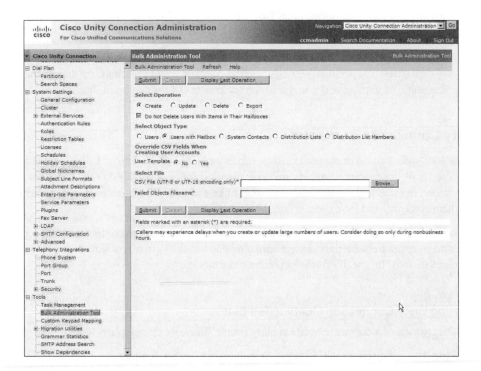

Figure 8-38   *Bulk Administration Tool*

Step 3.   Select the **Create** radio button under the **Select Operation** heading.

Step 4. Select the **User with Mailbox** radio button under the **Select Object Type** heading.

Step 5. When the CSV file contains information already defined in the template, Unity Connection must be aware of the information to be used. This process is accomplished by selecting **No** next to the **User Template** heading. If you choose to have the information in the template used, select **Yes**.

Step 6. Click the **Browse** button. Navigate to the CSV file and click **Open**.

Step 7. In the **Failed Objects Filename** field, enter the name that will be implemented for the error log in the event of problems that can occur with the creation of objects.

> **Note** If errors occur, you can view the errors by clicking the **Download the Failed Objects File** link. The link appears just below the **Status** heading. If there are no errors, the link does not appear on the page.

Step 8. Click the **Submit** button.

Step 9. After the import is complete, a summary of the results appears at the top of the page below the **Status** heading.

Now that the users are added, your system is ready for basic voicemail use. Users can now configure their personal settings, such as passwords and greetings, by dialing the voicemail pilot number and going through the process of user self-enrollment.

Unity Connection Contacts

Before you move on to managing users, take a look at another type of Unity Connection object called a contact. Contacts are typically used for people who do not have a voicemail account on your system, but you would like users on the system to be able to send them voicemail and look them up on the directory.

Contacts are created in much the same way that users are, but the configuration process is much easier because they do not have a mailbox in the system. As with users, a contact template must be specified when creating a contact.

Creating Unity Connection Contact Templates

The creation of a contact template is fairly simple. To create the template, follow these steps:

Step 1. From within UCA, select **Templates > Contact Templates**.

Step 2. Click the **Add New** button.

Step 3. Enter a unique name for the template in the **Alias** field.

Step 4. Enter a descriptive name in the **Description** field.

Step 5.   If this user is a VPIM contact, select a location from the **Delivery Location** drop-down list.

Step 6.   Click **Save**.

Step 7.   A new screen appears. From the **Partition** drop-down list, select the partition you want to assign to contacts that are created using this template.

Step 8.   If desired, you can also enter the contact's city and department information in the appropriate fields.

Step 9.   Click **Save**.

Creating Unity Connection Contacts

The following steps illustrate how to create a Unity Connection contact:

Step 1.   From within UCA, select **Contacts > Contacts**.

Step 2.   Click the **Add New** button.

Step 3.   A window like that shown in Figure 8-39 displays.

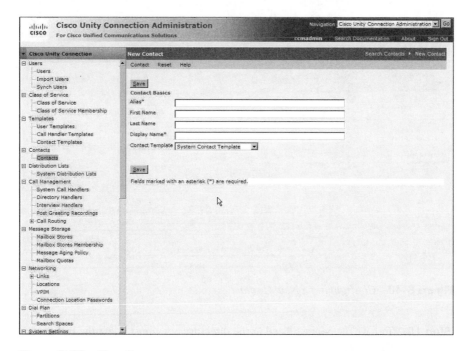

Figure 8-39   *New Contact*

Step 4.   Enter an alias for the user in the **Alias** field. The alias must be unique.

Step 5.   Enter the first and last name of the new user in the appropriate fields.

Step 6.   The display name is used by the voice recognition server when a caller speaks the name of the person he is trying to reach. It is also used to play the name of the contact if there is no recorded name. The display name is automatically generated based on the settings you define in the template. You can change it if you desire by entering the desired name in the **Displayed Name** field.

Step 7.   Select the template this contact should be based on from the **Contact Template** drop-down list.

Step 8.   Click **Save**.

Step 9.   A new screen similar to Figure 8-40 appears. The information you entered in the previous screen is used to populate the first four fields. To record the contact's name, click the **Play/Record** button. A recording panel opens. Click the red button on the panel. Enter your extension when prompted. When the phone rings, answer it and record the greeting.

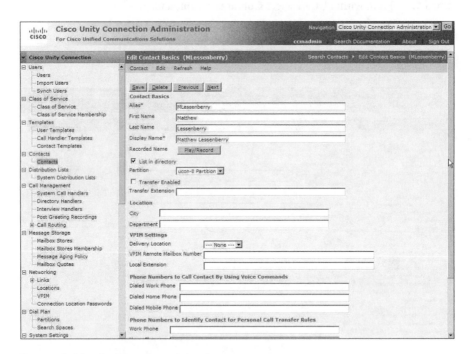

Figure 8-40   *Configuring a New Contact*

Step 10.   To have the contact listed in the directory, you must select the **List in Directory** check box.

Step 11.   The partition that you assigned to the template is assigned to the contact. If you want to change it, select the desired partition from the **Partition** drop-down list.

Step 12. To allow a call to be transferred to the contact, select the **Transfer Enable** check box and enter the number that the call should be transferred to in the **Transfer Extension** field.

Step 13. The **City** and **Department** fields are populated by the information in the contact template. You can change these if you want.

Step 14. When configuring a VPIM contact, select the VPIM delivery location from the **Delivery Location** drop-down list.

Step 15. When configuring a VPIM contact, enter the remote mailbox number in the **VPIM Remote Mailbox Number** field.

Step 16. When configuring a VPIM contact, a local extension can be assigned. Enter the desired extension the **Local Extension** field.

Step 17. Users on the system can reach contacts by using the voice recognition "Call" command. Enter the contact's work, home, and cell phone number in the **Dialed Work Phone, Dialed Home Phone**, and **Dialed Mobile Phone** fields.

Step 18. Users can set up personal call-routing rules in Unity Connection. These rules can be based on incoming phone numbers. To allow Unity to recognize the contact so that rules can be set up against their numbers, you must enter their work, home, mobile, and up to two other numbers in the **Phone Numbers to Identify Contact for Personal Call Transfer Rules** section.

Step 19. Click the **Save** button.

Alternate names can be assigned to contacts that might be known by a name other than their actual name, such as a maiden name. This allows them to be found in the directory if someone searches using a variation of their name. To configure alternate names for a Unity Connection contact, use the following steps:

Step 1. From the previous steps, select **Alternate Names** from the drop-down **Edit** menu. Otherwise, from within UCA, select **Contacts > Contacts**. Select the contact you want to manage from the list that appears. After the contact is active, select **Alternate Names** from the drop-down **Edit** menu.

Step 2. Enter the first and last name in the appropriate fields and click **Add New**.

Step 3. Click **Save**.

STMP proxy addresses are used to map a contact's email address to his Unity Connection account. To configure an SMTP proxy address for a Unity Connection contact, simply add his email address to the STMP proxy field. The following steps illustrate the process:

Step 1. From the previous steps, select **SMTP Proxy Addresses** from the drop-down **Edit** menu. Otherwise, from within UCA, select **Contacts > Contacts**. Select the contact you want to manage from the list that appears. After the contact is active, select **SMTP Proxy Addresses** from the drop-down **Edit** menu.

Step 2. Click **Add New**.

Step 3.   Enter the user's email address in the blank field.

Step 4.   Click **Save**.

Managing Users

After users are created, there might be some basic day-to-day administration required. For the most part, as long as things don't change, the user administration tasks should be minimal. Then again, things don't tend to go unchanged for long. The following sections are a collection of common user administrative tasks. No task discussed in these sections is difficult and, if performed often, can be done without reference to the sections. The goal is to provide a quick reference for you when you are required to perform an unfamiliar administrative task. Use this reference the first few times you perform any of these tasks. Although they are not difficult, some tasks can cause hours of troubleshooting if incorrectly configured. The tasks are divided into four categories:

■   User access

■   Call transfer and greetings

■   Message access and notification

■   Conversation management settings

Note   The steps shown for each task are designed so that they can stand on their own. That is, each individual set of steps is not dependent upon other sets of steps. This is designed intentionally so that the reader does not have to jump back and forth between multiple sections to complete one task. This format does, however, require the repetition of the same steps in multiple tasks. The text might seem repetitive, but to offer a task-independent reference, this format is required.

Managing User Access

A subscriber can access Unity in a number of ways. The following sections cover administrative tasks that are associated with subscriber access, such as passwords, CoS, and licensed features. Because the exact steps differ between Unity and Unity Connection, the steps for each are offered.

Unlocking an Account

Users often lock themselves out by entering the incorrect password too many times. These thresholds are configured on the **Subscriber > Account Policy > Phone Password Restrictions** page in Unity and on the **System Settings > Authentication Rules** page on Unity Connection.

There are two types of accounts that can become locked. The first is the voice mailbox. When this is locked, the user cannot access her messages from the phone. She still has access to messages through CPCA and viewmail, if she has these features. The second type of account, web access, when locked, prohibits all access. This also prevents any user from accessing the administrate interfaces.

To unlock either of these in Unity, follow these steps:

Step 1. From within SA, select **Subscribers > Subscribers**. Click the **Find** icon and search for the user you want to manage.

Step 2. When the name of the desired subscriber appears in the title strip, select **Account** from the menu that appears on the left side of the screen.

Step 3. To allow the subscriber access to messages from a phone, deselect the **Cisco Unity TUI Account Status** check box.

Step 4. To allow the subscriber access to CPCA and viewmail, deselect the **Cisco Unity GUI Access Status** check box. Remember, only subscribers who have a CoS that allows them access to these interfaces are able to access them regardless of what this setting is.

Step 5. Click the **Save** icon in the title strip.

To unlock either of these in Unity Connection, follow these steps:

Step 1. From within UCA, select **Users > Users**. Enter the appropriate search criteria and click the **Find** button to search for the user you want to manage.

Step 2. Click the name of the user you want to manage.

Step 3. Navigate to **Edit > Password Settings**.

Step 4. Select the type of account you want to unlock from the **Choose Password** drop-down list.

Step 5. If the account is locked because of invalid sign-in, the time that the account was locked is shown in the **Time Locked Due to Failed Sign-In Attempts** field. If the account is locked because of an administrative locking, the time that the account was locked is shown in the **Time Locked by Administrator** field.

Step 6. Click the **Unlock Password** button to unlock the account.

Step 7. Click **Save**.

Resetting Passwords

Another common issue is when the user forgets his/her password. This phenomenon has baffled system administrators for years. However, with the average person having to keep track of numerous passwords, it is a common occurrence.

To change a subscriber's password in Unity, follow these steps:

Step 1. From within SA, select **Subscribers > Subscribers**. Click the **Find** icon and search for the user you want to manage.

Step 2.   When the name of the desired subscriber appears in the title strip, select **Phone Password** from the menu that appears on the left side of the screen.

Step 3.   In the **Password** field, enter the new password.

Step 4.   In the **Confirm Password** field, enter the new password again.

Step 5.   Click the **Save** icon.

To change a subscriber's password in Unity Connection, follow these steps:

Step 1.   From within UCA, select **Users > Users**. Enter the appropriate search criteria and click the **Find** button to search for the user you want to manage.

Step 2.   Click the name of the user you want to manage.

Step 3.   Navigate to **Edit > Change Password**.

Step 4.   Select **Voice Mail** or **Web Application** from the **Choose Password** drop-down list.

Step 5.   In the **Password** field, enter the new password.

Step 6.   In the **Confirm password** field, enter the new password again.

Step 7.   Click **Save**.

Changing a Subscriber's Extension

A user's extension might need to be changed if they move to a different office or department.

To change a subscriber's extension in Unity, follow these steps:

Step 1.   From within SA, select **Subscribers > Subscribers**. Click the **Find** icon and search for the user you want to manage.

Step 2.   When the name of the desired subscriber appears in the title strip, select **Profile** from the menu that appears on the left side of the screen.

Step 3.   In the **Extension** field, enter the new extension number.

Step 4.   Click the **Save** icon.

To change a subscriber's extension in Unity Connection, follow these steps:

Step 1.   From within UCA, select **Users > Users**. Enter the appropriate search criteria and click the **Find** button to search for the user you want to manage.

Step 2.   Click the name of the user you want to manage.

Step 3.   Navigate to **Edit > User Basics**.

Step 4.   In the **Extension** field, enter the new extension number.

Step 5.   Click **Save**.

Changing a Subscriber's CoS

Many of the features that you want to allow a user access to are configured in the CoS. If you want to give the feature to all users in the CoS, you can simply edit their current CoS. However, if you want to grant certain features to only a subset of users that share the same CoS, you need to create a new CoS based on the current CoS, edit the new CoS, and assign it to those users. This section includes the steps required to add various features to CoS.

The following steps show how to change a Unity subscriber's CoS:

Step 1. From within SA, select **Subscribers > Subscribers**. Click the **Find** icon and search for the user you want to manage.

Step 2. When the name of the desired subscriber appears in the title strip, select **Profile** from the menu that appears on the left side of the screen.

Step 3. In the **Class of Service** field, select the desired class of service from the drop-down list.

Step 4. Click the **Save** icon.

The following steps show how to change a Unity Connection user's CoS:

Step 1. From within UCA, select **Users > Users**. Enter the appropriate search criteria and click the **Find** button to search for the user you want to manage.

Step 2. Click the name of the user you want to manage.

Step 3. Navigate to **Edit > User Basics**.

Step 4. In the **Class of Service** field, select the desired class of service from the drop-down list.

Step 5. Click **Save**.

Granting Access to Licensed Features (FaxMail, Text-to-Speech, CPCA)

To allow subscribers to have access to various licensed features, you must grant them rights. These rights are authorized based on the subscriber's CoS. If you want to permit all the subscribers of a particular CoS these rights, you can simply edit their current CoS. However, if you do not want to authorize these rights to all subscribers in a CoS, you need to create a new CoS, grant the rights to that CoS, and assign the new CoS to the selected subscribers.

To add access to the features of an exiting CoS in Unity, follow these steps:

Step 1. From within SA, select **Subscribers > Class of Service**.

Step 2. Click the **Find** icon, and a list of CoSs displays.

Step 3. Highlight the CoS you want to edit and click **View**.

Step 4. Select **Features** from the left side of the screen.

Step 5.   To allow subscribers to manage faxes using the phone, select the **FaxMail** check box. This feature requires that your organization has a supported third-party fax solution.

Step 6.   To allow subscribers to listen to their email over the phone, select the **Text-to-Speech for E-mail Messages** check box.

Step 7.   To allow subscribers to configure their personal setting through a web browser, select the **Cisco Unity Assistant** check box.

Step 8.   To allow subscribers to check their voicemail through a web browser, select the **Cisco Unity Inbox (Visual Messaging Interface)** check box.

Note   All of these features require a license for each subscriber who is assigned to the feature.

To add access to the features of an existing CoS in Unity Connection, follow these steps:

Step 1.   From within UCA, select **Class of Service > Class of Service**.

Step 2.   Click the name of the CoS you want to edit.

Step 3.   To allow users to access voicemails for an email client, select the **Allow Users to Access Voice Mail Using an IMAP Client** check box. If this feature is enabled, you must also select which part of the message they can receive through email. To let them receive all messages, select the **Allow Users to Access Message Bodies** radio button. If you do not want them to be able to receive messages marked private through email, select the **Allow Users to Access Message Bodies Except on Private Messages** radio button. To permit them to only see the header information such as time stamp and sender, select the **Allow Users to Access Message Headers Only** radio button.

Step 4.   To allow users to use the Unity Connection Messaging Inbox (CPCA), select the **Allow Users to Use the Messaging Inbox and RSS Feeds** check box.

Step 5.   To provide users with the ability to access email or use voice recognition, you must first select the **Allow Access to Advanced Features** check box. To allow access to email, select the **Allow Access to Email in Third-Party Message Stores** check box. To allow a user to use voice recognition, select the **Allow Users to Use Voice Recognition** check box.

Step 6.   If a transcription service is configured in your environment, you must grant users access to that service for them to be able to use it. To enable this feature, select the **Provide Transcriptions of Voice Messages** check box. By default, secure messages will not be transcribed. To enable transcription of secure messages, select the **Allow Transcriptions of Secure Messages** radio button. While this will enable transcription of secure messages, they will not be sent to notification devices unless you select the **Allow Transcriptions of Secure Messages to Be Sent to Notification Devices** radio button.

Step 7.   Click **Save**.

Granting Additional System Access Rights

Unity enables you to assign subscribers limited administrative rights that allow them to deal with certain administrative tasks. These rights are strictly Unity rights and do not correspond to any AD rights. By assigning limited rights to some subscribers, you can enable them to assist in various tasks such as unlocking accounts, changing passwords, and running reports. These rights are based on the subscribers' CoS.

Unity connection also enables you to grant users administrative rights, but this is done by assigning roles to user. It is not a function of the CoS. Roles have already been discussed in detail. This section simply shows how to change the role assignment.

The following steps describe the process of adding administrative rights to an existing CoS:

Step 1.   From within SA, select **Subscribers > Class of Service**.

Step 2.   Click the **Find** icon, and a list of CoSs displays.

Step 3.   Highlight the CoS you want to edit and click **View**.

Step 4.   Select **System Access** from the left side of the screen.

Step 5.   Figure 8-41 shows the various rights that can be assigned to a CoS. Based on what tasks you want the subscriber to perform, select the appropriate check boxes. For the most part, these rights are self-explanatory. Keep in mind that when you grant one right, another right can be inherited. For example, when you select the **Can Unlock Subscriber Accounts and Change Passwords** check box, the **Subscriber Access > Read** right is granted. Inherited rights are not automatically removed when you remove the parent right. You need to manually remove any inherited rights.

Step 6.   Click the **Save** icon in the title strip.

The following steps describe how to add administrative rights to Unity Connection users by assigning roles:

Step 1.   From within UCA, select **Users > Users**. Enter the appropriate search criteria and click the **Find** button to search for the user you want to manage.

Step 2.   Click the name of the user you want to manage.

Step 3.   Navigate to **Edit > Roles**.

Step 4.   To add roles to this user, select the desired roles from the **Available Roles** box and click the up arrow above that box to move them to the **Assigned Roles** box.

Step 5.   To remove roles from this user, select the roles you want to remove from the **Assigned Roles** box and click the Up Arrow above that box to move them to the **Available Roles** box.

Step 6.   Click **Save**.

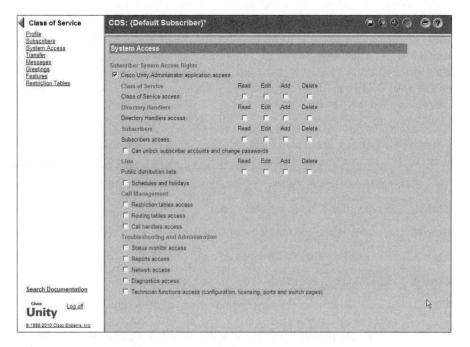

Figure 8-41   *Subscriber >CoS >System Access.*

Managing Call Transfer and Greetings

The following sections explore how to adjust a user's settings that affect the outside caller's experience when they are transferred to a user. This includes things such as call-screening options and one-key transfer settings.

Allowing Screening and Hold Options

Using screening options, a user can have the system request the caller's name and play it to the user before transferring the call. The user can then choose to take the call or send it to voicemail. The system can also be configured so that the user can choose to have the system ask callers to hold if they are on other calls. When either of these features is used, the voicemail port is held open until the call is transferred to a phone. It is best to use these options sparingly to enable call-screening and holding options.

The following steps demonstrate how to configure these features in Unity:

Step 1.   From within SA, select **Subscribers > Class of Service**.

Step 2.   Click the **Find** icon, and a list of CoSs displays.

Step 3.   Highlight the CoS you want to edit and click **View**.

Step 4. Select **Transfer** from the left side of the screen.

Step 5. To allow subscribers to enable call-screening options, select the **Subscribers Can Change Call Screening Options** check box.

Step 6. To allow subscribers to enable call-holding options, select the **Subscribers Can Change Call Holding Options** check box.

Step 7. Click the **Save** icon in the title strip.

The following steps demonstrate how to configure these features in Unity Connection:

Step 1. From within UCA, select **Class of Service > Class of Service**.

Step 2. Click the name of the CoS you want to manage.

Step 3. Scroll down to the **Call Transfer** section.

Step 4. To allow subscribers to enable call-screening options, select the **Allow Users to Change Call Screening Options** check box.

Step 5. To allow subscribers to enable call-holding options, select the **Allow Users to Change Call Holding Options** check box.

Step 6. Click **Save**.

Changing Maximum Greeting Length

The maximum length of a user's greeting is determined by the CoS. Follow these steps to change this value in Unity:

Step 1. From within SA, select **Subscribers > Class of Service**.

Step 2. Click the **Find** icon, and a list of CoSs displays.

Step 3. Highlight the CoS you want to edit and click **View**.

Step 4. Select **Greetings** from the left side of the screen.

Step 5. Enter the desired number of seconds in the **Maximum Greeting Length, in Seconds** field.

Step 6. Click the **Save** icon in the title strip.

Follow these steps to change the value in Unity Connection:

Step 1. From within UCA, select **Class of Service > Class of Service**.

Step 2. Click the name of the CoS you want to manage.

Step 3. Enter the desired number of seconds in the **Maximum Length Seconds** field located under the **Greetings** heading.

Step 4. Click **Save**.

Enabling and Disabling Greetings

A user can have up to five greetings configured. Both the subscriber and the administrator have the ability to enable or disable these greetings. The steps for doing this from within SA in Unity are as follows:

Step 1.   From with SA, select **Subscribers > Subscribers**.

Step 2.   Click the **Find** icon and enter search criteria that will match the subscriber account you plan to edit, and click **Find**.

Step 3.   Choose the subscriber from the list that displays.

Step 4.   Select **Greetings** from the left side of the screen.

Step 5.   Choose the greeting you want to enable/disable from the **Greeting** drop-down list, as shown in Figure 8-42.

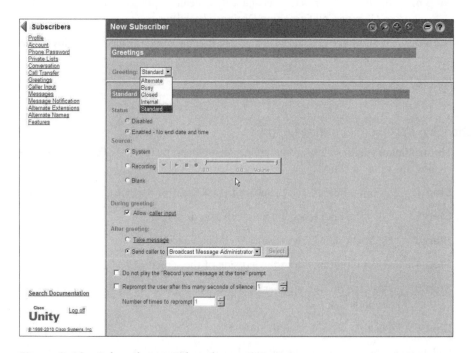

Figure 8-42   *Subscribers > Subscribers > Greetings*

Step 6.   Select either the **Enabled - No End Date and Time** or the **Disabled** radio button. You can also enable it with an automatic end date and time by selecting **Enable Until** and entering the time and date it should automatically become disabled.

Step 7.   Click the **Save** icon in the title strip.

The steps for configuring the process with UCA in Unity Connection are as follows:

Step 1.   From within UCA, select **Users > Users**. Enter the appropriate search criteria and click the **Find** button to search for the user you want to manage.

Step 2.   Click the name of the user you want to manage.

Step 3.   Navigate to **Edit > Greetings**.

Step 4.   Choose the desired greeting from the list that displays.

Step 5.   Select either the **Greeting Enabled with No End Date and Time** or the **Disabled** radio button. You can also enable it with an automatic end date and time by selecting **Enable Until** and entering the time and date it should automatically become disabled.

Step 6.   Click **Save**.

Modifying Caller Input Options

Users' greetings can include options that allow an outside caller to be transferred to another number by pressing a key on the dial pad. These are referred to as *one-key transfers*. For these to work, the administrator must configure the caller input options, which is the same as configuring caller input for a template. The steps that follow show how to configure these options in Unity:

Step 1.   From within SA, select **Subscribers > Subscribers**.

Step 2.   Click the **Find** icon and enter search criteria that will match the subscriber account you plan to edit, and click **Find**.

Step 3.   Choose the subscriber from the list that displays.

Step 4.   Select **Caller Input** from the left side of the screen.

Step 5.   To allow callers to enter another extension while listening to a greeting, select the **Allow Callers to Dial an Extension During Greeting** check box.

Step 6.   If the option to allow callers to dial another extension during the greeting is enabled, an interdigit timeout must also be configured. This is the amount of time Unity waits before deciding that the caller has finished pressing digits. This setting is **Milliseconds to Wait for Additional Digits**. The default value is 1500 milliseconds, which is a second and a half. Typically, this value is adequate. If, during a greeting, callers are transferred or receive error messages from Unity before they are finished dialing an extension, increase this value.

Step 7.   From the dial pad on the screen, configure the action that will be taken when a digit is pressed. A button can be configured for the following five types of actions:

- **Ignore Key:** No action is taken when digit is pressed.

- **Skip Greeting:** The greeting is skipped and Unity proceeds to the after-greeting action.

- **Take Message:** The caller can press this key to cause Unity to take a message.

- **Say Goodbye:** Unity plays a good-bye message and disconnects the call.

- **Send Caller To:** You can select various destinations. Table 8-10 lists the available options.

Step 8.   Click the digit you want to configure, and then select the action by clicking the appropriate radio button.

Note   When you choose to send the call to a call handler, directory handler, interview handler, or another subscriber, you have to designate the specific handler or subscriber.

Step 9.   If the **Lock This Key to the Action (Don't Wait for an Additional Keypress)** check box is selected, an extension that begins with this digit cannot be entered. Unity then transfers the call to the destination assigned to the key. This occurs without checking whether the caller will input additional digits. Only enable this field on digits that are not leading digits for any extensions.

Step 10.   After you have all the digits configured as desired, click the **Save** icon in the title strip.

The steps that follow show how to configure these options in Unity Connection:

Step 1.   From within UCA, select **Users > Users.** Enter the appropriate search criteria and click the **Find** button to search for the user you want to manage.

Step 2.   Click the name of the user you want to manage.

Step 3.   Navigate to **Edit > Caller Input.**

Step 4.   On the first screen that appears, select the key you want to configure as well as the **Wait for Additional Digits** and **Prepend Digits to Dialed Extensions** settings. The **Wait or Additional Digits** setting is the amount of time Unity Connection waits before deciding whether the caller has finished pressing digits. The default value is 1500 milliseconds, which is a second and a half. Typically, this value is adequate.

Step 5.   The **Prepend Digits** setting determines whether any digits are prepended to the extension that a caller enters. This is useful if your callers are accustomed to entering four digits but the actual extension number is seven digits. For example, the caller can enter 3322 but the full extension that the call needs to be transferred to is 5423322. By entering 542 in the **Digits to Prepend** field and selecting the **Enable** check box, the call would be transferred to 5423322.

Table 8-10 *Send Caller to Options*

Action	Description
Alternate Contact Number	Sends the call to the number that you specify in the **Number to Dial** field.
Broadcast Message Administrator	Sends the call to a conversation for sending broadcast messages.
CVM Mailbox Reset	Enables the caller to reset the mailbox (available with Community Voice-mail package).
Call Handler	Sends the call to the selected call handler.
Caller System Transfer	Enables the caller to transfer to another extension after he logs in with subscriber credentials. He can then transfer to any number that his restriction table allows.
Directory Handler	Sends the call to the directory handler you select.
Easy Sign-In	Sends the call to a login process that asks for the password for this mailbox.
Greetings Administrator	Sends the call to a conversation that allows users to manage the greetings of call handlers that they own.
Hang Up	Disconnects the call.
Hotel Checked Out	This option works in concert with Cisco Unity's Hospitality and Property Management Integration. It allows guests to archive their messages when checking out.
Interview Handler	Sends the call to the interview handler you select.
Sign-In	Sends the call to the subscriber sign-in.
Sign-In Archived Mailbox	Enables subscribers to access messages on the Cisco Unity server by entering their old Cisco Unity primary extension.
Subscriber	Sends the call to another subscriber's greeting or extension, depending upon how it is configured.
Subscriber System Transfer	Enables callers to transfer to another extension after they log in with subscriber credentials. They can then transfer to any number that their restriction table allows.

Step 6. Now you can start configuring the caller input keys. Select the key you want to configure. A screen similar to that shown in Figure 8-43 appears.

Step 7. The **Key** field is static and simply displays the number of the key you are configuring.

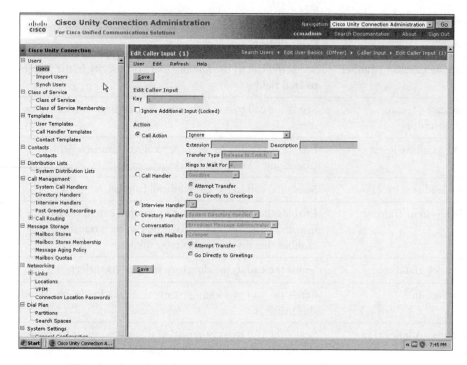

Figure 8-43   *Edit Caller Input*

Step 8.   The next field determines whether the key is locked. If the **Ignore Additional Input (Locked)** check box is selected, an extension that begins with this digit cannot be entered. Unity Connection transfers the call to the destination assigned to that key without waiting to see whether the caller is going to enter other digits. Only enable this field on digits that are not leading digits for any extensions.

Step 9.   The **Action** section determines where the call is sent when the key is pressed. Table 8-11 lists the available options.

Step 10.   Click **Save**. Return to the Caller Input page to select other keys to configure.

Managing Message Access, Notification, and Indication

Unity/Connection enables subscribers to manage their messages from both the phone and an email client. To do this efficiently, the system offers many features that impact how messages can be sent, received, and managed. The following sections discuss various settings that affect these features.

Table 8-11 *Caller Input Actions*

Action	Function
Call action such as hang-up	A specific action must be selected from the drop-down list.
Call handler	A specific call handler must be selected from the drop-down list. When sending to a call handler, you must select either **Attempt Transfer** or **Go Directly to Greeting**. Typically, **Greeting** is selected.
Interview handler	A specific interview handler must be selected from the drop-down list.
Directory handler	A specific directory handler must be selected from the drop-down list.
Conversation such as sign-in or greetings administrator	A specific conversation must be selected from the drop-down list.
Another user's mailbox	A specific user must be selected from the drop-down list. When sending to another user, you must select either **Attempt Transfer** or **Go Directly to Greeting**. To have the user's phone ring, select **Attempt Transfer**.

Allowing Subscribers to Send to Distribution Lists

You can choose to allow or prohibit subscribers to send messages to public distribution lists. This setting is based on a subscriber's CoS. The following steps explain how to configure this in Unity:

Step 1.   From within SA, select **Subscribers > Class of Service**.

Step 2.   Click the **Find** icon, and a list of CoSs displays.

Step 3.   Highlight the CoS you want to edit and click **View**.

Step 4.   Select **Messages** from the left side of the screen.

Step 5.   To allow subscribers with this CoS to send messages to distribution lists, select the **Subscribers Can Send Messages to Public Distribution Lists** check box. Deselect this box if you do not want subscribers with this CoS to send messages to distribution lists.

Step 6.   Click the **Save** icon in the title bar.

The following steps explain the configuration process for Unity Connection:

Step 1.   From within UCA, select **Class of Service > Class of Service**.

Step 2. Click the name of the CoS you want to manage.

Step 4. Scroll down to the **Messages Options** section.

Step 5. To allow subscribers with this CoS to send messages to distribution lists, select the **Allow Users to Send Messages to System Distribution Lists** check box. Deselect this box if you do not want subscribers with this CoS to send messages to distribution lists.

Step 6. Click **Save.**

Allowing Messages Deleted from the Phone to Be Saved in the Deleted Items Folder

By default, when a Unity subscriber deletes a message from the phone, the message is deleted from the system after the phone is hung up. However, in Unity Connection, the opposite is true. You can configure Unity to store the message in a subscriber's Deleted Items folder. Subscribers can then retrieve messages they have deleted from the phone through Outlook or Unity Inbox (version 4.03 or later). The following steps explain how to enable this feature:

Step 1. From within SA, select **Subscribers > Class of Service.**

Step 2. Click the **Find** icon, and a list of CoSs displays.

Step 3. Highlight the CoS you want to edit and click **View.**

Step 4. Select **Messages** from the left side of the screen.

Step 5. Select the **Deleted Messages Are Copied to the Deleted Items Folder** check box.

Step 6. Click the **Save** icon in the title bar.

Enabling Live Reply for a Subscriber

A feature called Live Reply allows subscribers to have Unity connect them with the extension of a subscriber that left a message by pressing 44 at the end of listening to the message. This feature is granted based on the subscriber's CoS. To enable these features in Unity, follow these steps:

Step 1. From within SA, select **Subscribers > Class of Service.**

Step 2. Click the **Find** icon, and a list of CoSs displays.

Step 3. Highlight the CoS you want to edit and click **View.**

Step 4. Select **Messages** from the left side of the screen.

Step 5. To allow subscribers access to Live Reply to reach other subscribers, select the **Subscribers Can Reply to Messages from Other Subscribers by Calling Them** check box.

Step 6. To allow subscribers access to Live Reply to reach unidentified callers, select the **Subscribers Can Reply to Messages from Unidentified Callers by Calling Them** check box.

Step 7. Click the **Save** icon in the title bar.

To enable these features in Unity Connection, follow these steps:

Step 1. From within UCA, select **Class of Service > Class of Service**.

Step 2. Click the name of the CoS you want to manage.

Step 3. Scroll down to the **Messages Options** section.

Step 4. To allow user to access Live Reply to reach other users, select the **Users Can Reply to Messages from Other Users by Calling Them** check box.

Step 5. To allow users to access Live Reply to reach unidentified callers, select the **Users Can Reply to Messages from Unidentified Callers by Calling Them** check box.

Step 6. Click **Save**.

Creating Private Lists

Private lists are similar to public distribution lists but are private to the users for whom they are created. Either the administrator or the user can create these lists. The following steps illustrate the process of list creation from SA in Unity:

Step 1. From within SA, select **Subscribers > Subscribers**.

Step 2. Click the **Find** icon and enter search criteria that will match the subscriber account you plan to edit, and click **Find**.

Step 3. Choose the subscriber from the list that displays.

Step 4. Select **Private Lists** from the left side of the screen.

Step 5. Select an unused list number from the **Private Lists** drop-down list.

Step 6. Enter a name for the list in the **Name of List** field.

Step 7. Click the **Change Members** button. A search criteria window displays. Enter search criteria that match the members you want to add to this list and click **Find**.

Step 8. A list of matching objects displays on the left side of the window. Highlight the objects you want to add to the private list and click the **>>** button.

Note You can choose multiple objects by holding the **Ctrl** key down as you click on the object's name.

Step 9.   After all desired members have been added, click the **Save** button.

Step 10.   Record a name for the list by clicking the red dot on the media master control panel. This should cause the phone to ring. Answer the phone and speak the name of the private list.

Step 11.   Click **Save**.

The following steps explain how to create these lists from UCA in Unity Connection:

Step 1.   From within UCA, select **Users > Users**. Enter the appropriate search criteria, and click the **Find** button to search for the user you want to manage.

Step 2.   Click the name of the user you want to manage.

Step 3.   Navigate to **Edit > Private Distribution Lists**.

Step 4.   A new window opens. Essentially, you are now logged in to the CPAC interface as the user you are configuring.

Step 5.   Click the **New Private List** button.

Step 6.   In the **Name** field, enter a name for the list.

Step 7.   You can record a name for the list by clicking the red button on the panel. Enter your extension if prompted. When the phone rings, answer it and record the name.

Step 8.   If you are using voice recognition in your environment, you can enter alternate names if the name assigned to the list is not pronounced like it is spelled. If needed, enter a phonetically spelled name as an alternate name.

Step 9.   To add users to the list, click the **Add Members** button.

Step 10.   A new window opens. The types of objects you can add appear near the top of the window. You can add users, distribution lists, private lists, and remote contacts to private lists. Select the type of object you want to add to the list.

Step 11.   Enter the appropriate search criteria and click **Find**.

Step 12.   Select the check box next to the name of object (user, list, and so on) that you want to add to the list.

Step 13.   Click **Add Members**.

Step 14.   The window closes and you return to the CPCA Private List page. The objects you added to the list are listed on the **Private List Members** heading. Click **Save** and close the window.

Configuring Message Notification

The user or the system administrator can configure message notification. If possible, encourage your users to control and configure their own message notification using CPCA. If it is necessary to configure message notification through the administrative interface, the process is very similar to configuration through a template. The following steps describe how to configure message notification for a Unity subscriber:

Step 1.   From within SA, select **Subscribers > Subscribers**. Click the **Find** icon, and search for the user you want to manage.

Step 2.   When the name of the desired subscriber appears in the title strip, select **Message Notification** from the menu that appears on the left side of the screen.

Step 3.   First you must select which device you want to configure. From the **Device** drop-down list, choose a device.

Step 4.   Depending on whether you choose a phone or an email device as the notification device, the next few configuration fields vary slightly. If you choose a phone or a pager, enter the phone number of that device in the **Phone Number** field. After dialing the phone number, enter any digits that still need to be dialed in the **Extra Digits** field. Extra digits are typically needed for pagers that use PINs.

Step 5.   If you choose a device that will use an email address as the delivery mechanism, such as a text pager or Text for VMI, enter the email address in the **To** field. Then enter the pilot number for Unity in the **From** field. Some cell phones act as pagers and can call back the number that is in this field.

Step 6.   When the notification device is a phone or pager, you can set it so that the extra digits are not sent until a connection is detected. To enable this option, select the **Try to Detect Connection** check box. If you want it to wait a specified number of seconds instead of trying to detect a connection, select the **Seconds to Wait Before Dialing Extra Digits** check box and enter the number of seconds to wait in the box to the right of that field. You can use the **Seconds to Wait** option if Unity is having trouble detecting a connection because of poor line quality. In some cases, you might need to use both the **Try to Detect a Connection** and the **Seconds to Wait** options. It might be necessary to set the parameters and then test these settings a few times before getting them to work properly with different paging companies.

When a device that uses an email address is selected, enter the text that you want to display in the notification in the **Text** field. A message count can be included in this notification by selecting the **Include Voice-mail, E-mail, and Fax Counts** check box.

Step 7.   To enable this device to be used for message notification, select the **Enabled** radio button. It is not enough to simply configure the device—you must ensure that the enable button is selected.

Step 8.   Under the **Notify Subscriber Of** heading, select the notification messages that you want to be accessible to the subscriber. You can select all messages or only one type, such as voicemail. You can further narrow it down by selecting only urgent messages.

Step 9. The next area of the screen is a grid that represents the days of the week. Each day is broken down into half-hour segments. This grid is used to define what hours of the day notifications will be sent. The boxes that have a check mark represent the time of day that notifications will be sent. Edit the schedule as needed.

Note You can copy the open/closed hours of one day to another day, all weekdays, or weekends by using the **Copy Day's Schedule** function found below the grid. Select the **Source Day** from the first drop-down list and the **Destination Day(s)** from the second drop-down list, and then click **Copy Day's Schedule**.

Step 10. The notification can be configured to be sent immediately or held a specified length of time before being sent. If cascading notification is being deployed, some devices are configured to wait for a certain number of minutes before being notified. Cascading notification occurs when a notification is sent, and if the message has not been retrieved after a specified number of minutes, a different device is notified. If, after an additional amount of time, the message is still not retrieved, another device is notified.

Step 11. Enter the number of minutes that Unity should wait before notifying this device in the **Send Initial Notification After How Many Minutes** field. Unity sends the notification only if the message is not retrieved after this amount of time.

Step 12. To have Unity send another notification to this device, only when a new message arrives, select the **Restart Notification Each Time a New Message Arrives** radio button. You can have the device notified every so many minutes until the message is retrieved by selecting the **Repeat Notification if There Are Still New Messages After This Many Minutes** radio button. If the **Repeat Notification if There Are Still New Messages After This Many Minutes** radio button is selected, enter the desired number of minutes in the field to the right of this label.

Note If the device you are configuring is a text pager or Text for VMI, none of the following settings display. Simply click the **Save** icon in the title strip to complete this task.

Step 13. Under the **If the Device Does Not Answer** heading, enter the number of rings Unity should wait before hanging up, how many times Unity should try again, and how many minutes should elapse between attempts in the appropriate fields.

Step 14. Under the **If Device Is Busy** heading, enter the number of times Unity should try again and how many minutes should elapse between attempts in the appropriate fields.

Step 15. If the notification fails, you can specify another device to be notified by selecting the device from the **If Notification Fails, Send Notification To** drop-down list.

Step 16. Click the **Save** icon in the title strip.

The following steps describe how to configure message notification for a Unity Connection User:

Step 1. From within UCA, select **Users > Users**. Enter the appropriate search criteria, and click the **Find** button to search for the user you want to manage.

Step 2. Click the name of the user you want to manage.

Step 3. Navigate to **Edit > Notification Devices**.

Step 4. A page appears that lists the five devices that can be configured. Select the device you want to configure.

Step 5. The **Enabled** check box must be selected for this device to receive notifications.

Step 6. The **Display Name** field is used to identify the device. In most cases, the existing display names are sufficient, but you can change them if you desire.

Step 7. Enter the number of minutes that Unity Connection should wait before notifying this device in the **Delay Before First Notification Attempt** field. Unity Connection only sends the notification if the message has not been retrieved after this amount of time.

Step 8. To invoke what some refer to as the "nag factor," you can have the device notified at selected intervals until the message is retrieved. Select the **Repeat Notification if There Are Still New Messages** check box, and then enter the number of minutes in the **Notification Repeat Interval** field.

Step 9. The **On Notification Fail** setting allows you to specify another device to be notified if the notification fails. To accomplish this, select the **Send To** radio button and select the device from the drop-down list. If you do not want to have another device notified, select the **Do Nothing** radio button.

Step 10. Under the **Notify User Of** heading, select the types of messages that you want to be accessible to the user. You can further narrow it down by selecting only urgent messages.

Step 11. The rest of the fields vary slightly depending on whether you choose a phone or an email as the notification device. If you choose SMTP as the delivery mechanism, you have the option to send transcriptions (if you are using a transcription service). You can choose to send them for all voicemails or only those marked urgent. Table 8-12 lists the rest of the fields that must be configured for STMP.

Step 12. If you choose a phone or a pager, additional configuration is necessary. Table 8-13 lists the required fields.

Step 13. Click **Save**.

Table 8-12   *SMTP Notification Fields*

Field	Description
To	Enter the address that the notification should be sent to.
From	Enter the address that should appear in the front field of the email.
Message Header	Enter the text that you want to appear at the top of the email notification.
Message Text	Enter the text that you want to appear in the body of the email notification.
Message Footer	Enter the text that you want to display below the body of the email notification.
Include Message Information in Message Text	Allows information like caller name, caller ID, urgency marking, and time message left to be included in the email.
Include Message Count in Message Text	The number of new messages the user has is included in the email.
Include a Link to Cisco PCA in Message Text	A link to CPCA is included in the email.

Adding Alternate Extensions

Alternate extensions are assigned to users to provide easy message access when calling Unity/Connection from a number other than that associated with their account. The administrator can add a maximum of nine alternate extensions for each user. To configure alternate extensions for a Unity subscriber, use the following steps:

Step 1.   From within SA, select **Subscribers > Subscribers**.

Step 2.   Click the **Find** icon and enter search criteria that match the subscriber account you plan to edit, and click **Find**.

Step 3.   Choose the subscriber from the list that displays.

Step 4.   Select **Alternate Extensions** from the left side of the screen.

Step 5.   Nine **Extension** fields appear. Enter the desired alternate extension(s) in the fields labeled 1 through 9. You can choose to configure as few as one or up to all nine alternate extensions.

Step 6.   Click the **Save** icon in the title strip.

Table 8-13 *Phone/Pager Notification Fields*

Field	Description
Phone Number	Enter the number to dial when sending notifications.
Extra Digits	If required, enter the digits that are sent after the call is connected. This can be used when sending a notification to a pager.
Duration to Wait Before Dialing Extra Digits	Enter the number of seconds to wait before sending the extra digits.
Ring to Wait	Enter the number of rings to wait before determining the call is left unanswered. This should be set lower than the number of rings that an answering machine or service (voicemail) waits before answering a call. This is to ensure that the notification is not answered by the service.
Busy Retry Limit	Enter the number of times that the notification will be tried when the device is busy.
Busy Retry Interval	Enter the number of minutes the between the notification retries when the device is busy.
RNA Retry Limit	Enter the number of times that the notification will be tried when the device does not answer.
RNA Retry Interval	Enter the number of minutes between the notification retries when the device does not answer.
Phone System	Select the phone system that is used for this notification device.
Prompt for User ID on Notification	If selected, the user will have to enter her ID (extension number) and PIN to retrieve the messages. Even if this is not selected, the user will have to enter her PIN.

Step 7.   The other field is simply a check box. This box is used when deleting alternate extensions. To delete an alternate extension, select the check box next to the one you want to delete and click the **Delete** button.

To configure alternate extensions for a Unity Connection user, use the following steps:

Step 1.   From within UCA, select **Users > Users**. Enter the appropriate search criteria, and click the **Find** button to search for the user you want to manage.

Step 2.   Click the name of the user you want to manage.

Step 3.   Navigate to **Edit > Alternate Extensions.**

Step 4.   Click the **Add New** button.

Step 5.   From the **Phone Type** drop-down list, select the device that it associated with the extension (phone number) you are going to add.

Step 6.   Enter a descriptive name in the **Display Name** field.

Step 7.   In the **Phone Number** field, enter the number you want to assign as an alternate extension.

Step 8.   From the **Partition** drop-down list, select the desired partition for the alternate extension.

Step 9.   Click **Save.**

Adding Alternate Names

Alternate names can be assigned to users who might be known by a name other than their given name such as a nickname. This allows them to be found in the directory if someone searches using a variation of their name or a nickname. To configure alternate names for a Unity subscriber, use the following steps:

Step 1.   From within SA, select **Subscribers > Subscribers.**

Step 2.   Click the **Find** icon and enter search criteria that match the subscriber account you plan to edit, and click **Find.**

Step 3.   Choose the subscriber from the list that displays.

Step 4.   Select **Alternate Names** from the left side of the screen.

Step 5.   Enter the first and last name in the appropriate fields and click **Add.**

Step 6.   Click the **Save** icon in the title strip.

To configure alternate names for a Unity Connection user, use the following steps:

Step 1.   From within UCA, select **Users > Users.** Enter the appropriate search criteria, and click the **Find** button to search for the user you want to manage.

Step 2.   Click the name of the user you want to manage.

Step 3.   Navigate to **Edit > Alternate Names.**

Step 4.   Enter the first and last name in the appropriate fields and click **Add New.**

Step 5.   Click **Save.**

Assigning External Service Accounts (Unity Connection Only)

External service accounts are required when services such as email, conferencing, and calendaring are integrated with Unity Connection. The tasks for adding and configuring these service accounts is beyond the scope of this book, but the following steps show how to assign an Exchange 2007 external service account to a user. These steps assume that the Exchange 2007 external service accounts have already been configured:

Step 1. From within UCA, select **Users > Users**. Enter the appropriate search criteria, and click the **Find** button to search for the user you want to manage.

Step 2. Click the name of the user you want to manage.

Step 3. Navigate to **Edit > External Service Accounts**.

Step 4. Click **Add New**.

Step 5. Select the Exchange 2007 service from the **External Service** drop-down list.

Step 6. The service type is defined when the external service account is initially configured. This can be left as it stands.

Step 7. Enter the email address for the user in the **Email Address** field.

Step 8. If the Windows domain user ID is the same as the Unity Connection alias, select **Use Connection Alias** from the **Sign-In Type** drop-down list. Otherwise, select **Use User ID Provided Below**.

Step 9. If you selected **Use User ID Provided Below** in the previous step, enter the user's Windows domain ID in the user ID field.

Step 10. Enter the user's Exchange password (if known) in the **Password** field.

Step 11. To allow users to access their Exchange calendar and personal contacts, select the **User Access to Calendar and Personal Contacts** check box.

Step 12. To allow users to access their Exchange email, select the **User Access to Email in Third-Party Message Store** check box.

Step 13. Click **Save**.

Add SMTP Proxy Addresses (Unity Connection Only)

STMP proxy addresses are used to map a user's email address to his Unity Connection mailbox. This is needed when users employ an email client to send and receive voicemail. To configure an SMTP proxy address for a Unity Connection user, simply add the user email address to the STMP proxy field. The following steps show how this is accomplished:

Step 1. From within UCA, select **Users > Users**. Enter the appropriate search criteria, and click the **Find** button to search for the user you want to manage.

Step 2. Click the name of the user you want to manage.

Step 3.   Navigate to **Edit > SMTP Proxy Addresses.**

Step 4.   Click **Add New.**

Step 5.   Enter the user's email address in the blank field.

Step 6.   Click **Save.**

Changing Maximum Outside Caller Message Length

As we have already discussed, the length of a message that a caller can leave for a user is based on his class of service. This section examines how to set the maximum length that an outside caller can leave on the system.

To configure this is Unity, follow these steps:

Step 1.   From within SA, select **Subscribers > Subscribers.**

Step 2.   Click the **Find** icon and enter search criteria that match the subscriber account you plan to edit. Click **Find.**

Step 3.   Choose the subscriber from the list that displays.

Step 4.   Select **Messages** from the left side of the screen.

Step 5.   Enter the maximum number of seconds that a message from an outside caller can be in the **Maximum Message Length, in Seconds** field.

Step 6.   Click the **Save** icon in the title strip.

To configure this in Unity Connection, follow these steps:

Step 1.   From within UCA, select **Users > Users.** Enter the appropriate search criteria, and click the **Find** button to search for the user you want to manage.

Step 2.   Click the name of the user you want to manage.

Step 3.   Navigate to **Edit > Message Settings.**

Step 4.   Enter the maximum number of seconds that a message from an outside caller can be in the **Maximum Message Length** field.

Step 5.   Click **Save.**

Adjusting Urgent Message Marking

You can allow or prohibit callers to mark messages urgent. You might find that you need to change this setting.

To change this in Unity, follow these steps:

Step 1.   From within SA, select **Subscribers > Subscribers.**

Step 2.   Click the **Find** icon and enter search criteria that match the subscriber account you plan to edit, and click **Find.**

Step 3.   Choose the subscriber from the list that displays.

Step 4.   Select **Messages** from the left side of the screen.

Step 5.   Under the **Mark Messages as Urgent** heading, you have three choices:

- To mark all incoming messages urgent, click the **Always** radio button.

- To mark incoming messages never urgent, click the **Never** radio button.

- To allow the caller to determine whether the messages should be marked urgent, click the **Ask Caller for Their Preference** radio button.

Step 6.   Click the **Save** icon in the title strip.

To change this in Unity Connection, follow these steps:

Step 1.   From within UCA, select **Users > Users**. Enter the appropriate search criteria, and click the **Find** button to search for the user you want to manage.

Step 2.   Click the name of the user you want to manage.

Step 3.   Navigate to **Edit > Message Settings**.

Step 4.   You have three choices when labeling a message:

- To allow the caller to label a message urgent, select the **Ask Caller** radio button under the **Message Urgency** heading.

- To mark a message always urgent without asking the caller, select the **Mark Urgent** radio button.

- To never mark the message urgent, select the **Mark Normal** radio button.

Step 5.   Click **Save**.

Enable MWI on Another Extension

There might be times you want an extension, other than the one associated with a user, to activate MWI when a new message arrives. This might be desirable if a user has phones in different physical locations with different extensions and wants to be able to receive an MWI for a single voice mailbox on both phones.

To configure this in Unity, follow these steps:

Step 1.   From within SA, select **Subscribers > Subscribers**.

Step 2.   Click the **Find** icon and enter search criteria that match the subscriber account you plan to edit, and click **Find**.

Step 3.   Choose the subscriber from the list that displays.

Step 4.   Select **Messages** from the left side of the screen.

Step 5.   Click the **Add** button, which is at the bottom of the screen under the **MWI Extension** field.

Step 6.   Enter the extension number for which you want to activate MWI in the new empty field that displays.

Step 7.   Click the **Save** icon in the title strip.

To configure this in Unity, follow these steps:

Step 1.   From within UCA, select **Users > Users**. Enter the appropriate search criteria, and click the **Find** button to search for the user you want to manage.

Step 2.   Click the name of the user you want to manage.

Step 3.   Navigate to **Edit > Message Waiting Indicators**.

Step 4.   Click the **Add New** button.

Step 5.   Select the **Enable** check box.

Step 6.   In the **Display** field, enter a descriptive name for the device that the MWI will be activated on.

Step 7.   If the **Inherit User's Extension** check box is selected, the MWI is sent to the primary extension of the user. If you want to activate an MWI on another extension, do not select this box.

Step 8.   In the **Extension** field, enter the extension you want the MWI activated on.

Step 9.   From the **Phone System** drop-down list, select the phone system that the selected extension is associated with.

Step 10.   The **Current Status** field displays the current status of the MWI.

Step 11.   Click **Save**.

Adding and Removing Users from a Distribution List

To view, add, or remove members from distribution lists in Unity, follow these steps:

Step 1.   From within SA, select **Subscribers > Public Distribution Lists**.

Step 2.   Click the **Find** icon in the title strip. Enter your search criteria and click the **Find** button. A list of PDLs displays. Click the PDL from which you want to add or remove subscribers.

Step 3.   Select **Members** from the left side of the screen.

Step 4.   You have the option to view, add, or remove members from the PDL. Select the action you want by clicking the appropriate radio button at the top part of the screen. If you choose to add members, you must select either **Selected Subscriber** or **Public Distribution Lists** from the drop-down list.

Step 5. Enter the search criteria for the subscriber you want to manage in the **Type a Subscriber Name to Find** field and click **Find**.

Step 6. If you are simply viewing, the PDL list displays. If you are adding or removing, a list displays with either an **Add to List** or **Remove** button. Select the subscriber you want to manage and click the **Add** or **Remove** button.

Step 7. Click **Save**.

To view, add, or remove members from distribution lists in Unity Connection, follow these steps:

Step 1. From within UCA, select **Distribution List > System Distribution Lists**.

Step 2. Select the distribution list you want to manage.

Step 3. Navigate to **Edit > Distribution List Members**.

Step 4. To add a user, click the **Add User** button. If you want to remove users from the list, skip to Step 8.

Step 5. Enter the search criteria for the user you want add and click **Find**.

Step 6. Select the check box next to the name of the user you want to add to the distribution list and click **Add Selected**.

Step 7. Click **Close** to close the available User Search Results window.

Step 8. To remove a user from the list, select the check box next to the name of the user and click **Remove Selected**.

Conversation Management Settings

One area of configuration that can greatly impact end-user satisfaction is the conversation. These settings define how Unity/Connection communicates with the user over the phone. If a user feels that the voicemail system is not offering her an efficient interface, she can become very frustrated. There is no such thing as a typical user, so Unity/Connection allows the conversation to be tailored to each end user's needs. The user can configure most of the conversation using CPCA. However, often the administrator is called upon to complete these tasks. The most common conversion configuration tasks are discussed in the following sections.

Changing Menus from Full to Brief

To change the menus from full to brief in Unity, follow these steps:

Step 1. From within SA, select **Subscribers > Subscribers**.

Step 2. Click the **Find** icon and enter search criteria that match the subscriber account you plan to edit, and click **Find**.

Step 3. Choose the subscriber from the list that displays.

Step 4.   Select **Conversation** from the left side of the screen.

Step 5.   Using the **Menu Style** drop-down list, select **Brief.**

Step 6.   Click the **Save** icon in the title strip.

To change the menus from full to brief in Unity Connection, follow these steps:

Step 1.   From within UCA, select **Users > Users.** Enter the appropriate search criteria and click the **Find** button to search for the user you want to manage.

Step 2.   Click the name of the user you want to manage.

Step 3.   Navigate to **Edit > Phone Menu.**

Step 4.   Using the **Touchtone Conversation Menu Style** drop-down list, select **Brief.**

Step 5.   Click **Save.**

Changing How a User Searches for Other Users

To configure how a Unity subscriber searches for another subscriber when addressing a message, follow these steps:

Step 1.   From within SA, select **Subscribers > Subscriber.**

Step 2.   Click the **Find** icon and enter search criteria that match the subscriber account you plan to edit, and click **Find.**

Step 3.   Choose the subscriber from the list that displays.

Step 4.   Select **Conversation** from the left side of the screen.

Step 5.   From the **Identify an Addressee By** drop-down list, select how a subscriber will be prompted to address messages to other subscribers. The available choices are as follows:

- Spelling the last name then first name

- Spelling the first name then last name

- Entering the extension

Step 6.   Click the **Save** icon from the title strip.

To configure how a Unity Connection user searches for another user when addressing a message, follow these steps:

Step 1.   From within UCA, select **Users > Users.** Enter the appropriate search criteria, and click the **Find** button to search for the user you want to manage.

Step 2.   Click the name of the user you want to manage.

Step 3.   Navigate to **Edit > Send Message Settings.**

Step 4.   From the **Enter a Recipient By** drop-down list, select how a subscriber will be prompted to address messages to other subscribers. The available choices follow:

- Spelling the last name then first name
- Spelling the first name then last name
- Entering the extension

Step 5.   Click **Save.**

Changing What Message Count Is Played to a User

To configure what message counts are played to a Unity subscriber, follow these steps:

Step 1.   From within SA, select **Subscribers > Subscribers.**

Step 2.   Click the **Find** icon and enter search criteria that match the subscriber account you plan to edit, and click **Find.**

Step 3.   Choose the subscriber from the list that displays.

Step 4.   Select **Conversation** from the left side of the screen.

Step 5.   The settings under the **For New Messages, Play** heading determine what message counts Unity plays when a subscriber logs in. To play the total number of new messages in a subscriber's mailbox (this includes voicemail, email, and faxes), select the **Message Count Totals** check box. Three other message count options are available:

- Voice message counts
- Email message counts
- Fax counts

To break down the message count by the type of message or limit the count to a particular type of message, select the check box next to the desired message count label.

Step 6.   To have Unity announce the total number of saved messages, select the **Saved Message Count** check box.

Step 7.   Click the **Save** icon in the title strip.

To configure what message counts are played to a Unity Connection user, follow these steps:

Step 1.   From within UCA, select **Users > Users.** Enter the appropriate search criteria, and click the **Find** button to search for the user you want to manage.

Step 2.   Click the name of the user you want to manage.

Step 3.   Navigate to **Edit > Playback Message Settings.**

Step 4. The settings under the **For New Messages, Play** heading determine what message counts Unity Connection plays when a subscriber logs in. To play the total number of new messages in a user's mailbox (this includes voicemail, email, and faxes), select the **Message Count Totals** check box. Four other message count options are available:

- Voice message counts

- Email message counts

- Fax counts

- Receipt message counts

To break down the message count by the type of message or limit the count to a particular type of message, select the check box next to the desired message count label.

Step 5. To have Unity Connection announce the total number of saved messages, select the **Saved Message Count** box check.

Step 6. Click **Save**.

Changing the Order in Which Messages Are Played

To change the order in which messages are played to a Unity subscriber, follow these steps:

Step 1. From within SA, select **Subscribers > Subscribers**.

Step 2. Click the **Find** icon and enter search criteria that match the subscriber account you plan to edit, and click **Find**.

Step 3. Choose the subscriber from the list that displays.

Step 4. Select **Conversation** from the left side of the screen.

Step 5. You can configure the order in which new messages are played. Under the **New Message Play Order** heading is a list of the various types of messages. The messages are played as they appear from top to bottom. To change the order, highlight the type of message you want to move and then click the **Move Up** or **Move Down** button. Configure all the message types until they are in the desired order.

Step 6. The default behavior of Unity is to play the oldest message first when playing new messages. To play the newest message first, choose **Newest First** from the **Then By** drop-down list found below the **New Message Play Order** list. In most cases, it is best to leave this setting at **Oldest First**.

Step 7. You can also configure the order in which saved messages are played. Under the **Saved Message Play Order** heading is a list of the various types of messages. The messages are played as they appear from top to bottom. To change the order, highlight the type of message you want to move and then click the

Move Up or **Move Down** button. Configure all the message types until they are in the desired order.

Step 8. The default behavior of Unity is to play the newest message first when playing saved messages. To play the oldest message first, choose **Oldest First** from the **Then By** drop-down list found below the **Saved Message Play Order** list. In most cases, it is best to leave this setting at **Newest First**.

Step 9. After changing these settings to the desired order, click the **Save** icon in the title strip.

To change the order in which messages are played to a Unity Connection user, follow these steps:

Step 1. From within UCA, select **Users > Users**. Enter the appropriate search criteria, and click the **Find** button to search for the user you want to manage.

Step 2. Click the name of the user you want to manage.

Step 3. Navigate to **Edit > Playback Message Settings**.

Step 4. You can configure the order in which new messages are played. Under the **New Message Play Order** heading is a list of the various types of messages. The messages are played as they appear from top to bottom. To change the order, highlight the type of message you want to move and then click the up or down arrows below the list. Configure all the message types until they are in the desired order.

Step 5. The default behavior of Unity Connection is to play the newest message first when playing new messages. To play the oldest message first, choose **Oldest First** from the **Then By** drop-down list found below the **New Message Play Order** list. In most cases, it is best to set this to **Oldest First**.

Step 6. You can also configure the order in which saved messages are played. Under the **Saved Message Play Order** heading is a list of the various types of messages. The messages are played as they appear from top to bottom. To change the order, highlight the type of message you want to move and then click the up or down arrows below the list. Configure all the message types until they are in the desired order.

Step 7. The default behavior of Unity Connection is to play the oldest message first when playing saved messages. To play the newest message first, choose **Newest First** from the **Then By** drop-down list found below the **Saved Message Play Order** list. In most cases, it is best to set this to **Newest First**.

Step 8. After changing these settings to the desired order, click **Save**.

Changing What Header Information Is Heard While Listening to Messages

To configure the header information that a Unity subscriber hears, follow these steps:

Step 1. From within SA, select **Subscribers > Subscribers.**

Step 2. Click the **Find** icon and enter search criteria that match the subscriber account you plan to edit, and click **Find.**

Step 3. Choose the subscriber from the list that displays.

Step 4. Select **Conversation** from the left side of the screen.

Step 5. Navigate to the **Before Playing Each Message, Play** heading near the bottom of the page. To have the sender's name played before the message is played, select the **Sender's Information** check box.

Step 6. To have the number of the current message played before the message, select the **Message Number** check box.

Step 7. To play the time the message was sent before the message is played, select the **Time Message Was Sent** check box.

Step 8. To play the length of the message, select the **Message Duration** check box.

Step 9. To play the time the message was sent after the message is played, select the **Time Message Was Sent** check box under the **After Playing Each Message, Play** heading.

Step 10. Click the **Save** icon in the title strip.

To configure the header information that a Unity Connection user hears, follow these steps:

Step 1. From within UCA, select **Users > Users.** Enter the appropriate search criteria, and click the **Find** button to search for the user you want to manage.

Step 2. Click the name of the user you want to manage.

Step 3. Navigate to **Edit > Playback Message Settings.**

Step 4. Navigate to the **Before Playing Each Message, Play** heading near the bottom of the page. To have the sender's name played before the message is played, select the **Sender's Information** check box. To include the sender's extension, select the **Include Extension** check box.

Step 5. To have the number of the current message played before the message, select the **Message Number** check box.

Step 6. To play the time the message was sent before the message is played, select the **Time the Message Was Sent** check box.

Step 7. To play the length of the message, select the **Message Duration** check box.

Step 8. To play the caller ID of an outside caller, select the **Sender's ANI** check box.

Step 9. To play the time the message was sent after the message is played, select the **Time Message Was Sent** check box under the **After Playing Each Message, Play** heading.

Although this chapter does not list every possible subscriber-related administrative task that you might need to perform, the most common tasks are covered. In future chapters, you can build on what you have learned here and apply this knowledge to other components found within Unity/Connection.

Summary

This chapter explored all the predeployment user-related tasks and the most common user-related administrative tasks. At this point, you should understand the role that templates play and know how to create them. A large portion of this chapter is dedicated to the creation and configuration of these templates. This is because a smooth, trouble-free deployment is heavily dependent upon the proper configuration of templates. Finally, you should feel comfortable with creating users and most of the common day-to-day subscriber administrative tasks. Now your system should be ready to handle your company's voicemail needs, but because Unity/Connection is more than just voicemail, it is important to understand its other capabilities. The next chapter explores the call-handling capabilities of Unity/Connection.

Chapter 9

Call Management

As stated previously, Unity/Connection is more than just a voicemail system. In addition to providing voice and unified messaging services, it can be configured as an auto-attendant. An auto-attendant is an application that answers incoming calls and plays a greeting to callers. The callers can then navigate through the voice prompts to reach desired destinations. This chapter discusses the components that make up an auto-attendant and describes how to configure them properly.

Today it is nearly impossible to call a large company and not be greeted by one of these systems. There are many horror stories about these systems, and for that reason, some companies choose not to deploy them. Even if you are not going to deploy an auto-attendant, this chapter is useful because it covers the system's call-handling capabilities. Although call-handling functions are typically used within an auto-attendant application, you can find other uses for them. With a solid understanding of the call-handling capabilities that the system offers, you can build a custom call-handling system.

Understanding Call Flow

Have you ever purchased one of those build-it-yourself desks or entertainment centers? It looks good in the store, and you figure it shouldn't be too difficult to build. The first thing you do is locate the instructions and put them in a nice safe place, just in case you need to refer to them later. Everyone knows that you don't use instructions the *first* time you try to build the item. Eventually, you have a screwdriver in one hand, the instructions in the other, and a look of total bewilderment on your face. Don't let this happen to you when it comes to building a call-handling application. It is best if you have a solid understanding of what you are going to build and understand the mechanics behind it.

The following sections discuss the mechanics behind Unity/Connection's call-handling capabilities, so that after you have created the application, it looks and acts the way you expect, unlike many of the build-it-yourself projects I have created.

Call Flow Architecture

An outside caller's experience with Unity/Connection is important because, in some cases, it is the first contact he has with your company. It is just as important that you spend time determining what type of conversation an outside caller will hear when calling as the time you spend time determining how Unity/Connection will interface with subscribers. Unity/Connection has the capability to determine how a call flows through the system based on a number of things, including time of day, called number, calling number, and caller input. The responsibility of the administrator is to determine the paths that calls take and the criteria to determine actual call flow—in other words, how the call will be handled.

We start by looking at a simple automated attendant flow. One of the simplest types of auto-attendant is one that asks callers to enter the extension of the parties with whom they want to speak. If they don't know the number, they can hold for an operator. Typically within Unity/Connection, the caller is also given the option of entering the person's name using the letters on the telephone keypad or by verbal request. In the following example, the verbal request option is not given.

When the caller reaches the auto-attendant, an opening greeting is heard. A sample greeting is "Thank you for calling Bailey's Guard Dogs. If you know your party's extension, you can enter it now. Otherwise, please hold for an operator." Now look at three call flows that can occur within this auto-attendant.

In the first path, a caller dials an extension and the called party answers. The flow looks like this:

1. During the greeting, the caller enters a user's extension.

2. The call is transferred to the user's extension.

3. The called party answers.

In the second path, a caller dials an extension, but the called party does not answer the call. The flow looks like this:

1. During the greeting, the caller enters a user's extension.

2. The call is transferred to the user's extension.

3. The called party does not answer.

4. After a certain number of rings, the call is forwarded to Unity/Connection on behalf of the called party's extension.

5. Because the call is forwarded to Unity/Connection from a known subscriber's extension, the user's greeting is played.

The final path, which the call can take, occurs when the caller does not enter anything. The flow looks like this:

1. During the greeting, the caller enters nothing.

2. After a certain number of seconds, the call is transferred to the operator's extension number.

The preceding examples are very simplistic, but they are designed to help you understand the call flow architecture.

Although a standard auto-attendant like this one might work for certain deployments, more can be accomplished by using call handlers. The following section begins to explore what call handlers are and how they are configured.

Call Handler Overview

Now that you understand how a standard auto-attendant works, you can explore more advanced call-handling capabilities.

At the core of Unity/Connection is call-handling capability components appropriately called *call handlers*. The job of a call handler is to route the call through the system based on caller input. There are three types of call handlers; a system call handler, a directory handler, and an interview handler.

The first is a system call handler. (Unity refers to system call handlers simply as call handlers.) Because this type of call handler has no predefined purpose, it is the most flexible. Most auto-attendant applications contain more of these call handlers than any other. Later in this section, more discussion is devoted to the various functions that this call handler can provide.

The second type of call handler is the directory handler. A directory handler enables the caller to search for the desired party by spelling a name using the letters on the telephone keypad. This feature is sometimes referred to as dial-by-name. Unity/Connection includes a default directory handler that normally contains all the users on the system. You can also create additional directory handlers. Later in this section, we discuss the benefits of added directory handlers.

The third and final type of call handler is the interview handler. An interview handler is used to request detailed information from the caller that might not be retrieved by asking only one question. An interview handler can be configured to ask the caller up to 20 questions and gives the caller time to answer between each question. An example of an interview handler is a class survey hotline. After students take a class, they are able to call a number and answer five questions. The answers are later transcribed and entered into the school's database.

Note The term *audio text* has been defined in many different ways. It is often used when referring to an advanced auto-attendant; however, in its purest sense, audio text is much more than that. It is defined in the Cisco Press book *Cisco Unity Deployment and Solutions Guide* as follows: "Audio text encompasses everything that you can do with a phone call in Unity other than leaving or retrieving messages."

An advanced feature that can be incorporated into an auto-attendant is the ability to make certain static information available to callers without the need for human intervention. This feature is sometimes referred to as an audio text application. For example, Figure 9-1 shows how you can allow callers to hear store hours or directions by using the auto-attendant. The audio text application is a number of call handlers configured so that the callers can navigate to the information they need without having to talk to a live person. Often this is not only a cost savings to the company but also a time saver for the caller. Instead of having to wait on hold to find out when the store opens, the caller simply presses a few buttons to hear the store hours.

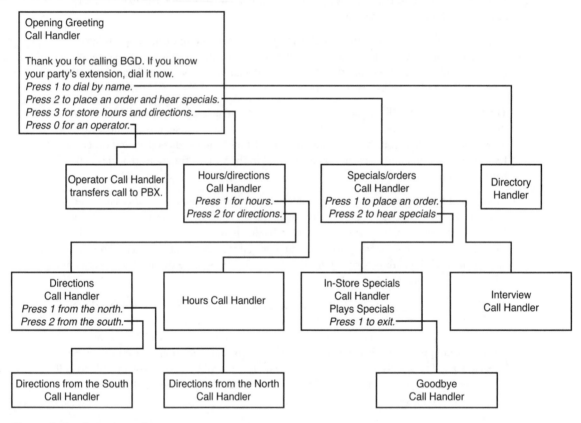

Figure 9-1   *Auto-Attendant*

The menu starts at what is called the opening greeting call handler. Most outside calls entering the system begin at a standard call handler. By default, there are three call handlers in Unity/Connection. The first is called the opening greeting and is the default entry point for outside calls. The opening greeting plays a greeting that offers the caller the available choices. In this example, if callers press 0 or hold on the line, they are transferred to the second default call handler, the operator call handler. Its job is to deliver the call to Communications Manager or a PBX with instructions to forward the call on to the operator's extension. The third default call handler is the goodbye call handler. This call handler politely ends a call. It gives the caller one last chance to dial an extension and then hangs up if an extension is not entered. In this example, if callers press 1 after hearing the in-store specials, they are sent to the goodbye call handler.

Now take a look at an example of an audio text application. Assume that a person who lives north of the store wants directions. When she reaches the opening greeting, she presses 3 for store hours and directions. Then she presses 2 for directions, and finally she presses 1 because she wants directions from the north. The caller was able to obtain the information she needed without having to wait to speak with someone.

Callers also have the option of dialing by name if they don't know their party's extension. By pressing 1 from the opening greeting, callers are sent to the directory handler, where they can enter the name of the person they want to reach.

This example also includes the use of an interview handler. If callers want to place an order, they press 2 from the opening greeting. They are transferred to the specials/orders call handler, from which they can press 1 to place an order. They are then transferred to an interview handler, which requests four pieces of information: name, customer number, product being ordered, and shipping method. The questions are not shown in Figure 9-1; they are simply part of the interview handler.

After reviewing this example, you should have a good understanding of how the different types of call handlers work together and how they can be tied to one another. The next section provides a more detailed look at these components and describes how each is configured.

Creating Basic Call-Routing Systems

Now that you have a basic understanding of the call-handling capabilities of Unity/Connection, it's time to put some of that knowledge to work. The first thing to do is to decide how advanced a call-handling system you want to provide. As discussed earlier, the system can be configured to offer a very simple call-handling system or a much more advanced one. The following sections discuss what steps are required to create a basic call-handling system.

The goal of these sections is to create the components needed for an auto-attendant system that allows outside callers to enter a subscriber's extension number, dial by name, or reach the operator. By default, these options are activated by using the opening greeting that comes with Unity/Connection. If these are the only features you require, little configuration is needed. However, these sections go into greater detail so that the auto-attendant provides the desired service and so that you will understand how to make changes as needed. Throughout these sections, each configuration setting is discussed so that you understand the impact that each setting will have on the system.

Call Handlers

Typically, calls are sent to the system in one of two methods. With the first method, each user has a Direct Inward Dial (DID) number. When an outside caller dials this number, the call is sent to the subscriber's phone. If the subscriber's phone is busy or is not answered, the call is forwarded to Unity/Connection, where the user's greeting is played. When DIDs are not available, calls are sent to the Unity/Connection system using the second method. With this method, a company can route calls to the main number on to Unity/Connection. A call handler, typically called opening greeting, is the entry point for calls that enter the system by dialing the company's main number. In some cases, there might be a need for multiple opening call handlers, such as for a company that wants a separate auto-attendant for each division of the company. In such cases, the greeting the caller hears depends on the number dialed to reach the company. The steps for providing this functionality are covered in the "Creating Advanced Call-Routing Systems" section, later in this chapter. In this example, you can assume that all incoming calls reach the same main greeting. Because all calls enter the system at a call handler, the first step is to create or modify a call handler. In most cases, you modify the call handler named opening greeting. Now look at the creation and configuration process for call handlers.

Logic tells you that before you can configure something, it must exist; therefore, before you can configure a call handler, one must be created. Because the steps required to create and configure call handlers in Unity are different than those in Unity Connection, the steps for both systems are covered in this chapter. Sstart with Unity configuration. If you are not using Unity, you can skip to the "Creating and Configuring Unity Connection Call Handlers" section, later in this chapter.

Creating and Configuring Unity Call Handlers

Three call handlers are created during the installation of Unity. In most environments, more need to be created. We begin with creating a call handler as outlined in the steps that follow:

Step 1.   From within SA, select **Call Management > Call Handlers**.

Step 2.   From the title strip, click the **Add** icon.

Step 3.   A new Add a Call Handler window displays, as shown in Figure 9-2. Enter a name for the new call handler.

Step 4.   Unity call handlers do not use templates to define their parameters. However, you can choose to create a new call handler based on an existing one. When you do this, the new call handler has all the attributes of the call handler on which it is based. To create the call handler with the same attributes as an existing call handler, select the **Based on Existing Handler** radio button and select the existing call handler from the **Based On** drop-down list. If you do not want the new call handler to copy the attributes of an existing call handler, select the **New Handler** radio button.

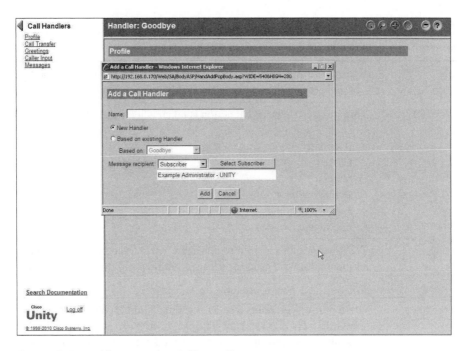

Figure 9-2 *Add New Unity Call Handler*

Step 5.   Call handlers can be configured to accept messages, but because a call handler does not have a mailbox on the system, you have to designate which subscriber will receive the messages. Using the **Message Recipient** drop-down
list, you can choose to have the message recipient classified as a subscriber or
a Public Distribution List (PDL). Typically, messages are sent to a single subscriber. If you need to have multiple subscribers receive the message, create a
PDL that contains the subscribers, and then select the PDL as the message
recipient.

Step 6.   Click the **Select Subscriber** or **Select Distribution List** button. A search criteria window displays. Enter the search criteria and click the Find button.
Highlight the desired subscriber/PDL from the list and click the Select button.

Step 7.   Click the **Add** button.

After the call handler is created, configuration is required to accomplish the task that you
designed for it. The next section covers the configuration process.

Table 9-1   *Call Handler Configurable Parameters*

Parameter	Details
Profile	General settings such as schedules and languages; recorded name for the call handler and the owner of the call handler are configured in this area.
Call transfer	This area determines what action is taken when this call handler is reached. There are six rules: • Alternate • Closed • Standard • Follow-me here • Follow-me home • Follow-me mobile
Greetings	The greetings area is used to configure which greetings are enabled, what action is allowed during the greeting, and what action is taken after the greeting.
Caller input	Often during a greeting, a caller is given a number of choices such as "press 1 for Sales, press 2 for Support, or to reach an operator, press 0." The caller input settings determine what action is taken if a digit is pressed during the greeting.
Messages	The settings in this area determine how long messages can be, whether callers can edit messages, and the action to be taken after receiving a message. Most important, this is where you configure which subscriber receives the message.

Configuring Unity Call Handlers

The creation of the call handler is simple. Many of the configuration steps are very similar to those you perform when you configure subscribers. Every subscriber has an associated call handler. Even though many of these steps seem identical, there are some subtle differences to highlight.

Each call handler has five configurable areas. Table 9-1 shows each of these areas and the types of parameters configured in each.

The following steps guide you through the configuration process described in Table 9-1.

Profile Settings

Figure 9-3 shows the parameters that can be configured on the Profile page of a call handler. The following steps explain how to configure these parameters and describe the effect of each.

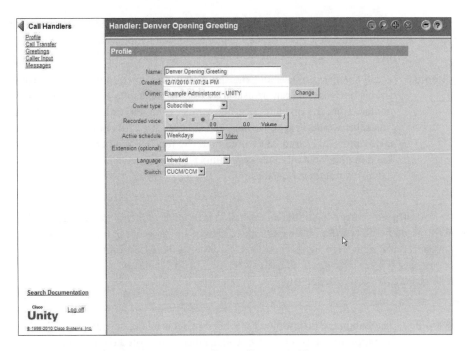

Figure 9-3 *Call Management > Call Handler > Profile.*

Step 1.   From within SA, select **Call Management > Call Handlers**. Click the **Find** icon, enter the search criteria, and click **Find**. Select the desired call handler from the list and click the **View** button. Click the **Profile** link on the left side of the screen.

Step 2.   The name of the call handler is shown in the **Name** field. The name can be changed in this field if needed.

Step 3.   The **Created** field on this page shows when the call handler was created.

Step 4.   Each call handler must have an owner. The current owner is shown in the **Owner** field. An owner can be either a subscriber or a Public Distribution List (PDL). The owner of a call handler can be allowed to change the greeting of the call handler remotely. To allow a group of subscribers to change the greeting, you should select a PDL that contains those subscribers as the owner. In the Owner Type field, select either a subscriber or PDL.

Step 5.   If you want to change the owner, click the **Change** button. A search criteria window displays. Enter criteria and click the **Find** button. A list of subscribers displays. Highlight a subscriber in the list and click the **Select** button.

Step 6.   Using the media master control panel or the Recorded Voice field, you can record a name for the call handler. This is not where you record the greeting. This is only the recorded name of the call handler. For example, if you name the call handler "Store hours," you would record the words **Store hours** here.

Step 7. From the **Active Schedule** drop-down list, select the schedule that you want to be associated with this call handler. The call handler transfer setting uses this schedule to determine how and where the call is transferred.

Step 8. A call handler can have an extension number assigned to it. This **Extension** field is optional but can be useful to outside callers. By entering the extension number from the opening greeting, a caller can jump right to this call handler. The caller would hear something like "In the future, to come directly to this menu, press 231," and 231 would be the extension number of the call handler. Keep in mind that all extension numbers in Unity must be unique. Enter the extension number if desired.

Note Another advantage to adding an extension is to manage the greeting of this call handler remotely. Unity offers the capability to change the greeting of a call handler by dialing into the system from any phone. This feature is called Cisco Unity Greetings Administrator (CUGA). However, to use this feature, the call handler you want to change must have an extension assigned to it.

Step 9. The **Language** drop-down list is used to set the language in which Unity prompts are played under this call handler. If Inherited displays in this field, whatever language was used in the previous call handler will continue to be used. Select the desired language from the drop-down list. When in doubt, set it to Inherited.

Step 10. From the drop-down list of the **Switch** field, specify which phone system the call handler uses.

Step 11. Click the **Save** icon in the title strip.

Call Transfer Settings

Call transfer settings determine how a call that reaches the call handler is treated. It determines whether the call is transferred to a phone and, if so, what type of transfer is used or whether the greeting is played. To configure a call handler's call transfer settings, follow these steps:

Step 1. From within SA, select **Call Management > Call Handlers**. Click the **Find** icon, enter the search criteria, and click **Find**. Select the desired call handler from the list and click the **View** button. Click the **Call Transfer** link on the left side of the screen.

Step 2. Figure 9-4 shows the Call Transfer page. At the top of the page is a Transfer Rule **Applies To** drop-down list. This field enables you to have a call handler transfer calls based on the schedule with which it is associated. For example, you could have a call handler transfer the call to a phone during open hours and go directly to a greeting during closed hours. Six types of transfer rules can be configured:

- Alternate

- Closed

- Follow-Me Here

- Follow-Me Home

- Follow-Me Mobile

- Standard

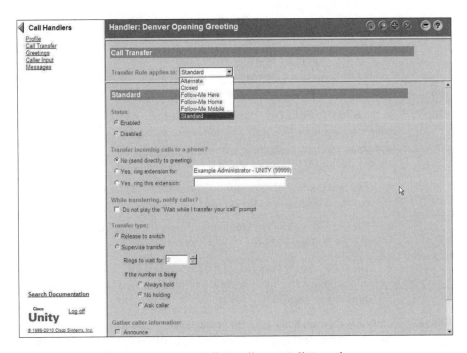

Figure 9-4 *Call Management > Call Handlers > Call Transfer.*

The most common is standard. This transfer rule applies during open hours. It also applies at all hours if no other transfer rule is enabled. If enabled, the closed transfer rule applies during closed hours. If the alternate transfer rule is enabled, it supersedes the other two transfer rules and is applied all hours on all days. The three other types of transfer rules are not normally used for call handlers. Select the transfer rule that you want to configure from the drop-down list.

Step 3. To enable the rule you just selected, click the **Enabled** radio button. To disable this rule, click the **Disabled** radio button. The standard rule is always enabled and cannot be disabled.

Step 4. Depending on the use of the call handler, you might want to configure it to play the greeting or transfer to a phone. In the case of a call handler applied to help guide a caller through the menu, click the **No (Send Directly to**

Greeting) radio button. The call handler can also be configured to transfer the call to a phone instead of playing a greeting. To transfer the call to the phone associated with the owner of the call handler, click the **Yes, Ring Extension For** radio button. To transfer the call to some other phone number, click the **Yes, Ring This Extension** radio button and enter the phone number in the field to the right of the label.

Step 5. By default, Unity plays a prompt to the caller for notification that the call is being transferred. To disable this prompt, select the Do Not Play the "Wait While I Transfer Your Call" Prompt check box.

Step 6. If the call is to be transferred to an extension, the type of transfer must be selected under the Transfer Type heading. If holding and screening options are desired, the **Supervise Transfer** radio button is selected. If these features are not needed, select the **Release to Switch** radio button. If Release to Switch is selected, the following steps do not apply.

Step 7. In the **Rings To Wait For** field, enter the number of rings that Unity waits before assuming that the call will not be answered. Unity has the capability to queue calls if the number to which Unity transfers a call is busy. You must choose one of three options under the If the Number Is Busy heading:

- The first choice, Always Hold, informs the caller that the extension is busy and places the caller on hold.

- The second option, No Holding, prompts the caller to leave a message or dial another extension.

- The third and final choice, Ask Caller, informs the caller that the extension is busy and offers the choice of holding, leaving a message, or dialing another extension.

Step 8. Unity has the capability to gather caller information for screening purposes on a supervised transfer. There are four options under the **Gather Caller Information** heading. These options are as follows:

- **Announce:** Unity says "Transferring call" when the subscriber answers the call.

- **Introduce:** Unity announces who the call is for when the subscriber answers the phone. This feature is used when more than one person receives calls on the same phone.

- **Confirm:** Asks the caller to press 1 to accept the call or 2 to send the call to voicemail.

- **Ask Caller's Name:** Unity asks callers to record their names and plays the name when subscribers answer their phones.

Select the options you want to enable by selecting the radio button next to each option.

Step 9. Click the **Save** icon in the title strip.

Greetings Settings

Each call handler can have up to five different greetings, the same five that can be configured for a subscriber: alternate, busy, closed, internal, and standard. Chapter 8, "User/Subscriber Reference," discusses the function of each of these greetings. These greetings can be configured using SA and can be managed by the owner of the call handler using CUGA. This feature is discussed later. For now, look at the following steps that show how to configure these setting using SA.

Step 1.   From within SA, select **Call Management > Call Handlers**. Click the **Find** icon, enter the search criteria, and click Find. Select the desired call handler from the list and click the **View** button. Click the **Greetings** link on the left side of the screen.

Step 2.   Figure 9-5 displays the call handler Greetings page. From this screen, you can enable and configure each of the five greetings. From the drop-down list, select the greeting you want to configure. Start with the standard greeting.

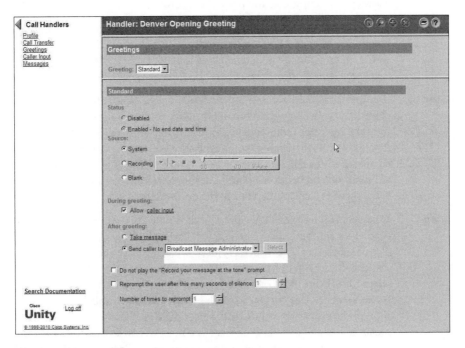

Figure 9-5   *Call Management > Call Handler > Greetings.*

Step 3.   Under the Status heading, the greeting can be enabled or disabled. If the greeting is disabled, it will not be used. The standard greeting is enabled by default and cannot be disabled. When configuring any greeting other than standard, you must select the **Enabled** radio button to enable this type of greeting.

Step 4.   Under the Source heading, the source of the message is chosen. The three choices for the source are as follows:

■   **System:** Plays the prerecorded greeting: "Sorry, <subscriber's name> is not available."

■   **Recording:** Plays the greeting that the subscriber recorded.

■   **Blank:** Plays no greeting and goes directly to the after-greeting action.

Typically Recording is chosen for this setting so that a custom greeting can be created for this call handler. Select the desired source by clicking the appropriately labeled radio button.

If Recording is chosen, you can use the media master control panel (the VCR-like panel next to the record label) to record a greeting. This interface also allows you to copy, cut, and paste the recording.

Step 5.   To allow callers to try to reach another extension or select options during a greeting, select the **Allow Caller Input** check box. You will notice that the words *caller input* are underlined; this is a link to the caller input page, which is covered later in this section.

Step 6.   Recall when you configured subscribers. In most cases, after the greeting was played, the caller was given the opportunity to leave a message by clicking the **Take Message** radio button. Depending on the type of call handler and its function in the application, you might want to send the caller to another call handler. If you want a different action to take place, click the **Send Caller To** radio button and select the desired destination from the drop-down list. Table 9-2 shows the available options in the drop-down list.

Step 7.   When choosing to send the call to a call handler, directory handler, interview handler, or another subscriber, you will have to specify the appropriate handler or subscriber. The Select <Type of Object You Selected> button becomes available to the right of the type of object you select. For example, if you select to send the call to a subscriber, click the **Select Subscriber** button. When you click this button, a search criteria window displays. Enter the appropriate criteria and click Find. Select the desired object from the list. If a subscriber or call handler is chosen, you must also select whether the call should be sent to the greeting or the phone. To send the call to the extension, select **Attempt Transfer For** from the Conversation drop-down list. To send the call to the subscriber's greeting, select **Send to Greeting For** from the Conversation drop-down list.

Note   Because you have to choose to send the call to the greeting or attempt to transfer has caused many administrators hours of frustration and troubleshooting. Make sure that if you want the phone of the subscriber to whom the call is transferred to ring, you must select **Attempt Transfer For.**

Table 9-2 *Send Caller To Options*

Destination	Action
Broadcast Message Administrator	Sends the call to a conversation for sending broadcast messages.
CVM Mailbox Reset	Sends calls to a conversation that allows the caller to reset the mailbox. This is available only when the Community Voice Mail (CVM) package is being used.
Call Handler	Sends calls to the selected call handler.
Caller System Transfer	Sends callers to a prompt that allows them to enter another extension to which they would like to be transferred.
Directory Handler	Sends calls to the directory handler you select.
Greetings Administrator	Sends callers to a conversation that allows them to manage the greetings of call handlers.
Hang Up	Disconnects calls.
Hotel Checked Out	This option works in concert with Cisco Unity's Hospitality and Property Management Integration. It allows guests to archive their messages when checking out.
Interview Handler	Sends calls to the interview handler you select.
Sign-in	Sends calls to the subscriber sign-in.
Sign-In Archived Mailbox	Enables subscribers to access messages on the Cisco Unity server by entering their old Cisco Unity primary extension.
Subscriber	Sends calls to another subscriber's greeting or extension depending upon how it is configured.
Subscriber System Transfer	Enables callers to transfer to another extension after they log in with subscriber credentials. They can then transfer to any number that their restriction table allows.

Step 8.   By default, Unity plays a prompt after the greeting that instructs the caller to leave a message after the tone. Because the greeting might already include these instructions, you might want to disable this prompt. You can do so by

selecting the **Do Not Play the "Record Your Message at the Tone" Prompt** check box.

Step 9.   If the caller remains silent after being offered the opportunity to leave a message, he can be reprompted. To have the caller reprompted, select the **Reprompt the User After This Many Seconds of Silence** check box and enter the number of seconds to wait for the caller to begin speaking. Then, enter the number of times that you want the caller to be reprompted. The maximum is 100.

Step 10. Click the **Save** icon in the title strip.

Configuring Call Handler Caller Input Settings

Call handlers are often used to guide a caller through the menu. To do this, the greeting informs the caller what number to press to be transferred to a certain destination. The call handler input settings are used to configure the call handler to transfer the calls when a touchtone is heard.

The following steps illustrate the configuration process of the Caller Input settings and are shown in Figure 9-6.

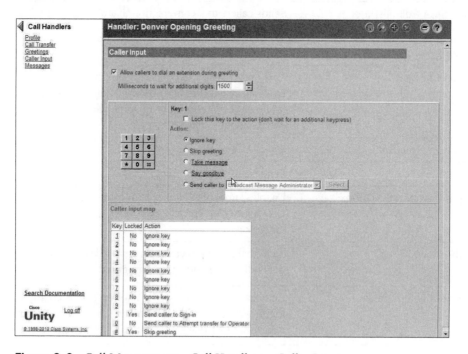

Figure 9-6   *Call Management > Call Handlers > Caller Input.*

Step 1.   From within SA, select **Call Management > Call Handlers**. Click the **Find** icon, enter the search criteria, and click **Find**. Select the desired call handler from the list and click the View button. Click the **Caller Input** link on the left side of the screen. A screen similar to that shown in Figure 9-6 appears.

Step 2. The first configuration setting determines whether callers can attempt to reach a different extension when listening to a greeting. To allow a caller to enter an extension while listening to a greeting, select the **Allow Callers to Dial an Extension During Greeting** check box.

Step 3. If the option to permit callers to dial another extension during the greeting is enabled, an interdigit time out must also be configured. The **Milliseconds to Wait for Additional Digits** setting is the amount of time that Unity waits before deciding that the caller is finished pressing digits. The default value is 1500 milliseconds, which is a second and a half. Typically this value is adequate. If you get comments that callers are transferred or receive error messages from Unity before they have finished dialing an extension during a greeting, increase this value.

Step 4. From the dial pad on the screen, you can configure the action to be taken when a digit is pressed. This is where the option in the spoken greeting is tied to the call handler. A button can be configured for five types of actions:

- **Ignore Key:** No action is taken when a digit is pressed.

- **Skip Greeting:** The greeting is skipped, and Unity proceeds to the after-greeting action.

- **Take Message:** The caller can press this key to cause Unity to take a message.

- **Say Goodbye:** Unity plays a good-bye message and disconnects the call.

- **Send Caller To:** There are various options you can select. Table 9-3 provides you with the available destinations.

Step 5. Click on the digit that you want to configure, and then select the action by clicking the appropriately labeled radio button. As with the Greetings settings, when choosing to send the call to a call handler, directory handler, interview handler, or another subscriber, you will have to specify the specific handler or subscriber.

Note If a subscriber or call handler is selected, you must also select whether the call should be sent to the greeting or the phone extension. To send the call to the extension, select Attempt Transfer For from the Conversation drop-down list. To send the call to the greeting, select Send to Greeting For from the Conversation drop-down list.

Step 6. If the **Lock This Key to the Action (Don't Wait for an Additional Keypress)** check box is selected, an extension that begins with this digit cannot be entered. This option causes Unity to transfer the call to the destination assigned to that key without waiting to see whether the caller is going to enter other digits. Only enable this field on digits that are not leading digits for any extensions.

Table 9-3 *Send Caller To Destination Options*

Action	Description
Broadcast Message Administrator	Sends the call to a conversation for sending broadcast messages.
CVM Mailbox Reset	Enables callers to reset their mailbox (available with the Community Voice Mail package).
Call Handler	Sends calls to the selected call handler.
Caller System Transfer	Sends callers to a prompt that allows them to enter another extension to which they would like to be transferred.
Directory Handler	Sends calls to the directory handler you select.
Greetings Administrator	Sends calls to a conversation that allows the caller to manage the greetings of call handlers that he or she owns.
Hang Up	Disconnects calls.
Hotel Checked Out	Used only with Unity's Hospitality and Property Management System.
Interview Handler	Sends calls to the interview handler you select.
Sign-in	Sends calls to the subscriber sign-in.
Sign-In Archived Mailbox	Enables subscribers to access messages on the Cisco Unity server by entering their old Cisco Unity primary extension.
Subscriber	Sends calls to another subscriber's greeting or extension, depending upon how it is configured.
Subscriber System Transfer	Enables callers to transfer to another extension after they log in with subscriber credentials. They can then transfer to any number that their restriction table enables.

Step 7. After you have all the digits configured as desired, click the **Save** icon in the title strip.

Configuring Call Handler Messages Settings

Unlike subscribers, call handlers do not have mailboxes. Therefore, when allowing a call handler to take messages, you must select a subscriber to receive them. By default, the creator of the call handler will be the message recipient. From the call handler Messages page, you can configure the message recipient and other message-related settings.

Figure 9-7 shows the call handler Messages page.

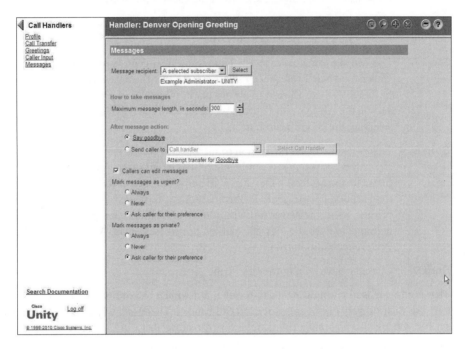

Figure 9-7   *Call Management > Call Handler > Messages.*

To configure the settings seen in this figure, follow these steps:

Step 1.   From within SA, select **Call Management > Call Handlers**. Click the **Find** icon, enter the search criteria, and click **Find**. Select the desired call handler from the list and click the **View** button. Click the **Messages** link on the left side of the screen.

Step 2.   Using the **Message Recipient** drop-down list, you can specify the message recipient as either a subscriber or a PDL. Typically, messages are sent to a single subscriber. If you need to have multiple subscribers receive the message, create a PDL that contains the subscribers and then select the PDL as the message recipient.

Step 3.   Click the **Select** button. A search criteria window displays. Enter the search criteria and click the Find button. Highlight the desired subscriber/PDL from the list and click the **Select** button.

Step 4. The maximum length of a message a caller can leave is set by entering the desired value in seconds in the **Maximum Message Length, in Seconds** box. Enter the desired value.

Step 5. Select the action to be taken after the message is recorded by selecting either the **Say Goodbye** or the **Send Caller To** radio buttons. When choosing **Send Caller To**, the destination must be chosen. The destinations are the same as those listed under Send Caller To in the caller input section.

Step 6. To let callers listen to, change, or delete the messages they leave, select the **Callers Can Edit Messages** check box.

Step 7. You can allow the caller to label a message as urgent by selecting the **Ask Caller for Their Preference** radio button under the Mark Messages as Urgent heading. You can choose to always mark it urgent without asking the caller by setting the Always radio button, or never have the message marked urgent by selecting the Never radio button.

Step 8. Callers can be given the option to mark a message as private. When messages are marked private, they can be encrypted based on the message security settings. To always have a message marked private, select the **Always** radio button in the Mark Messages as Private section. To never have a message marked private, select the **Never** radio button. To allow the caller to decide whether he wants to have the message marked private, select the **Ask Caller for Their Preference** radio button.

Step 9. Click the **Save** icon in the title strip.

That is all there is to configuring a call handler. It is similar to configuring a subscriber because each subscriber has an associated call handler. Therefore, when you create a subscriber you are also creating a call handler for that subscriber.

This section focused on the standard type of call handler. The other two types of call handlers were briefly discussed: the directory handler and the interview handler. In the next section, take a closer look at the directory handler.

Creating and Configuring Unity Connection Call Handlers

Three call handlers are created during the installation of Unity Connection. In most environments, additional call handlers need to be created. Begin with creating a call handler as outlined in the steps that follow:

Step 1. From within Unity Connection Administration, select **Call Management > System Call Handlers**.

Step 2. Click the **Add New** button.

Step 3. A window similar to Figure 9-8 displays. Enter a name for the call handler in the Display Name field.

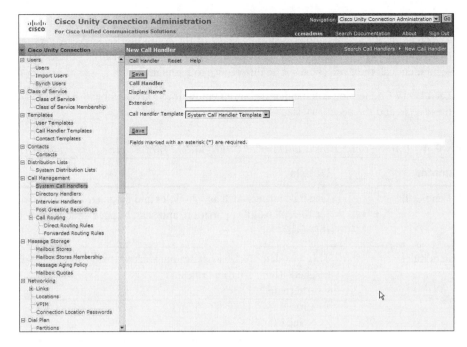

Figure 9-8 *Add New Unity Connection Call Handler*

Step 4. A call handler can have an extension number assigned to it. This Extension field is optional, but it can be useful to outside callers. By entering the extension number from the opening greeting, a caller can jump right to this call handler. The caller would hear something like "In the future, to come directly to this menu, press 231," and 231 would be the extension number of the call handler. Keep in mind that all extension numbers in Unity must be unique. Enter the extension number, if desired.

Step 5. Just as with users, Unity connection uses templates when creating call handlers. If you are going to create a number of call handlers that have similar attributes, you should first create a call handlers template. Select the desired template from the **Call Handler Template** drop-down list.

Note The steps to create a call handler template are very similar to those required to create a user template, which was covered in detail in Chapter 8. If you understand how to create a user template, it will be simple to create a call handler template. To create a call handler template, navigate to **Templates > Call Handler Templates** and proceed as you do when you are creating a user template. Because the steps are so similar, they will not be covered in this section. Instead you explore call handler configuration.

Step 6. Click **Save**.

After the call handler is created, you need to configure it to accomplish the task you designed for it. The next section covers the configuration process.

Configuring Unity Connection Call Handlers

The creation of the call handler is simple. Many of the configuration steps are very similar to those you perform when you configure users. Even though many of these steps seem identical, there are some subtle differences to highlight.

Each Unity Connection call handler has seven configurable areas. Table 9-4 shows each of these areas and the necessary steps for configuration.

Table 9-4   *Unity Connection Call Handler Configurable Parameters*

Parameter	Details
Call Handler Basics	General settings such as schedules and languages, recorded name for the call handler, partition, and search space are configured in this area.
Transfers Rules	This area determines what action is taken when this call handler is reached. There are three rules: • Alternate • Closed • Standard
Caller Input	Often during a greeting, a caller is given a number of choices such as "press 1 for Sales, press 2 for Support, or to reach an operator, press 0." The caller input settings determine what action is taken if a digit is pressed during the greeting.
Greetings	The greetings area is used to configure which greetings are enabled, what activity is allowed during the greeting, and what action is taken after the greeting.
Post Greeting Recording	This area enables you to determine whether an additional greeting is played after the user's greeting and, if so, which greeting to play.
Message Settings	The settings in this area determine how long messages can be, whether callers can edit messages, and the action to be taken after receiving a message. Most important, this is where you configure which user receives the message.
Call Handler Owners	This section enables you to assign users as owners of the call handler.

Configuring Call Handler Basics Settings

Figure 9-9 shows the parameters that can be configured on the Edit Call Handler Basics page. The following steps explain how to configure these parameters and describe the effect of each.

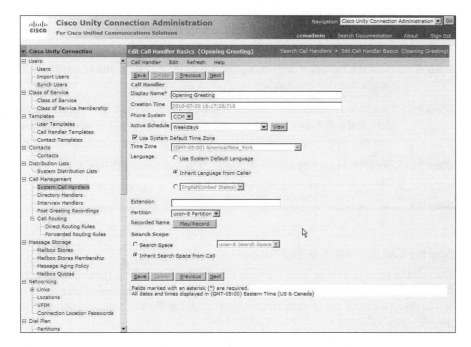

Figure 9-9   *Call Management>System Call Handler>Edit>Call Handler Basics.*

Step 1.   From within Unity Connection Administration, select **Call Management > System Call Handler**. Select the call handler you want to manage from the list that appears. After the template is active, select **Call Handler Basics** from the **Edit** drop-down menu.

Step 2.   The name of the call handler is defined when the call handler is created. You can change it by entering the desired name in the **Display Name** field.

Step 3.   The **Creation Time** field on this page displays when the call handler was created.

Step 4.   The **Phone System** field is defined when the template is created. You can change it now, but in most cases, it is left alone.

Step 5.   From the **Active Schedule** drop-down list, select the schedule you want to have associated with this call handler. The call handler transfer rules apply this schedule to determine how and where the call is transferred.

Step 6.   Because call handlers can route calls differently based on time and date, the call handler must be associated with a time zone. To link it with the system's time zone, select the **Use System Default Time Zone** check box. Otherwise, deselect this box and select the desired time zone from the **Time Zone** drop-down list.

Step 7.   The extension is normally assigned when the call handler is created. You can change the extension number by entering the desired number in the **Extension** field.

Step 8.   From the **Partition** drop-down list, select the partition you want to have assigned to this call handler.

Step 9.   To record a spoken name for the call handler, click the **Play/Record** button. A recording panel opens. Click the red button on the panel. If prompted, enter your extension number. When the phone rings, answer it and record the name.

Step 10.   From the **Search Space** drop-down list, select the search space that is associated to objects created using this template.

Step 11.   Click **Save**.

Configuring Call Handler Transfer Rules

The transfer rules determine what happens to a call when it reaches the call handler. It decides whether the call is transferred to a phone and, if so, what type of transfer is used or whether the greeting is played. To configure a call handler's call transfer settings, use the steps that follow.

Figure 9-10 shows the standard Edit Transfer Rule page. The following steps describe how to configure the various settings and indicate the effect they have on transferred calls:

Step 1.   From within Unity Connection Administration, select **Call Management > System Call Handler**. Select the call handler that you want to manage from the list that appears. After the call handler is active, select **Transfer Rules** from the **Edit** drop-down menu.

Step 2.   There are three rules that can be configured. The standard rule determines how the transfer is handled during open hours. The closed rule, if enabled, determines how the transfer is handled during closed hours. If the alternate rule is enabled, it will override the standard and closed rule, and the transfer will be handled according to its settings. Select the transfer rule you want to configure.

Step 3.   The **Rule Name** field is static and cannot be changed.

Step 4.   The Status section determines whether the rule is enabled. The standard rule is always enabled and cannot be disabled. If you are configuring one of the other rules, you must enable it for it to take effect. You can select **Enable with No End Date and Time** to have it always enabled. If you want to have it

enabled until a specific time and date, select **Enable Until** and enter the
desired date and time.

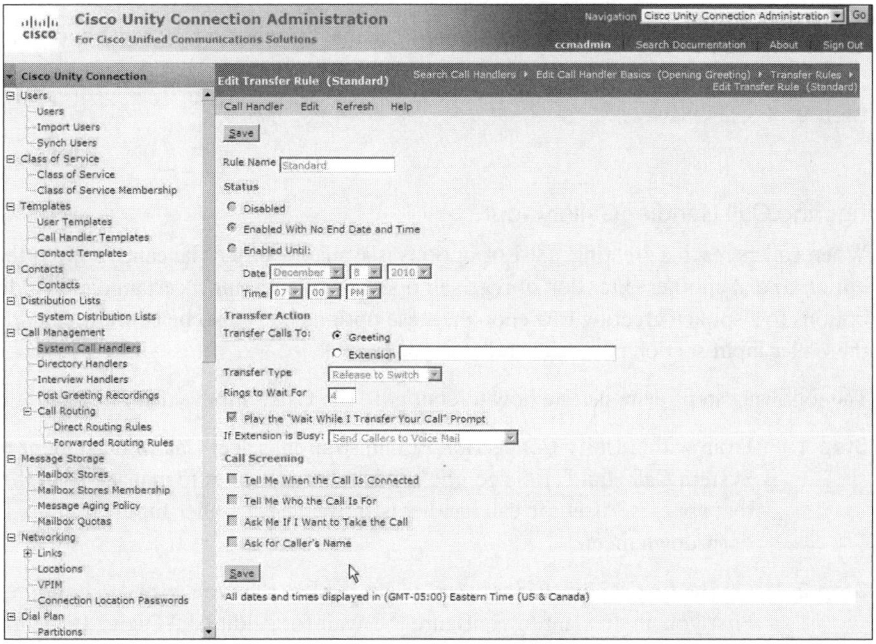

Figure 9-10   *Call Management > System Call Handler > Edit > Transfer Rules.*

Step 5.   In the Transfer Action section, select **Greeting** to transfer the call directly to
the greeting of the call handler. This is the most common setting for this
parameter. If you want to send the call to an extension, select **Extension** and
enter the number you want the call to be sent to.

Step 6.   If the call is transferred to an extension, the type of transfer must be selected
under the Transfer Type heading. If holding and screening options are desired,
select the **Supervise Transfer** radio button. If these features are not needed,
select the **Release to Switch** radio button. If Release to Switch is selected, the
remaining steps, other than Step 8, do not apply.

Step 7.   In the **Rings to Wait For** field, enter the number of rings that Unity
Connection should wait before sending the call to the voicemail greeting.

Step 8.   Unity Connection can inform the caller. Unity Connection announces
"Transferring call" when the user answers the call, as follows:

- **Tell Me Who the Call Is For:** Unity Connection announces the intended
recipient when the user answers the phone. This feature is used when
more than one person receives calls on the same phone.

- **Ask Me if I Want to Take the Call:** Unity Connection asks the user to
press 1 to accept the call or press 2 to send the call to voicemail.

■ **Ask Caller's Name:** Unity Connection asks the caller to record his or her name and plays the recorded name to the user when the phone is answered.

Select the options that you want to enable by selecting the radio button next to each option.

Step 9.   Click **Save.**

Configuring Call Handler Caller Input

When callers reach a greeting, a list of options is available. Often the caller is given the option to dial another extension or reach an operator by pressing a certain digit. Adding options to a spoken greeting isn't enough; these options must also be configured under the Caller Input section of a call handler.

The following steps demonstrate how to configure the Caller Input settings:

Step 1.   From within Unity Connection Administration, select **Call Management > System Call Handler.** Select the call handler you want to manage from the list that appears. After the call handler is active, select **Caller Input** from the **Edit** drop-down menu.

Step 2.   On the first screen that appears, select the key that you want to configure. First you might want to configure the Wait for Additional Digits, Prepend Digits to Dialed Extensions setting. The **Wait for Additional Digits** setting is the amount of time Unity Connection waits before deciding that the caller has finished pressing digits. The default value is 1500 milliseconds, which is a second and a half. Typically, this value is adequate.

Step 3.   The **Prepend Digits** setting determines whether any digits are prepended to the extension a caller enters. This is useful if your callers are accustomed to entering four digits but the actual extension number is seven digits. For example, the caller might enter 3322, but the full extension that the call needs to be transferred to is 5423322. By entering 542 in the Digits to Prepend field and selecting the Enable check box, the call would be transferred to 5423322.

Step 4.   Now you can start configuring the caller input keys. Select the key that you want to configure. A screen similar to that shown in Figure 9-11 appears.

Step 5.   The **Key** field is static and simply displays the number of the key that you are configuring.

Step 6.   The next field determines whether the key is locked. If the **Ignore Additional Input (Locked)** check box is selected, an extension that begins with this digit cannot be entered. Unity Connection transfers the call to the destination assigned to that particular key without waiting to see whether the caller is going to enter other digits. Only enable this field on digits that are not leading digits for any extensions.

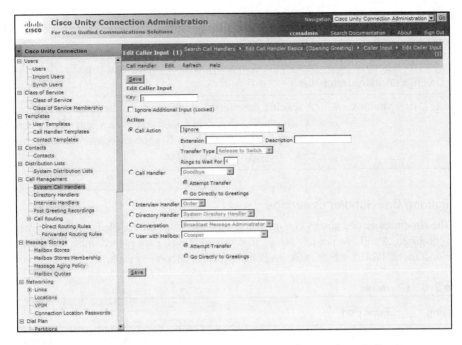

Figure 9-11 *Call Management > System Call Handler > Edit > Caller Input.*

Step 7.   The **Action** section determines where the call is sent when the key is pressed. Table 9-5 provides the available options. Configure as desired and click **Save**.

Table 9-5 *Caller Input Key Actions*

Action	Description
Call Action	A specific action must be selected from the drop-down list. If you choose to send the call to an alternate contact number, you must enter the extension number and define the type of transfer.
A Call Handler	A specific call handler must be selected from the drop-down list. When sending to a call handler, you must select either **Attempt Transfer** or **Go Directly to Greeting**. Typically, **Greeting** is selected.
An Interview Handler	A specific interview handler must be selected from the drop-down list.
A Directory Handler	A specific directory handler must be selected from the drop-down list.

Table 9-5 *Caller Input Key Actions*

Action	Description
A Conversation Such as Sign-In or Greetings Administrator	A specific conversation must be selected from the drop-down list.
Another User's Mailbox	A specific user must be selected from the drop-down list. When sending to another user, you must select either **Attempt Transfer** or **Go Directly to Greeting**. To have the user's phone ring, select **Attempt Transfer**.

Configuring Call Handler Greetings

The Greetings setting allows you to define what greetings are enabled and how they are configured. A call handler can use up to seven greetings, each played under different circumstances. Table 9-6 lists these greetings and the function of each.

Table 9-6 *Greetings*

Greeting	Function
Standard	Plays during open hours unless overridden by another greeting. If a closed greeting is not enabled, standard plays after hours.
Closed	Plays during closed hours as defined in the schedule associated with the user.
Busy	Plays when the call is transferred to Unity because the user's extension was busy.
Internal	Plays when the caller is another user on the system.
Alternate	When enabled, overrides all other greetings. This greeting plays all hours, all days until disabled.
Error	Plays when a caller presses an invalid key.
Holiday	Plays on dates defined as holidays.

Figure 9-12 shows the call handler Edit Greeting configuration screen. The following steps discuss the effects of these settings and describe how to configure them:

Step 1. From within Unity Connection Administration, select **Call Management > System Call Handler**. Select the call handler you want to manage from the list that appears. After the call handler is active, select **Greetings** from the **Edit** drop-down menu.

Step 2. A list of greetings appears. Select the greeting that you want to configure.

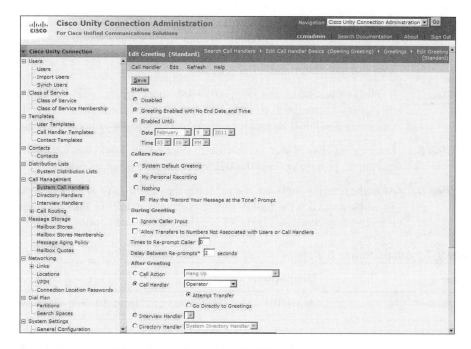

Figure 9-12   *Call Management>System Call Handler>Edit>Greetings>.*

Step 3.   The Status section determines whether the greeting is enabled. The standard greeting is always enabled and cannot be disabled. If you are configuring one of the other greetings, you must enable it for it to take effect. You can select **Enable with No End Date and Time** to have it always enabled. If you want to have it enabled until a specific time and date, select **Enable Until** and enter the desired end date and time.

Step 4.   Under the **Callers Hear** heading, the source of the message is chosen. The three choices for the source are as follows:

■   **System Default Greeting:** Plays the prerecorded default greeting

■   **My Personal Recording:** Plays the greeting that you record

■   **Nothing:** Plays no greeting and goes directly to the after-greeting action

Typically, My Personal Recording is chosen for this setting so that you can create your own greetings. If this is chosen, you can disable the "Record your message at the tone" prompt by deselecting the **Play the "Record Your Message at the Tone" Prompt** check box. Select the desired source by clicking the appropriate radio button.

Step 5.   To prevent the caller from transferring to another extension during the greeting or trying to skip the greeting, select **the Ignore Caller Input** check box. Typically this is not selected, but it can be useful in some situations.

Step 6.   By default, Unity Connection will only transfer calls to numbers that are assigned to users or call handlers. To allow Unity Connection to transfer calls to other numbers, select the **Allow Transfers to Numbers Not Associated with Users or Call Handlers** check box.

Step 7.   If callers remain silent after being offered the opportunity to leave a message, they can be reprompted. To have a caller reprompted, enter the number of times that she should be reprompted in the **Times to Re-prompt Caller** field.

Step 8.   Enter the number of seconds that Unity Connection should wait between playing the prompt again in the **Delay Between Re-prompts** field.

Step 9.   After the greeting is played, the caller has the opportunity to leave a message. To enable this, click the **Call Action** radio button and select **Take Message** from the drop-down list. Table 9-7 illustrates additional options.

Table 9-7   *After-Greeting Actions*

Action	Description
Call Action	A specific action must be selected from the drop-down list.
Call Handler	A specific call handler must be selected from the drop-down list. When sending to a call handler, you must select either **Attempt Transfer** or **Go Directly to Greeting**. Typically, **Greeting** is selected.
Interview Handler	A specific interview handler must be selected from the drop-down list.
Directory Handler	A specific directory handler must be selected from the drop-down list.
A Conversation Such as Sign-In or Greetings Administrator	A specific conversation must be selected from the drop-down list.
Another User's Mailbox	A specific user must be selected from the drop-down list. When sending to another user, you must select either **Attempt Transfer** or **Go Directly to Greeting**.

Step 10.   If more than one language is installed, greetings can be recorded in multiple languages. To record a greeting, select the language from the Select Language drop-down list and click the **Play/Record** button. A recording panel opens. Click the red button on the panel. Enter your extension when prompted. When the phone rings, answer it and record the greeting.

Step 11.   Click **Save**.

Configuring Call Handler Post-Greeting Recording

Unity Connection enables you to configure a greeting to be played after the user's greeting. You can also select whether all callers hear the recording or just unidentified callers hear it. To configure the post-greeting settings, follow these steps:

Step 1.   From within Unity Connection Administration, select **Call Management > System Call Handler**. Select the call handler that you want to manage from the list that appears. After the call handler is active, select **Post Greeting Recording Settings** from the **Edit** drop-down menu.

Step 2.   If you do not want Unity Connection to play a post-greeting recording, simply select the **Do Not Play Recording** radio button, and click **Save**. If you do want a post-greeting recording to play, go to Step 3.

Step 3.   To have the post-greeting recording played to everyone, select the **Play Recording to All Callers** radio button. To play it only to unidentified callers, click the **Play Recording Only to Unidentified Callers** radio button.

Step 4.   Select the desired greeting from the **Post Greeting Recording Selection** drop-down list.

Step 5.   Click **Save**.

Configuring Call Handler Messages Settings

The Message Settings section enables you to configure message-specific attributes, such as message length, caller options, and caller instructions following the message.

Figure 9-13 shows the various settings that are configured from this screen. The following steps illustrate the configuration and describe the effect of each setting:

Step 1.   From within Unity Connection Administration, select **Call Management > System Call Handler**. Select the call handler that you want to manage from the list that appears. After the call handler is active, select **Message Settings** from the Edit drop-down menu.

Step 2.   To set the maximum length of a message that an outside caller can leave, enter the value in seconds in the **Maximum Message Length, in Seconds** box.

Step 3.   If you want to let callers listen to and change or delete the message they leave, select the **Callers Can Edit Messages** check box.

Step 4.   The Language setting defines what language is used to play the system. When **Inherit Language from Caller** is selected, the language that was set by the handler or rule that transferred the call is used. If it is set to **Use System Default Language**, the system default language is used. To indicate a specific language, choose the radio button next to the drop-down list of languages. If only one language is installed on this system, the drop-down box is not available.

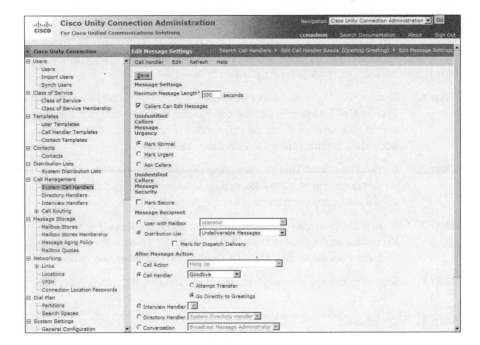

Figure 9-13   *Call Management > System Call Handler > Edit > Message Settings.*

Step 5.   Allow the caller to label a message urgent by selecting the **Ask Caller** radio button under the Message Urgency heading. To mark a message always urgent without asking the caller, select the **Mark Urgent** radio button, or to never mark the message urgent, select the **Mark Normal** radio button.

Step 6.   To have messages marked secure, select the **Mark Secure** check box.

Step 7.   After the message is recorded, the call can be sent to a number of destinations. Typically, the call is sent to the goodbye call handler. Table 9-8 lists additional options.

Step 8.   Click **Save**.

Configuring Call Handler Owners

For someone to be able to record or change the greeting of a call handler, that person must be an owner of the call handler. The following steps show how to assign a user as the owner of a call handler:

Step 1.   From within Unity Connection Administration, select **Call Management > System Call Handler**. Select the call handler that you want to manage from the list that appears. After the call handler is active, select **Call Handler Owners** from the **Edit** drop-down menu.

Table 9-8 *After-Message Action*

Action	Description
Call Action	A specific action must be selected from the drop-down list.
Call Handler	A specific call handler must be selected from the drop-down list. When sending to a call handler, you must select either **Attempt Transfer** or **Go Directly to Greeting**. Typically, **Greeting** is selected.
Interview Handler	A specific interview handler must be selected from the drop-down list.
Directory Handler	A specific directory handler must be selected from the drop-down list.
Conversation Such as Sign-In or Greetings Administrator	A specific conversation must be selected from the drop-down list.
User with Mailbox	A specific user must be selected from the drop-down list. When sending to another user, you must select either **Attempt Transfer** or **Go Directly to Greeting**. To have the user's phone ring, select **Attempt Transfer**.

Step 2.   Click **Add User**.

Step 3.   Enter the desired search criteria to limit the number of user that appear in the new window and click Find.

Step 4.   Select the check box next to the name(s) of the user(s) you want to make owners of the call handler.

Step 5.   Click **Add Selected User**.

That is all there is to configuring call handler. It is similar to configuring a subscriber because each subscriber has an associated call handler. Therefore, when you create a subscriber, you are also creating a call handler for that subscriber.

This section focused on the standard type of call handler. We briefly discussed the other two types of call handlers: the directory handler and the interview handler. In the next section, we take a closer look at the directory handler.

Directory Handlers

When callers dial the subscriber's name, they are sent to a directory handler. The directory handler "listens" to the keys that are pressed and, using the letters assigned to each key, searches for possible matches. After the caller has finished entering digits, the directory handler either plays the possible matches or routes the call directly to the matched subscriber. In earlier versions of Unity, there was only one directory handler, which made it impossible to search a selected group of subscribers for a match. In environments with multiple departments where each wants a separate auto-attendant, multiple directory handlers are often requested. As of Unity version 4.0, it is possible to create multiple directory handlers that resolve this limitation.

By default, one directory handler exists, called Directory Handler. For companies that do not need multiple directory handlers, just use the default. A directory handler is created using nearly the same steps used to create a new call handler. The next section demonstrates the steps needed to create a directory handler in Unity. To see how to create a directory for Unity Connection, refer to the "Configuring Unity Connection Directory Handlers" section, later in this chapter.

Configuring Unity Directory Handlers

Configuring a directory handler involves four elements: profile, search options, match list options, and caller input. The profile is used to assign an owner, recorded voice, extension, and language. The search options define if and how the search is limited. The match options determine how Unity acts upon finding matches. The caller input in the directory handler determines timeout thresholds and reprompt settings, which is different than the caller input setting in standard call handlers.

Directory Handler Profile Settings

Figure 9-14 shows the settings found on the Profile page of a directory handler. The following steps explain these settings and describe how to configure each of them:

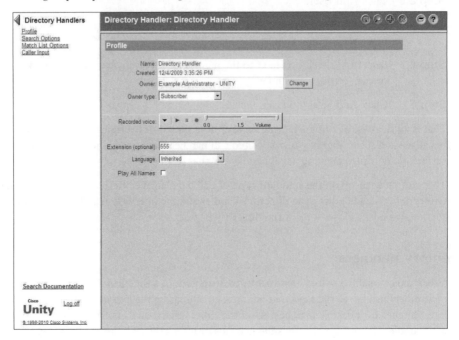

Figure 9-14 *Call Management > Directory Handler > Profile.*

Step 1.   From within SA, select **Call Management > Directory Handlers.** Click the
Find icon, enter the search criteria, and click Find. Select the desired call handler from the list and click the View button. Click the **Profile** link on the left
side of the screen.

Step 2.   The first two fields cannot be edited. They show the name of the directory
handler and the date and time it was created.

Step 3.   As with standard call handlers, directory handlers must have an owner. The
owner can be a subscriber or a PDL. If you need to change the owner type,
select the new type from the Owner Type drop-down list. To change the
owner, click the **Change** button next to the current owner. A search criteria
window displays. Enter the search criteria and click the **Find** button. Highlight
the desired subscriber/PDL from the list and click the **Select** button.

Step 4.   The Recorded Voice media master control panel is used to create a recorded
name for this directory handler.

Step 5.   Although optional, you can add an extension to a directory handler by entering a unique extension number in the **Extension (Optional)** field. By giving
the directory an extension, a caller can jump to the directory handler from
anywhere in the system's menu by entering the extension.

Step 6.   The **Language** drop-down list is used to set the language in which Unity
prompts are played under this call handler. If Inherited displays in this field,
whatever language was employed in the previous call handler will continued
to be used. Select the desired language from the drop-down list. When in
doubt, set it to Inherited.

Step 7.   If you select the **Play All Names** check box, Unity plays all the names in the
directory instead of having the caller spell the name using the phone keypad.
If more than five subscribers are in the directory, Unity offers the caller the
choice of spelling the name. If more than 50 subscribers are in the directory,
Unity will not play all the names and the caller must spell the name. Unless
you have a very small directory, leave this box deselected.

Step 8.   Click the **Save** icon in the title strip.

Directory Handler Search Options Settings

In larger companies that are using a single Unity system for multiple divisions, more than
one directory handler is often necessary. In current versions of Unity, multiple directory
handlers can be created. When creating a directory handler, you can configure the search
options so that Unity searches only a selected group of subscribers' names.

Figure 9-15 shows the directory handler Search Options page. The following steps
demonstrate the requirements to configure these options:

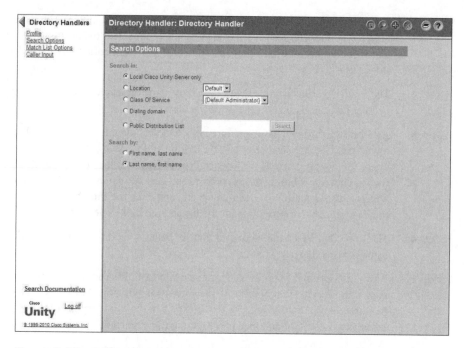

Figure 9-15   *Call Management > Directory Handlers > Search Options.*

Step 1.   From within SA, select **Call Management > Directory Handlers**. Click the **Find** icon, enter the search criteria, and click **Find**. Select the desired call handler from the list and click the **View** button. Click the **Search Options** link on the left side of the screen.

Unity can limit its search by searching only the subscribers who match the criteria selected under the Search In heading. Table 9-8 provides the search options.

Note   A PDL is an easy way to configure a directory handler to search a specific group of subscribers. If you have multiple directory handlers, it might be because of multitenant or multiple departments—these tenants/departments will most likely have a PDL that is associated with the group. So, using this for directory handlers makes maintenance easier because you only have to keep the PDL updated.

Table 9-8 *Caller Input Key Actions*

Search Option	Description
Local Cisco Unity Server Only	The directory handler searches only subscribers associated with the Unity server on which the call came in.
Location	The directory handler searches only subscribers associated with the primary and local delivery locations for this Unity server.
Class of Service	The directory handler searches only subscribers associated with the selected class of service (CoS) on the local Cisco Unity server.
Dialing Domain	Expands directory handler searches to include subscribers associated with other Unity servers within a dialing domain. Dial domains is discussed in further detail in Chapter 10, "Implementing Unity Networking." If you have subscribers with the same name in multiple locations, it is better not to have the directory handler search based on the dialing domain. Instead, use Local Cisco Unity Server Only, a PDL, or CoS.
Public Distribution List	The directory handler searches only subscribers associated with the selected PDL. Subscribers in the PDL that do not have recorded names will not be presented when the matches are played.

Step 2. Select which of these options you want the directory handler to use by clicking the radio button next to the desired option. If **Location** or **Class of Service** is chosen, use the drop-down list to choose the specific object. If **Public Distribution List** is selected, click the **Select** button. A window displays that allows you to choose the domain that you want to search. Select the domain from the drop-down list and click the **Find** button. A list of PDLs displays; click the correct one.

Step 3. The outside caller will be asked to enter either the first name first or the last name first. To configure Unity to request the first name, select the **First Name, Last Name** radio button. To have Unity request the last name first, select the **Last Name, First Name** radio button.

Step 4. Click the **Save** icon in the title strip.

Directory Handler Match List Options Settings

After the directory handler has found a match or possibly multiple matches, it will present those matches to the caller based on the settings configured under Match List Options. Figure 9-16 shows these settings. The following steps explain the settings and describe how to configure them:

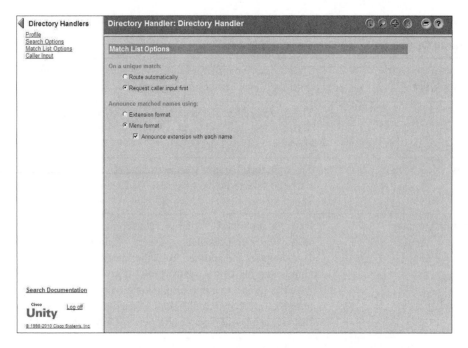

Figure 9-16   *Call Management > Directory Handlers > Match List Options.*

Step 1.   From within SA, select **Call Management > Directory Handlers**. Click the
Find icon, enter the search criteria, and click **Find**. Select the desired call handler from the list and click the **View** button. Click the **Match List Options**
link on the left side of the screen.

Step 2.   If the directory handler finds only one match, you can configure it to send the
call directly to the subscriber, or play the subscriber's name and ask callers to
confirm that they want to be connected with this subscriber. To have the
directory handler transfer the call without caller verification, select the **Route
Automatically** radio button. To have the directory handler ask the caller for
verification, select the **Request Caller Input First** radio button.

Step 3.   When the directory handler finds multiple matches, Unity plays the list of
subscribers and asks the caller to select the subscriber by entering the subscriber's extension or by pressing a single digit. To configure the directory
handler to announce the extensions, and ask the caller to enter the desired
extension, click the **Extension Format** radio button. The prompt that the
caller hears is something like, "For Roger Roberts, press 602, for John Roberts
press 610, . . ." To have the directory handler announce the subscribers' names
and have the caller press a single digit to transfer, select the **Menu Format**
radio button. The prompt that the caller hears is something like, "For Roger
Roberts, press 1, for John Roberts press 2, . . ." If the Announce Extension
with Each Name check box is selected, the caller hears the matching names
and their extension but still presses a single digit to transfer.

Step 4.   Click the **Save** icon in the title strip.

Directory Handler Caller Input Settings

Timeouts must be set within a directory handler so that it can determine when the caller has finished entering digits. If no timeouts are configured, the caller has to press the pound key (#) when finished entering digits. Timeouts also tell the directory handler how long to wait for the caller to begin entering digits. Figure 9-17 illustrates the timeout values that can be configured. The following steps explain how to configure these values and describe the effect that each will have:

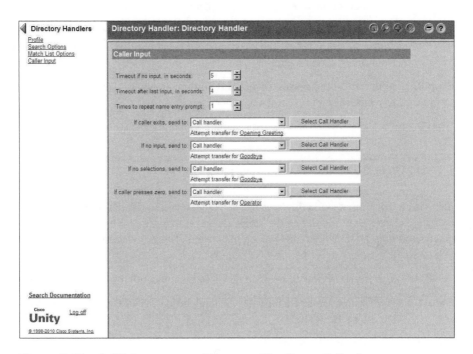

Figure 9-17   *Call Management > Directory Handlers > Caller Input.*

Step 1.   From within SA, select **Call Management > Directory Handlers.** Click the **Find** icon, enter the search criteria, and click **Find.** Select the desired call handler from the list and click the **View** button. Click the **Caller Input** link on the left side of the screen.

Step 2.   The **Timeout if No Input, in Seconds** field is the number of seconds that the directory waits for the caller to begin entering digits. Enter the desired time in the field.

Step 3.   The **Timeout After Last Input, in Seconds** field is the number of seconds that the directory handler waits after a digit is pressed. If no more digits are pressed within this time, the directory handler assumes that the caller has finished entering digits and searches for a match.

Step 4.   If the caller enters nothing within the allotted time, the directory handler can reprompt them. Enter the number of times an outside caller will be reprompted in the **Times to Repeat Name Entry Prompt** field.

Step 5.   When a caller leaves the directory handler, the call must be sent to a location. Select the type of destination to which the call will be sent from the **If Caller Exits, Send To** drop-down list.

Step 6.   In the **If No Input, Send To** drop-down list, select the destination to which the caller is sent when no number is entered.

Step 7.   In the **If No Selections, Send To** drop-down list, enter the destination to which the call is sent if the caller enters a name but does not select anything from the resulting menu.

Step 8.   In the **If Caller Presses Zero, Send To** drop-down list, select the destination to which the call is sent if the caller presses 0.

Step 9.   Click the **Save** icon in the title strip.

Configuring Unity Connection Directory Handlers

Configuring a Unity Connection directory handler involves three elements: directory handler basics, caller input, and edit greeting. The Directory Handler Basics section is used to assign an extension and define the language and search scope. The Caller Input section determines timeout thresholds and reprompt settings. The Edit Greeting section allows you to create a custom greeting for the directory.

The following steps show how to create a new Unity Connection directory handler:

Step 1.   From within Unity Connection Administration, select **Call Management > Directory Handler**.

Step 2.   Click the **Add New** link.

Step 3.   Enter a name for the directory handler in the **Display Name** field.

Step 4.   An extension can be assigned to a directory handler. This allows users to reach the directory handler by entering the extension number. If desired, enter a directory number in the **Extension** field.

Step 5.   From the **Partition** drop-down list, select the partition you want to have assigned to this directory handler. If you do not select a partition, the default partition is assigned. Keep in mind that only objects (users, call handlers, and so on) with a search space that has access to that partition will be permitted to reach the directory handler.

Step 6.   If the **Voice Enabled** check box is selected, a caller has the ability to search the directory handler by speaking the person's first and last name. Voice recognition services must be running for this feature to work.

Step 7.   Click **Save**.

The following three sections show how to configure a directory handler for Unity Connection.

Unity Connection Directory Handler Basic Settings

Figure 9-18 illustrates the settings found on the Edit Directory Handler Basics page of a directory handler. The following steps explain the settings and configuration processes for each of them:

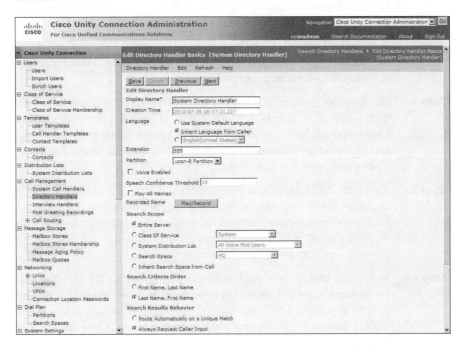

Figure 9-18   *Call Management > Directory Handlers > Edit > Directory Handler Basics.*

Step 1.   From within Unity Connection Administration, select **Call Management > Directory Handler**. Select the directory handler that you want to manage from the list that appears. After the directory handler is active, select **Directory Handler Basics** from the **Edit** drop-down menu.

Step 2.   The display name was defined when the directory handler was created. You can change it by entering a new name in the **Display Name** field.

Step 3.   The next field displays the time and date that the directory handler was created.

Step 4.   The Language section defines what language is used to play the system prompts. To use the system default language, select **Use System Default Language**. To use the language assigned to the object that sent the call to this handler, select **Inherit Language from Caller**. To specify a language, select the radio button next to the drop-down list of languages and select the desired language from the list.

Step 5.   Although optional, you can add an extension to a directory handler by entering a unique extension number in the **Extension (Optional)** field. By giving the directory an extension, a caller can jump to the directory handler from anywhere in the system's menu by entering the extension.

Step 6.   From the **Partition** drop-down list, select the partition you want to have assigned to this directory handler. If a partition is assigned, only objects (users, call handlers, and so on) with a search space that has access to that partition will be permitted to reach the directory handler.

Step 7.   If the **Voice Enabled check** box is selected, a caller is able to search the directory handler by speaking the person's first and last name. Voice recognition services must be running for this feature to work.

Step 8.   The **Speech Confidence Threshold** field can be adjusted to allow the voice recognition to be more or less liberal. If users complain that it is not detecting names, you can lower this number. If users complain that there are too many matches, this number should be increased. This field can only be edited if the Voice Enable check box is selected.

Step 9.   If the **Play All Names** check box is selected, Unity Connection will play all the names in the directory, up to five. If there are more than five and less than 51, Unity Connection will play all the names if the caller so chooses. If there are more than 51 names in the directory, the caller has to dial by name. This system is not applicable when the directory is voice enabled.

Step 10.   To record a spoken name for the directory handler, click the **Play/Record** button. A recording panel opens. Click the red button on the panel. If prompted, enter your extension number. When the phone rings, answer it and record the name. Spoken names are useful when managing handlers through the phone interface.

Step 11.   Unity Connection can limit its search by searching only the user that matches the criteria selected under the **Search Scope** heading. Table 9-9 illustrates the options under this heading. Select the desired setting.

Step 12.   The caller will be asked to enter either the first name first or the last name first. To configure Unity Connection to request the first name first, select the **First Name, Last Name** radio button. To have Unity Connection request the last name first, select the **Last Name, First Name** radio button.

Step 13.   If the directory handler finds only one match, you can configure it to send the call directly to the user, or play the user's name and ask callers to confirm that they want to be connected with this user. To have the directory handler transfer the call without caller verification, select the **Route Automatically on a Unique Match** radio button. To have the directory handler ask the caller for verification, select the **Always Request Caller Input** radio button.

Table 9-9 *Search Scope Options*

Search Scope	Description
Entire Server	The directory handler searches only subscribers associated with the Unity server on which the call came in.
Class of Service	The directory handler searches only users associated with the selected class of service (CoS).
System Distribution List	The directory handler searches only users associated with the selected system distribution list.
Search Space	The directory handler searches users that are in partitions located in the selected search space.
Inherit Search Space from Call	The directory handler uses the search space that was assigned by the object that sent the call to the directory handler.

Step 14. When the directory handler finds multiple matches, Unity Connection plays the list of users and asks the caller to select the user by entering the user's extension or by pressing a single digit. To configure the directory handler to announce the extensions and request the caller to enter the desired extension, click the **Announce Matched Names Using Extension Format** radio button. The prompt that the caller hears is something like "For Roger Roberts press 602, for John Roberts press 610, . . ." To have the directory handler announce the users' names and have the caller press a single digit to transfer, select the **Announce Matched Names Using Menu Format** radio button. The prompt that the caller hears is something like "For Roger Roberts, press 1, for John Roberts, press 2, . . ." If the Announce Extension with Each Name check box is selected, the caller hears the matching names and their extension, but still presses a single digit to transfer.

Step 15. Click the **Save**.

Unity Connection Directory Handler Caller Input Settings

Timeouts must be set within a directory handler so that it can determine when the caller has finished entering digits. Timeouts also instruct the directory handler how long to wait for the caller to begin entering digits. Figure 9-19 illustrates the timeout values that can be configured. The following steps explain the configuration and effects of each value:

Step 1. From within Unity Connection Administration, select **Call Management > Directory Handler**. From the list that appears, select the directory handler that you want to manage. After the directory handler is active, select **Caller Input** from the **Edit** drop-down menu.

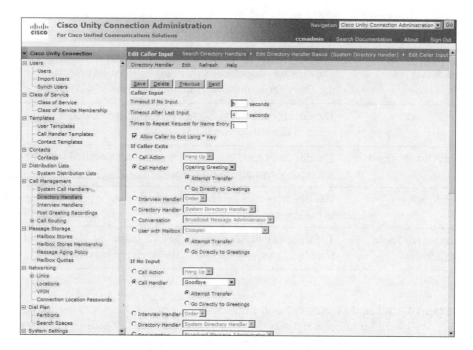

Figure 9-19   *Call Management > Directory Handlers > Edit > Caller Input.*

Step 2.   The **Timeout if No Input** field is the number of seconds the directory waits for the caller to begin entering digits. Enter the desired time in the field.

Step 3.   The **Timeout After Last Input** field is the number of seconds the directory handler waits after a digit is pressed. If no more digits are pressed within this time, the directory handler assumes that the caller has finished entering digits and searches for a match.

Step 4.   If the caller enters nothing within the allotted time, the directory handler can reprompt them. Enter the number of times that a caller will be reprompted in the **Times to Repeat Request for Name Entry** field.

Step 5.   When a caller leaves the directory handler, the call must be sent to a location. Select the type of destination to which the call will be sent from the **If Caller Exits, Send To** drop-down list.

Step 6.   To allow a caller to exit the directory handler by pressing the asterisk key, select the **Allow Caller to Exit Using * Key** check box.

Step 7.   When a caller leaves the directory handler, the call must be sent to a location. Select the type of destination to which the call will be sent from the **If Caller Exits** section. Table 9-10 lists the valid choices for this section.

Table 9-10   *If Caller Exits Options*

Action	Description
Call Action	A specific action must be selected from the drop-down list.
Call Handler	A specific call handler must be selected from the drop-down list. When sending to call handler, you must select either **Attempt Transfer** or **Go Directly to Greeting**. Typically, **Greeting** is selected.
Interview Handler	A specific interview handler must be selected from the drop-down list.
Directory Handler	A specific directory handler must be selected from the drop-down list.
Conversation Such as Sign-In or Greetings Administrator	A specific conversation must be selected from the drop-down list.
User with Mailbox	A specific user must be selected from the drop-down list. When sending to another user, you must select either **Attempt Transfer** or **Go Directly to Greeting**. To initiate the user's phone to ring, select **Attempt Transfer**.

Step 8. In the **If No Input** section, select the destination to which the caller is sent when no number is entered. The choices are the same as shown in Step 7.

Step 9. In the **If No Selections** section, select the destination to which the call is sent if the caller enters a name but does not select anything from the resulting menu. The choices are the same as shown in Step 7.

Step 10. In the **If Caller Presses Zero** section, select the destination to which the call is sent if the caller presses 0. The choices are the same as shown in Step 7.

Step 11. Click the **Save**.

Now that you understand how to configure the components that make up an auto-attendant, we move on and create one.

Unity Connection Directory Handler Greeting

Unity Connection allows you to create a custom greeting for each directory handler, although it is not required. If a custom greeting is not recorded, the system directory handler is used. To record a custom greeting, follow these steps:

Step 1. From within Unity Connection Administration, select **Call Management > Directory Handler**. From the list that appears, select the directory handler that you want to manage. After the directory handler is active, select **Greeting**

from the **Edit** drop-down menu.

Step 2. Select the **Use Custom Greeting** check box.

Step 3. If more than one language is installed, greetings can be recorded in multiple languages. To record a greeting, select the language from the **Select Language** drop-down list and click the **Play/Record** button. A recording panel opens. Click the red button on the panel. Enter your extension if prompted. When the phone rings, answer it and record the greeting.

Configuring Auto-Attendant

The components required for a basic auto-attendant are simple. The previous sections explained how to create and configure call handlers and directory handlers. Now you see how to create a basic auto-attendant.

First, you need to sketch on paper the flow of the auto-attendant that you are planning. Having a map expedites the actual configuration process, just as using a map on a trip helps avoid being delayed or lost. The auto-attendant you create in this section is basic. It enables an outside caller to enter the extension of a subscriber, to dial by name, or to reach an operator. Later you create a more advanced auto-attendant. The flow chart in Figure 9-20 is an example of a flow chart that is created before actually configuring anything in SA.

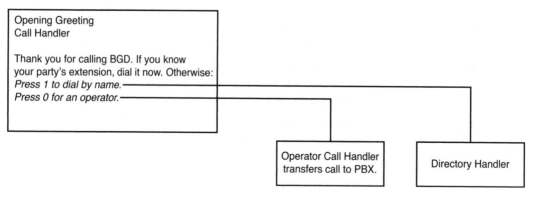

Figure 9-20 *Auto-Attendant Flow Chart*

There are only three objects required for this auto-attendant: two standard call handlers and one directory handler. All of these objects are automatically created when Unity is installed, so you only need to configure a few things.

Because the detailed steps for any of the configurations that you need to perform were covered in the previous sections, we will just look at the summary of the steps required. If you are uncertain of how to perform the specific steps, refer to the previous sections in this chapter for more details.

The configuration process should begin at the lowest level of the menu you are creating: in our example, the operator call handler or the directory handler. Don't start at the highest level because those objects will point to objects in lower levels, which must first exist. We start with the operator call handler.

The operator call handler already exists, so you don't need to create it. This handler determines what happens to a call when a caller presses 0 while in the auto-attendant. Only a few procedures need to be accomplished.

If you use Unity, follows these steps to verify/configure the operator call handler:

Step 1. From within SA, select **Call Management > Call Handlers**. Click the **Find** icon, enter the search criteria, and click **Find**. Select the operator call handler from the list and click the **View** button.

Step 2. On the Profile page, verify that the extension number assigned to the operator call handler is 0.

Step 3. On the Call Transfer page, select the standard transfer rule. Click the **Yes, Ring This Extension** radio button and enter the extension number in the field to the right of this button. When callers press 0 from within the auto-attendant, they will be transferred to the extension you entered here.

Step 4. All other settings can be left at default. Click the **Save** icon in the title strip.

If you use Unity Connection, follows these steps to verify/configure the operator call handler:

Step 1. From within Unity Connection Administration, select **Call Management > System Call Handlers**. Select the operator call handler from the list.

Step 2. On the Call Handler Basics page, verify that the extension number assigned to the operator call handler is 0.

Step 3. On the Transfer Rules page, select the standard transfer rule. Click the **Extension** radio button and enter the extension number in the field to the right of this label. When callers press 0 from within the auto-attendant, they will be transferred to the extension you entered here.

Step 4. All other settings can be left at the default. Click **Save**.

Because the default directory handler will list all the users we have added, there is no need to edit the handler.

The opening greeting call handler is the last handler that should be configured because all other handlers are beneath it.

If you use Unity, the following settings must be configured/verified:

Step 1. From within SA select **Call Management > Call Handlers**, click the **Find** icon, enter the search criteria, and click **Find**. Select the opening greeting call handler from the list and click the **View** button.

Step 2. On the Call Transfer page, select the standard transfer rule. Verify that **the No (Send Directly to Greeting)** radio button has been selected.

Step 3. From the Greetings page, record the desired greeting using the media master control panel. This greeting should reflect all options to a caller. In the example shown in Figure 9-20, the greeting would be "Thank you for calling BGD. If you know your party's extension, dial it now. Otherwise, press 1 to dial by name or press 0 for an operator."

Step 4. On the Caller Input page, configure the keys so that they are in line with the recorded greeting. For this example, key number 1 is configured to "send caller to directory handler" and key 0 is configured to "send caller to attempt transfer for operator."

Step 5. No other settings for this call handler need to be changed. Click the **Save** icon in the title strip.

If you use Unity Connection, the following settings must be configured/verified:

Step 1. From within Unity Connection Administration, select **Call Management > System Call Handlers** and select the opening greeting call handler from the list.

Step 2. On the Call Transfer page, select the standard transfer rule. Verify that **the No (Send Directly to This Handler's Greeting)** radio button has been selected.

Step 3. Navigate to the standard greeting. Record the desired greeting. This greeting should reflect all options that a caller has. In the example shown in Figure 9-20, the greeting would be "Thank you for calling BGD. If you know your party's extension, dial it now. Otherwise, press 1 to dial by name or press 0 for an operator."

Step 4. On the Caller Input page, configure the keys so that they are in line with the recorded greeting. For this example, key number 1 is configured to "send caller to directory handler" and key 0 is configured to "send caller to attempt transfer for operator."

Step 5. No other settings for this call handler should need to be changed. Click **Save**.

That's all there is to it. Pretty easy, isn't it? Now that you have mastered the basic auto-attendant, we will move on to creating a more advanced system.

Creating Advanced Call-Routing Systems

A basic auto-attendant is useful for some companies, but Unity/Connection has the ability to offer more advanced services. The following sections discuss some of these features but mainly cover the components and concepts that are needed to create an advanced auto-attendant. An advanced auto-attendant can allow a caller to navigate through a menu and retrieve prerecorded information. An example given earlier in this chapter allowed the caller to get directions without having to wait to speak with someone. Later in these sections, the steps required to build an auto-attendant with some of the more advanced features are discussed. First, we look at one more type of call handler, the interview call handler.

Using Interview Handlers

The interview call handler is used when you need to have the caller answer a number of specific questions. You can use an interview call handler to allow a caller to request a catalog or a similar task. The interview handler asks questions such as name, street address, city, zip code, and so on. The following two sections show how to create and configure interview handlers in Unity and Unity Connection. We start by looking at how to configure an interview handler on Unity. If you are using Unity Connection, you can move ahead to the section "Creating and Configuring Interview Handlers in Unity Connection."

Creating and Configuring Interview Handlers in Unity

To create an interview handler, follow these steps:

Step 1. From within SA, select **Call Management > Interview Handlers**.

Step 2. From the title strip, click the **Add** icon.

Step 3. In the Add an Interview Handler window, enter a name for the new interview handler.

Step 4. Interview handlers do not use templates to define their parameters. However, you can choose to create a new interview handler based on an existing one. When you do this, the new interview handler has all the attributes of the one that you based it on. To create the interview handler with the same attributes as an existing one, select the **Based on Existing Interview Handler** radio button and select the existing interview handler from the Based On drop-down list. If you do not want the new interview handler to copy the attributes of an existing interview handler, select the **New Interview Handler** radio button.

Step 5. Click the **Add** button.

After the interview handler is created, it must be configured. To configure the interview handler's profile settings, follow the steps for the settings shown in Figure 9-21.

Step 1. From within SA, select **Call Management > Interview Handlers**. Click the **Find** icon, enter the search criteria, and click **Find**. Select the desired interview handler from the list and click the **View** button. Click the **Profile** link on the left side of the screen.

Step 2. The name of the interview handler is shown in the **Name** field. The name can be changed in this field if needed.

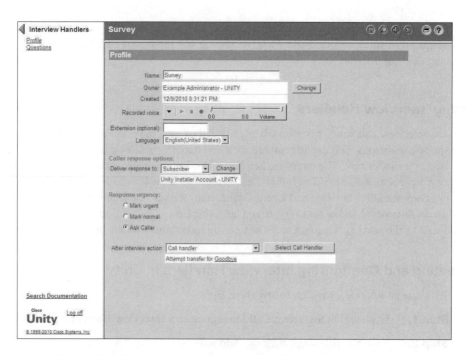

Figure 9-21   *Call Management > Interview Handlers > Profile.*

Step 3.   Each interview handler must have an owner. The current owner is shown in the Owner field. If you want to change the owner, click the **Change** button. A search criteria window displays. Enter criteria and click the Find button. A list of subscribers displays. Highlight a subscriber in the list and click the **Select** button.

Step 4.   The **Created** field displays the date and time that the interview handler was created.

Step 5.   Using the Recorded Voice media master control panel, you can record a name for the interview handler. This is not where you record the greeting. This is only the recorded name of the interview handler.

Step 6.   In the **Extension (Optional)** field, an interview handler can have an extension number assigned to it. Although optional, it can be useful to outside callers. By entering the extension number from the opening greeting, a caller can jump directly to this interview handler. Enter the extension number if desired.

Step 7.   The **Language** drop-down list is used to set the language in which Unity prompts are played under this interview handler. If Inherited displays in this field, whatever language was implemented in the previous call handler will continue to be used. Select the desired language from the drop-down list. When in doubt, set it to Inherited.

Step 8.   The responses can be delivered to either a subscriber or a PDL. Select either subscriber or distribution list from the **Deliver Response To** drop-down list. Click the Change button. A search criteria window displays. Enter the search criteria and click the **Find** button. Highlight the desired subscriber/PDL from the list and click the **Select** button.

Step 9.   You can allow the caller to label a message urgent by selecting the **Ask Caller** radio button under the Response Urgency heading. You can choose to always label it urgent without asking the caller by selecting the **Mark Urgent** radio button, or not label the message urgent by selecting the **Mark Normal** radio button.

Step 10.   In the **After Interview Action** field, choose the destination to which the call will be sent after the caller has answered all the questions.

Step 11.   Click the **Save** icon in the title strip.

Next, you must configure the questions required for the interview handler. Figure 9-22 illustrates this configuration page. The following steps explain how these settings are configured:

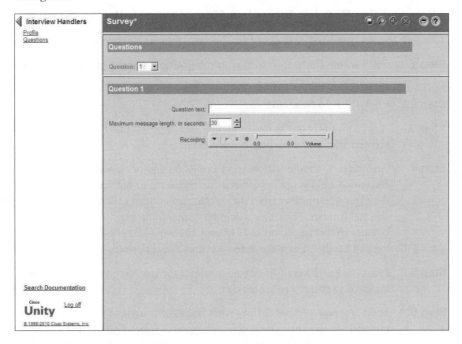

Figure 9-22   *Call Management > Interview Handlers > Questions.*

Step 1.   From within SA, select **Call Management > Interview Handlers**. Click the **Find** icon, enter the search criteria, and click **Find**. Select the desired interview handler from the list and click the **View** button. Click the **Questions** link on the left side of the screen.

Step 2.   From the **Question** drop-down list, select the number 1.

Step 3.   In the **Question Text** field, type the question that the caller will be asked. This text is just for reference. You still need to record the actual question that the caller will hear in Step 5.

Step 4.   In the **Maximum Message Length, in Seconds** field, enter the maximum number of seconds a caller's response can be.

Step 5.   Using the Recording media master control panel, record the question.

> **Note**   When recording a question, it is recommended that you to notify callers that they can press the pound key (#) when finished with each response. This prevents callers from having to wait for the silence timeout, which sometimes causes issues in noisy environments.

Step 6.   Click the **Save** icon in the title strip.

Creating and Configuring Interview Handlers in Unity Connection

To create an interview handler in Unity Connection, follow these steps:

Step 1.   From within Unity Connection Administration, select **Call Management > Interview Handlers**.

Step 2.   Click the **Add New** button.

Step 3.   A screen similar to the one in Figure 9-23 appears. Enter a name for the interview handler in the Display Name field.

Step 4.   An interview handler can have an extension number assigned to it. This **Extension** field is optional, but it can be useful to outside callers. By entering the extension number from the opening greeting, a caller can jump directly to this call handler. The caller would hear something like "In the future, to come directly to this menu, press 231," and 231 would be the extension number of the call handler. Enter the extension number, if desired.

Step 5.   From the **Partition** drop-down list, select the partition you want to have assigned to this interview handler.

Step 6.   The **Language** section defines what language is used to play the system prompts. To use the system default language, select **Use System Default Language**. To use the language assigned to the object **that sent the call** to this handler, select Inherit **Language from Caller**. To specify a language, select the radio button next to the drop-down list of languages and select the desired language from the list.

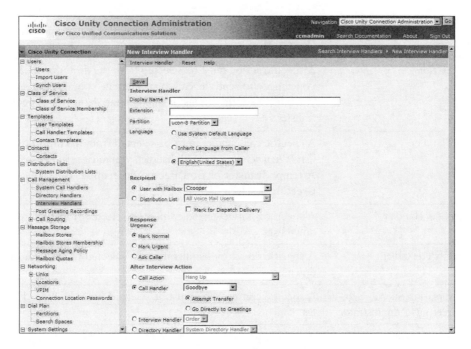

Figure 9-23 *Call Management>Interview Handlers>Add New.*

Step 7. The responses of an interview handler can be sent to a user or a distribution list. To send the responses to a user, select the **User with Mailbox** radio button and select a user from the drop-down list. To send the response to a distribution list, select the **Distribution List** radio button, and select a distribution list from the drop-down list.

Step 8. You can allow the caller to label a response as urgent by selecting the **Ask Caller** radio button under the Response Urgency heading. You can choose to always label it urgent without asking the caller by selecting the **Mark Urgent** radio button, or never label the message urgent by selecting the **Mark Normal** radio button.

Step 9. The After Interview Action section determines where the call is sent after all the interview handler questions have been answered. Table 9-11 illustrates the after-interview choices.

Table 9-11 *After Interview Actions*

Action	Description
Call Action	A specific action must be selected from the drop-down list. If you choose to send the call to an alternate contact number, you must enter the extension number and define the type of transfer.
Call Handler	A specific call handler must be selected from the drop-down list. When sending to a call handler, you must select either **Attempt Transfer** or **Go Directly to Greeting**. Typically, **Greeting** is selected.
Interview Handler	A specific interview handler must be selected from the drop-down list.
Directory Handler	A specific directory handler must be selected from the drop-down list.
Conversation Such as Sign-In or Greetings Administrator	A specific conversation must be selected from the drop-down list.
User with Mailbox	A specific user must be selected from the drop-down list. When sending to another user, you must select either **Attempt Transfer** or **Go Directly to Greeting**. To have the user's phone ring, select **Attempt Transfer**.

Step 10. Click **Save**.

Next, the questions need to be configured for the interview handler. The following steps explain how these settings are configured:

Step 1. From within Unity Connection Administration, select **Call Management > Interview Handler**. Select the interview handler that you want to manage from the list that appears. After the call handler is active, select **Interview Question** from the **Edit** drop-down menu.

Step 2. A question summary page appears. Select the number of the question that you want to manage. If you are creating a new list of questions, select 1.

Step 3. A screen similar to Figure 9-24 appears. The first field, **Question Number**, displays the number of the question that you are currently editing.

Step 4. In the **Maximum Reply Message Length** field, enter the maximum number of seconds for a caller's response.

Step 5. In the **Question Text** field, type the question that the caller will be asked.

Step 6. To record the question, click the **Play/Record** button. A recording panel opens. Click the red button on the panel. If prompted, enter your extension number. When the phone rings, answer it and record the name.

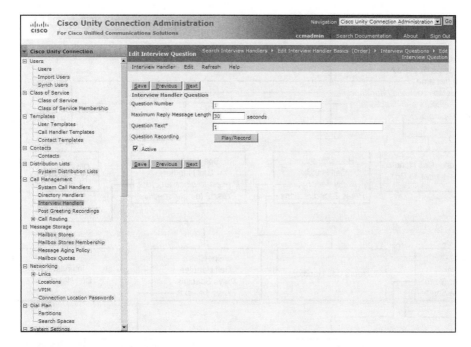

Figure 9-24   *Call Management > Interview Handlers > Edit > Interview Questions.*

Note   When recording a question, it is a good idea to notify callers that they can press the pound key (#) when finished with each response. It eliminates the wait for the silence timeout, which sometimes causes issues in noisy environments.

Step 7.   Click **Save**. If you want to record another question, click the Next button to be taken to the next question.

You have now learned how to create each type of object that will be needed for an advanced auto-attendant. Now review the steps required to build one.

Creating an Audio Text Application

In this section, you take a look at an example auto-attendant and the steps required to build it. This exercise combines the information that you have learned so far in this chapter.

Figure 9-25 presents the flow chart of the advanced auto-attendant that we examined earlier in this chapter. The section introduces the steps required to build the advanced auto-attendant.

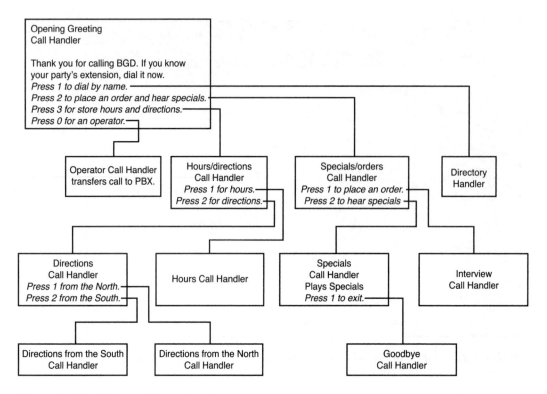

Figure 9-25 *Advanced Auto-Attendant*

When building an auto-attendant, remember that it is best to begin at the bottom. Of course, before you start any configuration, you should have the design on paper. In Figure 9-25, notice that there are three call handlers at the lowest level of the menu. One is the goodbye call handler, which is a default call handler, so no configuration is required. The other two are the call handlers that offer directionsto a caller. These are standard/system call handlers, which are created using the steps in the section "Creating Basic Call-Routing Systems," earlier in this chapter. These call handlers can be viewed as the last call handlers in the auto-attendant. After these call handlers are created and you confirm that the proper greeting has been recorded, you can move up to the next level.

The next level up has four call handlers. Three of them are standard/system call handlers, and the fourth is an interview handler. You can start with any call handler at the same level. You begin with the interview handler. The interview handler is created using the steps found in the section "Using Interview Handlers," earlier in this chapter. Keep in mind that before creating this handler, you should have the list of questions created and a knowledge of the recipients of the delivered responses.

Next, you build the three standard call handlers. They are as follows: the hours call handler, which states the store hours; the specials call handler, which plays this week's store specials; and the directions call handler, which requests the direction of the caller's location. These call handlers are created just like any standard call handler. Note that because the directions and specials call handlers enable callers to press a single digit to transfer elsewhere, the caller input page must be configured to reflect this.

The next level up has four call handlers. Three of them are standard/system call handlers, and the fourth is a directory handler. In this example, there is only one directory handler, so the default can be used. If you need multiple directory handlers, you can use the steps in the section "Directory Handlers," earlier in this chapter. The operator call handler shown in this example is created during the installation process, so it already exists. It does need to be configured the same way it was configured in the section "Configuring Auto-Attendant," earlier in this chapter.

The other two call handlers, the hours/directions and the specials/orders, are standard call handlers and are created the same way as the others. These call handlers navigate the caller through the system. Their purpose is to prompt the caller for input to determine where the call is transferred.

The top level of the menu is the opening greeting. Because an opening greeting call handler already exists, just rerecord the greeting and configure the caller input page to link to the call handlers. This is described in the "Configuring Call Handler Caller Input Settings" section, earlier in this chapter.

This is a high-level overview of the configuration tasks required to create an advanced auto-attendant. The following sections, in combination with previous instructions, should have you well on your way to being able to create an auto-attendant of which Alexander Graham Bell would be proud.

Remotely Managing Call Handlers

Unity offers the capability to allow owners of call handlers to remotely manage and change the greeting of the call handler. This is a popular feature, and it is fairly easy to configure.

First, the call handler being changed remotely must have an assigned extension number. Second, the person capable of making the greeting must be the owner of the call handler. After these two tasks are completed, you need to configure a way for a user to access the remote greeting administrator, known as CUGA.

Note There is an additional benefit when an extension is assigned to a call handler. By entering the extension number from the opening greeting, a caller can proceed directly to the call handler. The caller would hear something like "In the future, to come directly to this menu, press 231," and 231 would be the extension number of the call handler.

The best method is to create a call handler that transfers the caller to CUGA. The following steps outline how this is accomplished:

Step 1.   Create a call handler called CUGA (or any name that you choose).

Step 2.   Assign an extension number far outside the range that a normal caller would ever dial. For example, if the company uses 4-digit extensions in the 3000 range, you could pick 5434632. This should ensure that the number is not dialed by accident. Keep in mind that this extension is only dialed from within Unity, so it does not need to exist in Communications Manager.

Step 3.   On the **Transfer** page, enable the alternate rule and set it to **Send the Call Directly to the Greeting**.

Step 4.   On the **Greetings** page, set the recording source to **Blank/Nothing**. Set the after-greeting action to **Send the Caller to the Greetings Administrator Conversation**.

Step 5.   Click **Save**.

Let the subscribers who are going to need access to CUGA know the extension of this call handler. They can then dial the Unity pilot number from any phone and enter this extension. They will be prompted for their ID and PIN, and then they can remotely manage the call handlers they own.

Configuring Call Routing

Often Unity/Connection is deployed in an environment that requires multiple opening greetings, for example, when Unity is providing service for multiple departments or locations. This can be accomplished by creating call-routing rules. Unity/Connection checks each incoming call against the call-routing rules. The first rule in the list that matches the criteria of the incoming call is used to route the call. These route call rules can be based on the following criteria:

- Whether the call is internal or external

- The port the call came in on

- The trunk the call came in on

- The dialed number

- The calling number

- The schedule (time of day)

- The phone system

Note   The criteria for routing rules are based on whether Unity or Unity Connection is being used.

After looking at this information, the call routing rules determine the language the caller hears and the destination to which the call will be sent.

There are two types of call-routing rules: direct calls rules and forwarded calls rules.

The following two sections show how to create and configure call routing rules in Unity and Unity Connection. You start by looking at how to create a Unity configuration. If you use Unity Connection, move ahead to the section "Creating and Configuring a Call Routing Rule in Unity Connection."

Creating and Configuring a Call Routing Rule in Unity

The following steps illustrate the process used to create and configure a call routing rule in Unity:

Step 1. From within SA, select **Call Management > Call Routing**.

Step 2. Select either **Direct Calls** or **Forwarded Calls** from the left side of the screen.

Step 3. Click the **Add** icon in the title strip.

Step 4. Enter a name for the new rule.

Step 5. Click the **Add** button.

Note Because you are adding something new to the database, you do not have to save it. This, however, can be problematic. In earlier versions of Unity, the moment you added a rule, it became active. This can create problems because every call that comes in will match this rule. When a new rule is created, it sends matched calls to the directory handler. Therefore, because every call will match this rule, every call will go to the directory handler until you edit or disable the new rule. Make sure that new rules are disabled as soon as you add them.

Step 6. A screen similar to Figure 9-26 appears. The name of the rule displays in the Rule Name field. It can be edited if needed.

Step 7. To disable the rule, select the **Disabled** radio button. To enable the rule, select the **Enabled** radio button.

Note It is not possible to disable the default rules from this screen.

Step 8. The rule can apply to internal, external, or both types of calls. Select the type of call to which the rule should apply from the **Call Type** drop-down list.

Step 9. The port through which a call enters is used to determine whether the rule is applied. This could be used in a dual-switch environment to limit the rule to affect only calls coming from one of the PBXs. If you want the rule to apply

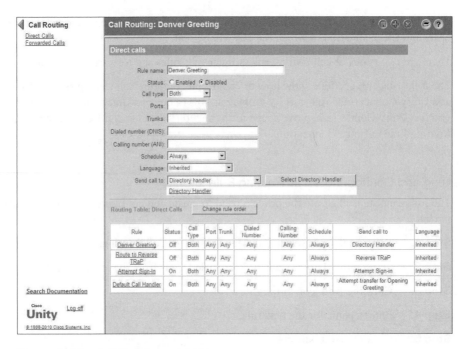

Figure 9-26   *Call Routing > Add New.*

to all calls regardless of the port they came in on, leave the **Ports** field blank. If you are configuring a forwarded calls rule, this field does not appear.

Step 10.   The trunk on which the call came in is also used to determine whether the rule will apply. If you want the rule to apply to all calls regardless of the trunk, leave the **Trunks** field blank. If you are configuring a forwarded calls rule, this field does not appear.

Step 11.   By using the dialed number to route a call, you can send calls to a different opening greeting based on the number the caller dialed. This is useful for companies that have multiple departments with different main numbers. Enter the dialed number in the **Dialed Number (DNIS)** field. The pattern for the dialed number can contain the digits 0 through 9 and the asterisk (*). The * is a wildcard that matches any digit and any number of digits. For example, to match any number that begins with 555, you enter 555*. Leave this field blank to have the rule match regardless of the dialed number.

Note   It is important to realize that the wildcards used in Unity differ from those used in Communications Manager. In Unity, an asterisk (*) stands for any digit and any number of digits, whereas in Communications Manager, an exclamation point (!) is the wildcard that matches any digit and any number of digits.

Step 12. Calls can also be routed based on the calling number. You can configure it so that all calls from a certain area code are routed to a specific call handler. The pattern for the calling number can contain the digits 0 through 9 and the *. The * is a wildcard that matches any digit and any number of digits. For example to match any number that begins with 555, enter 555*. Enter the calling number pattern in the **Calling Number (ANI)** field.

Step 13. The rule will be active during open hours of the schedule assigned to it. Select the desired schedule using the **Schedule** drop-down list.

Step 14. Using the **Language** drop-down list, select the language in which Unity prompts will be played for calls that match this rule.

Step 15. After you have determined the criteria that will match this rule, you must assign a destination for the call. Using the **Send Call To** drop-down list, select a destination. Table 9-12 lists the available destinations, which are the same as those found under caller input for a call handler.

When choosing to send the call to a call handler, directory handler, interview handler, or another subscriber, you have to specify the particular handler or subscriber.

Table 9-12   *Send Call To Options*

Destination	Action
Attempt Forward	Forwards the call to an extension of a subscriber.
Attempt Sign-in	Sends the call to the login prompt.
CVM Mailbox Reset	Allows the caller to reset the mailbox (available with Community Voice Mail package)
Broadcast Message Administrator	Sends the caller to a conversation that allows him or her to send broadcast messages.
Call Handler	Sends the call to the selected call handler.
Caller System Transfer	Sends callers to a prompt that allows them to enter another extension to which they would like to be transferred.
Directory Handler	Sends the call to the directory handler you select.
Greetings Administrator	Sends the call to a conversation that allows the caller to manage the greetings of call handlers that they own.
Hotel Checked Out	Used only with Unity's Hospitality and Property Management System.
Interview Handler	Sends the call to the interview handler you select.

Table 9-12 *Send Call To Options*

Destination	Action
Sign-in	Sends the call to a subscriber sign-in.
Start Live Record	Starts recording the call in the subscriber's mailbox. This feature is not supported on all phone systems.
Subscriber	Sends the call to another subscriber's greeting or extension, depending upon how it is configured.
Subscriber System Transfer	Enables callers to transfer to another extension after they log in with subscriber credentials. They can then transfer to any number that their restriction table enables.

Note   If a subscriber or call handler is selected, you must also choose whether the call should be sent to the greeting or the phone. To send the call to the phone, select **Attempt Transfer For** from the Conversation drop-down list. To send the call to the greeting, select **Send to Greeting For** from the Conversation drop-down list.

Step 16.   Click the **Save** icon in the title strip.

Step 17.   The rule that has just been added displays at the top of the routing table. Because Unity sends the call to the first match in the table, the order in which the rules display is important. Change the order by clicking the **Change Rule Order** button. The window shown in Figure 9-27 displays.

To change the order, click the name of the rule that you want to move, and then click **Up** or **Down** to move it to the desired level in the list.

Note   You cannot move the last rule in this list using this interface. This last rule should send calls to the opening greeting. Think of this as an "if all else fails" route.

Based on the previous steps, you should now be able to route calls depending on incoming call criteria. For example, if you wanted all calls that entered the system by dialing 5551122 to be sent to a call handler called "BGD greeting," you would create a rule that has 5551122 in the Dialed Number (DNIS) field and select the call handler named "BGD greeting" in the Send Call To field. Using these rules, you can configure Unity to handle a number of call-routing tasks.

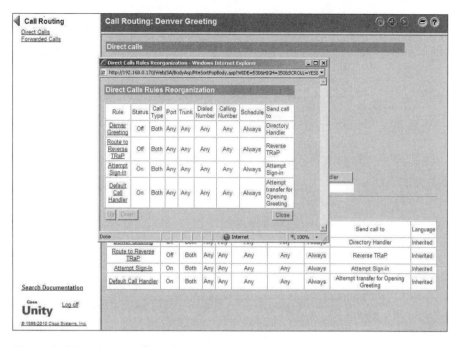

Figure 9-27 *Direct Calls Rules Reorganization*

Creating and Configuring a Call Routing Rule in Unity Connection

The following steps show how to create and configure a call routing rule in Unity Connection:

Step 1. From within Unity Connection Administration, expand **Call Management > Call Routing** by clicking the plus sign to the left of the Call Routing heading.

Step 2. Select either **Direct Routing Rules** or **Forwarded Routing Rules** under the Call Routing heading.

Step 3. Click the **Add New** link.

Step 4. Enter a name for the new rule.

Step 5. Click **Save**.

Step 6. A screen similar to Figure 9-28 appears. The name on the rule displays in the Display Name field. It can be edited, if needed.

Step 7. To disable the rule, select the **Inactive** radio button. To enable the rule, select the **Active** radio button. If Unity Connection determines that the rule is corrupt, it will mark it Invalid.

Step 8. The Language section defines what language is used to play the system prompts. To use the system default language, select **Use System Default Language**. To use the language assigned to the object that sent the call to this

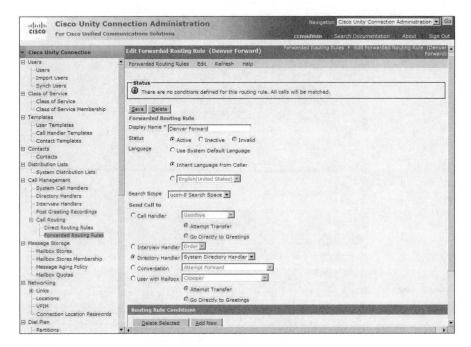

Figure 9-28   *Call Routing > Add New*

handler, select **Inherit Language from Caller**. To specify a language, select the radio button next to the drop-down list of languages and select the desired language from the list.

Step 9.   A search scope is assigned to this rule. It will determine the reachable matches for objects (for example, users) and calls. Select the desired search scope from the **Search Scope** drop-down list.

Step 10.   The Send Call To section defines the location of a call that matches this rule. Table 9-13 lists the options.

Step 11.   Now that the action to be taken has been defined, routing rule conditions must be set. If no conditions are set, all calls will match the rule. To add a condition, click the **Add New** button under the Routing Rule Conditions heading.

Step 12.   A screen similar to Figure 9-29 appears. From this screen, you can define one condition that must be met. To create a condition that matches calls based on the calling number, select the **Calling Number** radio button. From the drop-down list to the right, an operator must be selected. In the last field to the right, enter the pattern that should be used in conjunction with the operator to determine whether the calling number is a match.

Table 9-13 *Send Call To Options*

Destination	Action
Call Handler	A specific call handler must be selected from the drop-down list. When sending to a call handler, you must select either **Attempt Transfer** or **Go Directly to Greeting**. Typically, Greeting is selected.
Interview Handler	A specific interview handler must be selected from the drop-down list.
Directory Handler	A specific directory handler must be selected from the drop-down list.
Conversation (Such as Sign-In or Greetings Administrator)	A specific conversation must be selected from the drop-down list.
User with Mailbox	A specific user must be selected from the drop-down list. When sending to another user, you must select either **Attempt Transfer** or **Go Directly to Greeting**. To have the user's phone ring, select **Attempt Transfer**.

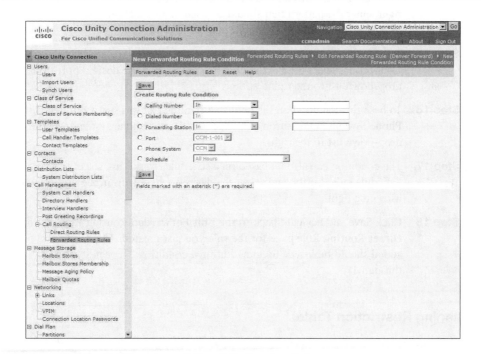

Figure 9-29 *Call Routing > Edit > Edit Routing Rule.*

Note   If you use the equals operator, the * and ? wildcards can be used. * matches any digit and any number of digits, and ? matches any single digit.

Note   For the most part, the operators are self-explanatory (such as greater than, less than, and so on). The one that sometimes confuses people is the operator called *in*. This is either a range or list of numbers. Ranges are separated by a dash, and lists are separated by a comma. For example, 2000-2100 matches all numbers between 2000 and 2100. If 2000,2100 is entered, only 2000 or 2100 is a match.

Step 13.   To create a condition that matches calls based on the number that was dialed, select the **Dialed Number** radio button. From the drop-down list to the right, an operator must be selected. In the last field to the right, enter the pattern that should be used in conjunction with the operator to determine whether the dialed number is a match.

Step 14.   If the **Forward Number** radio button is selected, the condition is based on the number for the object that forwarded the call. To use this type of condition, select an operator from the drop-down list to the right. In the last field to the right, enter the pattern that should be used in conjunction with the operator to determine whether the forward number is a match.

Step 15.   To base the condition on the port through which a call entered Unity Connection, select the **Port** radio button and select the desired port from the drop-down list to the right.

Step 16.   To base the condition on the phone system the call was sent from, select the **Phone System** radio button and select the desired phone system from the drop-down list to the right.

Step 17.   The condition can also be based on a schedule. To do this, select the **Schedule** radio button and select the desired schedule from the drop-down list to the right.

Step 18.   Click **Save** and navigate back to the **Edit Forwarded Routing Rule** or **Edit Direct Routing Rule** page for the rule you just created. The condition you added should be listed. To add additional conditions, repeat Steps 11 through 18.

Managing Restriction Tables

The majority of this chapter focuses on the capability of call handlers to provide call routing and management. Another area of call management needs to be addressed. As you know, Unity/Connection has the capability to enable some fairly advanced call-routing capabilities at both the call handler level and the subscriber level. This is one of the system's great strengths, but as with any power, if exploited, it can cause unexpected repercussions.

Users have the ability to assign Unity/Connection to make outbound calls. Because Unity/Connection is not bound by the same calling rights and restrictions as the caller might have on his phone, the user could configure any of the systems to dial to locations that are unauthorized. This opens up the possibly of unexpected long-distance charges and possible toll fraud.

To prevent this, the CoS to which the user is assigned has a restriction table for each of the three types of calls. Now take a look at how restriction tables are created and configured.

When you look at the default restriction tables, you see that a number of patterns already exist that block various types of calls. Here are two examples: 91???????*, which matches on long-distance numbers assuming that 9 is an outside line access code, and 9011???????*, which matches international numbers dialed from the United States.

Configuring Unity Restriction Tables

The following steps show how to create your own restriction tables in Unity. To see how this is designed in Unity Connection, refer to the next section in this chapter.

To create a new restriction table, follow these steps:

Step 1.   From within SA, select **Call Management > Restriction Tables.**

Step 2.   From the title strip, click the **Add** icon.

Step 3.   In the Add a Restriction Table window, enter a name for the new restriction table.

Step 4.   Restriction tables do not use templates to define their parameters. However, you can choose to create a new restriction table based on an existing one. When you do this, the new restriction table has all the attributes of the one on which you based it. To create the restriction table with the same attributes as an existing one, select the **Based on Existing Restriction Table** radio button and select the existing restriction table from the Based On drop-down list. If you do not want the new restriction table to copy the attributes of an existing restriction table, select the **New Restriction Table** radio button.

Step 5.   Click the **Add** button.

Figure 9-30 shows the Restriction Tables configuration page. The following steps show how these settings are configured:

Step 1.   From within SA, select **Call Management > Restriction Tables.** Click the **Find** icon, enter the search criteria, and click **Find**. Select the desired restriction table from the list and click the **View** button.

Step 2.   The name of the restriction table is in the **Restriction Table Name** field. The name can be changed here.

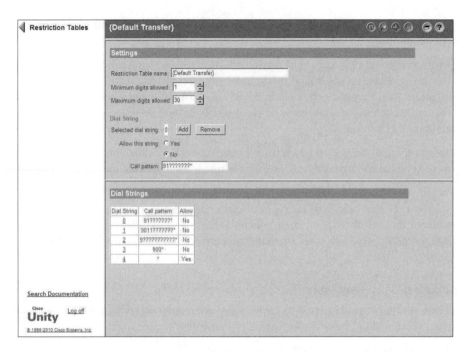

Figure 9-30   *Call Management > Restriction Tables.*

Step 3.   The **Minimum Digits Allowed** field determines the minimum number of digits that must exist in a string for this restriction table to apply. If there are
fewer digits, the call is not permitted. For example, if this value is set to 4,
three-digit numbers would not be permitted.

Step 4.   The **Maximum Digits Allowed** field determines the maximum number of digits that must exist in a string for this restriction table to apply. If there are a
greater number of digits, the call is restricted.

Step 5.   The **Selected Dial String** field identifies which of the dial strings listed in
the Dial Strings section of the page is the one being edited. To add a new
string, click the **Add** button. To remove the current dial string, click the
Remove button.

Step 6.   A dial string can be blocked or permitted based on the **Allow This String**
selection. If **Yes** is selected, the dial string is permitted, and if **No** is selected,
the dial string is blocked.

Step 7.   The dial string that you want to block or permit is entered in the **Call Pattern**
field. The pattern that you enter here is similar to the patterns discussed in the
Communications Manager section of this book. The wildcards that are used
are the question mark (?), which stands for any single digit, and the asterisk
(*), which matches any number of digits. For example, the call pattern 50?
would match 500, 501, 502, 503, 504, 505, 506, 507, 508, and 509. The call

pattern 54* would match any dial string that begins with 54. Enter the call pattern that you want to block or permit.

Step 8.   The order of the dial strings is important. Cisco Unity sequentially compares a phone number to the call pattern in the restriction table, starting with Dial String 0. If the number does not match this string, it is compared to the next string. When a match is found, Unity either permits or restricts the number depending on how the string is configured. After the pattern is entered and configured, click the **Save** icon in the title strip.

Step 9.   Remember that for these restriction tables to be active, they must be assigned in the subscriber's CoS. To assign a restriction table to a CoS, navigate to **Subscribers > Class of Service** and find the CoS for which you want to configure restriction tables. Click **Restriction Tables** from the list on the left side of the screen. Now simply assign the desired restriction table to each of the three types of calls. The following is a list of the three types of calls that Unity can place on behalf of a subscriber:

- **Outcalling:** Restricts numbers that Unity will allow for message delivery

- **Transfers:** Restricts numbers that Unity will allow for call transfer settings

- **Fax:** Restricts numbers that Unity will allow for fax dial strings

Configuring Unity Connection Restriction Tables

Unity Connection is preconfigured with five restriction tables, which in most cases are sufficient. But, there might be a time that you need to create or change one. The following steps illustrate how to change the Default Transfer restriction table:

Step 1.   From within Unity Connection Admininistration, navigate to **System Settings > Restriction Tables**.

Step 2.   Select Default Transfer (or the restriction table that you want to modify) for the list. A screen similar to the one shown in Figure 9-31 appears.

Step 3.   The **Display Name** field should contain a descriptive name.

Step 4.   In the **Maximum Length of Dial String** field, enter the maximum number of digits allowed in a single dial string. If a user enters a string larger than this number, it is rejected before it is even checked against the patterns defined in the table.

Step 5.   In the **Minimum Length of Dial String** field, enter the minimum number of digits allowed in a single dial string.

Step 6.   When you create a new pattern, you can set it to be blocked or allowed. To set all new patterns to be blocked, select the **New Restriction Patterns Are Blocked by Default** check box.

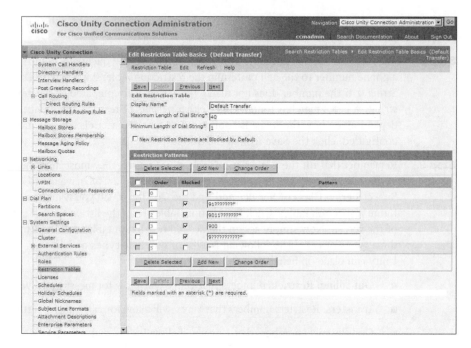

Figure 9-31   *Unity Connection Restriction Tables*

Step 7.   The **Restriction Patterns** section of this page is where you configure the patterns that will be blocked and allowed. The wildcards used for the restriction table are different than those used in Communications Manager. A **?** matches a single digit, and a * matches any digit and any number of digits. For example, the first pattern in Figure 9-31 is 91???????*. This pattern matches a pattern that starts with a 91 and is followed by at least seven digits. To modify an existing pattern, simply edit the pattern field.

Note   New patterns are put at the top of the list and, by default, are allowed. Because the pattern of * is entered automatically, when you add a new pattern, you need to be careful. If you accidentally save this pattern, you have, in effect, allowed nearly any pattern to be entered by a user.

Step 8.   To add a new pattern, click the **Add New** button below the patterns. A new pattern appears at the top of the list. Edit this pattern and select the **Block** check box. If you are creating a pattern that you want to allow, do not select the Block check box. When you are done creating the pattern click **Save**.

Step 9.   You can also delete patterns by selecting the check box to the far left of the pattern and then clicking the **Delete Selected** button.

Step 10.   To change the order of the patterns, click the **Change Order** button. All the patterns appear in a box in their current order. Highlight the pattern that you want to move and use the up and down arrows below the box to move it. After you are done rearranging the patterns, click the **Save** button.

Step 11.   If you did not change the order of the patterns, click the **Save** button to save the changes.

Summary

In this chapter, you learned how to create both basic and advanced auto-attendant systems. The three types of call handlers discussed in this chapter were the standard/system call handler, the directory call handler, and the interview call handler. At this point, you should be comfortable with creating and configuring these three types of call handlers and using them to create an auto-attendant.

In addition, this chapter discussed the steps necessary to implement call routing and restriction tables. These features allow you to route calls based on incoming call criteria and prevent Unity/Connection from sending calls to destinations that have been blocked.

Chapter 10

Implementing Unity Networking

Some companies need to connect Unity with their existing voicemail system. This is a common request during a migration period. Often customers choose to test the new system by deploying a pilot group of users. These users still need to send and forward voicemail to users on the existing voicemail server. This is where Unity/Connection networking comes in. Networking enables companies to almost seamlessly integrate Unity/Connection with an existing voicemail server. Not only does networking enable you to connect with a traditional voicemail server, but it also permits multiple Unity/Connection servers to be connected together and act as a single system.

This chapter discusses the various components of Unity/Connection networking and explores the types of networking that are available. Throughout this chapter, you become familiar with the features that Unity/Connection networking offers, and by the end, you can determine the proper type of networking needed within a given environment.

This chapter is spilt into two sections: Unity Networking and Unity Connection Networking, and Unity Connection to Unity Networking.

Unity Networking Overview

Unity networking is a rather broad term that is easily misunderstood. The term *networking* can suggest anything from connecting a few PCs together to the art of making contacts with other professional people. Because the term *networking* has taken on many definitions in today's world, it is understandable that assumptions about its meaning are sometimes incorrect. In short, Unity networking is the capability to interconnect a Unity server with another voicemail system. That, of course, is the short answer. Networking enables connections with other voicemail systems and the creation of an environment that enables the two systems to appear to function as one.

Networking Components

Although the configuration tasks for each type of networking are specific to the type of system to which Unity is connecting, they all share various components. The following sections provide an overview of the components that are found in each type. Each component is discussed in more detail in the individual networking sections.

Locations

Locations are objects that are stored in SQL and Active Directories (AD). By default, each Unity server has a primary location to which subscribers of that server belong as members. The location information is used to determine how to route the voicemail. Delivery locations can also be created that contain information about other voicemail servers to which Unity is networked. The information contained within the location includes the server's domain name or phone number, the location Dial ID, the search options, the recorded name, and the addressing options. If a message is sent to a subscriber who belongs to a delivery location, Unity uses the location information to determine how to route the call. The simplest way to define a location is as an object that assigns the route that Unity will use to connect to other servers.

Message Addressing

Messages can be addressed using blind addressing, creating external network subscribers, or using a combination of the two methods. When blind addressing is used, subscribers on networked systems cannot be searched from a directory handler. In this case, a message can only be addressed to a user on a networked voicemail server if the sender knows both the user's extension and the Dial ID of the delivery location associated with the networked server.

Network Subscribers

If you want users on a networked voicemail server to be listed in the Unity directory, a network subscriber must be created for each user. Network subscribers do not have access to Unity. The subscribers do not have mailboxes within the Unity system; their mailboxes reside in the voicemail server to which Unity is networked. Each type of networking has its own type of subscriber, as discussed later.

Note   Network subscribers do not need to be created when Unity servers are networked together using Digital Networking.

Voice Connector

The Voice Connector (VC) is used to ensure that a voicemail message is formatted properly so that when it reaches the other voicemail system, it is recognized as voicemail. In some cases, without the use of VC, messages are delivered but cannot be recognized as voicemail. In other cases, messages fail to be delivered. The VC is installed on the

Exchange server and is used whenever a voicemail is sent to or received from another voicemail system.

The VC can be used with Audio Messaging Interchange Specification (AMIS), bridge, and Voice Profile for Internet Mail (VPIM) networking. It is not required for Digital Networking. VC cannot be installed on Exchange 2007 or later versions. For Exchange 2007 or later, the interoperability gateway can be used.

Interoperability Gateway

The interoperability gateway is similar to the VC, but it supports only VPIM networking, trusted Internet subscribers, and Cisco Unity Connection networking. It can be installed on Exchange 2010, 2007, and 2003. While it is used when implementing networking, it does not support bridge or AMIS networking. For bridge and AMIS networking, the VC must be used. Because the VC is only supported on Exchange 2000 and 2003, you must use one of these versions when implementing bridge or AMIS networking.

Schema Extensions

The schema of the Active Directory (AD), of which Unity is a part, must be extended to add networking-specific attributes. Although the schema is extended before Unity is loaded, the networking-specific attributes might not have been added. When running the schema extension utility, you must choose which type of networking to use. If Digital or AMIS networking is used, the core schema extensions that were created before Unity was installed will be adequate. If bridge or VPIM networking is used, the schema might need to be extended further.

Although the previously mentioned components play a part in Unity networking, the manner in which these components are implemented depends on which type of networking is deployed. The next two sections break Unity networking into two broad categories. These are Unity-to-Unity networking and Unity-to-legacy (traditional) voicemail networking.

Unity-to-Unity Networking Overview

Companies that have multiple Unity servers might prefer to network the Unity servers together. There are certain advantages in doing so. The benefits offer both the subscriber and the outside caller additional functionality. Subscribers will now have the capacity to easily send, forward, and reply to messages from subscribers on other Unity servers. Networking also offers the ability to add subscribers on a different Unity server to local distribution and private lists. Depending on how the search options are configured, the outside caller might be able to search for subscribers who are on other Unity servers.

Unity-to-Unity networking is accomplished by using Digital Networking or VPIM networking. The type of networking is determined by whether the Unity systems share the same directory.

If the Unity servers share the same directory, Digital Networking should be used. Because the Unity servers share the same directory, it is easy to have these systems communicate and determine the delivery location of subscribers. Digital Networking is considered a standard feature. It is included as a feature starting with the base voicemail system.

If the Unity servers do not share the same directory, VPIM networking can be used. Because the Unity systems do not share a common directory, this type of networking requires more work on behalf of the administrator to make the system function as seamlessly as possible.

Unity-to-Legacy Voicemail Networking Overview

In a perfect world, there would be only one voicemail solution, and that solution would be Unity. That statement might be considered slightly biased, but the idea of using only one type of voicemail system would make connecting systems together easier. You do not live in a homogeneous world, so you must create ways to allow dissimilar systems to communicate with one another. The technology that is deployed to enable Unity systems to communicate with non-Unity voicemail systems is based on standards that have been used to connect voicemail systems together for years.

Typically, three types of networking are used to connect Unity and non-Unity systems. They are VPIM, AMIS, and bridge. Each is described in greater detail in the following sections, but a brief description of each follows:

- **VPIM:** Enables messaging between Cisco Unity and other voice-messaging systems using some type of IP connection. The other voice-messaging system must support the VPIM version 2 protocol. Messages are sent over an IP network using the VPIM messaging format.

- **AMIS:** Enables messaging between Cisco Unity and other voice-messaging systems over an analog connection. The other voicemail system must support AMIS, which is an industry-standard protocol.

- **Bridge:** Bridge networking enables messaging between Cisco Unity and Octel systems. This solution requires an additional server known as a bridge server. Messaging between Cisco Unity and the bridge is done by using a digital protocol that is based on the VPIM protocol and is sent over an IP connection. Messaging between the Octel servers and the bridge is done by using the Octel analog networking protocol. Cisco Unity and the Octel systems maintain separate voicemail directories.

Now that you have a basic understanding of the different types of networking and when each is used, you can better understand the next section. Take a closer look at each type and learn how the networking components are used.

Unity Networking Configuration

Most tasks discussed so far are considered administrative. However, the implementation of Unity networking can prove to be involved and should only be attempted by someone with a solid understanding of Unity and the remote voicemail system with which Unity will be integrated. Explaining the specific integration steps for each type of networking is outside of the scope of this book. However, it is important that you understand each type of networking so that you can properly manage a networked system.

The following sections can help you become familiar with the specific components and requirements of each type of networking. Begin by looking at the fundamentals of networking Unity to other Unity systems.

Defining Digital Networking

Cisco Unity Digital Networking is the feature that enables subscribers associated with one Cisco Unity server to exchange voice messages with subscribers associated with other Cisco Unity servers. One requirement of Digital Networking is that all Cisco Unity servers connected to a network share a single, global directory.

Digital Networking also enables calls to be transferred from the automated attendant or directory assistance to subscribers who are associated with the other Unity server.

Subscriber information is stored in SQL on the Unity server with which the subscriber is associated. Some of this information is replicated to the global directory. This information includes things such as distribution lists, locations, and certain subscriber information. Because this information is stored in the directory, the other Unity servers have access to it, which provides the means for Digital Networking. A process running on each Unity server scans the directory for information that relates to other Unity servers and adds it to its database. This enables subscribers on one Unity server to address messages to subscribers on the other Unity server.

The directory in which Cisco Unity stores data is specified when Cisco Unity is set up. When integrating with Dominos, you specify through which Dominos server Unity (the partner Dominos server) communicates to the other servers. When using Exchange, each server is part of the same directory, which enables this information to be shared.

Now that you have a basic understanding of what Digital Networking provides, take a closer look at the components required. The setup of Digital Networking is rather easy. You must first verify that your environment meets the minimum requirements for Digital Networking that are outlined in the following list:

- Unity partner servers must be in the same AD forest and be running Exchange 2000, Exchange 2003, Exchange 2007, or Exchange 2010.

- The AD schema must be extended with the Exchange Directory Monitor selected.

- Version compatibility:

  - 8.0(3), 7.0(2), and 5.0(1)

  - 7.0(2), 5.0 (1), 4.2(1), 4.1(1), and 4.0(5)

- No additional license is required for Digital Networking.

After you have confirmed that the preceding requirements have been met, a minimal amount of additional configuration is required. However, before moving forward, you need to have a good understanding of your existing dial plan and that of any other Unity server with which you plan to network.

Because Digital Networking enables multiple Unity servers to share the same directories, overlapping extensions can cause problems. By fully examining existing dial plans, you can avoid these problems. Because all extensions within a Unity system must be unique, a component known as dialing domains can be implemented to allow environments with overlapping extensions to participate in Digital Networking. An example is shown in Figure 10-1.

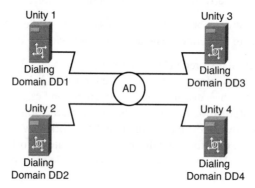

Figure 10-1 *Dialing Domains*

In Figure 10-2, each PBX has a phone with the extension of 2002 attached. Unity searches its local server first and allows the subscriber attached to the local PBX to be reached by subscribers on that server. Hence, if a caller wants to reach the 2002 on the other PBX and dials 2002, Unity sends the call to the 2002 in its local directory, which is not what is desired. By putting each Unity server in its own dialing domain and assigning unique Dial IDs, a caller can reach 2002 in the other dialing domain by preceding the extension number with the Dial ID. In this example, if a caller on Unity 1 wants to reach extension 2002 on Unity 2, he dials 2222002, which is the Dial ID of dialing domain 2 followed by the extension number of 2002. In this example, dialing domains can be used to limit the search when overlapping extensions exist. Dialing domains can also be used to enlarge the search capabilities of Unity. The process to broaden Unity searches is described next.

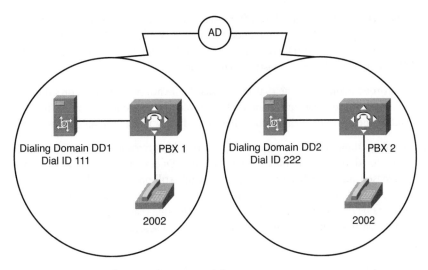

Figure 10-2 *Dialing Domain Example*

Because Digital Networking enables subscribers from one Unity server to be searched from another Unity server's auto-attendant, you must decide how broad you will allow these searches to be. There are three choices when determining the size of the search area. The available search parameters are as follows:

■ **Local Server:** This limits the directory search to the subscribers associated with the server itself.

■ **Dialing Domain:** Dialing domains are used to expand the directory search to include other Unity servers. When choosing this type of search, Unity first searches its local directory. If no match is found in the local directory, the search expands to other servers in the same dialing domain as the local server.

■ **Global Catalog (referred to in the pull-down list as Global Directory):** This search option enables all servers that are part of the global directory to be searched. Unity begins by searching the local server, then expands to the dialing domain (if one exists), and finally searches all other servers in the Global Address List (GAL).

The searching parameters are defined in the primary location of the Unity server. Each Unity server has a primary location that is created during the installation and cannot be deleted. This location can and should be modified when networking is implemented.

A primary location consists of two areas: profile and addressing options. Now examine the profile. Within the profile the following are defined:

■ **Display Name:** This is the name of the location. By default, the name of the default location is Default. It is recommended that you change this name to represent the physical location of this server. For example, if the server is located in Detroit, you might name the location DTW (Detroit airport code).

- **Dial ID:** A Dial ID is used to differentiate between locations. Each location must have a unique ID. It is recommended that the fixed-length IDs be used throughout the network for Dial IDs. Dial IDs must also be unique. Make certain that the Dial IDs do not overlap with existing extensions.

- **Recorded Name:** A name that represents the location must be recorded here. For example, if the location is named Detroit, record the name Detroit in this field. Subscribers will hear this name when they dial by name and match the location.

- **Dialing Domain:** The example in Figure 10-1 illustrates how dialing domains are used to address overlapping extension issues. Dialing domains are also used to increase Unity searches to other servers while still preventing all servers from being searched. Figure 10-2 shows an environment with four Unity servers. All of these servers belong to the same AD. Applying the same dialing domain to servers 1 and 2 limits Unity's search to these two servers when a search is initiated by a call on either of these systems.

  Dialing domains are created based on dial plans that exist within the telephony infrastructure. If a particular company has many PBXs interconnected to one another through trunking, they can all have one dial plan and need only one dialing domain. However, there are times when multiple dialing domains are necessary. It is best to start with one dialing domain and then expand if needed.

- **SMTP Information:** This field is required for VPIM networking and is discussed in the "Defining VPIM Networking" section, later in this chapter.

The second area is the addressing options. In this area, you configure where Unity searches for matches. Two types of searches must be configured:

- **Subscriber searches:** This parameter defines where Unity searches when a subscriber addresses a message from a phone. It also defines the search parameter used when adding subscribers to a public or private distribution list.

- **Blind addressing:** Blind addressing enables a subscriber to send a message to another subscriber by entering the Dial ID of the delivery location and the other subscriber's extension. For example, if another subscriber location Dial ID is 222 and his extension is 2002, the subscriber sending the message enters 2222002 from the telephone to address the message. The Blind Addressing Allowed Locations field determines where Unity will search for valid IDs when addressing messages using blind addressing.

After primary locations are configured on each server, Digital Networking for all intents and purposes is functioning. For Digital Networking to work, not only must the primary location be configured, but the server must also know about all its delivery locations. When implementing Digital Networking, there is no need to configure the delivery locations because location information is stored in AD; the other server's primary location is learned and added as a delivery location. If you look at the delivery locations defined on the Unity server, you see that the locations created on all the Unity servers within the common directory are present. When primary location information is changed, it can take up to 15 minutes for this information to replicate to the other servers.

Figures 10-3 and 10-4 show the location configuration screens within SA.

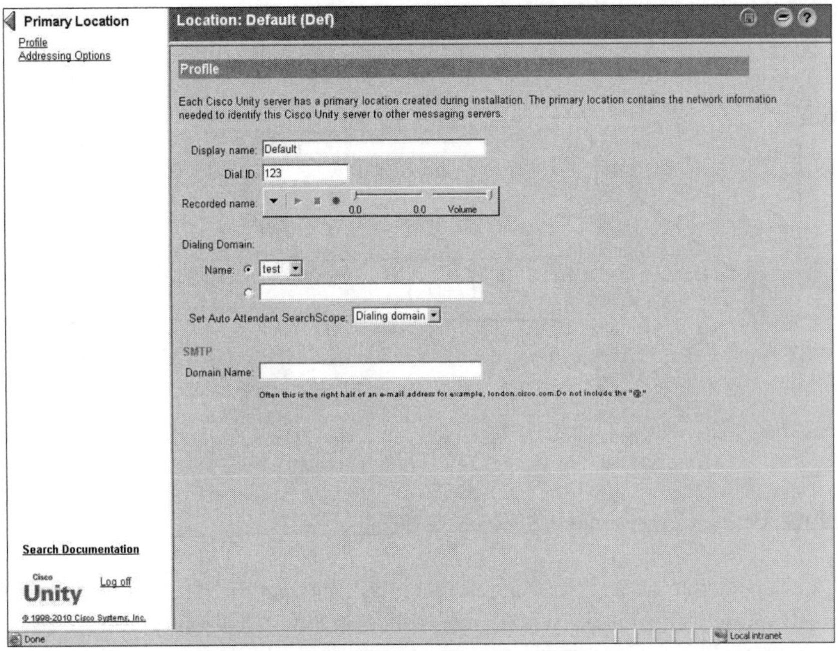

Figure 10-3   *Network > Primary Location > Profile*

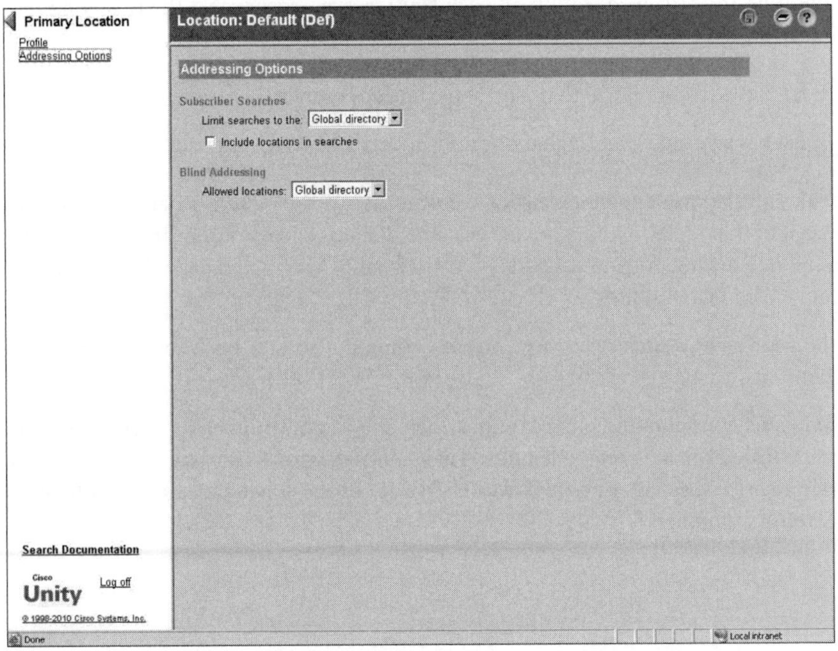

Figure 10-4   *Network > Primary Location > Addressing Options*

Now that you understand the components required for Digital Networking, explore the example shown in Figure 10-5.

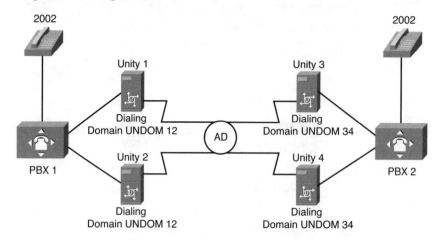

Figure 10-5 *Digital Networking Overview*

In this example, four Unity servers are running Exchange on-box. They all belong to the same AD forest: Unity 1 and 2 service subscribers on PBX 1, and Unity 3 and 4 service subscribers on PBX 2. Overlapping extensions exist on the PBXs. To allow Digital Networking to function, certain requirements must be configured.

To configure the primary location on each Unity server, ensure that the following requirements are met:

■ Each has a display name that represents its geographical location.

■ Each has a unique Dial ID that does not overlap with existing extensions.

To deal with the overlapping extensions, ensurethat Unity 1 and 2 are in the same dial domain and that Unity 3 and 4 are in the same dialing domain. For example, Unity 1 and 2 can be in a dialing domain called UNDOM12, and Unity 3 and 4 can be in a dialing domain called UNDOM34.

Set the addressing search options to be the dialing domain for both subscriber searches and blind addressing.

The previous configuration enables subscribers to search for other subscribers that are on the same PBX from a directory handler. They can also address messages to subscribers on the other PBX by entering the location Dial ID of the other Unity server followed by the extension number.

This section examined the requirements for networking Unity together with other Unity servers using Digital Networking, which requires all Unity servers to be part of the same directory. Other means of networking are required to network Unity servers that do not share a common directory.

Unity to Non-Unity Networking Concepts

Unity has the capability to connect to other voicemail systems, which enables subscribers to send messages to users on the other systems. The exact features available within a networked solution vary, based on the type of networking that is deployed. The goal of the following sections is to introduce you to the three types of networking that are used to connect Unity to other voicemail systems: AMIS, VPIM, and bridge networking.

The required networking tasks are quite involved. They should only be attempted by an individual who is trained on Unity networking tasks and has experience and a solid understanding of the other voicemail system to which Unity will be networked. If you are up to this task, refer to the networking integration guides available on Cisco.com, because these sections do not describe the actual integration process, only the concepts.

Defining AMIS Networking

AMIS networking enables Unity to network with non-Unity voicemail systems that also support AMIS. As with all types of networking, the goal is to allow users on both systems to exchange voicemails with one another as if they were using the same system.

AMIS networking is a licensed Unity feature that must be purchased from Cisco. In most cases, the other voicemail system will also require a license, which is purchased from that voicemail system's manufacturer.

Unity sends the messages to the other voicemail servers through analog lines. To accomplish this, Unity must have analog lines at its disposal.

Because the messages are sent through analog lines, the transmission speed of these messages is not fast. In short, it takes the message duration time, in addition to setup and teardown time, to transmit the message. If sending a single message to multiple recipients, the time it takes to deliver each message is multiplied. For example, if you want to send a 2-minute message to five people, it takes at least 10 minutes to deliver the messages.

To implement AMIS networking, a few components must be configured in Unity. This section provides a high-level overview of these components.

A mailbox called UAMIS must be created in the Exchange server. This mailbox is used to store all messages sent to and from the remote voicemail system while they are being processed and awaiting delivery. Because the transmission mechanism is not that efficient, the messages might queue up in this mailbox for some time. Therefore, you need to make sure that the storage limits for this mailbox are adequate to accommodate a large number of queued messages. Be sure to review this mailbox's limits and increase them as needed. If this mailbox becomes full, it can cause inbound and outbound AMIS messages to fail.

The ports used to deliver AMIS messages must be configured. It is possible to use more than one port for message transport functions. You can also configure schedules that allow AMIS message delivery to occur only at certain times of the day. This leaves the ports available for other functions if required.

The Voice Connector must be installed on the Exchange server. The Voice Connector is used to format the outbound message and deliver it to the UAMIS mailbox.

The primary location and delivery locations must be configured. A delivery location must be configured for each remote system. The delivery location will include the remote system's AMIS Node ID and the delivery phone number.

If you want the remote system user to appear in Unity's directory, you must create AMIS subscribers. These subscribers are contacts in AD. Because they do not have a mailbox on the Unity system, these subscribers have no direct access to the Unity system.

When an AMIS subscriber is created, a special email address is associated with that subscriber. This address contains the information that Unity needs to determine where the message is to be delivered. This address is associated with the Dial ID of the location to which the subscriber belongs. Previous to Unity 4.03, it was necessary to update this information if the Dial ID was changed using a utility called the Extension Address Utility. In current versions of Unity, this is automatically updated.

This section provided you with a brief overview of the components required to implement AMIS networking. However, only the Unity side of the configuration was discussed. The remote side also needs to be configured. Make sure that only a qualified engineer performs this implementation. For additional information on AMIS networking, refer to the AMIS sections of the "Networking in Cisco Unity Guide" on Cisco.com, along with a number of other excellent AMIS documents.

Defining VPIM Networking

VPIM networking enables Unity to send and receive messages from a non-Unity voicemail server through an IP connection. The goal of this networking is the same as any type of Unity networking: to allow users on both systems to easily exchange voicemails.

Note VPIM can be used to connect Unity to Unity Express and Unity Connection. With Unity 8.0 and Unity Connection 8.0, VPIM is no longer necessary. Digital Networking is now supported in such an environment.

VPIM is an industry-standard protocol that enables the exchange of voice, fax, and text messages between voice-messaging systems over an IP network. This protocol is based on the Simple Mail Transfer Protocol (SMTP) and the Multi-Purpose Internet Mail Extension (MIME) protocol.

After VPIM networking is implemented, companies can send, receive, forward, and reply to messages among different systems. Because VPIM uses SMTP as its transport, it is not susceptible to the delays that are often associated with AMIS networking. Transport costs might be less than those of AMIS, because toll charges might not be incurred.

The VPIM specification defines how the messages are transferred and the required format of the messages. VPIM is a Unity-licensed feature that must be purchased from Cisco. Remember that the remote voicemail system might also require licensing for VPIM. This must be purchased from the manufacturer of that voicemail system.

As with any type of networking, a number of components must be configured when implementing VPIM. The following is an overview of the required components.

Because VPIM uses SMTP as its transport mechanism, connectivity to an SMTP server must be configured. This means that the Exchange server used with Unity must be able to send and receive email to and from the mail server of the remote voicemail system.

The AD schema must be extended to allow specific VPIM attributes. The schema is extended during the installation of Unity, but if the VPIM option was not selected (it is not by default), the required attributes do not exist. In this case, the schema extension utility must be run again with the VPIM option selected.

The Voice Connector can be installed if using Exchange 2000 or Exchange 2003. If using Exchange 2003 or Exchange 2007, the Interoperability Gateway is used. These handle all VPIM messages. They are responsible for properly formatting the message so that it can be delivered to the other system. To do this, it transforms outbound messages from the Messaging Application Programming Interface (MAPI) format (Exchange's native format) to MIME format. VPIM checks the delivery location to determine whether it must convert that message to G.726 and implements it if necessary. The Voice Connector or Interoperability Gateway also handles inbound messages by converting them from MIME to MAPI format.

You must configure the primary location and create delivery locations. A delivery location must be configured for each remote system. The delivery location includes the SMTP domain name of the remote system. If multiple Unity servers exist within the same AD forest, delivery locations need to be configured only on one Unity system. The search options must also be configured with the location.

If you want the user on the remote system to appear in Unity's directory, VPIM subscribers must be created. They can be developed manually using Unity Administrator or the bulk import wizard. Automatic creation is configured under **Network > Delivery Locations > Subscriber Creation**. These subscribers are created as contacts in AD. Because they do not have a mailbox on the Unity system, they have no direct access to the Unity system.

When a VPIM subscriber is created, a special email address is associated with that subscriber, as with AMIS subscribers. The address contains the information that Unity requires to determine where the message is delivered. The address is associated with the Dial ID of the location to which the subscriber belongs. Previous to Unity 4.03, it was necessary to update this information if the Dial ID was changed using a utility called the Extension Address Utility. In current versions of Unity, this is automatically updated.

In addition to the configuration of these components, the remote system must be configured for VPIM. It is recommended that only a qualified engineer perform this type of networking. For additional information on the VPIM protocol, check out http://www.ema.org/vpim. There are also a number of VPIM networking documents on Cisco.com.

Defining Bridge Networking

Bridge networking is used to connect Unity to Octel voicemail systems. This solution is unique, but the overall goal is the same: to provide a way for users on both systems to easily and effectively use all the features of each system.

Bridge networking is unique because it is the only type of networking that requires an additional server. The server, referred to as a bridge server, is a gateway between Unity and Octel. This solution uses two protocols to accomplish its job. A Digital Networking protocol based on VPIM with a proprietary extension is used to communicate between Unity and the bridge server. Octel's Analog Networking protocol is used to communicate between the bridge server and the Octel system.

Figure 10-6 shows an overview of how the bridge server is connected to the voicemail systems. The connectivity used between the Unity's Exchange server and the bridge is IP, so an Ethernet connection is required on the bridge server. The Octel system communicates with the bridge server through analog lines that are connected to the PBX. A Brooktrout voice board must be installed in the bridge server for this connectivity.

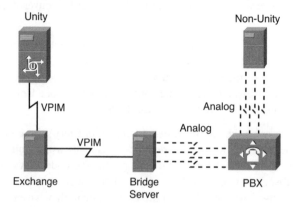

Figure 10-6 *Bridge Server*

As with the other types of networking mentioned in this section, bridge networking is a licensed feature of Unity. If multiple Unity systems networked together are required to network with an Octel system, a single Unity server is used to communicate with the bridge server. In addition to requiring licensing on Unity, the Octel server must be licensed for Octel's analog networking.

For bridge networking to work, certain components must be configured on the Unity system. We now look at the required components.

As with VPIM networking, the AD schema must be extended. This is done by running a schema extension utility that is included with Unity. This is the same utility used when Unity was first installed, but this time the bridge networking option must be chosen.

The Voice Connector must be installed. The Voice Connector is used to transform the outbound messages to VPIM and handle inbound VPIM messages.

A mailbox called UOmni must be created on the Exchange server. Unlike the UAMIS mailbox, this mailbox is not used to queue messages but to handle administrative messages received from the bridge server.

Locations must be configured. The primary location must be customized and delivery locations created for each Octel system with which Unity will be communicating. Delivery locations need to be created only on the Unity server that communicates with the bridge server. Search options must also be defined within the location.

If you want to have users who have mailboxes on the Octel system appear in the directory of Unity, bridge subscribers must be created for each of these users. Subscribers are created in three different ways. They can be manually created on the Unity server or bridge server, or they can automatically be configured utilizing usage-based NameNet emulation. Because bridge subscribers do not have a mailbox on the Exchange server and are only contacts in AD, they do not have access to the Unity server.

This section has outlined the components required for bridge networking and provided a summary of its application. For more information, you are encouraged to read the various Unity bridge release notes and installation guides found on Cisco.com.

Now that you have a good understanding of the different types of networking Unity supports, take a look at Unity Connection networking.

Unity Connection Networking Overview

The goal of Unity Connection networking is the same as Unity networking: to connect two or more voicemail systems together. There are basically three types of networking supported by UC:

- **Networking Unity Connection servers with other Unity Connection servers:** This is fairly simple and involves connecting multiple locations together to form Unity Connection sites.

- **Networking Unity Connection with Unity:** As you read earlier in this chapter, Unity supports Digital Networking, which enables Unity servers to network with other Unity servers if they are part of the same AD forest. When connecting Unity

Connection with UC, it is also sometimes referred to as Digital Networking, but it does not require Unity Connection to be part of the AD.

■ **VIPM networking:** This is implemented when you need to network Unity Connection with a voicemail system other than Unity or UC. The process is similar to Unity's VPIM networking methods.

The following sections offer a brief overview of the networking techniques and describe their configuration. The details required for implementing these features are beyond the scope of this book. The goal of these sections is to provide you with enough information to know the type of networking that you might require and to provide a high-level understanding of the requirements.

Networking Unity Connection to Unity Connection

You can connect up to ten Unity Connection servers (or clusters) together by creating a *connection site*. Sites are made up of locations. A location is a single Unity Connection server (or cluster). In addition, in Unity Connection 8.0, you can connect two sites together using intersite links. This allows up to 20 Unity servers (10 per site) to be connected. Although you can connect Unity Connection 7.0 servers with Unity Connection 8.0 servers, you cannot use intersite links to do so. Intersite links require all the Unity Connection servers to be at a minimum version 8.0.

After the servers are configured, users within the site can send, reply, and forward messages to other users in the site. A standalone Unity Connection can handle 20,000 users, but by implementing sites, you can enable a system that can handle many more users. The user information for all locations in the site is replicated to all other locations. Although it seems that you could theoretically have 200,000 users (because you can have ten locations and 20,000 users per location), the maximum is really 100,000 because that is the maximum that the Unity directory can handle.

In addition to replicating users across the locations in the site, the following information is also replicated:

■ Recorded names

■ Partitions and search spaces

■ Locations

■ System contacts

■ System distribution lists

The connection between two locations (servers) is an intrasite link. Before you implement such a link, you must acknowledge the following requirements:

■ The location display name for each serve must be unique.

■ The SMTP domain of each server must be unique.

- IP connectivity between the servers must be active.

- TCP port 25 must be open between the servers.

Note UC servers communicate with one another using STMP, which is a standard protocol used for messaging and operates on port 25.

Setting up the link can be done using one of two methods: automatic and manual.

The automatic method is fairly simple, but it requires that the server you want to connect to be up and running and have IP connectivity. If these requirements are met, joining a site is a simple matter of clicking a button and entering the IP address and login information of the server you want to connect to.

If the other server is not accessible, you can still configure an intrasite link using the manual method. The manual process is almost as simple as the automatic method. Download the location configuration from each server and upload it to the other. The manual method is useful if you want to prestage a server before shipping to a remote location.

Note If any of the locations are clusters, you also need a smart host. A smart host assists in routing the messages to a subscriber if the publisher is down.

Earlier in this section, it was stated that intersite links can be created that have the capability to connect two connection sites together. Because intersite links are also used to connect Unity Connection to Unity, they are discussed in more detail in the next section.

Networking Unity Connection to Unity

As discussed earlier, Unity uses Digital Networking to connect multiple Unity systems together. When networking Unity Connection to Unity, the same concepts are used on the Unity side. On the Unity Connection side, the same concepts are used as those used to connect the Unity Connection site together. Before we take a look at what is required on both systems, look at a high-level overview of the communication process.

Figure 10-7 shows a Unity Connection site networked to a Unity digital network. The Unity Connection site uses intrasite links to connect the servers to one another. An intersite link connects the Unity Connection site to the interoperability gateway, which is connected to the Unity digital network. When a user on the Unity side sends a message to a Unity Connection user, the message is sent to the interoperability gateway, which forwards it to the Unity Connection site using SMTP. The interoperability gateway is only required when a message is transferred between the Unity and Unity Connection sites; it is not used for messages sent within either site. As discussed earlier in this chapter, the interoperability gateway resides on the Exchange server and is used to allow Unity to connect to other voicemail systems.

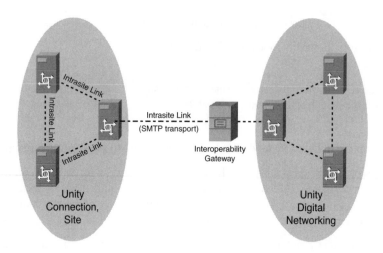

Figure 10-7   *Unity to Unity Connection Networking*

Now that you know what components are required, take a look at the requirements. First, look at the Unity server. You can connect a single Unity server or an entire Unity digital network to a Unity Connection site. Because Unity Connection is not part of AD, it is necessary to create a method of connection to the Unity digital network. The interoperability gateway provides the link. Because you do not need an interoperability gateway for digital networking, you might need to install this.

Before you install the interoperability gateway, make sure that the following requirements are met:

■   Primary location has been defined.

■   Permissions Wizard has been run with the Set Permissions Required by AMIS, Cisco Unity Bridge, and VPIM check box selected.

■   ADSchemaSetup has been run with the Exchange VPIM and Connection Networking Connector check box selected.

On the Unity Connection side, the Unity Connection that is acting as the site gateway must be configured to accept SMTP connections from the interoperability gateway. This is accomplished by adding the IP address to the access IP address list on the Unity Connection server.

The actual creation of the intersite link is a fairly simple process.

First, download the Unity gateway configuration file from the Unity server and the Unity Connection site configuration file from the UC. Now upload the Unity gateway configuration file to the Unity Connection gateway server, and upload the Unity Connection site configuration file to the Unity server.

As stated previously in this chapter, intersite links are used to connect Unity Connection sites together and to connect Unity Connection sites to Unity digital networks. The manual method for creating an intersite link between Unity Connection sites is nearly the same process as creating one to connect to a Unity digital network.

Simply download the configuration file from each site and upload to the other. After the file is uploaded, each site has the information required to connect to the other site. You can also choose to use the automatic method, which works similarly to the automatic method for intrasite links. You enter the IP address and login information of the other site, and the link is automatically created. This method requires that both sites are active and have IP connectivity between them.

Now that you have a good understanding of how networking between Unity Connection and Unity works, look at how Unity Connection can be networked to other voicemail systems.

Networking Unity Connection to Other Systems

When you need to network Unity Connection with a voicemail system other than Unity or another UC, you have one option, which is VPIM. VPIM was already discussed in the Unity networking section of this chapter, but for those of you who skipped that part, here is a brief introduction to VPIM.

Voice Profile for Internet Mail (VPIM) is an industry-standard protocol that allows the exchange of voice, fax, and text messages among voice-messaging systems over an IP network. This protocol is based on SMTP and the MIME protocol. The VPIM specification defines how the messages are transferred and their required formats.

It is important to understand that VPIM is not free. It is a licensed feature for Unity Connection, which means there is a cost associated with it. Also keep in mind that the other voicemail system might require VPIM licenses. Be sure to obtain all required licenses before you start configuring VPIM.

Because VPIM uses SMTP as its transport mechanism, you need to confirm that there is STMP connectivity to the remote system. After this has been verified, the configuration process can begin.

Within Unity Connection, a VPIM delivery location has to be created for each remote voicemail server. A VPIM location contains the following parameters:

- Display Name
- Dial ID
- Partition
- STMP Domain Name
- IP Address
- Remote Phone Prefix

VPIM contacts must be now be developed. VPIM contacts are created for users who have a voice mailbox on the remote system. You can think of them as pointers. When a message is addressed to the contact, it is routed to the remote system. VPIM contact also permits users that have a remote mailbox to appear in the directory of UC. VPIM contacts can be created manually or automatically. If automatic creation is used, Unity Connection checks to see whether the sender of a message from a VPIM location exists in the directory. If it does not, a contact is automatically created.

If VPIM contacts are not created, the VPIM users will not appear in the directory, but users can still send messages to them using *blind addressing*. The user enters the Dial ID of the VPIM location and the user's extension number. For example, if the Dial ID is 213 and the extension number is 423, the user would enter 213423 when addressing the message.

Because messages are sent using SMTP, the address that is used has the same format as an email address. In the previous example, assume that 213 was the Dial ID for the Chicago office. Furthermore, assume that the SMTP domain name for the Chicago office is chicagocmp.com. The message would be addressed to 423@chicagocmp.com.

For additional information on VPIM or any Unity Connection networking, search for "Networking Guide for Cisco Unity Connection" at Cisco.com.

Summary

This chapter explored the various types of networking that can be used to connect with other voicemail systems. Initially, you examined how Unity can easily integrate with other Unity systems that share the same directory by implementing Digital Networking, and the types of networking used to connect Unity to non-Unity systems. Later in this chapter, networking Unity Connection to Unity Connection and Unity Connection to Unity was explored. In conclusion, how VPIM is used to connect Unity Connection to other voicemail systems was discussed. Now that you have a high-level overview of the different types of networking and the environments for which each is designed, you can determine the type of networking required for a given deployment. Be sure to refer to the various networking integration guides and white papers available at Cisco.com for additional information on these topics.

Chapter 11

Exploring Unity/ Connection Tools

So far in this book, you have learned how to tackle many of the day-to-day configuration tasks that must be performed to create and maintain an efficient unified messaging solution. This chapter examines the monitoring and reporting capabilities that are accessible from the web-based administration interface.

In addition to web-based tools, developers of the Unity application have created a number of devices that help make the job of the integrator and administrator much easier. These tools assist in a wide scope of tasks that range from bulk editing to integration monitoring. These tools are available from the desktop of the Unity server by clicking the Unity Tools Depot icon.

The beginning of this chapter explores Unity's web-based tools and reports as well as offer a brief overview of many of the tools found in the tools depot. Next you explore Unity Connection's web-based tools and documentation.

Using Unity Tools

Unity offers both web-based and standalone tools. The web-based tools are accessible from any PC that has IE installed and has access to the Unity server. The standalone tools are installed on the Unity server and, for the most part, are run from the server. This first section in this part of the chapter explores the web-based tools. The second section offers an overview of some of the tools found in the Cisco Unity Tools Depot.

Unity Web-Based Tools

Many of the tools explored in this chapter must be run from the Unity server console; however, reports and limited monitoring are accomplished through IE.

From SA, you can generate a number of reports that enable valuable information to be gathered and presented in a web page or stored in a comma-separated value (CSV) file for later manipulation. An IE-based monitoring tool called Status Monitor is also available.

Through this interface, you can monitor the current status of Unity. Confusion often surrounds the IE-based Status Monitor utility because there is an .exe application with a similar name. To reduce the confusion, the IE-based Status Monitor is often referred to as "Status Monitor (HTML)."

The following sections explore the various reports that can be generated from SA and also examine the monitoring capabilities of Status Monitor (HTML). Start by taking a look at the monitoring capabilities.

Monitoring

The Status Monitor (HTML) enables you to view the current status of the system, ports, reports, and disk drives through a web browser. This utility is useful because you can access it from any PC on a network with IP connectivity to Unity and IE. Accessing Status Monitor (HTML) is quite simple. If you are logged on at the Unity console, simply click the **Status Monitor** icon on the desktop. Be aware that by default, Status Monitor will overtake the last active web page you have open. So if you have SA open when you start Status Monitor, it will cause your SA session to disappear. To prevent this, open Status Monitor by right-clicking the **Unity** icon in the system tray next to the clock. When you right-click this icon, a menu of options displays. One option is Launch Status Monitor. Clicking this selection causes Status Monitor to begin in a new window.

Figure 11-1 is the Status Monitor (HTML) screen. This figure shows five icons at the top of the page. Clicking the icons reveals the status of the various processes. When Status Monitor (HTML) is opened, the system status screen displays.

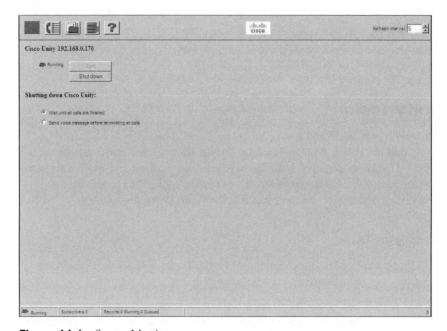

Figure 11-1 *Status Monitor*

The following figures and descriptions explain the icons and provide information pertaining to each screen presented.

Figure 11-2 demonstrates the icon used to select the System Status screen.

Figure 11-2   *System Status Icon*

Figure 11-3 shows the System Status screen. This screen confirms whether Unity is currently running and enables you to shut it down. If you want to shut the system down from this screen, you must first select whether you want to send out a notification. If you want to notify active users of the system shutdown before shutting down the system, click the **Send Voice Message Before Terminating All Calls** radio button. This causes a message to be played on all active ports informing the caller that the system is going to disconnect them and shut down. If you would rather wait for all calls to complete before the system shuts down, click the **Wait Until All Calls Are Finished** radio button. After you have chosen one of the radio buttons, simply click the **Shut Down** icon. If the system is shut down, you can start the system up by clicking the **Start** button.

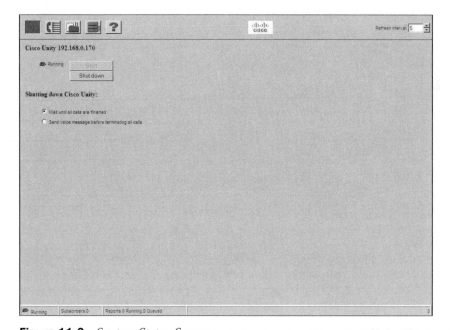

Figure 11-3   *System Status Screen*

Note   By default, the Status Monitor screen updates every 5 seconds. This can be changed by entering the desired value in the **Refresh Interval** field.

By clicking the Ports Status icon shown in Figure 11-4, you can view the current status of each port.

Figure 11-4   *Ports Status Icon*

Figure 11-5 shows the Ports Status screen. By default, this screen refreshes itself every 5 seconds. The screen displays the port number and extension of each port, the state of each port, and any available details. For example, the details portion might show which call handler is being played. From this screen, you can reset the port by highlighting the port and clicking the **Reset Port** button.

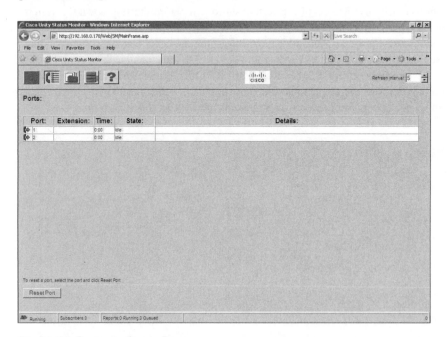

Figure 11-5   *Ports Status Screen*

> **Tip**   You can use the Status Monitor to check for ports that are locked up. By monitoring the **Time** field, you can easily see whether a port has been active for an inordinate amount of time.

By clicking the Reports Status icon shown in Figure 11-6, you can view the status of the reports that are queued.

Figure 11-7 shows the Reports Status screen. For each report that is generated, this screen displays the type of report and indicates the time it was queued, started, and finished.

Figure 11-6   *Reports Status Icon*

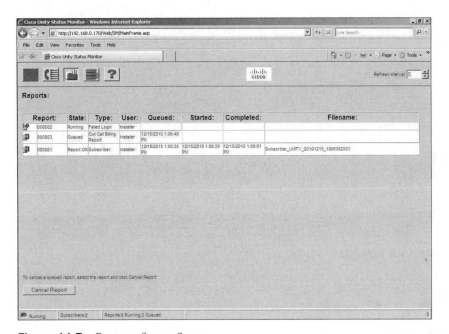

Figure 11-7   *Reports Status Screen*

Information about the disk drives in the system can be viewed by clicking the Disk Drive Status icon, shown in Figure 11-8.

Figure 11-8   *Disk Drive Status Icon*

Figure 11-9 shows the Disk Drive Status screen. This screen shows the total amount of space and the available space for each drive on the system.

When the Help icon in Figure 11-10 is clicked, a new window displays that contains online help for the Status Monitor (HTML) interface.

The Status Monitor enables you access to rudimentary tracking on Unity. A later section in this chapter explores more advanced utilities that offer more detailed monitoring capabilities, but exploring the reporting capabilities of Unity comes first.

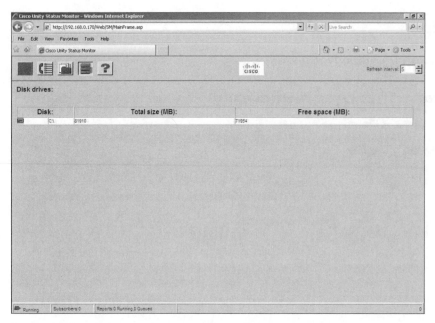

Figure 11-9   *Disk Drive Status Screen*

Figure 11-10   *Help Icon*

Reports

Unity offers the ability to run a number of reports for the SA interface. The reports are separated into two categories: subscriber and system.

As the name implies, subscriber reports deal with subscriber-related information, and the system reports deliver data related to system issues. This section explores the information that can be obtained from each report and describes the various times and reasons you might want to run certain reports.

Before various reports are explored, a few basic concepts regarding reports need to be addressed. One of the most common questions regarding reports is "How do you schedule reports to run?" The short answer is "You don't. All reports run from SA must be run interactively; that is, you must run them manually."

When generating reports, you have the choice of saving them as HTML pages or CSV files. Most often, reports are saved as CSV files so that the data can be imported into a spreadsheet application and manipulated. When the report is complete, it is delivered to the email account of the person who ran the report. In addition, reports can be found in the Commserver/Reports folder of the Unity server.

Some types of reports require a date range input. They use the data stored in the log files to create the report. When running these reports, you can only select a date within the number of days for which the Unity server was configured to store log files. Other reports do not require a date range, because they report on the system at the point in time when the report is run.

Subscriber Reports

Now we look at the subscriber reports. There are six different types of subscriber-related reports that can be run: Subscribers, Subscriber Message Activity, Distribution Lists, Failed Login, Transfer Call Billing, and OutCall Billing. Table 11-1 lists the benefit of each and the data that is provided for each report.

Each report is discussed in detail in the sections that follow.

Table 11-1   *Subscriber Reports*

Report Type	Benefit	Data Provided
Subscriber	Provides subscriber information	First/last name, Exchange alias, location, Windows domain, billing ID, class of service, extensions, inbox size
Subscriber Message Activity	Details voicemail activity	Date and time action was taken, source of the message, response action, number of new messages, sender's name, dual-tone multifrequency (DTMF), date and message arrival, dialout number, and dialout result
Distribution Lists	Provides a list of all distribution lists and the members of each list	List creation date, list alias, number of subscribers, distribution list name, owner, members (optional)
Failed Login	Lists failed logins	Subscriber, alias, caller ID, subscriber DTMF, date/time, maximum failures exceeded, and failure number
Transfer Call Billing	Reports calls that were transferred on behalf of subscribers	Name, extension, billing ID, date/time, dialed number, transfer result
OutCall Billing	Reports outgoing calls that were placed on behalf of subscribers	Name, extension, billing ID, time, dialed number, call time, and delivery device

Subscribers

This report provides the following information for selected subscribers: first and last name, Exchange alias, location, Windows domain, billing ID, class of service, extensions, and inbox size. This report can be saved as a CSV file and used to import this information into other programs.

Subscriber Message Activity

This report shows detailed information for a selected subscriber by providing useful data to help troubleshoot voicemail problems. This report determines whether the problems that subscribers encounter are self-created. The report shows each action that has taken place within a mailbox. When running this report, you must select a subscriber and a date and time range. The following details are provided for each message: date and time action was taken, source of the message, response action, number of new messages, sender's name and dual-tone multifrequency (DTMF), date and message arrival, dialout number, dialout result.

Distribution Lists

This report provides a list of all distribution lists and the members of each list. You can generate this report for all distribution lists or select a single list. The details in each report include list creation date, list alias, number of subscribers, distribution list name, owner, and members (optional). This report can be saved as a CSV file and used to import this information into other programs.

Failed Login

If subscribers are often locked out of their accounts, and they insist they have not entered an incorrect password, this report can be helpful. It lists all failed logins and the caller ID of the device from which the unsuccessful login occurred. This can help determine whether someone is trying to gain unauthorized access to the system. The information included in this report is subscriber, alias, caller ID, subscriber DTMF, date and time, maximum failures exceeded, and failure number.

The report also includes the following information for each failed SA login: username, computer, user domain, event ID, date and time, and failure number. This information can be used to determine whether someone is trying to gain unauthorized administrative access.

Transfer Call Billing

When Unity transfers a call from a subscriber account or call handler, the PBX simply records it as a call made by Unity. Some companies need to know which subscriber or call handler requested the transfer so that the call can be billed back to the proper department. This report shows all outbound calls made by Unity on behalf of a subscriber or call handler. The information in this report includes name, extension, billing ID, date, time, dialed number, and transfer result.

This report requires you to select an object for which to run this report. The valid object choices are subscriber, distribution list, billing ID, and call handler. You must also select a date and time range. You can generate this report on all subscribers at one time if you want.

OutCall Billing

This report is similar to the Transfer Call Billing reports except that it provides details on all message notification calls. The report includes the following information: name, extension, billing ID, time, dialed number, call time, and delivery device.

The report requires that you select an object in which to generate this report. The valid object choices are subscriber, distribution list, billing ID, and call handler. You must also select a date and time range. You can run this report on all subscribers at one time if you want.

System Reports

In addition to subscriber reports, you can generate seven system reports. These reports can be used to help monitor the status and health of the system. Table 11-2 provides a list and explanation of the various system reports. The sections that follow describe each system report in more detail.

Administrative Access

Use this report to track all changes made within SA. In a properly configured system, administrators are required to use their own login to access SA. This makes it possible to track the action of each administrator, which proves helpful when determining who made certain changes and why. The report includes the following information: administrative action, administrator's first and last name, administrator's Exchange alias, date and time of action, property changed, and new value.

Event Log

This report is generated from the information found in the Windows application log. You can choose to create the report based on all application data or only Unity data. The following information is included in this report: date and time, type of event, source component and computer, and message ID. Although information found in the report can be obtained from the Windows event viewer, the report format is sometimes more convenient, such as when you want to send the information to another person for review.

Port Usage

Use this report to determine whether the ports on the system are running close to capacity. A more advanced tool called Port Analyzer, which is discussed later in the chapter, can deliver more detail, but this report is helpful because it can be generated from any PC on the system. The information in this report includes port number, time, date range, number of calls, length of calls, average length of calls, percentage of ports used, average calls per hour, and average calls per day.

Table 11-2 *System Reports*

Type	Benefit	Details Provided
Administrative Access	Tracks administrative actions	Administrative action, administrator's first/last name, administrator's Exchange alias, date/time of action, property changed, new value
Event Log	Convenient to send to other reviewers	Date/time, type of event, source component, and computer message ID
Port Usage	Evaluates port capacity levels	Port number, time, date range, number of calls, length of calls, average length of calls, utilization, average calls per hour, and average calls per day
System Configuration	Provides server and software information	Serial number, Original Equipment Manufacturer (OEM) code, number of voice ports, languages, available license, total license, leading silence, trailing silence, minimum length of recording, domain name, hard drive space
Unresolved References	Identifies defunct subscriber accounts/associated call handlers	Handler name, handler ID, handler type, owner, and message recipient
Call Handler Traffic	Provides accessibility and exit strategies	Start time, total calls, key, DTMF ID, invalid DTMF ID, after-greeting action, and hang-ups
AMIS	Shows detailed information about each Audio Messaging Interchange Specification (AMIS) message sent or received	Date and time, importance, senders'/recipients' extension, target number, start time, duration, status, port number, total successes, and total failures

System Configuration

This report provides information about the server and software. The following data is included in this report: serial number, Original Equipment Manufacturer (OEM) code, number of voice ports, languages, version numbers, available license, total license, leading silence, trailing silence, minimum length of recording, domain name, hard drive space, and other system settings.

Print this report and keep it as a paper backup in case you are unable to access the system and need this information.

Unresolved References

All call handlers are associated with a subscriber account. If the subscriber account is deleted and the associated call handlers are not removed or reassociated with other subscribers, problems can occur. This report lists all call handlers that are associated with subscribers who no longer exist. The data in this report includes handler name, handler ID, handler type, owner, and message recipient.

Call Handler Traffic

After a system is up and running, check to see whether the call handlers you created are being used. The Call Handler Traffic Report shows the number of times a call handler was accessed and how calls exited the call handler. Use this information to determine whether the call handler flow is working as expected. The information detailed in this report is the total calls that enter a call handler over time and the total calls that exit a call handler for each exit method over time.

Audio Messaging Interchange Specification (AMIS) Out-Traffic and AMIS In-Traffic

If AMIS networking is implemented, inbound and outbound traffic reports can be generated. The reports show detailed information about each AMIS message sent or received. The following information is included in these reports: date and time, importance, senders'/recipients' extension, target number, start time, duration, status, port number, total successes, and total failures.

In total, 14 different reports can be generated; however, the process for running each report is similar. It would be a waste of paper and time to detail the steps required to run each report. However, the generic steps for generating a report are described in this section. Refer to these steps the first time or two you need to run a report, but you will soon find that the process is rather simple and intuitive:

Step 1. From within SA, select the type of report you want to run by selecting either **Reports > Subscribers** or **Reports > System. Reports > Subscribers** is used in this example.

Step 2. From the menu on the left side of the screen, shown in Figure 11-11, select the report you want to run. In this example, the Subscribers report is selected.

Step 3. After the type of report is selected, choose the criteria that the report will use to gather data. The specific criteria needed will vary based on the report. For example, you might need to select which subscribers this report should include.

Step 4. Choose the file format in which the report will be saved. CSV format is the most flexible because you can easily import this data into other programs.

Step 5. Depending on the type of report, you might need to enter a date and time range if required. Some reports rely on the system's log files to gather data. Because these logs are kept only for a specified number of days (which is configured on the **System > Configuration > Settings** page within SA), you might not be able to select a date that is beyond this range. By default, log files are stored for seven days.

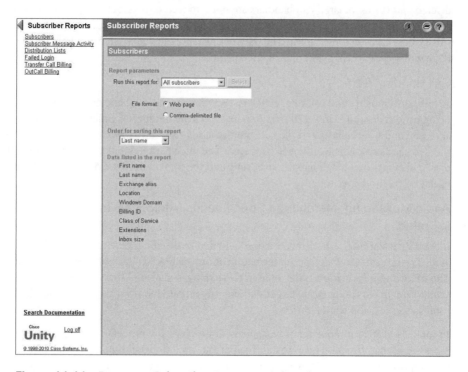

Figure 11-11   *Reports > Subscriber Reports > Subscribers*

Step 6.   After all the criteria is entered, click the **Run** icon, which is the icon of a man running, located in the title strip.

Step 7.   A window displays informing you that the report is queued.

Step 8.   After the report is complete, an email is sent to the person who started the report. You can check the status of all reports from within Status Monitor (HTML).

Warning   Running reports can create a draw on the system, so it is recommended that they are generated only during nonpeak hours.

Now that you understand the tools that are available through a browser, we look at some of the more advanced devices. These tools are often more powerful than those just discussed, so use caution when implementing them.

Using Advanced Tools

Over the years, many advanced tools have been developed that aid administrators and engineers in management and troubleshooting of Unity systems. These tools are divided into five major categories:

■   Administration

■   Audio management

■   Diagnostic

■   Reporting

■   Integration

To access these tools, click the **Cisco Unity Tools Depot** icon, which is on the desktop of the Unity server. This icon opens a common interface that enables you access to both the tools and some excellent help files for each. Figure 11-12 shows this application. There are two sections to this interface; the left side is a list of the tools, and the right side displays information about the highlighted tool.

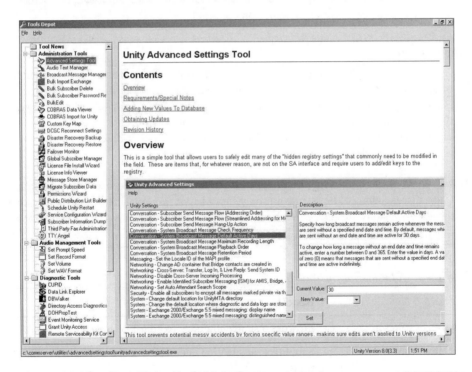

Figure 11-12   *Cisco Unity Tools Main Screen*

To run any tool in the Tools Depot, you must double-click it. If you click the tool just once, the online help displays in the right side of the window. By using online documentation that accompanies these tools, you should be able to understand how to use them. This chapter introduces you to the various tools and offers an overview of each one. Some of the tools are useful, and you will use them frequently, whereas you might never implement others. The high number of tools makes it impossible to provide a step-by-step guide on how to generate each one. However, as mentioned earlier, each of these tools includes an excellent online help screen for assistance.

Take a few minutes to see a quick review of what tools are available and how they function. This can help you save time when resolving issues because you will know what tools are at your disposal.

Note The tools available to you vary depending on the version of Unity employed. If any of the listed tools are not available on your system, they can be downloaded from http://www.ciscounitytools.com. However, be certain to read the "Requirements/Special Notes" section of the online help for each of these tools, which lists the required version of Unity for that specific tool.

Also, note that many of these tools must be run on-box (on the Unity server), whereas others are recommended to be run off-box (on a system other than the Unity server). Because these recommendations and requirements change as the utilities are improved, check the help file for the current recommendations on each tool.

Administration Tools

As of this writing, there were more than 25 administration-based tools. The exact number of tools that are available varies slightly depending on the version of Unity. These tools assist in tasks ranging from common administration to very specialized tasks. Because they are listed in alphabetical order in the Tools Depot, the tools are presented in the same order here. Table 11-3 lists administration tools with a brief description. The sections that follow describe each of the tools in more detail.

Note Some of these tools might not appear in the Tools Depot because of the version of Unity that is running. This is true not only for older versions of Unity but also for some of the newer versions. In some cases, tools have been removed or moved in later versions of Unity.

Table 11-3 *Administration Tools*

Tool	Benefit
Advanced Settings	Provides a simple interface to adjust settings
Audio Text Manager	Simplifies the creation and management of Audio Text applications
Broadcast Manager	Enables an administrator to manage broadcast messages
Bulk Import Exchange	Provides the ability to import a large number of users

Table 11-3   *Administration Tools*

Tool	Benefit
Bulk Subscriber Delete	Provides the ability to remove a large number of subscribers
Bulk Password Reset	Collectively resets passwords for multiple users
Bulk Edit	Collectively allows you to edit the attributes of a large number of subscribers or call handlers
COBRAS Data Viewer	Enables backup for subscribers, call handlers, PTLs, and schedules on Unity
COBRAS Import for Unity	Enables import data of information previously exported using the Consolidated Object Backup and Restore Application Suite (COBRAS) Export tool
Custom Key Map	Enables an administrator to edit a custom keypad mapping conversation
DCGC Reconnect Settings	Enables a user to view or change current settings for the Domain Controller (DC) or Global Catalog (GC) server reconnect feature
Disaster Recovery Backup	Provides backup and migration of all Unity-specific data
Disaster Recovery Restore	Restores backup data
Failover Monitor	Enables a user to view and force failover configuration
Global Subscriber Monitor	Enables administrators to access subscribers through a single interface regardless of server location
License File Install Wizard	Installs license files
License Information Viewer	Shows the current license on the server
Message Store Manager	Enables administrators to schedule various routine tasks in a single interface
Migrate Subscriber Data	Enables the migration of various data
Permissions Wizard	Sets the appropriate permission on accounts used by Unity
Public Distribution List Builder	Enables administrators to add subscribers to new or existing PDLs
Schedule Unity Restart	Enables system rebooting at a designated time
Service Configuration Wizard	Associates accounts to certain Unity processes
Subscriber Information Dump	Enables an administrator to create CSV files
Third Party Fax Administrator	Configures Unity to integrate with a fax server
TTY Angel	Creates WAV files

Advanced Settings Tools

A number of Unity's settings are stored in the Windows Registry and are hidden. Issues arise from time to time that require adjustments to these settings. As you might know, editing Registry settings on any Windows system can result in disaster if done incorrectly. The Advanced Settings tool offers a friendly, safe interface from which to adjust these settings. Tasks you can accomplish using this tool are varied, but a few examples follow:

- Enable Reply to All warning.

- Set maximum recording time higher than 20 minutes.

- Check to see whether the mailbox is full before taking messages.

Audio Text Manager

The main purpose of this tool is to simplify the task of creating and managing Audio Text applications. Audio Text Manager can also be used for many common administrative tasks and as a troubleshooting aid. From within this tool, you can manage call handlers and subscribers. Most tasks that you commonly perform from within SA can be achieved here.

This interface enables you to see a tree view of the call handlers and subscribers, illustrating how the call handlers and subscribers are connected through one-key dialing. A grid view is also available from within this interface, which displays a list of call handlers and subscribers.

Many administrators find this tool a more efficient interface for managing existing subscribers and call handlers. Although many of the common tasks accomplished in SA can be performed here, certain tasks cannot. This is easily remedied because the interface has a hyperlink that takes you directly to the selected object within SA when you need to complete such a task.

This tool can save hours of administration time after you fully understand its capabilities. If you use only one of the advanced tools, make it this one. However, as you explore the rest of the tools, I am sure you will find many others to be useful.

Broadcast Message Monitor

This tool enables you to manage broadcast messages. It enables you to view messages that are currently configured and the users that have listened to the messages. You can also use this tool to send and delete broadcast messages.

Bulk Import Exchange

This tool is also called Cisco Unity Bulk Import tool, which is discussed in Chapter 8, "User/Subscriber Reference." This tool enables you to import a large number of users from either a CSV file or an existing Exchange server. Refer to Chapter 8 for more information on this tool.

Bulk Subscriber Delete

The Bulk Subscriber Delete tool enables you to easily remove a large number of subscribers at one time. This tool is significantly faster than using SA and deleting subscribers individually.

A wizard enables you to remove only the subscriber from Unity and leave the directory and mailstore account, or remove the directory and mailstore account and the subscriber information.

Bulk Password Reset

The Bulk Password Reset tool enables you to reset passwords for a large number of users. The interface is similar to that of Bulk Edit. This tool enables you to assign trivial passwords even if it is prohibited in the Unity configuration.

Bulk Edit

Bulk Edit enables you to edit the attributes of a large number of subscribers or call handlers at one time.

Note   I know a person who went to each subscriber's account and manually changed the transfer rule to ring the phone first. She used this method because her integrator used the default subscriber template, which sent all subscriber calls directly to voicemail without ringing the phone first. It took more than 3 days to accomplish this task using SA. When I showed her how to accomplish this task in a matter of minutes using the Bulk Edit tool, she was pleased but also somewhat frustrated with her integrator.

This tool is fairly intuitive and enables you to change many attributes ranging from transfer settings to editing and adding alternate extensions. After using it, the tool will soon become one of your favorites. Keep in mind that it saves you time even if you only need to change the same attributes on a few objects. The tool enables you to complete tasks in a number of minutes versus hours.

COBRAS Data Viewer

Consolidated Object Backup and Restore Application Suite (COBRAS) is a set of utilities that enables you to back up all the subscribers, call handlers, PDLs, and schedules on Unity. It is often used when upgrading to a different version of Unity or when migrating to Unity Connection. The COBRAS data viewer is a tool that enables TAC or integration engineers to view the data in the COBRAS export file. It is most often used when troubleshooting import issues.

COBRAS Import for Unity

This tool enables import data that was exported using the COBRAS export tool. There are approximately 20 screens that must be configured when this tool is implemented. It is important that care is taken when using this tool to ensure that the import operation is successful. This tool is typically used by system engineer-level individuals.

Custom Key Map

The Custom Key Map tool enbles you to edit the custom keypad mapping conversation. Custom keypad maps enable you to chart voicemail functions to the keys you desire. For example, if you want users to press 0 to play messages, it can be accomplished with this tool. It also enables you to change the order in which options are presented to users. For example, "Hear new messages" is normally the first option callers hear at the main menu. It can be changed so that it is the third option they are offered.

DCGC Reconnect Settings

The tool enables you to view or change the current settings for Unity's Domain Controller (DC) and Global Catalog (GC) server reconnect feature. It is recommended that you leave this setting set to the default.

Disaster Recovery Backup

Often referred to as DIRT, or DIsaster Recovery Tool, this tool can back up all Unity-specific data. The tool can also be used for migration. The data is backed up from one server and restored to another; however, the Unity versions must be the same on both servers. Data is restored using the next tool, Disaster Recovery Restore. Current versions of the Disaster Recovery Backup tool can also back up subscriber messages. This should be done only in small voicemail-only environments, because it can require a large amount of disk space for the backup.

Note   It is recommended that all deployments have an approved backup solution for their primary means of backup.

Disaster Recovery Restore

This tool is used to restore the backup data that was made using the Disaster Recovery Backup tool. To do this, Unity must first be installed and running on the server. Remember that these two tools only back up Unity-specific data and not the entire system.

Failover Monitor

Failover Monitor enables you to view the current status of the failover configuration. You can also use this tool to force failover. This is useful if you want to perform maintenance on the primary server.

Global Subscriber Manager

Managing subscribers can become difficult in larger environments where there is more than one Unity server or a large number of subscribers. The Global Subscriber Manager tool helps make managing such environments easier. This interface enables administrators to access subscribers through a single interface, regardless of the server on which they are located. Imagine having five servers, each with 500 subscribers. Keeping track of which server each subscriber is on could be quite an undertaking. This interface enables you to search all servers for the subscriber you want to manage. There are two methods to find subscribers. The first approach is by starting the tool where a tree view displays. The servers and dialing domains in the Unity network display on the left side of the screen. Click a server, and you can display the subscribers of that server on the right side of the screen. Click the subscriber you want to manage, and the SA interface opens and brings you directly to this subscriber. The second method enables you to search for a subscriber by pressing F2. A search criteria box displays, which enables you to search based on any of the following:

- Alias
- Display name
- First name
- Last name
- DTMF ID
- Subscriber type

Using this interface, you can also accomplish more advanced tasks such as move, delete, or import subscribers. The Import feature of this utility enables you to import AD users. Although useful, if you need to import a large number of users, the Cisco Unity Bulk Import utility is a more efficient tool. The Delete feature of this tool assists in cleanly removing a subscriber. When you right-click a subscriber, a menu displays and one of the options is Delete. Click this and a Delete Object Wizard walks you through cleanly removing the user. You can also move a subscriber from one Unity server to another, as long as the servers are on the same dialing domain. To do this, right-click the subscriber, and choose Move from the menu that displays. A Move Wizard walks you through the move process. The move, delete, and import features require at least Unity 4.0 (1).

License File Install Wizard

Each Unity system must have a license file properly installed. This license file determines how many subscribers and for what features the system is licensed. The license is loaded during the installation of the system. This utility can be used when adding new licenses. When you run this utility, you are given the opportunity to select a license file(s). Make sure that you select all license files; this includes any that might have been previously loaded on the system.

License Info Viewer

The License Info Viewer tool shows the current license on the server. This tool is used with Unity 4.x and later. The information includes

- Serial number

- Version number

- Number of licensed ports

- Languages

- Subscribers

- Networking features

To retrieve similar information in Unity 3.x and 2.x, use the Key Dump tool.

Message Store Manager

Many routine tasks can consume an administrator's valuable time. This utility enables an administrator to perform a number of these tasks within a single interface. In addition, after it is configured, these tasks can be set to run automatically using Microsoft's Tasks Scheduler. The tasks that can be performed using this tool are as follows:

- Detailed CSV file of subscribers accounts.

- Move messages.

- Delete messages.

- Restore messages that are in the Deleted Items folder.

- Set mailbox limits.

- Hide mailbox from address list.

Migrate Subscriber Data

This tool enables you to associate an existing subscriber account to a mailstore account. This is useful when migrating from voicemail only to unified messaging. It can also be used to migrate bridge subscribers to Exchange subscribers.

Permissions Wizard

The Permissions Wizard is run during the installation of Unity and is used to set the appropriate permission on the accounts used by Unity. Normally this does not need to be run again; however, it has been known to resolve issues created by someone changing the rights on accounts after the installation. Before running this tool, make sure that the AD users, which are used by Unity, already exist. These accounts include

- Installation

- Administration

- Directory service

- Message store accounts

After these accounts are created, the Permissions Wizard walks you through, selecting each account for the proper role and assigning the proper permissions to the accounts.

Public Distribution List Builder

This tool enables an administrator to quickly add subscribers to new or existing public distribution lists (PDL). You can search for subscribers based on

- Class of service (CoS)

- Extension range

- CSV file

- Home mail server

- Switch with which they are associated

You can select all the subscribers who match certain criteria or pick them from the list that displays.

Schedule Unity Restart

As with most systems running Windows, occasionally the system needs to be rebooted. There never seems to be an opportune time. If you are fortunate, the system will need to be rebooted eventually but not immediately. If so, the Schedule Unity Restart tool comes in handy. Using this tool, Unity can be set to reboot at a given time. You can configure it to reboot the server, restart Unity, or restart only certain Unity services.

Note   Although highly unlikely, it is always possible that a server will not come back up after a reboot. For this reason, it is always recommended that a complete backup be done on a regular basis.

Service Configuration Wizard

This wizard runs during the installation process. Its function is to associate accounts to certain Unity processes. These are the same accounts to which the Permissions Wizard assigns rights. If someone changes or deletes these accounts, it might become necessary to run this wizard again.

Subscriber Information Dump

This tool enables an administrator to create a CSV file that contains many subscriber attributes. The attributes sent to the CSV range from the subscriber alias to the transfer type. Most of the subscriber attributes you can see within SA can be exported using this tool.

Third Party Fax Administration

Unity has the capability to work with a number of fax servers that integrate with Exchange. This tool is used to configure Unity to integrate with the fax server.

TTY Angel

The TTY Angel tool can be used to create WAV files that can be played to TTY devices. Type in text and the tool converts it to a WAV file. This produces a WAV file that should be understood by any TTY device that supports the Baudot protocol.

Audio Management Tools

Because Unity is responsible for handling many audio-related tasks, such as recording messages and greetings, it might be necessary to modify some of its audio handling functions. Table 11-4 lists the audio-related tools with a brief description of benefits. The sections that follow discuss the audio-related tools that are included within the Tools Depot in greater detail.

Set Prompt Speed

From time to time, customers might request that the Unity prompts either slow down or speed up. This tool enables you to change the speed of Unity prompts. Make sure to back up existing prompts before using this tool.

Set Record Format

This utility enables you to change the default codec that Unity uses to record all recordings. Any codec that is installed on the server can be selected. The default for record formats is 8-kb MuLaw. Remember that the format selected is used for *all* recordings, so be sure that you are happy with the quality before selecting it.

Set Volume

In Unity 3.1(1), Automatic Gain Control (AGC) was introduced. It is used to normalize the volume of all recordings. However, prior to 3.1(1), depending upon the volume of the incoming stream, there were issues with varying volume levels. If you have upgraded from a version earlier than 3.1, it is possible that some of the older recordings will be at varying volume levels. This tool enables you to quickly set all recordings at the same vol-

Table 11-4   *Audio Management Tools*

Tool	Benefit
Set Prompt Speed	Allows an administrator to change the speed of Unity prompts
Set Record Format	Allows an administrator to change Unity's default codec for recordings
Set Volume	Allows an administrator to set all recordings at the same volume level
Set WAV Format	Allows an administrator to convert all existing greetings to a new codec

ume level. By default, –26 dB is used, and it is strongly recommended that you use the default. Running the conversion process several times can cause the recordings to become distorted.

Set WAV Format

As mentioned earlier, Unity can use G.711 or G.729 codecs for recording. If the codec is changed, you might want to convert all existing greetings to the new codec. The Set WAV Format tool enables you to do this. Select the greeting you want to change and the desired codec. This tool offers you the option of saving the original greetings to a backup location. You are encouraged to do this.

Note Some people argue that converting all greetings to the same codec is not necessary because Unity has the capability to transcode between G.711 and G.729 on-the-fly. Keep in mind, however, that each time Unity must transcode, it takes CPU cycles away from other processes.

Diagnostic Tools

As with any system, there are times when you need to troubleshoot issues occurring within the Unity system. Troubleshooting is more of an art than a science, and often the hardest part of fixing a problem is finding the problem, or more accurately, the cause of the problem. The Tools Depot includes some excellent diagnostic tools that assist in many troubleshooting exercises. The following are the diagnostic tools available from within the Tools Depot. Table 11-5 lists the diagnostic tools with a brief description of benefits. The sections that follow discuss the diagnostic tools that are included within the Tools Depot in greater detail.

CUPID

Cisco Unified Performance Information and Diagnostics (CUPID) is used to monitor Windows performance counters. The data that is collected is written to a CSV file that can be imported later into a spreadsheet for analysis. Although the information you obtain using this utility is the same information that you see in the performance monitor, this tool has many added benefits. An XML configuration file is used to determine what counters this tool reads. The counters are then read every few seconds based on the time interval you define. You can define the maximum size of a log file. After reaching the defined size, a new file is created and automatically named based on the time and date.

DataLink Explorer

The data stored in Unity is in an SQL database. The Cisco Unity DataLink Explorer is an interface that enables you to view the tables in the database and offers definitions for the various tables and columns. This tool can be helpful when trying to determine the exact purpose of an object.

Table 11-5   *Diagnostic Tools*

Tool	Benefit
Cisco Unified Performance Information and Diagnostics (CUPID)	Monitors Windows performance counters
DataLink Explorer	Enables an administrator to view tables in a database and offers definitions for tables and columns
DBWalker	Checks for errors and inconsistencies
Directory Access Diagnostics	Tests to determine the proper rights to import by users
DOH Prop Test	Usually only accessible by a TAC engineer
Event Monitoring Service	Monitors event logs
Grant Unity Access	Reassociates the AD account to the subscriber
Remote Serviceability Kit Configuration	Enables an administrator to add Simple Network Management Protocol (SNMP), syslog, and Cisco Discovery Protocol (CDP) support to a Unity server
SysCheck	Tests to ensure that the Unity account has the proper rights to create Unity subscribers
Unity Diagnostic Tool (UDT)	Enables an administrator to enable traces and gather log files
Unity Diagnostic Viewer	Analyzes the log's output from UDT

DBWalker

DBWalker can "walk" through the database and check for errors and inconsistencies. You can configure the tool to check for errors or to fix certain errors automatically when found. It is a good idea not to allow the automatic correction of errors on the first run so that you can explore them and determine how they occurred. After the tool runs, it creates a report that shows the results and lists all errors and warnings found. Run this tool before backing up the data in preparation for an upgrade.

Directory Access Diagnostics

This tool, which is also known as DAD, is used when you experience errors when trying to import AD users into Unity. Errors can occur when the account used for services to enable importing does not have the proper rights. DAD is used as a test to determine whether the proper rights have been granted to allow the import to the user.

DOH Prop Test

Because this tool is so powerful, it is password protected. If a Technical Assistance Center (TAC) engineer needs you to access this tool, he will supply the password. This tool can be used without a password, but it will operate in a read-only mode.

Warning   This is a low-level database editor and requires the user to have an extensive understanding of the database structure.

Event Monitoring Service

When certain events occur, an entry is written to the Windows event log. You can configure the Event Monitoring Service to monitor the event log and alert an administrator when specified events occur.

Grant Unity Access

When individuals log in to SA, the AD account they use to log in to the domain determines what rights they will have within SA. This account is associated with a subscriber account that has administrator access in Unity. If the AD account has somehow lost this association, the Grant Unity Access tool is used to reassociate the AD account to the subscriber. This is a command-line utility that is run from a DOS prompt. The following is the syntax used and shows an example for each:

- GrantUnityAccess–u <Domain>\<UserAlias> -s <UnitySubscriberAlias>

- GrantUnityAccess–u DTW\Jsmith -s Jsmith

This example would associate the AD account Jsmith in the DTW domain to the Unity subscriber Jsmith.

This utility is also used to associate multiple AD accounts with a single Unity subscriber.

Remote Serviceability Kit Configuration

This tool enables you to add Simple Network Management Protocol (SNMP), syslog, and Cisco Discovery Protocol (CDP) support to a Unity server.

SysCheck

Run the SysCheck tool to test to see whether the account Unity is using has the proper rights to create Unity subscribers. This tool can also check to see whether Unity is properly configured to communicate with the mailstore. This tool reports any issues it finds and offers possible resolutions.

Unity Diagnostic Tool (UDT)

When troubleshooting problems within a Unity environment, it might be necessary to enable trace files. Trace files record detailed information of each Unity action. The exact information logged is based on the traces that you enable. Typically, you enable traces on the request of a TAC engineer. This tool enables you to allow traces and gather log files. This information is sent to a TAC engineer for analysis; however, you can also use the Unity Diagnostic Viewer to view this information.

Unity Diagnostic Viewer (UDV)

This tool is used to analyze the log's output from the Unity Diagnostic Tool. It enables you to filter out unneeded data and view only what is important to you.

Note Because filtering large amounts of data can burden the processor, it is recommended that you load and run this tool on a PC other than the Unity server.

Reporting Tools

After the system is up and running, it is important to monitor the system. As you learned earlier, Unity has a number of reports that can be run from within the SA. As good as these reports are, sometimes more detailed information is needed. The Tools Depot includes a number of tools that are able to offer more detailed information. Table 11-6 lists the reporting tools, with a brief description of benefits. The sections that follow discuss the reporting tools that are included within the Tools Depot in greater detail.

- Bridge Traffic Analyzer
- Gather Unity System Info
- Port Usage Analyzer

Table 11-6 *Reporting Tools*

Tool	Benefit
Bridge Traffic Analyzer	Provides the ability to monitor the amount of traffic being sent through the server
Gather Unity System Information	Facilitates the gathering of information for TAC
Port Usage Analyzer	Delivers detailed information about port usage reports

Bridge Traffic Analyzer

If you have implemented bridge networking, you want the ability to monitor the amount of traffic that is being sent through the server. The Bridge Traffic Analyzer does just that. This tool has the capability to produce reports on port usage, the number of messages passing through message queues, the length of time messages took to arrive, the number of failures, the source server, and the number of messages delivered.

Gather Unity System Information

When a TAC engineer is assisting you in troubleshooting an issue, certain information needs to be sent to the TAC engineer. This tool facilitates the gathering of this information by creating a cabinet (CAB) file that contains the following information about the system:

- Application and system event logs (5 days)
- System information
- All services, startup options, and associated accounts

Port Usage Analyzer

As mentioned in the Reports section of this chapter, there is a tool that can deliver more detailed information about port usage reports. The Port Usage Analyzer is that tool. This tool can deliver information on the following:

- **Port availability:** This information can be displayed by the day or hour.

- **Call distribution:** This displays the types of calls that each port handled.

- **Port time use:** This displays the amount of time that each port spent handling each type of call.

- **Call traffic:** This displays the number of each type of call that each port handled for each minute of the day. This report can display by the day or by the hour.

Switch Integration Tools

On occasion, it might be necessary to view or edit the way the switch is communicating with Unity. The Switch Integration tools, available with the Tools Depot, are listed in Table 11-7, with a brief description of benefits. The sections that follow discuss the Switch Integration tools in greater detail.

Table 11-7   *Switch Integration Tools*

Tool	Benefit
Integration Monitor	Shows details for call from traditional phone systems
Port Status Monitor	Enables user to view all events taking place on any port in real time
Telephone Integration Manager	Enables user to edit integration settings

Integration Monitor

The Integration Monitor tool can only be used with Simplified Message Desk Interface (SMDI) and DTMF integration. It shows details for calls from traditional phone systems. This tool displays the time, packet number, port number, origin, reason, trunk number, calling number, and forwarding extension. This tool does not work in a Communications Manager integration.

Port Status Monitor

The Port Status Monitor enables you to view all events taking place on any port in real time, and to create a log of these events. You can select any or all ports. This tool is useful when troubleshooting call flow issues. You can view what keys are pressed and see whether the expected action occurs.

Telephone Integration Manager

This tool enables you to edit the integration settings configured during the installation of the system and add additional integrations. This tool is often referred to as Unity Telephony Integration Manager (UTIM) and was covered in great detail earlier in this book. Refer to Chapter 7, "Unity Predeployment Tasks," for more details on this tool.

Using Unity Connection Tools

Unity Connection administration offers web-based access to tools and reports. The tools are available from within the Cisco Unity Connection Administration web page, whereas the reports are accessible through the Cisco Unity Connection Serviceability web page. We start by looking at the tools found in Cisco Unity Connection Administration.

Unity Connection Administration Tools

If you scroll down to the bottom of the list on the left side of the Unity Connection Administration web page, you will find a heading labeled Tools. If you are familiar with Unity, you can expect to find tools similar to those found in the Cisco Unity Tools Depot. However, that is not what you will find. You will find seven "tools" available to you. Table 11-8 lists the tools with a brief description of benefits. The sections that follow discuss the administration tools in greater detail.

Table 11-8   *Unity Connection Administration Tools*

Tool	Benefit
Task Management	Provides management options and data to review maintenance tasks
Bulk Administration Tool	Used to create, delete, and update multiple users, contacts, distribution lists, and distribution lists/members
Custom Keypad Mapping	Enables an administrator to configure a custom keypad mapping conversation
Migration Utilities	Used when migrating from Unity to Unity Connection
Grammar Statistics	Shows the number of object names that Unity Connection has built
SMTP Address Search	Enables an administrator to search Unity Connection for a Simple Mail Transfer Protocol (SMTP) address and locates the object it is associated with
Show Dependencies	Enables the administrator to identify objects that are connected (dependent) to other objects

Task Management

Unity Connection has a number of system maintenance tasks. Many of these are set to run automatically. To view the tasks that are predefined, navigate to **Tools > Task Management**. The number of tasks you see depends on the version of Unity Connection you are running. To view the details of any task, click the name of the task. Figure 11-13 shows the screen that appears when **Check System Configuration** is selected. Although it is possible to change the schedule of these tasks, in most cases, it is not required. The Task Execution Results section lists the start and end times of each task that was run. You can view results of the task by clicking the start time or end time. The icon in the Severity column alerts you to the type of results the task produced. There are three types of alerts:

- Error (**X** in a red circle)

- Warning (**!** In a yellow triangle)

- Information (**i** in a gray circle)

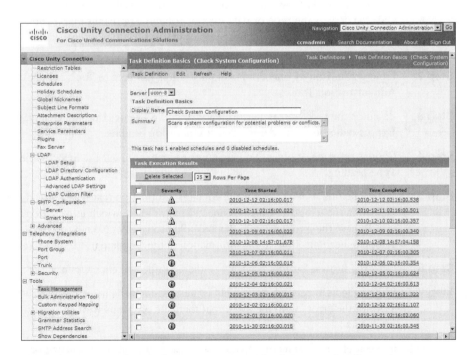

Figure 11-13   *Tools> Task Management > Check System Configuration.*

Bulk Administration Tool

The Bulk Administration tool found in Unity Connection is similar to that found in Communications Manager, but it is not the same tool. It is used for the create, delete and update:

■   Users

■   Contact

■   Distribution list

■   Distribution list members

The steps to add users using this tool were covered in Chapter 8. The steps are similar for any of the tasks that can be accomplished by using this tool. The following are general steps that can be applied to any Bulk Administration tools task:

Step 1.   Create a CSV file. The CSV file contains the information that will be added to the system, such as usernames, extensions, and so on. The top row of the CSV file defines the type of data for that column. For details on creating CSV, search "Constructing the Input CSV Files in Cisco Unity Connection" at Cisco.com.

Step 2.   From within Unity Connection Administration, navigate to **Tools > Bulk Administration Tool.**

Step 3.   Based on the task you are performing, select the **Create, Update, Delete**, or **Export** radio button under the **Select Operation** heading.

Step 4.   Choose the type of object you are going to manage under the **Select Object Type** heading.

Step 5.   When creating users, the CSV file contains information that might already be defined in the template. Unity Connection must know which information to use. To have the information in the CSV file used, select **No** next to the **User Template** heading. To have the information in the template used, select **Yes.**

Step 6.   Click the **Browse** button. Navigate to the CSV file and click **Open.**

Step 7.   If the **Failed Objects Filename** field is present, enter the name that will be used for the error log in the event that there are problems with the creation of objects.

Although this is a useful tool, sometimes you might just want to change a setting on a number of objects and not want to have to deal with creating a CSV file. If you are familiar with Unity, you might have heard of the Bulk Edit tool. Unity Connection offers the same function, but it is built into Unity Connection Administration. To edit multiple objects, first navigate to the list that displays the objects. For example, if you want to edit multiple users, navigate to **Users > Users.** Select the check box next to each object you want to edit, and click the **Bulk Edit** button. Now make the desired changes the same way as when managing a single object and click **Submit.** At the top of the page, there is a link to task management from which you can access the log by clicking the **Time Completed** link.

Custom Keypad Mapping

The Custom Keypad Mapping tool enables you to configure the custom keypad mapping conversation. A custom keypad map enables you to chart voicemail functions to the keys you desire. For example, if you want users to press 0 to delete messages, you could do that using this tool. You can configure up to six different keypad maps. For custom keypad maps to be of use, they must be assigned to a user. To assign a custom keypad map, navigate to **Edit > Phone Menu** of the desired user, and select the custom keypad map from the **Touchtone Conversation dropdown list**.

The configuration of the custom keypad map is fairly straightforward. First navigate to **Tools > Custom Keypad Mapping**. Choose one of the six custom keypad mappings. A screen similar to Figure 11-14 appears.

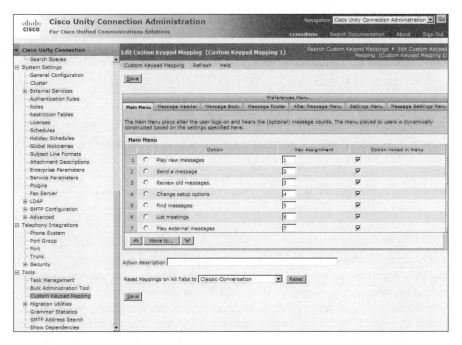

Figure 11-14   *Tools > Custom Keypad Mapping > Custom Keypad Mapping 1.*

There are eight sets of options that can be configured. Each is active based on the location of the user in the conversation. For example, the **Main Menu** is active when the user first logs in, while the **Message Body** options are available while the message is being played. The following steps describe how to configure a custom keypad mapping:

Step 1.   From within Unity Connection Administration, select **Tools > Custom Keypad Mapping**.

Step 2.   Select the custom keypad mapping you want to configure.

Step 3.   To configure the options, select the tab for the set of options you want to configure. For example, to configure the **Main Menu** options, click the **Main Menu** tab. The options that are available are listed.

Step 4.   To change the associated key, enter the desired key in the **Key Assignment** field. To have the key spoken in the menu, select the **Option Voiced in Menu** check box.

Step 5.   The options are played in the order that they appear. To change the order in which they are played, select the radio button next to the option and use the Up and Down Arrows to move it. You can also use the **Move To** button to move it above or below a specified option. This can save time when moving an option several places up or down.

Step 6.   To set the key mappings to the same mapping of an existing conversation, select the desired conversation from the **Reset Mappings on All Tabs To** drop-down list.

Step 7.   Click **Save**.

Step 8.   Repeat these steps for each set of options you want to configure.

Migration Utilities

There are two migration utilities found under **Tools > Migration Utilities**. They are Migrate Users and Migrate Messages. These utilities can be used when migrating from Unity to UC. However, Cisco recommends that Cisco Object Backup and Restore Application Suite (COBRAS) be used instead of these tools. This topic is not discussed in any further depth because migrating is beyond the scope of this book.

Grammar Statistics

The Grammar Statistics tool shows the number of object names that Unity Connection has built. Each time an object is added, Unity Connection adds the name to its grammar so that the name can be used with voice recognition functions. This page also shows whether there are updates pending or whether the grammar is currently being rebuilt. The grammar is updated when an object is added to the system unless a large numbers of objects are being added (more than five in a minute or through the Bulk Administration tool). When this occurs, Unity Connection waits 10 minutes after the objects have been added and then adds them to the grammar. The date and time next to each type of object display the last time the grammar for that object was updated.

The Rebuild Grammars button enables you to force a rebuild of the grammar. Because the grammar is updated when an object is added, this feature is only used if the voice recognition update schedule is changed or if you do not want to wait 10 minutes for the grammar to update after adding a user through the Bulk Administration tool.

SMTP Address Search

The STMP Address Search tool is a simple tool that enables you to search Unity Connection for an STMP address and locate the object it is associated with. To use this search feature, navigate to **Tools > SMTP Address Search**, enter the STMP address in the field, and click **Find**. A list of objects with that address appears. You can navigate to that object by clicking the name of the object.

Show Dependencies

Dependencies are objects that are connected (dependent) to other objects. For example, the dependencies of a user can be the call handlers he owns. Before removing an object, it is good to see whether there are any dependencies. This is accomplished by navigating to the list that displays the objects. For example, if you want to see the dependencies for a user, navigate to **Users > Users**. Now select the check box next to each object you want to check the dependencies for and click the **Show Dependencies** button. A list of dependences is displayed.

The **Show Dependencies** option under **Tools** enables you to view the most recent dependencies search. You cannot search for dependencies from this page; you can only view the results for the most recent search.

To view the results for the most recent dependencies search, navigate to **Tools > Show Dependencies** and click the **Display Previous Result** button.

Unity Connection Reports

If you take a close look at the Unity Connection Administration interface, you might notice that there doesn't seem to be any mention of reports. That is because reports are generated from Unity Connection Serviceability. This section explores each of the 19 reports that can be run.

Before you can run any of the reports, you need to log in to Unity Connection Serviceability and access the Reports page. The following steps show how this is accomplished:

Step 1. From within Unity Connection Administration, select **Cisco Unity Connection Serviceability** from the **Navigation** drop-down list in the upper-right corner of the page.

Step 2. A screen similar to Figure 11-15 should appear. Select **Tools > Reports**.

Note   If you are prompted for a username and password when attempting to access Unity Connection Serviceability, it is because the user you are currently logged in as does not have access to Unity Connection Serviceability. Log in as a user that has the system administrator role assigned.

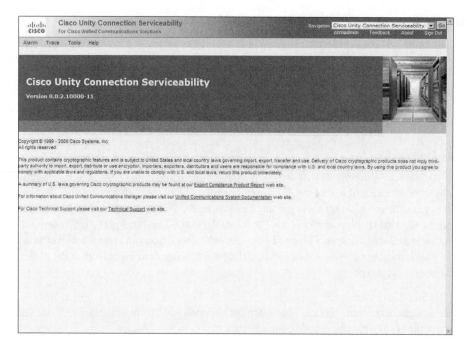

Figure 11-15 *Cisco Unity Connection Serviceability*

Step 3.   A list of reports appears. You can select the report you want to run.

Before various reports are explored, a few basic concepts regarding reports need to be covered. One of the most common questions regarding reports is "How do you schedule reports to run?" The short answer is "You don't. All reports run from Unity Connection Administration must be run interactively, that is, you must generate them manually."

When running reports, you have the choice of saving them as a web page, CSV file, or PDF file. Most often, reports are saved as CSV files so that the data can be imported into a spreadsheet application and manipulated. When the report is complete, it will appear in the web browser if you choose **Web Page** as the file format. If you choose **Comma-delimited File** or **PDF File** as the file format, a window appears that allows you to save the report to your computer.

Some types of reports require a date range input. They use the information stored in the log files to create the report. When running these reports, you can only select a date within the number of days for which the Unity Connection server was configured to store log files. Other reports do not require a date range because they report on the system at the point in time when the report is run.

The steps for running a report are pretty much the same for all reports. First navigate to the Reports page as described in the previous set of steps. Then select the type of report you want to generate and select a date range, if required. Then click the **Generate Report** button.

Note   For some reports, you can select which objects you want to run the report for. For example, the Phone Interface Failed Logon report allows you to select which users you want to run the report against.

Table 11-9 lists 19 Unity Connection reports that you can generate. The sections that follow provide more detailed information.

Table 11-9   *Unity Connection Reports*

Report	Benefit
Phone Interface Failed Logon Report	Lists all failed logins and the caller ID of the device
Users Report	Provides the first/last name, alias, location, home mail server, billing ID, class of service, extensions, whether the account is locked, and whether personal call transfers rules are enabled
Message Traffic Report	Lists totals for voice, fax, email, and so on
Port Activity Report	Determines the activity level of the ports in the system
Mailbox Store Report	Displays data regarding the mail store
Dial Plan Report	Displays a list of search spaces and partitions configured on Unity Connection
Dial Search Scope Report	Provides a list of all users and their extensions for all partitions
User Phone Login & MWI Report	Displays data regarding phone logins
User Message Activity Report	Provides data to assist in troubleshooting voicemail problems
Distribution List Report	Provides a list of all distribution lists and their members
User Lockout Report	Displays data for blocked user accounts
Unused Voicemail Accounts Report	Displays accounts that have not been accessed
Transfer Call Billing Report	Provides data for billing purposes
Outcall Billing Report	Reports on calls such as message notification for billing purposes
Outcall Billing Summary Report	Displays a summary of outbound calls for billing purposes

Table 11-9 *Unity Connection Reports*

Report	Benefit
Call Handler Traffic Report	Enables a user to review how often created call handlers are being used
System Configuration Report	Offers very detailed information regarding the Unity Connection system
Speech View Activity Report by User	Displays detailed activity for a selected user or CoS
Speech View Activity Summary Report	Displays detailed activity for the entire system

Phone Interface Failed Logon Report

If users are often locked out of their accounts and they insist they have not entered an incorrect password, this report can be helpful. This report lists all failed logins and the caller ID of the device from which the unsuccessful login occurred. This can help determine whether someone is trying to gain unauthorized access to the system. The information included in this report is the name of the user, alias, caller ID, extension of user, date and time, and whether the maximum failures were exceeded.

Users Report

This report provides the following information for selected users: first and last name, alias, location, home mail server, billing ID, class of service, extensions, whether the account is locked, and whether personal call transfers rules are enabled.

Message Traffic Report

This report includes totals for voice, fax, email, non-delivery receipts (NDR), delivery receipts, read receipt traffics as well as hourly totals and daily totals.

Port Activity Report

Use this report to determine the activity level of the ports on the system. The information in this report includes port name, number of inbound calls handled, number of outbound MWIs, outbound AMIS, outbound notification, and outbound TRAP calls handled as well as the total number of calls handled.

Mailbox Store Report

This report will display information about mail store that includes the mail database name, display name, server name, mailbox store size, number of mailboxes, current size, maximum size warning, last error, status, and whether the mail database can be deleted.

Dial Plan Report

This report displays a list of the search spaces configured on the connection and the partitions assigned to each search space.

Dial Search Scope Report

This report provides a list of all users and their extensions assigned to the selected partition. A list of all users and their extensions for all partitions is displayed when a partition is not selected.

User Phone Login and MWI Report

This report displays information about phone logins, MWI activity, and message notifications to phone devices per user and includes the following information:

- Name, extension, and class of service

- The source, date, and time for each activity.

- Action (for example, login, MWI on or off, and phone dialout)

- Dialout number and results

- Number of new messages at login

User Message Activity Report

Useful for providing information to help troubleshoot voicemail problems, this report shows detailed information for a selected subscriber. The information found in this report determines whether the problems subscribers are running into are self-created. The report shows each action that has taken place within a mailbox. When running this report, you must select a subscriber, and a date and time range. The following details are provided for each message: name, extension, class of service, date and time action was taken, type of message, action taken, and sender information.

Distribution Lists Report

This report provides a list of all distribution lists and members of each list. Generate this report for all distribution lists or selected lists. The details in each report include list creation date, name, display name, number of users, owner, location, and members (optional).

User Lockout Report

This report displays information about user accounts that are locked. It includes user alias, number of failed logon attempts, date and time that the account was locked, and credential type.

Unused Voice Mail Accounts Report

This report displays accounts that have not been accessed and includes the user alias, display name, and date and time that the user account was created.

Transfer Call Billing Report

When Unity Connection transfers a call from a user account or call handler, the Communications Manager simply records it as a call made by UC. Some companies require this data for billing purposes. It is necessary to identify which subscriber or call handler requested the transfer so that the call can be billed back to the proper department. This report reflects all outbound calls made by Unity Connection on behalf of a user or call handler. The information in this report includes name, extension, billing ID, date, time, dialed number, and transfer result.

This report requires you to select an object in which to run this report. The valid object choices are user, distribution list, billing ID, or call handler, class of service, or caller system transfer. You must also select a date and time range.

Outcall Billing Detail Report

This report is similar to the Transfer Call Billing report except that it reports on other types of calls such as message notification. The report includes the following information: name, extension, billing ID, time, dialed number, call duration, and result of the call (connected, ring-no-answer [RNA], busy, or unknown).

The report requires that you select an object in which to run this report. The valid object choices are user, distribution list, billing ID, and class of service. You must also select a date and time range.

Outcall Billing Summary Report

This report displays a summary of outbound calls Unity Connection placed, other than transfers, such as message notification. It includes the name, extension, and billing ID of the user who placed the call. It is sorted by date.

Call Handler Traffic Report

Use this report to see how often the call handlers you created are being used. Use this information to determine whether the call handler flow is working as expected. The information detailed in this report includes the total number of calls, extension, number of times the after-greeting action occurred, number of times the caller hung up, and number of times each key on the phone keypad was pressed.

System Configuration Report

This report offers detailed information about the Unity Connection system. It is typical for this report to be several pages in length. Although it is a good idea to have a copy of this report in hand in case Cisco TAC asks for it, it is not a report that you will find useful in day-to-day operations.

SpeechView Activity Report By User

This report displays the total number of transcribed messages, failed transcriptions, and truncated transcriptions for a selected user or class of service.

The report requires that you select an object in which to run this report. The valid object choices are user and class of service. You must also select a date and time range.

The report can be run for all users, and the information is displayed by the users.

SpeechView Activity Summary Report

This report displays the total number of transcribed messages, failed transcriptions, and truncated transcriptions for the entire system during a selected period of time.

Note   If a message is sent to multiple users, it is only transcribed once and therefore is only counted as a single transcription.

Summary

This chapter focused on the monitoring and reporting tools for Unity/Connection. For Unity, two types of reports are run from within SA, subscriber and system reports. Another web-based tool, Status Monitor, shows the status of the system, ports, queued reports, and disk drives. Reports for Unity Connection are accessed through Cisco Unity Connection Serviceability. There are 19 reports available in UC.

Included with Unity are additional tools that are accessed from the Unity Tools Depot icon on the server's desktop. These tools offer detailed information on many Unity processes. They are divided into five categories:

- Administration

- Audio management

- Diagnostic

- Reporting

- Switch integration

Unity Connection tools are accessible from within Unity Connection Administration and include the Bulk Administration tool and the Task Management tool.

After reading this chapter, you should feel comfortable running the various reports and tools available within both Unity and Unity Connection.

Chapter 12

Maximizing CUCM and Unity/Connection

This book has examined the configuration tasks required for the most commonly used features and functions of Communications Manager and Unity. Unfortunately it is not possible to include all features in every conceivable configuration in a book of this size. This chapter introduces you to a few of the more advanced features available in each application. In addition, this chapter encourages you to take what you have learned to create innovative solutions for unique issues by offering a few examples of what others have done.

The first section discusses some of the advanced features found in Communications Manager. These components include administrative access, time-of-day routing, and hunt lists. The next section discusses how Unity is configured to provide a few enhanced call-handling features such as call screening and call queuing. The final section illustrates how the features of both Communications Manager and Unity are configured to work together to offer a number of advanced features.

Advanced Communications Manager Features

As Communications Manager evolves as a product, new features are added and existing features are enhanced. Some but not all added components are unique to Communications Manager. The following sections take a look at some of these features.

Configuring Administrative Rights

After you log in to CCMAdmin, you can configure nearly every aspect of Communications Manager. This ability can prove disastrous in the wrong hands. Often administrators want the ability to hand certain configuration tasks over to the assistant administrators but might not want them to have full access to all administrator functions. This can be accomplished by defining administrative rights to certain Communications Manager users.

The components used to define these rights are roles and user groups. Roles offer the capability to enable varying degrees of access and administration rights to others. This is accomplished by configuring users, user groups, and roles. The roles are assigned to the user groups. Therefore, the groups a user belongs to determine the rights of that user.

There are a number of predefined roles that are assigned to predefined user groups. For most environments, these roles and groups should be adequate. Take time to review the existing roles and groups before creating your own. If you find that you need to create a level of access that does not exist, you can do so by creating custom roles and user groups.

Roles are assigned access to *resources*, which relate to web pages or specific functions. For example, one resource is the Enterprise Parameter web page. This resource enables access to the Enterprise Parameters page. Another resource is called Dial Plan, which can provide access to dial plan configuration when applied to a user group. To assign a resource to a role, you must choose to grant read and update rights.

Figure 12-1 shows the configuration page for a preconfigured role called Standard CCM Phone Management. In this figure, you can see a few of the resources that you can select when configuring roles. In total, there are more than 250 roles to select from. As you can see, Figure 12-1 shows only that the BLF Speeddial resources are selected, and both read and update rights are selected. By contrast, Figure 12-2 shows the configuration page for a preconfigured role called Standard CCMADMIN Administration. As you can see, all resources are assigned to this role.

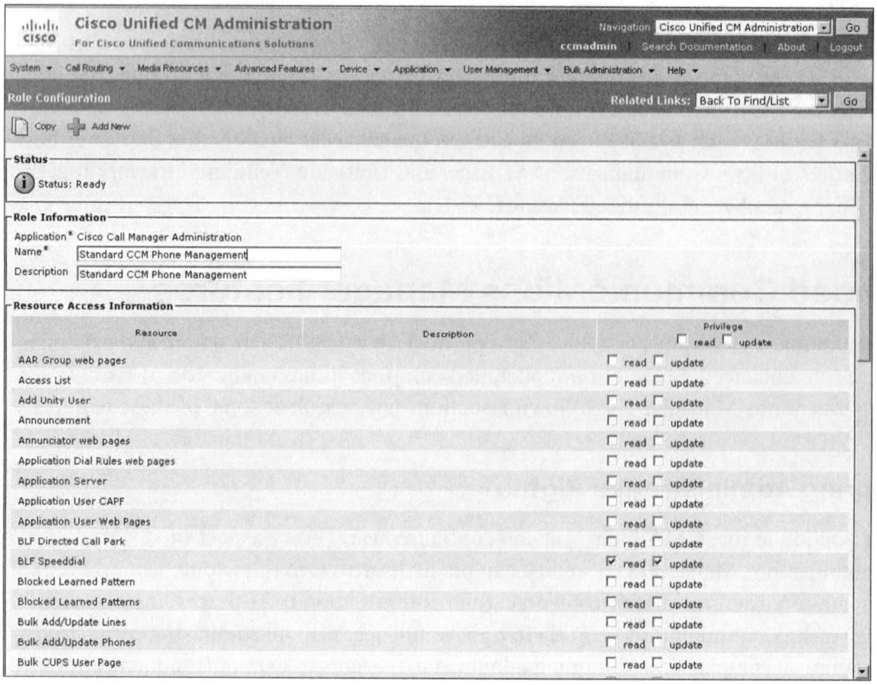

Figure 12-1 *Standard CCM Phone Management Role*

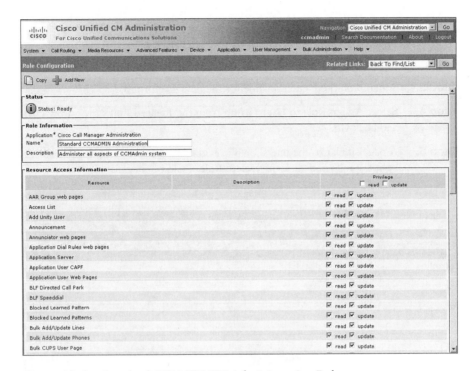

Figure 12-2 *Standard CCMADMIN Administration Role*

Note It is important to understand the exact rights that a role contains. For example, the Standard CCM Gateway Administrator group grants the right to read and update gateways. However, it also permits read rights to all pages in the Communications Manager administrative interface. This might not be what you want. Make sure that you take the time to understand all the rights that a role grants.

Now that you understand what roles are, look at how they are configured and assigned to user groups. Although you can create custom roles and groups, you might find that a group already exists that almost offers the right you want to assign. In cases like this, it is more efficient to simply copy the existing group and modify it. The following steps explain how to do this.

Warning It is recommended that you do not change any preconfigured roles. Instead, create a new role by copying an existing role and then make any desired changes to the new role.

Step 1.   From within CCMAdmin, select **User Management > User Group**.

Step 2.   Locate the group you want to make a copy of, and click the Copy icon that is located on the right side of the page.

Step 3.   When prompted, enter a name for the new user group.

Step 4.   Select **Assign Role to User Group** from the **Related Links** drop-down list, and click **Go**.

Step 5.   A page similar to the one shown in Figure 12-3 appears. To delete a role, highlight the role, and click the **Delete Role Assignment** button.

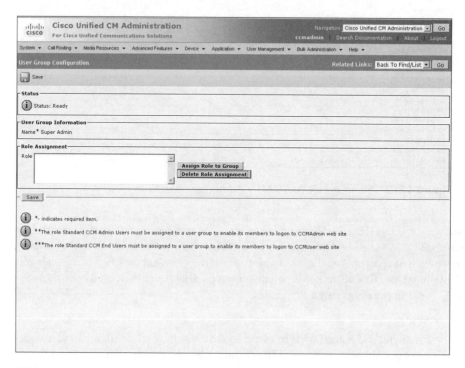

Figure 12-3   *User Group Configuration - Roles*

Step 6.   To add a role, click the **Assign Role to Group** button.

Step 7.   A window appears that should list the roles. If the roles do not appear in the list, click the **Find** button. Select the check box next to the roles you want to assign to this group.

Step 8.   Click the **Add Selected** button.

Step 9.   Click **Save**.

If you determine that you need to create roles that do not exist, you can do so using the following steps:

Step 1.   From within CCMAdmin, select **User Management > Role**.

Step 2.   To add a new role, click the **Add New** button.

Step 3.   Select the application that the resources you want to configure reside in. For most administrative roles, you will select **Cisco Call Manager Administration**.

Step 4.   Click **Next**.

Step 5.   In the **Name** field, enter a name for the new role.

Step 6.   In the **Description** field, enter a description for this new role.

Step 7.   Select the resources you want to assign to this role. To assign read-only privileges, select the **Read** check box next to the desired resource. To assign edit privileges as well, select the **Update** check box.

Step 8.   Now that you have selected all the desired privileges, click the **Save** button.

After roles are created, you must assign them to groups. Roles can only be assigned to groups that you create; that is, they cannot be assigned to the default preconfigured groups. The following steps explain how to create a new group and assign roles to it.

Step 1.   From within CCMAdmin, select **User Management > User Group**.

Step 2.   Click the **Add New** button.

Step 3.   In the **Name** field, enter a name for the user group.

Step 4.   Click **Save**.

Step 5.   Select **Assign Role to User Group** from the **Related Links** drop-down list and click **Go**.

Step 6.   A page similar to the one shown in Figure 12-3 appears. Click the **Assign Role to Group** button.

Step 7.   A window appears that should list the roles. If the roles do not appear in the list, click the **Find** button. Select the check box next to the roles you want to assign to this group.

Step 8.   Click the **Add Selected** button.

Step 9.   Click **Save**.

Time-of-Day Routing

The ability to route calls based on time of day is a feature that is available in Communications Manager 4.1 and later versions. This added function enables certain calls to be permitted and restricted based on time of day. It works in concert with Calling Search Space (CSS) and partitions, which enable you to apply certain time-of-day routing rules to one group of users and other rules to other groups.

In the simplest terms, a time frame is assigned to a partition. During that time frame, the partition is accessible by any device that has a CSS that includes the partition. Outside that time frame, no device has access to the partition.

To configure time-of-day routing, time periods and time schedules must be created. Time periods define a time range and the days to which it applies. Time schedules are groups of time periods. Time schedules are then assigned to the partitions. By using time schedules, you can assign more than one time period to a partition.

Now take a look at how these two components are configured. Because time schedules contain time periods, time periods must be configured first.

Creating a Time Period

The following steps explain how to configure a time period:

Step 1.   From within CCMAdmin, select **Call Routing > Class of Control > Time Period**.

Step 2.   Click the **Add New** button.

Step 3.   A screen similar to that shown in Figure 12-4 displays.

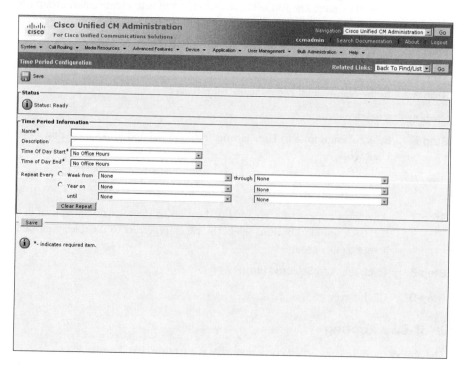

Figure 12-4   *Time Period Configuration*

Step 4.   Enter the name of this time period in the **Name** field.

Step 5. Enter a description that is helpful in identifying the purpose of this time period in the **Description** field.

Step 6. From the **Start Time** and **End Time** drop-down lists, select the time range for this time period.

Step 7. You can choose to apply this time range to days of the week or to a specific date. To apply it to days of the week, select the **Week From** radio button. Select the day range by selecting the beginning day from the first drop-down list and the end day of the range from the second drop-down list.

Step 8. To select a specific date instead of a weekday range, select the **Year On** radio button. Select the month from the first drop-down list and the date from the second drop-down list. Then select the end date from the next two drop-down lists.

Note The **Clear Repeat** button clears the day or date ranges that were specified.

Step 9. Click the **Save** button.

Repeat these steps to add all the time periods that are required. After all are created, they need to be assigned to a time schedule.

Creating a Time Schedule

Step 1. From within CCMAdmin, select **Call Routing > Class of Control > Time Schedule.**

Step 2. Click the **Add New** button.

Step 3. Enter the name of this time schedule in the **Name** field.

Step 4. Enter a description that is helpful in identifying the purpose of this time schedule in the **Description** field.

Step 5. Click **Save**.

Step 6. A screen similar to that shown in Figure 12-5 displays.

Step 7. Select a time period from the **Available Time Periods** box, and click the down arrow to add it to the **Selected Time Periods** box.

Step 8. After all the desired time periods are listed in the **Selected Time Period** box, click the **Save** button.

After the time schedule is created, it needs to be assigned to a partition, as explained in the section that follows.

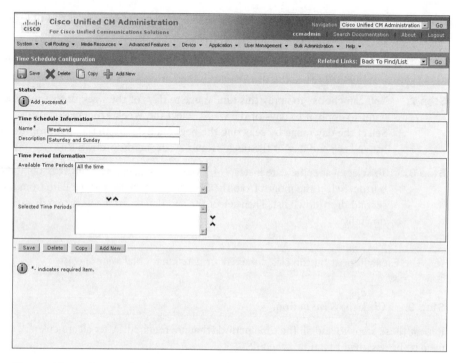

Figure 12-5   *Time Schedule Configuration*

Assigning a Time Schedule to a Partition

Step 1.   From within CCMAdmin, select **Call Routing > Class of Control > Partition.**

Step 2.   Enter search criteria to limit the partition results in the search field, and click the **Find** button.

Step 3.   Click the partition to which you want to assign a time schedule.

Step 4.   From the **Time Schedule** drop-down list, select the desired time schedule.

Step 5.   You can choose to apply the time schedule based on the time zone of the device that is placing the call or another time zone of your choosing. To base it on the time zone of the calling device, select the **Originating Device** radio button. To select another time zone, select the **Specific Time Zone** radio button, and select the desired time zone from the drop-down list.

Step 6.   Click the **Save** button.

After a time schedule is applied to a partition, time-of-day routing is active for any pattern to which that the partition is assigned.

Hunt List

Often it is desirable to have an unanswered call roll from one directory number to another. This is accomplished by creating a hunt list. A hunt list is a list of directory numbers that a call is routed through until it is answered. Make sure that you don't confuse this with hunt groups, which are specific to the Attendant Console.

A hunt list is made up of three components:

- **Line group:** A list of directory numbers
- **Hunt lists:** A list of line groups
- **Hunt pilot:** A pilot number that points to a hunt list

A hunt list works when a call is placed to the number assigned to the hunt pilot. For example, if an outside caller calls the main number, the hunt pilot points to the hunt list, which in turn sends the call to a member of the line group. The member to which the call is sent depends on how the line group is set up.

The following are the steps required to configure a hunt list. These components must be created in this order: line group, hunt list, and then hunt pilot.

Creating a Line Group

The following steps illustrate how to create a line group:

Step 1. From within CCMAdmin, select **Call Routing > Route/Hunt > Line Group**.

Step 2. Click the **Add New** button.

Step 3. A screen similar to that shown in Figure 12-6 displays. Enter a descriptive name for this line group in the **Line Group Name** field.

Step 4. The **RNA Reversion Timeout** field determines the length of time that a line will ring before it is sent to the next member of the group. RNA stands for Ring No Answer. This value is set in seconds, not rings. Enter the number of seconds you want each line in the group to ring.

Step 5. The next field determines how the call is distributed to the members of the line group. The available options are as follows:

- **Top Down:** Rings the first idle member on the line group regardless of all other factors
- **Circular:** Rings the member of the group that follows the member that had received the last call
- **Longest Idle Time:** Extends the call only to idle members, starting with the member that has been idle the longest
- **Broadcast:** Sends the call to all idle members

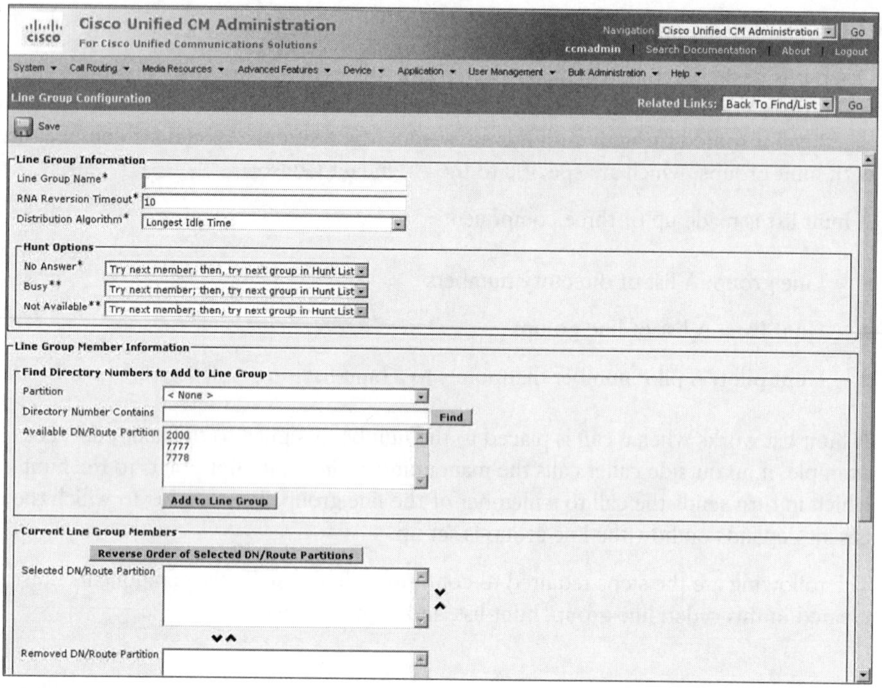

Figure 12-6   *Line Group Configuration*

Step 6.   Select the desired distribution method from the **Distribution Algorithm** drop-down list.

The next three fields determine what happens when a member of the group does not answer, is busy, or when the line is not available. The available options are as follows:

- **Try next member; then, try next group in hunt list:** Tries all the idle members of the group. If none answer, the call is sent to the next line group in the hunt list.

- **Try next member; but do not go to next group:** Tries all the idle members of the group. If none answer, the call is not sent to the next line group in the hunt list.

- **Skip remaining members, and go directly to next group:** If the member that the call is extended to does not answer, the call is sent to the next group.

- **Stop hunting:** Tries to sends the call to the first idle member of the line group. If the call is not answered, it will not be sent to another member and stops hunting.

Step 7.   Select the desired setting for each of the three conditions (**No Answer, Busy,** or **Not Available**) from the drop-down list.

Step 8.   Select a partition from the **Route Partition** drop-down list if one is required for this line group.

Step 9.   To limit the numbers that display in the **Available DN/Route Partition** box, enter search criteria in the **Directory Numbers Contains** field. For example, if you want to add lines 2020, 2030, 2040, and 2050 to a line group, you can enter 20[2-5]0 in this field. Remember that the wildcard [ ] matches a single number in a range.

Step 10.   In the **Available DN/Route Partition** box, highlight a line you want to add to this line group and click the **Add to Line Group** button. Repeat this step until all desired lines display in the **Selected DN/Route Partition** box.

Step 11.   To adjust the order in which the lines display in the group, highlight a line and use the up and down arrows to the right of the **Selected DN/Route Partition** box.

Note   The order of the DNs can be reversed by clicking the **Reverse Order of Selected DN/Route Partitions** button.

Step 12.   To remove a member from the line group, highlight the member and click the down arrow beneath the **Available DN/Route Partition** box. This moves the line to the **Removed DN/Route Partition** box.

Step 13.   Click the **Save** button to add this line group.

Creating a Hunt List

After the line groups are added, they need to be assigned to hunt lists. The following steps guide you through this process:

Step 1.   From within CCMAdmin, select **Call Routing > Route/Hunt > Hunt List.**

Step 2.   Click the **Add New** button.

Step 3.   Enter a name for this hunt list in the **Name** field.

Step 4.   Enter a description in the **Description** field.

Step 5.   Select the Communications Manager group to which this hunt list will register from the **Cisco Unified Communications Manager Group** drop-down list.

Step 6.   If this hunt list is going to be used for voicemail, select the **For Voice Mail Usage** check box.

Note   You do not need to select the **Enable This Hunt List** check box. This box will automatically be selected when you click the **Save** button.

Step 7.   Click the **Save** button.

Step 8.   A screen similar to that shown in Figure 12-7 displays.

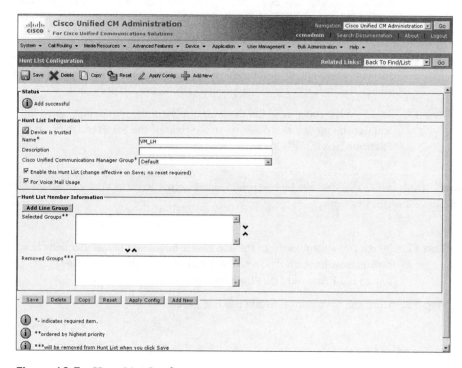

Figure 12-7   *Hunt List Configuration*

Step 9.   To add a line group to this hunt list, click the **Add Line Group** button. A new screen displays. From the drop-down list, select the line group you want to add and click **Save**. A window displays stating that the line group has been added and the hunt list must be reset. Click **OK**.

Step 10.   Repeat Step 9 to add all desired line groups to this hunt list.

Step 11.   To adjust the order in which the line groups display in the hunt list, highlight a line group, and use the Up and Down Arrows to the right of the **Selected Groups** box.

Step 12.   To remove a line group from the hunt list, highlight the line group, and click the down arrow beneath the **Selected Groups** box. This moves the line to the **Removed Groups** box.

Step 13.   Click the **Save** button to save changes made to this hunt list. A window displays stating that the hunt list must be reset for changes to take effect. Click **OK**.

Step 14.   Click the **Reset** button. A window displays informing you that you are about to reset the hunt list; this can cause Communications Manager to reject calls to this hunt list during the process. Click **Reset**.

Note   Because resetting a hunt list can cause calls to be rejected, it is recommended that you do this during off hours.

Step 15.   Click **Close**.

After the line groups and hunt lists are configured, hunt pilots need to be created that send calls to the hunt lists.

Creating Hunt Pilots

The process of creating hunt pilots is identical to that for creating route patterns. Most of the parameters configured when creating a hunt pilot have already been discussed in the "Creating Basic Patterns" section of Chapter 4, "Implementing a Route Plan."

To create a hunt pilot, follow these steps:

Step 1.   From within CCMAdmin, select **Call Routing > Route/Hunt > Hunt Pilot**.

Step 2.   Click the **Add New** button.

Step 3.   A screen similar to that shown in Figure 12-8 displays. Enter a directory number for this hunt pilot in the **Hunt Pilot** field.

Step 4.   Select the desired partition from the **Partition** drop-down list.

Step 5.   In the **Description** field, enter a description that helps identify the purpose of this hunt pilot.

Step 6.   Determine the precedence level to be assigned to this hunt pilot by selecting it from the **MLPP Precedence** drop-down list.

Step 7.   The directory number assigned to the hunt pilot should be sent to a hunt list. Select the list from the **Hunt** drop-down list.

Step 8.   The hunt pilot now has directory numbers assigned to it. You need to designate the hunt list where you want to have the calls sent. Select an option from the **Hunt List** drop-down list.

Step 9.   To allow calls that match this hunt pilot to be routed, select the **Route This Pattern** radio button.

Step 10.   If you want to have a secondary dial tone played after the first digit is dialed, select the **Provide Outside Dial Tone** check box.

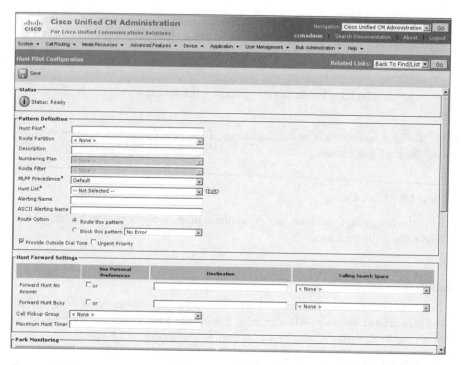

Figure 12-8   *Hunt Pilot Configuration*

Step 11.   If you want to route a call as soon as it matches this route pattern, select the **Urgent Priority** check box. Take caution when selecting this option. It could cause patterns that are similar to fail. For example, if the hunt pilot pattern was 5246 and another pattern was 524XXXX, when someone tried to dial 5426000, the call would match the 5426 hunt pilot and ignore the 000 if the hunt pilot for 5246 was set to urgent priority.

Step 12.   In the **Forward Hunt No Answer** field, enter the directory number to which you want calls to be sent if no member of the line groups answers the call. Also enter a CSS from the **Calling Search Space** drop-down list if one is needed.

Step 13.   In the **Forward Hunt Busy** field, enter the directory number to which you want calls to be sent if all destinations of the hunt list are busy. Also enter a CSS from the **Calling Search Space** drop-down list if one is needed.

Step 14.   Select a call pickup group from the **Call Pickup Group** drop-down list.

Step 15.   To limit how long the hunt pilot number rings, you can enter a value in the **Maximum Hunt Timer** field. This value is set in seconds, not number of rings.

Step 16.   When a call to a hunt pilot is parked, the **Park Monitoring Forward No Retrieve** field determines what number the call is forwarded to when the call is not retrieved within the amount of time specified by the **Park Monitoring**

Forward No Retrieve Timer service parameter. Enter the DN that the call should be forwarded to.

Step 17. If you want to manipulate caller ID information, configure the fields found under the **Calling Party Transformations** heading. The first field is labeled **Use Calling Party's External Phone Number Mask**. This field determines whether the mask configured on the directory number is used for calls that are routed through this hunt pilot.

Step 18. In the **Calling Party Transform Mask** field, enter any mask you want to affect the caller ID.

Step 19. In the **Prefix Digits (Outgoing Calls)** field, enter any digits that you want to have added to the front of the caller ID.

Step 20. The **Calling Line ID Presentation** field determines whether caller ID information is to be blocked for outbound calls that match this hunt pilot. To block caller ID, select **Restricted** from the drop-down list. To allow caller ID, select **Allowed** from the drop-down list.

Step 21. The **Calling Name Presentation** field determines whether caller name information is to be blocked for outbound calls that match this hunt pilot. To block calling name ID, select **Restricted** from the drop-down list. To allow calling name ID, select **Allowed** from the drop-down list.

Step 22. By default, the **Calling Party Number Type** and the **Calling Party Number Plan** fields are set to **Cisco Unified Communications Manager**. Only an individual that has extensive knowledge and experience using the dialing plans such as the NANP or the European dialing plan should change this field. It is recommended that this field be left at the default.

Step 23. The **Connected Line ID Presentation** field determines whether the connected party's ID information will display on the calling party's phone. To block the connected party's ID, select **Restricted** from the drop-down list. To allow the connected party's ID, select **Allowed** from the drop-down list.

Step 24. The **Connected Name Presentation** field determines whether the connected party's name information is displayed on the calling party's phone. To block the connected party's name, select **Restricted** from the drop-down list. To allow the connected party's name, select **Allowed** from the drop-down list.

Step 25. From the **Discard Digits** drop-down list, select the digit discard instruction that should be applied to calls that match this hunt pilot.

Step 26. In the **Called Party Transform Mask** field, enter the mask you want to use for calls that match this hunt pilot. If no mask is to be used, leave this field empty.

Step 27. In the **Prefix Digits (Outgoing Calls)** field, enter any digits that you want to have added to the front of a dialed number before it is sent to the hunt list.

Step 28. By default, the **Called Party Number Type** and the **Called Party Number Plan** fields are set to **Cisco Unified Communications Manager**. Only an individual that has extensive knowledge and experience using the dialing plans such as the NANP or the European dialing plan should change this field. It is recommended that this field be left at the default.

Step 29. From the **AAR Group** drop-down list, select the AAR group that the hunt pilot belongs to.

Step 30. In the **External Number Mask** field, enter the mask required to expand the hunt pilot number to a fully qualified number.

Step 31. Click **Save** to add the hunt pilot.

After the Hunt Pilot is created, the configuration for hunt lists is complete.

Now that you are familiar with some of the advanced features in Communications Manager, move on to a few features in Unity that can also enhance call-handling capabilities.

Advanced Unity/Unity Connection Features

Unity and Unity Connection have a number of advanced features that are not always used. The goal of these products is to provide voicemail and auto-attendant services, which they do quite well. However, they can also provide other services that are not always thought of as being a function of a voicemail system. The following sections explore a couple of these features. Although all the configuration tasks required to implement these services have been discussed in previous chapters, this chapter enables you to take a closer look at how you can use the features for some additional functionality.

Enabling Call Queuing

One of the underused features these products provide is that of call queuing. The queuing capabilities enable callers to decide whether they want to be placed on hold or transferred to voicemail if the number they are trying to reach is busy. Although this can be a handy feature, remember that if a caller chooses to hold, a voicemail port will be consumed for the entire time that the call is on hold. Therefore, this feature should be used only in environments in which an ample number of voicemail ports exist. Furthermore, this feature is normally configured for a small number of subscribers.

To configure call queuing in Unity, follow these steps:

Step 1. From within UA, select **Subscribers > Subscribers**.

Step 2. Click the **Find** icon, enter search criteria that will narrow the search results, and click the **Find** button.

Step 3. Select the subscriber for whom you are enabling call queuing.

Step 4. Click the **Call Transfer** link.

Step 5. Make sure that the **Transfer Incoming Calls to Subscriber's Phone** field is set to **Yes, Ring Subscriber's Extension** or **Yes, Ring Subscriber at This number**. The name of the field you see is dependent on the version of Unity used.

Step 6.   Select the **Supervise Transfer** radio button.

Step 7.   Set the **Rings to Wait For** value to a value that is less than that set in Communications Manager for this subscriber. Keep in mind that the value in Communications Manager is in seconds, whereas the value in Unity is in number of rings.

Step 8.   Select the **Ask Caller** radio button under the **If the Call Is Busy** options.

Step 9.   Click the **Save** icon.

To configure call queuing in Unity Connection, follow these steps:

Step 1.   From within Unity Connection administration, select **Users > Users**.

Step 3.   Select the subscriber for whom you are enabling call queuing.

Step 4.   Select **Edit > Transfer Rules**.

Step 5.   Select the **Standard** rule.

Step 6.   Make sure that the **Transfer Action** field is set to **Extension** and that the user's extension appears in the field.

Step 7.   From the **Transfer Type** drop-down list, select **Supervise Transfer**.

Step 8.   Set the **Rings to Wait For** value to a value that is less than that set in Communications Manager for this subscriber. Keep in mind that the value in Communications Manager is in seconds, whereas the value in Unity Connection is in number of rings.

Step 9.   From the **If Extension Is Busy** drop-down list, select **Ask Callers to Hold**.

Step 10.   Click the **Save** button.

After this is accomplished, callers attempting to reach the extension through the auto-attendant that find the extension busy are given the opportunity to be placed on hold or leave a message. The caller is informed of how many callers are ahead of him and then, every 30 seconds, is offered an opportunity to leave a message. If callers want to stay on hold instead of leaving a message, they must press 1 each time they are asked if they want to continue to hold.

Configuring Destination Call Screening

Unity and Unity Connection also provide the option to screen calls before they are transferred. The idea of allowing a called party to screen calls is often associated with avoiding phone calls. However, it is possible to use this feature to add functionality to a system.

Call screening can allow the recipient of a call to not only find out who the incoming call is coming from but also who it is intended for. For example, in a warehouse with multiple workers and only a single phone, it might be helpful for the person answering to know whom the call is for before the call is connected. This way, if the intended recipient of the call is not in, the call can be directed to that person's voicemail by pressing 2, saving time for the person answering. For this to work, a voice mailbox must be created for each person.

To configure this feature, create a user for each user with a unique extension that is different than the one assigned to the phone that he or she shares. Apply the following call transfer settings to each of these subscribers:

1.   Ring the extension of the shared phone. In Unity, select **Yes, Ring Subscriber at This Number** and enter the extension number. For Unity Connection, enter the share phone DN in the **Extension** field.

2.   Set up **Supervise Transfer** with a ring value less than that set in Communications Manager.

3.   In Unity, under the **Gather Caller Information** heading, select the **Introduce** and **Confirm** check boxes. In Unity Connection, select **Tell Me Who the Call Is For** and **Ask Me If I Want to Take the Call** under the **Call Screening** section.

After this is configured, all calls transferred from Unity or Unity Connection to the shared phone will announce who the call is for and allow the person who answered the call to press 1 to accept the call or press 2 to send the call to voicemail.

This is only a small sampling of some of the advanced features of Unity and Unity Connection. Additional features of Unity are discussed in the Cisco Press book *Cisco Unity Deployment and Solutions Guide*.

Unique Solutions

From time to time, a client wants a feature that isn't available or wants an existing feature with an enhancement or two. In these cases, find out the true functionality that the customer is seeking and see whether you can offer that functionality by leveraging the features found in Communications Manager, Unity, and Unity Connection. The following sections offer a few examples of real-world requests and how each was solved.

These sections do not offer a step-by-step solution but rather introduce you to a few unique solutions with the hope that it will encourage you to go beyond what you have learned in this book and create your own solutions with Communications Manager, Unity, and Unity Connection.

Enhanced Vacation Schedules

Although Unity enables you to define holidays, it has a few shortcomings. Unity plays the standard closed greeting for holidays. It doesn't notify the caller why you are closed. It would seem that if the caller called on a holiday, it would be obvious as to why your company is closed. That is not always the case. For example, if someone is calling from a different country, that person might not be aware that it is a holiday. It is also important that in addition to knowing that the company is closed for a holiday, you should let the caller know when the company will be open again. The second shortcoming is that it does not allow half-day holidays. Often a company might close early the day before a holiday, such as on Christmas Eve.

Although Unity has these shortcomings, there is a way to overcome them. Earlier in this chapter, you learned about time-of-day routing. By using this feature, you can configure Communications Manager and Unity to route the call to a specific call handler on holidays. The greeting for that call handler will inform the caller that the company is closed for the holiday.

The way this works is that there are two DNs that match the main incoming number. Each is assigned to a partition. The administrator should assign the DN that will route the call to a holiday call handler to a partition called Holiday. A time schedule is assigned to the Holiday partition. As you recall, a partition that has a time schedule assigned to it is only active during the hours of the time schedule. Transformation must be applied to the DN that is in the Holiday partition so that when the call reaches Unity, it can be handled differently than a call reaching Unity through the nonholiday DN. A favorable method is to set the calling party transformation mask to something unique like 7777777. Next, create a call-routing rule in Unity that routes calls with an ANI of 7777777 to the holiday call handler. This is a high-level overview of the process. It can be confusing, so we use a figure to show the pieces and describe how they fit together.

Figure 12-9 shows the components and flow of this solution. The following steps illustrate the flow in more detail:

Step 1. The calling search space of the gateway is used to determine what DN the call is routed to.

Step 2. The first partition in the CSS is Holiday, so that is the first partition to be searched. However, because the Holiday partition has a time schedule assigned to it, it is only active during the hours of the time schedule. If it is outside of those hours, the standard partition is searched.

Step 3. If it is outside of the holiday time schedule, the call is routed to Unity. Unity then sends the call through the call-routing rules, and the call ends up at the opening greeting.

Step 4. If the call enters the system during the holiday time schedule hours, the calling party transformation mask of 7777777 is assigned, and the call is routed to Unity. Unity then sends the call through the call-routing rules. Because the ANI is 7777777, the call ends up at the holiday call handler.

Now that you understand how this solution works, we take a look at what needs to be configured. The following steps describe the Communications Manager components that must be configured:

Step 1. Create a Holiday partition.

Step 2. Create a DN with the same number as the main line. Assign a calling party transformation mask of 7777777. Place the DN in the Holiday partition. Set it up to forward all calls to Unity.

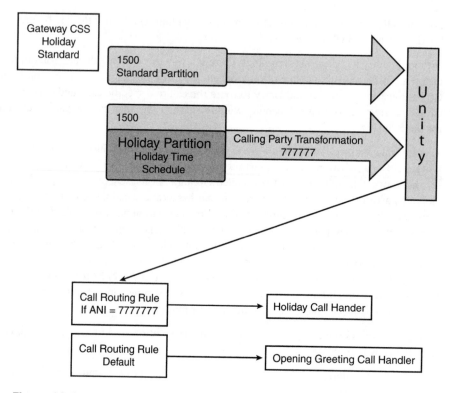

Figure 12-9   *Unity Holiday Call Routing*

Step 3.   Create time periods that match the hours you will be closed for the holiday.

Step 4.   Create a time schedule called Holiday, and assign the time periods you just created for it.

Step 5.   Assign the Holiday time schedule to the Holiday partition.

Step 6.   Modify the CSS assigned to the public switched telephone network (PSTN) gateway so that the Holiday partition is at the top of the list.

After the Communications Manager components are configured, a few things must be configured in Unity. The following steps describe the components that must be configured in Unity:

Step 1.   Create a call handler called Holiday.

Step 2.   Record a greeting for the Holiday call handler.

Step 3.   Create a call-routing rule in Unity that sends calls with a calling number (ANI) to the Holiday call handler.

After these tasks are completed, you should test this to make sure that it is working. The recommended testing method is to modify one of the time periods assigned to the Holiday time schedule so that it includes the current time. Dial in to the main number, and you should hear the greeting of the Holiday call handler. Because this testing will affect all incoming calls, testing should only be done after hours.

Configuring Unity/Connection as a Meet-Me Conference Manager

Communications Manager's meet-me conferences allow multiple people to dial in to a conference call. However, meet-me does not have any way to announce who has joined the conference or offer the option of prohibiting certain individuals from joining. Of course, using CSS and partitions, devices can be blocked from meet-me numbers, but this is often impractical because you might not want to block callers from all meet-me calls.

By using CSS, partitions, and call handlers, this functionality can be added to a Communications Manager and Unity/Connection environment. The steps that follow outline the tasks that are required:

Step 1.   Create a MEETME_PT partition and a MEETME_CSS CSS that contains the MEETME_PT partition.

Step 2.   Assign the MEETME_PT partition to the meet-me numbers.

Step 3.   Assign the MEETME_CSS CSS to all voicemail ports and to the phones that will initiate the conference. At least one phone must have this CSS or another CSS that allows access to the MEETME_PT partition. The meet-me conference can only be initiated from a phone that has access to the MEETME_PT partition.

Step 4.   Create a call handler for each meet-me number and assign it the same extension number as the meet-me conference. Set the call handler to ring the extension of the meet-me conference. This is the same number that is entered for this call handler's extension. Also, set up the call handler to do a supervise transfer with a ring value less than that set in Communications Manager. Under the **Gather Caller Information** section of the call handler heading, select the **Confirm and Ask Caller's Name** check box.

The result is that the phone allowed to initiate a meet-me conference will be successful. All other participants then dial in to Unity/Connection and enter the meet-me number. You might want to change the opening greeting so that outside callers know to enter the meet-me number. When the caller dials the meet-me number, Unity/Connection sends the call to the call handler with the same extension as the meet-me number. The call handler then asks the callers to record their names. The call is then forwarded to the conference and the caller's name is played. Unity/Connection then instructs participants in the conference to press 1 to accept the call or press 2 to send the call to voicemail. You might want to set the greeting for the call handlers to say something like "I'm sorry, but you are not authorized to enter this conference call" and then have the call handler send the caller back to the opening greeting.

Note   You need to be aware of a few things before deploying this. First, you must create a call handler for each meet-me pattern that exists in Communications Manager. Also, any member of the conference will be able to allow callers into and prohibit callers from the conference by pressing 1 or 2. Finally, if a caller tries to join the meet-me call and it has not been set up, the call can drop. For this reason, the host of the call must start the call at least five minutes early.

Managing Multilocation Overlapping Extensions

This section examines an actual problem faced by a client who failed to plan properly for the future. As mentioned earlier in this book, poor planning, or the entire lack of planning, causes failed deployments. As the saying goes, "He who fails to plan is planning to fail."

The client's problem was that the company had overlapping and duplicate extension numbers at multiple locations. All the phones were registered to a single cluster, and all voice mailboxes were on the same Unity system. That by itself can cause problems, but the main issue was that all incoming calls from each location were routed over the WAN to the Unity auto-attendant. Therefore, when an outside caller dialed the Memphis office, the call was routed to the Unity that resided in New York. The outside caller would then enter 324 to be transferred to extension 324. The problem was that there was a 324 extension in both Memphis and New York, so it was unclear to which location the call would be sent.

Note   Although this example involves Unity, the same principles apply to Unity Connection.

To solve this problem, you need to call upon the CSS and partitions again. The resolution of a number of issues requires the use of CSS and partitions.

The NYC_PT partition must be assigned to the New York 324 and the Memphis_PT partition to the Memphis 324. Indeed, all the directory numbers in NYC must be assigned a partition other than that of the Memphis directory numbers. In most cases, this is desirable even if this issue does not exist. To accomplish this, use two hunt lists: one to direct calls to voicemail ports that have a CSS with access to the lines in NYC_PT but not in Memphis_PT and the other to direct calls to voicemail ports that have a CSS with access to the lines in Memphis_PT but not in NYC_PT. All incoming calls from Memphis are directed to the hunt list that points to the ports that have access to Memphis_PT. All NYC incoming calls are directed to the hunt list that points to the ports that have access to NYC_PT.

Although this is by no means the ideal solution, it solved the immediate problem, which gave the company time to rework its entire dial plan. The major drawback to this solution is that the voicemail ports must be dedicated to specific sites instead of being shared.

Summary

This chapter introduced you to some of the new and more advanced features of Communications Manager and showed how the features within Communications Manager and Unity/Connection are used to provide more functionality.

The tasks required to configure administrative access rights, time-of-day routing, and hunt lists in Communications Manager were explained, and step-by-step procedures were provided for each. The steps to enable call queuing and destination call screening in Unity/Connection were discussed as well as enhancing Unity holiday greetings. Finally, you learned how issues such as meet-me conference limitations and overlapping extensions can be addressed.

At this point, you should feel comfortable with the majority of the day-to-day configuration and administration tasks that a Communications Manager and Unity/Connection deployment require. Because you will not have to perform all these tasks on a daily basis, you can refer to this book when confronted with an unfamiliar task.

Appendix

Additional Reference Resources

A large number of concepts and technologies have been discussed throughout this book. The presentation of these topics was designed to help you understand how to configure various components and see how each component fits into a Cisco IP communications solution. However, you might have found places in the book where you wanted more detail. Because the size of the book is limited, this appendix has been added to outline a list of additional references.

The appendix has two sections; the first is a list of concepts and components in alphabetical order. After each item, a pointer to additional documentation discusses each topic in further detail. The second section is a list of additional interesting reading. This section lists Cisco Press books that deal with this technology and a brief description of each.

Additional References

Have you ever wanted information on a topic and been told that you could find it on the web? It's like asking someone for the best way to get somewhere and being told the best way is to drive. Although driving might be the best way, you were probably hoping for a little more detail. That is what this section offers you. Instead of just referring you to Cisco.com for more details, each topic offers a specific link or book from which you can find more information. The hope is that this can save you time and allow you to gain a better understanding of a given topic.

However, don't stop here. Always continue to increase your knowledge. A favorite quote of a friend of mine seems to become truer with each passing year. Alvin Toffler writes that the illiterate of the future "will not be those who cannot read and write, but those who cannot learn, unlearn, and relearn."

Automatic Alternate Routing

Understanding Route Plans, found in Cisco Unified Communications Manager System Guide:

http://www.cisco.com/en/US/docs/voice_ip_comm/cucm/admin/8_0_2/ccmsys/a03rp.html

Audio Message Interface Standard (AMIS) Networking

AMIS Networking section in the Networking Guide for Cisco Unity:

http://www.cisco.com/en/US/docs/voice_ip_comm/unity/8x/networking/guide/8xcunet050.html

Annunciators

Annunciator section in Cisco Unified Communications Manager System Guide:

http://www.cisco.com/en/US/docs/voice_ip_comm/cucm/admin/8_0_2/ccmsys/a05ann.html

Audio Text Application

Cisco Unity Deployment and Solutions Guide: Chapter 18: "Audio-Text Application"
Cisco Press 2004, ISBN: 1-58705-118-4

Bulk Administration Tool (BAT)

Bulk Administration Tool Administration Guide:

http://www.cisco.com/en/US/docs/voice_ip_comm/cucm/bat/8_0_2/bat-802-cm.html

Bridge Networking

Networking Guide for Cisco Unity:

http://www.cisco.com/en/US/docs/voice_ip_comm/unity/8x/networking/guide/8xcunet060.html

Call Handlers

Cisco Unity Fundamentals: Chapter 5: "Cisco Unified Communication System Customization"
Cisco Press 2004, ISBN: 1-58705-098-6

Calling Search Space (CSS)

Cisco CallManager Fundamentals: A Cisco AVVID Solution
Cisco Press 2001, ISBN: 1-58705-008-0

Dial Plan

Dial Plan section of Cisco Unified Communications System SRND:
http://www.cisco.com/en/US/docs/voice_ip_comm/cucm/srnd/8x/dialplan.html

Digital Networking

Digital Networking section of Networking Guide for Cisco Unity:

http://www.cisco.com/en/US/docs/voice_ip_comm/unity/8x/networking/guide/8xcunet020.html

Emergency Responder

Cisco Emergency Responder User's Guide:

http://www.cisco.com/en/US/docs/voice_ip_comm/cer/8_5/english/users/guide/CERUG_85.html

Extension Mobility

Extension Mobility section in Cisco Unified Communications Manager Features and Services Guide:

http://www.cisco.com/en/US/docs/voice_ip_comm/cucm/admin/8_0_2/ccmfeat/fsem.html

Gatekeeper

Understanding H.323 Gatekeepers:

http://www.cisco.com/en/US/tech/tk1077/technologies_tech_note09186a00800c5e0d.shtml

H.323

Understanding H.323 Gatekeepers:

http://www.cisco.com/en/US/tech/tk1077/technologies_tech_note09186a00800c5e0d.shtml

Inter-Cluster Trunks (ICT)

Understanding Cisco Unified Communications Manager Trunk Types:

http://www.cisco.com/en/US/docs/voice_ip_comm/cucm/admin/8_0_2/ccmsys/a08trnk.html#wpmkr1099909

IP Phone Services

Developing Cisco IP Phone Services

Cisco Press 2002, ISBN: 1-58705-060-9

Locations

Location Configuration in Cisco Unified Communications Manager Administration Guide:

http://www.cisco.com/en/US/docs/voice_ip_comm/cucm/admin/8_0_2/ccmcfg/b02locat.html#wpxref86363

Media Resource Management

Media Resource Management section of Cisco Unified Communications Manager System Guide:

http://www.cisco.com/en/US/docs/voice_ip_comm/cucm/admin/8_0_2/ccmsys/a05media.html

Media Gateway Control Protocol (MGCP)

Understanding MGCP Interactions with Cisco CallManager:

http://www.cisco.com/en/US/tech/tk1077/technologies_tech_note09186a00801da84e.shtml

Multi-Level Access (MLA)

Cisco CallManager Best Practices: Chapter 9: "Using Multilevel Administration"

Cisco Press 2004, ISBN : 1-58705-139-7

Multi-Level Precedence and Preemption MLPP

Multi-Level Precedence and Preemption section of Cisco Unified Communications Manager Features and Services Guide:

http://www.cisco.com/en/US/docs/voice_ip_comm/cucm/admin/8_0_2/ccmfeat/fsmlpp.html#wpmkr1087240

Music on Hold (MOH)

Music on Hold section of Cisco Unified Communications Manager Features and Services Guide:

http://www.cisco.com/en/US/docs/voice_ip_comm/cucm/admin/8_0_2/ccmfeat/fsmoh.html

Media Termination Points (MTP)

Media Termination Points section of the Cisco Unified Communications Manager Features and Services Guide:

http://www.cisco.com/en/US/docs/voice_ip_comm/cucm/admin/8_0_2/ccmsys/a05mtp.html#wpmkr1078662

Partitions

Cisco CallManager Fundamentals: A Cisco AVVID Solution

Cisco Press 2001, ISBN: 1-58705-008-0

Patterns

Understanding Route Plans in Cisco Unified Communications Manager Features and Services Guide:

http://www.cisco.com/en/US/docs/voice_ip_comm/cucm/admin/8_0_2/ccmsys/a03rp.html#wp1100819

Phone Models

http://www.cisco.com/en/US/prod/collateral/voicesw/ps6788/phones/ps10326/IP_Phones_Positioning_External_December2009.pdf

Quality of Service (QoS)

Cisco QoS Exam Certification Guide, Second Edition

Cisco Press 2004, ISBN: 1-58720-124-0

Restriction Tables

Restriction Tables section in System Administration Guide for Cisco Unity:

http://www.cisco.com/en/US/docs/voice_ip_comm/unity/8x/administration/guide/
8xcusag070.html#wp1040314

Route Filters

Cisco CallManager Fundamentals: A Cisco AVVID Solution: Chapter 2: "Call Routing"

Cisco Press 2001, ISBN: 1-58705-008-0

Security Concerns (CallManager and Unity)

Cisco CallManager Best Practices: Chapter 6: "Securing the Environment"

Cisco Press 2004, ISBN: 1-58705-139-7

Session Initiation Protocol (SIP)

Understanding Session Initiation Protocol (SIP) section of the Cisco Unified
Communications Manager System Guide:

http://www.cisco.com/en/US/docs/voice_ip_comm/cucm/admin/8_0_2/ccmsys/
a08sip.html#wpmkr1164509

Survivable Remote Site Telephony (SRST)

Ensuring IP Telephony High Availability in the Branch Office:

http://www.cisco.com/en/US/products/sw/voicesw/ps2169/products_white_paper
09186a008009264e.shtml

Spanning Tree Protocol (STP)

Configuring Spanning Tree:

http://www.cisco.com/en/US/docs/switches/lan/catalyst4000/7.4/configuration/guide/
spantree.html

Tool for Auto-Register Phones Support (TAPS)

Cisco Unified Communications Manager Bulk Administration Guide:

http://www.cisco.com/en/US/docs/voice_ip_comm/cucm/bat/8_0_2/bat-802-cm.html

Voice Profile for Internet Mail (VPIM) Networking

VPIM Networking section of the Networking Guide for Cisco Unity:

http://www.cisco.com/en/US/docs/voice_ip_comm/unity/8x/networking/guide/
8xcunet070.html

Interesting Reading

Have you read any good books lately—aside from the one in your hands? Well, I have, and they are listed next. This is by no means a list of all the great Cisco Press books on the subject of IP telephony. It is simply a list of a few books I have in my library that I have found helpful. It doesn't matter how long you have been involved with the industry; there is always more to learn. So if you plan to grow your Cisco IP telephony library, I suggest the following books:

Voice Over IP *Fundamentals*, 2nd Edition

ISBN: 1-58705-257-1; Published July 27, 2006

Whether you come from a voice background and are trying to learn the data side or you come from a data background and are trying to ramp up on voice, this book is an excellent resource.

It offers a comparison of traditional voice systems to VoIP, which helps you gain a solid understanding of how the public switched telephone network (PSTN) works and how VoIP fits into modern solutions.

An excellent explanation of many of the traditional telephony signaling protocols and PSTN services are covered in the first portion of the book.

This book includes an IP primer, which can be a great help to anyone who is new to this data world. It helps you to understand the basics of the OSI model and routing protocols.

Additional topics are covered in this book, such as VoIP protocols, dial plans, and QoS. A great deal of information is packed into this book, which is just more than 400 pages. It is a great book for anyone who is either new to, or has experience with, this industry.

Cisco Unity Deployment and Solutions Guide

ISBN: 1-58705-118-4; Published Aug. 3, 2004

Many people have a limited view of Unity, which they display by saying, "It's just voice-mail." As I have stated, time and again, Unity is so much more. If you need any proof of this, next time you are at a bookstore, pick up a copy of this book and leaf through it.

You shouldn't have much trouble finding it among the other books. It is large. I feel that the size speaks volumes (please excuse the pun) as to how complex Unity can be.

The topics covered in this book range from design through installation to managing and beyond. It is touted as the definitive guide to Unity, which is no understatement.

This book is written by some of the most respected names in the Unity world. If you want an exhaustive resource that covers the inner workings of Unity, look no further.

Cisco Unity Connection

ISBN: 1587142813; Published May 2011

This newly released book is a comprehensive guide to designing networks using Cisco Unity Connection and implementing and configuring the various features that users require in today's business environments. This text includes detailed descriptions of the new features that Cisco has introduced in the current version of the product along with a detailed approach for the configuration of each feature and application. Although it covers some of the same topics as this book, it focuses on topics that are more of an engineering level versus administration tasks level.

Index

T

transfer rules, configuring call handlers, 518-520

translation patterns, creating, 179-183

trunks, gatekeeper-controlled, configuring, 215-217

U

Unity

account policies, defining, 334-337

administration tools, 600-608

audio management tools, 608-609

authentication settings, configuring, 331-332

call flow, 25-26

call handlers, 26-29

interview call handlers, configuring, 543-546

call queuing, enabling, 642-643

call screening, configuring, 643-644

configuration settings, defining, 322-330

CoS, configuring, 337-347

directory handlers, configuring, 528-534

holidays, adding, 321-322

meet-me conference manager, configuring, 647-648

networking

components, 568-569

configuring, 571-577

PDLs, creating, 349

ports, configuring, 332-334

reporting tools, 612-613

restriction tables, configuring, 561-563

schedules, creating, 318-322

security, 38-39

software architecture, 23-25

Status Monitor (HTML)

monitoring capabilities, 588-591

reports, 592-593

subscribers, 30

creating, 414-417

templates, creating, 381-414

supported networking, 33-35

switch integration tools, 613-614

Unity Administrator

accessing, 296-300

navigating, 296-300

Unity Connection

administration tools, 614-619

administrative interface, accessing, 301-303

authentication rules, configuring, 363-365

call flow, 25-26

call handlers, 26-29

configuring, 514-516

call queuing, enabling, 642-643

call screening, configuring, 643-644

CoS, configuring, 368-371

diagnostic tools, 609-612

dial plans, defining, 372-375

directory handlers, configuring, 534-540

general configuration settings, 355-358

integration, verifying for Communications Manager integration, 351-357

interview call handlers, configuring, 546-549

V

W-Z

·il|·il|·
CISCO™

ciscopress.com: Your Cisco Certification and Networking Learning Resource

CISCO
Cisco Learning Network
Free Test Prep and Beyond.
Access review questions
Watch Quick Learning Modules (QLMS)
Search for jobs and network with others
Take self-assessments
Participate in study groups
Play online learning games
Register for a free membership
and get started now.
www.cisco.com/go/learningnetwork
Cisco Learning Network
A social learning site brought to you by Learning@Cisco

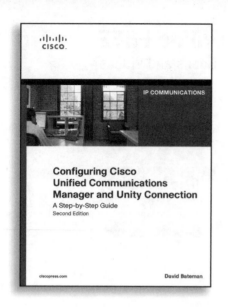

FREE Online Edition

Your purchase of **Configuring Cisco Unified Communications Manager and Unity Connection** includes access to a free online edition for 45 days through the Safari Books Online subscription service. Nearly every Cisco Press book is available online through Safari Books Online, along with more than 5,000 other technical books and videos from publishers such as Addison-Wesley Professional, Exam Cram, IBM Press, O'Reilly, Prentice Hall, Que, and Sams.

SAFARI BOOKS ONLINE allows you to search for a specific answer, cut and paste code, download chapters, and stay current with emerging technologies.

Activate your FREE Online Edition at www.informit.com/safarifree

> **STEP 1:** Enter the coupon code: TABAHAA.

> **STEP 2:** New Safari users, complete the brief registration form.
> Safari subscribers, just log in.

If you have difficulty registering on Safari or accessing the online edition, please e-mail customer-service@safaribooksonline.com